W9-AAL-770

THE ARCTIC
p 143

GERMANY &
THE ALPINE STATES
pp 100-101

THE LOW
COUNTRIES
pp 84-85

...land
83

NORTHERN EUROPE
pp 82-83

RUSSIA & KAZAKHSTAN
pp 118-119

EUROPEAN RUSSIA
pp 110-111

THE BRITISH
ISLES
pp 86-95

CENTRAL
EUROPE
pp 104-105

ASIA
pp 114-133

EUROPE
pp 78-111

EASTERN
EUROPE
pp 108-109

FRANCE
pp 96-97

ITALY
pp 102-103

SOUTHEAST
EUROPE
pp 106-107

TURKEY &
THE CAUCASUS
pp 120-121

CENTRAL
ASIA
pp 124-125

EAST
ASIA
pp 128-129

JAPAN &
KOREA
pp 132-133

SPAIN &
PORTUGAL
pp 98-99

Malta
p 112

Cyprus
p 112

THE
MEDITERRANEAN
pp 112-113

Israel
p 123

SOUTHWEST
ASIA
pp 122-123

SOUTH
ASIA
pp 126-127

Ryukyu
Islands
p 133

PACIFIC

OCEAN

NORTH AFRICA
pp 70-71

WEST AFRICA
pp 72-73

EAST
AFRICA
pp 74-75

Andaman
& Nicobar
Islands
p 127

SOUTHEAST
ASIA
pp 130-131

AFRICA
pp 68-77

SOUTHWEST
PACIFIC
pp 140-141

SOUTHERN
AFRICA
pp 76-77

INDIAN

OCEAN

AUSTRALASIA
& OCEANIA
pp 134-141

Samoa
p 140

AUSTRALIA
pp 136-137

NEW ZEALAND
pp 138-139

ANTARCTICA
p 142

STUDENT
ATLAS

LONDON • NEW YORK • MUNICH • MELBOURNE • DELHI
www.dk.com

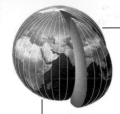

LONDON, NEW YORK, MELBOURNE, MUNICH, DELHI

FOR THE FIFTH EDITION
Publishing Director Jonathan Metcalf   Managing Cartographers David Roberts • Simon Mumford
Art Director Bryn Walls   Managing Editor Debra Wolter
Cartographers Paul Eames • Iorwerth Watkins   Jacket Designers Lee Ellwood • Duncan Turner
Systems Co-ordinator Philip Rowles   Production Rita Sinha

DORLING KINDERSLEY CARTOGRAPHY

MANAGING EDITOR   MANAGING ART EDITOR
Lisa Thomas   Philip Lord

PROJECT EDITORS   PROJECT DESIGNERS
Debra Clapson, Wim Jenkins, Jill Hamilton (US)   Rhonda Fisher, Karen Gregory

EDITORIAL CONTRIBUTORS   DESIGNERS
Thomas Heath, Kevin McRae, Constance Novis,   Carol Ann Davis, David Douglas,
Iris Rossoff (US), Siobhan Ryan   Nicola Liddiard

MANAGING CARTOGRAPHER   SENIOR CARTOGRAPHIC EDITOR
David Roberts   Roger Bullen

CARTOGRAPHERS
Pamela Alford, James Anderson, Chris Atkinson, Dale Buckton, Tony Chambers, Jan Clark,
Martin Darlison, Damien Demaj, Paul Eames, Sally Gable, Jeremy Hepworth, Michael Martin,
Ed Merritt, Simon Mumford, John Plumer, Gail Townsley, Julie Turner,
Sarah Vaughan, Jane Voss, Peter Winfield

DATABASE MANAGER   DIGITAL MAPS CREATED IN DK CARTOPIA BY
Simon Lewis   Phil Rowles, Rob Stokes

PLACENAMES DATABASE TEAM EDITORIAL DIRECTION
Natalie Clarkson, Julia Lynch,   Andrew Heritage

PICTURE RESEARCH
Louise Thomas

EDUCATIONAL CONSULTANTS
Dr. David Lambert, Institute of Education, University of London, David R Wright, BA MA

TEACHER REVIEWERS
US: Ramani DeAlwis; UK: Kevin Ball, Pat Barber, Stewart Marson

First American Edition, 1998.
Reprinted with Revisions, 1999.
Second Edition (revised) 2002, Reprinted 2003, Third Edition (revised) 2004,
Fourth Edition (revised) 2006, Fifth Edition (revised) 2008

Published in the United States by DK Publishing Inc.
375 Hudson Street, New York, New York, 10014

A Penguin Company

Student Atlas.
p.   cm.
Summary: Maps, illustrations and text describe various aspects of
countries of the world including physical features, population,
standards of living, natural resources, industries, environmental
issues and climate.
ISBN: 978-0-7566-3818-4
1. Children's atlases.   [1. Atlases.] I. DK Publishing, Inc.
G1021 .S78 1998 <G&M>
912--DC21
97-45730
CIP
MAPS

Reprographics by Altaimage Ltd, London, UK.

Printed and bound in Singapore by Star Standard Industries (Pte) Ltd.

See our complete catalog at www.dk.com

ACKNOWLEDGMENTS
The publishers are grateful for permission to reproduce the following photographs:
t=top, b=bottom, a=above, l=left, r=right, c=center
Axiom: Jiri Rezac 64br; J Spaull 92br. Bridgeman Art Library: Hereford Cathedral, Trustees of the Hereford Mappa Mundi 8tr. J Allan
Cash: 120cr. Bruce Coleman Ltd: C Ott 28cr (below); Dr E Pott 4bc; H Reinhard 19cr; J Murray 130bl; Peter Terry 19crr. Colourific: Black
Star/R Rogers 113br; Frank Herrmann 119bc. Comstock: 17tc. Corbis: Bob Daemmrich 30bl. James Davis Travel Photography: 44tr,
119tr. Robert Harding Picture Library: 6tr (below), 21c, 21cr, 22br, 92cr (above), 28bl, 30cr, 30br, 31bl, 38tr, 118bl; A Tovy 120br; Adam
Woolfitt 62br; C Bowman 112tr; Charcrit Boonson 90cr (below); David Lomax 20tr; Franz Joseph Land 19tr; G Boutin 120cl (below); G
Renner 17c, 118cr(above); Gavin Hellier 31tr; Geoff Renner 39cr (above); H P Merten 23tl; Jane Sweeney 23bl; Louise Murray 93tr; Peter
Scholey 91tr; Robert Francis 23cr; Schuster/Keine 62cr (above); Simon Westcott 90br. Hutchison Library: A Zvoznikov 19cl; J Nowell 93bl;
R Ian Lloyd 10cl. Image Bank: Carlos Navajas 17bl; M Isy-Schwart 17bc; P Grumann 64cr (below); Steve Proehl 30cr (below); Terje Rakke
17br. Images Colour Library: 19c, 62cr (below), 118br. Impact: Jeremy Nicholl 121cl (below); Mark Henley 20bl; Paul O'Driscoll 63cr;
Robin Lubbock 118br. Frank Lane Picture Agency: D Smith 19bc; W Wisniewsli 17cr. Magnum: Chris Steele Perking 120tr (below); Jean
Gaumy 65cl. N.A.S.A: 9tc. N.H.P.A: M Wendler 4cl, 110bl. Oxford Scientific Films: Konrad Wothe 19tc; L Gould 4tr; Nobert Rosing 28cl.
Panos Pictures: Alain le Garsheur 92cr; Alain le Garsmeur 31cl (below); Alberto Arzoz 63tr; Bruce Paton 121bl; Jeremy Hartley 120bl;
Maria Luiza M Cavalho 112cl (below); Paul Smith 111cr; Rhodri Jones 113bl; Ron Gilling 119cr; Trygve Bolstad 22bl. Edward Parker:
17cr (above). Pictor International: 4tc, 10bc, 18tr, 20br, 36bc, 38br. Planet Earth Pictures: J Waters 113bc. South American Pictures:
Robert Francis 29br; Tony Morrison 110cr, 111cl. Spectrum Colour Library: 29br. Frank Spooner Pictures: Gamma/E Baitel 91cl.
Still Pictures: J Frebet 113cr; R Seitre 90cr (above). Tony Stone Images: 17tr, 112cl; A Sacks 28cr; Alan Levenson 92cr; Charles Thatcher
39cr; D Austen 131cr; D Hanson 17cl; Donald Johnson 62bc; Earth Imaging 6tr (above); G Johnson 90bl; H Strand 113tr; Hans Schlapfer
38bc; J Jangoux 19bcr; J Warden 110bc; John Garrett 121br; L Resnick 121tr; Larry Ulrich 37br; P Chesley 130tr; Paul Chesley 36br; Randy
Wells 19br; Robert Frerck 65tr; Tom Walker 36bl; Tony Craddock 65cr. Telegraph Colour Library: 29tr. Travel Ink: Colin Marshall 22bc.
Trip: A Kuznetsov 92bc; H Rogers 90cr; M Barlow 112bl; N Ray 10tr; Robert Belbin 92bl; V Kolpakov 93cr (below); V Sidoropolev 64cr; W
Jacobs 130c. World Pictures: 131bl. ZEFA Picture Library: 19bcl, 19cll, 63bc; Damm 119cl; Heilman 110cr (below); K Siewert 110cl; Kitchen
19bll; Sunak 91cr; Surpress 111tr. JACKET IMAGES: Front: Corbis: Richard Berenholtz br; Bob Krist tc, bl; JamesRandklev tr, bl; Keren Su
tl.; Science Photo Library/NOAA. Back: Corbis: Robert Y. Ono bc; James Randklevbl; Paul A. Souders br; Royalty Free Images: Cobis tc;
Corbis tr. Spine: Corbis: Robert Y. Ono

CONTENTS

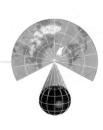

LEARNING MAP SKILLS

THE WORLD ABOUT US

THE WORLD ATLAS

NORTH AMERICA

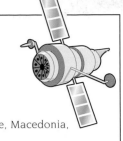

☐ KEY TO MAP SYMBOLS ON FRONT ENDPAPER

☐ FLAGS ON BACK ENDPAPER

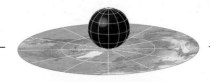

AMAZING EARTH

Earth is unique among the nine planets that circle the Sun. It is the only one that can support life, because it has enough oxygen in its atmosphere and plentiful water. In fact, seen from space, the Earth looks almost entirely blue. This is because about 70% of its surface is under water, submerged beneath four huge oceans: the Pacific, Atlantic, Indian and Arctic oceans. Land makes up about 30% of the Earth's surface. It is divided into seven landmasses of varying shapes and sizes called continents. These are, from largest to smallest: Asia, Africa, North America, South America, Antarctica, Europe, and Australia.

THE SHAPE OF THE EARTH

Photographs taken from space by astronauts in the 1960s, and more recently from orbiting satellites, have proven beyond doubt what humans had worked out long ago – that the Earth is shaped like a ball. But it is not perfectly round. The force of the Earth's rotation makes the world bulge very slightly at the Equator and go a little flat at the North and South Poles. So the Earth is actually a flattened sphere, or a "geoid."

WET EARTH

Tropical rain forests grow in areas close to the Equator, where it is wet and warm all year round. Although they cover just 7% of the Earth's land, these thick, damp forests form the richest ecosystems on the planet. More plant and animal species are found here than anywhere else on Earth.

DRY EARTH

Deserts are among the most inhospitable places on the planet. Some deserts are scorching hot, others are freezing cold, but they have one thing in common – they are all dry. Very few plant and animal species can survive in these harsh conditions. The world's coldest and driest continent, Antarctica (*left*), is a cold desert.

WATERY WORLD

The Earth's oceans and seas cover more than 142 million sq miles – that is twice the surface of Mars and nine times the surface of the moon.

Beneath the ocean waves lies the biggest and most unexplored landscape on Earth. Here are coral reefs, enormous, open plains, deep canyons, and the longest mountain range on Earth – the Mid-Atlantic Ridge – which stretches almost from pole to pole.

☐ HEIGHTS AND DEPTHS

The Pacific Ocean contains the deepest places on the Earth's surface – the ocean trenches. The very deepest is Challenger Deep in the Mariana Trench which plunges 36,201 ft into the Earth's crust. If Mount Everest, the highest point on land at 29,035 ft, was dropped into the trench, its peak wouldn't even reach the surface of the Pacific.

☐ WATER

Over 97% of the Earth's water is salt water. The total amount of salt in the world's oceans and seas would cover all of Europe to a depth of three miles. Less than 3% of the Earth's water is fresh. Of this, 2.24% is frozen in ice sheets and about 0.6% is stored underground as groundwater. The remainder is in lakes and rivers.

☐ COASTS

The total length of the Earth's coastlines is more than 300,000 miles – that is the equivalent of 12 times around the globe. A high percentage of the world's people live in coastal zones: of the ten most populated cities on Earth, seven are situated on estuaries or the coast.

☐ BIODIVERSITY

Today, almost 6,500,000,000 humans, approximately one million animal species, and 355,000 known plant species depend on the air, water, and land of planet Earth.

☐ VANISHING FORESTS

10,000 years ago, thick forests covered about half of the Earth's land surface. Today, 33% of those forests no longer exist, and more than half of what remains has been dramatically altered. During the 20th century, more than 50% of the Earth's rain forests have been felled.

DIFFERENT WORLD VIEWS

Because the Earth is round, we can only see half of it at any one time. This half is called a hemisphere, which means "half a sphere." There are always two hemispheres – the half that you see and the other half that you don't see. Two hemispheres placed together will always make a complete sphere.

Equator 0°

NORTH AND SOUTH

The Equator is an imaginary line drawn around the middle of the Earth, where its circumference is greatest. If we cut along the Equator, the Earth separates into two hemispheres: the Northern and Southern Hemispheres. Most of the Earth's land is the Northern Hemisphere. Europe and North America are the only continents that lie entirely in the northern hemisphere. Australia and Antarctica are the only continents that lie entirely in the southern hemisphere.

The Southern Hemisphere contains three of the Earth's four great oceans: the Pacific, Indian, and Atlantic Oceans.

Prime Meridian (0°)

North Pole

EAST AND WEST

The Earth can also be divided along two other imaginary lines – the Prime Meridian (0°) and 180° – which run opposite each other between the North and South Poles. This creates eastern and western hemispheres. The continents in the eastern hemisphere are traditionally called the Old World, while those in the western hemisphere – the Americas – were named the New World by the Europeans who explored them in the 15th century.

180°

PLANET WATER, PLANET LAND

The Earth can also be divided into land and water hemispheres. The land hemisphere shows most of the land on the Earth's surface. The water hemisphere is dominated by the vast Pacific Ocean – from this view, the Earth appears to be almost entirely covered by water.

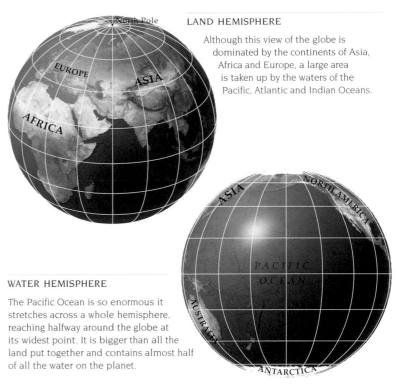

LAND HEMISPHERE

Although this view of the globe is dominated by the continents of Asia, Africa and Europe, a large area is taken up by the waters of the Pacific, Atlantic and Indian Oceans.

WATER HEMISPHERE

The Pacific Ocean is so enormous it stretches across a whole hemisphere, reaching halfway around the globe at its widest point. It is bigger than all the land put together and contains almost half of all the water on the planet.

THE SEASONS

As the Earth orbits the Sun, it is also spinning around an imaginary line called its axis, which joins the North and South Poles. The Earth's axis is not quite at right angles to the Sun, but tilts over at an angle of 23.5°. As a result, each place gradually moves closer to the Sun and then farther away from it again. Summer in the Northern Hemisphere is when the north is closest to the Sun. In winter, the Northern Hemisphere tilts away from the Sun, receiving far less heat and light. In the Southern Hemisphere the seasons are reversed, with summer in December and winter in June.

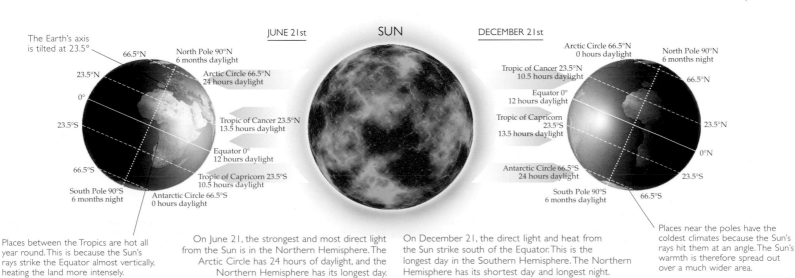

The Earth's axis is tilted at 23.5°
66.5°N
23.5°N
0°
23.5°S
66.5°S

JUNE 21st
North Pole 90°N
6 months daylight
Arctic Circle 66.5°N
24 hours daylight
Tropic of Cancer 23.5°N
13.5 hours daylight
Equator 0°
12 hours daylight
Tropic of Capricorn 23.5°S
10.5 hours daylight
South Pole 90°S
6 months night
Antarctic Circle 66.5°S
0 hours daylight

SUN

DECEMBER 21st
Arctic Circle 66.5°N
0 hours daylight
North Pole 90°N
6 months night
Tropic of Cancer 23.5°N
10.5 hours daylight
66.5°N
Equator 0°
12 hours daylight
Tropic of Capricorn 23.5°S
13.5 hours daylight
23.5°N
0°N
Antarctic Circle 66.5°S
24 hours daylight
South Pole 90°S
6 months daylight
66.5°S
23.5°S

Places between the Tropics are hot all year round. This is because the Sun's rays strike the Equator almost vertically, heating the land more intensely.

On June 21, the strongest and most direct light from the Sun is in the Northern Hemisphere. The Arctic Circle has 24 hours of daylight, and the Northern Hemisphere has its longest day.

On December 21, the direct light and heat from the Sun strike south of the Equator. This is the longest day in the Southern Hemisphere. The Northern Hemisphere has its shortest day and longest night.

Places near the poles have the coldest climates because the Sun's rays hit them at an angle. The Sun's warmth is therefore spread out over a much wider area.

MAPPING THE WORLD

The main purpose of a map is to show, or locate, where things are. The only truly accurate map of the whole world is a globe – a round model of the Earth. But a globe is impractical to carry around, so mapmakers (cartographers) produce flat paper maps instead. Changing the globe into a flat map is not simple. Imagine cutting a globe in half and trying to flatten the two hemispheres. They would be stretched in some places, and squashed in others. In fact, it is impossible to make a map of the round Earth on flat paper without some distortion of area, distance, or direction.

MODELS OF THE WORLD

Satellite images can show the whole world as it appears from space. However, this image shows only one half of the world, and is distorted at the edges.

A globe (*right*) is the only way to illustrate the shape of the Earth accurately. A globe also shows the correct positions of the continents and oceans and how large they are in relation to one another.

LATITUDE

We can find out exactly how far north or south, east or west any place is on Earth by drawing two sets of imaginary lines around the world to make a grid. The horizontal lines on the globe below are called lines of latitude. They run from east to west. The most important is the Equator, which is given the value 0°. All other lines of latitude run parallel to the Equator. and are numbered in degrees either north or south of the Equator.

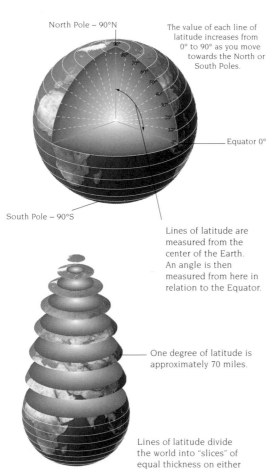

North Pole – 90°N

The value of each line of latitude increases from 0° to 90° as you move towards the North or South Poles.

Equator 0°

South Pole – 90°S

Lines of latitude are measured from the center of the Earth. An angle is then measured from here in relation to the Equator.

One degree of latitude is approximately 70 miles.

Lines of latitude divide the world into "slices" of equal thickness on either side of the Equator.

LONGITUDE

The vertical lines on the globe below run from north to south between the poles. They are called lines of longitude. The most important passes through Greenwich, England, and is numbered 0°. It is called the Prime Meridian. All other lines of longitude are numbered in degrees either east or west of the Prime Meridian. The line directly opposite the Prime Meridian is numbered 180°.

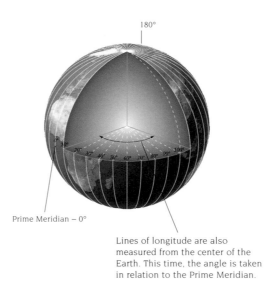

180°

Prime Meridian – 0°

Lines of longitude are also measured from the center of the Earth. This time, the angle is taken in relation to the Prime Meridian.

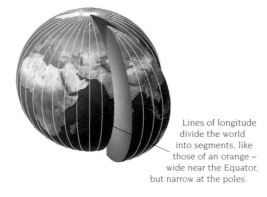

Lines of longitude divide the world into segments, like those of an orange – wide near the Equator, but narrow at the poles.

WHERE ON EARTH?

When lines of latitude and longitude are combined on a globe, or as here, on a flat map, they form a grid. Using this grid, we can locate any place on land, or at sea, by referring to the point where its line of latitude intersects with its line of longitude. Even when a place is not located exactly where the lines cross, you can still find its approximate position.

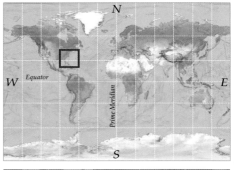

N

W   Equator   E

Prime Meridian

S

Boston
New York
Philadelphia
WASHINGTON DC

ATLANTIC OCEAN

Miami

The map above is of the eastern US. It is too small to show all the lines of latitude and longitude, so they are given at intervals of 5°. Miami is located at about 26° north of the Equator and 80° west of the Prime Meridian. We write its location 26°N 80°W.

MAKING A FLAT MAP FROM A GLOBE

Cartographers use a technique called projection to show the Earth's curved surface on a flat map. Many different map projections have been designed. The distortion of one feature – either area, distance, or direction – can be minimized, while other features become more distorted. Cartographers must choose which of these things it is most important to show correctly for each map that they make. Three major families of projections can be used to solve these questions.

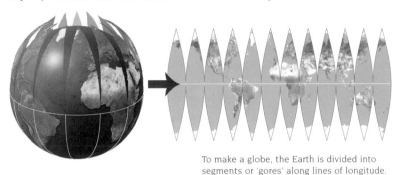

To make a globe, the Earth is divided into segments or 'gores' along lines of longitude.

1 CYLINDRICAL PROJECTIONS

These projections are "cylindrical" because the surface of the globe is transferred onto a surrounding cylinder. This cylinder is then cut from top to bottom and "rolled out" to give a flat map. These maps are very useful for showing the whole world.

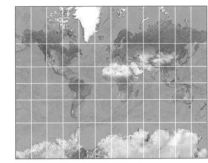

The cylinder touches the globe at the Equator. Here, the scale on the map will be exactly the same as it is on the globe. At the northern and southern edges of the cylinder, which are farthest away from the surface of the globe, the map is most distorted. The Mercator projection (*above*), created in the 16th century, is a good example of a cylindrical projection.

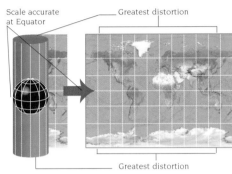

Scale accurate at Equator — Greatest distortion

Greatest distortion

2 AZIMUTHAL PROJECTIONS

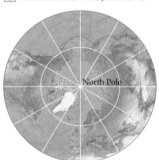

North Pole

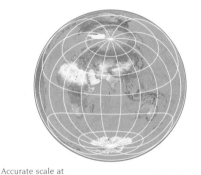

Azimuthal projections put the surface of the globe onto a flat circle. "Azimuthal" means that the direction or "azimuth" of any line coming from the center point of that circle is correct. Azimuthal maps are useful for viewing hemispheres, continents, and the polar regions. Mapping any area larger than a hemisphere gives great distortion at the outer edges of the map.

Accurate scale at central point — Greatest distortion

The circle only touches the globe's surface at one central point. The scale is only accurate at this point and becomes less and less accurate the farther away the circle is from the globe. This kind of projection is good for maps centering on a major city or on one of the poles.

3 CONIC PROJECTIONS

Conic projections are best used for smaller areas of the world, such as country maps. The surface of the globe is projected onto a cone which rests on top of it. After cutting from the point to the bottom of the cone, a flat map in the shape of a fan is left behind.

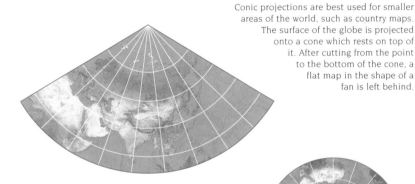

The conic projection touches the globe's surface at one latitude. This is where the scale of the map will be most accurate. The parts of the cone farthest from the globe will be the most distorted and are usually omitted from the map itself.

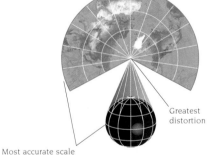

Greatest distortion

Most accurate scale

PROJECTIONS USED IN THIS ATLAS

The projections that are appropriate for showing maps at a world, continental, or country scale are quite different. The projections for this atlas have been carefully chosen. They are ones that show areas as familiar shapes that are distorted as little as possible.

1 World Maps

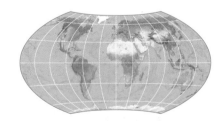

The Wagner VII projection is used for our world maps as it shows all the countries at their correct sizes relative to one another.

2 Continents

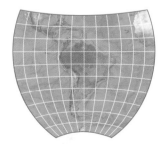

The Lambert Azimuthal Equal Area is used for continental maps. The shape distortion is relatively small and countries retain their correct sizes relative to one another.

3 Countries

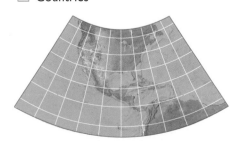

The Lambert Conformal Conic shows countries with as little distortion as possible. The angles from any point on the map are the same as they would be on the surface of the globe.

HOW MAPS ARE MADE

New technologies have revolutionized mapmaking. Computers and information from satellites have replaced drawing boards and drafting pens, and the process of creating new maps is now far easier. But mapmaking is still a skilled and often time-consuming process. Information about the world must be gathered, sorted, and checked. The cartographer must make decisions about the function of the map and what information to select in order to make it as clear as possible.

THE MAPPA MUNDI

Maps have been made for thousands of years. The 13th-century Mappa Mundi, meaning "known world" shows the Mediterranean Sea and the Don and Nile rivers. Asia is at the top, with Europe on the left, and Africa to the right. The oceans are shown as a ring surrounding the land. The map reflects a number of biblical stories.

HISTORICAL MAP MAKING

This detailed hand-drawn map of the southern coast of Spain was made in about 1750. The mountains are illustrated as small hills and the labels have been hand lettered.

For centuries, maps were drawn by hand. Very early maps were no more than a pictorial representation of what the surface of the ground looked like. Where there were hills, pictures were drawn to represent them. Later maps were drawn using information gathered by survey teams. They would carefully mark out and calculate the height of the land, the positions of towns, and other geographical features. As knowledge and techniques improved, maps became more accurate.

NEW TECHNIQUES

Computers make it easier to change map information and styles quickly. This map of the southern coast of Spain, made in 1997 has been made using digital terrain modeling (see below) and traditional cartography.

Today, cartographers have access to far more data about the Earth than in the past. Satellites collect and process information about its surface. This is called remote-sensed data. Further information may be drafted in the traditional way. Locations can be verified by GPS (Global Positioning Systems) linked to satellites. Computers are now widely used to combine different kinds of map information. Any computerized map is produced using a GIS (Geographical Information System).

MODERN MAP MAKING

1. **Measuring the Earth's surface**

The surface of the Earth is divided up into squares. Satellites take measurements of the height of the land in each square. The data collected can then be manipulated on a computer to produce a digital terrain model (DTM).

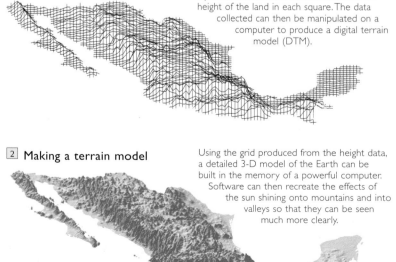

2. **Making a terrain model**

Using the grid produced from the height data, a detailed 3-D model of the Earth can be built in the memory of a powerful computer. Software can then recreate the effects of the sun shining onto mountains and into valleys so that they can be seen much more clearly.

3. **Adding detail to the land surface**

The height of the land can be shown using bands of color, or by contour lines, which are applied to the digitally created surface of the Earth. Color can also be used to show different kinds of vegetation, such as deserts, forests, and grasslands.

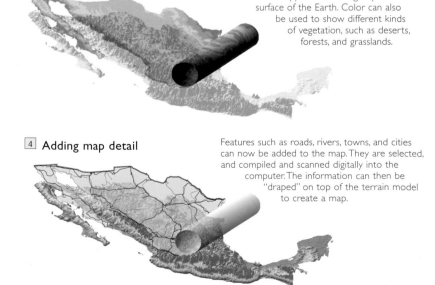

4. **Adding map detail**

Features such as roads, rivers, towns, and cities can now be added to the map. They are selected, and compiled and scanned digitally into the computer. The information can then be "draped" on top of the terrain model to create a map.

SHOWING INFORMATION ON A MAP

A map is a **selective diagram** of a place. It is the cartographer's job to decide what kind of information to show on a map. They can choose to highlight certain kinds of features – such as roads, rivers, and land height. They can also show other features such as sea depth, place names, and borders that would be impossible to see either on the ground or from a photograph. The information that can be shown on a map is influenced by a number of factors, most notably by its scale.

This is a satellite photograph of the harbor area of Rio de Janeiro in Brazil. Although you can see the bay and where most of the housing is, it is impossible to see roads or get any sense of the position of places relative to one another.

This is a map of the same area as you can see in the photograph. Much of the detail has been greatly simplified. Towns are named and marked; contours indicate the height of the land; and roads, railways and borders between districts have been added.

SCALE

To make a map of an area it needs to be greatly reduced in size. This is known as drawing to scale. The scale of the map shows us by how much the area has been reduced. The smaller the scale, the greater the area of land that can be shown on the map. There will be far less detail and the map will not be as accurate. The maps below show the different kinds of information that can be shown on maps of varying scales.

WAYS TO SHOW SCALE

When using a map to work out what areas or distances are in reality, we need to refer to the scale of that particular map. Map scales can be shown in several ways.

1 Representative fraction

One unit on the map would be equal to 1,000,000 units on the ground.

1:1,000,000

2 Linear scale

The line is marked off in units which represent the real distances of the map, given in both miles and kilometers.

SCALE BAR

0 km   10   20

0 miles   10   20

3 Statement of scale

It means that 1 inch on the map represents 1 mile on the ground.

1 inch represents 1 mile

LONDON 1:21,000,000

This small-scale map shows the position of London in relation to Europe. Very little detail can be seen at this scale – only the names of countries and the largest towns.

LONDON 1:5,500,000

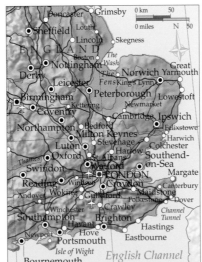

At a scale of 1 to 5,500,000 you can see the major road network in the southeast of the UK. Many towns are named and you can see the difference in size and status.

LONDON 1:900,000

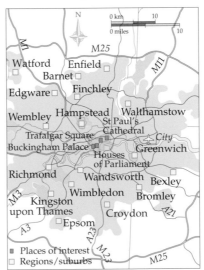

This map is at a much larger scale. You can see the major roads that lead out from London and the names of many suburbs, places of interest, and airports.

LONDON 1:12,500

This is a street map of central London. The streets are named, as are places of interest, train and subway stations. The scale is large enough to show plenty of detail.

READING MAPS

Maps use a unique visual language to convey a great deal of detailed information in a relatively simple form. Different features are marked out using special symbols and styles of print. These symbols are explained in the key to the map and you should always read a map alongside its key or legend. This page explains how to look for different features on the map and how to unravel the different layers of information that you can find on it.

PHYSICAL FEATURES

All the regional and country maps in this atlas are based on a model of the Earth's surface. The computer-generated relief gives an accurate picture of the surface of the land. Colors are used to show the relative heights of the land; green is for low-lying land, and yellows, browns, and grays are for higher land. Water features like streams, rivers, and lakes are also shown.

1 WATER FEATURES

On this map extract, the blue lines show a number of rivers, including the Salween and the Irrawaddy. The Irrawaddy forms a huge delta, splitting into many streams as it reaches the sea.

2 RELIEF

These mountains are in the north of Southeast Asia. The underlying relief on the map and the colored bands help you to see the height of the land.

HUMAN FEATURES

Maps also reveal a great deal about the human geography of an area. In addition to showing the location of towns and roads, different symbols can tell you more about the size of towns and the importance of a road. Borders between countries or regions can only be seen on a map.

3 BORDERS

Borders on the map are marked by a thick purple line. The boundary between Laos and Vietnam is in sparsely populated mountainous terrain, with the border generally running along a mountain range.

KEY TO MAP SYMBOLS

BOUNDARIES

▭▭▭	Full international border
▬ ▬ ▬	Disputed border

COMMUNICATION FEATURES

▬▬	Major road
▬▬	Minor road
▬▬	Railway
✈	International airport

DRAINAGE FEATURES

▬▬	Major river
◠	Minor river
◯	Lake
▦	Wetland

LANDSCAPE FEATURES

△	Mountain

POPULATED PLACES

●	Capital city
⊡	Greater than 500,000
◉	100,000–500,000
○	50,000–100,000
∘	Less than 50,000

NAMES

MYANMAR	Country
PARACEL ISLANDS (disputed by China, Taiwan & Vietnam)	Dependent territory
JAKARTA	Capital city
Sarawak	Cultural region
Chin Hills	Landscape feature
Puncak Jaya 16,535ft	Mountain/pass
Red River	River/lake
Java Sea	Sea feature

4 SETTLEMENTS

The symbol for a settlement can tell you its position, population, and political status. Most towns are shown by a circle or a square. These represent the size of their population. Where the dot for a town is colored red, this shows that it is a capital city such as Kuala Lumpur in Malaysia.

FINDING PLACES

Alphanumeric grid references

All the maps in this book are indexed using their alphanumeric grid reference – for example, G4. To find a place you must first look up its page number and then its grid reference. Read the letters and numbers off the bottom and side of the grid. Using rulers held at right angles to one another you will find the point where the lines meet. The place will be located within this square.

Latitude and longitude references

The lines of latitude and longitude are known as graticules. They are shown on the map as thin blue lines with the value of their latitude or longitude given as a blue number at the edge of the map.

LAND HEIGHT

	Above 13,120ft
	6,560–13,120ft
	3,280–6,560ft
	1,640–3,280ft
	820–1,640ft
	330–820ft
	0–330ft

SEA DEPTH

	0–820ft
	820–1,640ft
	1,640–3,280ft
	3280–6,560ft
	6,560–9,840ft
	9,840–13,120ft
	Below 13,120ft

CITIES AND TOWNS

⊡	Over 500,000 people
◉	100,000–500,000
○	50,000–100,000
∘	Less than 50,000

5 ROADS AND RAILROADS

a The major road and railroad links between Hue and Nha Trang hug the Vietnamese coast. A string of coastal towns is often connected by road and rail in this manner.

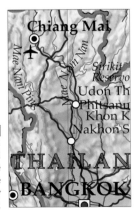

Chiang Mai, in northern **b** Thailand, is linked to the capital Bangkok to the south by railroad and road. At Chiang Mai, the mountains are too high for the railroad to continue, and only roads go north into Myanmar.

USING THE ATLAS

This Atlas has been designed to develop map-reading skills and to introduce readers to a wide range of different maps. It also provides a wealth of detailed geographic information about the world today. The Atlas is divided into four sections: **Learning Map Skills**; **The World About Us**, covering global geographic patterns; the **World Atlas**, dealing with the world's regions and an **Index**.

LEARNING MAP SKILLS

Maps show the Earth – which is three-dimensional – in just two dimensions. This section shows how maps are made; how different kinds of information are shown on maps; how to choose what to put on a map and the best way to show it. It also explains how to read the maps in this Atlas.

THE WORLD ABOUT US

These pages contain a series of world maps that show important themes, such as physical features, climate, life zones, population, and the world economy, on a global scale. They give a worldwide picture of concepts that are explored in more detail later in the book.

Text introduces themes and concepts in each spread.

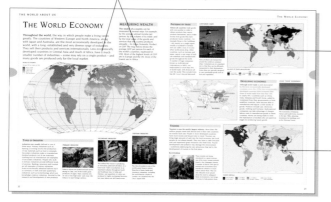

Photographs illustrate examples of places or topics shown on the main map.

World maps show geographic patterns on a global scale.

Introduction to projections: different projections and how they work.

Choosing the best projections: the map projections used in this book.

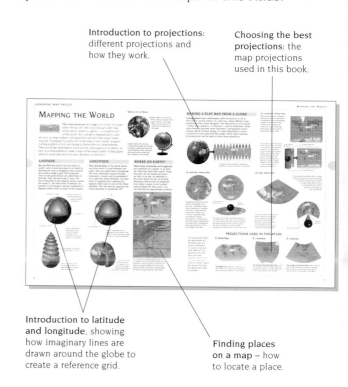

Introduction to latitude and longitude, showing how imaginary lines are drawn around the globe to create a reference grid.

Finding places on a map – how to locate a place.

CONTINENTAL MAPS

A cross section through the continent shows the relative height of certain features.

A detailed physical map of the continent shows major natural geographic features, including mountains, lakes and rivers.

Photographs and locator maps illustrate the main geographic regions and show you where they are.

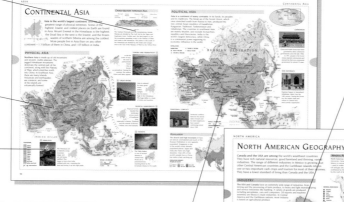

The industry map shows the main industrial towns and cities and the main industries in each continent. It also shows the wealth of each country relative to the rest of the world.

The political map of the continent shows country boundaries and country names.

CONTINENTAL GEOGRAPHY PAGES

Humans have colonized and changed all the continents except Antarctica. These pages show the factors which have affected this process: climate, the availability of resources such as coal, oil, and minerals, and varying patterns of land use. Mineral resources are directly linked to many industries, and most agriculture is governed both by the quality of the land and the climate.

The climate map shows the main types of climate across the continent and where the hottest and coldest, wettest and driest places are.

The mineral resources map shows where the most important reserves of minerals, including coal and precious metals, are found.

CONTINENTAL PAGES

These pages show the physical shape of each continent and the impact that humans have made on the natural landscape – building towns and roads and creating borders between countries. They show where natural features such as mountain ranges and rivers have created physical boundaries, and where humans have created their own political boundaries between states.

The land use map shows different types of land and the main kinds of farming that take place in each area.

REGIONAL MAPS

The main part of the Atlas contains detailed maps of countries and regions. Each of these is accompanied by a series of small thematic maps, models, and charts, which give information about the climate, where people live, how they use the land, the different kinds of industry, and important environmental issues.

TERRAIN MODEL

A computer-generated landscape model shows what the land really looks like. There are no roads or towns to mask the physical geography of the country or region. Mountain ranges, plains, and river basins can be easily seen.

COLOURED THUMB TAGS

Each section has its own colour code.

Learning Map Skills

The World About Us

North America

South America

Africa

Europe

Asia

Australasia and Oceania

Antarctica and the Arctic

CLIMATE MAPS

These maps show the temperature and rainfall patterns in January and July. Colored bands indicate temperatures: blue for low temperatures, orange for high ones. Rainfall is represented by black lines with a number giving the average amount of rain. These are called isohyets.

Isohyets show the rainfall patterns in inches per year. The areas between the lines are either over or under the figures shown on the isohyets.

The hottest areas are colored orange.

Here the rainfall is between 2 and 4 inches per year.

LOCATOR GLOBE

This shows the location of the country or region both within its continent and in relation to the rest of the world.

MAP GRID

Each main map has a grid. Using the grid will help you to find a place on the map. Grid references are expressed as letters (running from left to right across the frame), and numbers (running from the top to the bottom of the frame), for example, A-4, G-6. Everything on the map is referenced in the **Index** at the back of the book.

REGIONAL MAPS

The main map on each regional page shows the main topographical features of the area: the height of the land, the major roads, the rivers and lakes. It also shows the main cities and towns in the region – represented by different symbols.

Railway

LAND HEIGHT
- 6,560–13,120ft
- 3,280–6,560ft
- 1,640–3,280ft
- 820–1,640ft
- 330–820ft
- 0–330ft

SEA DEPTH
- 0–160ft
- 160–330ft
- 330–820ft
- 820–1,640ft
- 1,640–3,280ft
- Below 3,280ft

CITIES AND TOWNS
- ▣ Over 500,000 people
- ◉ 100,000–500,000
- ◎ 50,000–100,000
- ○ Less than 50,000

Longitude line

Latitude line Road

Major city

Minor town

Mountains

River

Compass rose used to indicate the orientation of each regional map.

THEMATIC MAPS

These small maps show various aspects of the geography of the country or region. The environment maps cover topics such as the effects of pollution. Industry, land use, and population maps locate the major industries, types of agriculture, and the distribution of population.

Diagrams are used to show the geographic information on the map statistically.

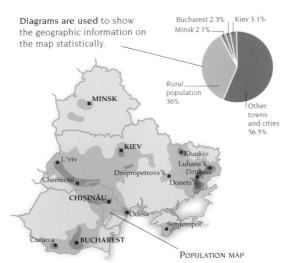

Bucharest 2.3%
Kiev 3.1%
Minsk 2.1%
Rural population 36%
Other towns and cities 56.5%

POPULATION MAP

INDUSTRY MAP

LAND USE MAP

LAND USE MAP

ENVIRONMENT MAP

THE PHYSICAL WORLD

This map shows the main physical features of the world: the mountain ranges, the great rivers and lakes, deserts, grassland plains, seas, and oceans. No human settlements are named on this map – only the physical or landscape features.

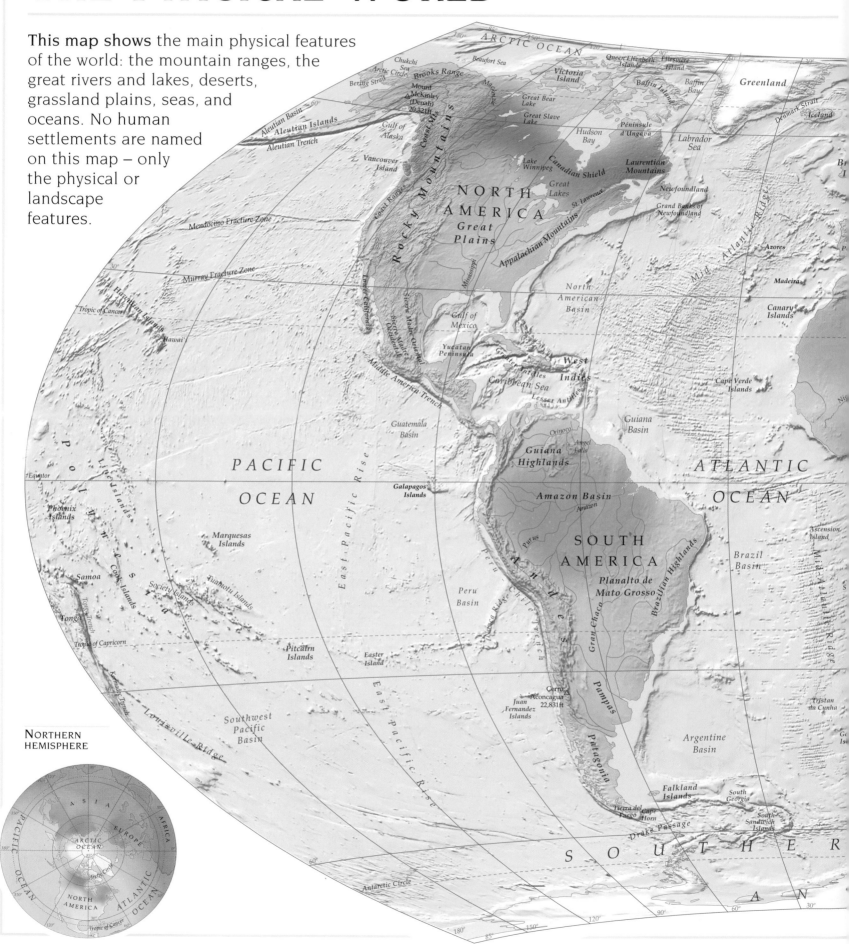

ARCTIC OCEAN

Chukchi Sea
Arctic Circle
Bering Strait
Beaufort Sea
Queen Elizabeth Islands
Ellesmere Island
Greenland

Brooks Range
Mount McKinley (Denali) 20,321ft
Mackenzie
Victoria Island
Baffin Island
Baffin Bay
Denmark Strait
Iceland

Aleutian Basin
Aleutian Islands
Aleutian Trench
Gulf of Alaska
Coast Mts
Great Bear Lake
Great Slave Lake
Hudson Bay
Péninsule d'Ungava
Labrador Sea

Vancouver Island
Coast Ranges
Lake Winnipeg
Canadian Shield
Laurentian Mountains
Newfoundland
Great Lakes

Mendocino Fracture Zone
NORTH AMERICA
Great Plains
St. Lawrence
Grand Banks of Newfoundland

Murray Fracture Zone
Rocky Mountains
Mississippi
Appalachian Mountains
North American Basin
Azores

Mid-Atlantic Ridge

Tropic of Cancer
Hawaiian Islands
Lower California
Sierra Madre Occidental
Gulf of Mexico
Madeira

Hawai'i
Sierra Madre Oriental
Yucatan Peninsula
West Indies
Canary Islands

Middle America Trench
Greater Antilles
Caribbean Sea
Lesser Antilles
Cape Verde Islands

Polynesia
Guatemala Basin
Guiana Basin

Equator
Orinoco
Angel Falls
Guiana Highlands

PACIFIC
Galapagos Islands
ATLANTIC

Phoenix Islands
OCEAN
Amazon Basin
OCEAN

Marquesas Islands
East Pacific Rise
Amazon
SOUTH AMERICA

Line Islands
Purus
Ascension Island

Samoa
Tuamotu Islands
Peru Basin
Planalto de Mato Grosso
Brazilian Highlands
Brazil Basin

Society Islands
Cook Islands
Andes
Peru-Chile Trench

Tonga
Tonga Trench
Gran Chaco

Tropic of Capricorn
Pitcairn Islands
Easter Island
Cerro Aconcagua 22,831ft
Pampas

Kermadec Trench
Nazca Ridge
Juan Fernandez Islands

Mid-Atlantic Ridge

East Pacific Rise
Argentine Basin
Tristan da Cunha

Louisville Ridge
Southwest Pacific Basin
Patagonia

Falkland Islands
South Georgia

Tierra del Fuego
Cape Horn
South Sandwich Islands

Drake Passage

Antarctic Circle
SOUTHERN
AN

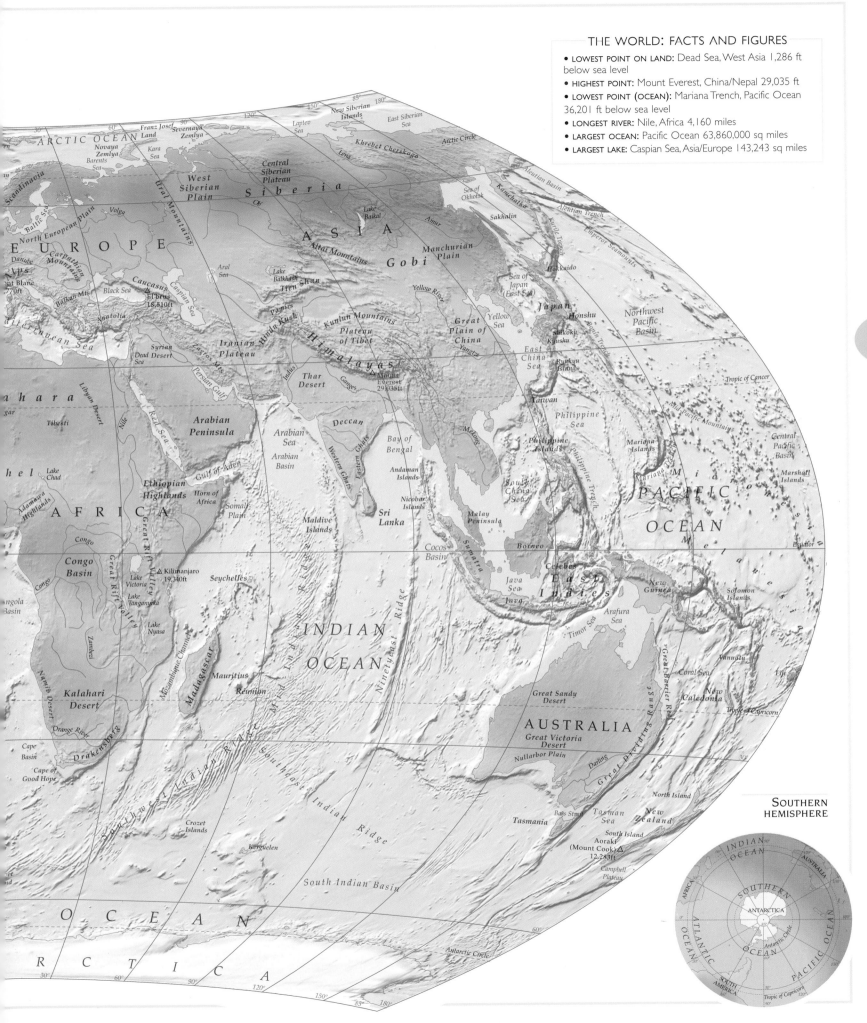

- **LOWEST POINT ON LAND:** Dead Sea, West Asia 1,286 ft below sea level
- **HIGHEST POINT:** Mount Everest, China/Nepal 29,035 ft
- **LOWEST POINT (OCEAN):** Mariana Trench, Pacific Ocean 36,201 ft below sea level
- **LONGEST RIVER:** Nile, Africa 4,160 miles
- **LARGEST OCEAN:** Pacific Ocean 63,860,000 sq miles
- **LARGEST LAKE:** Caspian Sea, Asia/Europe 143,243 sq miles

ARCTIC OCEAN

Franz Josef Land
Severnaya Zemlya
Novaya Zemlya
Barents Sea
Kara Sea
Laptev Sea
New Siberian Islands
East Siberian Sea
Arctic Circle

West Siberian Plain
Central Siberian Plateau
Siberia
Khrebet Cherskaga
Lena
Ob

Baltic Sea
North European Plain
Volga
Ural Mountains
ASIA
Lake Baikal
Amur
Sea of Okhotsk
Kamchatka
Aleutian Basin
Aleutian Trench

EUROPE
Danube
Carpathian Mountains
Alps
ont Blanc
770ft
Balkan Mts
Black Sea
Caucasus
Elbrus
18,510ft
Aral Sea
Caspian Sea
Lake Balkhash
Altai Mountains
Tien Shan
Gobi
Manchurian Plain
Sakhalin
Kurile Trench
Emperor Seamounts
Hokkaido

Anatolia
Syrian Desert
Dead Sea
Zagros Mts
Pamirs
Hindu Kush
Iranian Plateau
Kunlun Mountains
Plateau of Tibet
Himalayas
Yellow River
Great Plain of China
Yellow Sea
Sea of Japan (East Sea)
Japan
Honshu
Shikoku
Kyushu
Northwest Pacific Basin

hara
Tibesti
Libyan Desert
Nile
Red Sea
Persian Gulf
Thar Desert
Ganges
Mount Everest
29,035ft
Yangtze
East China Sea
Ryukyu Islands
Taiwan
Tropic of Cancer

gar
Mediterranean Sea
Arabian Peninsula
Deccan
Indus
Arabian Sea
Arabian Basin
Western Ghats
Eastern Ghats
Bay of Bengal
Andaman Islands
Philippine Sea
Philippine Islands
Mariana Islands
Mid-Pacific Mountains
Central Pacific Basin
Marshall Islands

hel
Lake Chad
Gulf of Aden
Ethiopian Highlands
Horn of Africa
Somali Plain
Maldive Islands
Sri Lanka
Nicobar Islands
Malay Peninsula
South China Sea
Mariana Trench
PACIFIC OCEAN

AFRICA
Adamawa Highlands
Congo
Congo Basin
Great Rift Valley
Lake Victoria
Kilimanjaro
19,340ft
Lake Tanganyika
Seychelles
Cocos Basin
Sumatra
Borneo
Celebes
East Indies
New Guinea
Solomon Islands

ngola Basin
Angola
Congo
Zambezi
Lake Nyasa
Mozambique Channel
Madagascar
Mauritius
Réunion
Mid Indian Ridge
Ninetyeast Ridge
INDIAN OCEAN
Java Sea
Java
Arafura Sea
Timor Sea
Coral Sea
Vanuatu
New Caledonia
Fiji

Namib Desert
Kalahari Desert
Orange River
Drakensberg
Cape Basin
Cape of Good Hope
Crozet Islands
Kerguelen
Southwest Indian Ridge
Southeast Indian Ridge
Great Sandy Desert
AUSTRALIA
Great Victoria Desert
Nullarbor Plain
Darling
Great Dividing Range
Great Barrier Reef
Tropic of Capricorn

South Indian Basin
Tasman Sea
North Island
New Zealand
Bass Strait
Tasmania
South Island
Aoraki (Mount Cook)
12,283ft
Campbell Plateau

OCEAN
RCTICA
Antarctic Circle

INDIAN OCEAN
AUSTRALIA
AFRICA
SOUTHERN OCEAN
ANTARCTICA
ATLANTIC OCEAN
PACIFIC OCEAN
SOUTH AMERICA
Antarctic Circle
Tropic of Capricorn

THE EARTH'S STRUCTURE

The shape and position of the Earth's oceans and continents make a familiar pattern. This is just the latest in a series of forms that the Earth has taken in the hundreds of millions of years since its creation. Massive forces inside the Earth cause the continents and oceans to move apart and together again, forming larger landmasses and then breaking them apart – a process known as plate tectonics. The movement is very slow – but over millions of years, the changes can be enormous.

DYNAMIC EARTH

The heart of the Earth is a solid core of iron surrounded by several layers of very hot – sometimes liquid – rock. The crust is relatively thin and is made up of a series of "plates" that fit closely together. Movement of the molten rock deep within the mantle of the Earth causes the plates to move, creating changes in the surface features of the Earth.

THE EARTH'S PLATES

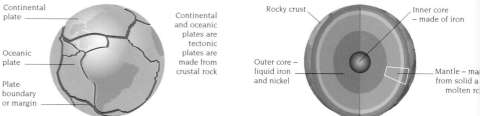

Continental plate

Oceanic plate

Plate boundary or margin

Continental and oceanic plates are tectonic plates are made from crustal rock

INSIDE THE EARTH

Rocky crust

Inner core – made of iron

Outer core – liquid iron and nickel

Mantle – ma from solid a molten ro

TECTONIC PLATES, VOLCANOES AND EARTHQUAKES

▲ Volcanic zone

▨ Earthquake zone on land

⇨ Direction of plate movement

〰 Rift valley

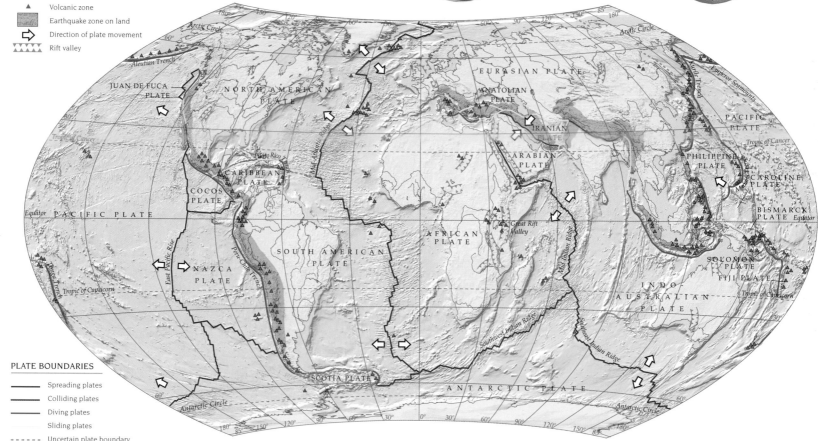

PLATE BOUNDARIES

─── Spreading plates

─── Colliding plates

─── Diving plates

─── Sliding plates

- - - Uncertain plate boundary

PLATE BOUNDARIES

The point where two plates meet is known as a plate boundary. As the Earth's plates move together or apart or slide alongside one another, the great forces that result cause great changes in the landscape. Mountains can be created, earthquakes occur, and there may be frequent volcanic eruptions.

SPREADING PLATES

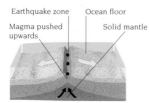

Earthquake zone   Ocean floor

Magma pushed upwards   Solid mantle

As plates move apart, magma rises through the outer mantle. When it cools, it forms new crust. The Mid-Atlantic Ridge is caused by spreading plates.

COLLIDING PLATES

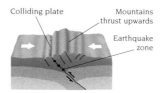

Colliding plate   Mountains thrust upwards

Earthquake zone

When two plates bearing landmasses collide with one another, the land is crumpled upward into high mountain peaks such as the Alps and the Himalayas.

DIVING PLATES

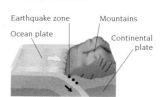

Earthquake zone   Mountains

Ocean plate   Continental plate

When an ocean-bearing plate collides with a continental plate it is forced downward under the other plate and into the mantle. Volcanoes occur along these boundaries.

SLIDING PLATES

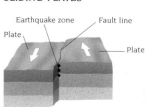

Earthquake zone   Fault line

Plate

Plate

As two plates slide past each other, great friction is set up along the fault line that lies between them. This can lead to powerful earthquakes.

SHAPING THE LANDSCAPE

The Earth's surface is made from solid rock or water. The land is constantly reshaped by external forces. Water flowing as rivers or in the oceans erodes and deposits material to create valleys and lakes and to shape coastlines. When water is built up and compressed into solid sheets of ice, it can erode more deeply, creating deeper, wider valleys. Wind also has a powerful effect: stripping away vegetation and transporting rock particles vast distances.

RIVERS

Most rivers have their sources in mountain areas. They flow fast through the mountains, eroding deep V-shaped valleys. As they reach flatter areas they begin to meander in great loops, both eroding and then depositing rock particles as they slow down.

GLACIERS

In cold areas, close to the poles or on mountaintops, snow is built up into rivers of ice called glaciers. They move slowly, eroding deep U-shaped valleys. When the glacier melts, ridges of eroded rock called moraines are left at the sides and end of the glacier.

SEA ACTION

The oceans change the landscape in two major ways. They batter cliffs, causing rock to break away and the land to retreat, and they carry eroded material along the coast, to make beaches and sandbars.

WIND

Wind can erode and break down rock into smaller boulders and stones and eventually into sand. Desert sand dunes are shaped by the force of the wind and vary from ripples to hills 650 ft high.

LANDSLIDES

Heavy rain can loosen soil and rock beneath the surface of slopes. As this moves, the top layers slip, forming heaps of rubble at the base of the slope.

THE WORLD'S OCEANS

Just over two-thirds of the Earth's surface is covered by water and more than 97% of this water is contained in the oceans. Movements within the Earth shape the ocean floor in the same way they do the land surface, creating mountain ranges, trenches, and plateaus, and changing the shape and size of the oceans. The difference between an ocean and a sea is simply its size; oceans are much bigger.

POLAR OCEANS

The Southern and Arctic Oceans contain large icebergs that have broken away from the ice shelf.

INDIAN OCEAN

The Indian Ocean covers about 20% of the world's surface. Ocean swells, starting deep in the Southern Ocean, often cause flooding in Sri Lanka and the Maldives.

PACIFIC OCEAN

The Pacific is the largest and deepest ocean in the world. It is surrounded by an arc of volcanoes, including Japan, Indonesia, and the Andes, known as the "Ring of Fire."

ATLANTIC OCEAN

The Atlantic Ocean was formed about 180 million years ago. The land that now forms Europe and Africa pulled apart from the Americas to create an ocean 1,900 miles wide.

CLIMATE AND LIFE ZONES

This map shows the different climates found around the world. Climates are particular combinations of temperature and humidity. Climates are affected by latitude, the height of the land, winds, and ocean currents. Climates can change, but not overnight. Weather is local and consists of short-term events such as thunderstorms, hurricanes, and blizzards.

HURRICANES

Hurricanes are violent cyclonic windstorms, driven by heat energy gathered from tropical seas. The Caribbean islands and the east coast of the US are particularly prone to hurricanes.

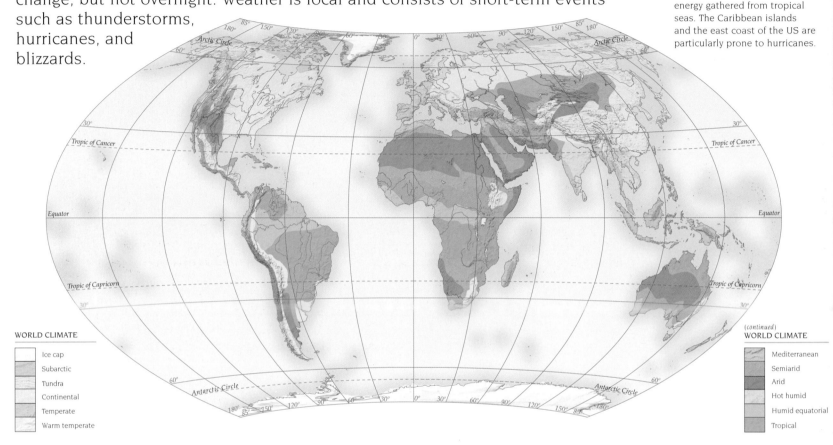

WORLD CLIMATE

	Ice cap
	Subarctic
	Tundra
	Continental
	Temperate
	Warm temperate

(continued) WORLD CLIMATE

	Mediterranean
	Semiarid
	Arid
	Hot humid
	Humid equatorial
	Tropical

WINDS

All over the Earth there are a series of large-scale wind patterns called prevailing winds that have a direct effect on weather and climate. The direction of the wind depends on global air pressure. Winds travel from areas of high pressure to areas of low pressure. The westerlies, polar easterlies, and northeast and southeast trade winds are all prevailing winds. The Equator is known for its light winds – referred to as the Doldrums. Changes in the direction of the prevailing winds can have a serious impact on the weather all over the planet.

WINDS

Cool wind

Warm wind

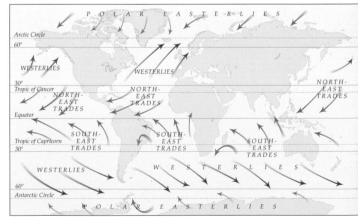

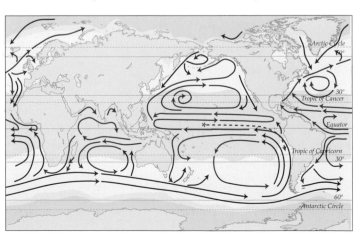

OCEAN CURRENTS

Ocean currents help distribute heat around the Earth and have a great influence on climate. Convection currents circulate massive amounts of warm and cold water around the oceans. Warm water is moved away from the tropics to higher latitudes and cold water is moved toward the tropics.

OCEAN CURRENTS AND SURFACE TEMPERATURES

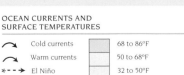

Cold currents	68 to 86°F
Warm currents	50 to 68°F
El Niño	32 to 50°F
	Seawater 28 to 32°F
	Sea ice (average) below 28°F

LIFE ZONES

The map below shows the Earth divided into different biomes – also called biogeographical regions. The combination of climate, the type of landscape, and the plants and animals that live there are used to classify a region. Similar biomes are found in very different places around the world.

POLAR REGIONS

The North and South Poles are permanently covered by ice. Only a few plants and animals can live here.

TUNDRA

Tundra is flat, cold, and dry, with few trees. Plants such as mosses and lichens grow close to the ground.

DESERTS
Very little rain falls in desert areas, whether they are hot deserts such as the Sahara or cold deserts like the Gobi.

CONIFEROUS FORESTS
Tall coniferous trees such as pine and spruce, with spines or needles instead of leaves, grow in the far north of Scandinavia, Canada, and the Russian Federation.

BROADLEAF FORESTS
Broadleaf or deciduous forests once covered temperate regions over most of the Northern Hemisphere. They contain trees of many varieties – all of which shed their leaves every year.

TEMPERATE RAINFORESTS
Evergreen, broadleaved trees need a warmer, wetter climate than deciduous trees. They are known as temperate rainforests.

MEDITERRANEAN
Close to the shores of the Mediterranean Sea, the vegetation consists mainly of herbs, shrubs, and drought-resistant trees.

BIOME TYPES
- Mountains
- Polar regions
- Tundra
- Tropical rainforests
- Dry woodlands
- Savannah
- Temperate grasslands

(continued)
BIOME TYPES
- Mediterranean
- Coniferous forests
- Temperate rainforests
- Broadleafs forests
- Cold deserts
- Hot deserts
- Wetlands

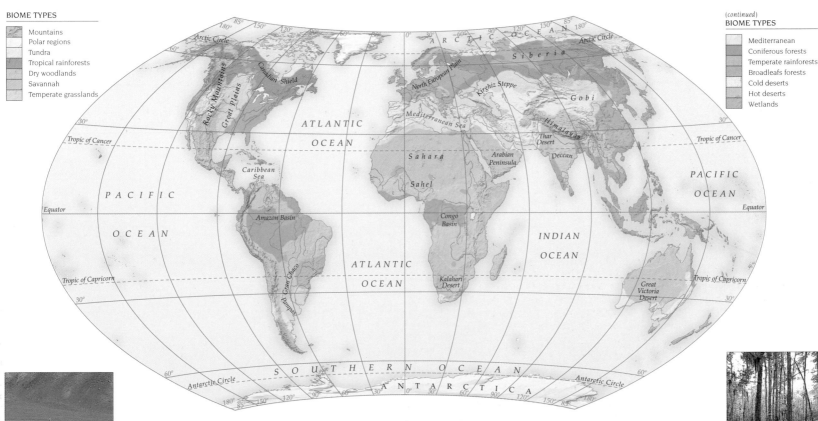

TEMPERATE GRASSLANDS
Grasslands cover the central areas of the continents. They are known in the middle latitudes as prairies, steppe, and pampas.

SAVANNA
The savanna consists of woodland interspersed with grassland. These regions lie between the tropical rain-forest and hot desert regions.

DRY WOODLANDS
Dry woodlands are found at the edge of grasslands. They contain small trees and shrubs adapted to dry conditions.

TROPICAL RAINFORESTS
Around the Equator, where temperatures are high and there is plenty of rain, tropical rainforests flourish. Trees grow continuously and are tall with huge, broad leaves.

WETLANDS
Low-lying swamps and marshes are known as wetlands. They are often home to a rich variety of animal, plant, and bird species.

WORLD POPULATION

Favelas – or shanty towns – have grown up around many South American cities because of overcrowding.

There are now nearly 6,500,000,000 people on Earth. The population has increased to nearly four times that of 1900. Before that date, the number of people increased slowly because people were born and died at similar rates. With improved living conditions, better medical care, and more efficient food production, more people survived to adulthood, and the population began to grow much faster. If growth continues at the present rate, the world's population is likely to reach 7.5 billion by the year 2020.

POPULATION STRUCTURES

Measuring the numbers of old and young people gives the age structure of a country or continent. If there are large numbers of young people and a high birthrate, the population is said to be youthful – as is the case in many African, Asian, and South American countries. If the birthrate is low but many people survive into old age, the population distribution is said to be aging – this is true of much of Europe, Japan, Canada, and the US. Extreme events like wars can distort the population, leading to a loss of population in certain age groups.

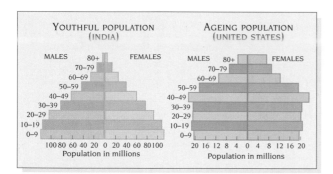

YOUTHFUL POPULATION
(INDIA)

MALES   80+   FEMALES
70–79
60–69
50–59
40–49
30–39
20–29
10–19
0–9
100 80 60 40 20 0 20 40 60 80 100
Population in millions

AGEING POPULATION
(UNITED STATES)

MALES   80+   FEMALES
70–79
60–69
50–59
40–49
30–39
20–29
10–19
0–9
20 16 12 8 4 0 4 8 12 16 20
Population in millions

POPULATION DENSITY

The main map (*center*) and the map below both show population density – the number of people who live in a given area. The map below shows the average population density per country. You can see that European countries and parts of Asia are very densely populated. The large map shows where people actually live. While the average population density in Brazil and Egypt is quite low, the coasts of Brazil and the areas close to the Nile River in Egypt are very densely populated.

DENSE POPULATION

Huge crowds near the Haora Bridge in Kolkata (Calcutta), India – one of the world's most densely populated cities.

POPULATION DENSITY

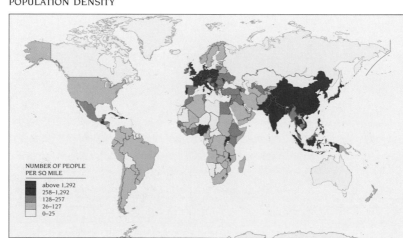

NUMBER OF PEOPLE
PER SQ MILE

above 1,292
258–1,292
128–257
26–127
0–25

SPARSE POPULATION

The cold north of Canada has one of the lowest population densities in the world. Some people live in extreme isolation, separated from others by lakes and forests.

URBAN GROWTH

The 20th century saw a huge increase in the number of people living in urban areas. This has led to more large cities and the development of some "super cities" such as Mexico City and Tokyo, each with more than 20 million people. In 1900, only about 10% of the population lived in cities. Now it is closer to 50% and soon the figure may be nearer two in three people. Some continents are far more "urbanized" than others: in South America nearly 80% of people live in cities, whereas in Africa the figure is only about 30%.

LEVELS OF URBANIZATION

URBANIZATION
- 90-100%
- 60-89%
- 40-59%
- 0-39%
- data unavailable

POPULATION GROWTH

The rate of population growth varies dramatically between the continents. Europe has a large population but it is increasing slowly. Africa is still sparsely populated, but in some countries such as Kenya, the population is growing very rapidly, increasing pressure on the land. China and India have the world's largest populations. Both countries now have laws designed to curb the birthrate.

CONTROLLING GROWTH

In 1980, fewer than 25% of women in less-developed countries used birth control. Education programs and more widely available contraceptives are thought to have doubled this figure. But many families still have no access to contraception.

AN AGING POPULATION

In some countries, a low birthrate and an increasingly long-lived elderly population have greatly increased the ratio of old people to younger people, putting a strain on health and social services. For example, in Japan, most people can now expect to live to at least 80 years of age.

POPULATION DENSITY
(People per sq mile)
- Below 3
- 3–13
- 13–29
- 30–51
- 52–130
- 131–260
- 261–520
- Above 520

BIRTHRATE

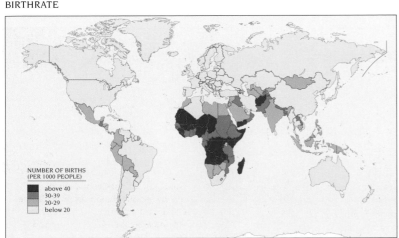

NUMBER OF BIRTHS
(PER 1000 PEOPLE)
- above 40
- 30-39
- 20-29
- below 20

LIFE EXPECTANCY

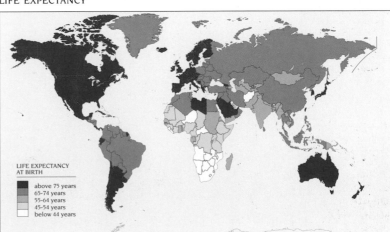

LIFE EXPECTANCY AT BIRTH
- above 75 years
- 65-74 years
- 55-64 years
- 45-54 years
- below 44 years

THE WORLD ECONOMY

Throughout the world, the way in which people make a living varies greatly. The countries of Western Europe and North America, along with Japan and Australia, are the most economically developed in the world, with a long- established and very diverse range of industries. They sell their products and services internationally. Less economically developed countries in Central Asia and much of Africa have a much smaller number of industries – some may rely on a single product – and many goods are produced only for the local market.

MEASURING WEALTH

The wealth of a country can be measured in several ways: for example, by the average annual income per person; by the volume of its trade; and by the total value of the goods and services that the country produces annually – its Gross Domestic Product or GDP. The map below shows the average GDP per person for each of the world's countries, expressed in US$. Most of the highest levels of GDP are in Europe and the US; most of the lowest are in Africa.

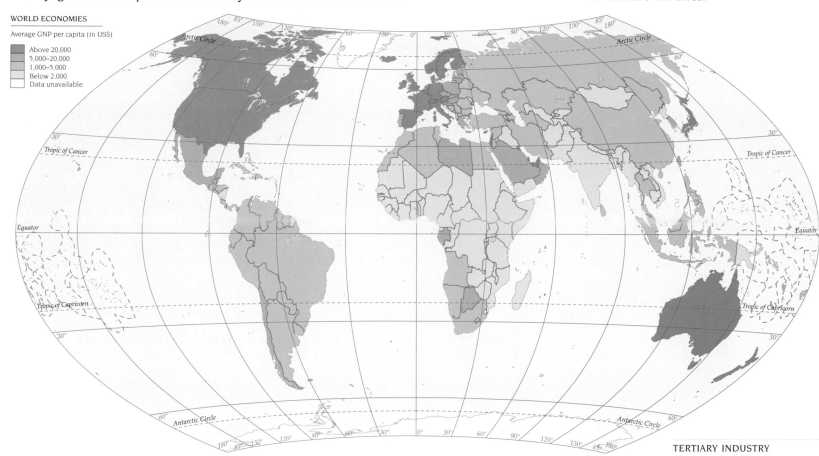

WORLD ECONOMIES

Average GNP per capita (in US$)

- Above 20,000
- 5,000–20,000
- 1,000–5,000
- Below 2,000
- Data unavailable

TYPES OF INDUSTRY

Industries are usually defined in one of three ways. Primary industries such as farming or mining involve the production of raw materials such as food or minerals. Secondary industries make or manufacture finished products out of raw materials: clothing and car manufacture are examples of secondary industries. People who work in tertiary industries provide different kinds of services. Banking, insurance, and tourism are all examples of tertiary industries. Some economically advanced nations such as Germany and the US now have quaternary industries, such as biotechnology which are knowledge-creation industries, devoted to the research and development of new products.

PRIMARY INDUSTRY

Tobacco leaves are picked and laid out for drying in Cuba, one of the world's great producers of cigars. Many countries rely on one or two high-value "cash crops" like tobacco to earn foreign currency.

SECONDARY INDUSTRY

This skilled Thai weaver is producing an intricately patterned silk fabric on a hand loom. Fabric manufacture is an important industry throughout South and Southeast Asia. In India and Pakistan, vast quantities of cotton are produced in highly mechanized factories, but many fabrics are still hand woven.

TERTIARY INDUSTRY

The City of London is one of the world's great finance centers. Branches of many banks and insurance companies, including the world-famous Lloyds of London, are clustered into the City's "square mile."

PATTERNS OF TRADE

Almost all countries trade goods with one another in order to obtain products they cannot produce themselves, and to make money from goods they have produced. Some countries – for example those in the Caribbean – rely mainly on a single export, usually a food or mineral, and can suffer a loss of income when world prices drop. Other countries, such as Germany and Japan, export a vast range of both raw materials and manufactured goods throughout the world. A number of huge companies, known as multinational corporations, are responsible for more than 70% of world trade, with divisions all over the world. They include firms like Exxon, Coca Cola, and Microsoft.

CONTAINER SHIPS

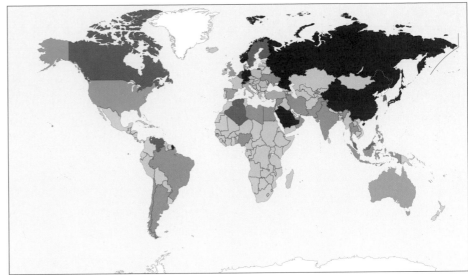

Many products are transported around the world on container ships. Containers are of a standard size so that they can be efficiently transported to their destinations. Some ships are specially designed to carry perishable goods such as fruit and vegetables.

BALANCE OF TRADE (MILLIONS US$)
Surplus: Over 30,000; 10,000–29,999; 1,000–9,999; 0–999
Deficit: 0–999; 1,000–9,999; 10,000–29,999; Over 30,000; Data unavailable

DEVELOPING ECONOMIES

Although world trade is still dominated by the more economically developed countries, since the 1970s, less economically developed countries have increased their share of world trade from less than 10% to nearly 30%. Countries such as China, India, Malaysia, and South Korea, aided by investment from their governments or from wealthier countries, have become able to manufacture and export a wide variety of goods. These products include cars, electronics, clothing, and footwear. Multinational companies can take advantage of cheaper labor costs to manufacture goods in these countries. Moves are being made to limit the exploitation of workers who are paid very low wages for producing luxury goods.

ASIAN 'TIGER' ECONOMIES

The economies of Malaysia, Taiwan, and South Korea boomed in the late 1980s, attracting investment for buildings such as the Petronas Towers (*above*).

TOURISM

Tourism is now the world's largest industry. More than 700 million people travel both abroad and in their own countries as tourists each year. People in more developed countries have more money and leisure time to travel. Tourism can bring large amounts of cash into the local economy, but local people do not always benefit. They may have to take low-paid jobs and experience great intrusions into their lives. Tourist development and pollution may damage the environment – sometimes destroying the very attractions that led to the development of tourism in the first place.

ECOTOURISM

These tourists are being introduced to a giant tortoise, one of the many unique animals found in the Galapagos Islands. A number of places with special animals and ecosystems have introduced programs to teach visitors about them. This not only educates people about the need to safeguard these environments, but brings in money to help protect them.

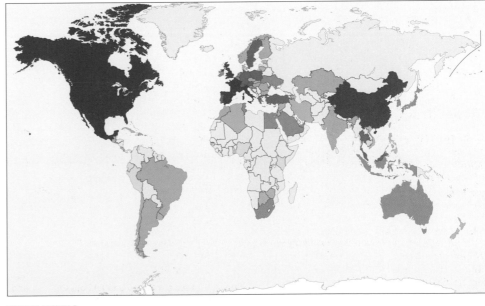

TOURIST ARRIVALS
Over 20 million; 10–20 million; 5–10 million; 2.5–5 million; 1–2.5 million; 700,000–1 million; Under 700,000; Data unavailable

BORDERS AND BOUNDARIES

There are more countries in the world today than ever before – over 190 – whereas in 1950, there were only 82. Since then, many former European colonies and Soviet states have become independent. The establishment of borders for each of these countries has often been the subject of disagreement.

Military borders
At the end of wars, new borders are often drawn up between the countries – frequently along cease-fire lines. They may remain there for many years. At the end of the Korean War in 1953, North and South Korea were divided close to the 38° line of latitude. This border has remained heavily fortified.

Enclaves
If part of a country's territory has become separated from the rest of the country, and is surrounded by foreign territory, it is called an enclave. Kaliningrad is part of the Russian Federation, but is cut off from it by Lithuania and Belarus.

River borders
Over one-sixth of the world's national borders are formed by rivers. Long stretches of the Danube form natural borders in southeastern Europe.

Long borders
The border between the USA and Canada is the second longest continuous border in the world. It cuts through the center of the Great Lakes. To the west of the Great Lakes, the border runs along the 49° line of latitude.

Mountain borders
Mountain ranges such as the Pyrenees, Alps and Himalayas form natural borders between many countries. In the Andes, border disputes between Chile and Argentina centered on finding the highest point in the mountain range that divided them.

Straight line borders
The borders of many countries in Africa and other former colonial territories are straight lines. This was the simplest solution for colonial administrators, who often knew little of the country's geography or population.

Lake boundaries
Countries which lie next to lakes usually fix their borders in the middle of the lake. Complicated agreements between colonial powers led to the awkward division of Lake Nyasa in Africa.

Territorial disputes
There are still many disputed territories and borders. One of the most serious territorial disputes is between India and Pakistan over Jammu and Kashmir, which has led to three wars since 1947.

THE ATLAS
OF THE
WORLD

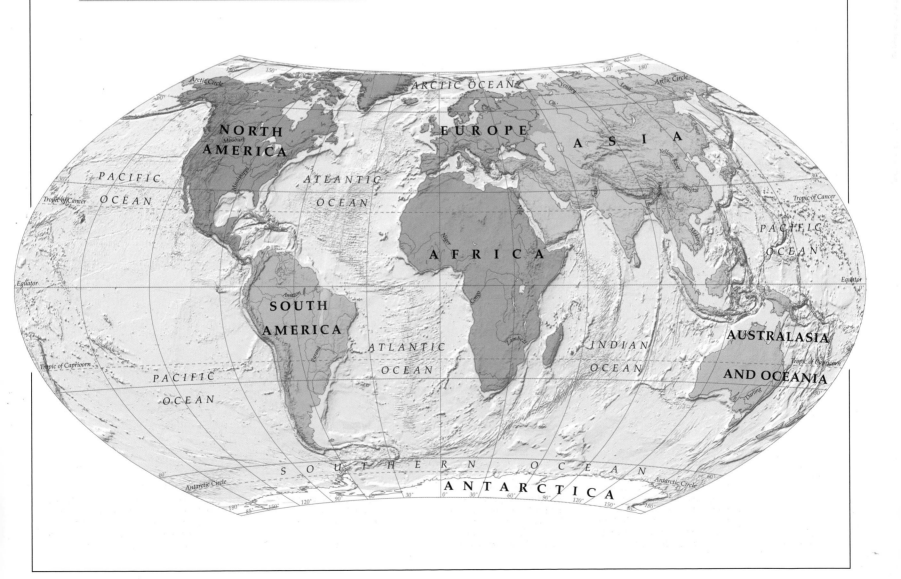

THE NATIONS OF THE WORLD

The world is divided into 194 independent countries, and about 60 overseas territories or dependencies. The largest country is the Russian Federation covering 6,592,735 sq miles; the smallest is Vatican City in Rome, with an area of 0.17 sq miles.

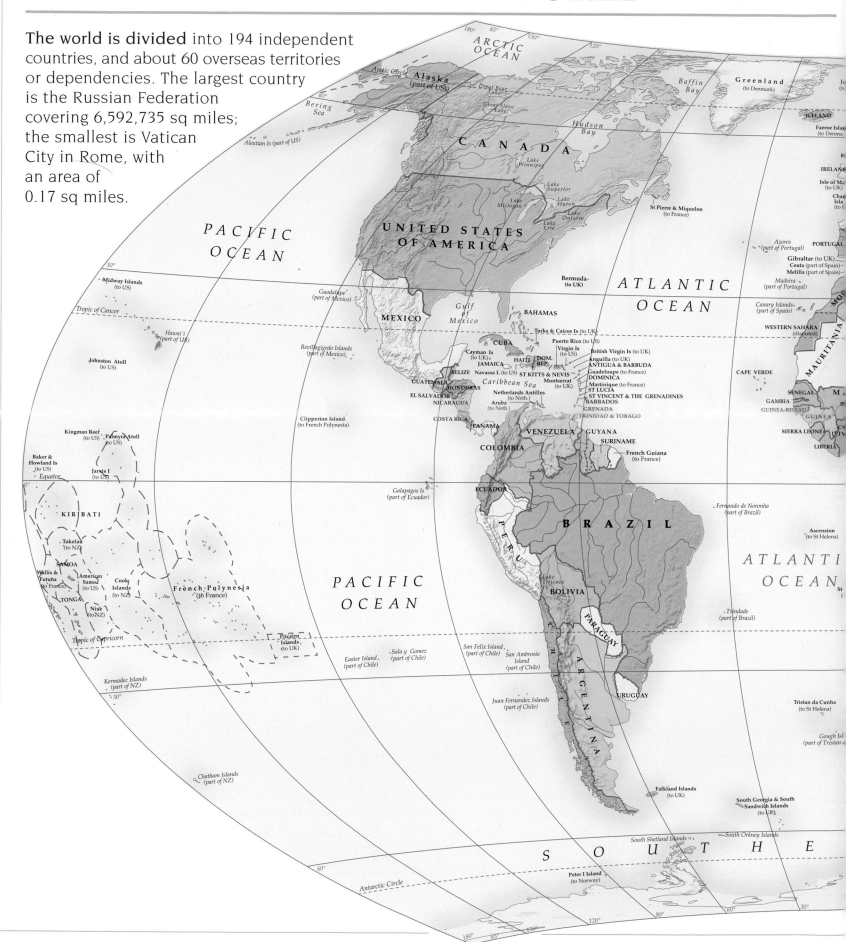

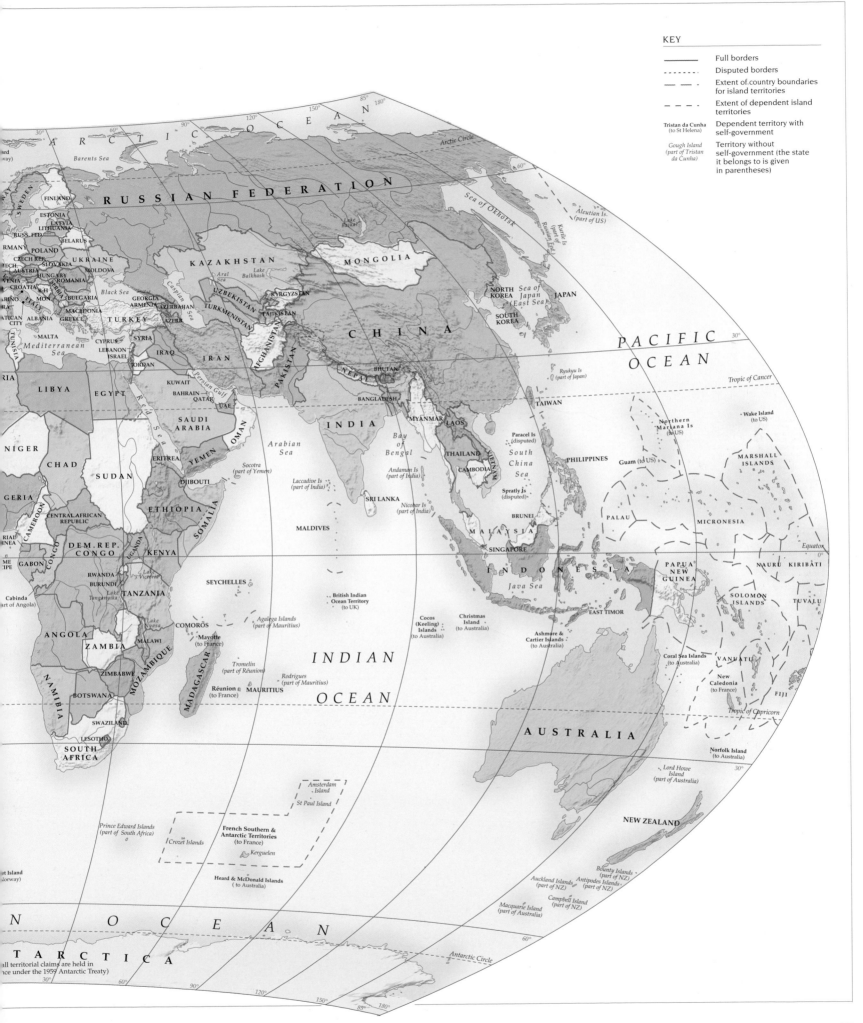

KEY

——————	Full borders
··········	Disputed borders
— · — · —	Extent of country boundaries for island territories
— — — —	Extent of dependent island territories
Tristan da Cunha (to St Helena)	Dependent territory with self-government
Gough Island (part of Tristan da Cunha)	Territory without self-government (the state it belongs to is given in parentheses)

ARCTIC OCEAN

Barents Sea

SWEDEN
FINLAND
ESTONIA
LATVIA
LITHUANIA
RUSS. FED.
BELARUS
POLAND
GERMANY
CZECH REP.
SLOVAKIA
AUSTRIA
HUNGARY
UKRAINE
MOLDOVA
CROATIA
ROMANIA
SAN MARINO
ITALY
MON.
BULGARIA
MACEDONIA
VATICAN CITY
ALBANIA
GREECE
MALTA
Mediterranean Sea
TUNISIA

RUSSIAN FEDERATION

Arctic Circle

Sea of Okhotsk

Aleutian Is. (part of US)

Kurile Is (part of Russian Fed.)

KAZAKHSTAN
Aral Sea
Lake Balkhash
MONGOLIA

Lake Baikal

Black Sea
Caspian Sea
GEORGIA
ARMENIA AZERBAIJAN
TURKEY
AZERB.
CYPRUS
SYRIA
LEBANON
ISRAEL
JORDAN
IRAQ
IRAN
UZBEKISTAN
KYRGYZSTAN
TURKMENISTAN
TAJIKISTAN
AFGHANISTAN
PAKISTAN

NORTH KOREA
Sea of Japan (East Sea)
JAPAN
SOUTH KOREA

CHINA

PACIFIC OCEAN

LIBYA
EGYPT
KUWAIT
BAHRAIN QATAR
UAE
SAUDI ARABIA
OMAN
Red Sea
Persian Gulf

NEPAL BHUTAN

Ryukyu Is (part of Japan)

Tropic of Cancer

BANGLADESH
INDIA
MYANMAR
LAOS
THAILAND
VIETNAM
CAMBODIA

TAIWAN

NIGER
CHAD
SUDAN
ERITREA
YEMEN
DJIBOUTI
ETHIOPIA
SOMALIA

Socotra (part of Yemen)
Arabian Sea
Bay of Bengal

Laccadive Is. (part of India)

Andaman Is (part of India)

Nicobar Is (part of India)

SRI LANKA

South China Sea

Paracel Is (disputed)

PHILIPPINES

Guam (to US)

Wake Island (to US)

Northern Mariana Is (to US)

MARSHALL ISLANDS

MALDIVES

Spratly Is (disputed)

BRUNEI
MALAYSIA
SINGAPORE

PALAU

MICRONESIA

CAMEROON
CENTRAL AFRICAN REPUBLIC
EQUATORIAL GUINEA
GABON
CONGO
DEM. REP. CONGO
UGANDA
KENYA
RWANDA
BURUNDI
TANZANIA
Lake Victoria
Lake Tanganyika
Cabinda (part of Angola)

SEYCHELLES

British Indian Ocean Territory (to UK)

INDONESIA
Java Sea

PAPUA NEW GUINEA

Equator

NAURU KIRIBATI

SOLOMON ISLANDS

TUVALU

Agalega Islands (part of Mauritius)

COMOROS
Mayotte (to France)
MADAGASCAR
ANGOLA
ZAMBIA
MALAWI
MOZAMBIQUE
ZIMBABWE
NAMIBIA
BOTSWANA
SWAZILAND
LESOTHO
SOUTH AFRICA
Lake Nyasa

Tromelin (part of Réunion)
Réunion (to France)
MAURITIUS
Rodrigues (part of Mauritius)

INDIAN OCEAN

Cocos (Keeling) Islands (to Australia)

Christmas Island (to Australia)

EAST TIMOR

Ashmore & Cartier Islands (to Australia)

Coral Sea Islands (to Australia)

VANUATU

New Caledonia (to France)

FIJI

Tropic of Capricorn

AUSTRALIA

Norfolk Island (to Australia)

Lord Howe Island (part of Australia)

Amsterdam Island
St Paul Island

Prince Edward Islands (part of South Africa)
Crozet Islands
French Southern & Antarctic Territories (to France)
Kerguelen

NEW ZEALAND

Heard & McDonald Islands (to Australia)

Bounty Islands (part of NZ)
Auckland Islands (part of NZ)
Antipodes Islands (part of NZ)
Campbell Island (part of NZ)
Macquarie Island (part of Australia)

OCEAN

Bouvet Island (to Norway)

ANTARCTICA

(all territorial claims are held in abeyance under the 1959 Antarctic Treaty)

Antarctic Circle

CONTINENTAL NORTH AMERICA

North America is the world's third largest continent, stretching from icy Greenland to the tropical Caribbean. The first people came from Asia more than 20,000 years ago. Their descendants spread across the continent, ate fish, meat, and wild and cultivated plants, and developed a wide variety of cultures and languages. About 500 years ago, immigrants from Europe, Africa, and Asia began to arrive in North America, bringing their own languages and cultures to the "New World."

CROSS-SECTION THROUGH NORTH AMERICA

In the west the land rises from the Pacific Ocean to the coastal ranges and the Rocky Mountains. Farther east, the continent flattens into the Great Plains and the Great Lakes – gouged out by glaciers at the end of the last Ice Age. The Appalachian Mountains are older than the Rockies, and are very worn down.

PHYSICAL NORTH AMERICA

The high peaks of the Rocky Mountains of Canada and the US tower above the lower ranges of the western coasts. These ranges stretch from the icy north of Alaska, south to Mexico and Central America. The heart of the continent is flatter, and much of it is drained by the mighty Mississippi-Missouri river system.

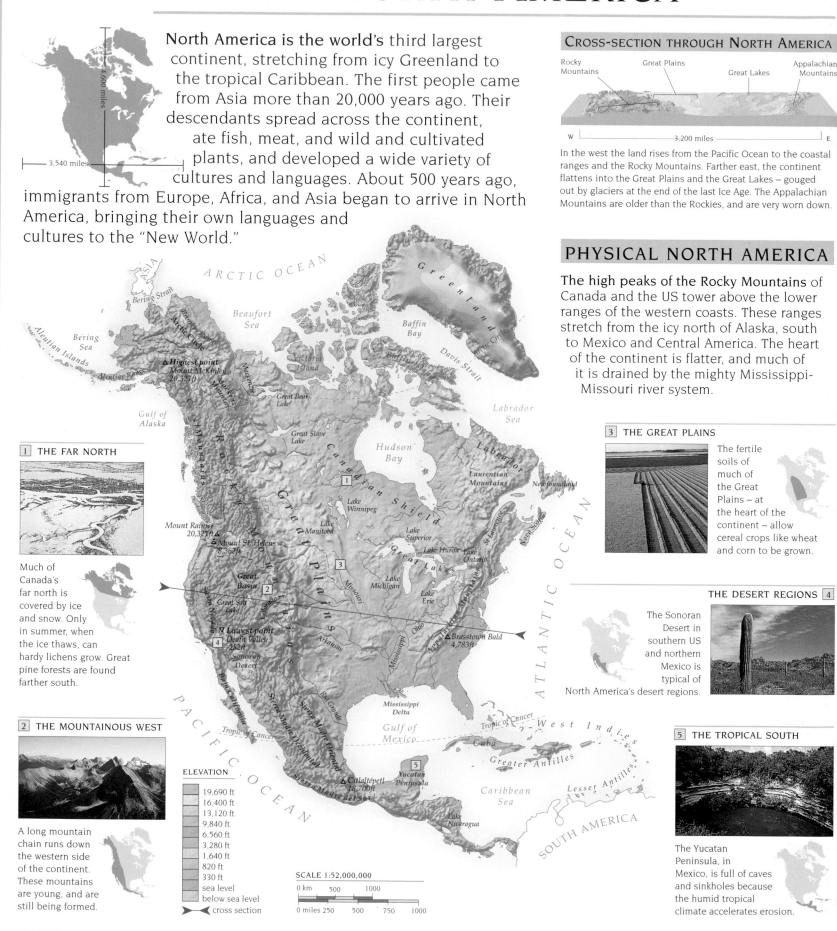

1 THE FAR NORTH

Much of Canada's far north is covered by ice and snow. Only in summer, when the ice thaws, can hardy lichens grow. Great pine forests are found farther south.

2 THE MOUNTAINOUS WEST

A long mountain chain runs down the western side of the continent. These mountains are young, and are still being formed.

3 THE GREAT PLAINS

The fertile soils of much of the Great Plains – at the heart of the continent – allow cereal crops like wheat and corn to be grown.

THE DESERT REGIONS 4

The Sonoran Desert in southern US and northern Mexico is typical of North America's desert regions.

5 THE TROPICAL SOUTH

The Yucatan Peninsula, in Mexico, is full of caves and sinkholes because the humid tropical climate accelerates erosion.

ELEVATION

19,690 ft
16,400 ft
13,120 ft
9,840 ft
6,560 ft
3,280 ft
1,640 ft
820 ft
330 ft
sea level
below sea level
cross section

SCALE 1:52,000,000

0 km   500   1000

0 miles 250   500   750   1000

28

POLITICAL NORTH AMERICA

The US, Canada, and Mexico are all federal countries. This means that political power is shared between the national government and the state or provincial governments. Canada and the US are democracies with a long history of freedom and equal rights. Governments in the countries south of the US have been less stable, often ruled by dictators or harsh regimes. Many people have suffered for their political beliefs. During the 1960s and 70s many of the Caribbean islands gained independence from their European colonial rulers.

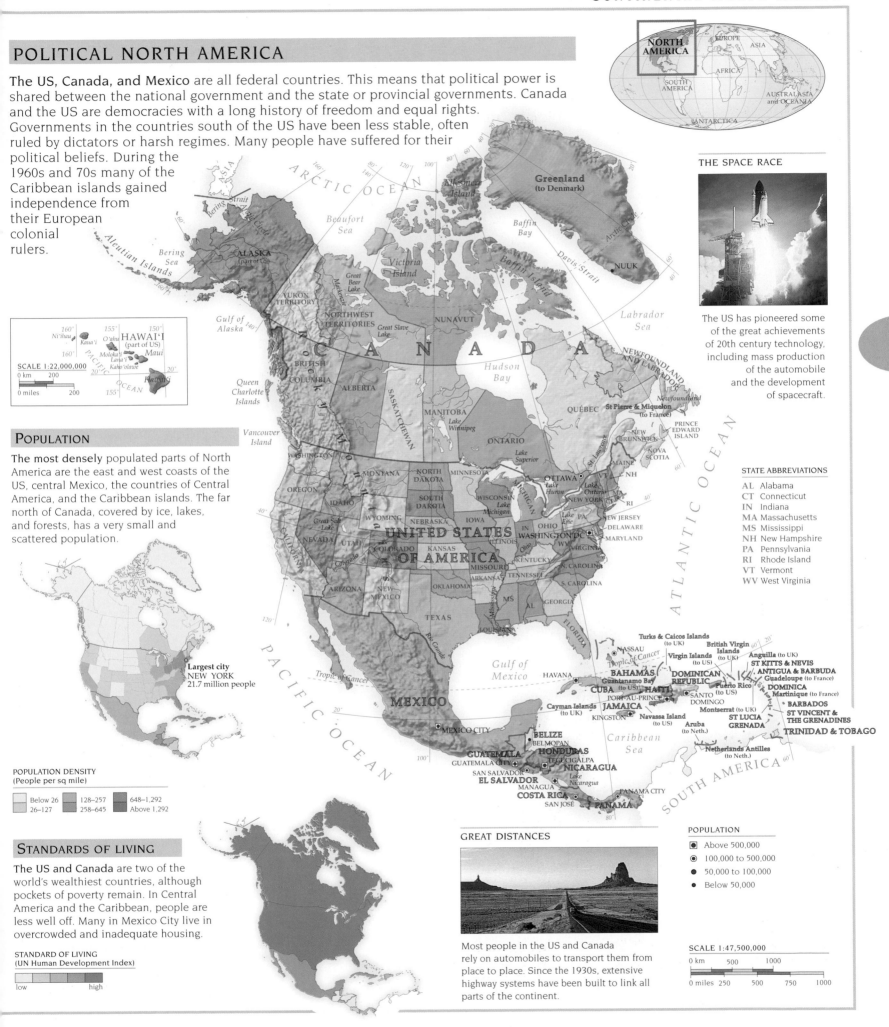

THE SPACE RACE

The US has pioneered some of the great achievements of 20th century technology, including mass production of the automobile and the development of spacecraft.

POPULATION

The most densely populated parts of North America are the east and west coasts of the US, central Mexico, the countries of Central America, and the Caribbean islands. The far north of Canada, covered by ice, lakes, and forests, has a very small and scattered population.

Largest city
NEW YORK
21.7 million people

POPULATION DENSITY
(People per sq mile)

Below 26	128–257	648–1,292
26–127	258–645	Above 1,292

STANDARDS OF LIVING

The US and Canada are two of the world's wealthiest countries, although pockets of poverty remain. In Central America and the Caribbean, people are less well off. Many in Mexico City live in overcrowded and inadequate housing.

STANDARD OF LIVING
(UN Human Development Index)

low   high

STATE ABBREVIATIONS

AL Alabama
CT Connecticut
IN Indiana
MA Massachusetts
MS Mississippi
NH New Hampshire
PA Pennsylvania
RI Rhode Island
VT Vermont
WV West Virginia

GREAT DISTANCES

Most people in the US and Canada rely on automobiles to transport them from place to place. Since the 1930s, extensive highway systems have been built to link all parts of the continent.

POPULATION

◉ Above 500,000
◉ 100,000 to 500,000
● 50,000 to 100,000
• Below 50,000

SCALE 1:47,500,000

0 km   500   1000

0 miles 250   500   750   1000

NORTH AMERICAN GEOGRAPHY

Canada and the US are among the world's wealthiest countries. They have rich natural resources, good farmland, and thriving, varied industries. The range of different industries in Mexico is growing, but other Central American countries and the Caribbean islands rely on one or two important cash crops and tourism for most of their incomes. They have a lower standard of living than the US and Canada.

INDUSTRY

The US and Canada have an extremely wide range of industries, from mining and the processing of farm produce, to heavy and light manufacturing and service industries like banking. A variety of goods are produced, including airplanes, cars, and computers. Oil exports and machine assembly are Mexico's main industries. In Central America and the Caribbean nations, most industry is based on agricultural produce.

MINERAL RESOURCES

North America still has large amounts of mineral resources. Canada has important nickel reserves, Mexico is renowned for its silver, and bauxite – used to make aluminum – is found in Jamaica. Oil and gas are plentiful, particularly in the Arctic northwest by the Beaufort Sea, and farther south by the Gulf of Mexico.

MINERAL RESOURCES
- Bauxite
- Copper
- Iron
- Nickel
- Phosphates
- Silver
- Uranium
- Oil/gas field
- Coal field

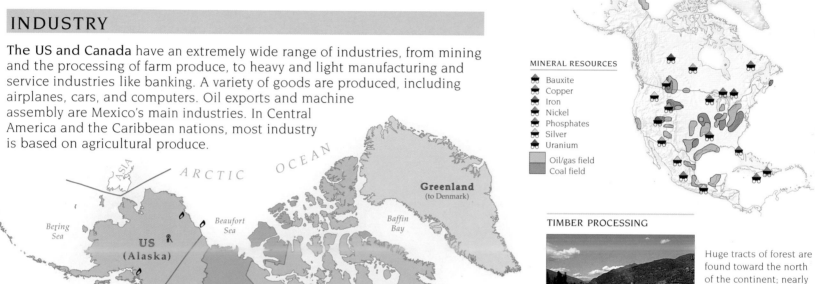

INDUSTRY
- ✈ Aerospace
- 🍺 Brewing
- 🚗 Car/vehicle manufacturing
- ⚗ Chemicals
- ⛏ Coal
- Defense
- ⚙ Engineering
- 🎥 Film industry
- S Finance
- Food processing
- 🖥 High-tech industry
- Iron and steel
- ⚫ Oil and gas
- Pharmaceuticals
- Printing and publishing
- ☢ Research and development
- Shipbuilding
- Textiles
- 🌲 Timber processing

GNI per capita (US$)
- Below 1,999
- 2,000–4,999
- 5,000–9,999
- 10,000–19,999
- 20,000–24,999
- Above 25,000
- • Industrial center

TIMBER PROCESSING

Huge tracts of forest are found toward the north of the continent; nearly 30% of Canada is covered by forest. Timber is processed to make paper in cities such as Portland and Vancouver.

HIGH-TECH INDUSTRY

The Santa Clara Valley, just south of San Francisco, is also known as Silicon Valley because of the number of firms producing computer hardware and software and microelectronics that have set up in the area.

FOOD PROCESSING

Jamaica has been famous for its rum since the 16th century. Syrup is extracted from sugarcane, which is then fermented to make rum.

MANUFACTURING

Mexico has many car part assembly plants. Labour costs in Mexico are low, making it cheap to assemble car parts here

CLIMATE

Much of northern Canada lies within the Arctic Circle and is permanently covered by ice or the sparse vegetation known as tundra. Southern Canada and much of central US have a continental climate, with hot summers and cold winters. The southern parts of the US, Central America, and the Caribbean have a hot, humid tropical climate. The Caribbean and the eastern and central states of the US often experience hurricane-force winds, waterspouts, and tornadoes.

EXTREME WEATHER EVENTS

Symbols indicate climatic extremes

CLIMATE
Ice cap
Tundra
Subarctic
Cool continental
Warm temperate
Mediterranean
Semiarid
Arid
Humid equatorial
Tropical
Hot humid

Coldest place
NORTHICE (Greenland)
Temp. -87°F

Wettest place
HENDERSON LAKE (BC, Canada)
Annual rainfall 262 in

Hottest place
DEATH VALLEY (CA, USA)
Temp. 135°F

Driest place
BATAQUES (Mexico)
Annual rainfall 1.2 in

NORTH AMERICA'S HOTTEST PLACE

Death Valley in California is the hottest and driest place in the US. Strong, dry winds sweep through the valley, constantly reshaping the sand and salt deposits that cover its floor.

LAND USE AND AGRICULTURE

On the Great Plains and prairies of the US and Canada, vast quantities of cereal crops, including corn and wheat, grow in the fertile soils. Cattle are also raised on great ranches throughout these regions and on the foothills of the Rocky Mountains. In California, vegetables and fruits are grown with the aid of irrigation. Bananas, coffee, and sugarcane are grown for export in Central America and the Caribbean, while sorghum and corn are grown as subsistence crops.

BANANA PLANTATION

Banana plantations are common in the Caribbean and Central America. The fruit is grown for local consumption and for export to the US and Europe, where they are valued for their flavor and nutritional qualities.

FISHING

The Grand Banks off the eastern coast of Canada were once home to almost limitless fish stocks. Overfishing has reduced the number of fish to very low levels. Quotas limiting the numbers of fish caught help the numbers to rise.

LAND USE AND AGRICULTURE
Cattle
Poultry
Pigs
Reindeer
Sheep
Bananas
Cereals
Citrus fruits
Coffee
Corn
Cotton
Fishing
Fruit
Peanuts
Rice
Shellfish
Soybeans
Sugarcane
Timber
Tobacco
Vineyards

Cropland
Desert
Forest
Ice cap
Mountain region
Pasture
Tundra
Wetland
Major conurbation

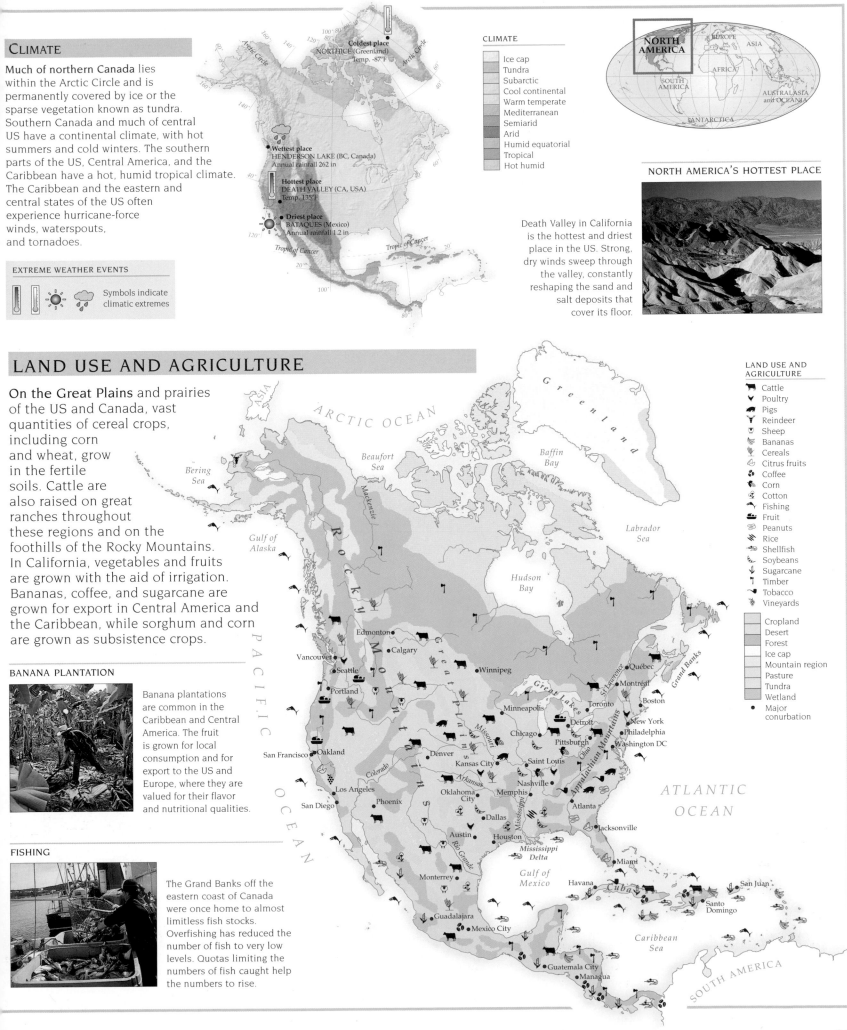

WESTERN CANADA

ALBERTA, BRITISH COLUMBIA, MANITOBA, NORTHWEST
TERRITORIES, NUNAVUT, SASKATCHEWAN, YUKON TERRITORY

The first inhabitants of Canada's western provinces
were Native Americans. By the late 1800s, the Canadian
Pacific Railroad was completed and European settlers
moved west, turning most of the prairie into huge grain
farms. North of the prairies lie the vast, empty territories
that have significant Native American populations.
In 1999, part of the Northwest Territories, known as
Nunavut, became a self-governing Inuit homeland.

INDUSTRY

The major industries in the prairie provinces
are related to agriculture, such as
meat-processing in Manitoba. Alberta
has huge reserves of fossil fuels,
and the other provinces are rich in
minerals, including zinc, nickel,
silver, and uranium. British
Columbia's economy depends
on manufacturing, especially
automobiles, chemicals, and
machinery, along
with paper and
timber industries.

STRUCTURE OF INDUSTRY

Primary 6%
Services 64%
Manufacturing 30%

INDUSTRY

🚗 Car manufacturing	△ Metal refining	⬡ Tourism
🧪 Chemicals	🛢 Oil and gas	▪ Major industrial center / area
⚙ Engineering	⛏ Mining	
🗃 Food processing	🌲 Timber processing	— Major road

ENVIRONMENTAL ISSUES

For hundreds of years sailors have searched in vain for
a route from Europe to Asia via the Northwest Passage,
through the north of this region. In recent summers the sea
ice has retreated further north, and in 2007 the route was
completely navigable.
Many of the extensive forests in
British Columbia are used for
commercial lumbering. The
province produces more than
half of Canada's timber.

ENVIRONMENTAL ISSUES

🦫 Lumbering activity

▦ Permafrost zone

● Major industrial center

---- Northwest Passage - direct route

FARMING AND LAND USE

More than 20% of the world's wheat is
grown in Canada's prairie provinces:
Manitoba, Alberta, and
Saskatchewan. Beef cattle graze
on the ranches of Alberta and
British Columbia. Fruits,
especially apples, flourish
in the sheltered southern
valleys of British Columbia,
and Pacific salmon and
herring are caught off
the west coast.

LAND USE

Pasture 5%
Cropland 4%
Forest 38%
Other (including mountains) 53%

FARMING AND LAND USE

🐄 Cattle		▨ Pasture
🌱 Fishing		▨ Cropland
🌾 Cereals		▨ Forest
🦐 Fruit		▨ Mountain region
🕎 Timber		▨ Barren
● Major conurbation		▨ Tundra

THE LANDSCAPE

The prairie provinces are mostly flat. Occasionally,
the level plains are broken up by river valleys such
as that of the Qu'Appelle in Saskatchewan. In the
west, the jagged peaks and steep passes of the Rocky
Mountains and the Coast Mountains are covered
in snow for months on end. West of the Rockies,
the land descends sharply toward the coast of
British Columbia. The far north is covered by dense
forests and many glacial lakes.

The Arctic
Most of Canada's northern
islands are within the Arctic
Circle. They are covered by
ice year-round.

Mount Logan (B 5)
Mount Logan is Canada's
tallest peak. It rises 19,551 ft.

Glacial lakes
The plains are
covered by
thousands of
lakes, many of
which are vast.
They are the
remains of great
glacial lakes left
after the last
Ice Age.

Islands and inlets (C 6, C7)
The British Columbia coast is peppered
with islands and fjordlike inlets, created
by the force of the Pacific Ocean.

River valleys
Prairie river valleys such as the Qu'Appelle (F 7)
(French for "who calls") were cut by glacial
meltwater thousands of years ago.

NORTH
AMERICA

Western
Canada

POPULATION

Most of the people in western
Canada live near the Canada/
US border, taking advantage
of the warmer climate
and convenient
transportation routes.
In the cold, forested
north, the population
is sparse, with only a
few people per 100 sq
miles – many of them
Native Americans such
as the Inuit.

Edmonton
Saskatoon
Winnipeg
Vancouver
Calgary
Regina

CLIMATE

Parts of northern Canada are frozen all
year round. The prairie provinces have
warm summers and cold winters. Coastal
British Columbia is mild and wet.

January

July

TEMPERATURE AND PRECIPITATION

More than 68°F	23 to 32°F
59 to 68°F	14 to 23°F
50 to 59°F	5 to 14°F
41 to 50°F	Less than 5°F
32 to 41°F	—4— Precipitation (in)

URBAN/RURAL POPULATION DIVISION

Vancouver 22.7%

Other towns
and cities 38%

Calgary
10.8%

Edmonton
10.5%

Rural population 18%

**INHABITANTS
PER SQ MILE**

More than 30

3–30

Less than 3

• Major city

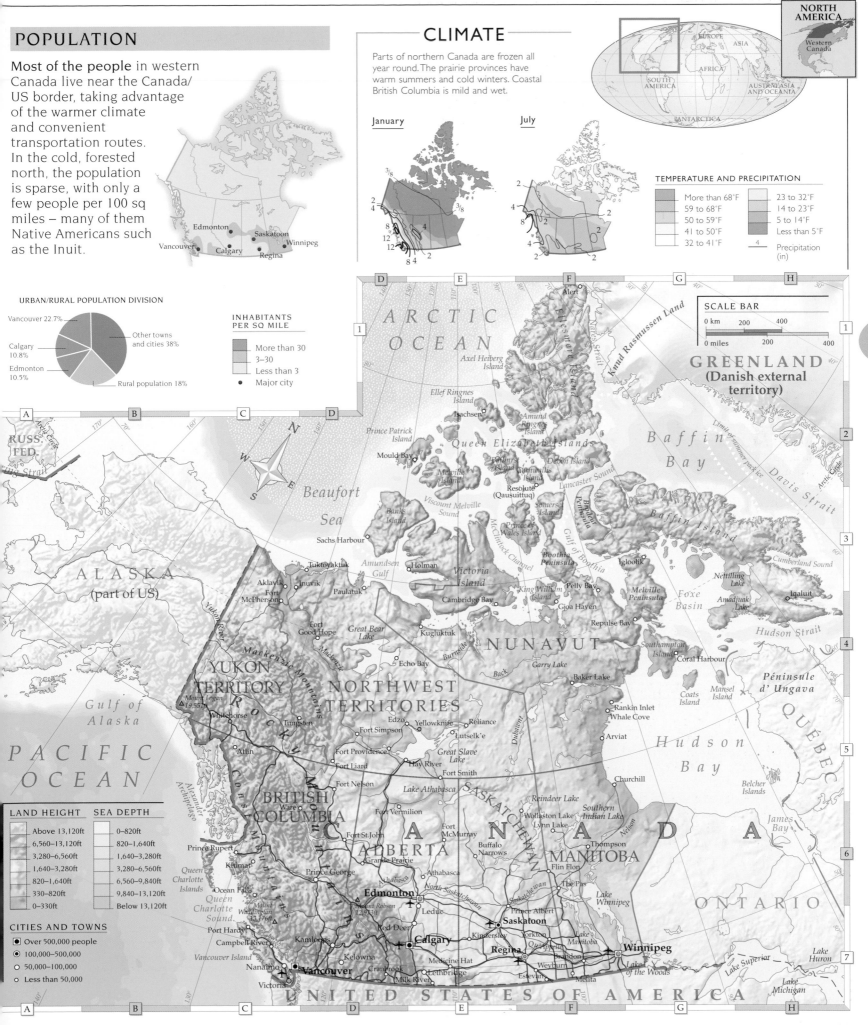

LAND HEIGHT

| Above 13,120ft |
| 6,560–13,120ft |
| 3,280–6,560ft |
| 1,640–3,280ft |
| 820–1,640ft |
| 330–820ft |
| 0–330ft |

SEA DEPTH

| 0–820ft |
| 820–1,640ft |
| 1,640–3,280ft |
| 3,280–6,560ft |
| 6,560–9,840ft |
| 9,840–13,120ft |
| Below 13,120ft |

CITIES AND TOWNS

◉ Over 500,000 people
● 100,000–500,000
▪ 50,000–100,000
○ Less than 50,000

SCALE BAR

0 km   200   400

0 miles   200   400

GREENLAND
(Danish external
territory)

ARCTIC
OCEAN

Alert

Axel Heiberg
Island

Ellef Ringnes
Island

Isachsen

Prince Patrick
Island

Mould Bay

Queen Elizabeth Islands

Amund
Ringnes
Island

Bathurst
Island Cornwallis
Island

Devon Island

Baffin
Bay

Limit of summer pack ice

Davis Strait

Arctic Circle

Beaufort
Sea

Banks
Island

Sachs Harbour

Viscount Melville
Sound

Resolute
(Qausuittuq)

Lancaster Sound

Prince
of Wales Island

Somerset
Island

Boothia
Peninsula

Gulf of
Boothia

Brodeur
Peninsula

Baffin Island

Cumberland Sound

Nettilling
Lake

Iqaluit

RUSS.
FED.

Bering Strait

Arctic Circle

ALASKA
(part of US)

Amundsen
Gulf

Holman

Victoria
Island

King William
Island

Pelly Bay

Melville
Peninsula

Foxe
Basin

Amadjuak
Lake

Hudson Strait

Tuktoyaktuk

Aklavik
Fort
McPherson

Inuvik

Paulatuk

Cambridge Bay

Gjoa Haven

Repulse Bay

Southampton
Island

Coral Harbour

Mansel
Island

Péninsule
d' Ungava

Yukon River

Fort
Good Hope

Great Bear
Lake

Kugluktuk

Burnside

NUNAVUT

Back

Garry Lake

Coats
Island

PACIFIC
OCEAN

Gulf of
Alaska

Mackenzie Mountains

Mackenzie

Echo Bay

Baker Lake

Rankin Inlet
Whale Cove

YUKON
TERRITORY

Mount Logan
△19,551ft

Whitehorse

Tungsten

NORTHWEST
TERRITORIES

Edzo

Yellowknife

Reliance

Dubawnt

Arviat

Hudson
Bay

QUEBEC

Alexander
Archipelago

Atlin

Fort Simpson

Lutselk'e

Rocky

Fort Providence

Great Slave
Lake

Fort Liard

Hay River

Fort Smith

Churchill

Fort Nelson

Lake Athabasca

SASKATCHEWAN

Reindeer Lake

Nelson

James
Bay

Prince Rupert

Queen
Charlotte
Islands

Ocean Falls

BRITISH
COLUMBIA

Ware

Columbia Mountains

Fort Vermilion

Fort St.John

CANADA

Fort
McMurray

Wollaston Lake

Southern
Indian Lake

Lynn Lake

Thompson

ONTARIO

ALBERTA

Buffalo
Narrows

MANITOBA

Flin Flon

Grande Prairie

Athabasca

North Saskatchewan

The Pas

Lake
Winnipeg

Kitimat

Queen
Charlotte
Sound

Mount
Waddington

Prince George

Athabasca

Mount Robson
△12,972ft

Edmonton

Ledue

Red Deer

Saskatchewan

Prince Albert

Saskatoon

Lake
Superior

Port Hardy

Campbell River

Vancouver
Island

Nanaimo

Kamloops

Kelowna

Cranbrook

Calgary

Kindersley

Medicine Hat

Lethbridge

Yorkton

Qu'Appelle

Regina

Brandon

Weyburn

Lake
Winnipegosis

Winnipeg

Lake
of the Woods

Lake
Huron

Victoria

Milk River

Estevan

Melita

Lake
Michigan

UNITED   STATES   OF   AMERICA

EASTERN CANADA

NEW BRUNSWICK, NEWFOUNDLAND AND LABRADOR,
NOVA SCOTIA, ONTARIO, PRINCE EDWARD ISLAND, QUÉBEC

The first European settlements grew up in the Atlantic provinces, and along the St. Lawrence River, where Québec City and Montréal were founded. People gradually migrated farther west along the St. Lawrence River and the Great Lakes, establishing other cities including Toronto. Although the majority of Canadians speak English, people in Québec speak mainly French, and both English and French are official languages in Canada.

INDUSTRY

In the Atlantic provinces the traditional fishing industry has declined, causing unemployment. However, Newfoundland has a thriving food processing industry. Ontario and Québec have a wide range of industries, including the generation of hydroelectricity, mining, and chemicals, car manufacturing and fruit canning in the great cities. Large amounts of wood pulp and paper are also produced.

STRUCTURE
OF INDUSTRY

Primary 7%
Services 64%
Manufacturing 29%

INDUSTRY

- 🚗 Car manufacturing
- ⚗ Chemicals
- 🐟 Fish processing
- 🥫 Food processing
- ⊣ Hydroelectric power
- △ Metal refining
- ⚒ Mining
- 🌲 Timber processing
- 💻 High-tech industry
- ⛩ Tourism
- ⊡ Major industrial center / area
- — Major road

FARMING AND LAND USE

The best farmland lies on the flat, fertile plains close to the St. Lawrence River and on the strip of land between Lake Erie and Lake Ontario. It is used to grow fruits such as grapes, cherries, and peaches, and to raise cattle. Nova Scotia has fruit farms, and the rich red soils of Prince Edward Island produce a big potato crop. The vast forests that grow across the north are a major source of timber.

LAND USE

Pasture 2% Cropland 2%
Other (including mountains) 32%
Forest 64%

FARMING AND LAND USE

- 🐄 Cattle
- 🐟 Fishing
- 🍇 Fruit
- ✽ Potatoes
- 🌲 Timber
- Pasture
- Cropland
- Forest
- Tundra
- ● Major conurbation

ENVIRONMENTAL ISSUES

Acid rain caused by emissions from factories in the US and along the St. Lawrence River destroys forests and kills marine life. Massive hydro-electric power projects in James Bay on Hudson Bay have flooded huge areas of land, affecting the environment and the local Cree people. Overfishing in the Atlantic has led to limits being set on the number of fish that can be caught.

ENVIRONMENTAL ISSUES

- Depleted fish stocks
- Major dam
- Urban air pollution
- Affected by acid rain
- Severe sea/lake pollution
- ● Major industrial center

THE LANDSCAPE

A huge, ancient mass of rock called the Canadian Shield lies beneath much of eastern Canada. It is covered by low hills, rocky outcrops, thousands of lakes, and huge areas of forest. Much of the Canadian Shield is permanently frozen. The St. Lawrence River flows out of Lake Ontario and into the Atlantic Ocean. It is surrounded by rolling hills and flat areas of very fertile farmland.

Scoured by ice

About 20,000 years ago, Labrador and northern Québec were completely covered by ice. The glaciers scraped hollows in the rock beneath. When the ice melted, lakes were left in the hollows that remained.

Lake Superior (B5)

Lake Superior is the largest freshwater lake in the world. It covers an area of 32,150 sq miles and lies between Canada and the USA.

St. Lawrence River (E5)

The St. Lawrence River is 744 miles long. Parts of it have become silted up, causing it to be braided into many different channels. Between December and mid-April the river freezes over.

Highlands

The highlands of New Brunswick, Nova Scotia, and Newfoundland are the most northerly part of the Appalachian mountain chain.

The Bay of Fundy (F5)

This bay has the world's highest tides. It is shaped like a funnel, and as the Atlantic flows into it, the ever narrowing shores cause the water level to rise 20–50 ft at every high tide.

NORTH AMERICA
Eastern Canada

POPULATION

Colonists from both France and Britain settled in Canada from the early 1600s onward. Ontario and the Atlantic provinces are mainly English speaking. Québec is the center of French settlement; 80% of the people there have French as a first language. Most people in eastern Canada now live in large towns and cities close to the St. Lawrence River.

Thunder Bay
St. John's
Québec
OTTAWA
Montréal
Halifax
Toronto
Windsor
London

URBAN/RURAL POPULATION DIVISION

Toronto 19.7%
Montréal 14.5%
Ottawa 3.7%
Other towns and cities 46.1%
Rural population 16%

INHABITANTS PER SQ MILE

- More than 260
- 130–260
- 3–130
- Less than 3
- ■ Capital city
- ● Major city

CLIMATE

Winters are very cold, but warm winds from the Gulf of Mexico can bring hot summers to southern Ontario and the areas bordering the St. Lawrence River.

January

July

TEMPERATURE AND PRECIPITATION

- More than 68°F
- 59 to 68°F
- 50 to 59°F
- 41 to 50°F
- 32 to 41°F
- 23 to 32°F
- 5 to 23°F
- -13 to 5°F
- Less than -13°F

— 4 — Precipitation (in)

CITIES AND TOWNS

- ■ Over 500,000 people
- ◉ 100,000–500,000
- ○ 50,000–100,000
- ○ Less than 50,000

LAND HEIGHT
- 1,640–3,280ft
- 820–1,640ft
- 330–820ft
- 0–330ft

SEA DEPTH
- 0–820ft
- 820–1,640ft
- 1,640–3,280ft
- 3,280–6,560ft
- 6,560–9,840ft
- 9,840–13,120ft
- Below 13,120ft

NUNAVUT

Ivujivik
Charles Island
Coats Island
Mansel Island
Baffin Island
Hudson Strait
Resolution Island
Akpatok Island
Button Islands

Péninsule d' Ungava

Ungava Bay

Labrador Sea

H U D S O N   B A Y

Churchill
Southern Indian Lake
Nelson
Hayes
MANITOBA
Fort Severn
Peawanuk
Severn
Belcher Islands
Inukjuak
Rivière aux Feuilles
Lac Minto
Kuujjuaq
Koksoak
Rivière à la Baleine
Caniapiscau
Nain
Hopedale
Makkovik
Cape Harrison
Cartwright
NEWFOUNDLAND & LABRADOR
Schefferville
Smallwood Reservoir
Lake Melville
Churchill
Lac Bienville
St.Anthony
Labrador City
Strait of Belle Isle

QUÉBEC

C A N A D A

Lake Winnipeg
Sandy Lake
Winisk
James Bay
Akimiski Island
Réservoir de Caniapiscau
Réservoir Manicouagan
Canadian Shield
Attawapiskat
Attawapiskat
Fort Albany
Albany
Moosonee
Eastmain
Rivière de Rupert
Moose
Eastmain
Lac Mistassini
Laurentian Mountains
Havre-St-Pierre
Corner Brook
Newfoundland
Gander
Grand Falls
St.John's

ONTARIO
Lake of the Woods
Kenora
Dryden
Rainy Lake
Fort Frances
Atikokan
MINNESOTA
Armstrong
Lake Nipigon
Nipigon
Longlac
Hearst
Kapuskasing
Cochrane
Marathon
Tip Top Mountain △2,100
Wawa
Foleyet
Timmins
Kirkland Lake
Amos
Rouyn-Noranda
Val-d'Or
Hurricana
Réservoir Gouin
Chibougamau
Lac St-Jean
Chicoutimi
Jonquière
Matane
Rimouski
Péninsule de Gaspé
Gaspé
Sept-Îles
Baie-Comeau
Gulf of St. Lawrence
Île d'Anticosti
Îles de la Madeleine
Channel-Port aux Basques
Cape Race
Cabot Strait
Cape Breton Island
Sydney
Glace Bay
ST PIERRE & MIQUELON (French territorial collectivity)

Thunder Bay
Lake Superior
MICHIGAN
WISCONSIN
Sault Ste.Marie
Sudbury
North Bay
La Tuque
Trois-Rivières
Québec
Charlesbourg
St Georges
Rivière-du-Loup
Edmundston
NEW BRUNSWICK
Bathurst
PRINCE EDWARD ISLAND
Charlottetown
Amherst
New Glasgow
NOVA SCOTIA
Cape Breton Island

Manitoulin Island
Georgian Bay
Lake Huron
Midland
Pembroke
Gatineau
Hull
Nepean
Laval
Montréal
OTTAWA
Sherbrooke
Drummondville
Fredericton
Moncton
Oromocto
Truro
Dartmouth
Halifax
MAINE
Saint John
Bay of Fundy
Liverpool
Yarmouth
Sable Island

UNITED STATES OF AMERICA
Lake Michigan
Peterborough
Brampton
Kitchener
Hamilton
London
Windsor
Leamington
Sarnia
Oshawa
Toronto
St. Catharines
Niagara Falls
Lake Ontario
Kingston
Appalachian Mountains
VERMONT
NEW HAMPSHIRE
MASSACHUSETTS
Cape Cod
RHODE ISLAND
CONNECTICUT
NEW YORK
PENNSYLVANIA
OHIO
INDIANA
ILLINOIS
IOWA
Mississippi River
Lake Erie

ATLANTIC OCEAN

SCALE BAR
0 km 150 300
0 miles 150 300

US: The Northeastern States

CONNECTICUT, DELAWARE, MAINE, MASSACHUSETTS, NEW-HAMPSHIRE, NEW JERSEY, NEW YORK, PENNSYLVANIA, RHODE ISLAND, VERMONT

The dynamic 200-year boom of the northeastern states has been the result of a combination of factors. Between 1855 and 1924, over 20 million people poured into the region from all over the world, hoping to build a new life. Natural resources, including coal and iron, fueled new industries and fertile farmland provided food for the region's growing population. The "gateway" cities of the Atlantic seaboard, New York and Boston, enabled manufacturers to export their goods worldwide.

INDUSTRY

Boston, New York, and Philadelphia are international centers of industry and commerce. Electronics and communications are growing throughout the Northeast alongside traditional industries such as fishing and wood products. Tourism is vital for the northeastern states, particularly along the Atlantic coast.

STRUCTURE OF INDUSTRY

Primary 0.5%
Manufacturing 16.5%
Services 83%

INDUSTRY

- Chemicals
- Engineering
- Food processing
- Iron and steel
- Pharmaceuticals
- Textiles
- Timber processing
- Defense
- Finance
- High-tech
- Research and development
- Tourism
- Major industrial center / area
- Major road

FARMING AND LAND USE

The varied landscape of the northeastern states supports a great range of farming. Livestock, including cattle, horses, poultry, and pigs, are raised throughout the region. The main crops are fruits and vegetables. Fishing is important, especially off the Atlantic coast of Maine.

FARMING AND LAND USE

- Cattle
- Pigs
- Poultry
- Fishing
- Cereals
- Cranberries
- Fruit
- Maple syrup
- Timber
- Cropland
- Forest
- Pasture
- Major conurbation

LAND USE

Pasture 6%
Cropland 14%
Other 16%
Forest 64%

THE LANDSCAPE

The Appalachian and Adirondack Mountains form a barrier between the marshy lowlands of the Atlantic coast and the lowlands farther west. The interior consists of rolling hills, fertile valleys, and thousands of lakes created by the movement of glaciers.

Appalachians (E3)
The Appalachian Mountains, which run through most of this region, are the eroded remnants of peaks that were once much higher.

Rocky coastline (G3)
The coast of Maine is made up of rocky bays, islands, and inlets. If the shoreline were stretched out, it would be 2,500 miles long.

Adirondacks (E3)
The Adirondacks are a broad, wide mountain range, formed when older rocks were forced into a "dome" shape by movements in the Earth's crust many millions of years ago.

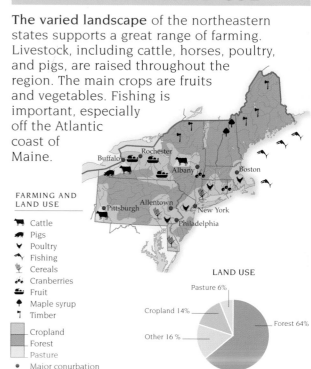

Long Island Sound (F5)
Long Island Sound is a river valley that was drowned by rising sea levels.

Finger Lakes (D3)
The long, narrow Finger Lakes lie in upper New York state. They were cut by glaciers.

Delaware Bay (D6)
Deep bays such as Delaware Bay are often surrounded by salt marshes and barrier beaches that create ideal breeding conditions for a wide variety of birds and animals.

ENVIRONMENTAL ISSUES

The high level of industry and the large population puts great pressure on the environment. Air pollution from automobiles and industry led to poor air quality in many cities and caused acid rain. The problem is worse toward the Great Lakes, where severe lake pollution has occurred.

ENVIRONMENTAL ISSUES

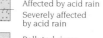

- Urban air pollution
- Wind farm
- Affected by acid rain
- Severely affected by acid rain
- Polluted rivers
- Sea/lake pollution
- Severe sea/lake pollution
- Major industrial center

POPULATION

The areas along the eastern seaboard were settled by some of the earliest European colonists. The Northeast is now one of the most densely populated parts of the US. A few of the largest cities in the US, such as New York and Philadelphia, are in this region, but in the six states known as New-England many towns and cities have populations of less than 30,000 inhabitants.

CLIMATE

Although the climate is mild during the spring and fall, summers can be hot and extremely humid, while winters are often very cold with heavy snowfall.

NORTH AMERICA

US: The Northeastern States

January

July

INHABITANTS PER SQ MILE

- More than 520
- 260–520
- 130–260
- 65–130
- Less than 65
- ● Major city

URBAN/RURAL POPULATION DIVISION

- New York 14.6%
- Philadelphia 2.7%
- Boston 1.1%
- Rural population 17%
- Other towns and cities 64.6%

TEMPERATURE AND PRECIPITATION

- More than 68°F
- 59 to 68°F
- 32 to 41°F
- 23 to 32°F
- 14 to 23°F
- Less than 14°F
- 4 Precipitation (in)

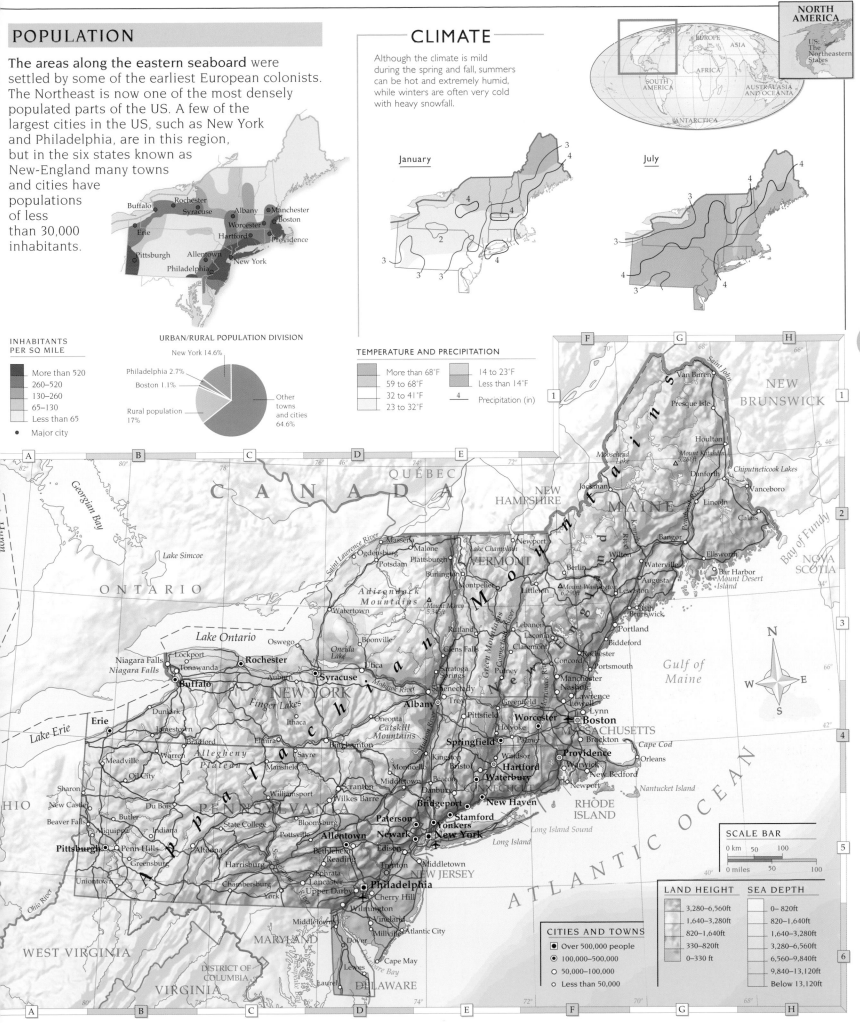

SCALE BAR
0 km 50 100
0 miles 50 100

CITIES AND TOWNS
- ■ Over 500,000 people
- ◉ 100,000–500,000
- ○ 50,000–100,000
- ∘ Less than 50,000

LAND HEIGHT
- 3,280–6,560ft
- 1,640–3,280ft
- 820–1,640ft
- 330–820ft
- 0–330 ft

SEA DEPTH
- 0– 820ft
- 820–1,640ft
- 1,640–3,280ft
- 3,280–6,560ft
- 6,560–9,840ft
- 9,840–13,120ft
- Below 13,120ft

US: THE SOUTHERN STATES

ALABAMA, ARKANSAS, DISTRICT OF COLUMBIA, FLORIDA, GEORGIA,
KENTUCKY, LOUISIANA, MARYLAND, MISSISSIPPI, NORTH CAROLINA,
SOUTH CAROLINA, TENNESSEE, VIRGINIA, WEST VIRGINIA

The southern states suffered great devastation and poverty
as a result of the Civil War (1861–65). Recovery has come
with the discovery and exploitation of resources and the
development of major commercial and industrial centers.
Yet these states retain the vibrant mix of cultures that
reflect their French, Spanish, English, and African heritage.

INDUSTRY

Tourism is a major industry in the "sunbelt" states, especially Florida,
and many people move to the area when they retire
to enjoy the climate. Oil and gas are extracted
along the coast of the Gulf of Mexico,
and there are many related
chemical industries. Textiles
are still produced in North
and South Carolina, but
aerospace and other high-
tech industries have been
established as well.

STRUCTURE OF INDUSTRY

Primary 2%
Services 78%
Manufacturing 20%

INDUSTRY

- ✈ Aerospace
- ⚗ Chemicals
- ⚙ Engineering
- 🏭 Food processing
- Iron and steel
- ⊤ Textiles
- ⚒ Coal
- ◌ Oil and gas
- ⌨ High-tech
- ☢ Research and development
- ⌂ Tourism
- ■ Major industrial center / area
- — Major road

POPULATION

Creoles, descended from
Spanish and French colonizers,
and Cajuns, of French-Canadian
ancestry, live in the south of
this region. Florida has a large
Hispanic population, increased by
migration from the Caribbean. In the
early 20th century, five million black
people, the descendants of slaves, left
the South for cities in the North.

INHABITANTS PER SQ MILE

- More than 520
- 260–520
- 130–260
- 65–130
- Less than 65
- ■ Capital city
- ● Major city

URBAN/RURAL POPULATION DIVISION

Louisville 0.9% Jacksonville 1%
Memphis 0.8%
Other towns and cities 65.3%
Rural population 32%

FARMING AND LAND USE

Cotton is still the South's main crop, but many old
cottonfields are now pastures where all types
of livestock are raised. Florida
is famous for citrus fruits,
while Georgia
is renowned
for peanuts.
Sugarcane,
soybeans,
tobacco, corn,
fruits, and rice
are grown in
other areas.

FARMING AND LAND USE

- 🐄 Cattle
- 🐟 Fishing
- 🐖 Pigs
- 🦃 Poultry
- 🦐 Shellfish
- 🍊 Citrus fruit
- 🌽 Corn
- Cotton
- 🍓 Fruit
- Peanuts
- 🌾 Rice
- Soybeans
- Sugarcane
- Timber
- Tobacco

- Cropland
- Forest
- Pasture
- Wetland
- ● Major conurbation

LAND USE

Pasture 12%
Cropland 15%
Forest 51%
Other 22%

THE LANDSCAPE

The South is a land of contrasts, the uplands of the
Appalachians, the foothills of the Piedmont, and low-lying coastal
regions are all featured. The interior lowlands are drained by the
Mississippi. Florida is dotted with thousands of lakes and is home
to the Everglades, a giant sawgrass swamp.

Mississippi River (C 4)
A major transportation artery,
the Mississippi was an essential
route in opening up the interior
region. With its main tributary,
the Missouri, it is nearly 3,800
miles long, making it the world's
fourth-longest river.

Kentucky Bluegrass (E 2)
The gently rolling
bluegrass landscape
of northern Kentucky
is ideal horse- and
livestock-raising country.

Barrier beaches (I 3)
Sandy barrier beaches and
islands line the eastern
and southern coasts, along
with sheltered lagoons
and salt marshes.

The Everglades (G 8)
The Everglades cover
5,000 sq miles and
support abundant
wild animals and
plants, many unique
to the area.

Thermal springs (B 4)
Hot Springs National
Park in Arkansas has
47 thermal springs
and is a popular
tourist and health
resort. Visitors relax
here in the hot
water that trickles
from the hillsides.

Tennessee River (D 4)
The Tennessee River is
625 miles long. Dams along
the river generate hydro-
electricity to provide
most of the region's
energy needs.

Limestone caves (E 4)
Cathedral Caverns in Alabama
is a collection of enormous
limestone caves. The main
entrance is more than 1,000 ft
high and 150 ft wide.

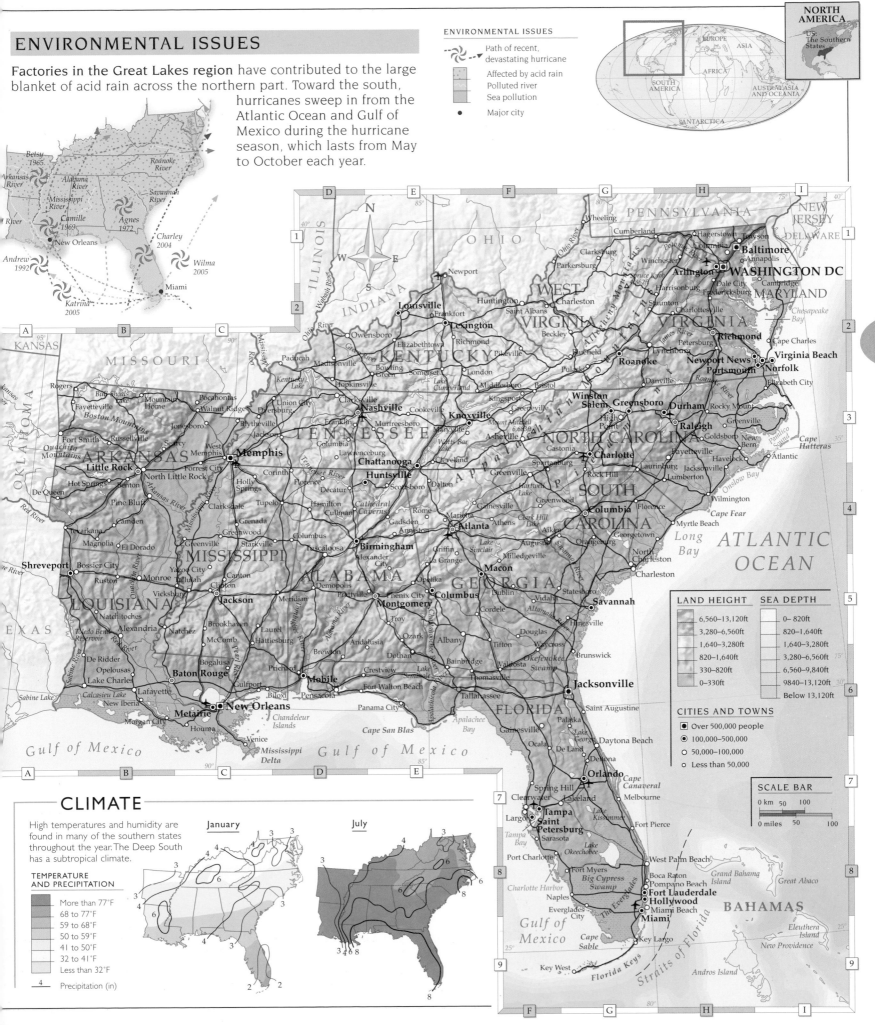

ENVIRONMENTAL ISSUES

Factories in the Great Lakes region have contributed to the large blanket of acid rain across the northern part. Toward the south, hurricanes sweep in from the Atlantic Ocean and Gulf of Mexico during the hurricane season, which lasts from May to October each year.

ENVIRONMENTAL ISSUES

- - - - Path of recent, devastating hurricane
- Affected by acid rain
- Polluted river
- Sea pollution
- Major city

NORTH AMERICA
US: The Southern States

Betsy 1965 · **Roanoke River** · **Arkansas River** · **Alabama River** · **Savannah River** · **Mississippi River** · **Camille 1969** · **New Orleans** · **Agnes 1972** · **Charley 2004** · **Andrew 1992** · **Wilma 2005** · **Miami** · **Katrina 2005**

LAND HEIGHT
- 6,560–13,120ft
- 3,280–6,560ft
- 1,640–3,280ft
- 820–1,640ft
- 330–820ft
- 0–330ft

SEA DEPTH
- 0–820ft
- 820–1,640ft
- 1,640–3,280ft
- 3,280–6,560ft
- 6,560–9,840ft
- 9840–13,120ft
- Below 13,120ft

CITIES AND TOWNS
- Over 500,000 people
- 100,000–500,000
- 50,000–100,000
- Less than 50,000

SCALE BAR
0 km 50 100
0 miles 50 100

CLIMATE

High temperatures and humidity are found in many of the southern states throughout the year. The Deep South has a subtropical climate.

January · **July**

TEMPERATURE AND PRECIPITATION
- More than 77°F
- 68 to 77°F
- 59 to 68°F
- 50 to 59°F
- 41 to 50°F
- 32 to 41°F
- Less than 32°F

—4— Precipitation (in)

US: THE GREAT LAKES STATES

ILLINOIS, INDIANA, MICHIGAN, OHIO, WISCONSIN

Good transportation links, excellent farmland, and a wealth of natural resources drew settlers from Europe and the south and east of the US to the Great Lakes states during the late 19th century. By the 1930s, they had become one of the world's most prosperous industrial and agricultural regions. In recent years, the decline in traditional heavy industries has hit some cities hard, leading to unemployment and a rising crime rate.

POPULATION

The Great Lakes states are one of the most densely populated parts of the US. Many of the largest cities in this region – Chicago, Detroit, and Milwaukee – grew up on the banks of the lakes and are connected to each other and the rest of the US by an impressive road and rail network.

INHABITANTS PER SQ MILE

- More than 520
- 260–520
- 130–260
- 65–130
- Less than 65
- ● Major city

URBAN/RURAL POPULATION DIVISION

- Detroit 2%
- Chicago 6.3%
- Indianapolis 1.7%
- Other towns and cities 66%
- Rural population 24%

CLIMATE

Plentiful rainfall waters the agricultural lands. In winter, strong winds sweep across the lakes, and water close to the shore may freeze.

January

July

TEMPERATURE AND PRECIPITATION

- More than 77°F
- 68 to 77°F
- 59 to 68°F
- 32 to 41°F
- 23 to 32°F
- 14 to 23°F
- Less than 14°F
- 4 Precipitation (in)

SCALE BAR

0 km 50 100

0 miles 50 100

CITIES AND TOWNS

- ■ Over 500,000 people
- ● 100,000–500,000
- ◉ 50,000–100,000
- ○ Less than 50,000

LAND HEIGHT

- 1,640–3,280ft
- 820–1,640ft
- 330–820ft
- 0–330ft

Map labels:

CANADA, MINNESOTA, IOWA, MISSOURI, KENTUCKY, WEST VIRGINIA, NEW YORK, PENNSYLVANIA, ONTARIO

Lake Superior, Lake Huron, Lake Michigan, Lake Erie, Lake Ontario, Georgian Bay, North Channel, Green Bay, Saginaw Bay, Lake Winnebago

WISCONSIN, MICHIGAN, ILLINOIS, INDIANA, OHIO

Isle Royale, Apostle Islands, Keweenaw Peninsula, Gogebic Range, Door Peninsula, Beaver Island, Seney Marsh

Superior, Ashland, Ironwood, Houghton, Marquette, Sault Sainte Marie, Grantsburg, Woodruff, Rice Lake, Rhinelander, Crystal Falls, Iron Mountain, Escanaba, Saint Ignace, Cheboygan, Ladysmith, Wausau, Eau Claire, River Falls, Stevens Point, Green Bay, Beulah, Traverse City, Alpena, Roscommon, Cadillac, Houghton Lake, Wisconsin Rapids, Appleton, Oshkosh, Tomah, La Crosse, Wisconsin Dells, Fond du Lac, Sheboygan, Ludington, Mount Pleasant, Midland, Bay City, Saginaw, Madison, West Bend, Muskegon, Waukesha, Milwaukee, Grand Rapids, Flint, Prairie du Chien, Racine, Wyoming, Lansing, Pontiac, Port Huron, Janesville, Kenosha, Livonia, Warren, Rockford, Waukegan, Kalamazoo, Ann Arbor, Detroit, Freeport, Evanston, Benton Harbor, Adrian, Ashtabula, Sterling, Elgin, Chicago, Euclid, Aurora, Hammond, Gary, South Bend, Elkhart, Toledo, Sandusky, Cleveland, Warren, Rock Island, Joliet, Valparaiso, Bowling Green, Fremont, Akron, Youngstown, Kewanee, Ottawa, Kankakee, Fort Wayne, Findlay, Canton, East Liverpool, Galesburg, Logansport, Wabash, Van Wert, Bucyrus, Macomb, Bloomington, Marion, Mansfield, Steubenville, Peoria, Pekin, Lafayette, Kokomo, Sidney, Delaware, Quincy, Champaign, Anderson, Muncie, Springfield, Cambridge, Springfield, Carmel, Columbus, Zanesville, Jacksonville, Decatur, Indianapolis, Dayton, Kettering, Marietta, Charleston, Terre Haute, Wilmington, Athens, Chillicothe, Alton, Effingham, Columbus, Bloomington, Cincinnati, Bedford, Vincennes, Portsmouth, Granite City, East Saint Louis, Belleville, Washington, New Albany, Mount Vernon, Evansville, Carbondale, Marion, Harrisburg

Rivers: Saint Croix River, Mississippi River, Chippewa River, Wolf River, Wisconsin River, Cedar River, Iowa River, Illinois River, Missouri River, Kaskaskia River, Wabash River, White River, Tippecanoe River, Maumee River, Scioto River, Hocking River, Ohio River, Manistee River, Muskegon River

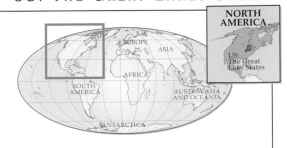
NORTH AMERICA

US: The Great Lake States

FARMING AND LAND USE

Michigan is renowned for its cherries and apples. Corn and soybeans are the main crops produced in the region's southern states. Livestock-rearing includes pig and poultry farms – many very large – in Illinois, Indiana, and Ohio. Cattle rearing and dairy farming are common in Michigan and Wisconsin.

Milwaukee
Detroit
Chicago
Cleveland
Indianapolis
Columbus

LAND USE

Pasture 8%
Other 16%
Cropland 47%
Forest 29%

FARMING AND LAND USE

Cattle	Vineyards
Pigs	Wheat
Poultry	
Corn	Cropland
Fruit	Forest
Soybeans	Pasture
Timber	• Major conurbation
Tobacco	

THE LANDSCAPE

Until about 10,000 years ago, much of this region was covered by great ice sheets that extended south to Illinois and Ohio. When the ice melted the Great Lakes were left in large hollows that the ice had scoured. The ice sheets changed the course of many rivers, so today most rivers flow south into the Mississippi/Missouri River system.

Lakes and marshes (B 3)
Wisconsin is scattered with thousands of smaller lakes and many marshy areas. Like the Great Lakes, they were formed by erosion by the retreating ice at the end of the last Ice Age.

Underground water
In northern Illinois much of the water is pumped from underground reservoirs. In some places, the water table has dropped by 700 ft over the last century, so many areas now face a water shortage.

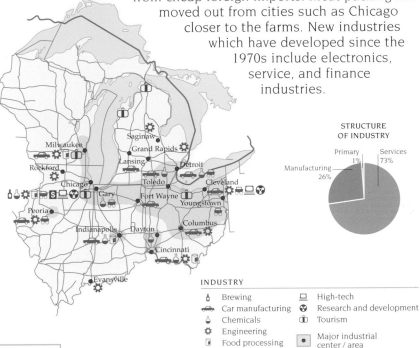

Moraines
When the last ice age ended, the retreating ice sheets left long ridges and piles of rock to the south of Lake Michigan. Some of these ridges, known as moraines, can be up to 300 ft high.

Limestone region
Limestone in the hills of southern Indiana has been dissolved by acid rainwater. This has produced features such as sinkholes and underground caves.

Lake Erie (F 5)
Lake Erie is the shallowest of the Great Lakes. Its average depth is about 62 ft. Storms that sweep across from Canada have eroded its shores and caused the silting of its harbors.

INDUSTRY

The US automobile industry grew up on the banks of the Great Lakes, supported by the manufacture of iron and steel. Both industries have suffered in recent years from competition from cheap foreign imports. Meat packing has moved out from cities such as Chicago closer to the farms. New industries which have developed since the 1970s include electronics, service, and finance industries.

Milwaukee
Saginaw
Grand Rapids
Rockford
Lansing
Detroit
Chicago
Toledo
Cleveland
Gary
Fort Wayne
Youngstown
Peoria
Columbus
Indianapolis
Dayton
Cincinnati
Evansville

STRUCTURE OF INDUSTRY

Primary 1%
Services 73%
Manufacturing 26%

INDUSTRY

Brewing	High-tech
Car manufacturing	Research and development
Chemicals	Tourism
Engineering	Major industrial center / area
Food processing	
Iron and steel	Major road
Finance	

ENVIRONMENTAL ISSUES

The heavy industries on the banks of the Great Lakes have caused terrible pollution over the last century. Industrial effluent has polluted the lakes themselves, and factory emissions have led to severely acidic rain, which affects forests and lakes both here and farther away in Canada.

Milwaukee
Detroit
Chicago
Gary
Cleveland
Mississippi River
Ohio River

ENVIRONMENTAL ISSUES

	Urban air pollution
	Wind farm
	Affected by acid rain
	Severely affected by acid rain
	Polluted rivers
	Lake pollution
	Severe lake pollution
•	Major industrial center

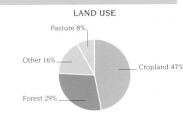

US: THE CENTRAL STATES

IOWA, KANSAS, MINNESOTA, MISSOURI, NEBRASKA,
NORTH DAKOTA, OKLAHOMA, SOUTH DAKOTA

The prairie states of the central US became one of America's richest agricultural regions in the mid-19th century. Despite the "Dustbowl" crisis of the 1930s, which led many farmers to leave their ruined lands, agriculture is still crucial to the economy, and one third of the people still live in rural areas rather than large cities.

FARMING AND LAND USE

Wheat and corn grow on the fertile plains. Kansas is the leading grower of wheat in the entire US, while Iowa is one of the leaders in corn and livestock. Irrigation projects to combat drought are crucial in large areas. Livestock – including cattle in vast herds; pigs, particularly in Iowa, the Dakotas, and Nebraska; sheep; and turkeys – are raised throughout these states.

LAND USE

Other 37%
Cropland 43%
Forest 11%
Pasture 9%

FARMING AND LAND USE

- Cattle
- Pigs
- Poultry
- Sheep
- Corn
- Soybeans
- Wheat
- Cropland
- Forest
- Pasture
- Major conurbation

INDUSTRY

Industries related to agriculture, such as food processing and the production of farm machinery, are traditional in these states but high-tech industries – such as aeronautical engineering – are increasing and large aerospace plants are found in Wichita and Saint Louis. Oil and gas are extracted in great quantities toward the south of the region, especially in Oklahoma and Kansas.

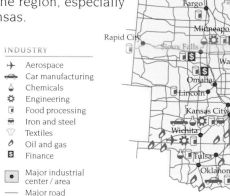

STRUCTURE OF INDUSTRY

Primary 4%
Services 76%
Manufacturing 20%

INDUSTRY

- ✈ Aerospace
- 🚗 Car manufacturing
- ⚗ Chemicals
- ⚙ Engineering
- 🏭 Food processing
- Iron and steel
- Textiles
- Oil and gas
- S Finance
- Major industrial center / area
- Major road

THE LANDSCAPE

Most of the eastern edge of this region is marked by the Mississippi River, while the Missouri bisects it, running from northwest to southeast. The Great Plains cover most of this area, gradually rising toward the Rocky Mountains at the far western edge of the Central States.

The Badlands (A 4)
The Badlands cover an area of about 2,000 sq miles in South Dakota. Heavily eroded by wind and water, almost nothing grows there.

Minnesota
Minnesota is filled with lakes, hills strewn with boulders, and mineral-rich deposits that have been left behind by the scouring movement of glaciers.

Chimney Rock (A-5)
Chimney Rock stands 500 ft above the plains. It is a remnant of an ancient land surface that was eroded by the North Platte River.

ENVIRONMENTAL ISSUES

Intensive agriculture requires large quantities of water to grow crops. Overintensive use of the land has destroyed the balance of soil and water in the past, leading to fertile farmland being turned into useless areas of "Dustbowl." These states have a great underground store of water known as the Ogallala Aquifer, but overextraction for irrigation is reducing the amount of available water.

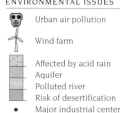

ENVIRONMENTAL ISSUES

- Urban air pollution
- Wind farm
- Affected by acid rain
- Aquifer
- Polluted river
- Risk of desertification
- Major industrial center

Great Plains (D 7)
Little more than a century ago the great flat plains that cover most of these states were home to wild grasses and massive herds of buffalo. In areas where lack of water has made farming impossible, large tracts of land are being allowed to return to grassland.

Great Salt Plains (D 7)
These arid salt plains cover about 45 sq miles of northern Oklahoma. An ancient salt lake once occupied the area. When the salt evaporated, only the salt flats were left.

NORTH AMERICA

POPULATION

The inhabitants are largely the descendants of Europeans who came to the region in the late 1800s. The entire region is primarily rural, with enormous tracts of land devoted to growing crops. North Dakota has no city with a population greater than 100,000.

URBAN/RURAL POPULATION DIVISION

Kansas City 1.9%   Oklahoma City 2.3%
Omaha 1.8%

Other towns and cities 60%

Rural population 34%

INHABITANTS PER SQ MILE

- More than 130
- 65–130
- Less than 65
- Major city

CLIMATE

The Central States have a continental climate, with hot, dry summers and long, cold winters. Unreliable rainfall can be a problem for farmers on the Great Plains.

January

July

TEMPERATURE AND PRECIPITATION

- More than 77°F
- 68 to 77°F
- 59 to 68°F
- 50 to 59°F
- 41 to 50°F
- 32 to 41°F
- 23 to 32°F
- 14 to 23°F
- 5 to 14°F
- Less than 5°F
- 4 Precipitation (in)

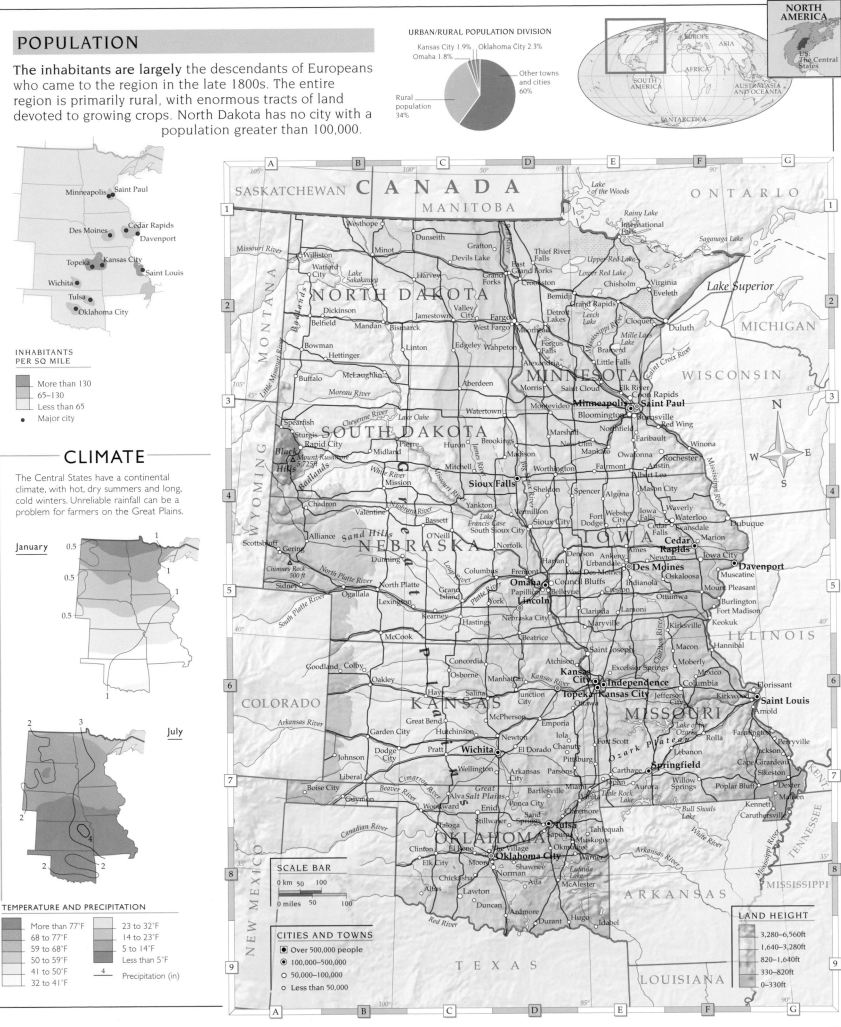

SCALE BAR

0 km 50 100

0 miles 50 100

CITIES AND TOWNS

- ◉ Over 500,000 people
- ◉ 100,000–500,000
- ○ 50,000–100,000
- ○ Less than 50,000

LAND HEIGHT

- 3,280–6,560ft
- 1,640–3,280ft
- 820–1,640ft
- 330–820ft
- 0–330ft

US: THE SOUTHWESTERN STATES

ARIZONA, NEW MEXICO, TEXAS

Large parts of the southwestern states were purchased from Mexico in 1848. This land of expansive plateaus, spectacular canyons, prairies, and deserts is home to several distinct peoples, whose customs and traditions are still practiced. The Navaho and Hopi own one-third of the land in Arizona, and the ruins of thousand-year-old cliff dwellings built by the Anasazi people are still preserved there today.

ENVIRONMENTAL ISSUES

Desertification is a serious problem in the southwestern states. Lack of water combined with intensive farming has allowed soils to erode. Drought is held at bay by irrigation, but falling water table levels are a cause for concern. New Mexico was the site for many early nuclear weapons tests, and some places remain contaminated.

ENVIRONMENTAL ISSUES

- Urban air pollution
- Former nuclear test site
- Path of recent, devastating hurricane
- Wind farm
- Desert area
- Risk of desertification
- Polluted river
- Major industrial center

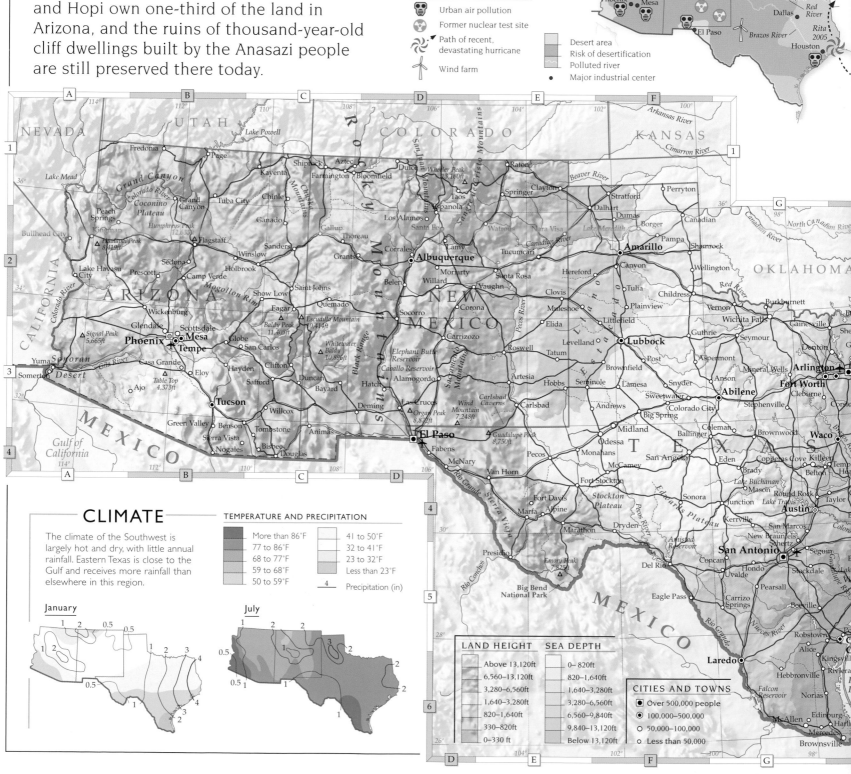

CLIMATE

The climate of the Southwest is largely hot and dry, with little annual rainfall. Eastern Texas is close to the Gulf and receives more rainfall than elsewhere in this region.

TEMPERATURE AND PRECIPITATION

- More than 86°F
- 77 to 86°F
- 68 to 77°F
- 59 to 68°F
- 50 to 59°F
- 41 to 50°F
- 32 to 41°F
- 23 to 32°F
- Less than 23°F
- 4 — Precipitation (in)

January

July

LAND HEIGHT
- Above 13,120ft
- 6,560–13,120ft
- 3,280–6,560ft
- 1,640–3,280ft
- 820–1,640ft
- 330–820ft
- 0–330 ft

SEA DEPTH
- 0–820ft
- 820–1,640ft
- 1,640–3,280ft
- 3,280–6,560ft
- 6,560–9,840ft
- 9,840–13,120ft
- Below 13,120ft

CITIES AND TOWNS
- Over 500,000 people
- 100,000–500,000
- 50,000–100,000
- Less than 50,000

NORTH
AMERICA
U.S.:
The Southwestern
States

THE LANDSCAPE

The arid, mountainous **Colorado Plateau** covers nearly half of Arizona, dipping toward the south to form desert basins. Parts of northern New Mexico are forested, but the south consists primarily of semiarid plains. Eastern Texas is bordered by the waters of the Gulf of Mexico, and the farmland of this area is well watered. Western Texas is covered by the Llano Estacado and, in the south, much of the land is arid.

Big Bend (E5)
Big Bend National Park gets its name from the 90° bend that the Rio Grande makes there.

Invading sea
The crust of southeastern Texas is warping, causing the land to subside and allowing the sea to invade. Hurricanes make the situation worse.

Grand Canyon (B1)
The Grand Canyon is a dramatic gorge cut in the rock by the Colorado River. It is about 217 miles long, 418 miles wide, and up to one-mile deep.

Carlsbad Caverns (B3)
Carlsbad Caverns are a series of underground caves, consisting of a three-level chain of limestone chambers studded with towering stalactites and stalagmites. They are millions of years old.

Rio Grande (G5)
The Rio Grande, or "Great River" forms all of the border between Texas and Mexico. It flows from its source high up in the Rocky Mountains, to the Gulf of Mexico.

INDUSTRY

Mining and related industries are one of the most important sources of income in the Southwest. Great deposits of oil lie under about 65% of Texas; copper and coal are mined in Arizona and New Mexico. Defense-related industries, including NASA have encouraged the development of many high-tech companies in Texas – and high-tech is also growing in larger cities such as Santa Fe and Phoenix.

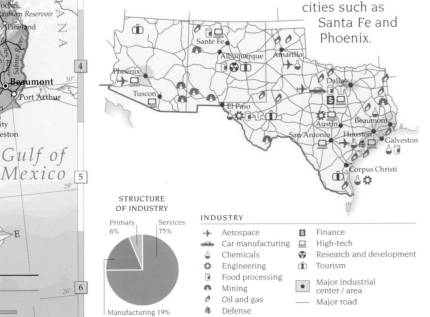

STRUCTURE OF INDUSTRY
- Primary 6%
- Services 75%
- Manufacturing 19%

INDUSTRY
- ✈ Aerospace
- 🚗 Car manufacturing
- ⚗ Chemicals
- ⚙ Engineering
- 🍴 Food processing
- ⛏ Mining
- 🛢 Oil and gas
- Defense
- $ Finance
- 💻 High-tech
- Research and development
- 🏛 Tourism
- ■ Major industrial center / area
- — Major road

FARMING AND LAND USE

Many cattle and sheep ranches have been set up on the open plateaus. Fruit and vegetables, grown in hothouses and cotton, hay, and wheat are among the major crops. Beef cattle and broiler chickens are raised on huge farms while sheep graze the drier parts of Texas. Extensive irrigation has made farming possible in even the most arid areas.

FARMING AND LAND USE
- 🐄 Cattle
- Poultry
- 🐑 Sheep
- Cotton
- Fruit and vegetables
- Irrigated crops
- Wheat
- Cropland
- Desert
- Forest
- Pasture
- • Major conurbation

LAND USE
- Other (including mountains) 80%
- Cropland 9%
- Pasture 5%
- Forest 6%

POPULATION

The descendants of Mexican and Spanish settlers and numerous groups of Native Americans live in the southwestern states. The great cities of Texas grew up on income from cattle-ranching and the oil industry. Much of Arizona and New Mexico is sparsely populated, but today people are moving to these states to escape the cold winters elsewhere.

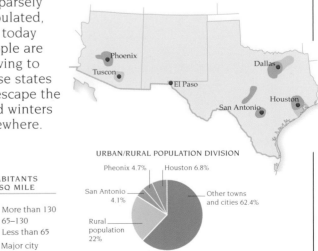

INHABITANTS PER SQ MILE
- More than 130
- 65–130
- Less than 65
- • Major city

URBAN/RURAL POPULATION DIVISION
- Pheonix 4.7%
- Houston 6.8%
- San Antonio 4.1%
- Other towns and cities 62.4%
- Rural population 22%

SCALE BAR

0 km   100
0 miles   100

US: THE MOUNTAIN STATES

COLORADO, IDAHO, MONTANA, NEVADA, UTAH, WYOMING

These states are home to some of the nation's most fantastic landscapes: endless treeless plains, craggy peaks, incredible desert landforms, and the salt flats of Utah. Although this was one of the last regions of the US to be settled, great mineral reserves have been exploited here in recent years, and new industries have grown up in some of the larger cities. Utah is the headquarters of the Mormon religion.

INDUSTRY

Rich mineral reserves, including coal, oil, and gas, are mined throughout the region and forests are a source of good-quality timber. In the larger cities of Colorado and Utah, growing industries include high-tech computer firms. Many tourists are drawn to this region to ski in the resorts of Colorado and to explore the wilderness.

INDUSTRY

- ⚗ Chemicals
- 📷 Food processing
- ☕ Textiles
- ⛏ Coal
- ⚒ Mining
- ⬧ Oil and gas
- ⚙ Timber processing
- ♨ Gambling
- 💻 High-tech
- ⚛ Research and development
- ⊕ Tourism

- ● Major industrial center / area
- — Major road

STRUCTURE OF INDUSTRY

- Primary 4%
- Manufacturing 16%
- Services 80%

FARMING AND LAND USE

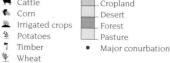

In the southern mountain states, cattle ranching is the main form of farming. Wheat and corn are grown in the eastern states, and the fertile soils of the Snake River valley in Idaho produce large crops of potatoes and many other vegetables. The northern states have many large commercial forests.

FARMING AND LAND USE

- 🐄 Cattle
- 🌽 Corn
- ⚘ Irrigated crops
- ⚘ Potatoes
- 🌲 Timber
- 🌿 Wheat

- Cropland
- Desert
- Forest
- Pasture
- ● Major conurbation

LAND USE

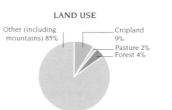

- Other (including mountains) 85%
- Cropland 9%
- Pasture 2%
- Forest 4%

POPULATION

Colorado, with the growing city of Denver, is the most populous of the mountain states. In other states, people have settled close to sources of water such as Great Salt Lake in Utah. Many towns have less than 10,000 people and are far apart.

INHABITANTS PER SQ MILE

- More than 130
- 65–130
- Less than 65
- ● Major city

URBAN/RURAL POPULATION DIVISION

- Las Vegas 4.3%
- Denver 4.7%
- Colorado Springs 3%
- Other towns and cities 64%
- Rural population 24%

THE LANDSCAPE

The great Rocky Mountains and many smaller mountain ranges cover almost all of this region.
Only eastern Montana is not mountainous. Here western parts of the Great Plains rise to meet the mountains. Parts of the southern mountain states are very arid with spectacular scenery, including blocklike *mesas*, formed by erosion.

Continental Divide
From this watershed, crossing the Lewis Range, rivers flow in different directions across North America. Some flow east to Hudson Bay, some south to the Gulf of Mexico and others west to the Pacific Ocean.

Yellowstone National Park (D 3)
Yellowstone was set up in 1872 as the first national park in the US. Water from hot springs has deposited minerals as it cools, forming white rock terraces close to the springs.

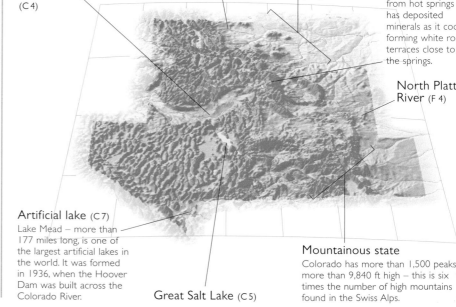

Snake River (C 4)

Great Plains (E 2)

North Platte River (F 4)

Artificial lake (C 7)
Lake Mead – more than 177 miles long, is one of the largest artificial lakes in the world. It was formed in 1936, when the Hoover Dam was built across the Colorado River.

Great Salt Lake (C 5)

Mountainous state
Colorado has more than 1,500 peaks more than 9,840 ft high – this is six times the number of high mountains found in the Swiss Alps.

NORTH
AMERICA

USA:
The Mountain
States

ENVIRONMENTAL ISSUES

Parts of the Rocky Mountains, including the National Parks, have become major centers for outdoor pursuits. The sheer number of people puts pressure on the land leading to soil erosion, and increasing the possibility of landslides. Nevada remains the main testing ground for the US nuclear arsenal, and there are many older, disused sites here.

Glacier

Yellowstone
Grand Teton

Salt Lake
City
Rocky
Mountains
Denver

Capitol Reef
Canyonlands

Zion   Bryce
Canyon   Mesa Verde

ENVIRONMENTAL ISSUES

Former nuclear test site
Nuclear test site
Urban air pollution
Wind farm
National Park
Winter tourist resort
Major industrial center

CLIMATE

In the lowland areas, particularly in the south, summers are often very hot and dry. Parts of the Rocky Mountains are permanently covered by snow, and some of the high passes are cut off by snow in the winter.

January

July

TEMPERATURE AND PRECIPITATION

More than 86°F	32 to 41°F
77 to 86°F	23 to 32°F
68 to 77°F	14 to 23°F
59 to 68°F	Less than 14°F
50 to 59°F	
41 to 50°F	4 Precipitation (in)

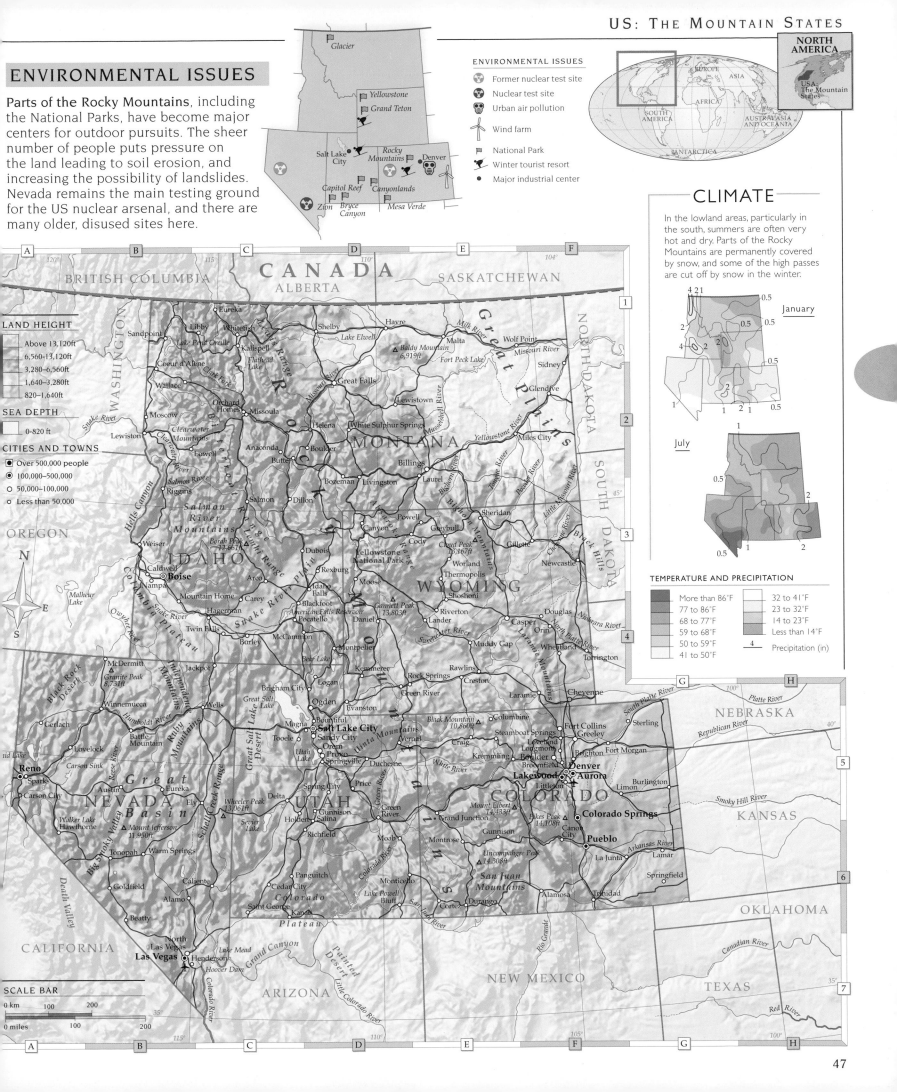

LAND HEIGHT

Above 13,120ft
6,560–13,120ft
3,280–6,560ft
1,640–3,280ft
820–1,640ft

SEA DEPTH

0–820 ft

CITIES AND TOWNS

Over 500,000 people
100,000–500,000
50,000–100,000
Less than 50,000

SCALE BAR

0 km   100   200
0 miles   100   200

CANADA

BRITISH COLUMBIA
ALBERTA
SASKATCHEWAN

WASHINGTON
OREGON
IDAHO
MONTANA
NORTH DAKOTA
SOUTH DAKOTA
WYOMING
NEBRASKA
NEVADA
UTAH
COLORADO
KANSAS
CALIFORNIA
ARIZONA
NEW MEXICO
OKLAHOMA
TEXAS

Great Plains
ROCKY MOUNTAINS

US: THE PACIFIC STATES

CALIFORNIA, OREGON, WASHINGTON

The earliest European visitors to the West Coast were fur-trappers and miners, but the Gold Rush of 1849 brought in the first major wave of settlers. Drawn by tales of the beautiful scenery, pleasant climate, and fertile valleys, more people arrived on the newly built railroads. People from all over the world are still moving into this region, seeking jobs in the dynamic economy and the famous laid-back lifestyle.

INDUSTRY

The Pacific States are the center of the high-tech computer industry with Silicon Valley between San Francisco and San Jose, and electronics industries growing in Portland and Seattle. Other major industries include research and development for the defense industry, filmmaking in Los Angeles, food processing and lumbering. Tourism is well developed throughout the Pacific States.

STRUCTURE OF INDUSTRY

Primary 2%
Services 81%
Manufacturing 17%

INDUSTRY

- ✈ Aerospace
- 🜨 Chemicals
- ⚙ Engineering
- 🍴 Food processing
- Iron and steel
- Shipbuilding
- ⌁ Textiles
- 🌲 Timber processing
- 🎬 Film industry
- 💻 High-tech
- ☢ Research and development
- 🎪 Tourism
- ■ Major industrial center / area
- — Major road

FARMING AND LAND USE

California's Central Valley and the river valleys of Washington and Oregon provide ideal conditions for a wide range of fruit and vegetables, including citrus fruit and grapes. Poultry farming is widespread in the northwest and there are many large cattle ranches. Millions of acres of commercial forest are located in this region.

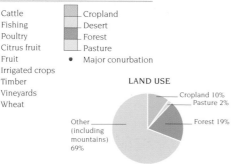

FARMING AND LAND USE

- 🐄 Cattle
- 🎣 Fishing
- 🦃 Poultry
- 🍊 Citrus fruit
- 🍓 Fruit
- Irrigated crops
- 🌲 Timber
- 🍇 Vineyards
- 🌾 Wheat
- Cropland
- Desert
- Forest
- Pasture
- • Major conurbation

LAND USE

Cropland 10%
Pasture 2%
Forest 19%
Other (including mountains) 69%

ENVIRONMENTAL ISSUES

Some of the great national parks of the US, including Yosemite and Sequoia, are found here. The immense numbers of visitors put great pressure on the landscape. Water is in short supply in large parts of California, and desertification, caused by overintense farming methods, is a problem. Wind farms have been set up on the hills above the San Joaquin valley to provide alternative energy.

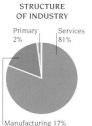

ENVIRONMENTAL ISSUES

- 🏴 National park
- 😷 Urban air pollution
- Wind farm
- Risk of wild fire
- Desert area
- Risk of desertification
- Severe risk of desertification
- Polluted rivers
- • Major industrial center

THE LANDSCAPE

The Coast and Cascade ranges run north–south through Oregon and Washington while further south, the high Sierra Nevada run along California's eastern fringes. Two broad valleys, the Sacramento and San Joaquin, are known as the Central Valley, and form a trough beneath the Sierra Nevada. The south is extremely dry – Death Valley is the hottest place in the entire US.

Northern rain forest (B 2)
The ocean-facing side of the Olympic Mountains receives 142 in of rain every year, supporting the only true temperate rain forest in the Northern Hemisphere.

Hells Canyon (D 3)
Hells Canyon is North America's deepest gorge. Running through part of Oregon, it was created as the Snake River cut down through the land.

Volcanic eruption (B 2)
Mount St. Helens erupted in 1980, killing 57 people and destroying a vast area.

San Andreas Fault
The San Andreas Fault runs for 650 miles underneath California. When both sides of the fault move at different rates, tremors and earthquakes result.

Hottest place (D 7)
In 1913, Death Valley set the record for the highest temperature ever recorded in the US, at 134° F.

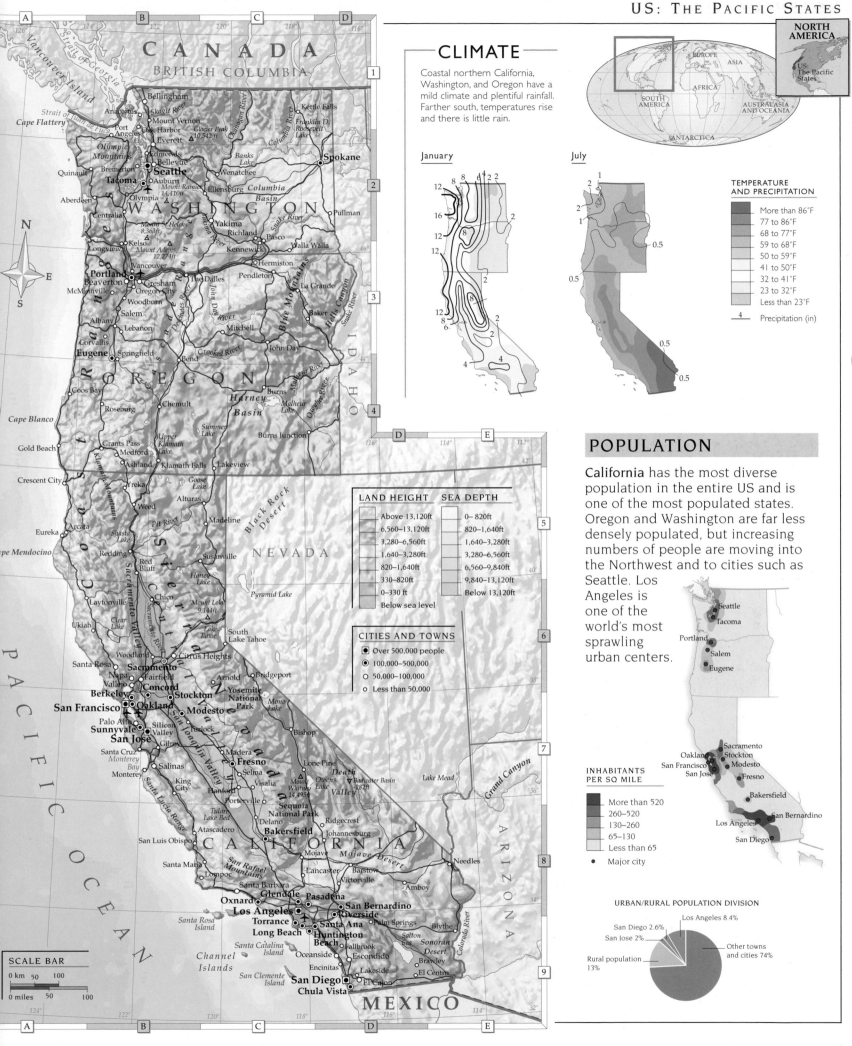

NORTH AMERICA

US: The Pacific States

CLIMATE

Coastal northern California, Washington, and Oregon have a mild climate and plentiful rainfall. Farther south, temperatures rise and there is little rain.

January

July

TEMPERATURE AND PRECIPITATION

More than 86°F
77 to 86°F
68 to 77°F
59 to 68°F
50 to 59°F
41 to 50°F
32 to 41°F
23 to 32°F
Less than 23°F

―4― Precipitation (in)

POPULATION

California has the most diverse population in the entire US and is one of the most populated states. Oregon and Washington are far less densely populated, but increasing numbers of people are moving into the Northwest and to cities such as Seattle. Los Angeles is one of the world's most sprawling urban centers.

INHABITANTS PER SQ MILE

More than 520
260–520
130–260
65–130
Less than 65

● Major city

URBAN/RURAL POPULATION DIVISION

Los Angeles 8.4%
San Diego 2.6%
San Jose 2%
Rural population 13%
Other towns and cities 74%

LAND HEIGHT

Above 13,120ft
6,560–13,120ft
3,280–6,560ft
1,640–3,280ft
820–1,640ft
330–820ft
0–330 ft
Below sea level

SEA DEPTH

0– 820ft
820–1,640ft
1,640–3,280ft
3,280–6,560ft
6,560–9,840ft
9,840–13,120ft
Below 13,120ft

CITIES AND TOWNS

▣ Over 500,000 people
● 100,000–500,000
◦ 50,000–100,000
○ Less than 50,000

CANADA

BRITISH COLUMBIA

Vancouver Island

Strait of Georgia

Strait of Juan de Fuca

Cape Flattery

Bellingham
Anacortes
Skagit River
Mount Vernon
Port Angeles
Oak Harbor
Edmonds
Everett
Glacier Peak 10,542ft
Banks Lake
Kettle Falls
Franklin D. Roosevelt Lake
Columbia River
Okanogan River
Bellevue
Seattle
Bremerton
Tacoma
Auburn
Mount Rainier 14,410ft
Olympia
Ellensburg
Wenatchee
Columbia Basin
Spokane
Quinault
Aberdeen
Centralia
Olympic Mountains

WASHINGTON

Mount St Helens 8,363ft
Yakima Richland
Snake River
Pasco
Pullman
Walla Walla
Kennewick
Hermiston
Mount Adams 12,274ft
Longview
Kelso
Vancouver
Portland
Beaverton
Gresham
Oregon City
The Dalles
Pendleton
La Grande
John Day River
McMinnville
Woodburn
Salem
Albany
Lebanon
Corvallis
Eugene
Springfield
Mitchell
Baker
Hells Canyon
Snake River
Bend
Crooked River
John Day
Blue Mountains

OREGON

Coos Bay
Roseburg
Chemult
Harney Basin
Malheur River
Malheur Lake
Owyhee River
Summer Lake
Burns
Cape Blanco
Upper Klamath Lake
Burns Junction
Gold Beach
Grants Pass
Medford
Ashland
Klamath Falls
Lakeview
Goose Lake

IDAHO

Crescent City
Yreka
Weed
Alturas
Black Rock Desert

Eureka
Arcata
Cape Mendocino
Shasta Lake
Redding
Red Bluff
Pit River
Susanville
Honey Lake
Madeline

NEVADA

Laytonville
Ukiah
Clear Lake
Chico
Mount Lola 9,144ft
Pyramid Lake

Santa Rosa
Napa
Vallejo
Berkeley
San Francisco
Oakland
Palo Alto
Sunnyvale
San Jose
Santa Cruz
Monterey Bay
Monterey
Woodland
Sacramento
Fairfield
Concord
Stockton
Modesto
Citrus Heights
Arnold
Bridgeport
Lake Tahoe
South Lake Tahoe
Yosemite National Park
Mono Lake
Turlock
Bishop
Gilroy
Madera
Salinas
King City
Fresno
Selma
Visalia
Hanford
Porterville
Lone Pine
Mount Whitney 14,495ft
Owens Lake
Death Valley
Badwater Basin −282ft
Lake Mead
Grand Canyon
Santa Lucia Range
San Luis Obispo
Tulare Lake Bed
Delano
Bakersfield
Ridgecrest
Johannesburg

CALIFORNIA

Santa Maria
Lompoc
San Rafael Mountains
Santa Barbara
Lancaster
Barstow
Victorville
Mojave
Mojave Desert
Needles
Amboy

ARIZONA

Glendale
Pasadena
Oxnard
Los Angeles
Torrance
Long Beach
Huntington Beach
Riverside
San Bernardino
Santa Ana
Palm Springs
Blythe
Salton Sea
Sonoran Desert
Colorado River
Santa Rosa Island
Santa Catalina Island
San Clemente Island
Channel Islands
Oceanside
Fallbrook
Escondido
Encinitas
Lakeside
Bradley
El Centro
San Diego
Chula Vista
El Cajon

PACIFIC OCEAN

MEXICO

SCALE BAR

0 km 50 100
0 miles 50 100

Sacramento River
Sacramento Valley
Sierra Nevada
San Joaquin Valley
Sequoia National Park

ALASKA

A **magnificent land** of mountains, forests, and snowfields, with rich oil and mineral reserves, Alaska was purchased from Russia for $1 million in 1867. Almost 650,000 people live here, many drawn by the oil industry. Some of Alaska's native peoples like the Aleuts and Inupiaq still live by hunting and fishing.

ENVIRONMENTAL ISSUES

Much of northern Alaska is covered by permafrost (permanently frozen ground). The Trans-Alaska Pipeline, which brings oil from Prudhoe Bay to Valdez, was built above ground to stop the permafrost melting. A number of major oil spills have threatened Alaska's unique environment.

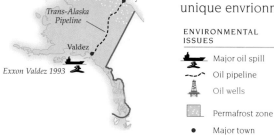

Trans-Alaska Pipeline
Prudhoe Bay
Valdez
Exxon Valdez 1993

ENVIRONMENTAL ISSUES
🚢 Major oil spill
— Oil pipeline
🛢 Oil wells
▨ Permafrost zone
● Major town

INDUSTRY

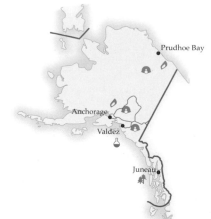

Prudhoe Bay
Anchorage
Valdez
Juneau

The Alaskan economy is dominated by the oil business. The oilfields of Alaska are of a similar size to those in the Persian Gulf. Minerals including gold are mined in the mountains, and paper products are exported to countries on the Pacific Rim.

INDUSTRY
⚗ Chemicals
⛏ Mining
💧 Oil and gas
🌲 Timber processing
■ Major industrial center
— Major road

FARMING AND LAND USE

Anchorage

Salmon are caught in great numbers in the waters of the north Pacific. Much of the state – more than 22.2 million acres – is covered by forest which is commercially lumbered. Most food must be imported, although fruit is grown in hothouses near the larger cities.

FARMING AND LAND USE
↰ Fishing
🦀 Fruit
🌲 Timber
▨ Barren
▨ Forest
▨ Mountains
▨ Tundra
● Major conurbation

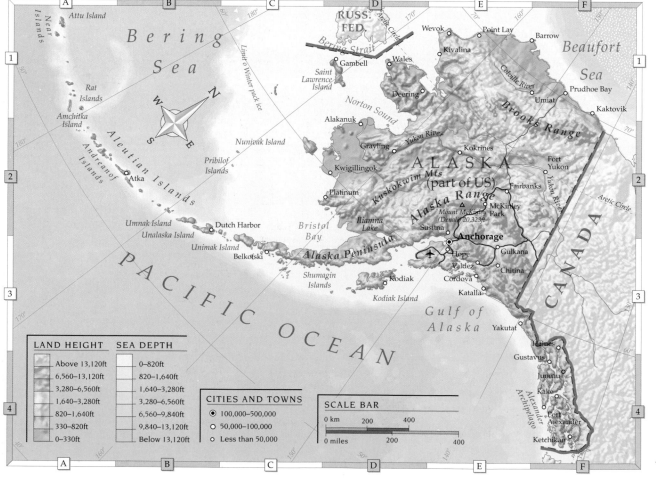

LAND HEIGHT
Above 13,120ft
6,560–13,120ft
3,280–6,560ft
1,640–3,280ft
820–1,640ft
330–820ft
0–330ft

SEA DEPTH
0–820ft
820–1,640ft
1,640–3,280ft
3,280–6,560ft
6,560–9,840ft
9,840–13,120ft
Below 13,120ft

CITIES AND TOWNS
◉ 100,000–500,000
○ 50,000–100,000
○ Less than 50,000

SCALE BAR
0 km 200 400
0 miles 200 400

CLIMATE

Parts of northern Alaska are frozen year-round and can be cut off entirely in the winter. Summers are milder – especially in the Aleutians.

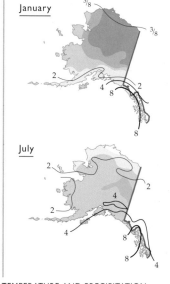

January

July

TEMPERATURE AND PRECIPITATION

More than 59°F
50 to 59°F
41 to 50°F
32 to 41°F
23 to 32°F
14 to 23°F
5 to 14°F
Less than 5°F
—4— Precipitation (in)

HAWAI'I

Hawai'i is the 50th US state. It lies far from the mainland in the middle of the Pacific Ocean. The island chain was formed by volcanoes, only one of which, Mauna Loa, remains active today. The islands' indigenous peoples are Polynesians, but continued immigration means that they now make up only 9% of the population.

INDUSTRY AND LAND USE

Tourism is the most important industry in Hawai'i, accounting for one in every three jobs. The naval base at Pearl Harbor also provides jobs for numerous people. The many large plantations grow sugarcane, bananas, and tropical fruit for export.

FARMING AND LAND USE

Cattle		Cropland
Fishing		Forest
Fruit		Mountain region
Sugarcane		Pasture

INDUSTRY

Tourism   • Major town

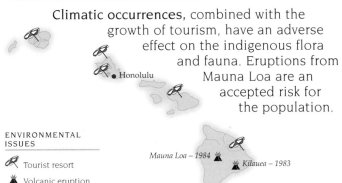

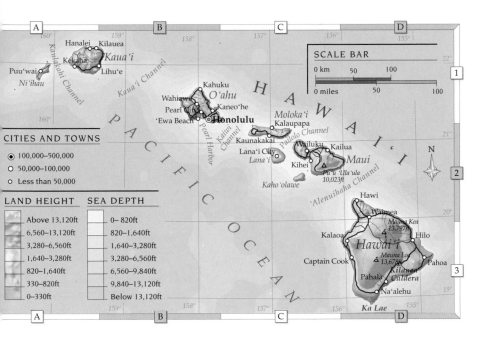

CITIES AND TOWNS

◉ 100,000–500,000
○ 50,000–100,000
○ Less than 50,000

LAND HEIGHT	SEA DEPTH
Above 13,120ft	0– 820ft
6,560–13,120ft	820–1,640ft
3,280–6,560ft	1,640–3,280ft
1,640–3,280ft	3,280–6,560ft
820–1,640ft	6,560–9,840ft
330–820ft	9,840–13,120ft
0–330ft	Below 13,120ft

ENVIRONMENTAL ISSUES

Climatic occurrences, combined with the growth of tourism, have an adverse effect on the indigenous flora and fauna. Eruptions from Mauna Loa are an accepted risk for the population.

ENVIRONMENTAL ISSUES

Tourist resort
Volcanic eruption
• Major town

Mauna Loa – 1984   Kilauea – 1983

US OVERSEAS TERRITORIES

America's overseas territories have traditionally been seen as strategically or economically important. In most cases, the local population has been given a say in deciding whether it wants to govern itself. A US commonwealth territory has a greater level of independence than a US unincorporated or external territory. The US has 13 overseas territories: the four largest are shown here.

AMERICAN SAMOA

American Samoa consists of five volcanic islands and two coral atolls in the south Pacific. The people are among the last true Polynesians.

US VIRGIN ISLANDS

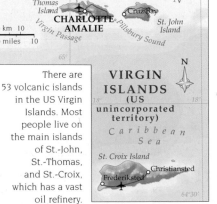

There are 53 volcanic islands in the US Virgin Islands. Most people live on the main islands of St.-John, St.-Thomas, and St.-Croix, which has a vast oil refinery.

PUERTO RICO

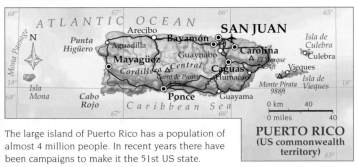

The large island of Puerto Rico has a population of almost 4 million people. In recent years there have been campaigns to make it the 51st US state.

GUAM

The US military base that covers one-third of the island makes Guam strategically important to the US. The Chamorro, the indigenous people, are in charge of political and social life.

MEXICO

Mexico is a large country with a rich mixture of traditions and cultures. The ancient civilization of the Aztecs that flourished here was crushed by Spanish invaders in the 16th century. Spain ruled Mexico until its independence in 1836, and today the country has the world's largest Spanish-speaking population. Mexico is mostly dry and mountainous, and farmland is limited, so the country has to import most of the basic foods it needs to feed its people.

FARMING AND LAND USE

Most of the land suitable for farming is planted with corn – a big part of the Mexican diet. Along the Gulf coast coffee, sugarcane, and cotton are grown on plantations for export. Parts of the dry north are irrigated to grow cotton, but most of the land is taken up by large cattle ranches. Fishing, especially for shellfish such as lobster and shrimp is important in coastal areas.

FARMING AND LAND USE

- Cattle
- Fishing
- Sheep
- Bananas
- Coffee
- Corn
- Cotton
- Fruit
- Grapes
- Shellfish
- Sugarcane
- Timber
- Cropland
- Desert
- Forest
- Pasture
- Wetland
- Major conurbation

LAND USE

Cropland 14%
Pasture 42%
Other 15%
Forest 29%

THE LANDSCAPE

Much of Mexico is made up of a high plateau. The climate there is very dry and varies between true desert in the north, and semidesert farther south. The plateau is separated from the coastal plains by two long, rugged mountain chains: the Eastern Sierra Madre and the Western Sierra Madre. Toward the south, the mountain ranges join, meeting in the region of high volcanic peaks that surround Mexico City.

The Rio Grande (D 2)
This river flows from Colorado in the US and forms much of Mexico's northern border. It crosses a vast arid area on its way to the Gulf of Mexico.

Earthquakes and volcanoes
Volcanic activity is common in Mexico. Popocatépetl (F 5) and Volcán El Chichónal (G 5) have erupted recently, and Mexico City was hit by a devastating earthquake in 1985.

Eastern Sierra Madre (D 5).

Yucatan Peninsula (H 4)
The Yucatan Peninsula is a low, wide tableland, formed by layers of limestone. Limestone absorbs water, so there are few rivers on the peninsula, and the tropical rainforests found there are fed mainly by streams and underground water.

Baja (Lower) California (B 3)
This long and very dry peninsula separates the Gulf of California from the Pacific Ocean. The Gulf was formed after the last Ice Age, when the sea rose to flood a major rift valley.

Western Sierra Madre (C 3).

POPULATION

Most of the north is sparsely populated due to the hot, dry climate and lack of cultivable farmland. As people have migrated from the countryside in search of work, the cities have grown dramatically; almost 75% of Mexicans now live in urban areas. Mexico City is home to almost a fifth of the population and is one of the world's largest cities.

INHABITANTS PER SQ MILE

- More than 520
- 260–520
- 130–260
- Less than 130
- ■ Capital city
- ● Major city

URBAN/RURAL POPULATION DIVISION

Mexico City 17.1%
Guadalajara 3.5%
Monterrey 3.1%
Other towns and cities 50.3%
Rural population 26%

ENVIRONMENTAL ISSUES

Fast, unplanned growth has led to poor sanitation and water supplies in Mexico City, while the wall of mountains that surrounds the city traps pollution from cars and factories, giving it some of the world's worst air pollution. Much of Mexico's tropical rainforest has been felled, leading to increased soil erosion. Land clearance farther north is also causing desertification.

ENVIRONMENTAL ISSUES

- Risk of desertification
- Deforested areas
- Remaining tropical forests
- Path of recent, devastating hurricane
- ● Major industrial city
- Volcanic eruption
- Urban air pollution
- Flooding

Emily 2005
Wilma 2005
Mitch 1998
Dean 2007
Guadalajara
Mexico City
Nevado de Colima 1994
Popocatépetl 1994
Volcán El Chichónal 1994
2007

CALIFORNIA

Tijuana Mexicali
Sa

Rosarito
Ensenada

Isla Cedros Sebas
Vizca
Guerrero Neg

Tropic of Cancer

Isla Clarión

INDUSTRY

Oil and gas on the Gulf coast are the biggest source of income. Mexico is also rich in other minerals; it is the world's top silver producer. Manufacturing is centered around Mexico City and along the US border, where mainly foreign-owned factories assemble products for export. Tourism is also very important to Mexico.

Mexicali
Ciudad Juárez
Chihuahua
Piedras Negras
Nuevo Laredo
Torreón
Monterrey
San Luis Potosí
Tampico
Mérida
Guadalajara
Veracruz
Mexico City
Puebla
Minatitlán
Manzanillo
Oaxaca
Salina Cruz

STRUCTURE OF INDUSTRY

Primary 4%
Services 70%
Manufacturing 26%

INDUSTRY

- Car manufacturing
- Electronics
- Engineering
- Food processing
- Iron and steel
- Oil refining
- Textiles
- Mining
- Oil and gas
- Tourism
- Major industrial center / area
- Major road

CLIMATE

Northern Mexico and the peninsula of Baja California are dry, hot, and largely desert. Toward the south, rainfall increases, especially in July. Moist, warm conditions allow rainforests to grow.

January

July

TEMPERATURE AND PRECIPITATION

- More than 86°F
- 77 to 86°F
- 68 to 77°F
- 59 to 68°F
- 50 to 59°F
- 41 to 50°F
- Less than 41°F
- 4 — Precipitation (in)

Map

ALABAMA
GEORGIA
FLORIDA
MISSISSIPPI
LOUISIANA
ARIZONA
NEW MEXICO
TEXAS
UNITED STATES OF AMERICA

Red River
Sabine River
Mississippi River
Brazos River
Colorado River
Pecos River
Río Grande del Norte

Mississippi Delta

Nogales
Ciudad Juárez
Agua Prieta
Samalayuca
Cananea
Magdalena
Cumpas
San Pedro de la Cueva
Nuevo Casas Grandes
El Sueco
Ojinaga
Villa Acuña
Boquillas
Piedras Negras
Hermosillo
Isla Tiburón
El Sáuz
Chihuahua
San Miguel
Nueva Rosita
Sabinas
Nuevo Laredo
Guaymas
Empalme
Esperanza
Delicias
Cuauhtémoc
Ciudad Camargo
Jiménez
Monclova
Sabinas Hidalgo
Ciudad Miguel Alemán
Padre Island
Ciudad Obregón
Navojoa
San Francisco del Oro
Hidalgo del Parral
Santa Barbara
Reynosa
Río Bravo
Matamoros
Huatabampo
San Blas
Los Mochis
Guamúchil
Gómez Palacio
San Pedro
Parras
Saltillo
Monterrey
Montemorelos
Linares
Laguna Madre
Isla Santa Margarita
La Paz
El Dorado
Bahía de La Paz
Navolato
Guasave
Ciudad Lerdo
Torreón
Miguel Auza
Juan Aldama
Río Grande
MEXICO
Loreto
Culiacán
Tropic of Cancer
Santa Genoveva
Miraflores
7894ft
San Lucas Cape
Durango
Fresnillo
Zacatecas
San Luis Potosí
Ciudad Victoria
Gulf of Mexico
Yucatan Channel
Rio Lagartos
Cancún
Tizimín
Isla Cozumel
Mazatlán
Guadalupe
Villanueva
Ciudad Mante
Ciudad Madero
Tampico
Progreso
Motul
Mérida
Umán
Valladolid
Escuinapa
Acaponeta
Lagos de Moreno
Río Verde
Pánuco
Ciudad Valles
Laguna de Tamiahua
Ticul
Peto
Oxkutzcab
Tekax
Islas Tres Marías
Tuxpan
Jalpa
Yahualica
Aguascalientes
Tamazunchale
Tuxpán
Bay of Campeche
Campeche
Yucatan Peninsula
Felipe Carrillo Puerto
Isla San Juanito
Isla María Madre
Isla María Magdalena
Isla María Cleofas
Tepic
León
Dolores Hidalgo
Poza Rica
Papantla
Champotón
Guanajuato
Querétaro
Tequila
Tulancingo
Laguna de Términos
Chetumal
Puerto Vallarta
Guadalajara
Irapuato
Pachuca
Teziutlán
Frontera
Carmen
Tlaquepaque
Zamora de Hidalgo
Morelia
MEXICO CITY
Tlaxcala
Xalapa
Veracruz
Comalcalco
Villahermosa
Ciudad Guzmán
Toluca
Puebla
Córdoba
Coatzacoalcos
Macuspana
BELIZE
Colima
Tuxpan
Uruapan
Cuernavaca
Cuautla
Tehuacán
San Andrés Tuxtla
Minatitlán
Teapa
Manzanillo
Tecomán
Aguililla
Taxco
Iguala
Zacatepec
Juxtepec
Isthmus of Tehuantepec
Volcán El Chichonal
Tuxtla
San Cristóbal de Las Casas
Presa del Infiernillo
Chilpancingo
Oaxaca
Matías Romero
Ixtepec
Ocozocuautla
Presa de la Angostura
Comitán
Lázaro Cárdenas
Ixtapa
Río Balsas
Sierra Madre del Sur
Tehuantepec
Juchitán
Pijijiapan
Arriaga
Tecpan
Pinotepa Nacional
Miahuatlán
Salina Cruz
Escuintla
Huixtla
GUATEMALA
HONDURAS
Acapulco
Puerto Escondido
Puerto Angel
Gulf of Tehuantepec
Tapachula
Ciudad Hidalgo
EL SALVADOR
Popocatépetl 17,888ft
Pérote

Revillagigedo (part of Mexico)
Isla San Benedicto
Isla Socorro
Isla Clarión (part of Mexico)

PACIFIC OCEAN

LAND HEIGHT
- Above 13,120ft
- 6,560–13,120ft
- 3,280–6,560ft
- 1,640–3,280ft
- 820–1,640ft
- 330–820ft
- 0–330ft

SEA DEPTH
- 0–820ft
- 820–1,640ft
- 1,640–3,280ft
- 3,280–6,560ft
- 6,560–9,840ft
- 9,840–13,120ft
- Below 13,120ft

CITIES AND TOWNS
- Over 500,000 people
- 100,000–500,000
- 50,000–100,000
- Less than 50,000

SCALE BAR
km 200
miles 200

CENTRAL AMERICA

BELIZE, COSTA RICA, EL SALVADOR, GUATEMALA, HONDURAS, NICARAGUA, PANAMA

Central America lies on a narrow bridge of land which links North and South America. All the countries here, except Belize, were once governed by Spain. Today, most of their people are *mestizos* – a mix of the original Maya Indian inhabitants and Spanish settlers. The hot, steamy climate is ideal for growing tropical crops, such as coffee and bananas, which are exported worldwide.

POPULATION

Central America's people live mainly in the valleys of the central highlands or along the Pacific coastal plains. Despite the threat of volcanic eruptions and earthquakes, towns and cities were developed in these areas because of the fertile volcanic soils found there. Around half the population still lives in rural areas, mostly in small villages or remote settlements, but the cities have expanded rapidly and overcrowding has become a serious problem.

INHABITANTS PER SQ MILE

More than 130
52–130
Less than 52
■ Capital city

URBAN/RURAL POPULATION DIVISION

San Salvador 3.3%
Tegucigalpa 3.2%
Managua 3.5%
Other towns and cities 37%
Rural population 53%

FARMING AND LAND USE

About half of all the agricultural products grown here are exported. The Pacific coast has fertile, well-watered land suitable for growing cotton and sugarcane. In the central highlands are big coffee plantations and ranches where beef cattle are raised. Bananas grow well along the humid Caribbean coastal plain, and shrimp and lobster are caught offshore.

FARMING AND LAND USE

- Cattle
- Shellfish
- Bananas
- Coffee
- Corn
- Cotton
- Sugarcane
- Timber

Cropland
Forest
Pasture
• Major conurbation

LAND USE

Pasture 27%
Forest 35%
Cropland 15%
Other 23%

THE LANDSCAPE

The Sierra Madre in the north and the Cordillera Central to the south form a mountainous ridge that stretches down most of Central America. Along the Pacific coast north of Panama is a belt of more than 40 active volcanoes. The mountains are broken by valleys and basins with large, fertile areas of rich, volcanic soil.

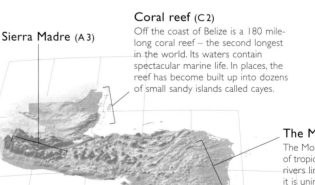

Sierra Madre (A 3)

Coral reef (C 2)
Off the coast of Belize is a 180 mile-long coral reef – the second longest in the world. Its waters contain spectacular marine life. In places, the reef has become built up into dozens of small sandy islands called cayes.

The Mosquito Coast (E 4)
The Mosquito Coast is a remote area of tropical rain forests, lagoons, and rivers lined with mangroves. Most of it is uninhabited by humans, but there is a huge variety of animal species, including monkeys and alligators.

Lake Nicaragua (E 5)
This large freshwater lake contains about 400 islands, some of which are active volanoes like Volcán Concepcion. The lake is also home to the world's only freshwater sharks.

Cordillera Central (G 6)

Panama Canal (H 6)
The Panama Canal links the Atlantic and Pacific oceans along a distance of 51 miles. Half of its route passes through Lake Gatún, a freshwater lake that acts as a reservoir for the canal, providing water to operate the locks.

ENVIRONMENTAL ISSUES

Central America's rain forests are rapidly being cut down for timber and to make way for farmland and land for building. Over half of Guatemala's forests have been felled, mostly in the last 30 years. The situation is also bleak in Honduras, Costa Rica, and Nicaragua. Central America has a line of volcanoes running through the region which, are still active.

Mitch 1998
Felix 2007
Volcán Tacaná 1986
Volcán de Fuego 1974
Volcán de Izalco 1958
Volcán San Cristobal 2000
Volcán Cerro Negro 1995
Volcán Masaya 2001
Volcán Concepcion 1986
Volcán Arenal 1998, 2000
Volcán Rincon de la Vieja 1998

ENVIRONMENTAL ISSUES

Volcanic eruption
Deforested areas
Remaining forests
Path of recent, devastating hurricane

NORTH
AMERICA

CLIMATE

Temperatures are high all year round, although in January the Caribbean side of Central America is cooler and wetter than the Pacific side. Summers are generally much wetter, especially in the Sierra Madre in Guatemala and on the Pacific coasts of Costa Rica and Panama.

**TEMPERATURE
AND PRECIPITATION**

More than 77°F
68 to 77°F
Less than 68°F

4 ─── Precipitation (in)

January

July

INDUSTRY

Coffee, fish, and timber processing, fruit exporting, and textile-weaving are typical of the small-scale industries found in Central America. Most industries are based in the capital cities and larger towns. In Panama, many people work at the Panama Canal, which is one of the world's busiest shipping routes. The country is also a major financial center, with many banking and insurance companies.

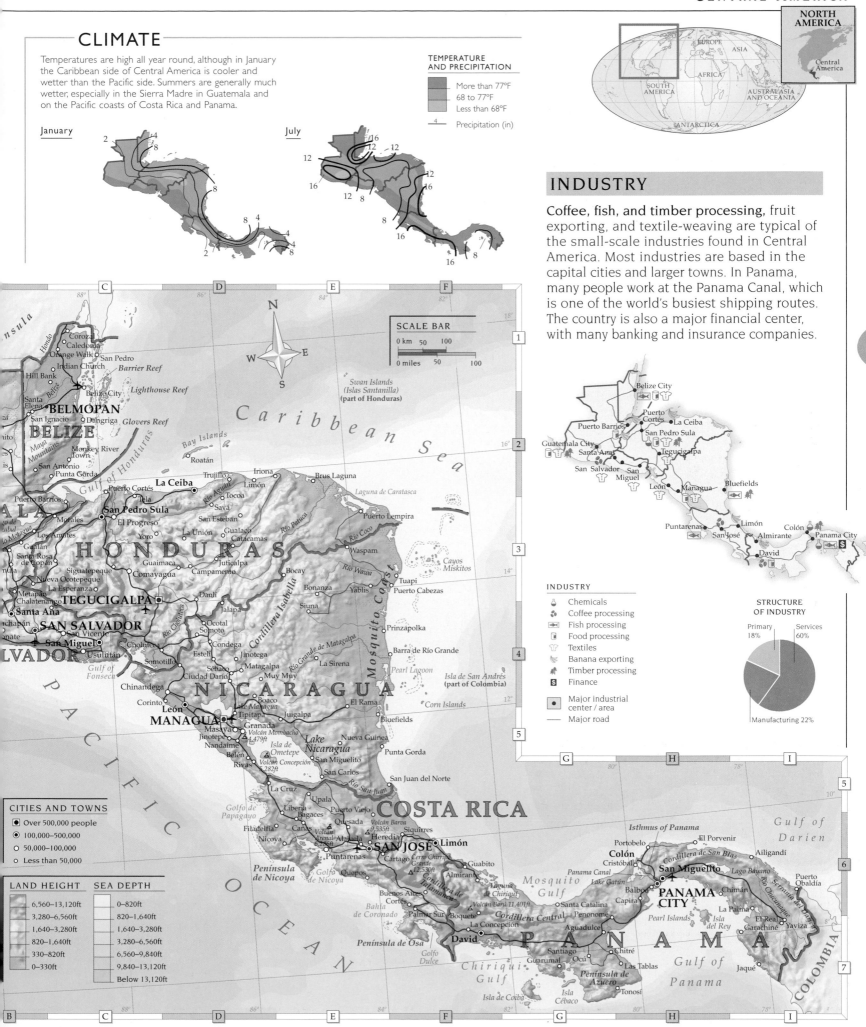

SCALE BAR

0 km   50   100

0 miles   50   100

INDUSTRY

🜨 Chemicals
☕ Coffee processing
🐟 Fish processing
🍽 Food processing
👕 Textiles
🍌 Banana exporting
🌲 Timber processing
Ⓢ Finance

▣ Major industrial
   center / area
── Major road

**STRUCTURE
OF INDUSTRY**

Primary
18%
Services
60%

Manufacturing 22%

CITIES AND TOWNS

■ Over 500,000 people
◉ 100,000–500,000
○ 50,000–100,000
∘ Less than 50,000

LAND HEIGHT

6,560–13,120ft
3,280–6,560ft
1,640–3,280ft
820–1,640ft
330–820ft
0–330ft

SEA DEPTH

0–820ft
820–1,640ft
1,640–3,280ft
3,280–6,560ft
6,560–9,840ft
9,840–13,120ft
Below 13,120ft

THE CARIBBEAN

The Caribbean Sea is enclosed by an arc of many hundreds of islands, islets, and offshore reefs that reach from Florida in the US, round to Venezuela in South America. From 1492, Spain, France, Britain, and the Netherlands claimed the islands as colonies. Most of the islands' original inhabitants were wiped out by disease and a wide mixture of peoples – of African, Asian, and European descent – now make up the population. The islands are prone to earthquakes, hurricanes, and volcanic eruptions.

THE LANDSCAPE

The Bahamas
The Bahamas are low-lying islands formed from limestone rock. Their coastlines are fringed by coral reefs, lagoons, and mangrove swamps. Some of the bigger islands are covered by forests.

The islands are formed from two main mountain chains: the Greater Antilles, which are part of a chain running from west to east, and the Lesser Antilles, which run from north to south. The mountains are now almost submerged under the Atlantic Ocean and Caribbean Sea. Only the higher peaks reach above sea level to form islands.

Hispaniola (F4)
Two countries, Haiti and the Dominican Republic, occupy the island of Hispaniola. The land is mostly mountainous, broken by fertile valleys.

Cuba (C3)
Cuba is the largest island in the Antilles. Its landscape is made up of wide, fertile plains with rugged hills and mountains in the southeast.

The Lesser Antilles
Most of these small volcanic islands have mountainous interiors. Barbados and Antigua & Barbuda are flatter, with some higher volcanic areas. Montserrat was evacuated in 1997, following volcanic eruptions on the island.

FARMING AND LAND USE

Agriculture is an important source of income, with over half of all produce exported. Many islands have fertile, well-watered land and large areas are set aside for commercial crops such as sugarcane, tobacco, and coffee. Some islands rely heavily on a single crop; in Dominica, bananas provide over half the country's income. Cuba is one of the world's biggest sugar producers.

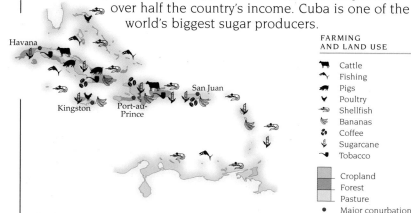

FARMING AND LAND USE

- 🐂 Cattle
- 🐟 Fishing
- 🐖 Pigs
- 🦃 Poultry
- 🦪 Shellfish
- 🍌 Bananas
- ☕ Coffee
- Sugarcane
- Tobacco

- Cropland
- Forest
- Pasture
- • Major conurbation

ENVIRONMENTAL ISSUES

The islands of the Caribbean are often under threat from hurricane storm systems which sweep in from the Atlantic Ocean between May and October. The winds can reach speeds of up to 185 miles per hour, devastating everything that lies in their path and causing severe flooding. The storms themselves are enormous; a hurricane can extend outward for 400 miles from its calm center, which is known as the "eye."

TOURISM

Tourism is thriving in the Caribbean, often bringing more income to the region than other, traditional industries. Long sandy beaches, clear, warm waters, and the climate are the main attractions. In Cuba and the Dominican Republic, tourism is expanding at some of the fastest rates in North America. As hotel complexes and new roads and airports are developed, the environment is often damaged. Local people who work in the industry often receive little of the extra cash brought in by the tourists.

TOURISM

🏖 Major tourist destinations

EUROPE
ASIA
AFRICA
SOUTH AMERICA
AUSTRALASIA AND OCEANIA
ANTARCTICA

ENVIRONMENTAL ISSUES

Path of recent, devastating hurricane

Hurricane Flora – over 7,000 dead
Hurricane Jeanne – 3,000 dead
Hurricane David – 2,000 dead
Hurricane Gordon – 1,100 dead
Hurricane Georges – 600 dead
Hurricane Gilbert – over 300 dead

Jeanne 2004
Gilbert 1988
Gordon 1994
David 1979
Flora 1963
Dennis 2005

INDUSTRY

Food processing – such as sugarcane refining and fruit exporting – and textiles, are typical of traditional Caribbean industry, which supplies mainly foreign markets. Cuba's economy has suffered from years of neglect and a trade ban imposed by the US government. Minerals and oil are also important. Jamaica has some of the world's largest reserves of bauxite – used to make aluminum – and oil is extracted and refined in Trinidad & Tobago and the Bahamas.

INDUSTRY

Chemicals
Engineering
Oil refining
Textiles
Mining
Sugar processing
Tobacco processing
Major industrial center / area
Major road

Freeport
Havana
Santa Clara
Camagüey
Santiago de Cuba
Santiago
San Juan
Port-au-Prince
Ponce
St Croix
Kingston
Santo Domingo
Willemstad
Port-of-Spain

ATLANTIC OCEAN

Harbour
Abaco
Eleuthera Island
Rock Sound
Cat Island
San Salvador
Exuma Sound
Town
Rum Cay
Exuma Island
Long Island
Tropic of Cancer
Clarence Town
Crooked Island Passage
Crooked Island
Island Range
Acklins Island
Mayaguana Passage
Mayaguana
Caicos Passage
Little Inagua
Lake Rosa
Matthew Town
Great Inagua
COCKBURN TOWN
TURKS & CAICOS ISLANDS
(UK dependent territory)

BAHAMAS

Holguín
Guantánamo
Santiago de Cuba
Bahía de Guántanamo (to US)
NAVASSA ISLAND
(US unincorporated territory)
Jérémie
Windward Passage
Hispaniola
Monte Cristi
Puerto Plata
Cap-Haïtien
Santiago
La Vega
San Francisco de Macorís
Gonaïves
HAITI
Pico Duarte 10,417ft
Cordillera Central
SANTO DOMINGO
Île de la Gonâve
PORT-AU-PRINCE
La Romana
Cayes
Jacmel
Isla Saona
DOMINICAN REPUBLIC
Isla Beata
KINGSTON
Jamaica Channel
Caribbean

BRITISH VIRGIN ISLANDS
VIRGIN ISLANDS (US unincorporated territory)
Sombrero (part of Anguilla)
ROAD TOWN
ANGUILLA (UK dependent territory)
THE VALLEY
St-Martin (part of Guadeloupe)
St-Barthélemy (part of Guadeloupe)
SAN JUAN
Caguas
CHARLOTTE AMALIE
Mayagüez
St Croix
NETH. ANTILLES (autonomous part of Neth.)
Barbuda
ANTIGUA & BARBUDA
ST JOHN'S
Antigua
Ponce
Mona Passage
Isla Mona
PUERTO RICO (US commonwealth territory)
BASSETERRE
SAINT KITTS & NEVIS
MONTSERRAT (UK dependent territory)
Grande Terre
GUADELOUPE (French overseas department)
Basse-Terre
Pointe-à-Pitre
Marie-Galante
BASSE-TERRE
Lesser Antilles
DOMINICA
ROSEAU
Martinique Passage
MARTINIQUE (French overseas department)
FORT-DE-FRANCE
St Lucia Channel
CASTRIES
ST LUCIA
Vieux Fort
BARBADOS
Saint Vincent Passage
Saint Vincent
KINGSTOWN
BRIDGETOWN
SAINT VINCENT & THE GRENADINES
The Grenadines
GRENADA
ST GEORGE'S
Tobago
Scarborough
TRINIDAD & TOBAGO
PORT-OF-SPAIN
Trinidad
San Fernando
Gulf of Paria

Leeward Islands
Windward Islands
Caribbean Sea

ARUBA (autonomous part of Netherlands)
ORANJESTAD
NETHERLANDS ANTILLES (autonomous part of Netherlands)
Curaçao
Bonaire
WILLEMSTAD
Isla La Orchila
Isla Blanquilla
Islas Los Testigos
Islas Los Roques
Isla de Margarita
Isla La Tortuga

COLOMBIA
Gulf of Venezuela
VENEZUELA

LAND HEIGHT
6,560–13,120ft
3,280–6,560ft
1,640–3,280ft
820–1,640ft
330–820ft
0–330ft

SEA DEPTH
0–820ft
820–1,640ft
1,640–3,280ft
3,280–6,560ft
6,560–9,840ft
9,840–13,120ft
Below 13,120ft

CITIES AND TOWNS
Over 500,000 people
100,000–500,000
50,000–100,000
Less than 50,000

CONTINENTAL SOUTH AMERICA

The towering peaks of the Andes stand high above the western side of South America. They act as a barrier to the sparsely inhabited interior of the continent, which includes the dense rain forest of the Amazon Basin – one of the Earth's last great wildernesses. Most people live on South America's coastal fringes. Brazil is both the largest country and the most populous. Over half the continent's land area and half of its people are found there.

3,100 miles
4,750 miles

CROSS-SECTION ACROSS SOUTH AMERICA

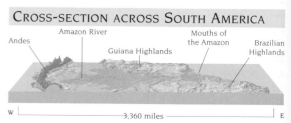

Andes · Amazon River · Guiana Highlands · Mouths of the Amazon · Brazilian Highlands

W — 3,360 miles — E

The high peaks of the Andes rise up from a narrow strip of land bordering the Pacific Ocean. East of the Andes, the land flattens into a broad, shallow basin into which the Amazon River flows. To the north are the older Guiana Highlands where rock has been eroded to form flat-topped "table" mountains.

PHYSICAL SOUTH AMERICA

Ancient masses of rocks, like the Guiana and Brazilian highlands, which are known as shields, form the core of South America. The Andes are the solid backbone of the continent. They are relatively young, formed by collisions between different plates of the Earth's crust. The major rivers: the Paraná and the mighty Amazon, flow in deep depressions to the east of the mountains.

ELEVATION

19,960ft
16,400ft
13,120ft
9,840ft
6,560ft
3,280ft
1,640ft
820ft
330ft
sea level
below sea level
cross section

SCALE 1:40,000,000

0 km   400   800
0 miles   400   800

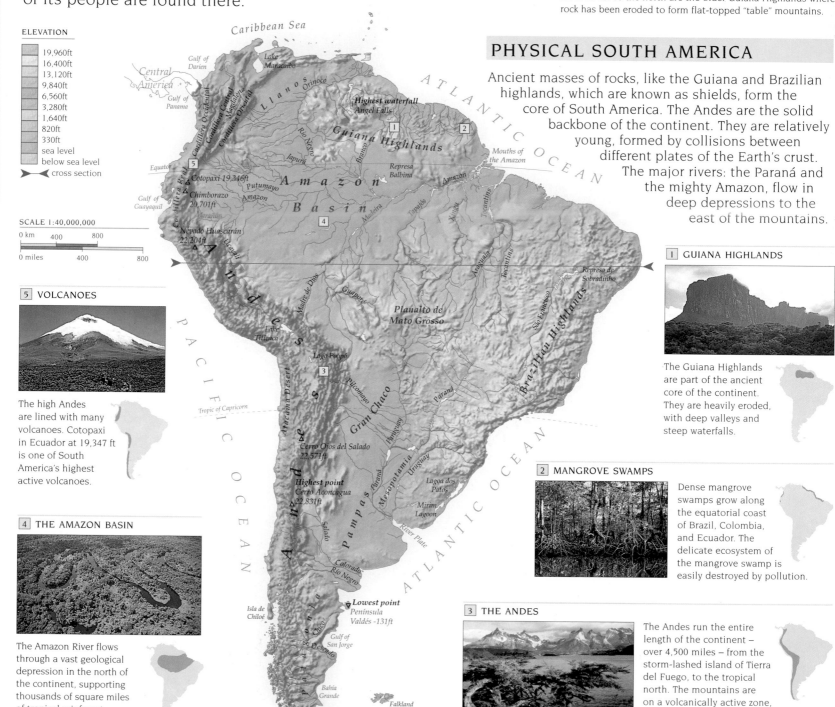

Caribbean Sea · Gulf of Darien · Lake Maracaibo · Central America · Gulf of Panama · Llanos · Orinoco · Highest waterfall Angel Falls · Guiana Highlands · ATLANTIC OCEAN · Equator · Cordillera Occidental · Cordillera Central · Cordillera Oriental · Rio Negro · Japurá · Branco · Represa Balbina · Mouths of the Amazon · Amazon · Cotopaxi 19,346ft · Putumayo · Amazon · Amazon Basin · Madeira · Tapajós · Xingu · Tocantins · Chimborazo 20,701ft · Gulf of Guayaquil · Marañón · Ucayali · Nevado Huascarán 22,204ft · Madre de Dios · Guaporé · Araguaia · Tocantins · Represa de Sobradinho · São Francisco · Brazilian Highlands · Planalto de Mato Grosso · Lake Titicaca · Lago Poopó · Pilcomayo · Gran Chaco · Paraná · Mesopotamia · Atacama Desert · Andes · Paraguay · Paraguay · Uruguay · Lagoa dos Patos · Tropic of Capricorn · Cerro Ojos del Salado 22,571ft · Pampas · Mirim Lagoon · Highest point Cerro Aconcagua 22,831ft · Salado · Colorado · Rio Negro · River Plate · Lowest point Península Valdés -131ft · ATLANTIC OCEAN · Isla de Chiloé · Chubut · Gulf of San Jorge · Patagonia · Bahía Grande · Falkland Islands · Strait of Magellan · Tierra del Fuego · Cape Horn · PACIFIC OCEAN

5 VOLCANOES

The high Andes are lined with many volcanoes. Cotopaxi in Ecuador at 19,347 ft is one of South America's highest active volcanoes.

4 THE AMAZON BASIN

The Amazon River flows through a vast geological depression in the north of the continent, supporting thousands of square miles of tropical rainforest.

1 GUIANA HIGHLANDS

The Guiana Highlands are part of the ancient core of the continent. They are heavily eroded, with deep valleys and steep waterfalls.

2 MANGROVE SWAMPS

Dense mangrove swamps grow along the equatorial coast of Brazil, Colombia, and Ecuador. The delicate ecosystem of the mangrove swamp is easily destroyed by pollution.

3 THE ANDES

The Andes run the entire length of the continent – over 4,500 miles – from the storm-lashed island of Tierra del Fuego, to the tropical north. The mountains are on a volcanically active zone, and earthquakes are common.

POLITICAL SOUTH AMERICA

In the 17th century, explorers from Spain and Portugal claimed most of South America for their rulers in Europe. Their influences are still strong today: Brazilians speak Portuguese, while much of the rest of the continent is Spanish-speaking. The small nations of the north, Suriname and Guyana, were Dutch and British colonies, and French Guiana is a French overseas department. The mix of peoples is mainly European, Native American, and African. Some native peoples still live in the dense Amazon rainforest.

SCALE 1:35,000,000

0 km 400 800
0 miles 400 800

TRANSPORTATION LINKS

The Pan American Highway is a vital transportation link, running from the far south of the continent, northward along the Pacific coast. Its route takes it through sparsely populated areas like the Atacama Desert.

POPULATION

Many South American countries have a similar pattern of population distribution. The largest concentrations of people are found near the coasts. Migration to the coastal cities has led to rocketing population figures and growing social problems. São Paulo is now one of the world's largest cities; its outskirts are fringed with sprawling, shanty town suburbs, known as *favelas*.

Largest city
SÃO PAULO
19.9 million people

POPULATION DENSITY
(People per sq mile)
Below 13
13–23
24–36
37–50
51–76
Above 76

BORDER DISPUTES

Many of South America's borders have been, or remain, disputed. Bolivia is landlocked as a result of a dispute with Chile in 1883, when it lost its lands bordering the Pacific Ocean.

URBAN GROWTH

Urban growth has transformed São Paulo into a major population and industrial center. Its rapid growth has created many problems, such as traffic congestion, overcrowding, and inadequate sewerage.

POPULATION

Capital cities
- Above 500,000
- 100,000 to 500,000
- 50,000 to 100,000
- Below 50,000

Other cities
- Above 500,000
- 50,000 to 100,000

STANDARDS OF LIVING

There are many inequalities in living standards across South America. Argentina's economy has suffered during the regional recession but living standards are still above those of Guyana and Bolivia, which have weak economies and are heavily reliant upon trade in raw materials. The booming black-market drugs trade increases crime and corruption.

STANDARD OF LIVING
(UN Human Development Index)
low   high   no data

SOUTH AMERICAN GEOGRAPHY

Agriculture is still the most common form of employment in South America. Cattle and cash crops of coffee, cocoa, and, in some places, coca for cocaine, provide the main sources of income. Brazil has the greatest range of industries, followed by Argentina, Venezuela, and Chile. The large coastal cities such as Rio de Janeiro, Lima, and Buenos Aires are where most of the jobs are found. This encourages people to migrate from the country to the city, in search of employment.

MINERAL RESOURCES

South America's mineral resources are highly localized. Few countries have both fossil fuels and metallic ores. The richest oilfields are in the north, especially in Venezuela. Coal, however, is scarce. When the Andes were formed, heat helped create the many metallic minerals that are mined today.

MINERAL RESOURCES
- Bauxite
- Copper
- Iron
- Lead
- Silver
- Tin
- Oil/Gas field
- Coal field

COPPER MINES

Metallic mineral reserves are abundant in the Andes. Chuquicamata, northern Chile, is one of the world's largest copper mines.

INDUSTRY

Brazil is the continent's leading industrial producer, and São Paulo is the major industrial city. Manufactured products include iron and steel, automobiles, chemicals, textiles, and meat and leather products from the continent's vast cattle herds. In the mountains of Bolivia and Colombia, coca plants are grown to make cocaine, which has created a black market for this illegal drug.

OIL AND GAS

Under the waters of Lake Maracaibo, Venezuela, lie some of South America's biggest oil reserves. Oil exploitation has brought great wealth to Venezuela. The money has helped the country to build new roads and develop other industries.

INDUSTRIAL CENTER

São Paulo, Brazil, is the largest city in South America and a leading industrial center. A wide range of goods is manufactured here, including automobiles, chemicals, textiles, and electronic products. São Paulo is also a leading financial center. Hundreds of people flock to the city daily in search of work.

TRADE AND EXPORTS

The Chilean port of Valparaíso ships many different products out of South America. Trade is growing with Japan and other countries around the Pacific Ocean.

Map labels

Caribbean Sea
Central America
Barranquilla
Maracaibo
Caracas
Cartagena
Barquisimeto
Valencia
Ciudad Guayana
VENEZUELA
Georgetown
Paramaribo
GUYANA
French Guiana (to France)
SURINAME
Medellín
Bogotá
COLOMBIA
Cali
ATLANTIC OCEAN
Quito
ECUADOR
Guayaquil
Amazon Basin
Manaus
Belém
Fortaleza
Chiclayo
Natal
Chimbote
Recife
BRAZIL
Lima
PERU
Cusco
Maceió
Salvador
Arequipa
BOLIVIA
La Paz
Brasília
Santa Cruz
Arica
Sucre
Iquique
Chuquicamata
Belo Horizonte
Antofagasta
PARAGUAY
São Paulo
Rio de Janeiro
Asunción
Curitiba
San Miguel de Tucumán
Corrientes
Córdoba
Porto Alegre
Valparaíso
Mendoza
Santa Fe
Rosario
URUGUAY
Rio Grande
PACIFIC OCEAN
Santiago
Buenos Aires
Montevideo
Talca
CHILE
Concepción
ARGENTINA
Neuquén
Bahía Blanca
Valdivia
ATLANTIC OCEAN
Comodoro Rivadavia
GNI per capita (US$)
Below 1,000
1,000-1,999
2,000-2,999
3,000-3,999
4,000-4,999
Above 5,000
• Industrial center
Falkland Islands (to UK)
Punta Arenas
Cape Horn

INDUSTRY
- ✈ Aerospace
- Brewing
- Car/vehicle manufacturing
- Chemicals
- Coal
- Electronics
- ✿ Engineering
- S Finance
- Fish processing
- Food processing
- High-tech industry
- Iron and steel
- △ Metal refining
- Narcotics
- Oil and gas
- Pharmaceuticals
- Printing and publishing
- Shipbuilding
- Textiles
- Timber processing
- Tobacco processing

CLIMATE

South America has four main climatic regions: tropical, arid, temperate, and the cold climate of the far south. The Amazon Basin, covered by massive rain forests, and the Guiana Highlands have a humid, tropical climate that allows vegetation to flourish. West of the Andes the climate tends to be very dry. Moist air flowing west from the Atlantic Ocean is prevented from reaching the shores of the Pacific Ocean by the Andes, and rain falls before it can pass over the mountains. This creates arid deserts like the Atacama.

Wettest place
QUIBDO (Colombia)
Annual rainfall 354in

Driest place
ARICA (Chile)
Annual rainfall 1/4in

Hottest place
RIVADAVIA (Argentina)
Temp 120°F

Coldest place
SARMIENTO (Argentina)
Temp -27°F

EXTREME WEATHER EVENTS

Symbols indicate climatic extremes

CLIMATE

- Subarctic
- Cool continental
- Warm temperate
- Semiarid
- Arid
- Temperate
- Tropical
- Humid equatorial

PATAGONIAN ICEFIELDS

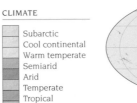

Toward the south of the continent, the climate becomes very cold. Large expanses of ice, forming glaciers, are found in southern Patagonia and on islands such as Tierra del Fuego at the tip of South America.

LAND USE AND AGRICULTURE

Many plants now found throughout the world originated in South America, like the tomato, potato, and cassava. Today, coffee, cocoa, rubber, soybeans, corn, and sugarcane are widely cultivated, and grapes are grown in sheltered valleys in the Andes. Much of the Amazon Basin is covered by dense rain forest and is unsuitable for cultivation, although some farmers practice "slash and burn" techniques to make land for crops and cattle farming, which destroy ancient forest.

LAND USE AND AGRICULTURE

- Cattle
- Pigs
- Sheep
- Bananas
- Corn
- Citrus fruits
- Coca
- Cocoa
- Cotton
- Coffee
- Fishing
- Oil palms
- Peanuts
- Rubber
- Shellfish
- Soybeans
- Sugarcane
- Vineyards
- Wheat

- Barren land
- Cropland
- Desert
- Forest
- Mountain region
- Pasture
- Wetland
- Major conurbation

COFFEE

South America, and Brazil in particular, is a major producer of coffee. The plants thrive in the rich red soils of southern Brazil and are grown on huge plantations on the mountain slopes.

LOCAL MARKETS

At traditional markets such as this one in Ecuador, high in the Andes, local people trade fruit, vegetables, and goods such as clothing, rugs, and blankets. Some goods produced by Ecuadorean Indians are now exported worldwide.

CATTLE

The vast plains of the Pampas, to the west of Buenos Aires, support large herds of cattle. Meat processing and canning is a major industry in Argentina, Paraguay, and Uruguay.

NARCOTICS

Coca, grown in forest clearings in remote mountain areas, is used to make the drug cocaine. Government troops burn any coca plants they discover to discourage production.

NORTHERN SOUTH AMERICA

BRAZIL, COLOMBIA, ECUADOR, GUYANA, PERU,
SURINAME, VENEZUELA

High mountains, rain forests, and hot, grassy plains
cover much of northern South America. From the 16th
century, after the conquest of the Incas, the western
countries were ruled by Spain. Brazil was governed
by Portugal, Guyana by Britain, and Suriname by
the Dutch. The more recent history of some of these
countries has included periods of civil war and military
rule. Most are still troubled by widespread poverty.

INDUSTRY

Important oil reserves are found in
Venezuela and parts of the Amazon
Basin; Venezuela is one of the world's
top oil producers. Brazil's cities have
a wide range of industries including
chemicals, clothes and shoes,
and textiles. Metallic minerals,
particularly iron ore, are mined
throughout the area and specially built
industrial centers like Ciudad Guayana
have been developed to refine them.

STRUCTURE OF INDUSTRY

Primary 11%
Services 50%
Manufacturing 39%

INDUSTRY

- ⚗ Chemicals
- 🥫 Food processing
- 🚂 Iron and steel
- △ Metal refining
- ♟ Textiles
- ⛏ Mining
- ⚓ Oil
- 🌲 Timber processing
- 🏛 Tourism
- ▪ Major industrial center / area
- — Major road

POPULATION

Most of the population lives in urban
areas. Many cities are extremely
overcrowded, with poor housing.
São Paulo in Brazil is one of
the world's fastest-growing
cities. The rain forests of
the interior and high Andes
are sparsely populated. The
few Native American peoples
live in remote areas.

INHABITANTS PER SQ MILE

- More than 520
- 260–520
- 130–260
- 30–130
- Less than 30
- ▪ Capital city
- ● Major city

URBAN/RURAL POPULATION DIVISION

Rio de Janeiro 4%
São Paulo 6.4%
Bogotá 2.6%
Rural population 21%
Other towns and cities 66%

FARMING AND LAND USE

The variety of climates allows a wide range
of crops, including sugarcane, cocoa,
and bananas, to be grown for export.
Coffee is the most important cash
crop; Brazil is the world's leading
coffee grower. Cattle are farmed
on the plains of Colombia,
Venezuela, and southern Brazil.
Much of the good farmland is
owned by a few rich landowners:
many peasant farmers do not have
enough land to make a living.

FARMING AND LAND USE

- 🐂 Cattle
- 🐟 Fishing
- 🐐 Goats
- 🐑 Sheep
- 🍌 Bananas
- 🌰 Cocoa
- Cotton
- ☕ Coffee
- Rubber
- ⚘ Sugarcane
- 🌲 Timber
- Cropland
- Forest
- Mountain region
- Pasture
- Wetland
- ● Major conurbation

LAND USE

Cropland 6%
Other (including mountains) 15%
Pasture 23%
Forest 56%

THE LANDSCAPE

The Andes run down the western side of South
America. There are many volcanoes among their peaks,
and earthquakes are common. The tropical rain forests
surrounding the Amazon River take up most of western
Brazil. Huge, dry, flat grasslands called *llanos* cover
central Venezuela and part of eastern Colombia.

Angel Falls (D 2)
Venezuela's Angel Falls is the
world's highest waterfall. Twenty
times as high as Niagara Falls, it
drops 3,212 ft from a spectacular
plateau deep in the Guiana Highlands.

Amazon River (D 4)
The Amazon is the longest
river in South America, and
the second longest in
the world. It flows over
4,049 miles from the
Peruvian Andes to the
coast of Brazil. One-fifth of
the world's freshwater is
carried by the river.

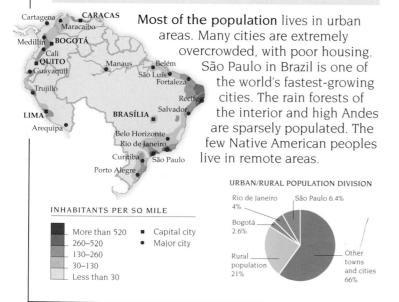

Andes (B 5)
The snow-capped
Andes are the
longest mountain
range on Earth.
They stretch
4,500 miles down
the whole length
of South America.

Lake Titicaca (C 6)
South America's
largest lake is the
highest navigable
lake in the world
at 12,500 ft
above sea level.
It lies across the
border between
Peru and Bolivia.

Pantanal (E 6)
This is the largest area of
wetlands in the world. It spreads
across 50,000 sq miles of Brazil.
Many hundreds of plant and
animal species are found here.

Amazon rain forest (D 4)
The enormous rain forest
surrounding the Amazon
River and its tributaries
covers 2,510,000 sq miles,
an area almost as big as
Australia. It is estimated
that at least half of all
known living species
are found in the forest.

ENVIRONMENTAL ISSUES

The destruction of the Amazon rain forest, which is being reduced by 1.2 sq miles every hour, is the most important environmental issue in this region. This is seriously threatening one of the world's most valuable resources and wiping out many species. The main causes of deforestation are clearance for farmland and commercial logging.

Colombia 181 sq miles of forest lost each year

Venezuela 1,112 sq miles of forest lost each year

Brazil 8% of Amazon forest lost since 1990. 11,981 sq miles of forest lost each year

Ecuador 765 sq miles of forest lost each year

Peru 363 sq miles of forest lost each year

ENVIRONMENTAL ISSUES
- Deforested areas
- Remaining forests

CLIMATE

Lowland areas are hot and humid all year round. The highlands are cooler, and the higher peaks of the Andes are permanently covered by snow.

TEMPERATURE AND PRECIPITATION
- More than 86°F
- 68 to 86°F
- 50 to 68°F
- 32 to 50°F
- Less than 32°F

Precipitation (in)

January   July

CITIES AND TOWNS
- Over 500,000 people
- 100,000–500,000
- 50,000–100,000
- Less than 50,000

LAND HEIGHT	SEA DEPTH
Above 13,120ft	0–820ft
6,560–13,120ft	820–1,640ft
3,280–6,560ft	1,640–3,280ft
1,640–3,280ft	3,280–6,560ft
820–1,640ft	6,560–9,840ft
330–820ft	9,840–13,120ft
0–330ft	Below 13,120ft

SOUTHERN SOUTH AMERICA

ARGENTINA, BOLIVIA, CHILE, PARAGUAY, URUGUAY

The southern half of South America forms a long, narrow cone, with landscapes ranging from barren desert in the west to frozen glaciers in the far south. The whole area was governed by Spain until the early 19th century, and Spanish is still the main language spoken, although the few remaining Native American groups use their own languages. Most people now live in vast cities such as Buenos Aires and Santiago.

INDUSTRY

Rich deposits of minerals – especially copper – in the Andes have led to the development of large metal refining industries in Chile. The capital cities, Buenos Aires and Santiago, are home to a wide range of industries, and Argentina is an important producer of processed foods like canned beef. There are fewer industries in the south, although oil and gas are extracted in southern Argentina and Chile.

INDUSTRY

- 🚗 Car manufacturing
- ⚗ Chemicals
- 🥫 Food processing
- △ Metal refining
- 🧵 Textiles
- ♦ Oil and gas
- 🌲 Timber processing
- ◉ Major industrial center / area
- — Major road

STRUCTURE OF INDUSTRY

Primary 10%
Services 55%
Manufacturing 35%

ENVIRONMENTAL ISSUES

Many of southern South America's rivers are polluted, particularly close to Buenos Aires. The Itaipú Dam on the Paraná River is the world's largest hydroelectric power plant. Deforestation is a persistent problem in Bolivia, Paraguay and northern Argentina with 2,320 sq miles cut down every year. Air quality in Buenos Aires and Santiago is poor, especially in Santiago, which is surrounded by mountains, making it difficult for pollution to escape.

ENVIRONMENTAL ISSUES

- 〰 Major dam
- 😷 Urban air pollution
- Deforested areas
- Polluted river
- • Major industrial center

POPULATION

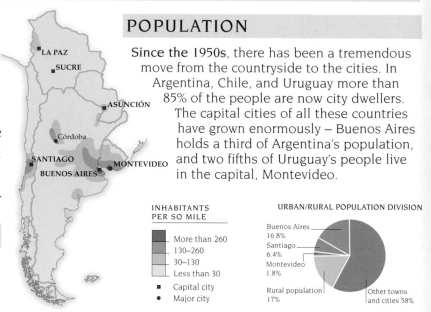

Since the 1950s, there has been a tremendous move from the countryside to the cities. In Argentina, Chile, and Uruguay more than 85% of the people are now city dwellers. The capital cities of all these countries have grown enormously – Buenos Aires holds a third of Argentina's population, and two fifths of Uruguay's people live in the capital, Montevideo.

INHABITANTS PER SQ MILE

- More than 260
- 130–260
- 30–130
- Less than 30
- ■ Capital city
- • Major city

URBAN/RURAL POPULATION DIVISION

- Buenos Aires 16.8%
- Santiago 6.4%
- Montevideo 1.8%
- Rural population 17%
- Other towns and cities 58%

THE LANDSCAPE

Southern South America's landscape varies from tropical forest and dry desert in the north to subantarctic conditions in the south. The towering Andes divide Chile from Argentina. East of the Andes lie forests and rolling grasslands. To the west is a thin coastal strip. The wet, windswept, freezing southern tip of the continent has volcanoes alongside glaciers and fjords.

Gran Chaco (C3)
This huge stretch of forest and grassland runs from Bolivia, through Paraguay and into Argentina. The south and east provide grazing for cattle.

Paraná River (C4)
South America's second-longest river is the Paraná. It stretches 2,485 miles from the Brazilian Highlands, finally flowing into the Plate River near Buenos Aires in Argentina.

Iguazu Falls (D4)
The Iguazu River drops 860 ft over the Iguazu Falls. When the river is at its fullest, the water flowing over the falls could fill six Olympic swimming pools every second.

Atacama Desert (A3)
The Atacama Desert in northern Chile is the driest place on Earth. In some parts, rain has not fallen for hundreds of years.

Pampas (B5)
The grassy plains in central Argentina – known as the Pampas – cover 251,000 sq miles. The western part is semidesert, but the east gets plenty of rain.

Chile
The far south of Chile has a dramatic landscape of fjords, lakes, jagged mountain peaks, and spectacular glaciers.

Patagonia (B8)
The high, windswept plateau of Patagonia covers 297,000 sq miles of southern Argentina. The south is dry and freezing cold, with very little vegetation.

SOUTH AMERICA
Southern South America

LAND HEIGHT
- Above 13,120ft
- 6,560–13,120ft
- 3,280–6,560ft
- 1,640–3,280ft
- 820–1,640ft
- 330–820ft
- 0–330ft

SEA DEPTH
- 0–820ft
- 820–1,640ft
- 1,640–3,280ft
- 3,280–6,560ft
- 6,560–9,840ft
- 9,840–13,120ft
- Below 13,120ft

CITIES AND TOWNS
- ◉ Over 500,000 people
- ● 100,000–500,000
- ○ 50,000–100,000
- ○ Less than 50,000

BOLIVIA'S TWO CAPITALS
LA PAZ – legislative and administrative capital
SUCRE – legal capital

CLIMATE

Temperature patterns are similar in January and July; warmer to the north and east, colder to the south and west, although January is much warmer than July. Temperatures are always low, high in the Andes.

January

July

TEMPERATURE AND PRECIPITATION
- More than 68°F
- 50 to 68°F
- 32 to 50°F
- Less than 32°F
- —4— Precipitation (in)

SCALE BAR
0 km 200 400
0 miles 200 400

FARMING AND LAND USE

The enormous grasslands to the east of the Andes provide good grazing for cattle and sheep, and Argentina is one of the world's leading suppliers of meat, milk, and hides. The country is also an important grower of wheat and fruit. Chile grows grapes for its successful wine industry, and for eating; it is also the world's top producer of fishmeal. The illegal growing of coca, used to make the drug cocaine, is a major source of income in Bolivia.

LAND USE
- Cropland 7%
- Pasture 43%
- Other (including mountains) 23%
- Forest 27%

FARMING AND LAND USE
- Cattle
- Fishing
- Sheep
- Cotton
- Fruit
- Sugarcane
- Timber
- Vineyards
- Wheat
- Barren land
- Cropland
- Desert
- Forest
- Mountain region
- Pasture
- Wetland
- ● Major conurbation

FALKLAND ISLANDS
(UK dependent territory)

CONTINENTAL AFRICA

Africa is the second-largest continent in the world. Its dramatic landscapes include arid deserts, humid rain forests, and the valleys of the east African rift – where humans may have first evolved. Today, there are 53 separate countries in Africa, and its people speak a rich variety of languages. The world's highest temperatures have been recorded in Africa's deserts.

4,510 miles
4,737 miles

CROSS-SECTION THROUGH AFRICA

Niger Delta
Congo Basin
Great Rift Valley
Ethiopian Highlands
Lake Victoria
Horn of Africa

W — 3,230 miles — E

In the west, the Niger River flows into the Atlantic Ocean through the swampy Niger Delta. Farther east is the immense Congo Basin, where the Congo River winds its way through thick rainforests. In the east is the Great Rift Valley and the Ethiopian Highlands. The Horn of Africa is Africa's most easterly point.

1 DESERTS

The Sahara covers much of north Africa. One-quarter of the desert is sandy dunes; the remainder consists of bare, rocky plains and mountainous outcrops. Other large deserts include the Namib and the Kalahari in the south.

2 GREAT RIFT VALLEY

Cracks beneath the Earth formed this valley, which runs from Lake Nyasa to the Red Sea. It is thought that East Africa – the Horn – will eventually split from the rest of Africa.

4 RAINFORESTS

Dense rainforests grow near the Equator, where rainfall is plentiful. Here, it is hot and humid enough for large areas of vegetation to flourish.

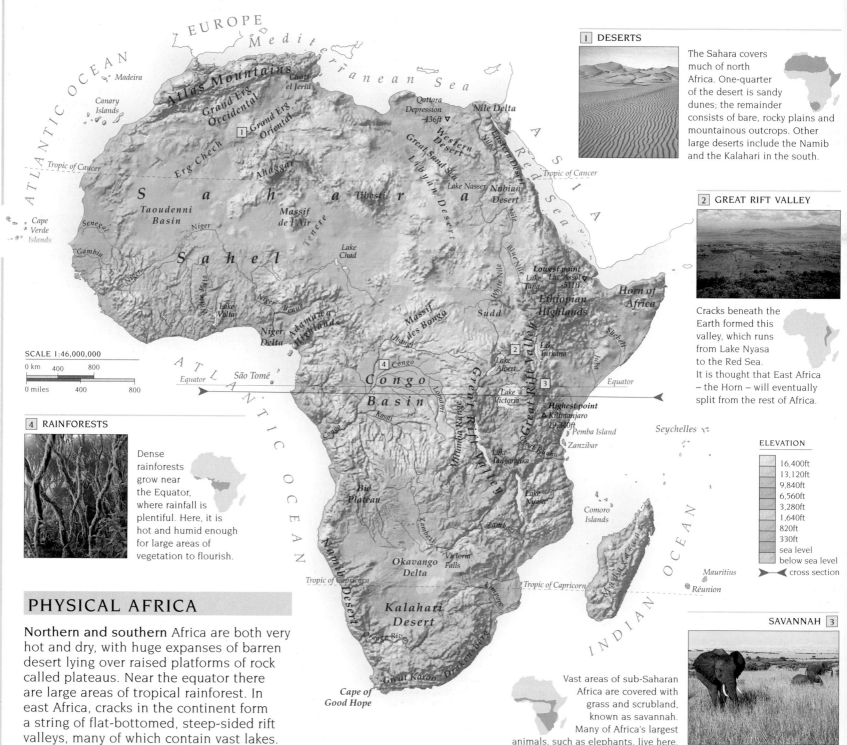

SCALE 1:46,000,000

0 km 400 800
0 miles 400 800

EUROPE
Mediterranean Sea
ATLANTIC OCEAN
Madeira
Canary Islands
Atlas Mountains
Grand Erg Occidental
Chott el Jerid
Grand Erg Oriental
Erg Chech
Tropic of Cancer
Qattara Depression -436ft ▽
Nile Delta
Western Desert
Great Sand Sea
Libyan Desert
Ahaggar
Tibesti
Cape Verde Islands
Taoudenni Basin
Senegal
Gambia
Niger
Massif de l'Air
Ténéré
Lake Chad
Lake Nasser
Nubian Desert
Nile
Red Sea
ASIA
Sahara
Sahel
Lake Volta
Niger
Benue
Adamawa Highlands
Niger Delta
São Tomé
Equator
ATLANTIC OCEAN
Congo
Ubangi
Massif des Bongo
Sudd
White Nile
Blue Nile
Lake Tana
Lowest point Lac Assal -511ft ▽
Ethiopian Highlands
Shebeli
Horn of Africa
Juba
Lake Turkana
Lake Albert
Great Rift Valley
Equator
4 Congo
Lomami
Kasai
Congo
Lake Victoria
Highest point △ Kilimanjaro 19,340ft
Pemba Island
Zanzibar
Seychelles
Great Ruaha
Rukwa River
Lake Tanganyika
Bié Plateau
Zambezi
Lake Nyasa
Comoro Islands
Namib Desert
Okavango Delta
Victoria Falls
Zambezi
Limpopo
Tropic of Capricorn
Madagascar
Mauritius
Réunion
INDIAN OCEAN
Kalahari Desert
Orange River
Great Karoo
Drakensberg
Cape of Good Hope

ELEVATION

16,400ft
13,120ft
9,840ft
6,560ft
3,280ft
1,640ft
820ft
330ft
sea level
below sea level
⪢⪡ cross section

PHYSICAL AFRICA

Northern and southern Africa are both very hot and dry, with huge expanses of barren desert lying over raised platforms of rock called plateaus. Near the equator there are large areas of tropical rainforest. In east Africa, cracks in the continent form a string of flat-bottomed, steep-sided rift valleys, many of which contain vast lakes.

SAVANNAH 3

Vast areas of sub-Saharan Africa are covered with grass and scrubland, known as savannah. Many of Africa's largest animals, such as elephants, live here.

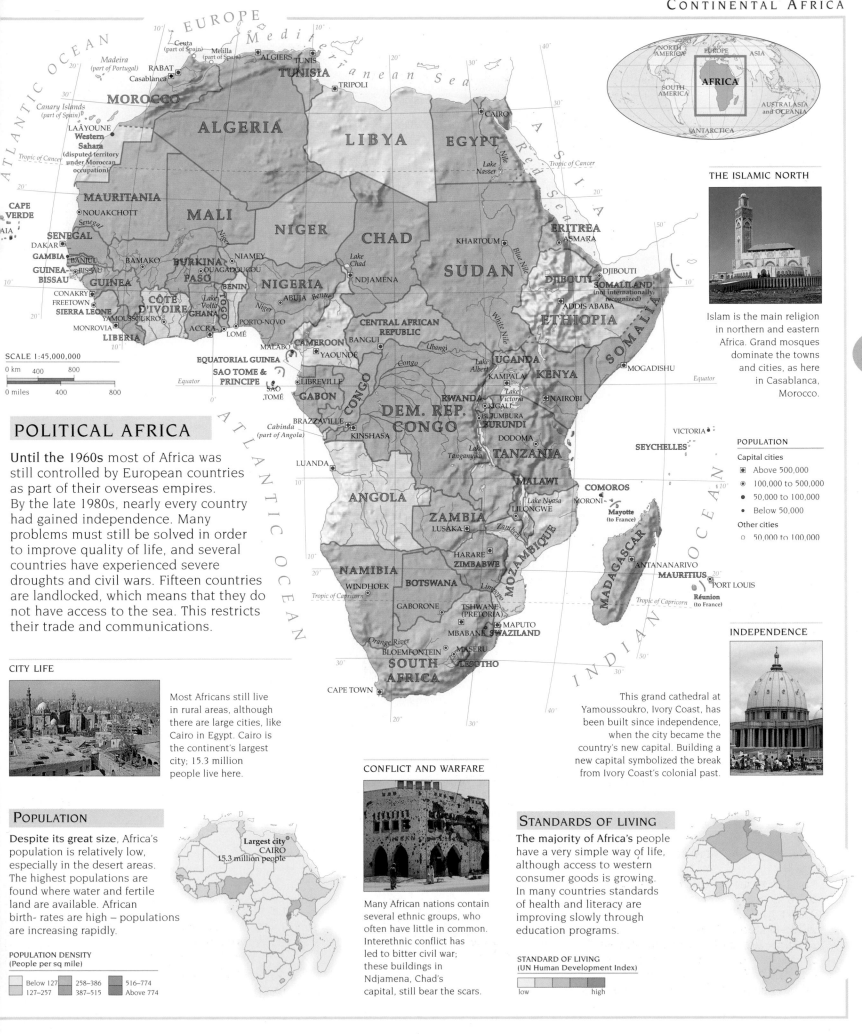

EUROPE

ATLANTIC OCEAN

Mediterranean Sea

Ceuta (part of Spain)
Melilla (part of Spain)
ALGIERS
TUNIS
TUNISIA
TRIPOLI
RABAT
Casablanca
Madeira (part of Portugal)
MOROCCO
Canary Islands (part of Spain)
Tropic of Cancer
LAÂYOUNE
Western Sahara (disputed territory under Moroccan occupation)
ALGERIA
LIBYA
EGYPT
CAIRO
Lake Nasser
Nile
Tropic of Cancer
Red Sea

ASIA

CAPE VERDE
MAURITANIA
NOUAKCHOTT
Senegal
MALI
NIGER
CHAD
KHARTOUM
Blue Nile
ERITREA
ASMARA
SENEGAL
DAKAR
GAMBIA
BANJUL
BAMAKO
Niger
NIAMEY
BURKINA FASO
OUAGADOUGOU
Lake Chad
NDJAMENA
SUDAN
DJIBOUTI
DJIBOUTI
SOMALILAND (not internationally recognized)
GUINEA-BISSAU
BISSAU
GUINEA
CONAKRY
FREETOWN
SIERRA LEONE
MONROVIA
LIBERIA
CÔTE D'IVOIRE
YAMOUSSOUKRO
Lake Volta
GHANA
BENIN
TOGO
ACCRA
LOMÉ
PORTO-NOVO
Niger
NIGERIA
ABUJA
Benue
PORTO-NOVO
CAMEROON
BANGUI
CENTRAL AFRICAN REPUBLIC
ADDIS ABABA
ETHIOPIA
White Nile
MALABO
EQUATORIAL GUINEA
YAOUNDÉ
SAO TOME & PRINCIPE
Equator
LIBREVILLE
SÃO TOMÉ
GABON
Congo
Ubangi
BRAZZAVILLE
KINSHASA
Cabinda (part of Angola)
DEM. REP. CONGO
Lake Albert
UGANDA
KAMPALA
RWANDA
KIGALI
BURUNDI
BUJUMBURA
Lake Victoria
KENYA
NAIROBI
MOGADISHU
SOMALIA
Equator

LUANDA
ANGOLA
DODOMA
TANZANIA
Lake Tanganyika
VICTORIA
SEYCHELLES
MALAWI
LILONGWE
Lake Nyasa
COMOROS
MORONI
Mayotte (to France)
ZAMBIA
LUSAKA
Zambezi
HARARE
ZIMBABWE
MOZAMBIQUE
MADAGASCAR
ANTANANARIVO
MAURITIUS
PORT LOUIS
Réunion (to France)
NAMIBIA
WINDHOEK
BOTSWANA
GABORONE
Limpopo
Tropic of Capricorn
TSHWANE (PRETORIA)
MBABANE
SWAZILAND
MAPUTO
Orange River
BLOEMFONTEIN
MASERU
LESOTHO
SOUTH AFRICA
CAPE TOWN

INDIAN OCEAN

ATLANTIC OCEAN

POLITICAL AFRICA

Until the 1960s most of Africa was still controlled by European countries as part of their overseas empires. By the late 1980s, nearly every country had gained independence. Many problems must still be solved in order to improve quality of life, and several countries have experienced severe droughts and civil wars. Fifteen countries are landlocked, which means that they do not have access to the sea. This restricts their trade and communications.

SCALE 1:45,000,000
0 km 400 800
0 miles 400 800

AFRICA
NORTH AMERICA
EUROPE
ASIA
SOUTH AMERICA
AFRICA
AUSTRALASIA and OCEANIA
ANTARCTICA

THE ISLAMIC NORTH

Islam is the main religion in northern and eastern Africa. Grand mosques dominate the towns and cities, as here in Casablanca, Morocco.

POPULATION

Capital cities
- ◙ Above 500,000
- ◉ 100,000 to 500,000
- ● 50,000 to 100,000
- • Below 50,000

Other cities
- ○ 50,000 to 100,000

CITY LIFE

Most Africans still live in rural areas, although there are large cities, like Cairo in Egypt. Cairo is the continent's largest city; 15.3 million people live here.

CONFLICT AND WARFARE

Many African nations contain several ethnic groups, who often have little in common. Interethnic conflict has led to bitter civil war; these buildings in Ndjamena, Chad's capital, still bear the scars.

INDEPENDENCE

This grand cathedral at Yamoussoukro, Ivory Coast, has been built since independence, when the city became the country's new capital. Building a new capital symbolized the break from Ivory Coast's colonial past.

POPULATION

Despite its great size, Africa's population is relatively low, especially in the desert areas. The highest populations are found where water and fertile land are available. African birth-rates are high – populations are increasing rapidly.

Largest city
CAIRO
15.3 million people

POPULATION DENSITY
(People per sq mile)
- Below 127
- 127–257
- 258–386
- 387–515
- 516–774
- Above 774

STANDARDS OF LIVING

The majority of Africa's people have a very simple way of life, although access to western consumer goods is growing. In many countries standards of health and literacy are improving slowly through education programs.

STANDARD OF LIVING
(UN Human Development Index)
low —— high

AFRICAN GEOGRAPHY

Africa's massive reserves of minerals, including oil, gold, copper, and diamonds, are among the largest in the world. Mining is a very important industry for many countries and has provided money for growth and development. Many different types of crops can be grown in Africa's wide range of environments. Rubber, bananas, and oil palms are grown for export in the Tropics, and east Africa is especially famous for its tea and coffee.

INDUSTRY

Most African industries are based on processing raw materials such as food crops or mineral ores. Some African countries depend on one product or crop for most of their income, but in many larger cities different industries are developing. Northern Africa, Nigeria, and South Africa have the widest range of industries.

MINERAL RESOURCES

The southern countries, in particular South Africa, have large reserves of diamonds, gold, uranium, and copper. The large copper deposits in Dem. Rep. Congo and Zambia are known as the "copper belt." Oil and gas are extracted in Algeria, Angola, Egypt, Libya, and Nigeria.

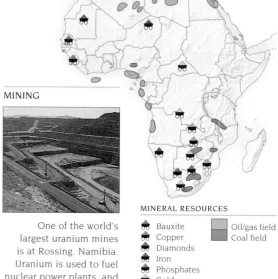

MINING

One of the world's largest uranium mines is at Rossing, Namibia. Uranium is used to fuel nuclear power plants, and is also mined in Niger and South Africa.

MINERAL RESOURCES

- ♠ Bauxite
- ♠ Copper
- ♠ Diamonds
- ♠ Iron
- ♠ Phosphates
- ♠ Gold
- ♠ Uranium
- Oil/gas field
- Coal field

OIL AND GAS

In the desert wastes of Algeria, a drilling rig searches for new sources of oil in the rich north African oilfields. There are several large oil fields in the Niger delta and North Africa.

INDUSTRY

- 🍶 Brewing
- 🚗 Car/vehicle manufacturing
- Cement
- Chemicals
- Coal
- Engineering
- Fish processing
- S Finance
- Food processing
- Iron & steel
- Mining
- Oil & gas
- Pharmaceuticals
- Shipbuilding
- Textiles
- Timber processing

GNI per capita (US$)

- Below 500
- 500-999
- 1,000-1,999
- 2,000-2,999
- 3,000-3,999
- Above 4,000
- • Industrial center

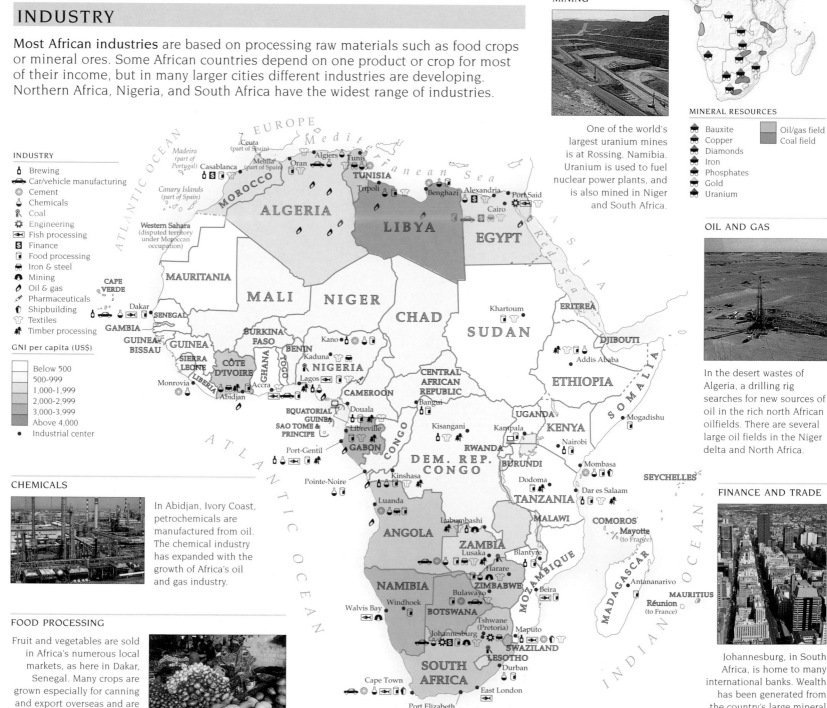

CHEMICALS

In Abidjan, Ivory Coast, petrochemicals are manufactured from oil. The chemical industry has expanded with the growth of Africa's oil and gas industry.

FOOD PROCESSING

Fruit and vegetables are sold in Africa's numerous local markets, as here in Dakar, Senegal. Many crops are grown especially for canning and export overseas and are known as "cash crops."

FINANCE AND TRADE

Johannesburg, in South Africa, is home to many international banks. Wealth has been generated from the country's large mineral resources, such as diamonds.

CLIMATE

Africa is the world's hottest continent: temperatures of more than 122°F have been recorded in the Sahara. The northern coast has a hot, dry climate with little rainfall. Farther inland, the Sahara is extremely arid, with strong, dry winds. South of the Sahara is the Sahel, where cutting down trees for fuel has turned farmland into desert. Close to the equator there is more rainfall, and huge rain forests can grow in western and central Africa. In the south, the climate is much drier, and drought is a problem.

EXTREME WEATHER EVENTS

Symbols indicate climatic extremes

CLIMATE

- Warm temperate
- Mediterranean
- Semiarid
- Arid
- Humid equatorial
- Tropical

Coldest place
IFRANE (Morocco) Temp. -11°F

Hottest place
AL 'AZIZIYAH (Libya) Temp. 136°F

Driest place
WADI HALFA (Sudan) Annual rainfall 1/8in

Wettest place
CAPE DEBUNDSHA (Cameroon) Annual rainfall 405in

Tropic of Cancer

Equator

Tropic of Capricorn

THE ENCROACHING DESERT

Africa has three main desert areas: the Sahara in the north and the Namib and Kalahari deserts in the south. They are a mixture of sandy dunes and bare, rocky plateaus. At the desert's edges, low rainfall and land clearance is causing the deserts to expand into areas that were once grassland.

LAND USE AND AGRICULTURE

The quality of land and the amount of rainfall has a great impact on the type of farming. In the mountain regions of countries such as Rwanda, Uganda, and Kenya, tea and coffee are grown. In the north, there is not enough water to produce staple crops such as wheat for all the population, but "cash crops" such as citrus fruits, dates, and olives are grown for export. Subtropical west Africa grows peanuts, cocoa, and coffee. In the southern part of the continent, South Africa grows many different crops: citrus fruits are grown for export, as well as grapes, which are used to make wine.

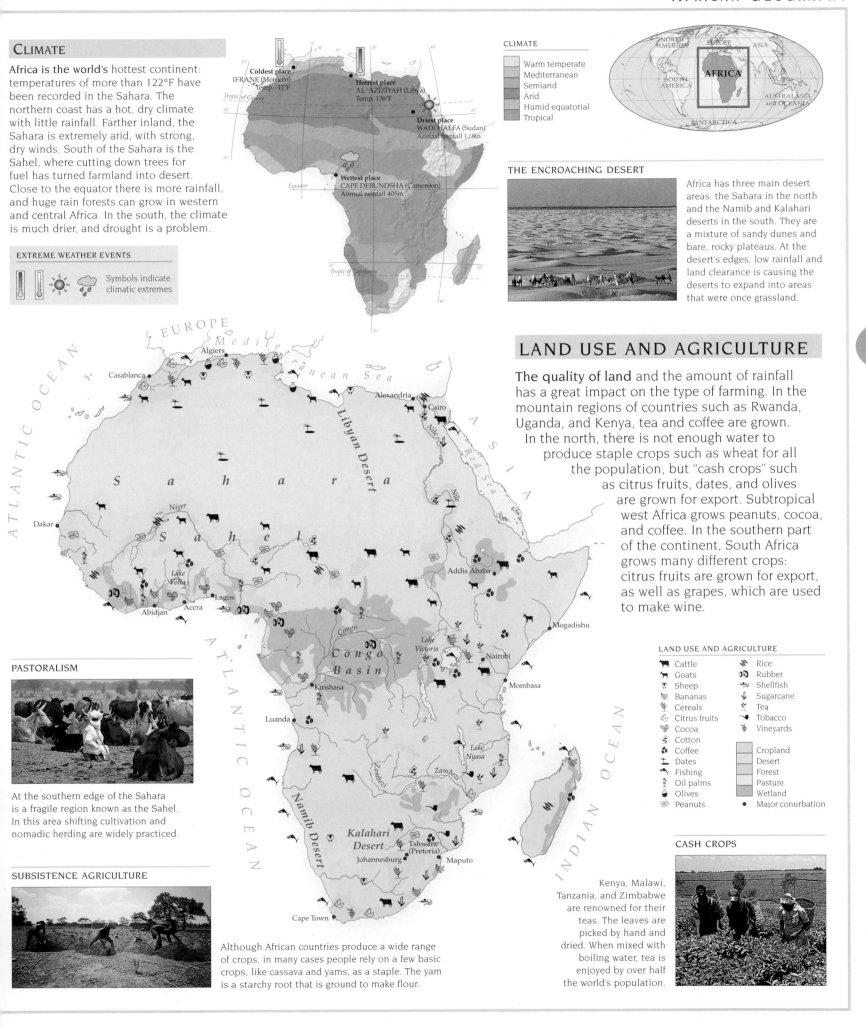

PASTORALISM

At the southern edge of the Sahara is a fragile region known as the Sahel. In this area shifting cultivation and nomadic herding are widely practiced.

SUBSISTENCE AGRICULTURE

Although African countries produce a wide range of crops, in many cases people rely on a few basic crops, like cassava and yams, as a staple. The yam is a starchy root that is ground to make flour.

LAND USE AND AGRICULTURE

- Cattle
- Goats
- Sheep
- Bananas
- Cereals
- Citrus fruits
- Cocoa
- Cotton
- Coffee
- Dates
- Fishing
- Oil palms
- Olives
- Peanuts
- Rice
- Rubber
- Shellfish
- Sugarcane
- Tea
- Tobacco
- Vineyards
- Cropland
- Desert
- Forest
- Pasture
- Wetland
- Major conurbation

CASH CROPS

Kenya, Malawi, Tanzania, and Zimbabwe are renowned for their teas. The leaves are picked by hand and dried. When mixed with boiling water, tea is enjoyed by over half the world's population.

NORTH AFRICA

ALGERIA, EGYPT, LIBYA, MOROCCO, TUNISIA.

Sandwiched between the Mediterranean and the Sahara, North Africa has a history dating back to the dawn of civilization. About 6,000 years ago, settlements were established along the banks of the Nile River. Since then, waves of settlers, including Romans, Arabs, and Turks, have brought a mix of different cultures to the area. In the 19th century, Spain, France, and Britain claimed colonies in the region, but today North Africa is independent, although Western Sahara is occupied by Morocco.

FARMING AND LAND USE

Most farming in North Africa is restricted to the fertile Mediterranean coastal strip, and the banks of the Nile where it relies heavily on irrigation. In spite of these seemingly inhospitable conditions, the region is a major producer of dates, which grow in desert oases, and of cork, made from the bark of the cork oak tree. A wide variety of other crops is also grown, including grapes, olives, and cotton.

FARMING AND LAND USE

Fishing
Goats
Sheep
Citrus Fruits
Cork
Cotton
Dates
Olives
Vineyards

Cropland
Desert
Forest
Pasture
• Major conurbation

CLIMATE

Most of north Africa is desert, and the climate is harsh. Rainfall is scarce, and drought is common. Temperatures are freezing at night, scorching by day and have been known to climb to over 120°F.

January

July

whole area has below 1in rainfall

LAND USE

Forest 1%
Pasture 13%
Cropland 5%
Other (including desert) 81%

TEMPERATURE AND PRECIPITATION

More than 95°F
86 to 95°F
77 to 86°F
68 to 77°F
59 to 68°F
50 to 59°F
41 to 50°F
Less than 41°F

4 — Precipitation (in)

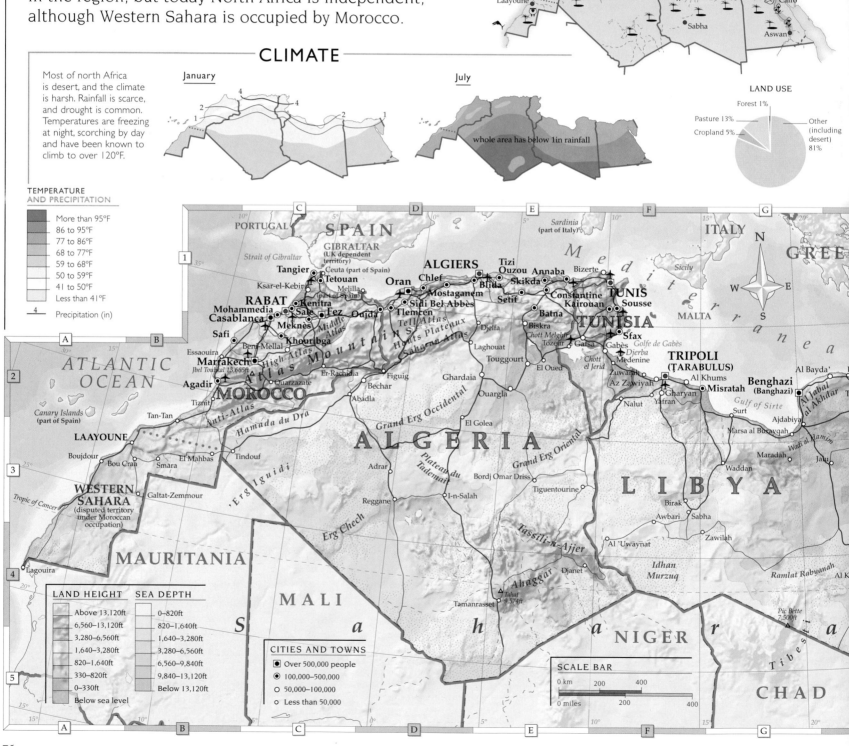

LAND HEIGHT

Above 13,120ft
6,560–13,120ft
3,280–6,560ft
1,640–3,280ft
820–1,640ft
330–820ft
0–330ft
Below sea level

SEA DEPTH

0–820ft
820–1,640ft
1,640–3,280ft
3,280–6,560ft
6,560–9,840ft
9,840–13,120ft
Below 13,120ft

CITIES AND TOWNS

■ Over 500,000 people
● 100,000–500,000
◉ 50,000–100,000
○ Less than 50,000

SCALE BAR

0 km   200   400
0 miles   200   400

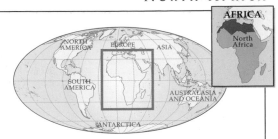

POPULATION

The majority of the population, and all of the big towns and cities, are found on the coastal plains, or along the banks of the Nile – about 99% of Egyptians live along the river. Egypt's capital, Cairo, is Africa's largest city, with over 15 million people. Western Sahara and the southern portions of Egypt, Algeria, and Libya are sparsely populated by Tuareg nomads who roam the desert.

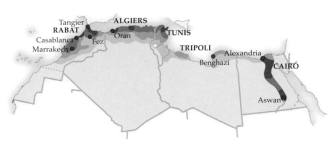

INHABITANTS
PER SQ MILE

- More than 520
- 260–520
- 130–260
- 30–130
- Less than 30
- ■ Capital city
- ● Major city

URBAN/RURAL POPULATION DIVISION

- Alexandria 2.2%
- Cairo 4.5%
- Casablanca 2%
- Rural population 46%
- Other towns and cities 45.3%

THE LANDSCAPE

The parched rocks and endless sandy expanses of the Sahara occupy much of North Africa. The only major river here is the Nile, with a delta that extends into the Mediterranean Sea. The old, eroded Atlas Mountains are the highest mountain range.

Sand dunes
Winds blowing across the Sahara cause the sand to build up into dunes which can reach heights of up to 1,411 ft.

Nile Delta (I 2)
As the Nile River nears the Mediterranean, it separates into many small streams, which flow over a fertile triangle of land. Mud and rock carried by the river and deposited in the delta have formed new land.

Red Sea (J3)
The Red Sea gets its name from red algae that live on the sea floor and make the water appear red.

Atlas Mountains (C 2)
The Atlas Mountains are made up of a number of different ranges – the Anti-Atlas, High Atlas, Middle Atlas, Tell Atlas, and Saharan Atlas. They stretch some 1,400 miles from the north of Tunisia to the Atlantic coast of Morocco.

Qattara Depression (I 3)
In the northwest of Egypt is a huge desert depression 200 miles long and 75 miles wide. Its floor, part of which is 440 ft below sea level, is covered with sand, brackish ponds and salt marshes.

Nile River (I 3)
The world's longest river flows 4,160 miles to the Mediterranean Sea. The system of rivers and lakes that flow into the Nile drain some 1,100,000 sq miles – about 10% of the entire African continent.

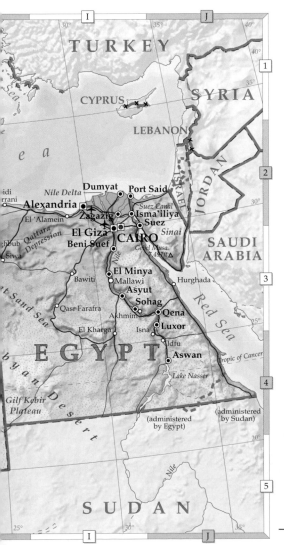

INDUSTRY

Oil and natural gas have brought wealth to the area, particularly to Libya, which has enough oil reserves to last into the middle of this century. Textile manufacture is widespread – North Africa is famous for its exotic cloths and rugs. Several large chemical refineries and steel plants have been established along the coast, especially in the major industrial cities like Alexandria and Cairo in Egypt.

STRUCTURE OF INDUSTRY

- Primary 16%
- Services 44%
- Manufacturing 40%

INDUSTRY

- Chemicals
- Food processing
- Iron and steel
- Textiles
- Oil and gas
- Tourism
- Major industrial center / area
- Major road

ENVIRONMENTAL ISSUES

Droughts, overgrazing, and the stripping of vegetation for firewood and animal food have caused the Sahara to expand northward. This has reduced the already limited amount of land available for farming. The risk of desertification is acute in many coastal areas. North Africa is very dry, and there are severe droughts periodically. Many of the larger cities like Alexandria and Cairo have very poor air quality.

ENVIRONMENTAL ISSUES

- Drought
- Urban air pollution
- Existing desert
- Risk of desertification
- Severe risk of desertification
- Unaffected area
- ● Major industrial center

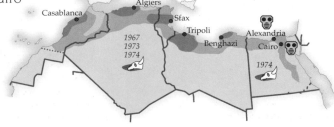

WEST AFRICA

BENIN, BURKINA FASO, CAMEROON, CENTRAL AFRICAN REPUBLIC, CHAD, CÔTE D'IVOIRE, EQUATORIAL GUINEA, GAMBIA, GHANA, GUINEA, GUINEA-BISSAU, LIBERIA, MALI, MAURITANIA, NIGER, NIGERIA, SAO TOME & PRINCIPE, SENEGAL, SIERRA LEONE, TOGO

West Africa's varied climate and agricultural and mineral wealth have provided the foundation for some of Africa's greatest civilizations, like those of the Malinke and Asante people. The area remains ethnically and culturally diverse today as well as densely populated. Nigeria is the most populous country in Africa. Since independence from European colonial powers in the 1960s, political instability has been a reality for many countries here.

INDUSTRY

Agricultural products still form the basis of most economies in West Africa. Food processing is widespread – oil palms and groundnuts are processed for their valuable vegetable oils. Oil and gas are found off the coast of Côte D'Ivoire and around the Niger delta, where a large chemical industry has developed.

INDUSTRY

- 🍶 Chemicals
- 🗄 Food processing
- ⊤ Textiles
- 🌲 Timber
- ⛏ Mining
- ◔ Oil and gas
- ■ Major industrial center / area
- — Major road

STRUCTURE OF INDUSTRY

Manufacturing 30%
Primary 34%
Services 36%

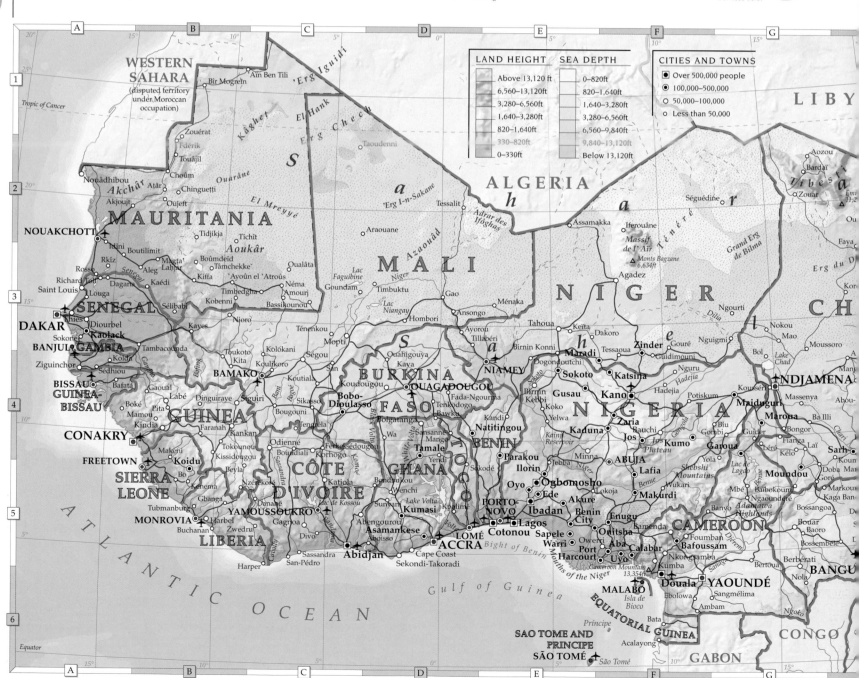

LAND HEIGHT
- Above 13,120 ft
- 6,560–13,120 ft
- 3,280–6,560 ft
- 1,640–3,280 ft
- 820–1,640 ft
- 330–820 ft
- 0–330 ft

SEA DEPTH
- 0–820 ft
- 820–1,640 ft
- 1,640–3,280 ft
- 3,280–6,560 ft
- 6,560–9,840 ft
- 9,840–13,120 ft
- Below 13,120 ft

CITIES AND TOWNS
- ■ Over 500,000 people
- ◉ 100,000–500,000
- ○ 50,000–100,000
- ∘ Less than 50,000

FARMING AND LAND USE

Plentiful rainfall along the coast allows a wide variety of crops to be grown, including cocoa and oil palms, both of which provide important cash crops. In the drier north, goats and sheep are grazed and subsistence crops such as yams, millet, and cassava are grown.

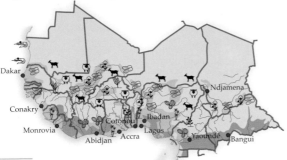

FARMING AND LAND USE

- 🐐 Goats
- 🐑 Sheep
- 🦪 Shellfish
- 🌿 Cassava
- 🌱 Cocoa
- 🌱 Cotton
- 🌾 Millet
- 🌴 Oil palms
- 🥜 Groundnuts
- ▬ Cropland
- ▬ Desert
- ▬ Forest
- ▬ Pasture
- ▬ Wetland
- • Major conurbation

LAND USE

Cropland 10%
Pasture 26%
Forest 16%
Other (including desert) 48%

CLIMATE

The climate differs immensely from the hot desert north to the tropical rainforest south. July is the wet season, and rainfall is heavy in the south. The desert areas remain dry throughout the year.

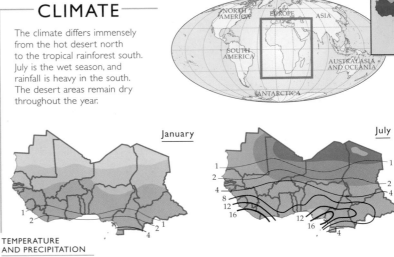

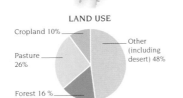
January

July

TEMPERATURE AND PRECIPITATION

- ▬ More than 95°F
- ▬ 86 to 95°F
- ▬ 77 to 86°F
- ▬ 68 to 77°F
- ▬ Less than 68°F
- —4— Precipitation (in)

ENVIRONMENTAL ISSUES

Persistent droughts are the main concerns in the north of the region. The problem is made worse by a shortage of wood needed for fuel, which leads to the cutting down of any available trees. In the tropical south, the timber industry is destroying much of the ancient forest. In 2007 huge floods affected almost all of the region.

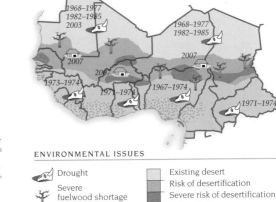

ENVIRONMENTAL ISSUES

- 🐟 Drought
- 🌳 Severe fuelwood shortage
- 🏠 Flooding
- ▬ Existing desert
- ▬ Risk of desertification
- ▬ Severe risk of desertification
- ▬ Deforested area

POPULATION

Most of the population lives in the southern coastal regions. In the drier north, settlement is sparser, and nomadic tribespeople are best suited to live in the desert north. Nigeria is the most populated country in Africa and Lagos is one of the continent's larger cities, although West Africa's population remains mainly rural.

INHABITANTS PER SQ MILE

- ▬ More than 520
- ▬ 260–520
- ▬ 130–260
- ▬ 30–130
- ▬ Less than 30
- ■ Capital city
- • Major city

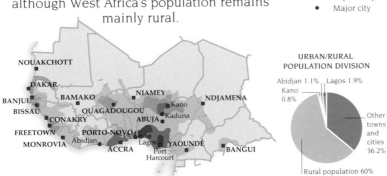

URBAN/RURAL POPULATION DIVISION

Abidjan 1.1%   Lagos 1.9%
Kano 0.8%
Other towns and cities 36.2%
Rural population 60%

EGYPT

Tropic of Cancer

SUDAN

CENTRAL AFRICAN REPUBLIC

DEM. REP. CONGO

Equator

SCALE BAR

0 km 200 400
0 miles 200 400

THE LANDSCAPE

Major differences in rainfall from north to south have led to a varied landscape. The wet coastal regions contain tropical rain forests. To the north, savanna grasslands, arid Sahel scrubland, and barren desert lie in successive bands. The Niger is one of the larger rivers and is unusual because it has two deltas: one at the sea and one inland.

Sahel (E 3)

The band of semidesert stretching from Senegal to Sudan along the southern boundary of the Sahara is called the Sahel. Frequent droughts in recent years and excessive cutting of trees have meant that much of the Sahel is turning to desert.

Tibesti mountains (G 2)

These mountains in north-western Chad are a chain of extinct volcanoes that now form solitary peaks in the midst of the Sahara.

River Niger (D 3)

The Niger River is West Africa's longest river. When it reaches the sea, it flows through a vast delta of mudflats and mangrove swamps. Great oil deposits have been found here.

Adamawa Highlands (G 5)

This mountainous spine separates West Africa from the vast Congo Basin to the southeast.

EAST AFRICA

BURUNDI, DJIBOUTI, ERITREA, ETHIOPIA, KENYA, RWANDA, SOMALIA, SUDAN, TANZANIA, UGANDA

Much of East Africa is covered by long grass, scrub, and scattered trees, called savanna. This land is grazed by both domestic animals and a great variety of wild animals including lions, giraffes and elephants. The east of the region is known as the Horn of Africa, because it is shaped like an animal horn. Sudan, and the other countries there have recently been devastated by civil wars, and periods of drought and famine. In contrast, Kenya in the south is more stable but still has to battle with corruption.

FARMING AND LAND USE

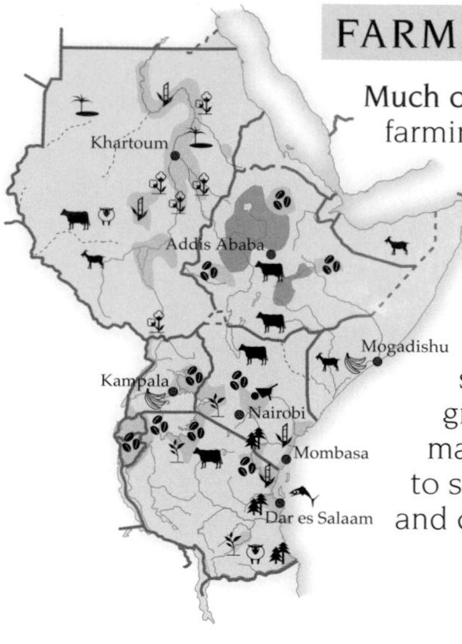

Much of the north and east is too dry for farming, but in Sudan, cotton is grown on land irrigated by the Nile River. The Lake Victoria basin and rich volcanic soils of the highlands in Kenya, Uganda, and Tanzania support staple food crops, and those grown for export, such as tea and coffee. Kenya also grows high-quality vegetables, like mangetout, and exports them by air to supermarkets abroad. Sheep, goats, and cattle are herded on the savanna.

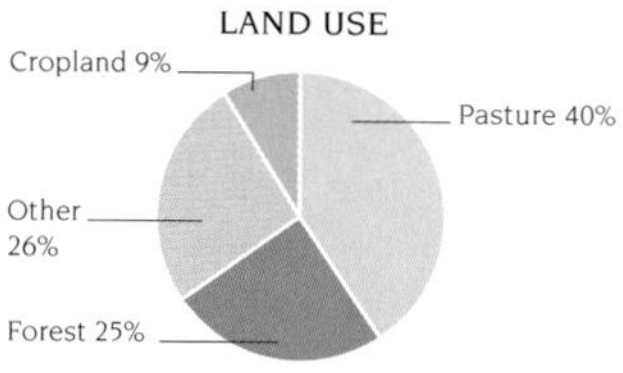

FARMING AND LAND USE

- Cattle
- Fishing
- Goats
- Sheep
- Bananas
- Coffee
- Cotton
- Dates
- Market gardening
- Sugarcane
- Sisal
- Tea
- Cropland
- Desert
- Forest
- Pasture
- Wetland
- Major conurbation

INDUSTRY

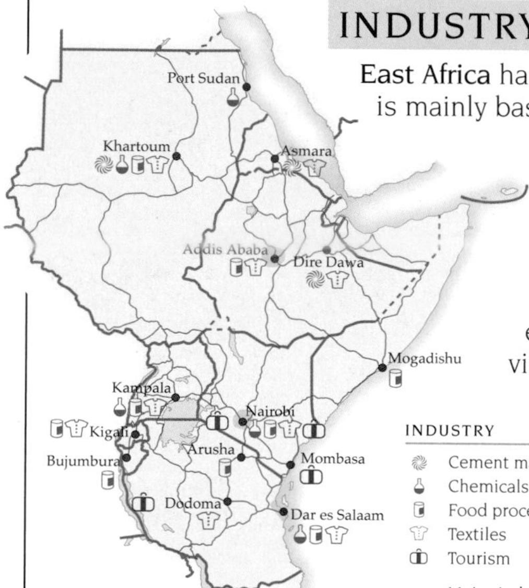

East Africa has few mineral resources, and industry is mainly based on processing raw materials. Coffee, tea, sugarcane, and sisal, are harvested and processed before being exported. Textile production is widespread, but is only on a small scale. Tourism is increasingly important in Kenya and Tanzania; each year, many thousands of people visit the wildlife reserves there.

INDUSTRY

- Cement manufacturing
- Chemicals
- Food processing
- Textiles
- Tourism
- Major industrial center / area
- Major road

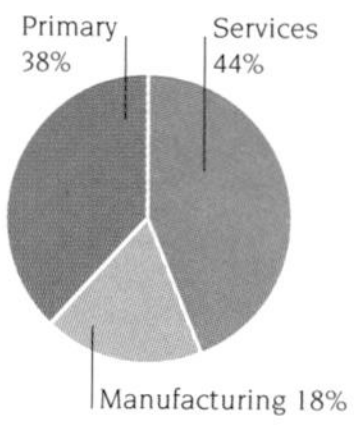

ENVIRONMENTAL ISSUES

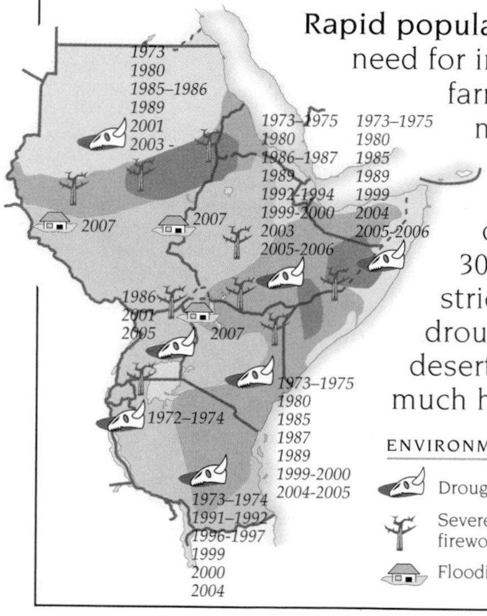

Rapid population growth has created a need for increasing amounts of land for farming. This, in addition to the need for firewood, has led to tree cover being stripped, allowing the soil to be washed or blown away. Over the past 30 years, East Africa has been stricken by many catastrophic droughts that have made desertification worse, and brought much human suffering.

ENVIRONMENTAL ISSUES

- Drought
- Severe firewood shortage
- Flooding
- Existing desert
- Risk of desertification
- Severe risk of desertification

THE LANDSCAPE

The south of East Africa is savanna grassland, broken by the rugged mountains – some of them active volcanoes – and large fresh and saltwater lakes that make up part of the Great Rift Valley. The Nile River has its source here, flowing through Lakes Victoria, Kyoga, and Albert as it takes much-needed water to the arid desert areas in the north.

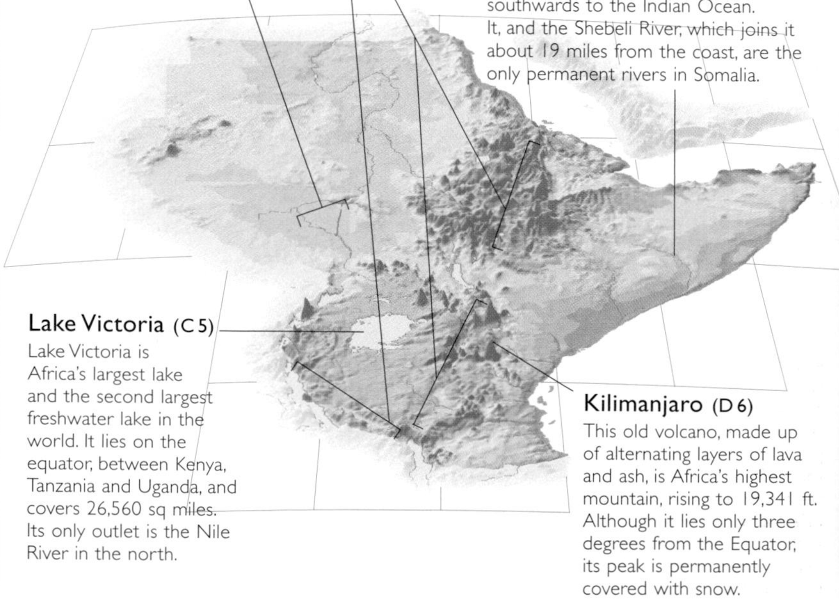

Great Rift Valley (D 6) (D 4)
The Great Rift Valley is like a deep scar running 4,300 miles from north to south through East Africa. It has been formed by the movements of two of the Earth's plates over millions of years. If these movements continue, East Africa may eventually become an island, separated by the ocean from the rest of the continent.

Sudd (B 4)
The north of Sudan is rocky desert, but in the south, the waters of the White Nile run into a swampy area called the Sudd where much of its water disperses and evaporates.

Juba River (E 5)
This river rises in the highlands of Ethiopia and flows some 750 miles southwards to the Indian Ocean. It, and the Shebeli River, which joins it about 19 miles from the coast, are the only permanent rivers in Somalia.

Lake Victoria (C 5)
Lake Victoria is Africa's largest lake and the second largest freshwater lake in the world. It lies on the equator, between Kenya, Tanzania and Uganda, and covers 26,560 sq miles. Its only outlet is the Nile River in the north.

Kilimanjaro (D 6)
This old volcano, made up of alternating layers of lava and ash, is Africa's highest mountain, rising to 19,341 ft. Although it lies only three degrees from the Equator, its peak is permanently covered with snow.

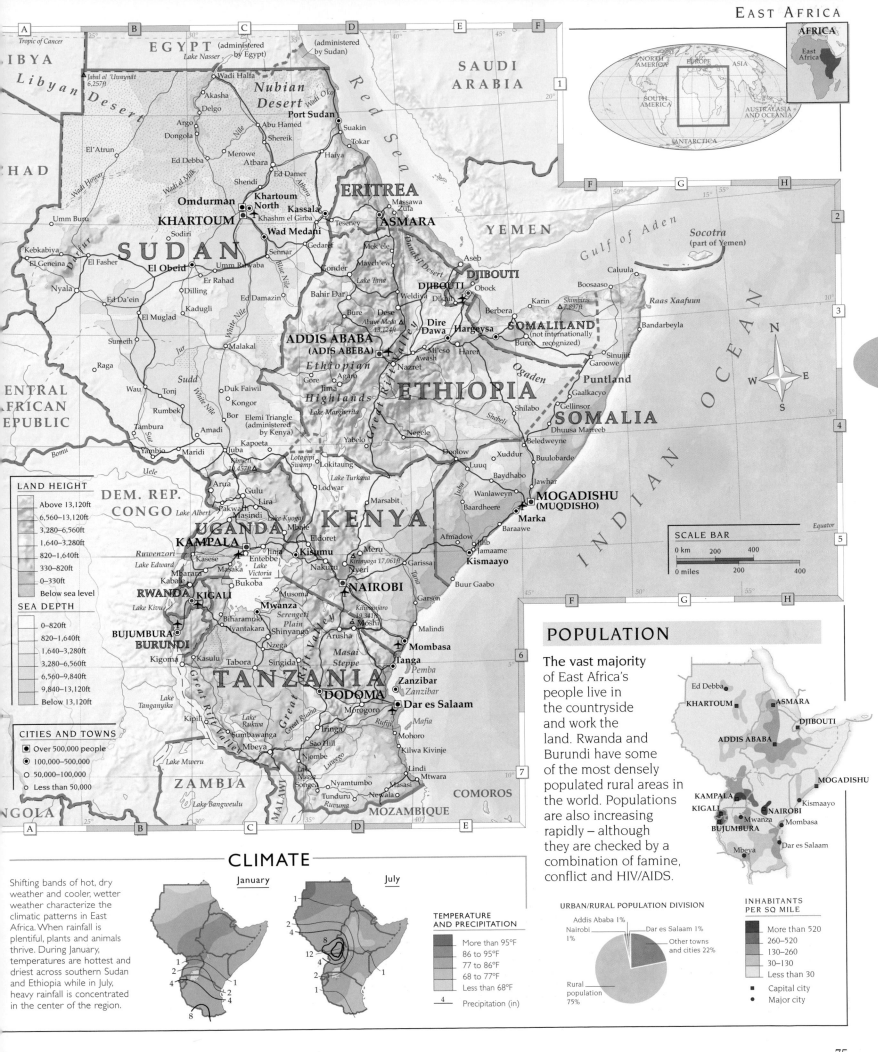

EAST AFRICA

POPULATION

The vast majority of East Africa's people live in the countryside and work the land. Rwanda and Burundi have some of the most densely populated rural areas in the world. Populations are also increasing rapidly – although they are checked by a combination of famine, conflict and HIV/AIDS.

URBAN/RURAL POPULATION DIVISION

Addis Ababa 1%
Nairobi 1%
Dar es Salaam 1%
Other towns and cities 22%
Rural population 75%

INHABITANTS PER SQ MILE
More than 520
260–520
130–260
30–130
Less than 30
■ Capital city
• Major city

CLIMATE

Shifting bands of hot, dry weather and cooler, wetter weather characterize the climatic patterns in East Africa. When rainfall is plentiful, plants and animals thrive. During January, temperatures are hottest and driest across southern Sudan and Ethiopia while in July, heavy rainfall is concentrated in the center of the region.

January

July

TEMPERATURE AND PRECIPITATION
More than 95°F
86 to 95°F
77 to 86°F
68 to 77°F
Less than 68°F
4 — Precipitation (in)

LAND HEIGHT
Above 13,120ft
6,560–13,120ft
3,280–6,560ft
1,640–3,280ft
820–1,640ft
330–820ft
0–330ft
Below sea level

SEA DEPTH
0–820ft
820–1,640ft
1,640–3,280ft
3,280–6,560ft
6,560–9,840ft
9,840–13,120ft
Below 13,120ft

CITIES AND TOWNS
■ Over 500,000 people
◉ 100,000–500,000
○ 50,000–100,000
○ Less than 50,000

SCALE BAR
0 km 200 400
0 miles 200 400

SOUTHERN AFRICA

ANGOLA, BOTSWANA, COMOROS, CONGO, DEM. REP. CONGO, GABON, LESOTHO, MADAGASCAR, MALAWI, MOZAMBIQUE, NAMIBIA, SOUTH AFRICA, SWAZILAND, ZAMBIA, ZIMBABWE

Southern Africa contains the richest deposits of valuable minerals on the continent. South Africa is the wealthiest and most industrialized country in the region. Most of the surrounding countries rely on it for trade and work. Racial segregation under apartheid operated from 1948 until 1994, when South Africa held its first multiracial elections.

FARMING AND LAND USE

Most of **southern Africa's** farmers grow just enough food to feed their families, although much of the farmland is in the hands of a few wealthy landowners. In the tropical north, oil palms and rubber are grown on large commercial plantations. Fruits are cultivated in the south, and tea and coffee are important in the east. Cattle farming is widespread across the dry grasslands.

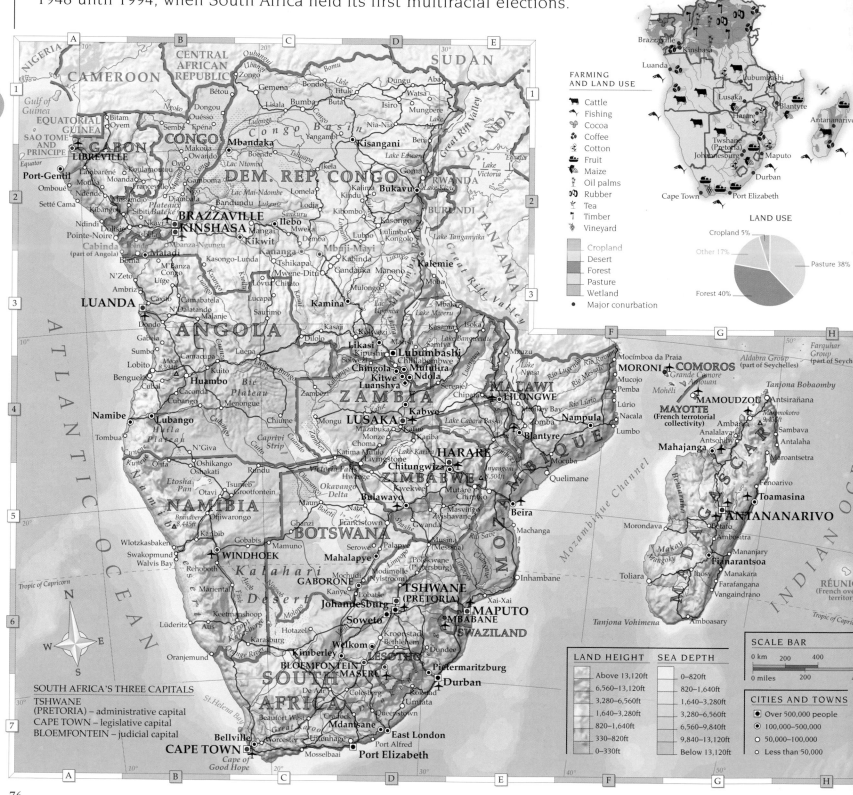

FARMING AND LAND USE

- Cattle
- Fishing
- Cocoa
- Coffee
- Cotton
- Fruit
- Maize
- Oil palms
- Rubber
- Tea
- Timber
- Vineyard

Cropland
Desert
Forest
Pasture
Wetland
● Major conurbation

LAND USE

Cropland 5%
Other 17%
Pasture 38%
Forest 40%

SOUTH AFRICA'S THREE CAPITALS

TSHWANE (PRETORIA) – administrative capital
CAPE TOWN – legislative capital
BLOEMFONTEIN – judicial capital

LAND HEIGHT

	Above 13,120ft
	6,560–13,120ft
	3,280–6,560ft
	1,640–3,280ft
	820–1,640ft
	330–820ft
	0–330ft

SEA DEPTH

	0–820ft
	820–1,640ft
	1,640–3,280ft
	3,280–6,560ft
	6,560–9,840ft
	9,840–13,120ft
	Below 13,120ft

SCALE BAR

0 km 200 400
0 miles 200

CITIES AND TOWNS

- ■ Over 500,000 people
- ● 100,000–500,000
- ○ 50,000–100,000
- ○ Less than 50,000

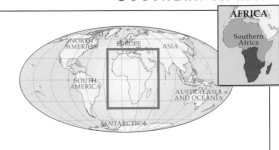

CLIMATE

During January, temperatures are highest in the Kalahari Desert and rainfall is plentiful in the center of southern Africa. July is cooler and drier, with rainfall concentrated in the north of Dem. Rep. Congo. The Atlantic coast of Namibia receives little rain all year round.

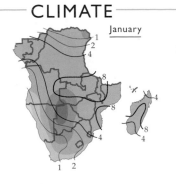

January — July

TEMPERATURE AND PRECIPITATION

- More than 95°F
- 86 to 95°F
- 77 to 86°F
- 68 to 77°F
- 59 to 68°F
- Less than 59°F
- 4 — Precipitation (in)

ENVIRONMENTAL ISSUES

The immense rainforests of the Congo Basin in the north remain relatively untouched, but deforestation is beginning to occur at its edges, with much more forest due to be cleared in the future. Large parts of Madagascar have also been deforested. Farther south, occasional drought and the clearing of bushlands for firewood can cause soil loss.

Congo Basin

1991–1992 2000–2002 2005
1971–1974 1979–1985 1991–1992 2002, 2005
1982–1984, 1992 1997–1998, 2001
1983–1985 1992–1993 2002–2003
1983 1985 2005 2007
2000

ENVIRONMENTAL ISSUES

- Drought
- Severe firewood shortage
- Flooding
- Existing desert
- Risk of desertification
- Severe risk of desertification
- Deforested area
- Remaining tropical forest

THE LANDSCAPE

Southern Africa stretches from just north of the equator down to the southern tip of the continent. It is an area with an extremely varied climate and geography. In the north are the tropical rainforests of the Congo Basin, while arid desert covers much of the southwest. The eastern regions are mostly grasslands, with lush vegetation found on the tropical coast of Mozambique.

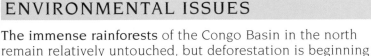

Congo Basin (C 1)
The Congo River is Africa's second longest river, flowing in an arc through the dense tropical forests of the Congo Basin before emptying into the Atlantic Ocean.

Namib Desert (B 5)
The Namib is one of the world's driest deserts. The only water it receives is from mists that roll in from the sea. Where the desert meets the coast is known as the Skeleton Coast because of sailors who were shipwrecked and died there.

Okavango Delta (C 5)
The Okavango River terminates in the Kalahari Desert, forming a vast, swampy inland delta.

Victoria Falls (D 5)
On its way to the Indian Ocean, the Zambezi River plunges over a 420 ft cliff, into a narrow chasm. The resultant spray rises up to 1,600 ft, and the thunder of the water can be heard up to 25 miles away.

Madagascar (G 5)
The world's fourth largest island lies in isolation 155 miles off the east coast of southern Africa. It became separated from the African continent 135 million years ago, and its plant and animal life are unique. The rich biodiversity of the rain forests is being threatened by uncontrolled lumbering.

Drakensberg (D 4)
The Drakensberg are a chain of mountains that lie at the edge of a broad plateau that has tilted because of the movement of the Earth's plates. Rivers have carved through the high mountains, creating dramatic gorges and waterfalls.

INDUSTRY

Southern Africa has extraordinary mineral resources. Angola has large deposits of oil, and diamonds are found in Angola, Botswana, Namibia, and South Africa. Copper is mined in the region known as the "copper belt," that runs from Dem. Rep. Congo into Zambia. South Africa is the world's largest gold producer. Manufacturing, such as fruit canning and steel production, is most developed in South Africa.

INDUSTRY
- Car manufacturing
- Chemicals
- Engineering
- Food processing
- Iron and steel
- Metal refining
- Textiles
- Oil and gas
- Mining
- Timber processing
- Tourism
- Major industrial center / area
- Major road

STRUCTURE OF INDUSTRY
- Primary 10%
- Services 59%
- Manufacturing 31%

POPULATION

The population is still mostly rural with two thirds of southern Africa's residents living in the countryside. Dense tropical rainforest in the north and arid desert in the southwest have kept habitation to a bare minimum. Malawi is the most densely populated country in the region.

INHABITANTS PER SQ MILE
- More than 260
- 130–260
- 30–130
- Less than 30
- ■ Capital city
- ● Major city

Luanda 1.4% Kinshasa 2.4%
Cape Town 1.2%
Other towns and cities 34%
Rural population 61%

CONTINENTAL EUROPE

Europe is the world's second smallest continent, occupying the western tip of the vast Eurasian landmass. To the north and west are old highlands, with the high peaks of the Alps in the south. Most people live on the densely populated North European Plain, which extends from southern England, through northern France, across Germany into Russia.

├─3,360 miles─┤
├─3,140 miles─┤ (vertical)

CROSS-SECTION THROUGH EUROPE

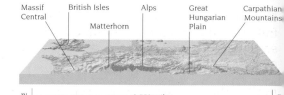

Massif Central | British Isles | Matterhorn | Alps | Great Hungarian Plain | Carpathian Mountains

W ├─────── 1,550 miles ───────┤ E

In the west, the land rises up from the Atlantic coast toward the Massif Central in France, and the high peaks of the Alps. Between the Alps and the Carpathian Mountains is the Great Hungarian Plain, where the Danube River flows on its way to the Black Sea.

PHYSICAL EUROPE

The ancient mountains of northwest Europe were scoured and smoothed by glaciers in the last Ice Age. The Alps are newer and more jagged – pushed up when Africa collided with Europe. In between is the North European Plain, where thick layers of fertile soils allow many different crops to be grown.

Novaya Zemlya

Barents Sea

Ostrov Kolguyev

Arctic Circle

Gora Narodnaya △ 6,217ft

Norwegian Sea

Kola Peninsula

White Sea

Arctic Circle

Iceland

Faeroe Islands

Shetland Islands

Outer Hebrides

Northern Dvina

Lake Onega

Lake Ladoga

Ural Mountains

Galdhøpiggen 8,100ft

Lake Vänen

Volga

Ben Nevis △ 4,406ft

North Sea

Ireland

British Isles

Jutland

Baltic Sea

Gulf of Bothnia

Western Dvina

North European Plain

Central Russian Upland

ASIA

Thames

English Channel

Elbe

Vistula

Pripet Marshes

Volga Upland

Seine

Rhine

Dnieper

Volga

Ardennes

Loire

Danube

Carpathian Mountains

Gerlachovský Štít 8,710ft

Don

Lowest point ▽ Volga Delta -92ft

Bay of Biscay

Massif Central

Alps

Matterhorn △ 14,691ft

Great Hungarian Plain

Sea of Azov

Caspian Sea

Pyrenees

Ebro

Rhône

Mt Blanc 15,770ft

Apennines

Po

Dinaric Alps

Danube

Crimea

Caucasus

Highest point El'brus 18,510ft

Black Sea

Iberian Peninsula

Corsica

Adriatic Sea

Balkan Mountains

Balearic Islands

Sardinia

Vesuvius 3,841ft

Tyrrhenian Sea

ASIA

Mediterranean Sea

Sicily

Etna △ 10,705ft

Ionian Sea

Malta

Peloponnese

Aegean Sea

Crete

AFRICA

ELEVATION

16,400ft
13,120ft
9,840ft
6,560ft
3,280ft
1,640ft
820ft
330ft
sea level
below sea level
◄ cross section

SCALE 1:31,000,000

0 km   300   600
0 miles   300   600

[1] THE FROZEN NORTH

Europe's northern coastline stretches deep into the Arctic Circle. Here in Norway, icebergs drift into the deep, wide-bottomed fjords.

THE NORTH EUROPEAN PLAIN [2]

The North European Plain has low, rolling hills and plains. Much of the area is cultivated and used for growing crops like wheat and sugarbeet.

[3] ANCIENT HIGHLANDS

Some of the world's oldest rocks are found in northwest Europe. Erosion by glaciers in the last Ice Age created smoothed hills like the mountains of Wales.

[4] THE ATLANTIC COAST

On Europe's Atlantic coast, the force of waves and winds has created striking landforms like this huge sand dune in southwest France.

THE ALPS [5]

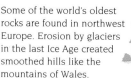

The Alps are Europe's major mountain chain. They formed about 65 million years ago. The Matterhorn is one of the most dramatic peaks.

POLITICAL EUROPE

Europe's population increased rapidly during the 18th and 19th centuries, following the Industrial Revolution. In the 20th century, Europe suffered a series of wars which redrew the political map. From 1989–1991, communist governments in eastern Europe and the former Soviet Union collapsed, as political reform swept through the countries behind the 'Iron Curtain'. In 2007 the European Union admitted two more states in a further expansion.

EUROPEAN UNION

- six original members, 1957
- nine further members, 1973 – 1995
- ten further members, 2004
- two new members, 2007

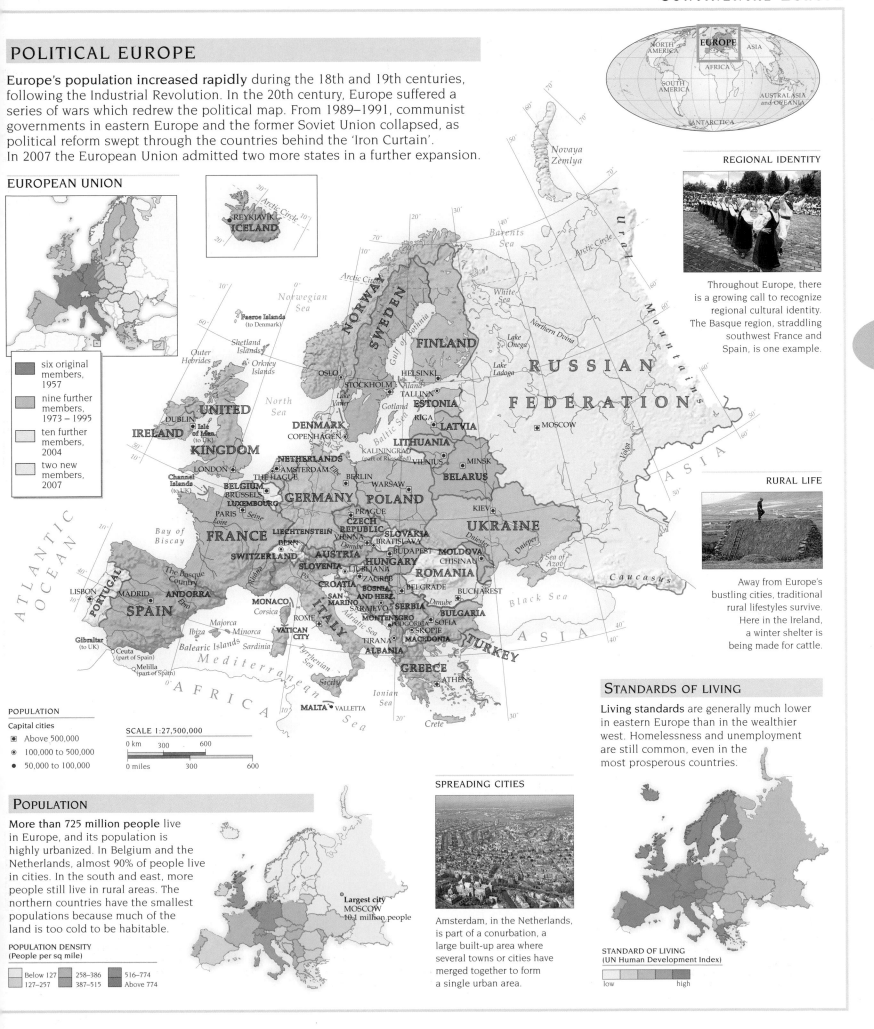

REGIONAL IDENTITY

Throughout Europe, there is a growing call to recognize regional cultural identity. The Basque region, straddling southwest France and Spain, is one example.

RURAL LIFE

Away from Europe's bustling cities, traditional rural lifestyles survive. Here in the Ireland, a winter shelter is being made for cattle.

STANDARDS OF LIVING

Living standards are generally much lower in eastern Europe than in the wealthier west. Homelessness and unemployment are still common, even in the most prosperous countries.

POPULATION

Capital cities
- ◉ Above 500,000
- ◉ 100,000 to 500,000
- ● 50,000 to 100,000

SCALE 1:27,500,000

0 km   300   600

0 miles   300   600

POPULATION

More than 725 million people live in Europe, and its population is highly urbanized. In Belgium and the Netherlands, almost 90% of people live in cities. In the south and east, more people still live in rural areas. The northern countries have the smallest populations because much of the land is too cold to be habitable.

Largest city
MOSCOW
10.1 million people

POPULATION DENSITY
(People per sq mile)
- Below 127
- 127–257
- 258–386
- 387–515
- 516–774
- Above 774

SPREADING CITIES

Amsterdam, in the Netherlands, is part of a conurbation, a large built-up area where several towns or cities have merged together to form a single urban area.

STANDARD OF LIVING
(UN Human Development Index)
low   high

EUROPEAN GEOGRAPHY

Europe is blessed with a temperate climate, ample mineral reserves, and good transportation links. During the 18th and 19th centuries the continent was transformed, as new methods of production made industry and farming more efficient and productive. Today, in many countries, heavy industries have been replaced by high-tech and service industries. Agriculture is still important, and many crops thrive on Europe's fertile plains.

INDUSTRY

Western Europe has some of the world's wealthiest countries. In countries such as France, Germany, and the UK, traditional industries like iron and steel-making are now being replaced by light industries, such as electronics, and services like finance and insurance. In Eastern Europe, industry was subsidized by the communist governments for years. Many factories are old-fashioned and need investment to improve their equipment and production methods.

MINERAL RESOURCES

Europe has few sizable reserves of metallic minerals; most were used up by industry during the 19th century. Oil, gas, and coal are found in large quantities – gas in the North Sea and oil in the Volga basin. Coal, although abundant, is being steadily depleted.

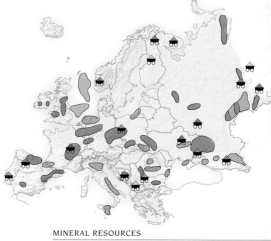

MINERAL RESOURCES

Bauxite	Manganese	Oil/gas field
Chromium	Nickel	Coal field
Copper	Uranium	
Iron		

OIL AND GAS

Oil and gas reserves are plentiful in the Russian Federation. South of Rostov-on-Don, oil is pumped from the ground and piped to nearby refineries.

CAR MANUFACTURING

Germany is one of the world's largest manufacturers of cars. Companies like BMW, Mercedes-Benz, and Volkswagen export cars across the world.

FINANCE

London, Frankfurt and Paris are among the most important financial centers in the world. Many banks and financial institutions have their headquarters here. At the London Stock Exchange, people buy and sell stocks and shares.

ECONOMIC ACTIVITY

- ✈ Aerospace
- Vehicle manufacturing
- Chemicals
- Coal
- Defense
- Electronics
- Engineering
- Finance
- Food processing
- High-tech industry
- Iron and steel
- Oil and gas
- Printing and publishing
- Textiles
- Timber processing

GNI per capita (US$)

- Below 1,999
- 2,000–4,999
- 5,000–9,999
- 10,000–19,999
- 20,000–24,999
- Above 25,000
- Industrial center

CLIMATE

Europe's climate is temperate with few climatic extremes. In the far north, Europe extends into the Arctic Circle and the climate is so cold that the Baltic Sea freezes over in the winter. Toward the Atlantic coast in the west, the climate becomes wetter and warmer because of a warm ocean current, known as the Gulf Stream. Countries such as Italy and Spain that border the Mediterranean Sea have long, hot summers and low rainfall, which can sometimes lead to such problems as drought.

EXTREME WEATHER EVENTS

Symbols indicate climatic extremes

CLIMATE
- Tundra
- Subarctic
- Cool continental
- Temperate/humid
- Mediterranean
- Semiarid

Coldest place
UST' SHCHUGOR (Russ. Fed.)
Temperature -67F

Driest place
ASTRAKHAN' (Russ. Fed.)
Annual rainfall 6 in

Wettest place
CRKVICE (Montenegro)
Annual rainfall 183 in

Hottest place
SEVILLE (Spain)
Temperature 122F

THE MEDITERRANEAN CLIMATE

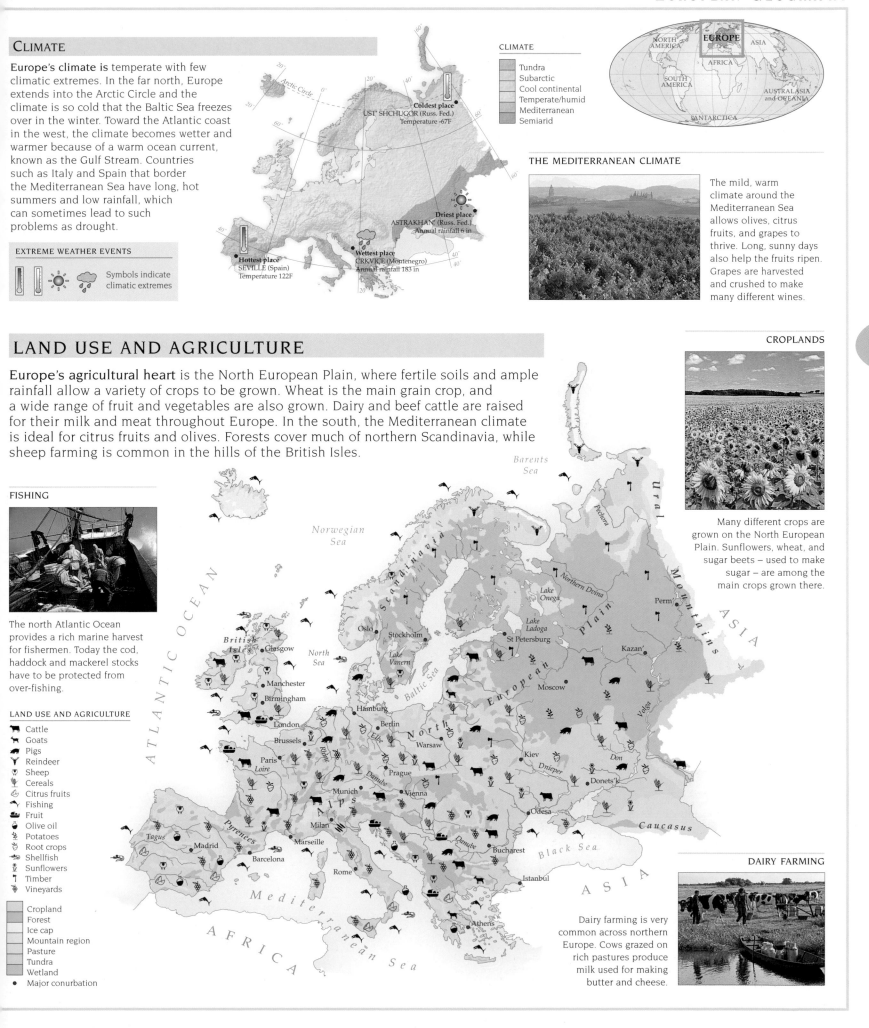

The mild, warm climate around the Mediterranean Sea allows olives, citrus fruits, and grapes to thrive. Long, sunny days also help the fruits ripen. Grapes are harvested and crushed to make many different wines.

LAND USE AND AGRICULTURE

Europe's agricultural heart is the North European Plain, where fertile soils and ample rainfall allow a variety of crops to be grown. Wheat is the main grain crop, and a wide range of fruit and vegetables are also grown. Dairy and beef cattle are raised for their milk and meat throughout Europe. In the south, the Mediterranean climate is ideal for citrus fruits and olives. Forests cover much of northern Scandinavia, while sheep farming is common in the hills of the British Isles.

CROPLANDS

Many different crops are grown on the North European Plain. Sunflowers, wheat, and sugar beets – used to make sugar – are among the main crops grown there.

FISHING

The north Atlantic Ocean provides a rich marine harvest for fishermen. Today the cod, haddock and mackerel stocks have to be protected from over-fishing.

LAND USE AND AGRICULTURE
- Cattle
- Goats
- Pigs
- Reindeer
- Sheep
- Cereals
- Citrus fruits
- Fishing
- Fruit
- Olive oil
- Potatoes
- Root crops
- Shellfish
- Sunflowers
- Timber
- Vineyards

- Cropland
- Forest
- Ice cap
- Mountain region
- Pasture
- Tundra
- Wetland
- Major conurbation

DAIRY FARMING

Dairy farming is very common across northern Europe. Cows grazed on rich pastures produce milk used for making butter and cheese.

NORTHERN EUROPE

DENMARK, ESTONIA, FINLAND, ICELAND, LATVIA,
LITHUANIA, NORWAY, SWEDEN

Denmark, Sweden, and Norway are together known
as Scandinavia. These countries, along with the North
Atlantic island of Iceland, have similar languages and
cultures. Finland has a very different language and
a separate identity from its Scandinavian neighbors.
Estonia, Latvia, and Lithuania, known as the Baltic
states, were part of the Soviet Union until 1989,
when each became an independent country.

INDUSTRY

In Scandinavia, many natural
resources are used in industry:
timber for paper and furniture;
iron ore for steel and cars; and
fish and natural gas from the seas.
Hydroelectric power is generated
by water flowing down steep
mountain slopes. The Baltic states
still rely on Russia to supply
their raw materials and energy.

INDUSTRY

- 🚗 Car manufacturing
- ⚗ Chemicals
- ⚙ Engineering
- 🐟 Fish processing
- ⚡ Hydroelectric power
- 🚢 Shipbuilding
- 🌲 Timber processing
- 🏛 Tourism

- ▪ Major industrial center / area
- — Major road

STRUCTURE
OF INDUSTRY

Primary 4%
Services 65%
Manufacturing 31%

Tromsø
Narvik
Reykjavík
Akureyri
Luleå
Kemi
Oulu
Trondheim
Umeå
Ålesund
Sundsvall
Jyväskylä
Tampere
Bergen
Oslo
Turku
Lappeenranta
Helsinki
Stockholm
Stavanger
Tallinn
Kristiansand
Tartu
Gothenburg
Linköping
Jönköping
Riga
Ålborg
Liepāja
Copenhagen
Daugavpils
Odense
Malmö
Kaunas
Vilnius
Kaliningrad

POPULATION

The population is distributed mainly along the warmer
and flatter southern and coastal areas. Population totals and
densities are low for all of the countries, and Iceland
has the lowest population density in
Europe, with just seven people per
sq mile. Many Scandinavians have
holiday homes on the islands, along
the lake shores, or in coastal areas.

REYKJAVÍK

Trondheim
Tampere
Bergen
Uppsala
HELSINKI
Espoo
OSLO
TALLINN
Gothenburg
STOCKHOLM
Århus
RIGA
COPENHAGEN
Malmö
VILNIUS
Kaliningrad

INHABITANTS
PER SQ MILE

- More than 520
- 260–520
- 130–260
- Less than 130
- ▪ Capital city
- ● Major city

URBAN/RURAL
POPULATION DIVISION

Copenhagen 3.4%   Stockholm 3.8%
Helsinki 3.3%
Other towns and cities 66.5%
Rural population 23%

FARMING AND LAND USE

Southern Denmark and Sweden are the most productive
areas, with pig farming, dairy farming, and crops such as
wheat, barley, and potatoes. Sheep farming is important
in southern Norway and Iceland. In the Baltic states,
cereals, potatoes, and sugar beets are the main crops, and
cattle graze on damp pasture.

FARMING AND LAND USE

- 🐄 Cattle
- 🐟 Fishing
- 🐖 Pigs
- 🐑 Sheep
- 🌾 Cereals
- 🥕 Root crops
- 🌲 Timber

- Pasture
- Cropland
- Forest
- Ice cap
- Mountain region
- Tundra
- ● Major conurbation

LAND USE

Pasture 3%
Cropland 11%
Forest 49%
Other (including mountains) 37%

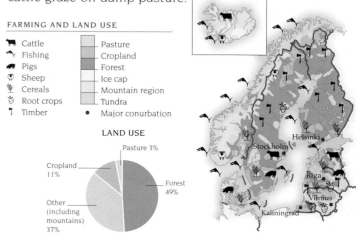

Helsinki
Stockholm
Riga
Vilnius
Kaliningrad

THE LANDSCAPE

The north and west of Scandinavia is extremely rugged
and mountainous, with landscapes eroded by ice. In the
south of Scandinavia the land is flatter, with fertile soils
deposited by glaciers. Much of Finland, Norway, and Sweden
is covered by dense forests. The Baltic states are much
lower, with rounded hills and many lakes and marshes.

The land of ice and fire.
Iceland is one of the world's most
active volcanic areas. There are about
200 volcanoes on the island, along
with bubbling hot springs, mud-holes,
and geysers that spurt boiling water
and steam high into the air.

Fjords
Norway has many
fjords: deep, wide
valleys carved by
glaciers, drowned by
seawater when the
ice melted at the end
of the last Ice Age.

Baltic Sea (D 7)
Ships from Finland, Sweden,
and the Baltic states use the
Baltic Sea as their route to the
north Atlantic Ocean. In winter,
much of the sea is frozen.

Glacial lakes
Finland and Sweden have many
thousands of lakes. During the
last Ice Age, glaciers scoured
hollows that filled with water
when the ice melted.

Courland Spit (D 7)
This wide sandspit runs f
62-miles along the Baltic
coast of Lithuania and the
Russian enclave of Kalinin
It encloses a huge lagoon

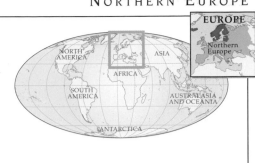

EUROPE
Northern
Europe

ENVIRONMENTAL ISSUES

Northern Europe has been badly affected by industrial pollution from other parts of Europe. Polluted air moves north and mixes with the rain to create acid rain. This poisons forests and lakes, destroying the plants and animals living in them. Renewable energy plays a major role in this region, hydro-electric, geothermal and wind power are all exploited.

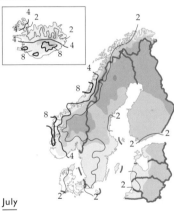

Vatnajökull
1996

▲ Surtsey 1963

● Stockholm   ● Helsinki
                    Tallinn
                        ● Riga

● Copenhagen

ENVIRONMENTAL ISSUES

- Major dams
- Urban air pollution
- Volcanic eruption
- Wind farm
- Geothermal power
- Affected by acid rain
- Sea pollution
- ● Major industrial center

CLIMATE

Warm ocean currents flowing north along the coasts of Norway and Iceland make the climate mild and wet. Away from the sea, the climate is generally colder and drier.

January

July

TEMPERATURE AND PRECIPITATION

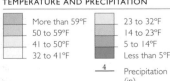

More than 59°F	23 to 32°F
50 to 59°F	14 to 23°F
41 to 50°F	5 to 14°F
32 to 41°F	Less than 5°F

—4— Precipitation (in)

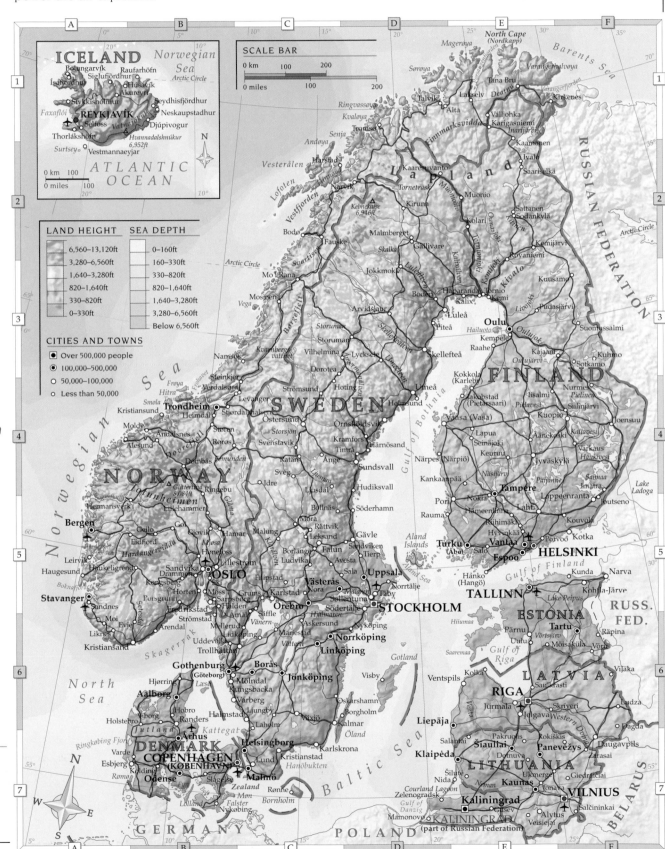

ICELAND

Norwegian Sea

Bolungarvík
Ísafjördhur
Siglufjördhur   Raufarhöfn
Stykkishólmur   Húsavík   Akureyri
                Seydhisfjördhur
Faxaflói   **REYKJAVÍK**   Neskaupstadhur
           Selfoss   Vatnajökull   Djúpivogur
Thorlákshöfn   Hvannadalshnúkur
               6,952ft
Surtsey   Vestmannaeyjar

ATLANTIC OCEAN

0 km   100
0 miles   100

SCALE BAR

0 km   100   200
0 miles   100   200

LAND HEIGHT   SEA DEPTH

LAND HEIGHT	SEA DEPTH
6,560–13,120ft	0–160ft
3,280–6,560ft	160–330ft
1,640–3,280ft	330–820ft
820–1,640ft	820–1,640ft
330–820ft	1,640–3,280ft
0–330ft	3,280–6,560ft
	Below 6,560ft

CITIES AND TOWNS

- ◼ Over 500,000 people
- ◉ 100,000–500,000
- ○ 50,000–100,000
- ○ Less than 50,000

RUSSIAN FEDERATION

North Cape (Nordkapp)
Magerøya   Barents Sea
Søroya   Varangerhalvøya
Talvik   Lakselv   Kirkenes
Kvaløya   Alta   Valjohka   Karigasniemi
Tromsø   Kaaresuvanto   Kaamanen   Ivalo   Saariselkä
Vesterålen   Harstad   Kiruna   Muonio   Sattanen   Sodankylä
Lofoten   Narvik   Torneträsk   Kolari   Kemijärvi   Kuusamo
Bodø   Malmberget   Gällivare   Rovaniemi
Fauske   Jokkmokk   Tornio   Kemi   Suomussalmi
Mo i Rana   Boden   Haparanda   Kalix   Oulu   Pudasjärvi
Mosjøen   Arvidsjaur   Luleå   Raahe   Kajaani   Sotkamo
Vega   Piteå   Skellefteå   Kokkola (Karleby)   **FINLAND**   Kuhmo
Namsos   Vilhelmina   Umeå   Jakobstad (Pietarsaari)   Iisalmi   Nurmes
Steinkjer   Dorotea   Holmsund   Vaasa (Vasa)   Kuopio   Siilinjärvi
Verdalsøra   Strömsund   Hoting   Närpes (Närpiö)   Seinäjoki   Joensuu
Trondheim   Levanger   Örnsköldsvik   Lapua   Äänekoski   Varkaus
Kristiansund   Östersund   Kramfors   Keuru   Jyväskylä
Molde   Storsjön   Härnösand   Kankaanpää   Näsijärvi
Åndalsnes   Storen   Timrå   Pori   **Tampere**   Lahti
Ålesund   Røros   Ånge   Rauma   Hämeenlinna   Lappeenranta   Imatra
Dombås   Idre   Sundsvall   Nokia   Riihimäki   Kouvola
Ringebu   Ljusdal   Hudiksvall   Turku (Åbo)   Hyvinkää   Porvoo   Kotka
Bergen   Lillehammer   Bollnäs   Söderhamn   Espoo   **Vantaa**   **HELSINKI**
Guol   Mora   Rättvik   Gävle   Åland Islands   Hanko (Hangö)   Kunda
Hermansverk   Hamar   Leksand   Sandviken   Tierp   **TALLINN**   Narva
Eidfjord   Gjøvik   Malung   Falun   Sala   Uppsala   **STOCKHOLM**   Kohtla-Järve   **RUSS. FED.**
Oslo   Filipstad   Ludvika   Avesta   Norrtälje   **ESTONIA**   Tartu   Räpina
Leirvik   Drammen   Karlstad   Västerås   Täby   Pärnu   Mõisaküla   Võru
Haukeligrend   Kongsberg   Örebro   Nora   Sollentuna   Hiiumaa   Viljaka
Haugesund   Porsgrunn   Grums   Askersund   Södertälje   Saaremaa   Gulf of Riga
Stavanger   Horten   Moss   Sarpsborg   Vänern   Nyköping   **Norrköping**   Ventspils   **LATVIA**
Sandnes   Fredrikstad   Amal   Mariestad   **Linköping**   Visby   Kolka   **RIGA**   Skriveri
Moi   Strömstad   Lidköping   Gotland   Jūrmala   Jelgava   Ludza
Evje   Uddevalla   Vättern   Liepāja   Dagda
Liknes   Trollhättan   **Borås**   Oskarshamn   Salacgriva   Daugavpils
Kristiansand   **Gothenburg (Göteborg)**   **Jönköping**   Borgholm   Pakruojis   Rokiškis
North Sea   Hjørring   Mölndal   Ventspils   Šiauliai   Panevėžys   Zarasai
Aalborg   Kungsbacka   Varberg   Kalmar   **Klaipėda**   Dotnuva   **LITHUANIA**
Holstebro   Hobro   Randers   Ljungby   Öland   Salantai   Šilute   Ukmergė   Giedraičiai
Varde   Viborg   Halmstad   Växjö   Nida   Neman   **Kaunas**   **VILNIUS**
Esbjerg   **Århus**   **Helsingborg**   Laholm   Kaliningrad   Gusev   Alytus   Salčininkai
Rønne   **DENMARK**   **COPENHAGEN (KØBENHAVN)**   Karlskrona   Zelenogradsk   Veisiejai
Odense   Slagelse   **Malmö**   Lund   Kristianstad   Courland Lagoon   **KALININGRAD** (part of Russian Federation)
Zealand   Møn   Baltic Sea   Mamonovo
Falster   Bornholm   Gulf of Danzig
Nykøbing

GERMANY   **POLAND**

BELARUS

THE LOW COUNTRIES

BELGIUM, LUXEMBOURG, NETHERLANDS

Belgium, Luxembourg, and the Netherlands are called the Low Countries because most of their land is flat and low-lying. Much of the Netherlands lies below sea level, and over hundreds of years the Dutch have built dikes and dams to prevent flooding, and have pumped water off large areas of land to reclaim them from the sea. The Low Countries are Europe's most densely populated countries, but most of their people have a high living standard.

ENVIRONMENTAL ISSUES

Huge land reclamation projects in the Netherlands, such as the IJsselmeer project, have created some new land for agricultural use, and also for houses, roads, and open spaces. However, because of this work, sea-level rise is a major threat to large parts of the Netherlands.

ENVIRONMENTAL ISSUES

- 😷 Urban air pollution
- Built-up areas
- Reclaimed land
- Polluted river
- • Major industrial center

CLIMATE

The Low Countries share a similar climate, with mild winters and warm summers. Only in the upland Ardennes region does rainfall increase and temperatures decrease.

TEMPERATURE AND PRECIPITATION

- More than 59°F
- 50 to 59°F
- 41 to 50°F
- 32 to 41°F
- Less than 32°F

— 4 Precipitation (in)

January — Less than 2

July — Less than 2

NETHERLANDS' TWO CAPITALS
AMSTERDAM - capital
THE HAGUE - seat of government

LAND HEIGHT
- 1,640–3,280ft
- 820–1,640ft
- 330–820ft
- 0–330ft
- Below sea level

SEA DEPTH
- 0–330ft

CITIES AND TOWNS
- ■ Over 500,000 people
- ● 100,000–500,000
- ◐ 50,000–100,000
- ○ Less than 50,000

SCALE BAR
0 km   25   50
0 miles   25   50

POPULATION

More than 27 million people live in the Low Countries, and nine out of every ten people live in a town or city. The largest urban area – known as the *Randstad Holland* – is in the Netherlands. It runs in an unbroken line from Rotterdam in the south, to Amsterdam in the west. Even most rural areas in the Low Countries are densely populated.

INHABITANTS
PER SQ MILE

- More than 520
- 260–520
- 130–260
- 0–130
- ■ Capital city
- ● Major city

URBAN/RURAL
POPULATION DIVISION

Amsterdam 2.8%
Rotterdam 2.3%
Brussels 3.9%
Rural population 8%
Other towns and cities 83%

INDUSTRY

The Low Countries are an important center for the high-tech and electronics industries. Good transportation links to the rest of Europe allow them to sell their products in other countries. The built-up area stretching from Amsterdam in the Netherlands to Antwerp in Belgium has the greatest number of factories. Luxembourg is also an important banking center; many international banks have their headquarters in its capital city.

STRUCTURE
OF INDUSTRY

Primary 2%
Services 73%
Manufacturing 25%

INDUSTRY

- ✈ Aerospace
- ♨ Chemicals
- ✿ Engineering
- ✎ Pharmaceuticals
- 👕 Textiles
- Ⓢ Finance
- 💻 High-tech industry
- 🏛 Tourism
- ● Major industrial center / area
- — Major road

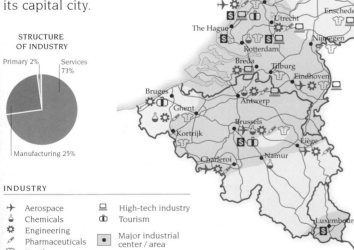

FARMING AND LAND USE

The Low Countries' fertile soils and flat plains provide excellent conditions for farming. The main crops grown are barley, potatoes, and flax for making linen. In the Netherlands, much farmland is used for dairy farming. The country is also famous for growing flowers, which are exported around the world. Flowers and vegetables are grown either in open fields or in enormous greenhouses, which allow production year-round.

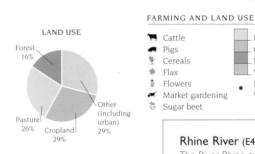

LAND USE

Forest 16%
Pasture 26%
Cropland 29%
Other (including urban) 29%

FARMING AND LAND USE

- 🐄 Cattle
- 🐖 Pigs
- 🌾 Cereals
- ✻ Flax
- ⚘ Flowers
- 🥬 Market gardening
- 🌱 Sugar beet
- Pasture
- Cropland
- Forest
- Wetland
- ● Major conurbation

THE LANDSCAPE

The Low Countries are largely flat and low-lying. The ancient hills of the Ardennes, in the far southeast, are the only higher region. They rise to heights of more than 1,640 ft. Two major rivers – the Meuse and the Rhine – flow across the Low Countries to their mouths in the North Sea. At the coast, the Rhine deposits large quantities of sediment to form a delta.

Polders
In the Netherlands, land has been reclaimed from the sea since the Middle Ages by building dikes and drainage ditches. These areas of land are called polders. They are very fertile.

Rhine River (E4)
The River Rhine erodes and carries large amounts of sediment along its course. When it reaches the Netherlands it divides into three rivers. As they approach the North Sea, the rivers slow down, depositing the sediment to form a delta.

Low-lying Netherlands
Over two-thirds of the Netherlands lies at or below sea level. This makes flooding a constant threat in coastal areas.

Flanders (B6)
The plains of Flanders in western Belgium have fertile soils which were deposited by glaciers during the last Ice Age. They provide excellent land for growing crops.

Heathlands
The heathlands on the Dutch-Belgian border have thin, sandy soils. The only plants that grow well here are heathers and gorse.

Ardennes (D8)
The hills of the Ardennes were formed over 300 million years ago. They have many deep valleys, which have been eroded by rivers like the Meuse.

THE BRITISH ISLES

IRELAND, UNITED KINGDOM

The British Isles lie off the northwest coast of mainland Europe. They are made up of two large islands and more than 5,000 smaller ones. Politically, the region is divided into two countries: the United Kingdom – England, Wales, Scotland, and Northern Ireland – and the Republic of Ireland. Geographically, the British Isles are divided between highlands to the north and west, and lowlands to the south and east.

THE LANDSCAPE

Low rolling hills, high moorlands, and small fields with high hedges are all typical of the British Isles. Ireland is known as the Emerald Isle because heavy rainfall gives it a lush, green appearance. Scotland and Wales are mountainous; the rocks forming the mountains there are some of the oldest in the world.

Indented coastlines
The west coast of the British Isles faces the Atlantic Ocean, and more than 1,860 miles of open sea to the North American continent. Storms and high waves constantly batter the hard, rocky coastline, giving it a jagged outline.

Ben Nevis (C 4)
This mountain is the highest point in the British Isles. It is 4,406 ft above sea level.

The Lake District (D 5)
The Lake District National Park has England's highest peak, Scafell Pike, at 3,209 ft, its deepest lake, Wast Water (260 ft), and its largest lake, Windermere (10 miles long).

The Pennines (D 6)
The Pennines are a chain of high hills, topped by moorland. They run for more than 250 miles, and are known as the "backbone of England."

The Burren (A 6)
The Burren is a large area of limestone in the west of Ireland. Its flat surfaces are known as limestone "pavements." There are also many caves and sinkholes in the area.

Rias
Rias are river valleys that have been drowned by rising sea levels. The southern coast of southwest England has many good examples.

The Fens (E 6)
This is the flattest area in England. Much of the land here has been reclaimed from the sea.

FARMING AND LAND USE

The English lowlands and the wide, flat stretches of land in East Anglia are the agricultural heartland of the United Kingdom. The country is no longer self-sufficient in food, but wheat, potatoes and other vegetables, and fruits, are widely grown. In Ireland, and in central and southern England, dairy and beef cattle feed off grassy pastures. In the hilly and mountainous areas, sheep farming is more usual.

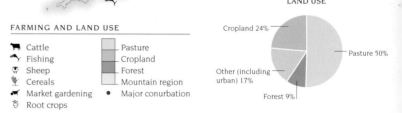

FARMING AND LAND USE

- Cattle
- Fishing
- Sheep
- Cereals
- Market gardening
- Root crops
- Pasture
- Cropland
- Forest
- Mountain region
- • Major conurbation

LAND USE
- Cropland 24%
- Pasture 50%
- Other (including urban) 17%
- Forest 9%

INDUSTRY

The United Kingdom's traditional industries, such as coal mining, iron- and steel-making, and textiles, have declined in recent years. Today, newer industries make cars, chemicals, and electronic and high-tech goods. Service industries, especially banking and insurance, have grown in importance. The country's most valuable natural resource is its large North Sea oil and gas fields.

INDUSTRY

- ✈ Aerospace
- 🚗 Car manufacturing
- Chemicals
- ⚙ Engineering
- Textiles
- S Finance
- High-tech industry
- Tourism
- ▪ Major industrial center / area
- — Major road

STRUCTURE OF INDUSTRY
- Primary 2%
- Services 67%
- Manufacturing 31%

POPULATION

The United Kingdom is densely populated, with most of the people living in urban areas. The southeast is the most crowded part of the country. The Scottish Highlands are less populated today than they were 200 years ago. Ireland is still mainly rural, with many Irish people making their living from farming.

URBAN/RURAL POPULATION DIVISION
- Birmingham 1.6%
- London 11.4%
- Glasgow 1%
- Rural population 12%
- Other towns and cities 74%

INHABITANTS PER SQ MILE
- More than 520
- 260–520
- 130–260
- Less than 130
- ▪ Capital city
- • Major city

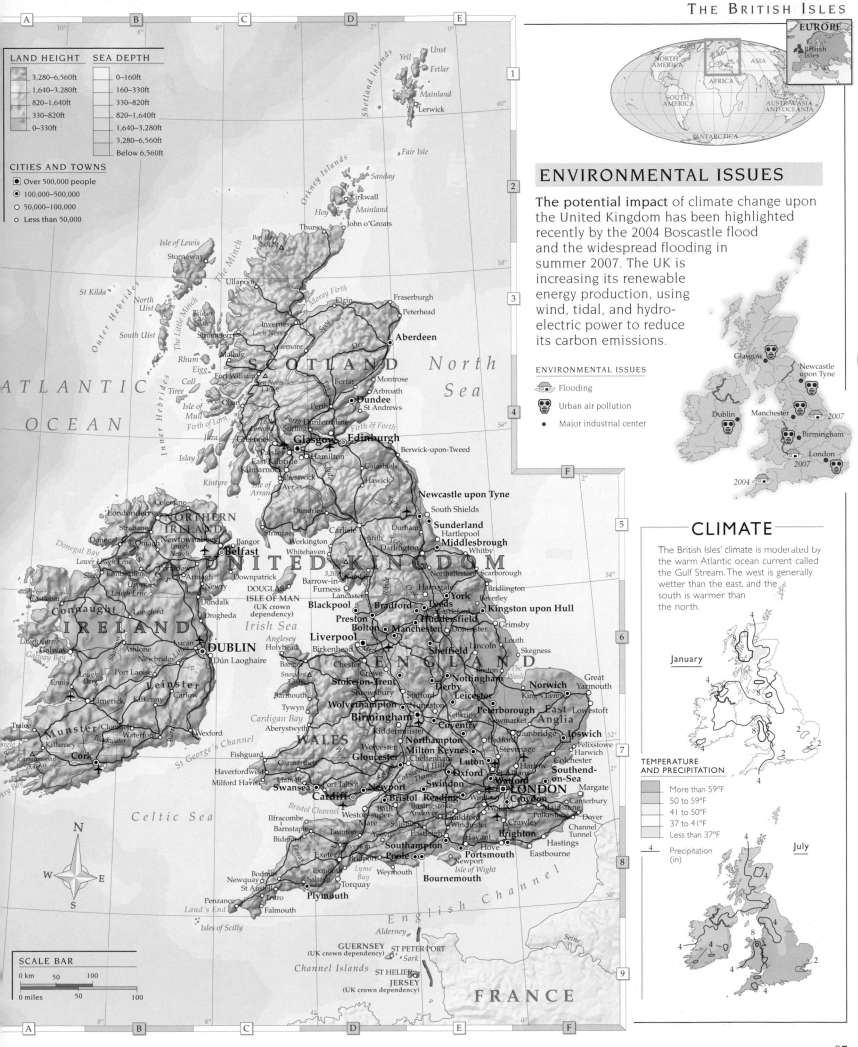

LAND HEIGHT
- 3,280–6,560ft
- 1,640–3,280ft
- 820–1,640ft
- 330–820ft
- 0–330ft

SEA DEPTH
- 0–160ft
- 160–330ft
- 330–820ft
- 820–1,640ft
- 1,640–3,280ft
- 3,280–6,560ft
- Below 6,560ft

CITIES AND TOWNS
- Over 500,000 people
- 100,000–500,000
- 50,000–100,000
- Less than 50,000

EUROPE
British Isles

ENVIRONMENTAL ISSUES

The potential impact of climate change upon the United Kingdom has been highlighted recently by the 2004 Boscastle flood and the widespread flooding in summer 2007. The UK is increasing its renewable energy production, using wind, tidal, and hydro-electric power to reduce its carbon emissions.

ENVIRONMENTAL ISSUES
- Flooding
- Urban air pollution
- Major industrial center

Glasgow
Newcastle upon Tyne
Dublin
Manchester
2007
Birmingham
London
2007
2004

CLIMATE

The British Isles' climate is moderated by the warm Atlantic ocean current called the Gulf Stream. The west is generally wetter than the east, and the south is warmer than the north.

January

July

TEMPERATURE AND PRECIPITATION
- More than 59°F
- 50 to 59°F
- 41 to 50°F
- 37 to 41°F
- Less than 37°F
- 4 — Precipitation (in)

SCALE BAR
0 km 50 100
0 miles 50 100

IRELAND

IRELAND, NORTHERN IRELAND

Ireland faces the north Atlantic Ocean and is one of the remotest parts of the European Union. Since 1921 the island has been divided into two separate states: Northern Ireland, which is part of the United Kingdom, and Ireland, which has its own government in Dublin. The eastern side of the island has more people and industry. In the west, traditional ways of life based on farming remain strong and the native Irish language is still spoken by some people.

INDUSTRY

Ireland has few mineral resources, around 15% of its electricity is produced by burning peat. In the last 20 years the European Union has given money to help the Irish economy and many new factories have been set up, mainly in the area around Dublin. Hi-tech industries expanded rapidly, as a result of low set-up costs and tax benefits.

INDUSTRY

- ✈ Aerospace
- ♠ Brewing
- ♧ Chemicals
- ⚙ Engineering
- ▣ Food processing
- 👕 Textiles
- ▭ Hi-tech industry
- ⊕ Tourism
- ▪ Major industrial center / area
- — Major road

POPULATION

The population of Ireland has actually fallen over the last century as a result of mass emigration, mainly to North America. The rate of people leaving the country to live abroad is still high, although one of Europe's highest birth rates and economic immigration are finally causing the population to rise again, with one person in every three being less than 20-years old.

INHABITANTS PER SQ MILE

- More than 650
- 260–650
- 130–260
- Less than 130
- ▪ Capital city
- ● Major city

FARMING AND LAND USE

Potatoes were once the traditional staple food of the Irish; potatoes and cereals flourish in the drier east. The climate is too wet for many types of crop, particularly in the west, where the soils are thin and the land is mostly used for sheep grazing. In bog areas a type of soil called peat is cut from the ground and dried to be burned as fuel.

FARMING AND LAND USE

- 🐄 Cattle
- 🐑 Sheep
- 🌾 Cereals
- 🌿 Potatoes
- Cropland
- Forest
- Pasture
- ● Major conurbation

THE LANDSCAPE

Ireland's mountains are nearly all close to the sea. They form a ring of high ground – broken in only a few places – encircling a lower-lying plain which fills the central areas. Hundreds of lakes, large areas of bogland, and low, grassy hills cover this central plain. The west coast follows an extremely irregular line, with many long bays and headlands.

High cliffs (C 2)
The cliffs of Donegal are some of the highest in Europe. Slieve League has been half cut away by sea erosion, so that the cliff rises vertically, all the way up from the shore to its 2,198 ft summit.

Lakes made by glaciers
The central plain is covered with lakes of many different sizes. Most of these lakes were formed by huge blocks of ice which remained lying around as the last Ice Age came to an end, slowly melting over hundreds of years to leave sunken pits in the land surface.

Flooded river valleys (A 6)
Dingle Bay extends deep inland. Rising seas have flooded the old river valley. Bays formed when the sea floods a river valley are known as rias.

Shannon (C 4)
The Shannon is Ireland's longest river and also its main source of hydroelectric power. The main power station lies to the north of Limerick.

Macgillycuddy's Reeks (B 6)
This is the highest mountain range in Ireland. The jagged peaks and steep-sided valleys were cut from the highly resistant rocks by glacial erosion, during the last Ice Age.

Burren (B 4)
The Burren is a large plateau of limestone rock. Limestone is permeable, which means that water sinks below the surface and flows underground. The bare rock is visible at the surface in many places, where it is called a limestone pavement.

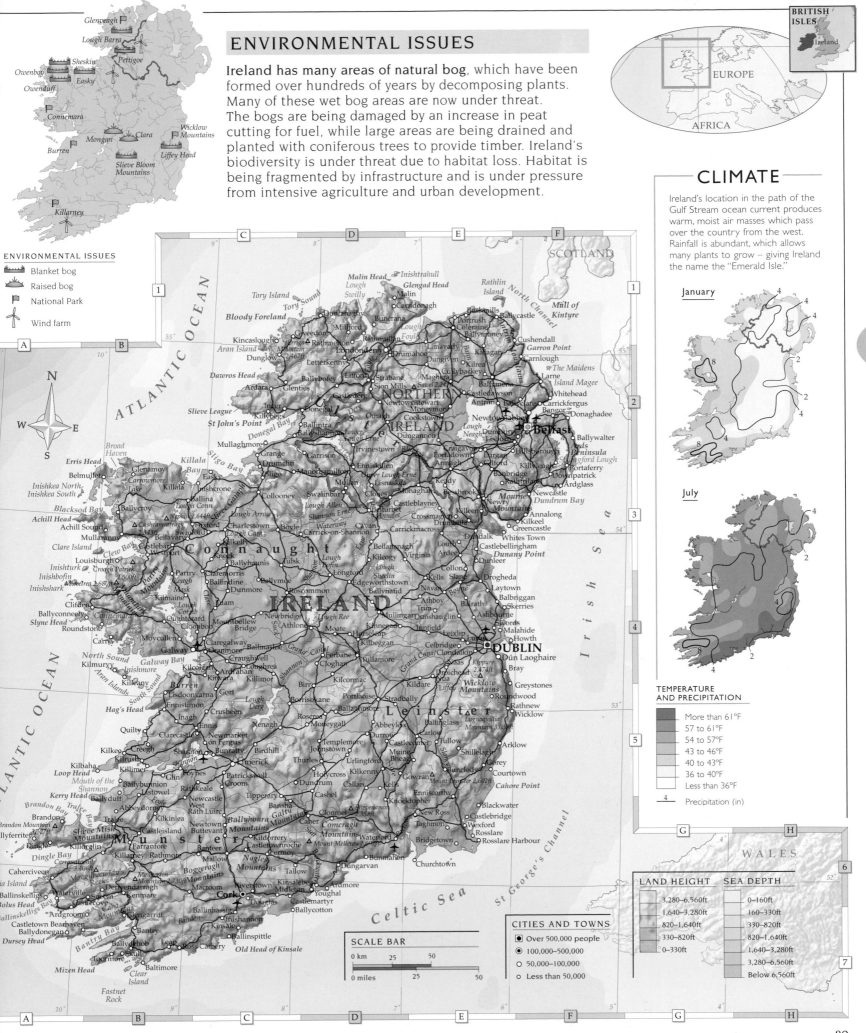

BRITISH ISLES
Ireland

EUROPE
AFRICA

ENVIRONMENTAL ISSUES

Ireland has many areas of natural bog, which have been formed over hundreds of years by decomposing plants. Many of these wet bog areas are now under threat. The bogs are being damaged by an increase in peat cutting for fuel, while large areas are being drained and planted with coniferous trees to provide timber. Ireland's biodiversity is under threat due to habitat loss. Habitat is being fragmented by infrastructure and is under pressure from intensive agriculture and urban development.

CLIMATE

Ireland's location in the path of the Gulf Stream ocean current produces warm, moist air masses which pass over the country from the west. Rainfall is abundant, which allows many plants to grow – giving Ireland the name the "Emerald Isle."

January

July

ENVIRONMENTAL ISSUES

- Blanket bog
- Raised bog
- National Park
- Wind farm

TEMPERATURE AND PRECIPITATION

- More than 61°F
- 57 to 61°F
- 54 to 57°F
- 43 to 46°F
- 40 to 43°F
- 36 to 40°F
- Less than 36°F
- —4— Precipitation (in)

CITIES AND TOWNS

- Over 500,000 people
- 100,000–500,000
- 50,000–100,000
- Less than 50,000

SCALE BAR

0 km 25 50
0 miles 25 50

LAND HEIGHT

- 3,280–6,560ft
- 1,640–3,280ft
- 820–1,640ft
- 330–820ft
- 0–330ft

SEA DEPTH

- 0–160ft
- 160–330ft
- 330–820ft
- 820–1,640ft
- 1,640–3,280ft
- 3,280–6,560ft
- Below 6,560ft

SCOTLAND

Scotland occupies the northern third of Britain and has three main regions: the northern highlands and islands, the Southern Uplands and, between these two mountain areas, the central lowlands, where around three-quarters of the population live and work. Scotland was once an independent country and, after nearly 300 years of union with England, has regained its own parliament, with certain autonomous powers. Scotland's economy has been boosted over the last 30 years by the North Sea oil industry.

INDUSTRY

A century ago, the area around the Clyde River was one of the great industrial regions of the world. The old heavy industries have since declined and been replaced by hi-tech and electronics industries, earning the area the name of "Silicon Glen." North Sea oil has brought many jobs and attracted new, oil-based industries such as chemicals and plastics production to the east coast.

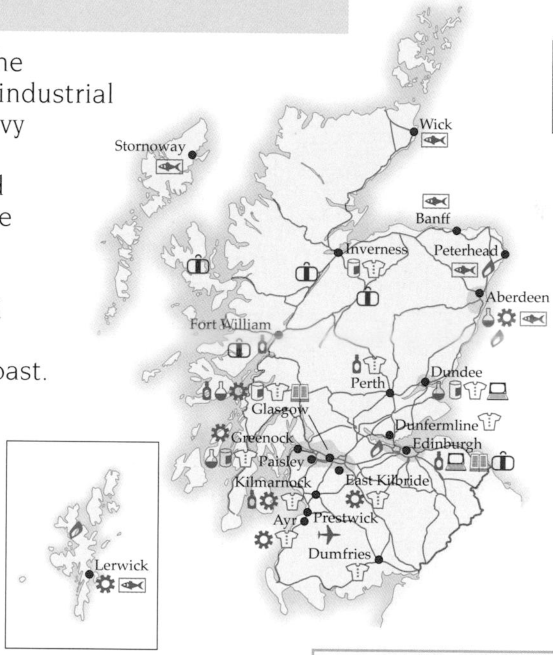

INDUSTRY

- ✈ Aerospace
- Brewing
- Chemicals
- Engineering
- Fish processing
- Food processing
- Textiles
- Oil and gas
- Hi-tech industry
- Printing and publishing
- Tourism
- • Major industrial center / area
- — Major road

Places on map: Stornoway, Wick, Banff, Inverness, Peterhead, Aberdeen, Fort William, Perth, Dundee, Glasgow, Greenock, Dunfermline, Edinburgh, Paisley, East Kilbride, Kilmarnock, Ayr, Prestwick, Dumfries, Lerwick

ENVIRONMENTAL ISSUES

During a storm in January 1993, the Braer oil tanker struck the cliffs of southern Shetland. The ship broke up, shedding its entire load of crude oil into the sea. Although the oil was washed away within weeks, it did have some long-term effects upon the shellfish industry. Due to its favorable landscape, Scotland has seen a significant rise in the number of wind farms built in recent years.

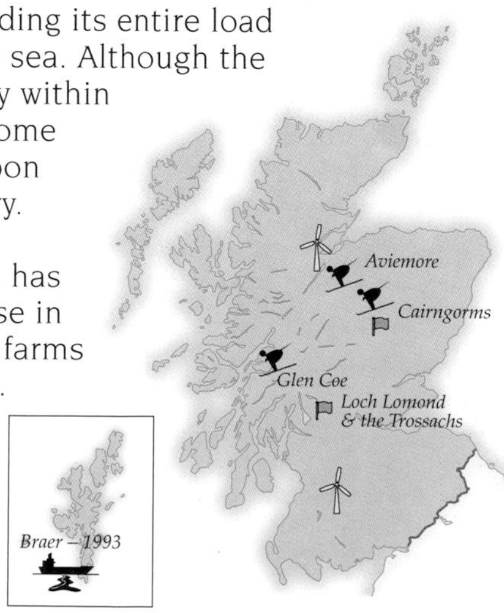

ENVIRONMENTAL ISSUES

- Major oil spill
- Skiing resort
- Wind farm
- National Park

Map labels: Aviemore, Cairngorms, Glen Coe, Loch Lomond & the Trossachs, Braer — 1993

FARMING AND LAND USE

The eastern side of Scotland has a drier climate than the west and is suitable for growing cereal crops and vegetables. Most of the mountain areas are too wet and barren for arable farming and are put to a variety of uses, which include sheep and deer farming, game-keeping, forestry, tourism, and recreation. Scottish fishermen currently land about two-thirds of all the fish caught by the UK.

FARMING AND LAND USE

- Cattle
- Deer
- Fishing
- Sheep
- Cereals
- Root crops
- Timber
- Cropland
- Forest
- Mountains
- Pasture
- • Major conurbation

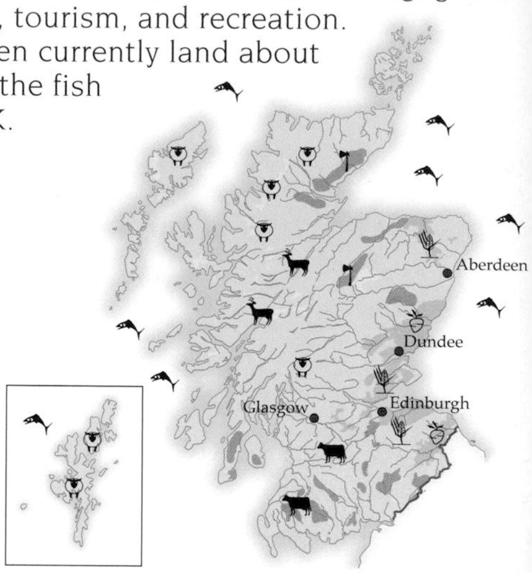

Map labels: Aberdeen, Dundee, Glasgow, Edinburgh

THE LANDSCAPE

Much of Scotland is rugged and mountainous. During the last Ice Age, around 18,000 years ago, glaciers and great sheets of ice attacked Scotland's hard, ancient rocks, leaving behind a landscape of high moorlands and steep-sided mountains separated by deep valleys, often filled by lakes known as lochs.

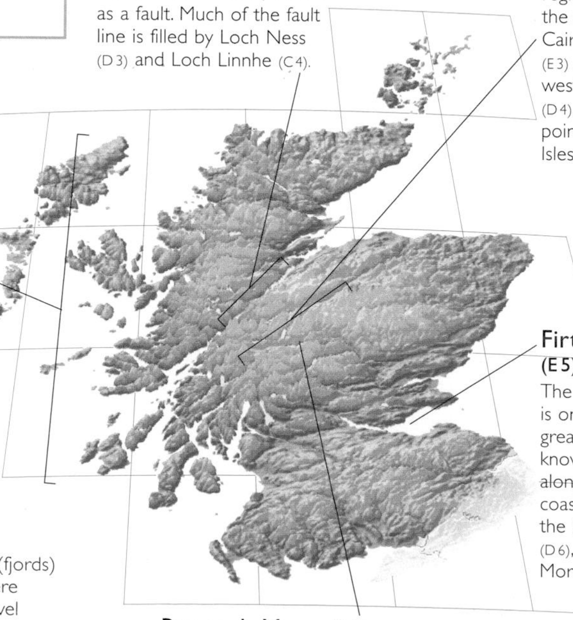

Glen Mor (D3)
Glen Mor is a deep valley which runs right across Scotland. It marks a major line of rock fracture, known as a fault. Much of the fault line is filled by Loch Ness (D3) and Loch Linnhe (C4).

Grampians (D4)
The Grampians are Britain's largest and highest mountain region. They include the spectacular Cairngorm range (E3) and, to the west, Ben Nevis (D4), the highest point in the British Isles, at 4,406 ft.

Hebrides (A2), (B6)
The Inner and Outer Hebrides comprise several large islands and hundreds of small ones. Many of these were formed following the last Ice Age, as the sea level rose, cutting off parts of the mountainous landscape from the mainland.

Firth of Forth (E5)
The Firth of Forth is one of several great sea inlets, known as firths, along the Scottish coast. They include the Firths of Clyde (D6), Tay (F5), and Moray (E3).

Lochs (D5)
The many sea lochs (fjords) of the west coast were formed as the sea level rose after the last Ice Age, flooding the deep valleys that had been cut by glaciers. The sea lochs cause the coast to follow a highly irregular line.

Rannoch Moor (D5)
Rannoch Moor is the largest wild moorland in Scotland. A great ice sheet covered the area during the last Ice Age, leaving behind a vast expanse of bleak, bare ground, pitted with small depressions.

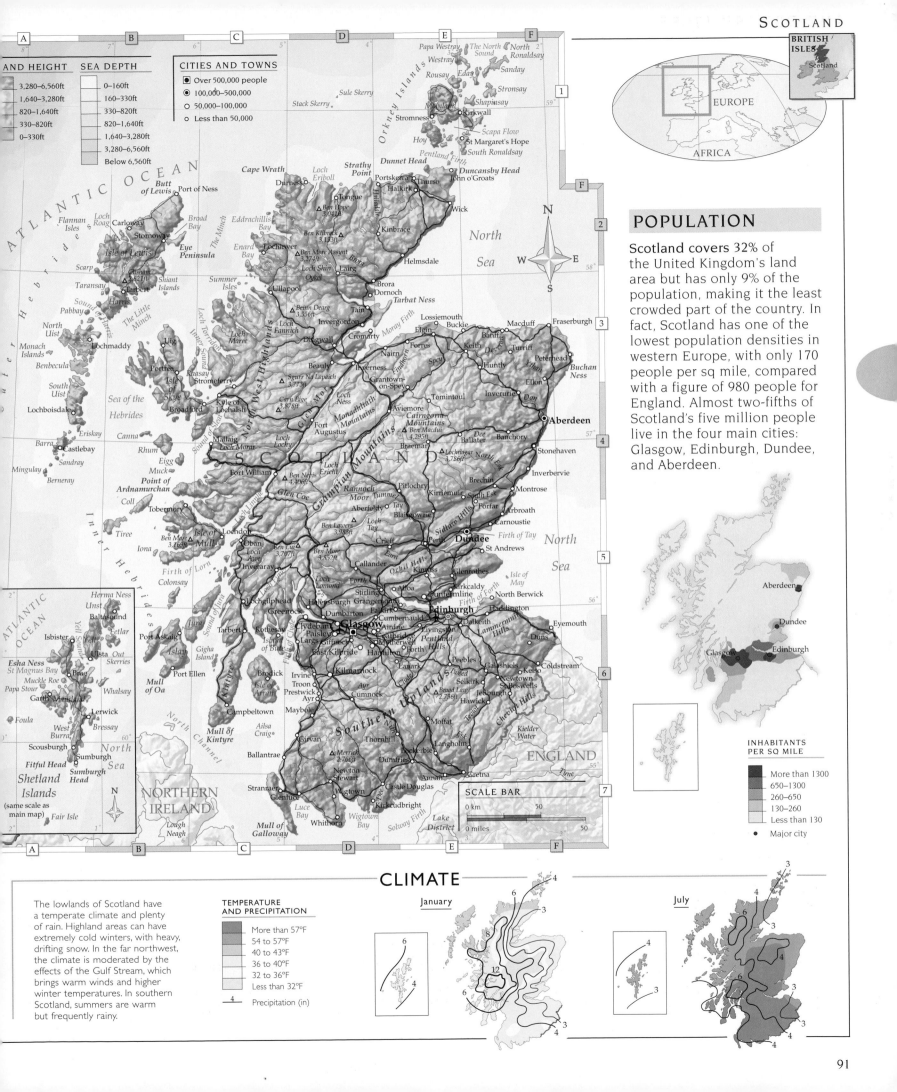

LAND HEIGHT / SEA DEPTH

LAND HEIGHT
- 3,280–6,560ft
- 1,640–3,280ft
- 820–1,640ft
- 330–820ft
- 0–330ft

SEA DEPTH
- 0–160ft
- 160–330ft
- 330–820ft
- 820–1,640ft
- 1,640–3,280ft
- 3,280–6,560ft
- Below 6,560ft

CITIES AND TOWNS
- ■ Over 500,000 people
- ◉ 100,000–500,000
- ○ 50,000–100,000
- ○ Less than 50,000

BRITISH
ISLES

Scotland

EUROPE

AFRICA

POPULATION

Scotland covers 32% of the United Kingdom's land area but has only 9% of the population, making it the least crowded part of the country. In fact, Scotland has one of the lowest population densities in western Europe, with only 170 people per sq mile, compared with a figure of 980 people for England. Almost two-fifths of Scotland's five million people live in the four main cities: Glasgow, Edinburgh, Dundee, and Aberdeen.

INHABITANTS PER SQ MILE
- More than 1300
- 650–1300
- 260–650
- 130–260
- Less than 130
- ● Major city

CLIMATE

The lowlands of Scotland have a temperate climate and plenty of rain. Highland areas can have extremely cold winters, with heavy, drifting snow. In the far northwest, the climate is moderated by the effects of the Gulf Stream, which brings warm winds and higher winter temperatures. In southern Scotland, summers are warm but frequently rainy.

TEMPERATURE AND PRECIPITATION
- More than 57°F
- 54 to 57°F
- 40 to 43°F
- 36 to 40°F
- 32 to 36°F
- Less than 32°F

4 ── Precipitation (in)

January

July

SCALE BAR
0 km ──────── 50
0 miles ──────── 50

91

NORTHERN ENGLAND & WALES

The **Industrial Revolution** of the 18th and 19th centuries began in northern England, exploiting rich local resources to begin a new era of mass production. Today, these industries have declined, but despite a number of difficult years, northern England is becoming more prosperous again. Similarly, south Wales was once a major coal-mining and heavy industrial area but this has largely been replaced by new service industries. The magnificent scenery throughout this region attracts many tourists and outdoor enthusiasts.

INDUSTRY

Traditional industries such as iron and steel, coal-mining, and textiles have been in decline for many years. More recently, the type of industries have changed to light engineering and hi-tech industries, producing microchips and computers, together with service industries such as insurance and retailing, printing and publishing. Tourism is important; large numbers of people visit the area's stunning national parks each year.

INDUSTRY

- ✈ Aerospace
- 🍺 Brewing
- 🚗 Car manufacture
- ⚙ Ceramics
- 🧪 Chemicals
- ⚙ Engineering
- 🐟 Fish processing
- 🥫 Food processing
- 🔩 Iron & steel
- △ Metal refining
- ✏ Pharmaceuticals
- ⚓ Shipbuilding
- 👕 Textiles
- 🛢 Oil refining
- 💻 Hi-tech industry
- 💻 Printing and publishing
- 🏛 Tourism
- ◼ Major industrial center / area
- — Major road

ENVIRONMENTAL ISSUES

Some of the UK's most dramatic scenery is found in this area, and national parks have long been established to protect the environment. These parks have proved so popular that in some places tourists are in danger of destroying the environment. Coal-fired power stations in the region power the large cities, but recently there has been an increase in renewable energy production.

ENVIRONMENTAL ISSUES

- Coal-fired power station
- Barrage scheme
- Major hydro-electric scheme
- National park
- Wind farm
- Major oil spill
- Major industrial city

Milford Haven – 1996
Cardiff Bay

FARMING AND LAND USE

The eastern lowlands have an ideal climate for arable crops, while oats and potatoes grow in the north and west. The southwest is used mainly for grazing cattle and sheep, which also graze rough in the upland areas of the Pennines and Wales. Forestry is increasingly important in mountain areas.

FARMING AND LAND USE

- Cattle
- Sheep
- Cereals
- Market gardening
- Root crops
- Cropland
- Forest
- Pasture
- Major conurbation

THE LANDSCAPE

The Pennines form the backbone of northern England. Likewise, the Cambrian Mountains, including the spectacular landscape of Snowdonia, run the length of central Wales. To the east, the Aire and Ouse rivers have cut a broad floodplain between the Pennines and the North York Moors, while in the far northwest, Cumbria's Lake District has many long, deep lakes, which were formed during the last Ice Age.

Limestone pavements
Bare "pavements" of weathered limestone are also known as karst scenery. They have a block like appearance, with deep cracks between the blocks that have been dissolved by rainwater.

Spurn Head (F4)
Spurn Head is a long sand bar (called a spit) at the mouth of the Humber estuary. It was formed by waves which deposited sand across the mouth of the bay. Constant erosion has often made Spurn Head almost inaccessible from the mainland.

Lake District (C3)
The Lake District covers a small area of the Cumbrian Mountains. The 15 lakes here form a radial pattern, spreading out from a central zone of volcanic rock.

The Pennines (D3)

North York Moors (E3)

Snowdonia (B5)
These spectacular mountains include Snowdon, the highest point in England and Wales, at 3,560 ft. The spectacular sheer sides and jagged ridges were carved by glaciers during the last Ice Age.

Cambrian Mountains (B6)
The Cambrian range runs the whole length of the country and contains some of the oldest rocks in Britain. The rock is rich in minerals. Slate was also once mined in great quantities in northern and central areas.

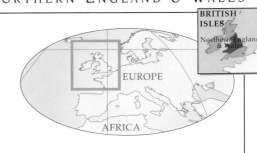

BRITISH ISLES
Northern England & Wales

POPULATION

The cities of Liverpool, Manchester, Leeds, and Bradford have spread out to form great conurbations. In the West Midlands, large populations grew up in and around the industrial cities of Coventry and Birmingham. The northeastern coast from Middlesbrough to Newcastle upon Tyne is also densely populated. The area around Newport, Cardiff, and Swansea is home to more than 60% of the population of Wales. Upland regions are sparsely populated.

INHABITANTS PER SQ MILE

- More than 1,200
- 650–1,200
- 250–650
- 125–250
- Less than 125
- • Major city

CLIMATE

Northern England tends to be cooler and wetter than the south, especially in the summer months. High rainfall totals are recorded in the upland areas of the west. The east, in the "rainshadow" of the Pennines, is drier.

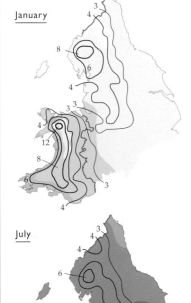

January

July

TEMPERATURE AND PRECIPITATION

- More than 61°F
- 57 to 61°F
- 54 to 57°F
- 40 to 43°F
- 35 to 40°F
- Less than 35°F
- —4— Precipitation (in)

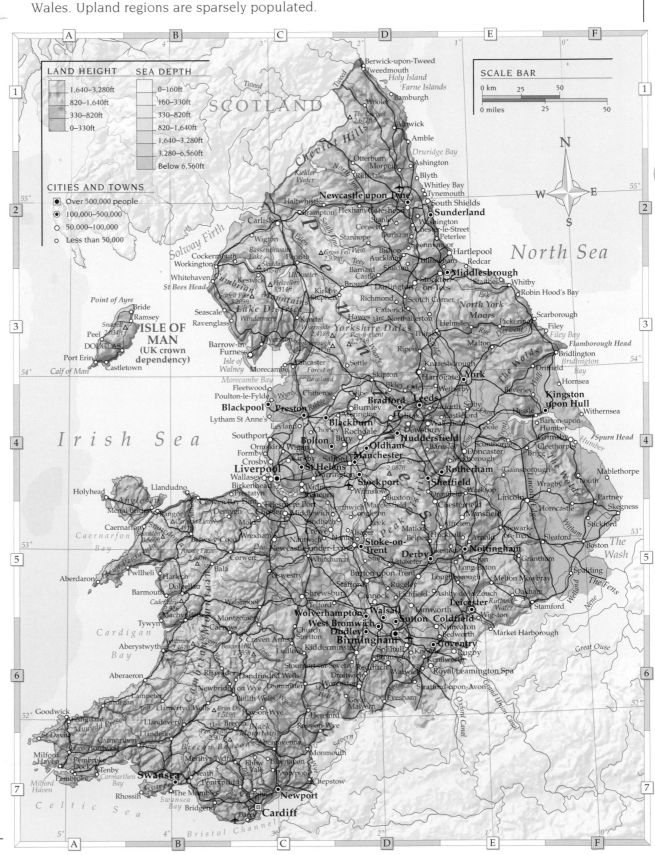

LAND HEIGHT
- 1,640–3,280ft
- 820–1,640ft
- 330–820ft
- 0–330ft

SEA DEPTH
- 0–160ft
- 160–330ft
- 330–820ft
- 820–1,640ft
- 1,640–3,280ft
- 3,280–6,560ft
- Below 6,560ft

CITIES AND TOWNS
- Over 500,000 people
- 100,000–500,000
- 50,000–100,000
- Less than 50,000

SCALE BAR

0 km 25 50

0 miles 25 50

SOUTHERN ENGLAND

The southern counties of England, and particularly Greater London, are the most densely populated part of the British Isles. There are more industries and more jobs here than anywhere else in the UK. In contrast, the counties of the far west and east are much less heavily populated and more rural, although towns in the eastern counties have been growing rapidly since the 1980s. Following the completion of the Channel Tunnel, the UK has had a direct rail link to Europe.

INDUSTRY

London is one of the world's top financial centers and is also a leading center for other service industries including insurance, the media, and publishing. Many car manufacturers are based in southern England, though the numbers of people employed have greatly decreased. Several cities, including Cambridge and Swindon, are centers for hi-tech industry. Thousands of tourists visit the historic and cultural centers in southern England every year.

INDUSTRY

- ✈ Aerospace
- 🍶 Brewing
- 🚗 Car manufacture
- 🧪 Chemicals
- ⚙ Engineering
- 🗋 Food processing
- 👕 Textiles
- S Finance
- 🖥 Hi-tech industry
- ▦ Printing and publishing
- 🧳 Tourism
- • Major industrial center / area
- — Major road

ENVIRONMENTAL ISSUES

The large and growing population of southern England has increased pressure for the development of "green belt" land, designed to protect the countryside surrounding large cities. Alternatives include infilling in urban areas, "brownfield" redevelopment, and building on floodplains. The proposed expansion of Heathrow airport has many environmental concerns.

ENVIRONMENTAL ISSUES

- 🔺 "Green belt" areas
- ✈ Proposed airport expansion
- ⚑ National Park
- 🌀 Wind farm
- • Major town/city

FARMING AND LAND USE

Fertile soils and reliable rainfall mean that a wide range of crops can be grown in southern England. Large arable farms growing wheat and barley are found in the flat eastern counties, and a great variety of soft and orchard fruits and vegetables are grown in market gardens in the far southeast. Beef and dairy cattle and large flocks of sheep are grazed throughout the south.

FARMING AND LAND USE

- 🐄 Cattle
- 🐟 Fishing
- 🐑 Sheep
- 🌾 Cereals
- 🥬 Market gardening
- ▨ Cropland
- ▨ Forest
- ▨ Pasture
- • Major conurbation

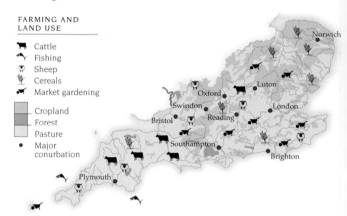

THE LANDSCAPE

The landscape of southern England is very varied. Cornwall in the far west has craggy hills, and a jagged coastline shaped by the Atlantic Ocean. The Cotswolds and the North and South Downs are gentle hills, while toward the east, the land becomes flatter. Near the east coast, low-lying areas are occasionally prone to flooding.

Chalk hills The rounded hills of the Chilterns (F 3) are made from chalk. Because chalk is a porous rock, water quickly seeps through it, so few rivers can be seen in chalk areas.

The Broads (H 2) The Broads in Norfolk are a series of wide waterways flowing across flat meadows. The channels were cut by peat cutters and are not "natural." They then flooded, forming shallow inland lakes.

Steep cliffs The coasts of north Devon and Cornwall are battered by great waves from the Atlantic Ocean. The force of the waves weakens the rock at the foot of the cliffs, causing them to be "undercut." The top layer of rock breaks off and the cliffs recede.

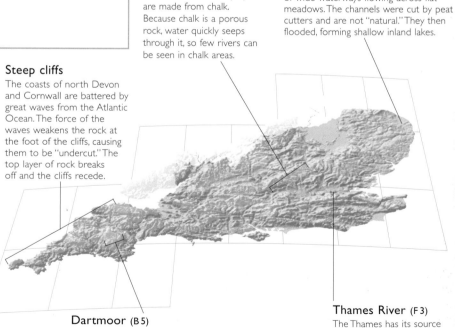

Dartmoor (B 5) Dartmoor is the visible part of a great dome of granite rock. It was formed when molten rock seeped into and cooled in the Earth's crust. Because granite is so hard it erodes very slowly, so outcrops of rock known as *tors* can be seen all over Dartmoor.

Thames River (F 3) The Thames has its source close to the Cotswolds, and meanders through Oxford and London before reaching the North Sea in a wide estuary.

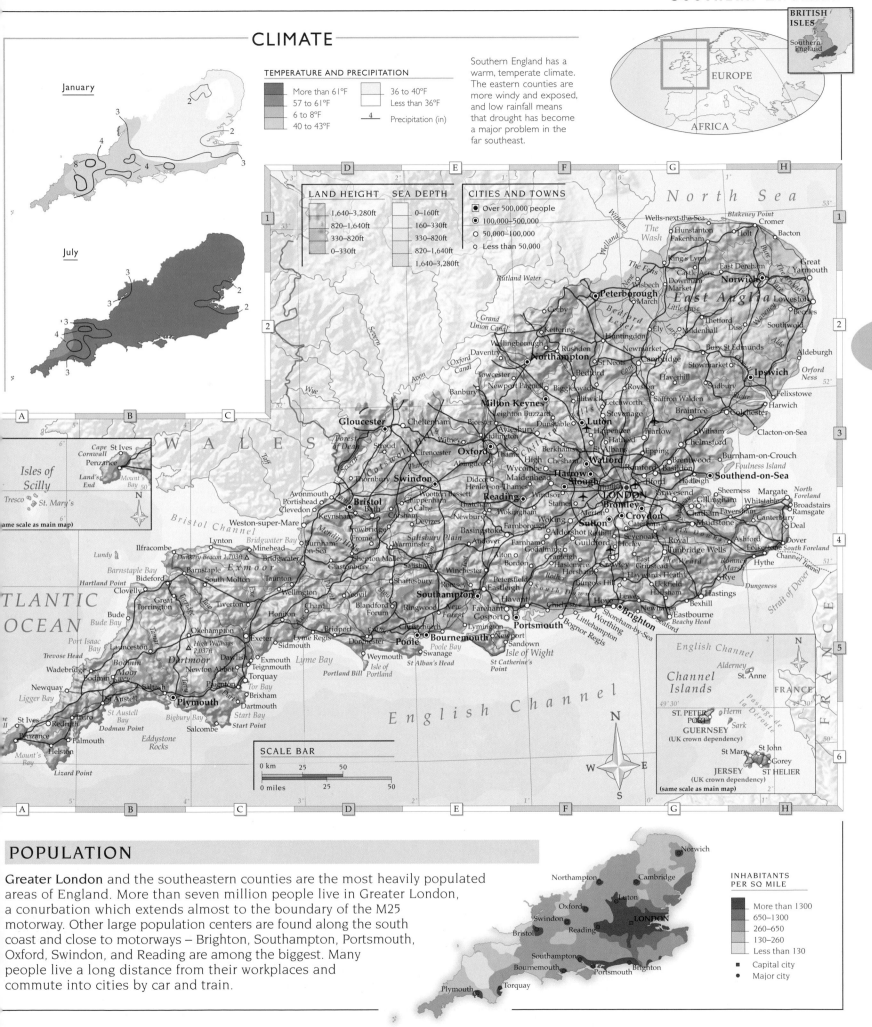

CLIMATE

TEMPERATURE AND PRECIPITATION

- More than 61°F
- 57 to 61°F
- 6 to 8°F
- 40 to 43°F
- 36 to 40°F
- Less than 36°F
- 4 — Precipitation (in)

Southern England has a warm, temperate climate. The eastern counties are more windy and exposed, and low rainfall means that drought has become a major problem in the far southeast.

January

July

LAND HEIGHT
- 1,640–3,280ft
- 820–1,640ft
- 330–820ft
- 0–330ft

SEA DEPTH
- 0–160ft
- 160–330ft
- 330–820ft
- 820–1,640ft
- 1,640–3,280ft

CITIES AND TOWNS
- ■ Over 500,000 people
- ◉ 100,000–500,000
- ○ 50,000–100,000
- ○ Less than 50,000

BRITISH ISLES
Southern England

EUROPE

AFRICA

SCALE BAR
0 km — 25 — 50
0 miles — 25 — 50

POPULATION

Greater London and the southeastern counties are the most heavily populated areas of England. More than seven million people live in Greater London, a conurbation which extends almost to the boundary of the M25 motorway. Other large population centers are found along the south coast and close to motorways – Brighton, Southampton, Portsmouth, Oxford, Swindon, and Reading are among the biggest. Many people live a long distance from their workplaces and commute into cities by car and train.

INHABITANTS PER SQ MILE
- More than 1300
- 650–1300
- 260–650
- 130–260
- Less than 130
- ■ Capital city
- ● Major city

FRANCE

ANDORRA, FRANCE, MONACO

France has helped shape the history and culture of Europe for centuries. Today, as a founder-member of the European Union, France is an avid supporter of the eventual political and economic integration of Europe's different countries. France is Western Europe's leading farming nation and one of the world's top industrial powers. Its cultural attractions and scenery draw tourists from around the world.

FARMING AND LAND USE

France is able to produce a variety of crops because of its rich soils and mild climate. Wheat is grown in many parts of the north, along with potatoes and other vegetables. Fields of corn and sunflowers and fruit orchards are found in the south, while grapes for the famous wine industry are grown across the country. Beef and dairy cattle are grazed on low-lying pasture.

FARMING AND LAND USE

- 🐂 Cattle
- 🐟 Fishing
- 🌾 Cereals
- 🐄 Market gardening
- Root crops
- Tobacco
- 🍇 Vineyards
- Pasture
- Cropland
- Forest
- Mountain region
- Wetland
- Major conurbation

LAND USE

Other (including urban) 18%
Cropland 35%
Forest 27%
Pasture 20%

THE LANDSCAPE

The north and west of France is made up of mainly flat, grassy plains or low hills. Wooded mountains line the country's borders in the south and east, and much of central France is taken up by the Massif Central, an enormous plateau cut by deep river valleys and scattered with extinct volcanoes. Three major rivers, the Loire, Seine, and Garonne, drain the lowland basins.

Paris Basin
The Paris Basin is a saucer-shaped hollow made up of layers of hard and soft rock, covered with very fertile soils. It runs across about 38,600 sq miles of northern France.

Alps (E 5)
The western end of the European Alpine mountain chain stretches into southeast France. The French Alps can be crossed by several passes, which give access to Italy and Switzerland.

Normandy
The coast of Normandy is lined with high chalk cliffs.

Pyrenees (C 7)
These mountains form a natural barrier between France and Spain. Several peaks reach heights of over 9,480 ft. The Pyrenees are difficult to cross, due to their height, and because they have few low passes.

Massif Central (D 5)
This vast granite plateau was formed over 200 million years ago. Volcanic activity here stopped only within the last 10,000 years, and the region's rounded hills are the worn-down remains of volcanic mountains.

Mont Blanc (E 5)
This mountain in the French Alps is the tallest in Western Europe. It is 15,771 ft high.

Camargue (D 7)
The Camargue is an area of marshes, pastures, sand dunes, and salt flats at the mouth of the Rhône River. Rare animal and plant species are found there.

INDUSTRY

France is one of the world's top manufacturing nations, with a variety of both traditional and high-tech industries. Cars, machinery, and electronic products are exported worldwide, along with luxury goods such as perfumes, fashions, and wines. Extensive use of nuclear power has allowed France to become the world's largest net exporter of electricity.

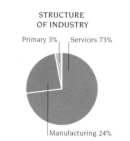

STRUCTURE OF INDUSTRY

Primary 3%
Services 73%
Manufacturing 24%

INDUSTRY

- ✈ Aerospace
- 🚗 Car manufacturing
- ⚗ Chemicals
- ⚙ Engineering
- Textiles
- 💻 High-tech industry
- Tourism
- Major industrial center / area
- Major road

POPULATION

In the past 50 years, most people have moved from the countryside into urban areas. Paris and its suburbs, the industrial cities, and the Côte d'Azur in the southeast are the most economically developed parts of France and now have the biggest populations.

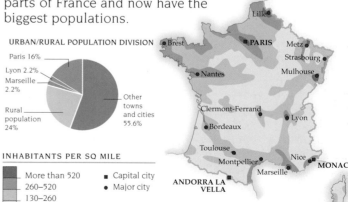

URBAN/RURAL POPULATION DIVISION

Paris 16%
Lyon 2.2%
Marseille 2.2%
Rural population 24%
Other towns and cities 55.6%

INHABITANTS PER SQ MILE

- More than 520
- 260–520
- 130–260
- Less than 130
- Capital city
- Major city

96

ENVIRONMENTAL ISSUES

Many of France's coastal areas have been polluted by industry and tourism. A summer heatwave in 2003 severeley affected France, with temperatures of up to 104°F contributing to the deaths of an estimated 15,000 people. France's reliance on nuclear energy – over 75% of its electricity is generated by nuclear power – means that it suffers less from the pollution caused by burning fossil fuels than many other countries in Europe.

ENVIRONMENTAL ISSUES
- Nuclear power station
- Sea pollution
- Polluted rivers
- Major industrial center

CLIMATE

In winter, the coldest areas of France are the mountains of the Massif Central and the Alps. Summers are hottest on the Mediterranean coast.

TEMPERATURE AND PRECIPITATION
- More than 68°F
- 59 to 68°F
- 50 to 59°F
- 41 to 50°F
- 32 to 41°F
- 23 to 32°F
- Less than 23°F
- 4 Precipitation (in)

January

July

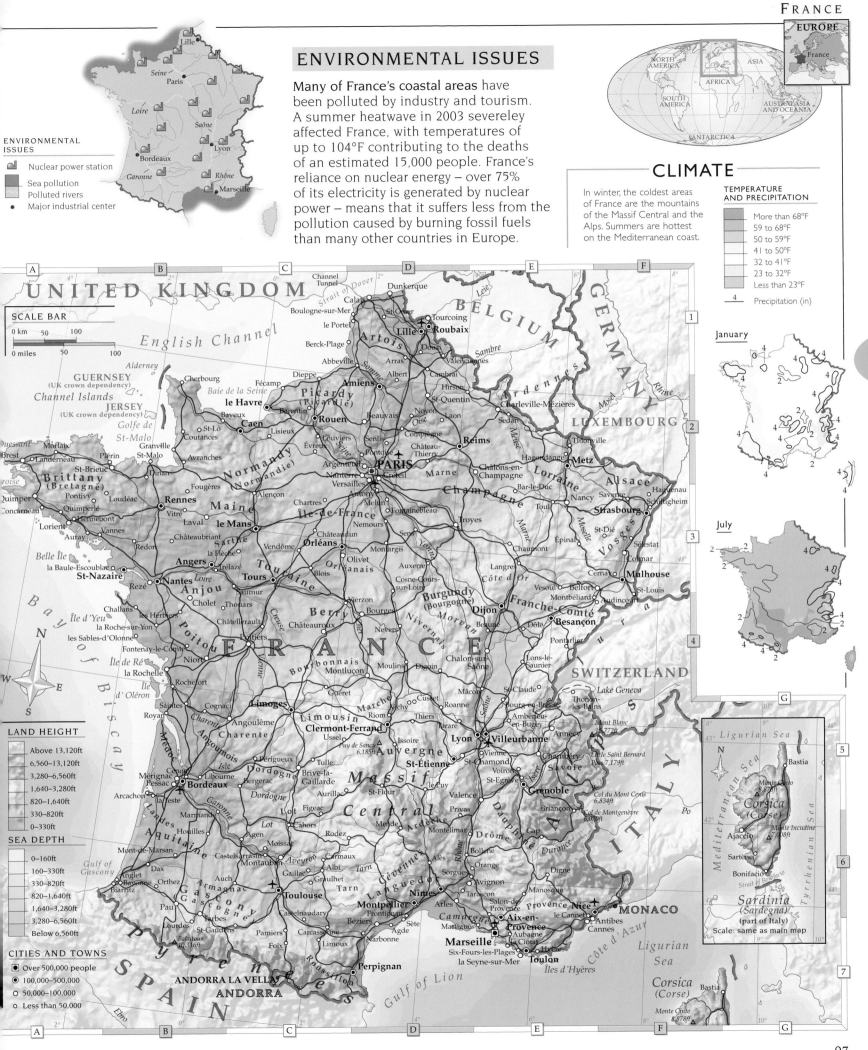

LAND HEIGHT
- Above 13,120ft
- 6,560–13,120ft
- 3,280–6,560ft
- 1,640–3,280ft
- 820–1,640ft
- 330–820ft
- 0–330ft

SEA DEPTH
- 0–160ft
- 160–330ft
- 330–820ft
- 820–1,640ft
- 1,640–3,280ft
- 3,280–6,560ft
- Below 6,560ft

CITIES AND TOWNS
- Over 500,000 people
- 100,000–500,000
- 50,000–100,000
- Less than 50,000

SPAIN AND PORTUGAL

PORTUGAL, SPAIN

Spain and Portugal occupy the Iberian Peninsula, which is cut off from the rest of Europe by the Pyrenees. Over the centuries, Iberia has been invaded and settled by many different peoples. The Moors, who arrived from North Africa in the 8th century, ruled much of Spain for almost 800 years, and their influence can still be seen in Spanish culture. Portugal has modernized its economy since joining the European Union, and both countries have changed their currencies to the euro.

INDUSTRY

Madrid, Barcelona, and the northern ports are Spain's industrial centers. Here, iron ore from Spanish mines is used to make steel, and factories produce cars, machinery, and chemicals. Portugal exports textiles, clothing, and footwear, along with fish, such as sardines and tuna, caught off the Atlantic coast. In both countries, tourism is very important to the economy.

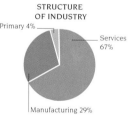

STRUCTURE OF INDUSTRY

Primary 4%
Services 67%
Manufacturing 29%

INDUSTRY

- Car manufacture
- Chemicals
- Engineering
- Fish processing
- Shipbuilding
- Steel
- Textiles
- Mining
- Publishing
- Tourism
- Major industrial center / area
- — Major road

POPULATION

In the first half of the 20th century, most Spaniards lived in villages or small towns scattered around the country. Today, tourism and industry have drawn most of the population to the cities and coastal areas. Most Portuguese live in cities, but one third still live in rural areas along the coast or in the river valleys.

URBAN/RURAL POPULATION DIVISION

Barcelona 3%
Lisbon 1%
Madrid 6%
Other towns and cities 65%
Rural population 25%

INHABITANTS PER SQ MILE

- More than 520
- 260–520
- 130–260
- Less than 130
- Capital city
- Major city

FARMING AND LAND USE

Cereals, especially wheat and barley, are Iberia's chief crops. In the dry south of Spain, the land is irrigated to citrus fruits, particularly oranges, and a variety of vegetables. In both countries, olive trees and vineyards occupy large areas of land; olive oil and wine are important exports. Cork oak trees from Iberia's forests supply 80% of the world's cork.

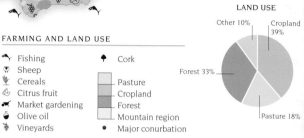

FARMING AND LAND USE

- Fishing
- Sheep
- Cereals
- Citrus fruit
- Market gardening
- Olive oil
- Vineyards
- Cork
- Pasture
- Cropland
- Forest
- Mountain region
- Major conurbation

LAND USE

Other 10%
Cropland 39%
Forest 33%
Pasture 18%

THE LANDSCAPE

Most of inland Spain is taken up by the Meseta, a dry, almost treeless plateau surrounded by steep mountain ranges. The only lowlands, apart from narrow strips along the Mediterranean coast, are the valleys of the Ebro, Tagus, Guadiana, and Guadalquivir Rivers. Portugal's coast is lined by wide plains. Inland, the Tagus River divides the country in two. To the north the land is hilly and wooded; to the south it is low-lying and drier.

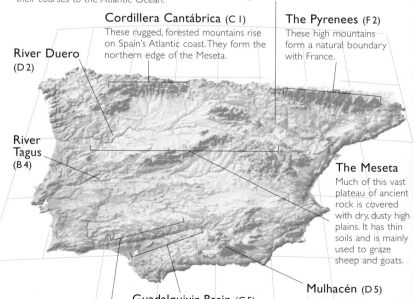

Westward-flowing rivers
The Duero, Tagus, and Guadalquivir Rivers flow across the Meseta on their courses to the Atlantic Ocean.

Ebro River (E 2)
The Ebro River carries vital irrigation water to Spain's northeastern plains before flowing into the Mediterranean Sea.

Cordillera Cantábrica (C 1)
These rugged, forested mountains rise on Spain's Atlantic coast. They form the northern edge of the Meseta.

The Pyrenees (F 2)
These high mountains form a natural boundary with France.

River Duero (D 2)

River Tagus (B 4)

The Meseta
Much of this vast plateau of ancient rock is covered with dry, dusty high plains. It has thin soils and is mainly used to graze sheep and goats.

Sierra Morena (C 5)
The southern end of the Meseta is marked by this low range of mountains.

Guadalquivir Basin (C 5)
The Guadalquivir River has deposited layers of rich soil called alluvium on its floodplain, making this one of Spain's most fertile regions.

Mulhacén (D 5)
Mulhacén, in the snow-capped Sierra Nevada range in southern Spain, is 11,421 ft high. It is Iberia's tallest mountain.

ENVIRONMENTAL ISSUES

Soil erosion – where the top layer of soil has been worn away by wind and rain – has affected much of the Iberian Peninsula. This is caused by farming, combined with drought and deforestation. In Spain, a national tree-planting program has been started to combat this problem. Industrial and tourist development along the Mediterranean coast of Spain and in the Balearic Islands has damaged natural habitats on both land and sea.

Aegean Sea 1992

Prestige 2002

Douro
Guadiana
Guadalquivir
Ebro
Segura
Ibiza
Majorca
Costa Brava
Costa Blanca
Costa del Sol

ENVIRONMENTAL ISSUES

- Major oil spill
- Overbuilding
- Soil degradation
- Severe soil degradation
- Polluted rivers
- Sea pollution

CLIMATE

Northern Spain is wetter and cooler than the south. On the central plateau, summers are very hot and dry, and winters often freezing. The north of Portugal is cooled by winds blowing off the Atlantic Ocean. The south is warmer, with dry, mild winters.

January

July

TEMPERATURE AND PRECIPITATION

- More than 77°F
- 68 to 77°F
- 59 to 68°F
- 50 to 59°F
- 41 to 50°F
- 32 to 41°F
- 23 to 32°F
- 14 to 23°F
- Less than 14°F

4 — Precipitation (in)

EUROPE

NORTH AMERICA
SOUTH AMERICA
ASIA
AFRICA
AUSTRALASIA AND OCEANIA
ANTARCTICA

Spain and Portugal

LAND HEIGHT
- 6,560–13,120ft
- 3,280–6,560ft
- 1,640–3,280ft
- 820–1,640ft
- 330–820ft
- 0–330ft

SEA DEPTH
- 0–820ft
- 820–1,640ft
- 1,640–3,280ft
- 3,280–6,560ft
- 6,560–9,840ft
- 9,840–13,120ft
- Below 13,120ft

CITIES AND TOWNS
- Over 500,000 people
- 100,000–500,000
- 50,000–100,000
- Less than 50,000

SCALE BAR
0 km 50 100
0 miles 50 100

GERMANY AND THE ALPINE STATES

AUSTRIA, GERMANY, LIECHTENSTEIN, SLOVENIA, SWITZERLAND

Germany lies at the heart of Europe and is the biggest industrial power in the continent. In 1945, Germany was divided into two separate countries, East and West Germany, which were reunited in 1990. To the south, the snow-capped peaks of the Alps, Europe's highest mountains, tower over the Alpine states – Switzerland, Austria, Liechtenstein, and the former Yugoslavian state of Slovenia.

INDUSTRY

Germany is a leading manufacturer of cars, chemicals, machinery, and transportation equipment. Switzerland and Liechtenstein make high-value products such as watches and pharmaceuticals and provide services such as banking. The Alpine states are a popular tourist location year-round.

INDUSTRY

- 🚗 Car manufacture
- ♨ Chemicals
- ⚙ Engineering
- ⚒ Iron & steel
- ⚓ Shipbuilding
- ✎ Pharmaceuticals
- S Finance
- 💻 Hi-tech industry
- 🏛 Tourism

- ▣ Major industrial center / area
- — Major road

STRUCTURE OF INDUSTRY

Primary 1%
Services 68%
Manufacturing 31%

POPULATION

Western and central Germany are the most densely populated areas in this region – particularly in and around the Rhine and Ruhr valleys, where there are many industries. In the south, the steep slopes of the Alps and permanent snow cover on the higher peaks means that most large towns and cities are in scattered lowland areas.

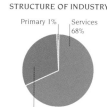

INHABITANTS PER SQ MILE

- More than 520
- 260–520
- 130–260
- Less than 130

- ■ Capital city
- ● Major city

URBAN/RURAL POPULATION DIVISION

Hamburg 1.8%
Berlin 3.5%
Vienna 1.7%
Rural population 16%
Other towns and cities 77%

FARMING AND LAND USE

Germany produces three-quarters of its own food. Crop farming is widespread, with cereals and root crops grown in flat, fertile areas. Cattle and pig farming supplies meat and dairy products. Across the Alps, the mountains limit farming, although grapes are grown on the warmer, south-facing slopes. The rich pastures of the lower slopes are used to graze beef and dairy cattle.

FARMING AND LAND USE

- 🐄 Cattle
- 🐖 Pigs
- 🌾 Cereals
- Root crops
- 🍇 Vineyards

- Pasture
- Cropland
- Forest
- Mountain region
- ● Major conurbation

LAND USE

Forest 33%
Other (including mountains) 20%
Pasture 18%
Cropland 29%

THE LANDSCAPE

To the north, flat plains and heathlands surround the North Sea coast. Farther south are Germany's central uplands, which are lower and older than the jagged peaks of the Alps, which began to form about 65 million years ago. From its source in the Black Forest, the Danube River flows eastward across Germany and Austria on its course to the Black Sea. The other major river, the Rhine, flows northward.

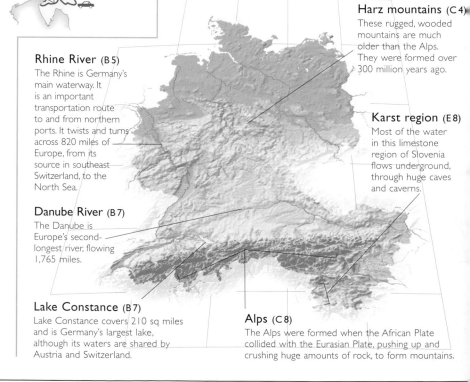

Harz mountains (C4)
These rugged, wooded mountains are much older than the Alps. They were formed over 300 million years ago.

Rhine River (B5)
The Rhine is Germany's main waterway. It is an important transportation route to and from northern ports. It twists and turns across 820 miles of Europe, from its source in southeast Switzerland, to the North Sea.

Karst region (E8)
Most of the water in this limestone region of Slovenia flows underground, through huge caves and caverns.

Danube River (B7)
The Danube is Europe's second-longest river, flowing 1,765 miles.

Lake Constance (B7)
Lake Constance covers 210 sq miles and is Germany's largest lake, although its waters are shared by Austria and Switzerland.

Alps (C8)
The Alps were formed when the African Plate collided with the Eurasian Plate, pushing up and crushing huge amounts of rock, to form mountains.

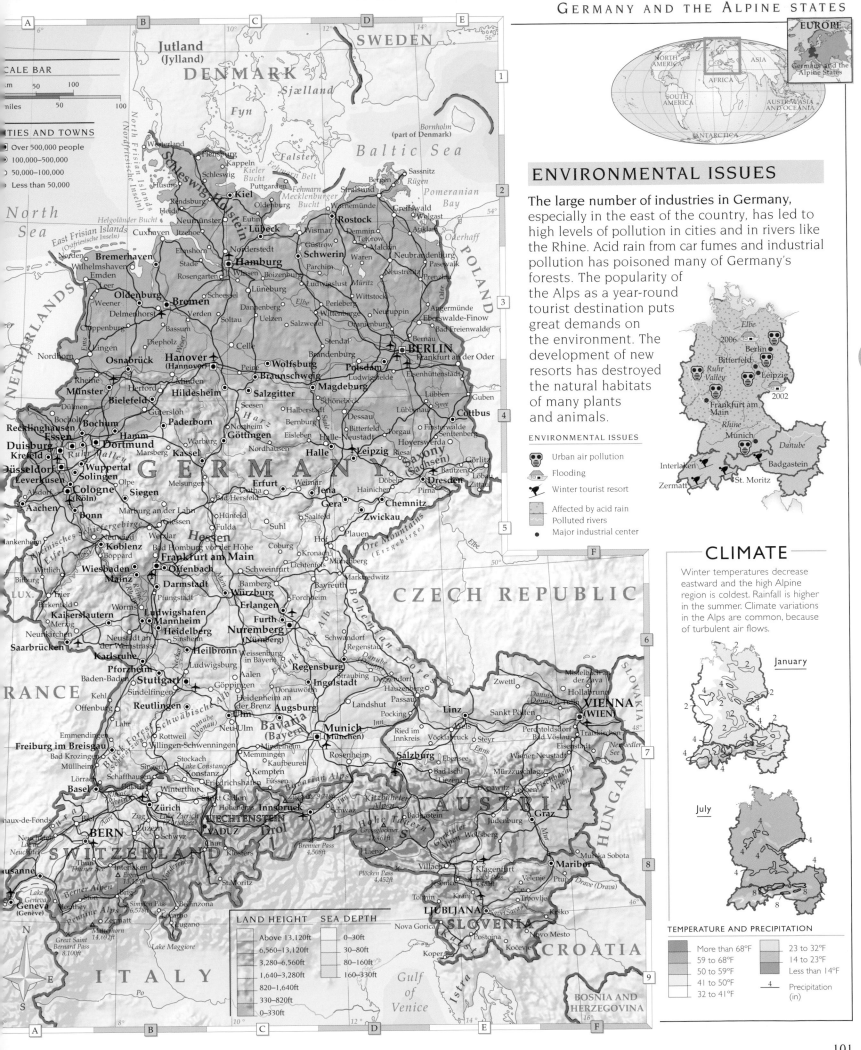

ENVIRONMENTAL ISSUES

The large number of industries in Germany, especially in the east of the country, has led to high levels of pollution in cities and in rivers like the Rhine. Acid rain from car fumes and industrial pollution has poisoned many of Germany's forests. The popularity of the Alps as a year-round tourist destination puts great demands on the environment. The development of new resorts has destroyed the natural habitats of many plants and animals.

ENVIRONMENTAL ISSUES

- Urban air pollution
- Flooding
- Winter tourist resort
- Affected by acid rain
- Polluted rivers
- Major industrial center

CLIMATE

Winter temperatures decrease eastward and the high Alpine region is coldest. Rainfall is higher in the summer. Climate variations in the Alps are common, because of turbulent air flows.

January

July

TEMPERATURE AND PRECIPITATION

- More than 68°F
- 59 to 68°F
- 50 to 59°F
- 41 to 50°F
- 32 to 41°F
- 23 to 32°F
- 14 to 23°F
- Less than 14°F
- 4 — Precipitation (in)

ITALY

ITALY, SAN MARINO, VATICAN CITY

Italy has played an important role in Europe since the Romans based their mighty empire here over 2,000 years ago. The famous boot shape divides into two very different halves. Northern Italy has a varied range of industries and agriculture. Beautiful cities like Venice, Florence, and Rome draw tourists from all over the world. Southern Italy is poorer and less developed than the north, with a hotter, drier climate and less productive land.

THE LANDSCAPE

Italy is a peninsula jutting south from mainland Europe into the Mediterranean Sea. In northern and central Italy the land is mainly mountainous. Most of the flat land is in the Po Valley and along the eastern coast. Italy lies within an earthquake zone, which makes the land unstable, and there are also a number of active volcanoes.

Italian lakes
Great lakes like Garda (B3) and Como (B2) fill several south-facing valleys once occupied by glaciers.

The Dolomites (D2)
These high mountains are part of the same range as the Alps. They were formed 65 million years ago.

Po Valley (C2)
The basin of the Po River has the best soils in Italy. Rich alluvium is washed from the mountains by the river to form a wide plain.

The Apennines (C4)
This mountain range forms the "backbone" of Italy, dividing the rocky west coast from the flatter, sandy east coast.

Tyrrhenian Sea (C6)
This sea, which divides the Italian mainland from Sardinia, is gradually filling with sediment from the rivers which flow into it.

Earthquakes
The southern Apennines, as well as coastal areas of southwestern Italy, often experience earthquakes and mudslides.

Sardinia
The island of Sardinia is made from very old rocks that were thrust up to form mountains.

Sicily
Sicily is the largest island in the Mediterranean. It has a famous active volcano called Mount Etna and often experiences earthquakes.

Gulf of Taranto (F7)
During earthquakes, great blocks of land have broken away and sunk into the sea, forming the Gulf's square shape.

FARMING AND LAND USE

The Po Valley is a broad, flat plain in the north of Italy. It contains the most fertile land in the country, and wheat and rice are the main cereal crops grown here. Grapes for wine are grown everywhere in Italy. In much of the south, the land must be irrigated to support crops. Where there is enough water, citrus fruits, olives, and many kinds of tomatoes are grown.

LAND USE
- Other 14%
- Cropland 37%
- Forest 34%
- Pasture 15%

FARMING AND LAND USE
- Cattle
- Pigs
- Sheep
- Cereals
- Citrus fruits
- Olive oil
- Rice
- Vineyards
- Pasture
- Cropland
- Forest
- Mountain region
- Major conurbation

INDUSTRY

Italian industry is located mainly in the north. Design is extremely important to Italians, and they are proud of the elegant designs of their furniture, clothes, and shoes. Although many firms are small, they are very efficient. Italy has few mineral resources, so it needs to import raw materials to make cars, engines, and other high-tech products.

INDUSTRY
- Car manufacture
- Chemicals
- Iron & steel
- Textiles
- Finance
- Hi-tech industry
- Tourism
- Major industrial center / area
- Major road

STRUCTURE OF INDUSTRY
- Primary 3%
- Services 66%
- Manufacturing 31%

POPULATION

Most of Italy's population lives in the north, mainly in and around the Po Valley, which is home to over 25 million people. Most people here have a high standard of living. Southern Italy is much more rural: towns are smaller and life is often much harder.

URBAN/RURAL POPULATION DIVISION
- Milan 2.2%
- Rome 4.4%
- Naples 1.7%
- Rural population 33%
- Other towns and cities 58.7%

INHABITANTS PER SQ MILE
- More than 520
- 260–520
- 130–260
- 0–130
- Capital city
- Major city

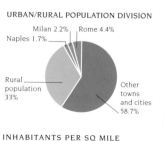

ITALY

EUROPE

ENVIRONMENTAL ISSUES

Sewage and chemical by-products from industry have polluted the Mediterranean and Adriatic Seas. Southern Italy is subject to natural dangers like volcanoes, earthquakes, and mudslides. Mount Etna is one of the most active volcanoes in the world.

ENVIRONMENTAL ISSUES
- Catastrophic earthquakes
- Urban air pollution
- Acid rain
- Sea pollution
- Severe sea pollution
- Major industrial center

CLIMATE

The Alpine north has cold winters, often with snow. Farther south, temperatures are higher. Sicily has Italy's highest temperatures, because of the warm African winds.

January

July

TEMPERATURE AND PRECIPITATION
- More than 77°F
- 68 to 77°F
- 59 to 68°F
- 50 to 59°F
- 41 to 50°F
- 32 to 41°F
- 23 to 32°F
- 14 to 23°F
- Less than 14°F
- 4 Precipitation (in)

LAND HEIGHT
- Above 13,120ft
- 6,560–13,120ft
- 3,280–6,560ft
- 1,640–3,280ft
- 820–1,640ft
- 330–820ft
- 0–330ft

SEA DEPTH
- 0–160ft
- 160–330ft
- 330–820ft
- 820–1,640ft
- 1,640–3,280ft
- 3,280–6,560ft
- Below 6,560ft

SCALE BAR

CITIES AND TOWNS
- Over 500,000 people
- 100,000–500,000
- 50,000–100,000
- Less than 50,000

103

CENTRAL EUROPE

CZECH REPUBLIC, HUNGARY, POLAND, SLOVAKIA

Central Europe has been invaded many times throughout history. The countries have changed shape frequently as their borders have shifted back and forth. From the end of World War Two until 1989, they were ruled by communist governments, which were supported by the Soviet Union. In 1993, the state of Czechoslovakia voted to split into two separate nations, called the Czech Republic and Slovakia.

FARMING AND LAND USE

Central Europe's main crops are cereals such as corn, wheat and rye, along with sugar beets and potatoes. Sweet peppers grow in Hungary, helped by the warm summers and mild winters. They are used to make paprika. Grapes are also grown, to make wine. Large areas of the plains of Hungary and Poland are used for rearing pigs and cattle. Trees for timber grow in the mountains of Slovakia and the Czech Republic.

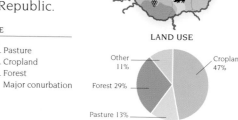

FARMING AND LAND USE

- 🐄 Cattle
- 🐖 Pigs
- 🌾 Cereals
- 🌱 Root crops
- 🌿 Potatoes
- 🌲 Timber
- 🍇 Vineyards
- Pasture
- Cropland
- Forest
- • Major conurbation

LAND USE

Other 11%
Forest 29%
Pasture 13%
Cropland 47%

INDUSTRY

Brown coal, or lignite, is central Europe's main fuel, and one of Poland's major exports. A variety of minerals are mined in the mountains of the Czech Republic and Slovakia. Hungary has a wide range of industries producing vehicles, metals, and chemicals, as well as textiles and electrical goods. The Czech Republic is famous for its breweries and glass-making.

STRUCTURE OF INDUSTRY

Primary 3%
Services 65%
Manufacturing 32%

INDUSTRY

- 🍶 Brewing
- 🚗 Car manufacturing
- ⚗ Chemicals
- ⚙ Engineering
- 🥫 Food processing
- Iron and steel
- ⛏ Coal mining
- ▣ Major industrial center / area
- — Major road

THE LANDSCAPE

The high Carpathian Mountains sweep across northern Slovakia. The lower Sudeten Mountains lie on the border of the Czech Republic and Poland. Together, these mountains form a barrier that divides the Great Hungarian Plain and the Danube River basin in the south from Poland and the vast rolling lowlands of the North European Plain.

Pomerania (C 2)
This is a sandy coastal area with lakes formed by glaciers. It stretches west from the River Vistula to just beyond the German border.

Vistula River (F 4)
Poland's largest river is the Vistula. It flows northward, passing through the capital, Warsaw, on its way to the Baltic Sea.

North European Plain

Hot springs
The Sudeten mountains (C5) are famous for their hot mineral springs. These occur where water heated deep within the Earth's crust finds its way to the surface along fractures in the rock.

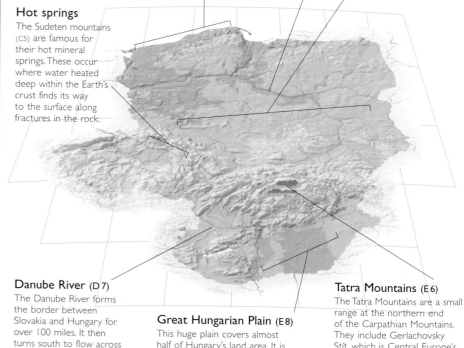

ENVIRONMENTAL ISSUES

The growth of heavy industries that took place under communist rule has caused terrible environmental pollution in some places. Hungary's oil and Poland's brown coal have a high sulfur content. Burning these fuels to produce electricity causes air pollution, and the sulfur dioxide produced combines with moisture in the air, leading to acid rain.

ENVIRONMENTAL ISSUES

- ☁ Severe industrial pollution
- 🏠 Flooding
- Urban air pollution
- Affected by acid rain
- Polluted rivers
- • Major industrial center

Danube River (D 7)
The Danube River forms the border between Slovakia and Hungary for over 100 miles. It then turns south to flow across the Great Hungarian Plain.

Great Hungarian Plain (E 8)
This huge plain covers almost half of Hungary's land area. It is a mixture of farmland and steppe.

Tatra Mountains (E 6)
The Tatra Mountains are a small range at the northern end of the Carpathian Mountains. They include Gerlachovsky Stít, which is Central Europe's highest point at 8,711 ft.

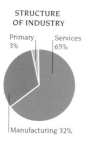

EUROPE
Central Europe

POPULATION

Most people in central Europe live in low-lying areas – for example, along the Vistula River in Poland, and in the lowlands of the Czech Republic. In mountainous Slovakia, many people still live in rural towns and villages. The industrial areas and capital cities have the highest population densities.

URBAN/RURAL POPULATION DIVISION

Warsaw 2.6%   Budapest 2.7%
Prague 1.7%
Other towns and cities 59%
Rural population 34%

NORTH AMERICA ASIA AFRICA SOUTH AMERICA AUSTRALASIA AND OCEANIA ANTARCTICA

INHABITANTS PER SQ MILE
More than 520
260–520
130–260
Less than 130
■ Capital city
● Major city

Gdynia
Łódź WARSAW
Rybnik Chorzów
PRAGUE Hradec Králové Kraków
Brno
BRATISLAVA
BUDAPEST

CLIMATE

The Carpathian Mountains are both the coldest and the wettest part of central Europe. Temperatures plunge below freezing across the whole region during winter. In summer, eastern Hungary is the hottest place.

January

July

TEMPERATURE AND PRECIPITATION
More than 68°F
59 to 68°F
50 to 59°F
41 to 50°F
32 to 41°F
23 to 32°F
Less than 23°F
— 4 — Precipitation (in)

LAND HEIGHT
6,560–13,120ft
3,280–6,560ft
1,640–3,280ft
820–1,640ft
330–82ft
0–82ft

SEA DEPTH
0–98ft
98–262ft

CITIES AND TOWNS
● Over 500,000 people
◉ 100,000–500,000
○ 50,000–100,000
○ Less than 50,000

SCALE BAR
0 km 50 100
0 miles 50 100

LITHUANIA
Baltic Sea
Bornholm (part of Denmark)
KALININGRAD (part of Russ. Fed.)
BELARUS
GERMANY
POLAND
WARSAW (WARSZAWA)
UKRAINE
CZECH REPUBLIC
PRAGUE (PRAHA)
SLOVAKIA
AUSTRIA
BRATISLAVA
HUNGARY
BUDAPEST
ROMANIA
SLOVENIA
ITALY
CROATIA
SERBIA

SOUTHEAST EUROPE

ALBANIA, BOSNIA AND HERZEGOVINA, BULGARIA, CROATIA, GREECE, MACEDONIA, MONTENEGRO, SERBIA

Southeast Europe extends inland from the coasts of the Aegean, Adriatic, and Black Seas. Ancient Greece was the birthplace of European civilization. Albania and Bulgaria were ruled by communists for over 50 years, until the early 1990s. The rest of the region was part of a communist union of states called Yugoslavia. The collapse of this union in 1991 led to a civil war, after which six separate countries emerged.

— THE LANDSCAPE —

Southeast Europe is largely mountainous, with ranges running from northwest to southeast. The Dinaric Alps run parallel to the Dalmatian coast, and the Pindus Mountains continue this line into Greece. In the Aegean Sea, the drowned peaks of an old mountain chain form thousands of islands.

Earthquakes
Bulgaria, Greece, and Macedonia lie in earthquake zones. Major earthquakes have hit the Ionian Islands in 1953 and Macedonia in 1963.

Great Hungarian Plain (D 1)
The Vojvodina region of Serbia is the southern part of the Great Hungarian Plain. The plain is flat, and fertile soil enables crops like corn and wheat to be grown.

Dinaric Alps (C 2)

Balkan Mountains (F 3)
The mountains form a spur running east to west through Bulgaria and separate the two main rivers, the Danube and the Maritsa.

Dalmatian coast (B 2)
The Dalmatian coast has many long, narrow islands near the shore. These were formed as the Adriatic Sea flooded the river valleys that ran parallel to the coast.

Greek Islands

The Peloponnese (E 6)
The Peloponnese is a mountainous peninsula linked to the Greek mainland only by a narrow strip of land, only 6 km wide, called the Isthmus of Corinth.

Greek Islands
There are two groups of Greek Islands, the Ionian Islands to the west of mainland Greece, and the more numerous islands to the east in the Aegean Sea.

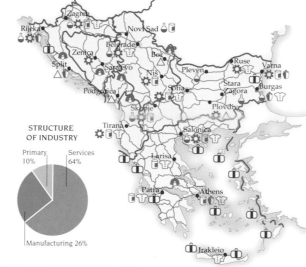

STRUCTURE OF INDUSTRY
Primary 10% • Services 64% • Manufacturing 26%

FARMING AND LAND USE

Cereals like wheat, and fruits, vegetables, and grapes are grown in the fertile north of the region. The band of mountains across southeast Europe is used mainly for grazing sheep and goats. Farther south, and in coastal areas, the warm Mediterranean climate is ideal for growing grapes, olives, and tobacco.

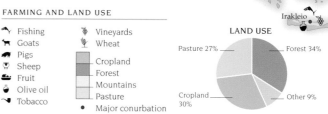

FARMING AND LAND USE
Fishing · Goats · Pigs · Sheep · Fruit · Olive oil · Tobacco · Vineyards · Wheat · Cropland · Forest · Mountains · Pasture · Major conurbation

LAND USE
Pasture 27% · Forest 34% · Cropland 30% · Other 9%

INDUSTRY

Mainland Greece and the many islands in the Aegean Sea are centers of a thriving tourist trade, while tourism on the Black Sea coast continues to grow. The Dalmatian coast's growing tourist industry is recovering, after the civil war in former Yugoslavia disrupted it, and other industries. Heavy industries like chemicals, engineering, and shipbuilding remain an important source of income in Bulgaria.

INDUSTRY
Chemicals · Engineering · Food processing · Metal refining · Shipbuilding · Textiles · Mining · Tourism · Major industrial center / area · Major road

POPULATION

Greece's population is two thirds urban; over 35% live in the capital, Athens, and in Salonica. In Bulgaria, most people live in cities. About half of Albania's and Macedonia's people are still rural. Since the civil war, the different ethnic groups in Bosnia and Herzegovina, Montenegro, Serbia, and Croatia have lived apart from one another.

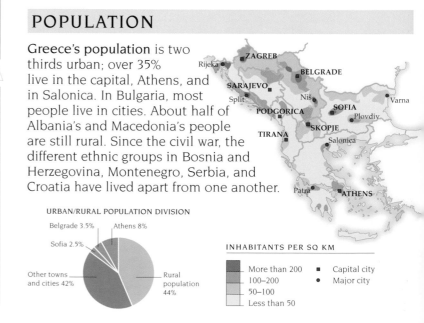

URBAN/RURAL POPULATION DIVISION
Belgrade 3.5% · Athens 8% · Sofia 2.5% · Other towns and cities 42% · Rural population 44%

INHABITANTS PER SQ KM
More than 200 · 100–200 · 50–100 · Less than 50 · Capital city · Major city

CLIMATE

Southeastern Europe's climate varies from north to south. Continental climates are found in the north; winters are cold and dry, while toward the south, winters are milder and summers much hotter. Europe's wettest place is found in the mountains in Bosnia and Herzegovina.

January

July

TEMPERATURE AND PRECIPITATION

More than 77°F
68 to 77°F
59 to 68°F
50 to 59°F
41 to 50°F
32 to 41°F
23 to 32°F
Less than 23°F

4 — Precipitation (in)

EUROPE

Southeast Europe

NORTH AMERICA
ASIA
AFRICA
SOUTH AMERICA
AUSTRALASIA AND OCEANIA
ANTARCTICA

ENVIRONMENTAL ISSUES

Emissions from industry and traffic fumes have polluted the air in Athens and Zagreb. In Athens, smog from vehicle exhausts can be severe as it gets trapped in the city's natural basin. The situation is made worse because many residents drive, rather than use public transportation. Earthquakes are possible; Macedonia's capital city, Skopje, was badly hit in 1963.

Zagreb
Belgrade
Danube
Sofia
Skopje 1963
Salonica 1978
Athens

ENVIRONMENTAL ISSUES

⊚ Catastrophic earthquake
🗹 Urban air pollution
✕ Risk of wild fire

Sea pollution
Severe sea pollution
Polluted river
• Major town

CITIES AND TOWNS

■ Over 500,000 people
■ 100,000–500,000
○ 50,000–100,000
○ Less than 50,000

SCALE BAR

0 km   50   100
0 miles   50   100

LAND HEIGHT

6,560–13,120ft
3,280–6,560ft
1,640–3,280ft
820–1,640ft
330–820ft
0–330ft

SEA DEPTH

0–160ft
160–330ft
330–820ft
820–1,640ft
1,640–3,280ft
3,280–6,560ft
Below 6,560ft

AUSTRIA
SLOVENIA
ITALY
HUNGARY
CROATIA
Drava
Mur
Sava
Varaždin
ZAGREB
Virovitica
Osijek
Subotica
Kikinda
VOJVODINA
Zrenjanin
Istra
Rijeka
Karlovac
Kolpa
Papuk
Vrbas
Novi Sad
Mures
Pula
Bosanska
Novi
Bihać
Banja Luka
REPUBLIKA SRPSKA
Vukovar
Slavonski Brod
Gradačac
Tuzla
Zemun
Pančevo
Vršac
Zadar
Dugi Otok
Kozara
BOSNIA AND HERZEGOVINA
Zenica
Šabac
BELGRADE (BEOGRAD)
Smederevo
Smederevska Palanka
Adriatic Sea
San Marino
Losinj
Pag
Vis
Split
Mostar
FEDERACIJA BOSNE I HERCEGOVINE
SARAJEVO
Foča
Valjevo
Kragujevac
Negotin
ROMANIA
Ialomița
Danube (Dunărea)
Silistra
Dulovo
Ruse
Razgrad
Dobrich
Kavarna
Hvar
Korčula
Mljet
Bijelo Polje
SERBIA
Kosovska Mitrovica
Kraljevo
Niš
Leskovac
Lom
Dimovo
Kozloduy
Vratsa
Montana
Danubian Plain
Pleven
Veliko Turnovo
Gabrovo
Shumen
Varna
Black Sea
Dubrovnik
PODGORICA
Nikšić
MONTENEGRO
Peć
Priština
Pernik
SOFIA (SOFIYA)
Balkan Mountains
Kazanluk
Sliven
Luda Kamchiya
Aytos
Burgas
Scutari
Shkodër
KOSOVO
Bujanovac
Kyustendil
Blagoevgrad
Musala 9,597ft
Pazardzhik
Stara Zagora
Dimitrovgrad
Plovdiv
Khaskovo
Kurdzhali
Yambol
Tsarevo
ALBANIA
Durrës
TIRANA (TIRANË)
Bitola
SKOPJE
MACEDONIA
Kumanovo
Prilep
Rhodope Mountains
Sandanski
Petrich
Drama
Xanthi
Komotini
Ergene Irmağı
Didymoteicho
Fier
Berat
Korçë
Lake Prespa
Lake Ohrid
Vlorë
Strait of Otranto
Gjirokastër
Sarandë
Kozani
Giannitsa
Kilkis
Salonica (Thessaloniki)
Kavala
Thasos
Alexandroupoli
Sea of Marmara
TURKEY
Corfu (Kerkyra)
Neapoli
Pindus Mountains
Metsovo
Chalkidiki
Thermaic Gulf
Katerini
Sarti
Thracian Sea
Samothraki
Myrina
Limnos
Lesbos
Mount Olympus
Ioannina
Igoumenitsa
Trikala
Larisa
Volos
Loutra
Karyes
Agios Efstratios
Mytilini
Paxoi
Preveza
Arta
Karditsa
Sourpi
Alonnisos
Northern Sporades
Kallonî
Gediz Nehri
Ionian Islands (Iónia Nisiá)
Lefkada
Ionian Sea
Vasiliki
Kefallonia
Nafpaktos
Lamia
Skyros
Kymi
Euboea (Evvoia)
Chalkida
Aiharios
Aegean Sea
Chios
Psara
Büyükmenderes Nehri
Samos
Ikaria
GREECE
Patra
Lechaina
Poros
Zakynthos
Pyrgos
Keri
Gulf of Corinth
Isthmus of Corinth
Corinth (Korinthos)
ATHENS (ATHINA)
Piraeus (Peiraías)
Natplio
Ermioni
Tzia
Andros
Tinos
Mykonos
Syros
Kythnos
Serifos
Sifnos
Paros
Naxos
Patmos
Leros
Agathonisi
Cyclades (Kyklades)
Amorgos
Kos
Dodecanese (Dodekánisa)
Nisyros
Kalamata
Tripoli
Leonídio
Sparti
Milos
Santorini
Anafi
Astypalaia
Chalki
Tilos
Rhodes (Rodos)
Koroni
Areopoli
Laknikos Kolpos
Neapoli
Mirtoan Sea
Kythira
Antikythira
Kasos
Karpathos
Lindos
Sária
Chania
Lefka Ori
Rethymno
Irakleio
Dikti
Agios Nikolaos
Sea of Crete (Kritikó Pélagos)
Tympaki
Crete (Kriti)
Mediterranean Sea
MOLDOVA
UKRAINE
Danube (Dunărea)

EASTERN EUROPE

BELARUS, MOLDOVA, ROMANIA, UKRAINE

Much of Eastern Europe, which extends north from the Danube River and the Black Sea, is covered by open grasslands called steppe. Ukraine's excellent farmland and large mineral reserves make it one of the strongest new countries to emerge from the former Soviet Union. Moldova and Belarus were also part of the USSR until they became independent in 1991. Romania was a strict communist regime from 1945 until 1989.

INDUSTRY

In Ukraine, most industry is based around the country's mineral reserves. The Donbass region has Europe's largest coalfield and is an important center for iron and steel production. The main industries of Belarus are chemicals, machine building, and food-processing. Romania's manufacturing industries are growing, with the help of foreign investment.

INDUSTRY

- 🚗 Car manufacturing
- ♨ Chemicals
- ⚙ Engineering
- ▤ Food processing
- ⚒ Iron and steel
- 👕 Textiles
- ⚒ Coal
- ⛏ Mining
- ◔ Oil and gas
- 🍺 Tourism
- ▣ Major industrial center / area
- — Major road

STRUCTURE OF INDUSTRY

Primary 15% Manufacturing 42%
Services 43%

FARMING AND LAND USE

The black soils found across much of Ukraine are very fertile and the country is a big producer of cereals, sugar beets, and sunflowers, which are grown for their oil. In Moldova and southern Romania, the warm summers are ideal for growing grapes for wine, along with sunflowers and a variety of vegetables. Cattle and pigs are farmed throughout Eastern Europe.

LAND USE

Other 11%
Forest 24%
Pasture 15%
Cropland 50%

FARMING AND LAND USE

- 🐄 Cattle
- 🐖 Pigs
- 🐑 Sheep
- 🥕 Root crops
- 🌻 Sunflowers
- 🍇 Vineyards
- 🌾 Wheat
- Cropland
- Forest
- Pasture
- Wetland
- • Major conurbation

POPULATION

Many Romanians still live in rural areas, although Bucharest, the capital, is home to six times as many people as the next largest city. In Ukraine, two-thirds of the population live in cities such as those in the Donbass industrial area. Most of Belarus's people are city dwellers. Moldova is the most rural country in Eastern Europe; over half live in the countryside.

URBAN/RURAL POPULATION DIVISION

Bucharest 2.3%   Kiev 3.1%
Minsk 2.1%
Rural population 36%
Other towns and cities 56.5%

INHABITANTS PER SQ MILE

- More than 520
- 260–520
- 130–260
- Less than 130
- ■ Capital city
- • Major city

THE LANDSCAPE

Flat or rolling grasslands, marshes, and river flood plains cover almost all of Ukraine and Belarus. The Carpathian Mountains cross the southwestern corner of Ukraine and continue in a large arc-shaped chain of high peaks at the heart of Romania. Along the southern part of this chain, the Carpathians are called the Transylvanian Alps.

Pripet Marshes (C 3)
The Pripet Marshes in Belarus and Ukraine form the largest area of marshland in Europe.

The steppes
The steppes are great, wide grasslands that are found across eastern Europe and central Asia. Over 70% of the Ukrainian landscape is steppe. Little rain falls throughout the steppes.

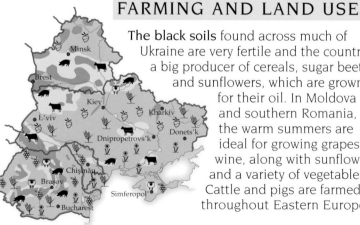

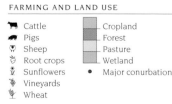

Carpathian Mountains (C 5)
The Carpathians are the largest mountain range in Eastern Europe. They are a rich source of timber and minerals.

Dnieper (E 5) and Dniester (D 5) Rivers
The Dnieper and Dniester run south and east toward the Black Sea. They flow slowly across huge areas of low-lying land.

The Crimea (F 6)
This peninsula divides the Sea of Azov from the Black Sea. The steep mountains of Kryms'ki Hory run along the southeastern coast of the Crimea.

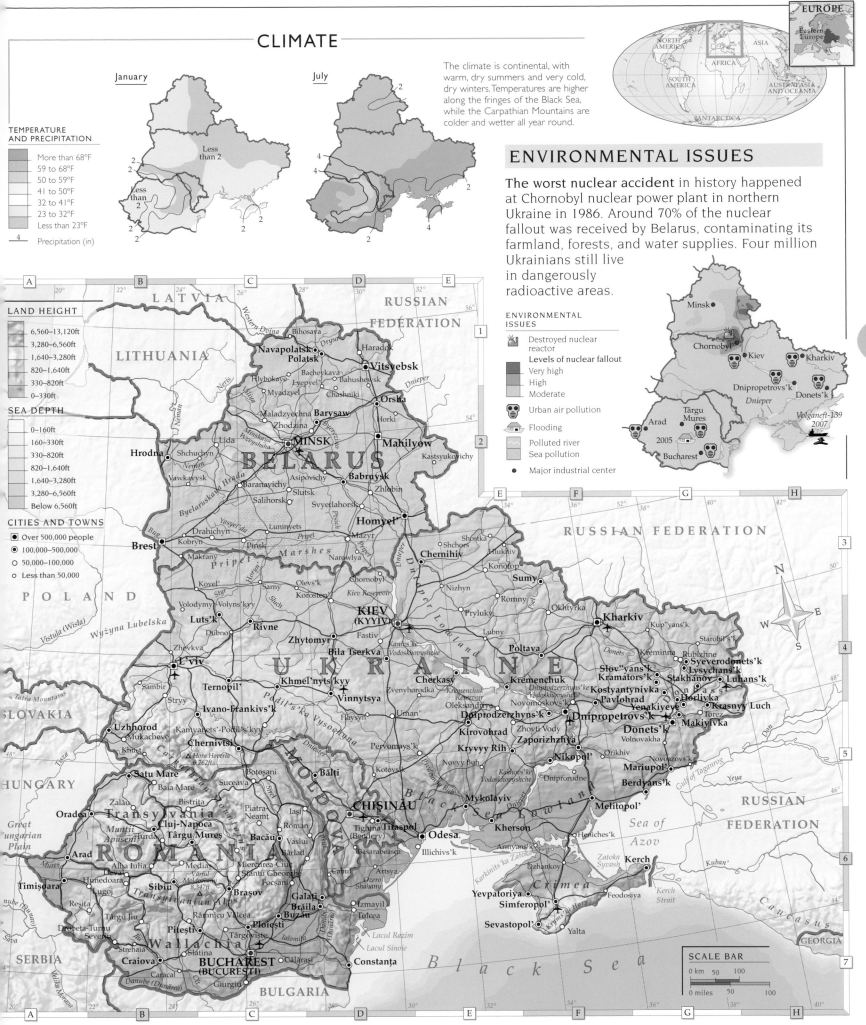

CLIMATE

January

July

The climate is continental, with warm, dry summers and very cold, dry winters. Temperatures are higher along the fringes of the Black Sea, while the Carpathian Mountains are colder and wetter all year round.

EUROPE

Eastern Europe

TEMPERATURE AND PRECIPITATION

More than 68°F
59 to 68°F
50 to 59°F
41 to 50°F
32 to 41°F
23 to 32°F
Less than 23°F

4 Precipitation (in)

Less than 2

ENVIRONMENTAL ISSUES

The worst nuclear accident in history happened at Chornobyl nuclear power plant in northern Ukraine in 1986. Around 70% of the nuclear fallout was received by Belarus, contaminating its farmland, forests, and water supplies. Four million Ukrainians still live in dangerously radioactive areas.

ENVIRONMENTAL ISSUES

Destroyed nuclear reactor

Levels of nuclear fallout
Very high
High
Moderate

Urban air pollution

Flooding

Polluted river

Sea pollution

● Major industrial center

Minsk
Chornobyl
Kiev
Kharkiv
Dnipropetrovs'k
Donets'k
Dnieper
Târgu Mures
Arad
2005
Volganeft-139
2007
Bucharest

LAND HEIGHT
6,560–13,120ft
3,280–6,560ft
1,640–3,280ft
820–1,640ft
330–820ft
0–330ft

SEA DEPTH
0–160ft
160–330ft
330–820ft
820–1,640ft
1,640–3,280ft
3,280–6,560ft
Below 6,560ft

CITIES AND TOWNS
● Over 500,000 people
● 100,000–500,000
○ 50,000–100,000
○ Less than 50,000

LATVIA
RUSSIAN FEDERATION
LITHUANIA
Bihosava
Navapolatsk
Polatsk
Haradok
Drysa
Vitsyebsk
Hlybokaye
Bacheykava
Lyepyel'
Bahushewsk
Dnieper
Myadzyel
Chashniki
Orsha
Maladzyechna
Barysaw
Horki
Zhodzina
Lida
MINSK
Mahilyow
Hrodna
Shchuchyn
Byarezhina
Kastsyukovichy
Neman
BELARUS
Asipovichy
Babruysk
Vawkavysk
Baranavichy
Zhlobin
Slutsk
Salihorsk
Svyetlahorsk
Byelaruskaya Hrada
Drahichyn
Luninyets
Homyel'
Brest
Kobryn
Pinsk
Mazyr
Pripet
Marshes
Narowlya
Shostka
POLAND
Makrany
Pripet
Shchors
Hlukhiv
Chernihiv
Olevs'k
Chornobyl
Konotop
Sumy
Sarny
Korosten'
Kiev Reservoir
Nizhyn
Volodymyr-Volyns'kyy
Romny
Okhtyrka
Luts'k
Rivne
KIEV (KYYIV)
Pryluky
Kharkiv
Dubno
Fastiv
Kup"yans'k
L'viv
Zhytomyr
Lubny
Starobil's'k
Zhovkva
Bila Tserkva
Poltava
Donets
Kreminna
Rubizhne
Ternopil'
Khmel'nyts'kyy
Cherkasy
Kremenchuk
Syeverodonets'k
Slov"yans'k
Kramators'k
Stakhanov
Lysychans'k
Luhans'k
Vinnytsya
Zvenyhorodka
Kostyantynivka
Ivano-Frankivs'k
Uman'
Oleksandriya
Novomoskovs'k
Pavlohrad
Yenakiyeve
Horlivka
Krasnyy Luch
Uzhhorod
Haysyn
Dniprodzerzhyns'k
Dnipropetrovs'k
Makiyivka
Mukacheve
Kirovohrad
Zhovti Vody
Torez
Chernivtsi
Khust
Kamyanets'-Podil's'kyy
Pervomays'k
Kryvyy Rih
Zaporizhzhya
Donets'k
Hora Hoverla
6,762ft
Dnister
Novyy Buh
Nikopol'
Orikhiv
Novoazovs'k
Satu Mare
Botosani
Bălţi
Kotovs'k
Mariupol'
Baia Mare
Suceava
Berdyans'k
Zalău
Transylvania
Piatra-Neamt
Iaşi
Dniprorudne
Mykolayiv
Melitopol'
Oradea
Cluj-Napoca
Roman
CHIŞINĂU
RUSSIAN FEDERATION
Muntii Apuseni
Turda
Târgu Mures
Bacău
Vaslui
Tighina (Bendery)
Tiraspol'
Kherson
Heniches'k
Arad
ROMANIA
Alba Iulia
Media
Bârlad
Basarabeasca
Odesa
Sea of Azov
Timişoara
Hunedoara
Deva
Sibiu
Miercurea-Ciuc
Sfântu Gheorghe
Focşani
Illichivs'k
Armyans'k
Dzhankoy
Kerch
Lugoj
Varful Moldoveanu
8,347ft
Braşov
Galaţi
Izmayil
Yevpatoriya
Crimea
Feodosiya
Reşita
Râmnicu Vâlcea
Brăila
Buzău
Tulcea
Simferopol'
Drobeta-Turnu Severin
Piteşti
Ploieşti
Lacul Rozim
Sevastopol'
Yalta
Wallachia
Târgovişte
Craiova
Caracal
Slatina
BUCHAREST (BUCUREŞTI)
Giurgiu
Constanţa
Black Sea
GEORGIA
SERBIA
BULGARIA

SCALE BAR
0 km 50 100
0 miles 50 100

109

EUROPEAN RUSSIA

RUSSIAN FEDERATION

European Russia is separated from the Asiatic part of the Russian Federation by the Ural Mountains. It is home to two-thirds of the country's population. Russia was the largest and most powerful republic of the communist Soviet Union, which collapsed in 1991. New businesses were set up when communism ended, but many old state industries closed down, causing unemployment and further hardship for many people.

INDUSTRY

European Russia is rich in natural resources. Minerals are mined on the Kola Peninsula and in the Urals, while dense forests are felled and processed in many of the larger northern cities. The Volga basin is one of Europe's largest sources of oil and gas. Moscow and the cities near the Volga are centers of skilled labor for a wide range of manufacturing industries like cars, chemicals, and heavy engineering and steel production.

INDUSTRY

🚗	Car manufacturing	🜂	Oil and gas
🜹	Chemicals	⚒	Timber processing
⚙	Engineering	⬛	Major industrial center/area
🜨	Iron and steel	—	Major road
👕	Textiles		
⚒	Mining		

FARMING AND LAND USE

Russia's best farmland lies within this region. Big crops of wheat, barley and oats, potatoes and sunflowers are produced in the fertile black soil that forms a thick band across the country to the south of Moscow. The far north is cold and frozen, with bare mountains and tundra making cultivation impossible. Farther south there are extensive forests, and rough pastures that are used for herding and hunting.

FARMING AND LAND USE

🐄	Cattle		Barren land
🐟	Fishing		Cropland
🐖	Pigs		Forest
🦌	Reindeer		Mountain region
🐑	Sheep		Pasture
🌾	Cereals		Tundra
🥔	Root crops		Wetland
🌻	Sunflowers	●	Major conurbation
🌲	Timber		

POPULATION

Three-quarters of European Russia's people live in towns and cities, most in a broad band stretching south from St. Petersburg to Moscow, and eastward to the Urals. The capital, Moscow, and St. Petersburg are very crowded cities. Living conditions there are cramped, with two families often sharing one apartment. The southeast is also heavily populated. Over 12 million people live in the cities and towns that line the banks of the Volga River.

INHABITANTS PER SQ MILE

	More than 260
	130–260
	30–130
	Less than 30
■	Capital city
●	Major city

THE LANDSCAPE

European Russia lies on the North European Plain, a huge, rolling lowland with wide river basins. The northern half of the plain, which was once covered by glaciers, has many lakes and swamps. The Volga River drains much of the plain as it flows south to the Caspian Sea. The Caucasus and Ural Mountains form natural boundaries in the south and east.

Northern European Russia (C 3)
Northern European Russia reaches into the Arctic Circle. It is a region of pine and birch forests, marshes, and tundra. There are also tens of thousands of lakes, including the biggest in Europe, Ladoga, which covers about 6,830 sq miles.

Ural Mountains (E 5)
The Ural Mountains run from north to south, stretching almost 2,500 miles.

Lake Ladoga (B 4)

Valdai Hills (A 5)
The Valdai Hills are a high, swampy region of the North European Plain. Two of Europe's biggest rivers, the Volga and the Western Dvina, have their sources here.

North European Plain (C 4)
The North European Plain sweeps west from the Ural Mountains, all the way to the Rhine River in Germany. In European Russia it includes a number of hill ranges, such as the Volga Uplands and the Central Russian Upland.

Caucasus (A 9)
This massive barrier of mountains stretches from the Black Sea to the Caspian Sea. It includes El'brus, the highest peak in Europe, at 18,511 feet.

Caspian Sea (C 9)

Volga River (C 7)
The Volga River flows for 2,292 miles, making it Europe's longest river and Russia's most important inland waterway. It is used for transportation and to generate hydro-electric power.

ENVIRONMENTAL ISSUES

The many factories in European Russia have caused widespread pollution, Dzerzhinsk is said to be the most polluted town on earth. Several of Russia's older nuclear power plants have been declared unsafe, but are yet to be shut down. Waste from these power plants, as well as from nuclear submarines, has for many years been dumped in the Barents Sea and off Novaya Zemlya.

ENVIRONMENTAL ISSUES

- Nuclear waste dump site
- Unstable nuclear reactor
- Urban air pollution
- Polluted rivers
- Sea pollution
- Major industrial center

CLIMATE

Winters are extremely cold and dry; temperatures plunge well below freezing in the north and east. Summer brings much warmer and wetter weather, especially in the south, while along the northern coast it remains relatively cold. Rainfall is highest in the Caucasus.

January

July

TEMPERATURE AND PRECIPITATION

- More than 68°F
- 59 to 68°F
- 50 to 59°F
- 41 to 50°F
- 32 to 41°F
- 23 to 32°F
- 14 to 23°F
- 5 to 14°F
- Less than 5°F
- 4 Precipitation (in)

CITIES AND TOWNS
- Over 500,000 people
- 100,000–500,000
- 50,000–100,000
- Less than 50,000

LAND HEIGHT	SEA DEPTH
Above 13,120ft	0–160ft
6,560–13,120ft	160–330ft
3,280–6,560ft	330–820ft
1,640–3,280ft	820–1,640ft
820–1,640ft	1,640–3,280ft
330–820ft	3,280–6,560ft
0–330ft	Below 6,560ft
Below sea level	

SCALE BAR

0 km 100 200

0 miles 100 200

THE MEDITERRANEAN

The Mediterranean Sea separates Europe from Africa. It stretches more than 2,500 miles from east to west and is almost completely enclosed by land. Many great civilizations, including the Greek and Roman empires, grew up around the Mediterranean. It has been a crossroads of international trade routes for many centuries. More than 100 million people live in the 28 countries that border the sea, and their numbers are increased by the large crowds of tourists who regularly visit the area.

ENVIRONMENTAL ISSUES

Water pollution is widespread in the Mediterranean, especially near the large coastal resorts where raw sewage and industrial effluent is pumped out to sea, and often ends up on the beaches. Oil refining and oil spills have also increased pollution.

ENVIRONMENTAL ISSUES

⬯ Oil spill

▢ Mild water pollution
▢ Severe water pollutio

LAND HEIGHT	SEA DEPTH
Above 13,120ft	0–820ft
6,560–13,120ft	820–1,640ft
3,280–6,560ft	1,640–3,280ft
1,640–3,280ft	3,280–6,560ft
820–1,640ft	6,560–9,840ft
330–820ft	9,840–13,120ft
0–330ft	Below 13,120ft
Below sea level	

CITIES AND TOWNS

◉ Over 500,000 people
● 100,000–500,000
◎ 50,000–100,000
○ Less than 50,000

THE LANDSCAPE

The Mediterranean Sea would be an enormous lake if it were not for the Strait of Gibraltar, a narrow opening only 8 miles wide, which joins it to the Atlantic Ocean. The Mediterranean lies over the boundary of two continental plates. Where they meet, earthquakes and volcanoes are common.

Strait of Gibraltar

Sandy beaches
The Mediterranean coasts are bordered by several thousand miles of sandy beaches.

Shallow shelves
The area of water off the coast of Tunisia, and also the Adriatic Sea, are shallower than the rest of the Mediterranean.

Greek islands
Greece has thousands of islands that lie both in the Mediterranean and in the smaller Aegean Sea. Some of them are the remains of old volcanoes which have left black sand on the beaches.

Suez Canal
The Suez Canal links the Mediterranean to the Gulf of Suez and the Red Sea. Before it was built, ships had to sail around all of Africa to reach Asia.

Atlas Mountains
The rugged Atlas Mountains run through most of Morocco and Algeria. They form a barrier between the Mediterranean coast and the Sahara, which lies to the south.

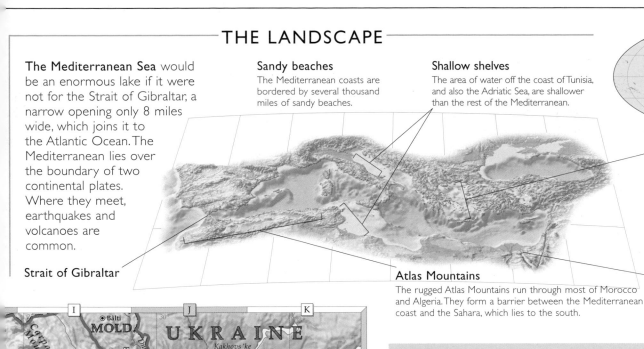

TOURISM

The tourist industry in and around the Mediterranean is one of the most highly developed in the world. More than half the world's income from tourism is generated here. Resorts have grown up along the northwest coast of Africa, and in Egypt, southern Spain, France, Italy, Greece, and Turkey. Tourism brings huge economic benefits, but the ever-increasing number of visitors has also damaged the environment.

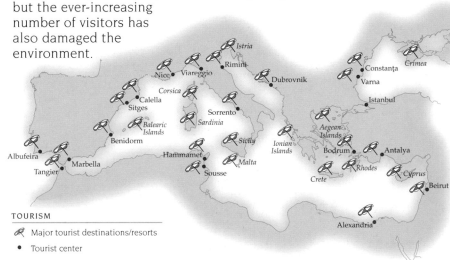

TOURISM

- Major tourist destinations/resorts
- Tourist center

INDUSTRY

The Mediterranean has a large fishing industry, although most of the fishing is small-scale. Tuna and sardines are caught throughout the region, and mussels are farmed off the coast of Italy. Fish canning and packing take place at most of the larger ports. Small oil and gas reserves are extracted off the coast of North Africa and near Greece, Spain, and Italy.

INDUSTRY

- Fishing ports
- Oil and gas
- Major city

113

CONTINENTAL ASIA

Asia is the world's largest continent, and has the greatest range of physical extremes. Some of the highest, lowest, and coldest places on Earth are found in Asia: Mount Everest in the Himalayas is the highest, the Dead Sea in the west is the lowest, and the frozen wastes of northern Siberia are among the coldest. More people live in Asia than on any other continent – 1.3 billion of them in China, and 1.07 billion in India.

4,040 miles

6,030 miles

CROSS-SECTION THROUGH ASIA

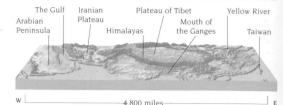

The Gulf | Iranian Plateau | Plateau of Tibet | Yellow River
Arabian Peninsula | Himalayas | Mouth of the Ganges | Taiwan

W ⊢――――4,800 miles――――⊣ E

The Arabian Peninsula and the mountainous Iranian Plateau are divided by the Persian Gulf, fed by the Tigris and Euphrates Rivers. Farther east, the land begins to rise, the mountains spreading north to the Plateau of Tibet, and south to the Himalayas. The plains to the south of the Himalayas are drained by the Indus and Ganges, and to the east of the Plateau of Tibet by the Yellow River.

PHYSICAL ASIA

Northern Asia is made up of old mountains and ancient, stable plateaus. The jagged Himalayan mountains dominate the central part of the continent, along with the Plateau of Tibet, which stretches north into China. In Southeast Asia, there are many islands. Volcanoes and earthquakes are common, and some of the islands are volcanically formed.

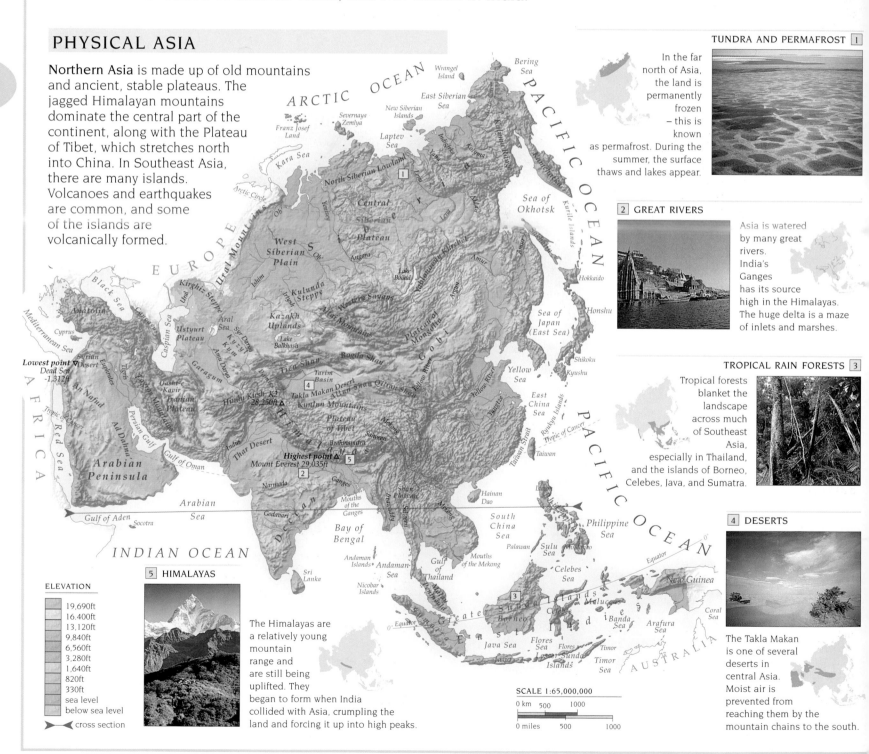

TUNDRA AND PERMAFROST 1

In the far north of Asia, the land is permanently frozen – this is known as permafrost. During the summer, the surface thaws and lakes appear.

2 GREAT RIVERS

Asia is watered by many great rivers. India's Ganges has its source high in the Himalayas. The huge delta is a maze of inlets and marshes.

TROPICAL RAIN FORESTS 3

Tropical forests blanket the landscape across much of Southeast Asia, especially in Thailand, and the islands of Borneo, Celebes, Java, and Sumatra.

4 DESERTS

The Takla Makan is one of several deserts in central Asia. Moist air is prevented from reaching them by the mountain chains to the south.

5 HIMALAYAS

The Himalayas are a relatively young mountain range and are still being uplifted. They began to form when India collided with Asia, crumpling the land and forcing it up into high peaks.

ELEVATION

19,690ft
16,400ft
13,120ft
9,840ft
6,560ft
3,280ft
1,640ft
820ft
330ft
sea level
below sea level

⊱⊰ cross section

SCALE 1:65,000,000

0 km   500   1000

0 miles   500   1000

POLITICAL ASIA

Asia is a continent of many contrasts: in its lands, its peoples, and its traditions. The break-up of the Soviet Union, which once stretched south from Russia to Iran, produced the new central Asian republics of Kazakhstan, Kyrgyzstan, Tajikistan, Turkmenistan, and Uzbekistan. The countries in southwest Asia are mainly Muslim, and include monarchies, republics and theocracies. India is the world's largest democracy, while China is a communist power regaining its economic influence in the world.

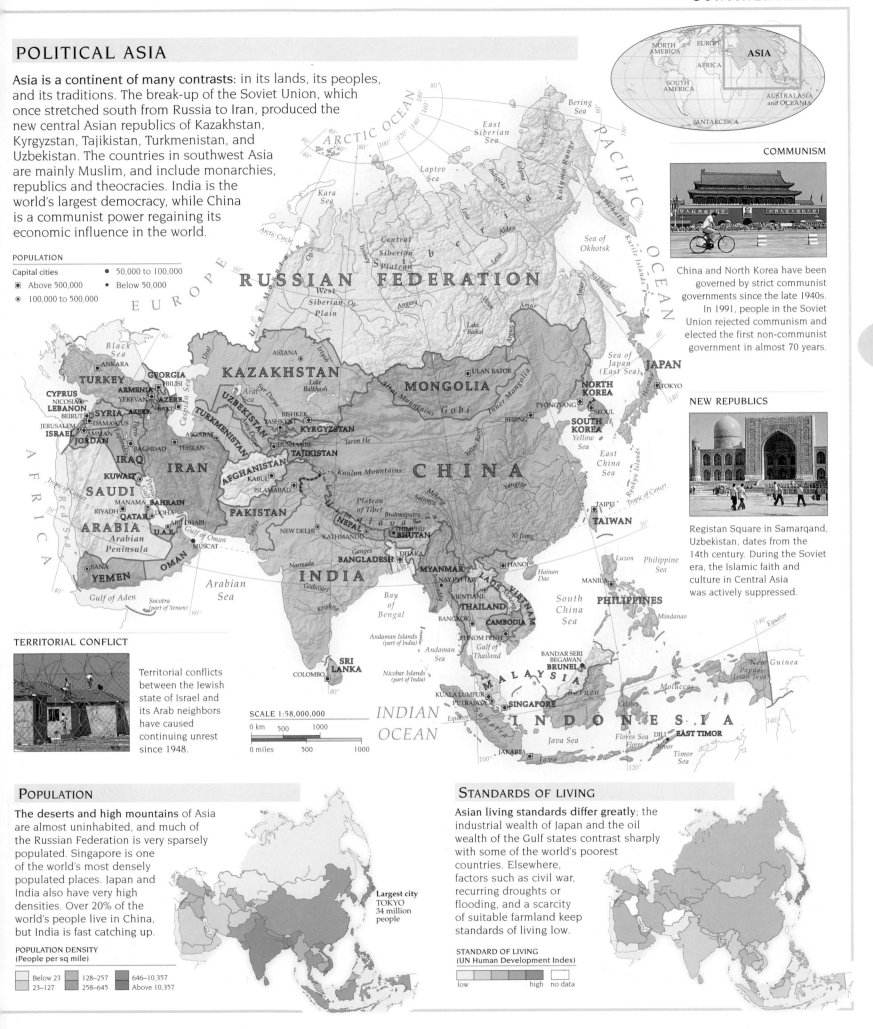

COMMUNISM

China and North Korea have been governed by strict communist governments since the late 1940s. In 1991, people in the Soviet Union rejected communism and elected the first non-communist government in almost 70 years.

NEW REPUBLICS

Registan Square in Samarqand, Uzbekistan, dates from the 14th century. During the Soviet era, the Islamic faith and culture in Central Asia was actively suppressed.

POPULATION

Capital cities
- Above 500,000
- 100,000 to 500,000
- 50,000 to 100,000
- Below 50,000

TERRITORIAL CONFLICT

Territorial conflicts between the Jewish state of Israel and its Arab neighbors have caused continuing unrest since 1948.

SCALE 1:58,000,000

POPULATION

The deserts and high mountains of Asia are almost uninhabited, and much of the Russian Federation is very sparsely populated. Singapore is one of the world's most densely populated places. Japan and India also have very high densities. Over 20% of the world's people live in China, but India is fast catching up.

Largest city TOKYO 34 million people

POPULATION DENSITY (People per sq mile)
- Below 23
- 23–127
- 128–257
- 258–645
- 646–10,357
- Above 10,357

STANDARDS OF LIVING

Asian living standards differ greatly; the industrial wealth of Japan and the oil wealth of the Gulf states contrast sharply with some of the world's poorest countries. Elsewhere, factors such as civil war, recurring droughts or flooding, and a scarcity of suitable farmland keep standards of living low.

STANDARD OF LIVING (UN Human Development Index)
low — high — no data

ASIAN GEOGRAPHY

Asia's forbidding mountain ranges, barren deserts and fertile plains have affected the way in which people settled the continent. Intensive agriculture is found in the more fertile areas, and the largest concentrations of people grew up near fertile land, and close to great rivers. Asia's mineral wealth has brought people to the more inhospitable parts of the continent; the deserts of southwest Asia for oil, and frozen Siberia for oil, gas, and minerals.

INDUSTRY

Many people in Asia still rely on agriculture as a source of income, and some countries have very few industries. Heavy industry dominates eastern China and Russia, but Japan is the most industrially productive country. In recent years, booming "tiger" economies have developed in countries such as Taiwan, which border the Pacific Ocean.

MINERAL RESOURCES

Over half of the world's oil and gas reserves are in Asia, most importantly around the Persian Gulf, and in western Siberia. Coal in Siberia and China has provided power for steel industries. Metallic minerals are also abundant: tin in Southeast Asia, and platinum and nickel in Siberia.

MINERAL RESOURCES

- Chromium
- Tin
- Nickel
- Iron
- Platinum
- Gold
- Lead
- Oil/gas field
- Coal field

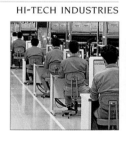

OIL AND GAS

The discovery of oil in the Persian Gulf has generated enormous wealth, and produced rapid industrial and social change in countries such as Saudi Arabia, U.A.E., and Kuwait which control the oil supplies.

HI-TECH INDUSTRIES

Japan is a world-leading producer of electronic and hi-tech goods like computers, cameras, and hi-fi equipment. Taiwan, South Korea, and Singapore also produce electronic goods.

INDUSTRY

- ✈ Aerospace
- Brewing
- Car/vehicle manufacture
- Cement
- Chemicals
- Coal
- Electronics
- Engineering
- Finance
- Food processing
- High-tech industry
- Iron and steel
- Mining
- Oil and gas
- Pharmaceuticals
- Printing and publishing
- Shipbuilding
- Textiles
- Timber processing

FINANCE

Mumbai (Bombay) is India's leading industrial city, and has a thriving stock market. Modern office blocks stand close to sprawling slums.

INDUSTRIAL COMPLEXES

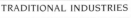

Noril'sk is one of several Soviet-era industrial complexes built in Russia. It is a processing centre for the rich mineral reserves found nearby.

GNI per capita (US$)

- Below 1,999
- 2,000-4,999
- 5,000-9,999
- 10,000-19,999
- 20,000-24,999
- Above 25,000
- • Industrial center

TRADITIONAL INDUSTRIES

Traditional industries and methods of working are still important to less industrialized nations. Here in Vietnam, sea water has been evaporated by the sun, and the salt is collected for market.

CLIMATE

Most of Asia has a continental climate, apart from coastal areas. Without the moderating effects of the ocean, temperatures can soar during the day, and plummet at night; while rainfall is generally low – producing several large deserts. Temperatures as low as −90°F have been recorded in the frozen wastes of Siberia, while the islands in Southeast Asia have tropical climates. Southern and eastern Asia are also affected by a seasonal wind called the monsoon. This originates in the Indian Ocean and brings heavy rainfall and high winds, often devastating small coastal and low-lying villages and towns.

Coldest place
VERKHOYANSK (Russ. Fed.)
Temp −90°F

Hottest place
TIRAT TSVI (Israel)
Temp 129°F

Driest place
ADEN (Yemen)
Annual rainfall 3/16in

Wettest place
CHERRAPUNJI (India)
Annual rainfall 45in

EXTREME WEATHER EVENTS

Symbols indicate climatic extremes

CLIMATE

- Tundra
- Subarctic
- Cool continental
- Warm temperate
- Mediterranean
- Semiarid
- Arid
- Humid equatorial
- Tropical
- Hot humid

RAIN FORESTS

The tropical climate across the islands of Southeast Asia produces warm, humid conditions in which rain forests flourish. Each island provides a slightly different habitat, so the animals and plants that have evolved on one island may be very different to those on the next.

RICE

China is the world's largest producer of rice, which is grown in muddy fields called paddy fields. Water buffaloes are used to plow the ground before planting.

LAND USE AND AGRICULTURE

Large expanses of Asia are uncultivated, because the soil is too poor, or the climate is too cold or dry for crops to grow. The Plateau of Tibet, much of Siberia, and the Arabian Peninsula have limited agriculture. Some of the most fertile land is found in eastern China and India, where rice is a staple. Elsewhere, cash crops are grown for profit, such as dates in southwest Asia, rubber in Southeast Asia, tea in India, China, and Sri Lanka, and coconuts throughout the island archipelago of Southeast Asia.

LAND USE AND AGRICULTURE

- Cattle
- Goats
- Pigs
- Sheep
- Cereals
- Coconuts
- Corn
- Cotton
- Dates
- Fishing
- Fruit
- Jute
- Groundnuts
- Rice
- Root crops
- Rubber
- Shellfish
- Sugarcane
- Soybeans
- Tea
- Timber

- Mountains
- Cropland
- Desert
- Forest
- Pasture
- Wetland
- • Major conurbation

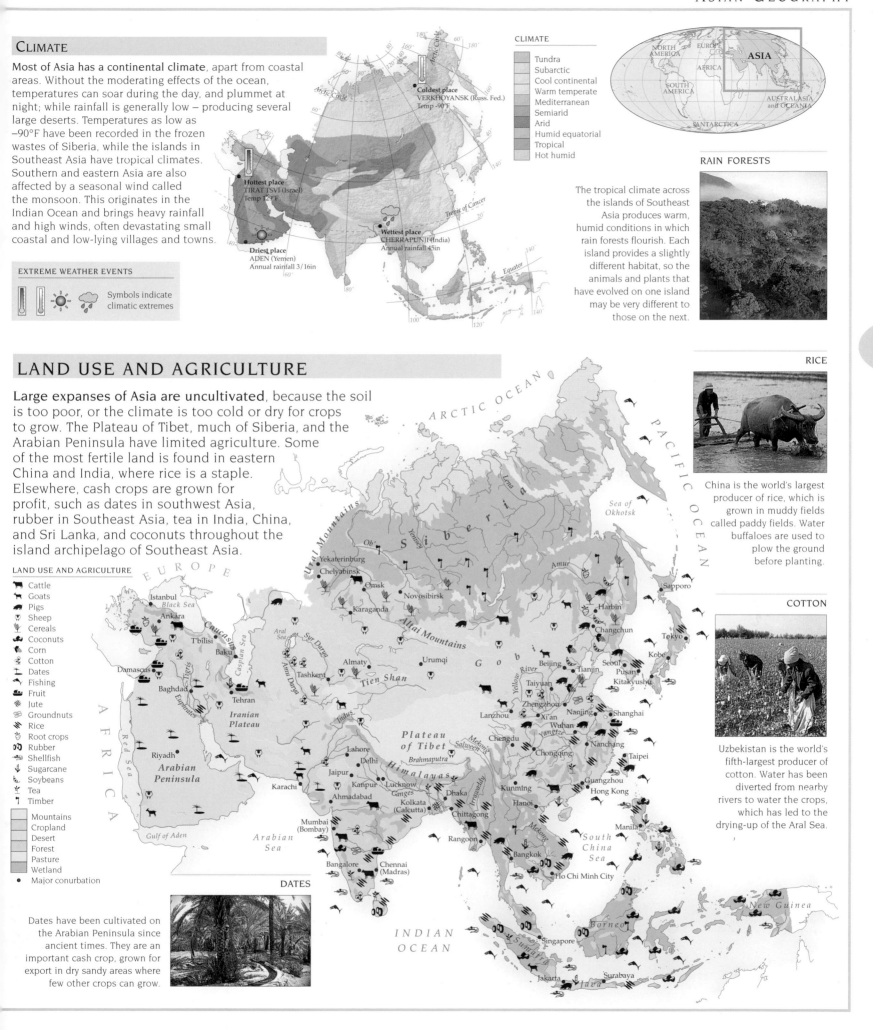

COTTON

Uzbekistan is the world's fifth-largest producer of cotton. Water has been diverted from nearby rivers to water the crops, which has led to the drying-up of the Aral Sea.

DATES

Dates have been cultivated on the Arabian Peninsula since ancient times. They are an important cash crop, grown for export in dry sandy areas where few other crops can grow.

RUSSIA AND KAZAKHSTAN

Russia lies partly in Europe but mostly in Asia. The land to the east of the Ural Mountains is called Siberia. This immense stretch of grasslands, thick, evergreen forest, and tundra is crossed by giant rivers. Vast areas of Siberia are almost untouched by human activity, yet in the industrial regions set up under communism (1922–1991), air, water, and soil are heavily polluted with harmful substances. Along with the former Soviet state of Kazakhstan, Siberia is rich in a huge variety of minerals.

INDUSTRY

The discovery of gold in the 19th century opened Siberia up to economic and industrial development. Later, vast reserves of oil, coal, and gas were found, especially in the west, which is now the main center for oil extraction. Gold and diamonds are mined in the east. In Kazakhstan, mining and other industries are growing with the help of foreign investors.

STRUCTURE OF INDUSTRY

Primary 5%
Services 60%
Manufacturing 35%

INDUSTRY

- Car manufacture
- Chemicals
- Engineering
- Iron & steel
- Textiles
- Diamonds
- Mining
- Oil and gas
- Timber manufacturing
- ▪ Major industrial center / area
- — Major road

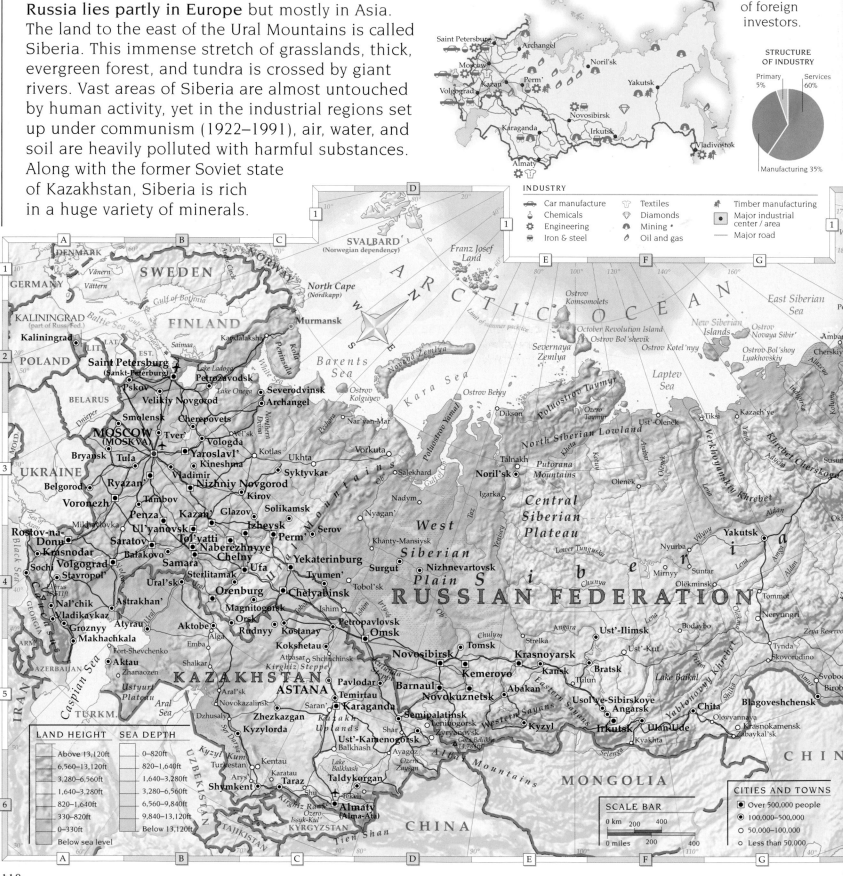

LAND HEIGHT
- Above 13,120ft
- 6,560–13,120ft
- 3,280–6,560ft
- 1,640–3,280ft
- 820–1,640ft
- 330–820ft
- 0–330ft
- Below sea level

SEA DEPTH
- 0–820ft
- 820–1,640ft
- 1,640–3,280ft
- 3,280–6,560ft
- 6,560–9,840ft
- 9,840–13,120ft
- Below 13,120ft

SCALE BAR
0 km 200 400
0 miles 200 400

CITIES AND TOWNS
- ● Over 500,000 people
- ● 100,000–500,000
- ○ 50,000–100,000
- ○ Less than 50,000

ASIA

Russia and Kazakhstan

THE LANDSCAPE

East of the Ural Mountains lies the West Siberian Plain – the world's largest area of flat ground. The plain gradually rises to the Central Siberian Plateau and then again to highlands in the southeast. Great coniferous forests called *taiga* stretch across most of this land. The far north of Siberia extends into the Arctic Circle. Here the landscape is made up of frozen plains called tundra. Much of Kazakhstan is covered by huge rolling grasslands, or steppe. In the south are arid sandy deserts.

Tundra and *taiga*
Stubby birch trees, dwarf bushes, moss and lichen huddle close to the ground in the frozen tundra wastes of northern Russia. They lie between the permanent ice and snow of the Arctic, and the thick *taiga* forests which cover an area greater than the Amazon rain forest.

The Caspian Sea (A 5)
The Caspian Sea covers 143,243 sq miles and is the world's largest expanse of inland water. It is fed by the Volga and Ural Rivers, which flow in from the plains of the north.

West Siberian Plain (D 4)
This vast, flat expanse is covered with a network of marshes and streams. The Ob' River, which winds its way north across the plains, is frozen for up to half the year.

Lake Baikal (F 5)
Lake Baikal is the deepest lake in the world, and the largest freshwater one – it is more than 1 mile deep and covers 12,500 sq miles. It is fed by 336 rivers and contains around 20% of all the fresh water in the world.

CLIMATE

Russia and Kazakhstan have continental climates, and their distance from seas and oceans means that temperatures fluctuate wildly, both daily and seasonally. Temperatures in eastern Siberia have been known to reach -90°F.

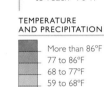

January

Less than 2

July

TEMPERATURE AND PRECIPITATION

- More than 86°F
- 77 to 86°F
- 68 to 77°F
- 59 to 68°F
- 50 to 59°F
- 41 to 50°F
- 32 to 41°F
- 23 to 32°F
- 14 to 23°F
- 5 to 14°F
- Less than 5°F
- —4— Precipitation (in)

FARMING AND LAND USE

Siberia's harsh climate has restricted farming to the south, where there are a few areas warm enough to grow cereal crops such as wheat and oats and to raise cattle on the small pockets of pasture. The rest of the region is used for hunting, herding reindeer, and forestry – the *taiga* forests contain the world's largest timber reserves. In Kazakhstan, big herds of cattle, goats, and sheep are raised for wool and meat, and wheat is cultivated in the fertile north.

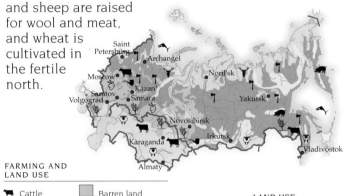

Saint Petersburg
Archangel
Moscow
Noril'sk
Kazan
Saratov
Samara
Volgograd
Yakutsk
Novosibirsk
Karaganda
Irkutsk
Vladivostok
Almaty

FARMING AND LAND USE

- 🐄 Cattle
- 🐟 Fishing
- 🐖 Pigs
- 🦌 Reindeer
- 🐑 Sheep
- Root crops
- Timber
- Tobacco
- Wheat
- Barren land
- Cropland
- Desert
- Forest
- Mountains
- Pasture
- Tundra
- Wetland
- ● Major conurbation

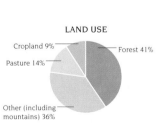

LAND USE

- Cropland 9%
- Pasture 14%
- Forest 41%
- Other (including mountains) 36%

POPULATION

Siberia has some of the world's largest areas of uninhabited land – the bitingly cold climate and harsh living conditions have kept the population small. The industrial cities in the west have the most people. Despite its huge size, Kazakhstan has only 16 million people, just over half live in urban areas.

Saint Petersburg
MOSCOW
Nizhniy Novgorod
Kazan'
Saratov
Samara
Volgograd
Omsk
Yakutsk
ASTANA
Novosibirsk
Khabarovsk
Karaganda
Irkutsk
Almaty
Vladivostok

INHABITANTS PER SQ MILE

- More than 260
- 13–260
- 30–130
- Less than 30
- ■ Capital city
- ● Major city

URBAN/RURAL POPULATION DIVISION

- Saint Petersburg 2.6%
- Moscow 6.4%
- Novosibirsk 1%
- Rural population 24%
- Other towns and cities 66%

ENVIRONMENTAL ISSUES

Decades of industrial development during the communist regime brought new industries to undeveloped parts of the region, such as Siberia. This industrial development has now led to environmental degradation on a massive scale: river, air, and land pollution in Russia is among the worst in the world.

Saint Petersburg
Archangel
Moscow
Noril'sk
Perm'
Ob'
Yekaterinburg
Volgograd
Chelyabinsk
Irtysh
Volga
Novosibirsk
Ishim
Irkutsk
Khabarovsk
Almaty

ENVIRONMENTAL ISSUES

- Urban air pollution
- Polluted rivers
- Sea pollution
- ● Major industrial center

(Left-hand map region)
ALASKA (part of US)
Arctic Circle
Bering Strait
Gulf of Anadyr
Anadyr
Bering Sea
Ostrov Karaginskiy
Ossora
Shelekhov Gulf
Ust'-Kamchatsk
Vulkan Klyuchevskaya Sopka 15,585ft
Magadan
Atlasovo
Mil'kovo
Koryak Range
Kamchatka
Petropavlovsk-Kamchatskiy
Sea of Okhotsk
Pervyy Kuril'skiy Proliv
Ostrov Paramushir
Sakhalin
Kurile Islands
Ostrov Urup
Ostrov Iturup
Komsomol'sk-na-Amure
Yuzhno-Sakhalinsk
Khabarovsk
La Pérouse Strait
Kurile Islands (administered by Russian Federation, claimed by Japan)
Lake Khanka
Ussuriysk
Nakhodka
Vladivostok
JAPAN
Sea of Japan (East Sea)
Honshu
Limit of winter pack ice

TURKEY AND THE CAUCASUS

ARMENIA, AZERBAIJAN, GEORGIA, TURKEY

Turkey and the Caucasus lie partly in Europe, and partly in Asia. Turkey has a long Islamic tradition, and although the country is now a secular (nonreligious) one, most. Turks are Muslims. Turkey is becoming more industrialized, although one third of its workforce is still employed in agriculture. The countries of the Caucasus were under Russian rule for 70 years, until 1991. They are home to more than 50 different ethnic groups.

INDUSTRY

Turkey has a wide range of industries, including tourism and growing trade links with Europe. Azerbaijan has large oil reserves and is able to export oil. The other states use imported fuel and hydro-electric power generated by their rushing rivers. Georgia produces industrial machinery and chemicals. Armenia's economy is recovering from the conflict with Azerbaijan.

FARMING AND LAND USE

With its warm climate and good soils, Turkey is able to produce all of its own food. Cattle and goats are kept on the central plateau. Along the Mediterranean coast, farmers grow olives, figs, grapes, and peaches. Hazelnuts are cultivated along the shores of the Black Sea. Across the Caucasus, the limited fertile land is used to grow wine grapes, tobacco, and cotton.

FARMING AND LAND USE

- 🐄 Livestock
- 🐟 Fishing
- 🌿 Cotton
- 🍈 Fruit
- 🌰 Hazelnuts
- 🌱 Root crops
- 🍇 Tobacco
- 🍇 Vineyards

- Pasture
- Cropland
- Forest
- • Major conurbation

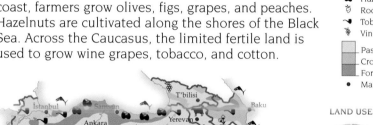

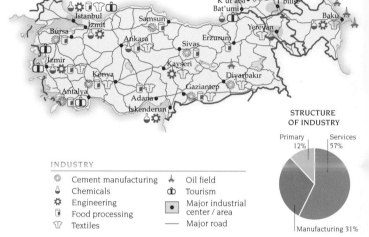

STRUCTURE OF INDUSTRY

Primary 12%
Services 57%
Manufacturing 31%

LAND USE

Other 31%
Cropland 34%
Forest 15%
Pasture 20%

INDUSTRY

- 🏭 Cement manufacturing
- 🧪 Chemicals
- ⚙️ Engineering
- 🗄 Food processing
- 👕 Textiles
- ⚓ Oil field
- 🏬 Tourism
- ▪ Major industrial center / area
- — Major road

THE LANDSCAPE

A huge semiarid plateau called Anatolia runs across the center of Turkey. It is rimmed by several mountain ranges along the Black Sea coast and the steep Taurus Mountains in the south. A narrow strip of lowland separates the Caucasus and the Lesser Caucasus mountains in the northeast.

Anatolia
Anatolia has large areas of soft limestone rock. Over a long period of time, layers of rock have been worn away by water to produce strange landscapes with caves and tall, isolated rock pinnacles.

Caucasus Mountains (H 1)

Lesser Caucasus (H 2)

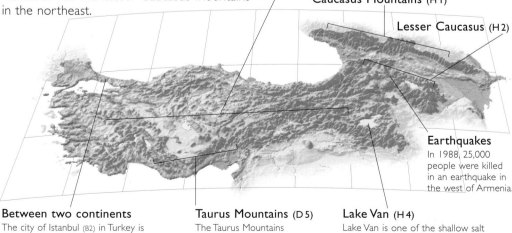

Earthquakes
In 1988, 25,000 people were killed in an earthquake in the west of Armenia.

Between two continents
The city of Istanbul (B2) in Turkey is divided in two by a narrow channel of water called the Bosporus. One part of the city is in Europe, the other in Asia. The two parts are linked by bridges.

Taurus Mountains (D 5)
The Taurus Mountains were formed around 60 to 65 million years ago. Weathering has formed caves and deep gorges.

Lake Van (H 4)
Lake Van is one of the shallow salt lakes found in Anatolia. Salt lakes develop in hot, dry areas where large quantities of water evaporate, leaving behind salty deposits.

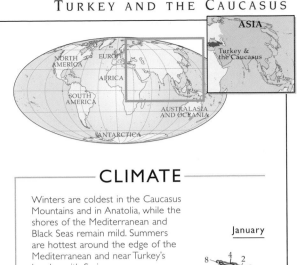

ASIA
Turkey & the Caucasus

POPULATION

Over 75% of Turks live in large towns or cities, mostly in the western half of the country. The eastern and southeastern parts of Anatolia are home to the Kurdish people. The Caucasian republics became more industrialized under Russian rule, and today, two thirds of their people live in urban places.

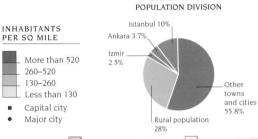

URBAN/RURAL POPULATION DIVISION

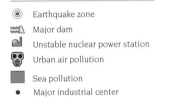

Istanbul 10%
Ankara 3.7%
Izmir 2.5%
Other towns and cities 55.8%
Rural population 28%

INHABITANTS PER SQ MILE

- More than 520
- 260–520
- 130–260
- Less than 130
- ■ Capital city
- ● Major city

ENVIRONMENTAL ISSUES

Turkey has built many large dams to use water from rivers – especially the Euphrates – to irrigate its farmland. Syria and Iraq, which lie downstream, have opposed the dams, because they will have less water flowing into their countries. The safety of old-style nuclear plants such as Metsamor in Armenia has caused concern.

ENVIRONMENTAL ISSUES

- ◎ Earthquake zone
- 〜 Major dam
- ⬔ Unstable nuclear power station
- 😷 Urban air pollution
- Sea pollution
- ● Major industrial center

CLIMATE

Winters are coldest in the Caucasus Mountains and in Anatolia, while the shores of the Mediterranean and Black Seas remain mild. Summers are hottest around the edge of the Mediterranean and near Turkey's border with Syria and Iraq.

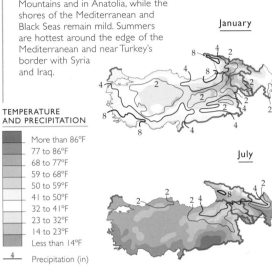

January

July

TEMPERATURE AND PRECIPITATION

- More than 86°F
- 77 to 86°F
- 68 to 77°F
- 59 to 68°F
- 50 to 59°F
- 41 to 50°F
- 32 to 41°F
- 23 to 32°F
- 14 to 23°F
- Less than 14°F
- —4— Precipitation (in)

SCALE BAR
0 km 75 150
0 miles 75 150

CITIES AND TOWNS
- ■ Over 500,000 people
- ◉ 100,000–500,000
- ◎ 50,000–100,000
- ○ Less than 50,000

LAND HEIGHT
- Above 13,120ft
- 6,560–13,120ft
- 3,280–6,560ft
- 1,640–3,280ft
- 820–1,640ft
- 330–820ft
- 0–330ft
- Below sea level

SEA DEPTH
- 0–160ft
- 160–330ft
- 330–820ft
- 820–1,640ft
- 1,640–3,280ft
- 3,280–6,560ft
- Below 6,560ft

SOUTHWEST ASIA

BAHRAIN, IRAN, IRAQ, ISRAEL, JORDAN, KUWAIT, LEBANON, OMAN, QATAR, SAUDI ARABIA, SYRIA, UNITED ARAB EMIRATES, YEMEN

Most of southwest Asia is barren desert, yet the world's first cities originated here over 5,000 years ago. It was the birthplace of three major religions: Islam, Judaism, and Christianity. In recent years, the discovery of oil has brought great wealth to much of the region, but it has also been torn by internal conflicts and wars between neighboring countries. Most people here are Muslims, although Israel is the world's only Jewish state.

INDUSTRY

Oil has made the previously poor Arab states very wealthy. It and natural gas continue to be the main sources of income for many of the countries here. Other industries are being developed to support the region's economies when these resources run out. Iran is famous for its carpets, which are woven from wool or silk.

INDUSTRY

- ⚙ Cement manufacturing
- 🥫 Food processing
- 🚂 Iron and steel
- 🛢 Oil refining
- 👕 Textiles
- ⬧ Oil and gas
- Ⓢ Finance
- ▪ Major industrial center / area
- — Major road

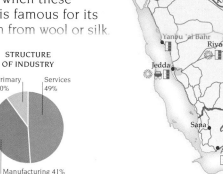

STRUCTURE OF INDUSTRY

- Primary 10%
- Services 49%
- Manufacturing 41%

FARMING AND LAND USE

The best farmland is found along the Mediterranean coast and in the fertile valleys of the Tigris, Euphrates and Jordan Rivers. Wheat is the main cereal crop, and cotton, dates, and citrus and orchard fruits are grown for export. Elsewhere, modern irrigation techniques have created patches of fertile land in the desert. Dates, wheat, and coffee are cultivated in the oases and along the Persian Gulf coast.

LAND USE

- Forest 2%
- Pasture 45%
- Other (including desert) 47%
- Cropland 6%

FARMING AND LAND USE

- 🐐 Goats
- 🎣 Fishing
- 🐑 Sheep
- 🍊 Citrus fruits
- ☕ Coffee
- 🌿 Cotton
- 🌴 Dates
- 🍎 Fruit
- 🌱 Tobacco
- 🌾 Wheat
- Cropland
- Desert
- Forest
- Pasture
- Wetland
- ● Major conurbation

ENVIRONMENTAL ISSUES

Water shortages are common because of the hot, dry climate and the lack of rivers. Desalination plants convert seawater into freshwater, and are found along the Red Sea and Gulf coasts. Lack of water also makes the risk of desertification greater. Iran has had many catastrophic earthquakes; in 2003 an earthquake in Bam killed 26,000 people.

ENVIRONMENTAL ISSUES

- 🚰 Area with many desalination plants
- ◎ Catastrophic earthquake
- 👹 Urban air pollution
- Existing desert
- Risk of desertification
- Sea pollution
- ● Major industrial center

THE LANDSCAPE

Great desert plateaus, both sandy and rocky, cover much of southwest Asia. On the enormous Arabian Peninsula, which covers an area almost the size of India, narrow, sandy plains along the Red Sea and south coast rise to dry mountains. In the center is a vast, high plateau that slopes gently down to the flat shores of the Persian Gulf. The mountainous areas of Iran experience frequent earthquakes.

Wadis

Valleys or riverbeds, called *wadis*, are found in the Saudi Arabian desert. They are usually dry, but after heavy rains, they are briefly filled by fast flowing rivers.

Syrian Desert (B 2)

The Syrian Desert extends from the Jordan valley in the west to the fertile plains of the Tigris and Euphrates Rivers in the east. It is mainly a rocky desert, because the sand has been swept away by winds and occasional heavy rainstorms.

Oases

Oases are areas within a desert where water is available for plants and human use. They are usually formed when a fault, or split, in the rock allows water to come to the surface. Oases can be no bigger than a few palm trees or cover several hundred sq miles.

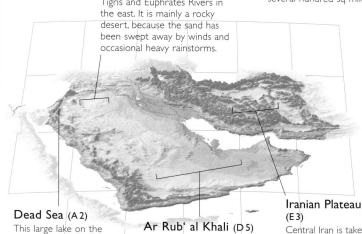

Dead Sea (A 2)

This large lake on the border between Israel and Jordan is the lowest point on the Earth's surface – its shores lie 1,286 ft below sea level. It is also the world's saltiest body of water, and cannot sustain any life.

Ar Rub' al Khali (D 5)

The Ar Rub' al Khali desert, also known as the "Empty Quarter," is the largest uninterrupted stretch of sand on Earth. It covers some 250,000 sq miles and is one of the world's driest and most hostile deserts.

Iranian Plateau (E 3)

Central Iran is taken up by a vast, semiarid plateau, that rises steeply from the coastal lowlands bordering the Persian Gulf. It is ringed by the high Zagros and Elburz mountains.

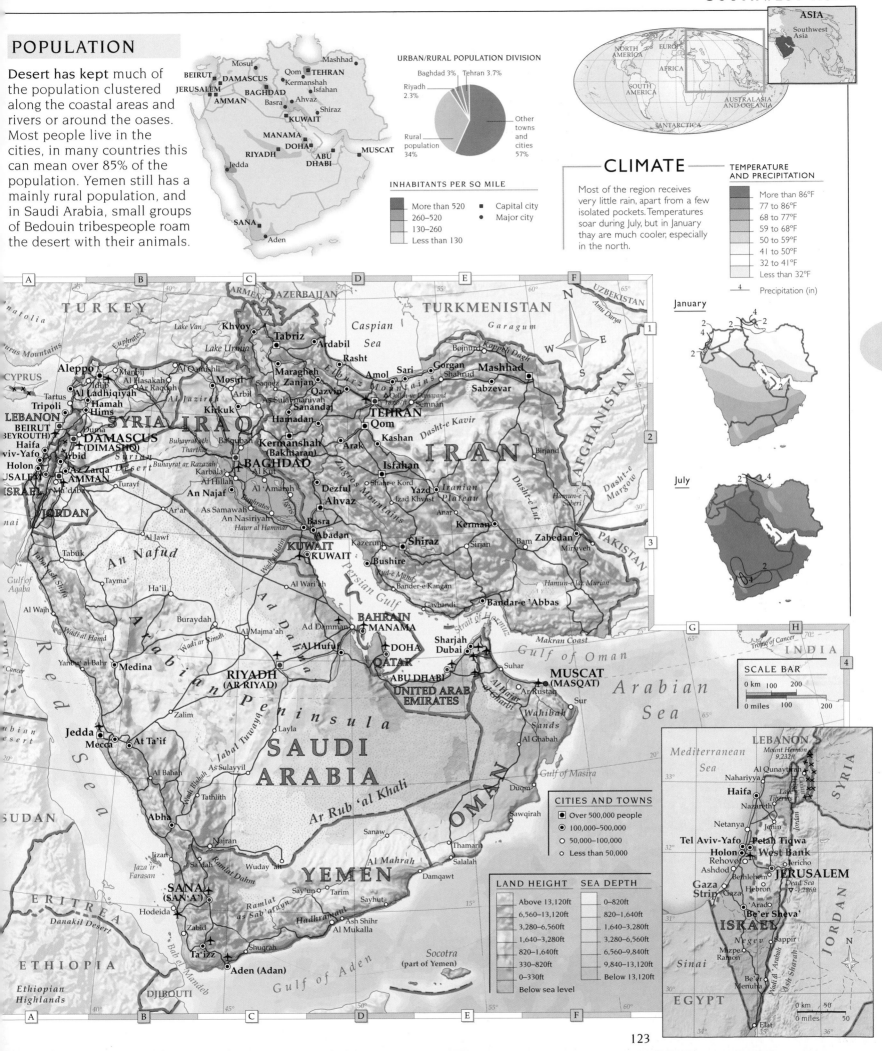

POPULATION

Desert has kept much of the population clustered along the coastal areas and rivers or around the oases. Most people live in the cities, in many countries this can mean over 85% of the population. Yemen still has a mainly rural population, and in Saudi Arabia, small groups of Bedouin tribespeople roam the desert with their animals.

URBAN/RURAL POPULATION DIVISION

Baghdad 3% Tehran 3.7%
Riyadh 2.3%
Rural population 34%
Other towns and cities 57%

INHABITANTS PER SQ MILE

More than 520
260–520
130–260
Less than 130

■ Capital city
● Major city

ASIA
Southwest Asia

NORTH AMERICA EUROPE ASIA
AFRICA
SOUTH AMERICA AUSTRALASIA AND OCEANIA
ANTARCTICA

CLIMATE

Most of the region receives very little rain, apart from a few isolated pockets. Temperatures soar during July, but in January thay are much cooler, especially in the north.

TEMPERATURE AND PRECIPITATION

More than 86°F
77 to 86°F
68 to 77°F
59 to 68°F
50 to 59°F
41 to 50°F
32 to 41°F
Less than 32°F

4 — Precipitation (in)

January

July

CITIES AND TOWNS

■ Over 500,000 people
◉ 100,000–500,000
◎ 50,000–100,000
○ Less than 50,000

LAND HEIGHT

Above 13,120ft
6,560–13,120ft
3,280–6,560ft
1,640–3,280ft
820–1,640ft
330–820ft
0–330ft
Below sea level

SEA DEPTH

0–820ft
820–1,640ft
1,640–3,280ft
3,280–6,560ft
6,560–9,840ft
9,840–13,120ft
Below 13,120ft

SCALE BAR

0 km 100 200
0 miles 100 200

Central Asia

AFGHANISTAN, KYRGYZSTAN, TAJIKISTAN, TURKMENISTAN, UZBEKISTAN

Central Asia is a land of hot, dry deserts and high, rugged mountains. It lies on the ancient Silk Road, an important trade route between China and Europe for over 400 years, until the 15th century. All of the countries here, except for Afghanistan, were part of the Soviet Union from the 1920s until 1991, when they gained independence. Since then, their people have reestablished their local languages and Islamic faith, which were restricted under Russian rule.

INDUSTRY

Fossil fuels, especially coal, natural gas, and oil, are extracted and processed throughout Central Asia. Agriculture supplies the raw materials for many industries, including food and textile processing, and the manufacture of leather goods and clothing. The region is famous for its colorful traditional carpets, hand-woven from the wool of the Karakul sheep. The Fergana Valley, southeast of Tashkent, is the main industrial area.

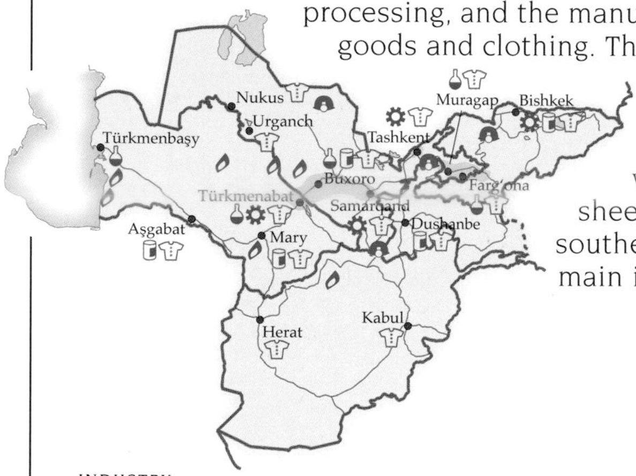

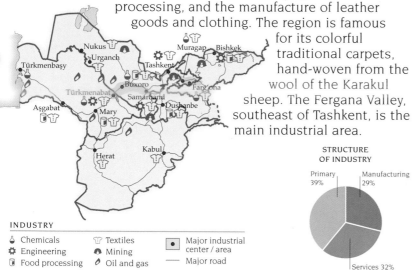

Nukus
Urganch
Türkmenbaşy
Muragap
Bishkek
Tashkent
Buxoro
Farg'ona
Türkmenabat
Samarqand
Dushanbe
Aşgabat
Mary
Kabul
Herat
INDUSTRY
Chemicals
Engineering
Food processing
Textiles
Mining
Oil and gas
Major industrial center / area
Major road

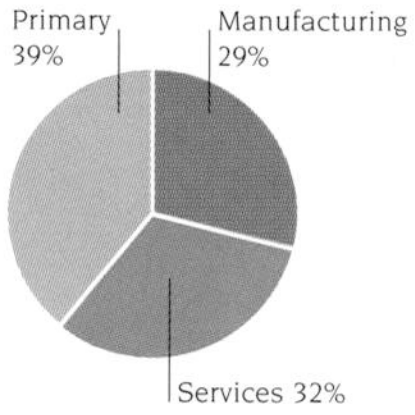

STRUCTURE OF INDUSTRY
Primary 39%
Manufacturing 29%
Services 32%

POPULATION

The peoples of Central Asia are mostly rural farmers, living in the river valleys and in oases. There are few large cities. A few still lead a traditional nomadic lifestyle, moving from place to place with their animals in search of new pastures. Large areas of Afghanistan, the western deserts, and the mountain regions in the east, are virtually uninhabited.

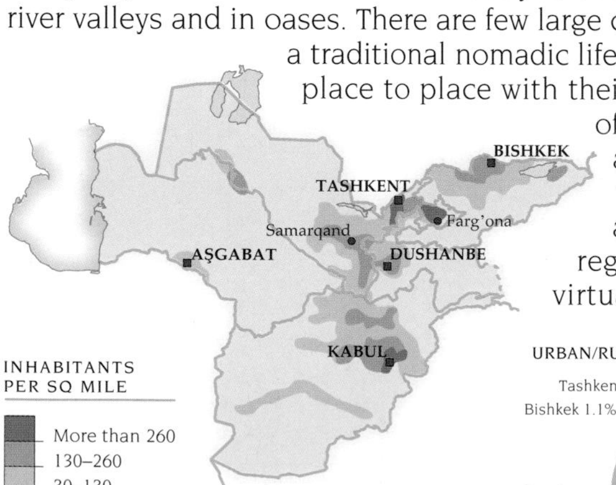

BISHKEK
TASHKENT
Farg'ona
Samarqand
AŞGABAT
DUSHANBE
KABUL
INHABITANTS PER SQ MILE
More than 260
130–260
30–130
Less than 30
Capital city
Major city

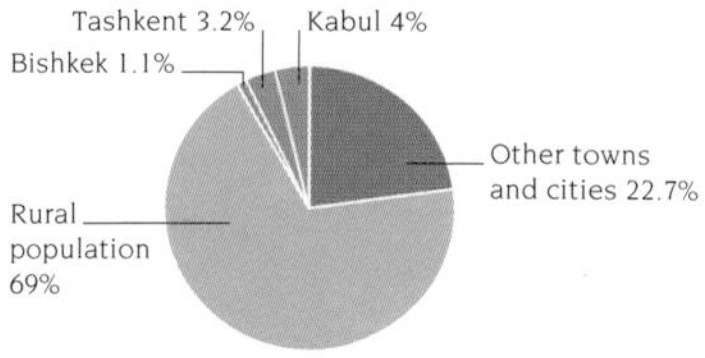

URBAN/RURAL POPULATION DIVISION
Tashkent 3.2%
Kabul 4%
Bishkek 1.1%
Other towns and cities 22.7%
Rural population 69%

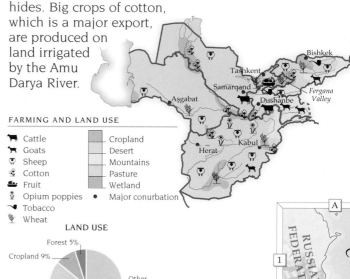

FARMING AND LAND USE

Farming is concentrated around the fertile river valleys in the east, like the Fergana Valley. A variety of cereals and fruits – including peaches, melons, and apricots – are grown. In drier areas, animal breeding is important, with goats, sheep, and cattle supplying wool, meat, and hides. Big crops of cotton, which is a major export, are produced on land irrigated by the Amu Darya River.

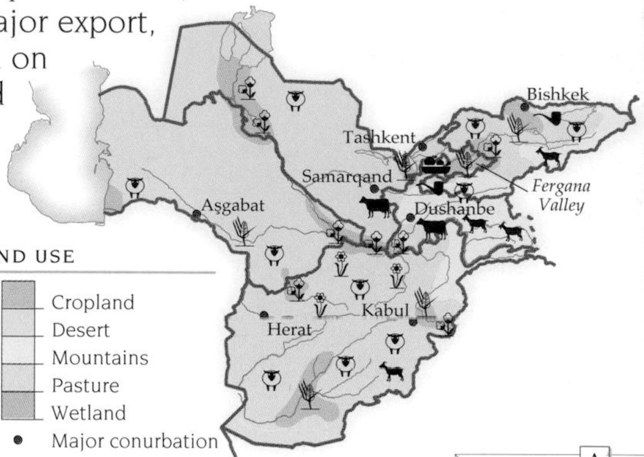

Bishkek
Tashkent
Samarqand
Fergana Valley
Aşgabat
Dushanbe
Herat
Kabul
FARMING AND LAND USE
Cattle
Goats
Sheep
Cotton
Fruit
Opium poppies
Tobacco
Wheat
Cropland
Desert
Mountains
Pasture
Wetland
Major conurbation

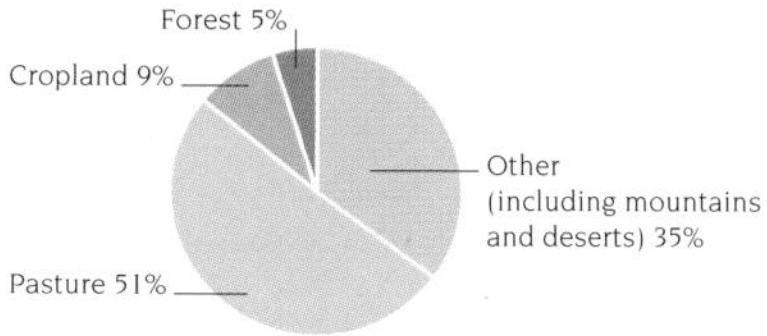

LAND USE
Forest 5%
Cropland 9%
Other (including mountains and deserts) 35%
Pasture 51%

THE LANDSCAPE

Two of the world's great deserts, the Kara Kum and the Kyzyl Kum, cover much of the western portion of Central Asia. In the east, a belt of high mountain ranges – the Hindu Kush, the Tien Shan, and the Pamirs – tower above the land. Few rivers cross the deserts, apart from the Amu Darya, which flows from the Pamirs to the shrinking Aral Sea.

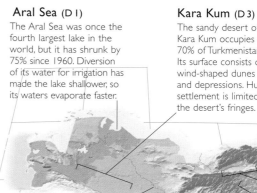

Aral Sea (D 1)
The Aral Sea was once the fourth largest lake in the world, but it has shrunk by 75% since 1960. Diversion of its water for irrigation has made the lake shallower, so its waters evaporate faster.

Kara Kum (D 3)
The sandy desert of the Kara Kum occupies over 70% of Turkmenistan. Its surface consists of wind-shaped dunes and depressions. Human settlement is limited to the desert's fringes.

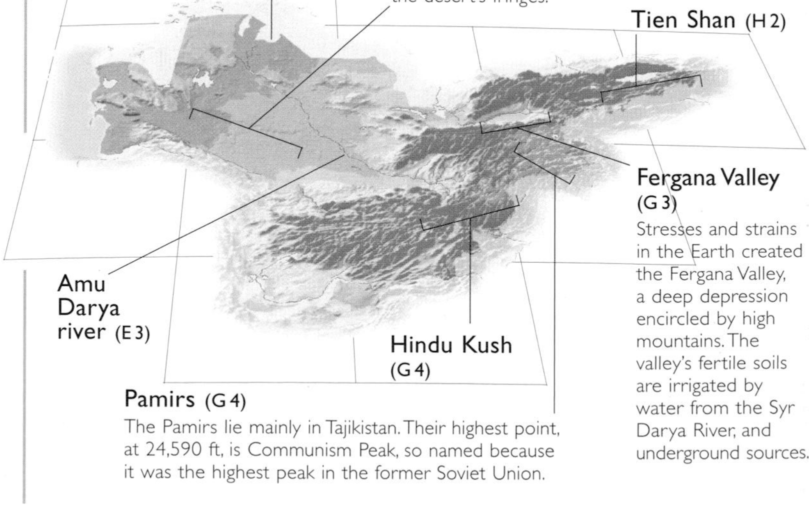

Tien Shan (H 2)

Fergana Valley (G 3)
Stresses and strains in the Earth created the Fergana Valley, a deep depression encircled by high mountains. The valley's fertile soils are irrigated by water from the Syr Darya River, and underground sources.

Amu Darya river (E 3)

Hindu Kush (G 4)

Pamirs (G 4)
The Pamirs lie mainly in Tajikistan. Their highest point, at 24,590 ft, is Communism Peak, so named because it was the highest peak in the former Soviet Union.

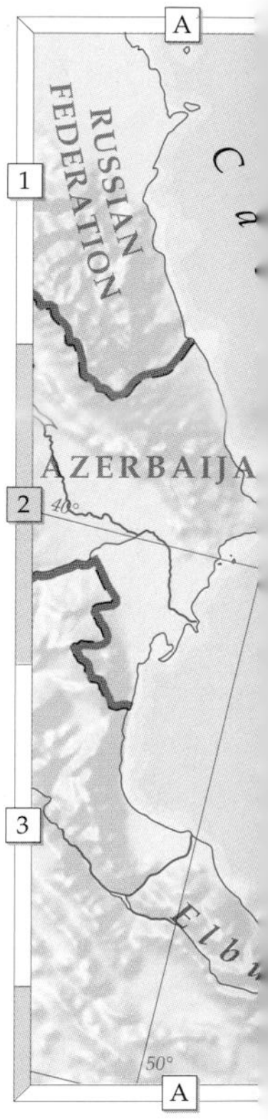

RUSSIAN FEDERATION
AZERBAIJA
A
1
2
3

Name_____ Class_____

LATITUDE/LONGITUDE EXERCISE ON INNER ASIA

Use your student atlas to help you find these **PHYSICAL FEATURES**.

#	CLUES	COORDINATES	ANSWERS
1	SEA	40°N 50°E	Caspian Sea
2	DESERT	40°N 57°E	Kara Kum
3	RIVER	42°N 60°E	Amu Darya
4	UPLANDS	48°N 76°E	

#	CLUES	COORDINATES	ANSWERS
5	RAINFALL (annual)	40°N 60°E	0-250 (mm.)
6	LAKE	52°N 105°E	Baikal
7	GROWING SEASON	40°N 60°E	months
8	MOUNTAINS	64°N 59°E	Urals

#	CLUES	COORDINATES	ANSWERS
9	GRASSLAND	51°N 50°E	
10	LOWLANDS	43°N 60°E	
11	SEA	45°N 60°E	Aral Sea
12	LAND USE	50°N 60°E	

#	CLUES	COORDINATES	ANSWERS
13	PLAIN	62°N 78°E	
14	VEGETATION (nat.)	60°N 80°E	
15	RIVER	63°N 66°E	Ob River
16	LAKE	47°N 75°E	Balqash

#	CLUES	COORDINATES	ANSWERS
17	VEGETATION (nat.)	40°N 60°E	
18	DEPRESSION	48°N 50°E	Caspian Depression
19	LAND USE	62°N 62°E	
20	MOUNTAINS	42°N 80°E	

GRADING AT 5 % PER ANSWER = %

ENVIRONMENTAL ISSUES

The Aral Sea is rapidly drying up, because the rivers feeding it are being diverted to irrigate cottonfields. Central Asia is a very dry area, and desertification is a constant threat, especially in Afghanistan. Severe urban and industrial air pollution is a legacy from the communist era, when heavy industries were established in the countries here.

ENVIRONMENTAL ISSUES

- Urban air pollution
- Existing desert
- Risk of desertification
- Severe risk of desertification
- Polluted river
- Sea pollution
- Major industrial center

Aral Sea
Amu Darya
Bishkek
Dushanbe
Fergana Valley

CLIMATE

Central Asia's climate is strongly inflenced by its position deep within Asia, far from the moderating effects of the oceans. Winters are cold, summers are very hot everywhere. Rainfall is virtually nonexistent all year round.

ASIA
Central Asia

NORTH AMERICA
EUROPE
ASIA
AFRICA
SOUTH AMERICA
AUSTRALASIA AND OCEANIA
ANTARCTICA

January
Less than 2in precipitation

July
Less than 2in precipitation

TEMPERATURE AND PRECIPITATION

- More than 86°F
- 77 to 86°F
- 41 to 50°F
- 32 to 41°F
- Less than 32°F

LAND HEIGHT
- Above 13,120ft
- 6,560–3,120ft
- 3,280–6,560ft
- 1,640–3,280ft
- 820–1,640ft
- 330–820ft
- 0–330ft
- Below sea level

SEA DEPTH
- 0–30ft
- 30–80ft
- 80–160ft
- 160–330ft
- 330–820ft

CITIES AND TOWNS
- Over 500,000 people
- 100,000–500,000
- 50,000–100,000
- Less than 50,000

SCALE BAR
0 km 100 200
0 miles 100 200

KAZAKHSTAN
Lake Balkhash
Ili
Peski Moyynkum
Khrebet Karatau
Sur Darya

Ustyurt Plateau
Aral Sea
Turan Lowland
Mo'ynoq
Chimboy
Taxtako'pir
Qo'ng'irot
Köneürgenç
Nukus
Taxiatosh
Gubadag
Gurbansoltan Eje
Urganch
Daşoguz
Xiva
Gazojak
Lebap
To'rtko'l
Zarafshon
Uchquduq
Kyzyl Kum
UZBEKISTAN

BISHKEK
Kara-Balta
Klyuchevka
Gora Manas 14,705ft
Talas
Tokmak
Kemin
Balykchy
Ozero Issyk-Kul'
Tyup
Dzhergalan
Karakol
Okyzyl-Suu
Kadzhi-Say
Kara-Say
Pik Pobedy 24,419ft
KYRGYZSTAN
Naryn
Chatyr-Tash
Kek-Art
Nordan
Daroot-Korgon
Qarokul

TASHKENT (TOSHKENT)
Chirchiq
Angren
Yangiyo'l
Olmaliq
Namangan
Andijon
Osh
Qo'qon
Fergona
Khujand
Farg'ona
Sulyukta
Khaydarkan

TURKMENISTAN
Türkmenbaşy
Balkanabat
Hazar
Türkmen Aylagy
Bereket
Garagum
Köpetdag Gerşi
Magtymguly
Gora Chapan 9,479ft
ASGABAT
Gökdepe
Abadan
Serdar
Baharly
Kaka
Tejen
Mary
Bayramaly
Murgap
Sarahs
Garagum Canal
Atamyrat
Zeydskoye Vodokhranilishche
Amyderya
Seýdi
Galkynyş
Türkmenabat
Sayat
Kogon

Nurota
Langar
Ayderko'l Ko'li
G'ijduvon
Gazli
Buxoro
Navoiy
Guliston
Jizzax
Bekobod
Oqtosh
Koson
Qarshi
Kattaqo'rg'on
Samarqand
Urgut
Uroteppa
Zeravshan
Kitob

DUSHANBE
TAJIKISTAN
Denov
Boyson
Qurghonteppa
Jarqo'rg'on
Termiz
Dusti
Aqchah
Balkh
Kholm
Mazar-e Sharif
Sheberghan
Kondoz
Talqon
Eshkamesh
Baghlan
Pol-e Khomri
Norak
Danghara
Kulob
Moskva
Parkhar
Khorugh
Ishkoshim
Qalaikhum
Chudara
Dzhelandy
Murghob
Qizilrabot
Barang
Pamir
Sarhad
Communism Peak 24,591ft
Gissar Range
Surkhob
Baroghil Pass 12,392ft

Takla Makan Desert
CHINA

IRAN
Mountains

Garabil Belentligi
Serhetabat
Towraghoudi
Bala Morghab
Meymaneh
Daryā-ye Morghāb
Qal'eh-ye Now
Herat
Ghurian
Shindand
Anar Darreh
Farah
Delaram
Kuh-e Sangan
Shahrak
Chaghcharan
Daryā-ye Āndarāb
Chārikār
Maydan Shahr
Ghazni
Uruzgan
Baghran
Zarghun Shahr
Khowst
Gardiz

KABUL (KABOL)
Mehtar Lām
Mahmud-e Raqi
Asmar
Barikowt
Asadabad
Jalalabad
Salang Tunnel
Hindu Kush
Khyber Pass 3,544ft
Kashmir

AFGHANISTAN
Farah Rud
Dasht-e Khash
Hamun-e Saberi
Zaranj
Chakhansur
Dasht-e Margow
Lashkar Gah
Gereshk
Darvishan
Kuchnay Darweyshan
Deh Shu
Daryā-ye Helmand
Rigestan
Chagai Hills
Kandahar
Spin Buldak
Qalat
Toba Kakar Range
Daryā-ye Arghandāb

PAKISTAN
Sulaiman Range
Indus

Aksai Chin (administered by China, claimed by India)
Demchok/ Demqog (administered by China, claimed by India)
(claimed by India)
(A 'line of control' was agreed between India and Pakistan in 1972)
Karakoram Range
Himalayas
INDIA
Ravi
Ganges

SOUTH ASIA

BANGLADESH, BHUTAN, INDIA, NEPAL, PAKISTAN, SRI LANKA

South Asia is a land of many contrasts. Its landscape ranges from the mighty peaks of the Himalayas in the north through vast plains and arid deserts, to tropical forests and palm-fringed beaches in the south. More than one-fifth of the world's people live here, and a long history of foreign invasions has left a mosaic of vastly different cultures, religions, and traditions and thousands of languages and dialects.

INDUSTRY

Industry has expanded in India in recent years. In the cities a variety of goods are produced and processed, including cars, airplanes, chemicals, food, and drink. Service industries such as tourism and banking are also growing. Elsewhere, small-scale cottage industries serve the needs of local people, but many products, mainly silk and cotton textiles, clothing, leather, and jewelry, are also exported.

STRUCTURE OF INDUSTRY

Primary 23%
Services 49%
Manufacturing 28%

INDUSTRY

- ✈ Aerospace
- 🚗 Car manufacture
- ⚗ Chemicals
- Electronics
- ⚙ Engineering
- Food processing
- Iron and steel
- 👕 Textiles
- ⛏ Mining
- Ⓢ Finance
- Tourism
- ▣ Major industrial center / area
- — Major road

POPULATION

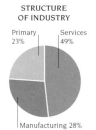

Most of South Asia's people live in villages scattered across the fertile river floodplains, in mountain valleys, or along the coasts, but increasing numbers are migrating to the cities in search of work. Overcrowding is a serious problem in both rural and urban areas; in many cities, thousands of people are forced to live in slums or on the streets.

INHABITANTS PER SQ MILE

- More than 520
- 260–520
- 130–260
- Less than 130
- ■ Capital city
- • Major city

URBAN/RURAL POPULATION DIVISION

Calcutta 1%
Delhi 0.8%
Mumbai 1.2%
Other towns and cities 23%
Rural population 74%

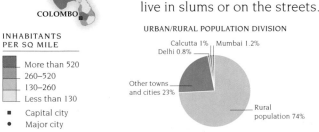

FARMING AND LAND USE

Over 60% of the population is involved in agriculture, but most farms are small and produce only enough food to feed one family. Grains are the staple food crops – rice in the wetter parts of the east and west, corn, and millet on the Deccan plateau, and wheat in the north. Groundnuts are widely grown as a source of cooking oil. Cash crops include tea, which is grown on plantations, and jute.

FARMING AND LAND USE

- 🐄 Cattle
- 🐟 Fishing
- 🐐 Goats
- Cereals
- Groundnuts
- Jute
- Rice
- Tea
- Cropland
- Desert
- Forest
- Pasture
- Wetland
- • Major conurbation

LAND USE

Pasture 5%
Forest 21%
Cropland 50%
Other 24%

THE LANDSCAPE

A massive, towering wall of snow-capped mountains stretches in an arc across the north, isolating South Asia from the rest of the continent. The huge floodplains and deltas of the Indus, Ganges, and Brahmaputra Rivers separate the mountains from the rest of the peninsula: a great rolling plateau, bordered on either side by coastal hills called the Eastern and Western Ghats.

Himalayas (E 2)
The Himalayas are the highest mountain system in the world. They were formed about 40 million years ago when two of the Earth's plates collided, thrusting up huge masses of land.

Mount Everest (F 3)
The northern ranges of the Himalayas average 23,000 ft in height. They include the highest point on Earth, Mount Everest on the Nepal–China border, which soars to 29,035 ft.

Thar Desert (C 3)
The border between India and Pakistan runs through the arid, sandy Thar Desert.

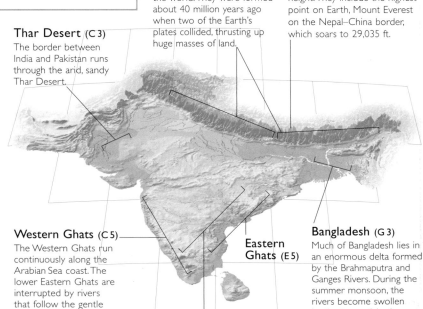

Western Ghats (C 5)
The Western Ghats run continuously along the Arabian Sea coast. The lower Eastern Ghats are interrupted by rivers that follow the gentle slope of the Deccan plateau and flow across broad lowlands into the Bay of Bengal. This is one of the wettest regions in the world.

Eastern Ghats (E 5)

Deccan plateau (D 5)
This giant plateau makes up most of central and southern India. Its volcanic rock has been deeply cut by rivers such as the Krishna, creating stepped valleys called *traps*.

Bangladesh (G 3)
Much of Bangladesh lies in an enormous delta formed by the Brahmaputra and Ganges Rivers. During the summer monsoon, the rivers become swollen by the torrential rains – and meltwater from the Himalayas – and the delta floods. Over the years, millions of people have drowned or been made homeless by heavy flooding.

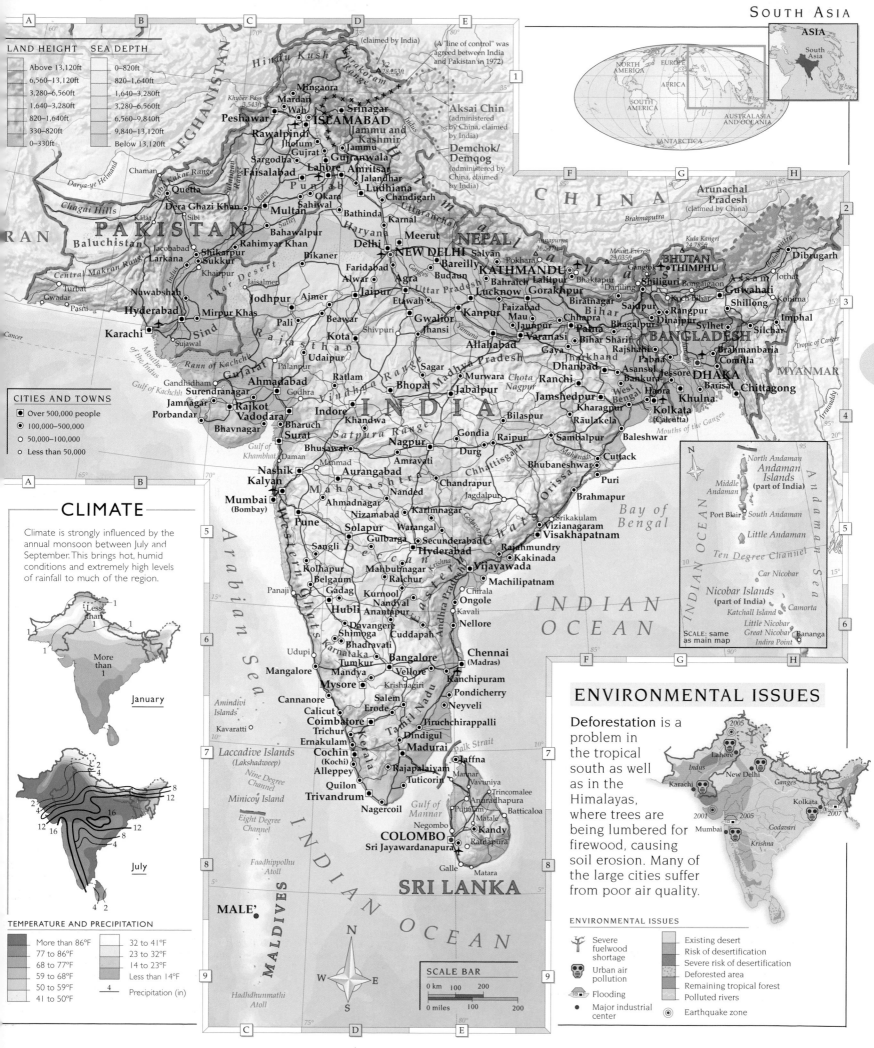

LAND HEIGHT
- Above 13,120ft
- 6,560–13,120ft
- 3,280–6,560ft
- 1,640–3,280ft
- 820–1,640ft
- 330–820ft
- 0–330ft

SEA DEPTH
- 0–820ft
- 820–1,640ft
- 1,640–3,280ft
- 3,280–6,560ft
- 6,560–9,840ft
- 9,840–13,120ft
- Below 13,120ft

ASIA
South Asia

NORTH AMERICA
EUROPE
ASIA
AFRICA
SOUTH AMERICA
AUSTRALASIA AND OCEANIA
ANTARCTICA

AFGHANISTAN

Hindu Kush
Karakoram Range
(claimed by India)
△ 28,253ft

A "line of control" was agreed between India and Pakistan in 1972

Khyber Pass 3,543ft
Mingaora
Mardan
Wah
Peshawar
Srinagar
ISLAMABAD
Rawalpindi
Jammu and Kashmir
Jhelum
Jammu
Gujrat
Gujranwala
Sargodha
Faisalabad
Lahore
Amritsar
Jalandhar
Ludhiana
Chandigarh

Aksai Chin (administered by China, claimed by India)
Demchok/Demqog (administered by China, claimed by India)

CHINA

Arunachal Pradesh (claimed by China)

Chaman
Kalat
Quetta
Kakar Range
Sibi
Dera Ghazi Khan
Multan
Okara
Sahiwal
Bathinda
Karnal
Meerut
NEW DELHI
Delhi
Bareilly
Bahawalpur
Haryana
Uttaranchal
Salyan
Pokhara
NEPAL
KATHMANDU
Bhaktapur
Lalitpur
Annapurna
Mount Everest 29,035ft
Gangtok
Darjiling
Shiliguri
BHUTAN
THIMPHU
Kula Kangri 24,785ft
Koch Bihar
Dibrugarh
Jorhat

Baluchistan
Central Makran Range
Chagai Hills
Rahimyar Khan
Bikaner
Faridabad
Alwar
Agra
Budaun
Bahraich
Lucknow
Gorakhpur
Biratnagar
Rangpur
Dinajpur
Sajdpur
Bongaigaon
Guwahati
Shillong
Kohima

IRAN
Turbat
Gwadar
Pasni
Jacobabad
Shikarpur
Larkana
Sukkur
Khairpur
Nawabshah
Hyderabad
Mirpur Khas
Karachi

Ludhiana
Sind
Thar Desert
Jaisalmer
Jodhpur
Ajmer
Jaipur
Etawah
Kanpur
Faizabad
Mau
Jaunpur
Chhapra
Patna
Bhagalpur
Bihar Sharif
Rajshahi
Pabna
Brahmanbaria
Comilla
Silchar
Imphal

Rajasthan
Pali
Beawar
Shivpuri
Jhansi
Gwalior
Allahabad
Varanasi
Gaya
Jharkhand
Dhanbad
Asansol
Bankura
Jessore
DHAKA
Barisal
Chittagong

MYANMAR

Mouths of the Indus
Udaipur
Kota
Ratlam
Sagar
Murwara
Chota Nagpur
Ranchi
Jamshedpur
West Bengal
Haora
Kolkata (Calcutta)
Khulna

Gandhidham
Surendranagar
Gujarat
Ahmadabad
Godhra
Bhopal
Madhya Pradesh
Jabalpur
Bilaspur
Raulakela
Kharagpur
Baleshwar

Jamnagar
Porbandar
Rajkot
Vadodara
Indore
Khandwa
Vindhya Range
Nagpur
Durg
Raipur
Chhattisgarh
Sambalpur
Mouths of the Ganges

Bhavnagar
Bharuch
Surat
Daman
Gulf of Khambhat
Satpura Range
Bhusawal
Amravati
Gondia
Bhubaneswar
Cuttack
Puri

Nashik
Kalyan
Mumbai (Bombay)
Aurangabad
Nanded
Chandrapur
Jagdalpur
Orissa
Brahmapur

Bay of Bengal

Pune
Ahmadnagar
Nizamabad
Karimnagar
Warangal
Srikakulam
Vizianagaram
Visakhapatnam

Solapur
Gulbarga
Secunderabad
Hyderabad
Rajahmundry
Kakinada

Sangli
Kolhapur
Mahbubnagar
Raichur
Krishna
Vijayawada
Machilipatnam

Belgaum
Gadag
Kurnool
Nandyal
Eastern Ghats
Andhra Pradesh
Chirala
Ongole
Kavali
Nellore

Panaji
Hubli
Anantapur
Deccan

Davangere
Shimoga
Cuddapah
Udupi
Bhadravati
Karnataka
Bangalore
Vellore
Chennai (Madras)
Kanchipuram

Mangalore
Tumkur
Mandya
Krishnagiri
Pondicherry

Cannanore
Mysore
Salem
Neyveli
Erode

Calicut
Coimbatore
Tiruchchirappalli
Tamil Nadu

Trichur
Dindigul
Ernakulam
Cochin (Kochi)
Madurai
Jaffna

Rajapalaiyam
Alleppey
Quilon
Tuticorin
Mannar
Vavuniya
Trincomalee

Trivandrum
Kerala
Nagercoil
Gulf of Mannar
Anuradhapura
Puttalam
Batticaloa

Negombo
Matale
Kandy

COLOMBO
Sri Jayawardanapura
Ratnapura

SRI LANKA

Galle
Matara

MALE'

MALDIVES

INDIAN OCEAN

Arabian Sea
Amindivi Islands
Kavaratti
Laccadive Islands (Lakshadweep)
Nine Degree Channel
Minicoy Island
Eight Degree Channel
Faadhippolhu Atoll
Hadhdhunmathi Atoll

Andaman Islands (part of India)
North Andaman
Middle Andaman
Port Blair
South Andaman
Little Andaman
Ten Degree Channel
Car Nicobar
Nicobar Islands (part of India)
Katchall Island
Little Nicobar
Great Nicobar
Bananga
Indira Point
Camorta

INDIAN OCEAN
Andaman Sea

SCALE: same as main map

CITIES AND TOWNS
- Over 500,000 people
- 100,000–500,000
- 50,000–100,000
- Less than 50,000

CLIMATE
Climate is strongly influenced by the annual monsoon between July and September. This brings hot, humid conditions and extremely high levels of rainfall to much of the region.

Less than 1
More than 1

January

July

TEMPERATURE AND PRECIPITATION
- More than 86°F
- 77 to 86°F
- 68 to 77°F
- 59 to 68°F
- 50 to 59°F
- 41 to 50°F
- 32 to 41°F
- 23 to 32°F
- 14 to 23°F
- Less than 14°F
- 4 — Precipitation (in)

ENVIRONMENTAL ISSUES
Deforestation is a problem in the tropical south as well as in the Himalayas, where trees are being lumbered for firewood, causing soil erosion. Many of the large cities suffer from poor air quality.

Lahore
Karachi
New Delhi
Mumbai
Kolkata
Indus
Ganges
Godavari
Krishna
2005
2001
2005
2007

ENVIRONMENTAL ISSUES
- Severe fuelwood shortage
- Urban air pollution
- Flooding
- Major industrial center
- Existing desert
- Risk of desertification
- Severe risk of desertification
- Deforested area
- Remaining tropical forest
- Polluted rivers
- Earthquake zone

SCALE BAR
0 km 100 200
0 miles 100 200

EAST ASIA

CHINA, MONGOLIA, TAIWAN

China is the world's fourth-largest country and its most populous – over one billion people live there. Under its communist government, which came to power in 1949, China has become a major industrial nation, but most of its people still live and work on the land as they have for thousands of years. Taiwan also has a booming economy and exports its products around the world. Mongolia is a vast, remote country with a small population, many of whom are nomads.

INDUSTRY

Chemicals, iron and steel, engineering, and textiles are the main industries in China's east coast cities, and in industrial centers like Shenyang. Shanghai, Hong Kong, and Beijing are also important financial centers. In the interior, large deposits of coal support the heavy industries in major cities such as Chengdu and Wuhan. Taiwan specializes in textiles and shoe manufacture, along with electronic goods. Mongolia's economy is mainly agricultural.

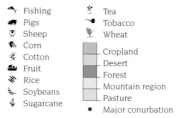

INDUSTRY

🚗	Car manufacture	👕 Textiles
🧪	Chemicals	⛏ Coal
🔌	Electronics	🔨 Mining
💻	Electronic goods	$ Finance
⚙	Engineering	
🥫	Food processing	⊡ Major industrial center / area
🚂	Iron & steel	— Major road
🛳	Shipbuilding	

STRUCTURE OF INDUSTRY

Services 37%
Manufacturing 50%
Primary 13%

POPULATION

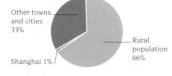

Most of China's people live in the eastern part of the country, where the climate, landscape and soils are most favorable. Urban areas there house more than 250 million people, but almost 70% of the population lives in villages and farms the land. Taiwan's lowlands are very densely populated. In Mongolia, one third of the people live in the countryside.

URBAN/RURAL POPULATION DIVISION

Other towns and cities 33%
Rural population 66%
Shanghai 1%

INHABITANTS PER SQ MILE

- More than 520
- 260–520
- 130–260
- Less than 130
- ■ Capital city
- ● Major city

FARMING AND LAND USE

Despite its size, about 90% of China is unsuitable for farming. Either the soils and climate are poor, or the landscape is too mountainous. In the north and west, most farmers make their living by herding animals. On the fertile eastern plains, soybeans, wheat, corn, and cotton are grown. Farther south, rice becomes the main crop, and pigs are raised in large numbers.

FARMING AND LAND USE

Fishing	🍵 Tea	
Pigs	🚬 Tobacco	
Sheep	🌾 Wheat	
Corn		Cropland
Cotton		Desert
Fruit		Forest
Rice		Mountain region
Soybeans		Pasture
Sugarcane	● Major conurbation	

LAND USE

Cropland 14%
Pasture 49%
Other (including mountains) 21%
Forest 16%

THE LANDSCAPE

China's landscape is divided into three areas. The vast Plateau of Tibet in the southwest is the highest and largest plateau on Earth. It contains both dry deserts and pockets of pasture surrounded by high mountains. Northwest China has dry highlands. The great plains of eastern China were formed from soils deposited by rivers like the Yellow River over thousands of years. Most of Mongolia is dry, grassland steppe and cold, arid desert.

Tien Shan mountains (B 2)

The Tien Shan, or "Heavenly Mountains" reach heights of 24,419 ft. They surround fields of permanent ice and spectacular glaciers.

Gobi (E 2) and Takla Makan (B 3) deserts

The arid landscapes of the Gobi and Takla Makan deserts are made up of bare rock surfaces and huge areas of shifting sand dunes. They are hot in summer, but unlike most other deserts, are extremely cold in winter.

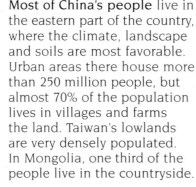

Takla Makan Desert

"The Roof of the World"

The cold, remote Plateau of Tibet averages 13,000 ft in height. Many of China's great rivers have their sources here. The world's highest human settlement, a town called Wenquan, is found in the east of the plateau. It lies 16,729 ft above sea level.

The Yellow River (E 3)

The Yellow River (Huang He) is the world's muddiest river, carrying hundreds of truckloads of sediment to the sea every minute. The river has burst its banks many times throughout history, causing enormous damage and claiming millions of human lives.

A handmade landscape

In the farming areas of eastern and southern China, terraces have been carved into the hillsides to make them flat enough to grow rice and other crops. This method of farming has been used for over 7,000 years.

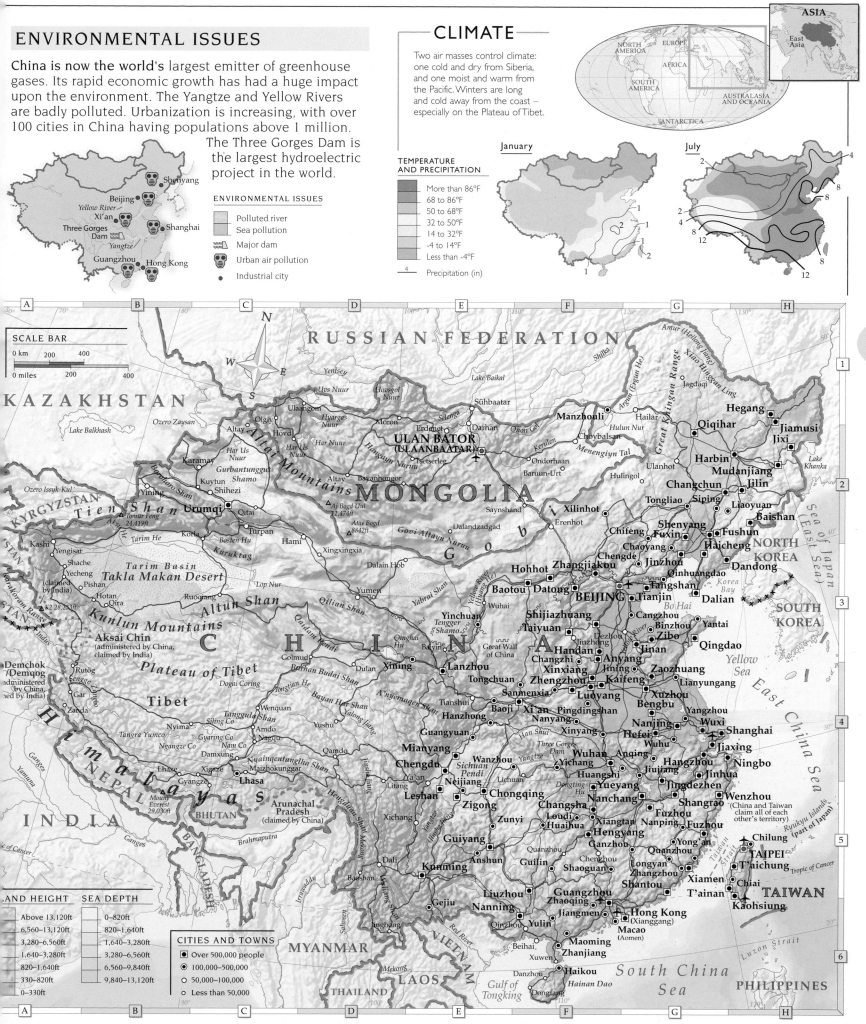

ENVIRONMENTAL ISSUES

China is now the world's largest emitter of greenhouse gases. Its rapid economic growth has had a huge impact upon the environment. The Yangtze and Yellow Rivers are badly polluted. Urbanization is increasing, with over 100 cities in China having populations above 1 million.

The Three Gorges Dam is the largest hydroelectric project in the world.

ENVIRONMENTAL ISSUES

- Polluted river
- Sea pollution
- Major dam
- Urban air pollution
- Industrial city

CLIMATE

Two air masses control climate: one cold and dry from Siberia, and one moist and warm from the Pacific. Winters are long and cold away from the coast – especially on the Plateau of Tibet.

TEMPERATURE AND PRECIPITATION

- More than 86°F
- 68 to 86°F
- 50 to 68°F
- 32 to 50°F
- 14 to 32°F
- -4 to 14°F
- Less than -4°F
- 4 — Precipitation (in)

January   July

ASIA
East Asia

CITIES AND TOWNS
- Over 500,000 people
- 100,000–500,000
- 50,000–100,000
- Less than 50,000

LAND HEIGHT

LAND HEIGHT	SEA DEPTH
Above 13,120ft	0–820ft
6,560–13,120ft	820–1,640ft
3,280–6,560ft	1,640–3,280ft
1,640–3,280ft	3,280–6,560ft
820–1,640ft	6,560–9,840ft
330–820ft	9,840–13,120ft
0–330ft	

SCALE BAR
0 km 200 400
0 miles 200 400

SOUTHEAST ASIA

BRUNEI, CAMBODIA, EAST TIMOR, INDONESIA, LAOS, MALAYSIA, MYANMAR, PHILIPPINES, SINGAPORE, THAILAND, VIETNAM

Southeast Asia is made up of a mainland area and many thousands of tropical islands. The region has great natural wealth – from precious stones to oil – and has recently experienced fast industrial growth. Some countries here, especially Singapore and Malaysia, have become prosperous, but Laos and Cambodia remain poor and are still recovering from years of terrible warfare.

ENVIRONMENTAL ISSUES

In Myanmar, Malaysia, and Indonesia, ancient rain forests are being cut down faster than they can grow back. On December 26th, 2004 a tsunami devastated the west of the region, it is estimated that over 225,000 people died around the Indian Ocean.

ENVIRONMENTAL ISSUES
- Urban air pollution
- Deforested area
- Remaining tropical forest
- Major industrial center

POPULATION

On the mainland, the population is concentrated in the river valleys, plateaus, or plains. Upland areas are inhabited by small groups of hill peoples. Most people still live in rural areas, but the cities are growing fast. In Indonesia and the Philippines, the population is unevenly distributed. Some islands, such as Java, are densely settled; others are barely occupied.

INHABITANTS PER SQ MILE
- More than 520
- 260–520
- 130–260
- Less than 130
- ■ Capital city
- ● Major city

URBAN/RURAL POPULATION DIVISION

Bangkok 1.2%
Jakarta 1.5%
Manilla 1.8%
Rural population 37%
Other towns and cities 58.5%

INDUSTRY

Industries based on the processing of raw materials, like metallic minerals, timber, oil and gas, and agricultural produce, are important here, but manufacturing has grown dramatically in recent years. Many foreign firms, attracted by low labor costs, have invested in the region. Malaysia and Singapore are major producers of electronic goods like disk drives for computers.

STRUCTURE OF INDUSTRY

Primary 19%
Services 45%
Manufacturing 36%

INDUSTRY
- Chemicals
- Engineering
- Food processing
- Textiles
- Mining
- Oil and gas
- Timber
- High-tech
- Tourism
- Major industrial center / area
- — Major road

THE LANDSCAPE

On the mainland, a belt of mountain ranges, cloaked in thick forest, runs north–south. The mountains are cut through by the wide valleys of five great rivers. On their way to the sea, these rivers have deposited sediment, forming immense, fertile flood plains and deltas. To the southeast of the mainland lies a huge arc of over 20,000 mountainous, volcanic islands.

Borneo (D 7)
Borneo is the world's third-largest island, with a total area of 292,298 sq miles. Lying on the Equator and in the path of two monsoons, the island is hot and one of the wettest places on Earth. The landscape contains thickly forested central highlands and swampy lowlands.

Asian Tsunami (A 6)
On December 26th, 2004 the second largest earthquake ever recorded occured under the sea off the west coast of Sumatra. This triggered a huge Tsunami wave, up to 100 ft high in places, that devastated coastal communities causing the deaths of over 225,000 people in eleven countries.

Philippines (E 4)
The Philippines' 7,000 islands are mountainous and volcanic with narrow coastal plains.

Irian Jaya (I 7)
Irian Jaya is a province of Indonesia. Its dense rain forests are some of the last unexplored areas on Earth and are inhabited by many rare plant and animal species.

Volcanoes
Indonesia is the most active volcanic region in the world. Java alone has over 50 active volcanoes out of the country's total of more than 220.

Indonesia (C 7)
Indonesia is an archipelago of 13,677 islands, scattered over almost 3,110 miles. The islands lie on the boundary between two of the Earth's tectonic plates and frequently experience earthquakes.

SCALE BAR

0 km 200 400
0 miles 200

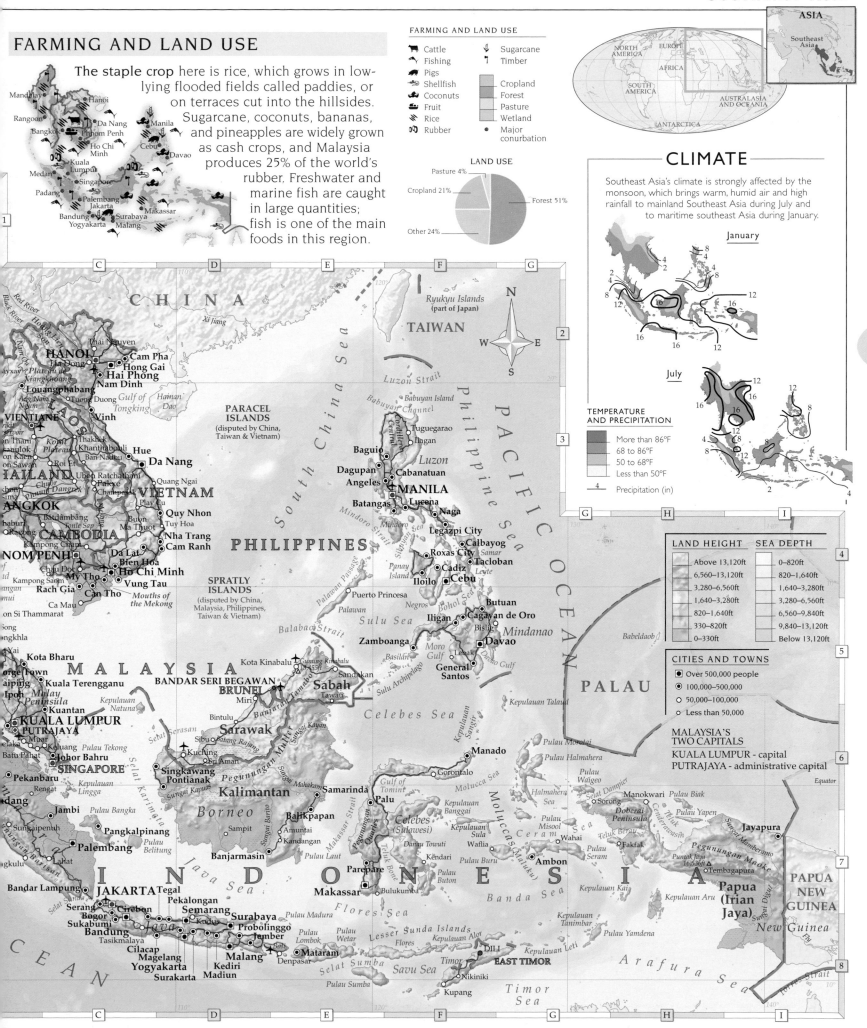

FARMING AND LAND USE

The staple crop here is rice, which grows in low-lying flooded fields called paddies, or on terraces cut into the hillsides. Sugarcane, coconuts, bananas, and pineapples are widely grown as cash crops, and Malaysia produces 25% of the world's rubber. Freshwater and marine fish are caught in large quantities; fish is one of the main foods in this region.

FARMING AND LAND USE

- Cattle
- Fishing
- Pigs
- Shellfish
- Coconuts
- Fruit
- Rice
- Rubber
- Sugarcane
- Timber
- Cropland
- Forest
- Pasture
- Wetland
- Major conurbation

LAND USE

Pasture 4%
Cropland 21%
Forest 51%
Other 24%

ASIA

Southeast Asia

NORTH AMERICA EUROPE ASIA AFRICA SOUTH AMERICA AUSTRALASIA AND OCEANIA ANTARCTICA

CLIMATE

Southeast Asia's climate is strongly affected by the monsoon, which brings warm, humid air and high rainfall to mainland Southeast Asia during July and to maritime southeast Asia during January.

January

July

TEMPERATURE AND PRECIPITATION

- More than 86°F
- 68 to 86°F
- 50 to 68°F
- Less than 50°F
- 4 — Precipitation (in)

LAND HEIGHT

- Above 13,120ft
- 6,560–13,120ft
- 3,280–6,560ft
- 1,640–3,280ft
- 820–1,640ft
- 330–820ft
- 0–330ft

SEA DEPTH

- 0–820ft
- 820–1,640ft
- 1,640–3,280ft
- 3,280–6,560ft
- 6,560–9,840ft
- 9,840–13,120ft
- Below 13,120ft

CITIES AND TOWNS

- Over 500,000 people
- 100,000–500,000
- 50,000–100,000
- Less than 50,000

MALAYSIA'S TWO CAPITALS

KUALA LUMPUR - capital
PUTRAJAYA - administrative capital

CHINA
Xi Jiang
Ryukyu Islands (part of Japan)
TAIWAN
Red River
Black River
Mandalay
Hanoi
Hong Yuen San
Rangoon
Bangkok
HANOI
Ha Dong
Cam Pha
Hong Gai
Hai Phong
Thai Nguyen
Nam Dinh
Plateau de Xiangkhoang
Louangphabang
Tuong Duong
Gulf of Tongking
Hainan Dao
Nam Ou
Ngum
VIENTIANE
Vinh
Hue
Da Nang
Thakhek
Khanthabouli
Ban Nadou
Quang Ngai
Ubon Ratchathani
Roi Et
THAILAND
Pakse
Champasak
VIETNAM
Pley Ku
BANGKOK
Battdambang
CAMBODIA
Buon Ma Thuot
Quy Nhon
Tuy Hoa
Nha Trang
Tonle Sap
Kampong Cham
Da Lat
Cam Ranh
Kampong Saom
NOM PENH
Chau Doc
Bien Hoa
Kampong Som
My Tho
Ho Chi Minh
Vung Tau
Rach Gia
Can Tho
Ca Mau
Mouths of the Mekong
Kota Bharu
George Town
MALAYSIA
Taiping
Ipoh
Malay Peninsula
Kuantan
Kuala Terengganu
KUALA LUMPUR
PUTRAJAYA
Muar
Kluang
Batu Pahat
Johor Bahru
SINGAPORE
Pekanbaru
Rengat
Jambi
Medan
Padang
Sungaipenuh
Bukit Barisan
Lahat
Bengkulu
Bandar Lampung

PARACEL ISLANDS (disputed by China, Taiwan & Vietnam)
South China Sea
PHILIPPINES
Babuyan Island
Babuyan Channel
Luzon Strait
Luzon
Cordillera Central
Baguio
Dagupan
Cabanatuan
Angeles
MANILA
Batangas
Lucena
Naga
Mindoro Strait
Mindoro
Sibuyan Sea
Tuguegarao
Ilagan
Legazpi City
Calbayog
Roxas City
Tacloban
Samar
Leyte
Cadiz
Iloilo
Cebu
Panay Island
Negros
Bohol Sea
SPRATLY ISLANDS (disputed by China, Malaysia, Taiwan & Vietnam)
Palawan Passage
Puerto Princesa
Palawan
Sulu Sea
Balabac Strait
Iligan
Butuan
Cagayan de Oro
Bislig
Mindanao
Zamboanga
Moro Gulf
Basilan
Davao
General Santos
Lebak
Davao Gulf
Sulu Archipelago
Kota Kinabalu
Gunung Kinabalu 13,455ft
Sandakan
Sabah
Tawau
Miri
BANDAR SERI BEGAWAN
BRUNEI
Bintulu
Sarawak
Kuching
Sri Aman
Sibu
Batang Rajang
Kepulauan Natuna
Singkawang
Pontianak
Pegunungan Muller
Kalimantan
Borneo
Samarinda
Balikpapan
Sampit
Amuntai
Kandangan
Banjarmasin
Sungai Barito
Sungai Kapuas
Selat Serasan
Pulau Tekong
Selat Karimata
Kepulauan Lingga
Pulau Bangka
Pangkalpinang
Palembang
Pulau Belitung

Philippine Sea
PACIFIC OCEAN
PALAU
Babeldaob
Kepulauan Talaud
Celebes Sea
Manado
Gorontalo
Kepulauan Sangir
Pulau Morotai
Pulau Halmahera
Pulau Waigeo
Pulau Moraiai
Gulf of Tomini
Palu
Pegunungan Quarles
Celebes (Sulawesi)
Kepulauan Banggai
Kepulauan Sula
Danau Towuti
Kendari
Pulau Buru
Wahai
Waflia
Pulau Seram
Ceram Sea
Ambon
Molucca Sea
Halmahera Sea
Pulau Waigeo
Selat Dampier
Sorong
Manokwari
Pulau Biak
Pulau Yapen
Doberai Peninsula
Fakfak
Teluk Berau
Teluk Cenderawasih
Sungai Mamberamo
Jayapura
Pegunungan Mnoke
Puncak Jaya 16,536ft
Tembagapura
Papua (Irian Jaya)
New Guinea
PAPUA NEW GUINEA

INDONESIA
Java Sea
JAKARTA
Tegal
Serang
Bogor
Cirebon
Pekalongan
Semarang
Sukabumi
Bandung
Tasikmalaya
Cilacap
Magelang
Yogyakarta
Surakarta
Kudus
Surabaya
Probolinggo
Jember
Malang
Kediri
Madiun
Java
Pulau Madura
Bali
Denpasar
Mataram
Pulau Lombok
Pulau Sumbawa
Lesser Sunda Islands
Flores
Pulau Sumba
Selat Sumba
Savu Sea
Flores Sea
Timor
DILI
EAST TIMOR
Nikiniki
Kupang
Timor Sea
Pulau Wetar
Kepulauan Alor
Kepulauan Leti
Pulau Yamdena
Kepulauan Tanimbar
Kepulauan Kai
Kepulauan Aru
Pulau Buton
Bulukumba
Parepare
Makassar
Pulau Laut
Banda Sea
Arafura Sea
Selat Makassar
Makassar Strait
Sungai Mahakam
Teluk Bone
Sungai Digul
Torres Strait
OCEAN
Equator

JAPAN AND KOREA

JAPAN, NORTH KOREA, SOUTH KOREA

Japan is a curved chain of over 4,000 islands in the Pacific Ocean. To the west, Korea juts out from northern China. Japan has few natural resources, but it has become one of the world's most successful industrial nations, due to investment in new technology and a highly efficient workforce. North Korea is a communist state with limited contact with the outside world, while South Korea is a democracy with major international trade links.

FARMING AND LAND USE

Modern farming methods allow Japan to grow much of its own food, despite a shortage of farmland. Rice is the main crop grown throughout the region. Japan has a large fishing fleet; the Japanese eat more fish than any other nation. In North Korea, farming is controlled by the government.

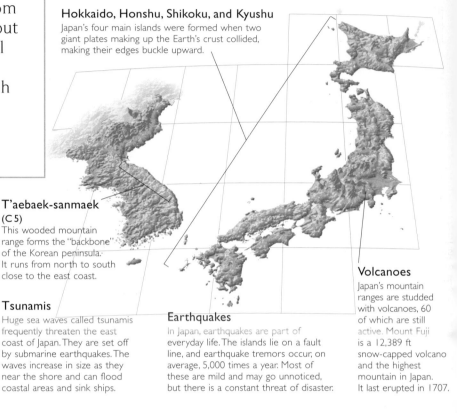

FARMING AND LAND USE

- 🐂 Cattle
- ↰ Fishing
- 🐗 Pigs
- 🍏 Fruit
- 〰 Rice
- Soybeans
- ⚘ Tea
- Tobacco
- Cropland
- Forest
- Pasture
- ● Major conurbation

LAND USE

Pasture 1%
Cropland 16%
Other (including mountains) 18%
Forest 65%

POPULATION

Most of Japan's 128 million people live in crowded cities on the coasts of the four main islands. The Kanto Plain around Tokyo is Japan's biggest area of flat land, and the most populous part of the country. In South Korea, a quarter of the population lives in the capital, Seoul. Most North Koreans live on the coastal plains.

URBAN/RURAL POPULATION DIVISION

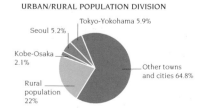

- Seoul 5.2%
- Tokyo-Yokohama 5.9%
- Kobe-Osaka 2.1%
- Rural population 22%
- Other towns and cities 64.8%

INHABITANTS PER SQ MILE

- More than 520
- 260–520
- 130–260
- Less than 130
- ■ Capital city
- ● Major city

THE LANDSCAPE

Most of Japan is covered by forested mountains and hills, among which are many short, fast-flowing rivers and small lakes. Only about a quarter of the land is suitable for building and farming, and new land has been created by cutting back hillsides and reclaiming land from the sea. North and South Korea are mostly mountainous, with some coastal plains.

Hokkaido, Honshu, Shikoku, and Kyushu

Japan's four main islands were formed when two giant plates making up the Earth's crust collided, making their edges buckle upward.

T'aebaek-sanmaek (C 5)

This wooded mountain range forms the "backbone" of the Korean peninsula. It runs from north to south close to the east coast.

Tsunamis

Huge sea waves called tsunamis frequently threaten the east coast of Japan. They are set off by submarine earthquakes. The waves increase in size as they near the shore and can flood coastal areas and sink ships.

Earthquakes

In Japan, earthquakes are part of everyday life. The islands lie on a fault line, and earthquake tremors occur, on average, 5,000 times a year. Most of these are mild and may go unnoticed, but there is a constant threat of disaster.

Volcanoes

Japan's mountain ranges are studded with volcanoes, 60 of which are still active. Mount Fuji is a 12,389 ft snow-capped volcano and the highest mountain in Japan. It last erupted in 1707.

INDUSTRY

Japan is a world leader in high-tech electronic goods like computers, televisions and cameras, as well as cars. South Korea also has a thriving economy. It produces ships, cars, high-tech goods, shoes, and clothes for worldwide export. Both countries have to import most of their raw materials and energy. North Korea has little trade with other countries, but it is rich in minerals such as coal and silver.

STRUCTURE OF INDUSTRY

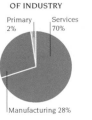

- Primary 2%
- Services 70%
- Manufacturing 28%

INDUSTRY

- 🚗 Car manufacture
- ⚗ Chemicals
- ⚙ Engineering
- Food processing
- 🚂 Iron & steel
- Shipbuilding
- 👕 Textiles

- Mining
- S Finance
- 💻 Hi-tech
- ☢ Research & Development
- Major industrial center / area
- — Major road

ASIA
Japan
and
Korea

ENVIRONMENTAL ISSUES

Industrial pollution from Korea and China has produced acid rain, and pollution in Japanese cities has led to people wearing masks to filter the air. Russia regularly dumps nuclear waste into the Sea of Japan. In 1995, an earthquake caused great destruction to the city of Kobe.

ENVIRONMENTAL ISSUES

- ⊚ Catastrophic earthquake
- ☢ Nuclear waste dump site
- ☠ Urban air pollution
- Affected by acid rain
- Site of nuclear accident
- • Major industrial center

Sea of Japan/ East Sea

1999
Tokyo
Seoul
Kobe 1995
Osaka

CLIMATE

Korea has hot summers and dry, very cold winters, especially in the north, where snow is common. In Japan, winters are less cold than on the Asian mainland; summers are hot, wet, and humid.

January

Less than 2

July

TEMPERATURE AND PRECIPITATION

More than 68°F	32 to 41°F
59 to 68°F	23 to 32°F
50 to 59°F	Less than 23°F
41 to 50°F	4 Precipitation (in)

SCALE BAR

km 0 100 200
miles 0 100 200

LAND HEIGHT

- 6,560–13,120ft
- 3,280–6,560ft
- 1,640–3,280ft
- 820–1,640ft
- 330–820ft
- 0–330ft

SEA DEPTH

- 0–820ft
- 820–1,640ft
- 1,640–3,280ft
- 3,280–6,560ft
- 6,560–9,840ft
- 9,840–13,120ft
- Below 13,120ft

CITIES AND TOWNS

- ▪ Over 500,000 people
- ◉ 100,000–500,000
- ◎ 50,000–100,000
- ∘ Less than 50,000

(North and South Korea have been divided by a ceasefire agreement since 1953)

Liancourt Rocks (claimed by Japan and South Korea)

Kurile Islands (administered by Russian Federation, claimed by Japan)

Sea of Okhotsk

Hokkaido

JAPAN

Honshu

Sea of Japan/ East Sea

NORTH KOREA

SOUTH KOREA

CHINA

Yellow Sea

East Korea Bay

Korea Strait

East China Sea

Philippine Sea

Ryukyu Islands (part of Japan)

Shikoku

Kyushu

PACIFIC OCEAN

AUSTRALASIA & OCEANIA

Australasia and Oceania encompasses the ancient landmass of Australia, the islands of New Zealand, and the scattering of thousands of small islands that stretch out into the Pacific Ocean. Indigenous peoples of the South Pacific, such as the Aborigines, Maoris, Polynesians, Micronesians, and Melanesians, inhabit the region. In Australia and New Zealand, they live alongside people of European origin who settled in the 18th century, and more recent arrivals from East and Southeast Asia.

PACIFIC ISLANDS

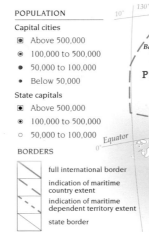

Micronesia is one of the Pacific's island nations, consisting of a group of volcanic islands, low-lying coral reefs, and lagoons. Many of the smaller Pacific islands are only a few feet above sea level.

LAND USE AND AGRICULTURE

Much of the center of Australia is a dry, barren desert and unsuitable for agriculture. At its fringes, sheep farming is practiced, and both Australia and New Zealand are massive producers of wool and lamb. The Pacific islands export many exotic fruits and crops – especially oil palms and coconut palms. Oil from the palms is processed and sold as well as the fruits themselves. Small-scale fishing is common, but larger operations are run by foreign fishing fleets, especially the Japanese, who fish for tuna in the deeper waters of the Pacific.

SHEEP FARMING

New Zealand and Australia are the world's biggest producers of wool. In New Zealand, sheep outnumber people by 12 to 1.

POPULATION

Capital cities
- ◼ Above 500,000
- ◉ 100,000 to 500,000
- ● 50,000 to 100,000
- • Below 50,000

State capitals
- ◼ Above 500,000
- ◉ 100,000 to 500,000
- ○ 50,000 to 100,000

BORDERS

- full international border
- indication of maritime country extent
- indication of maritime dependent territory extent
- state border

SCALE 1:37,250,000

0 km 300 600

0 miles 300 600

COCONUTS

Coconuts are grown throughout the islands of the Pacific, and the white flesh is dried in the sun to produce copra. Copra is a valuable export crop for many islands.

LAND USE AND AGRICULTURE

- Cattle
- Sheep
- Coconuts
- Coffee
- Fishing
- Fruit
- Shellfish
- Sugarcane
- Timber
- Vineyards
- Wheat

- Cropland
- Desert
- Forest
- Mountain region
- Pasture
- • Major conurbation

MINERAL RESOURCES

Mineral resources are not widespread, but where they are found, they are in great abundance. Most of the small Pacific islands have no mineral resources, but Australia has enormous reserves of bauxite and iron ore, and also sizable reserves of gold and zinc. Copper is found in Papua New Guinea, and New Caledonia has large nickel reserves. There are ample supplies of fossil fuels, and although coal is plentiful in eastern Australia, oil and gas are found only in isolated pockets around Australia's coast.

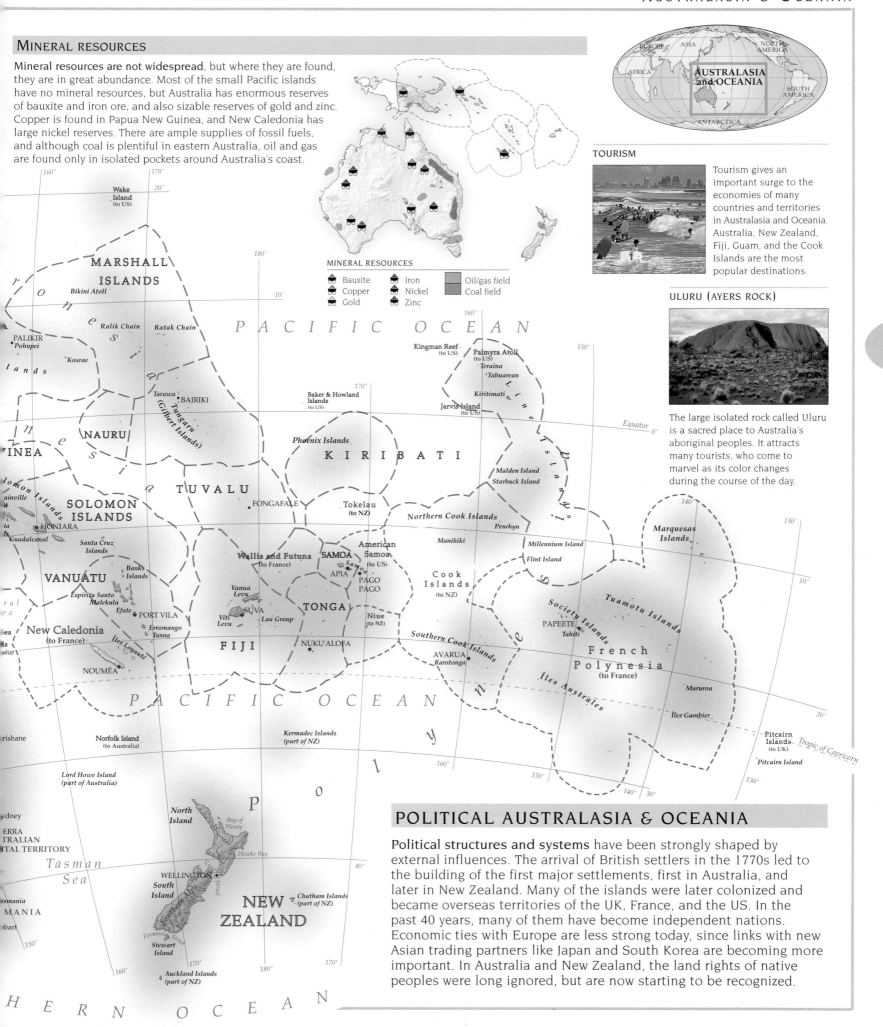

AUSTRALASIA and OCEANIA

MINERAL RESOURCES

- ⬢ Bauxite
- ⬢ Copper
- ⬢ Gold
- ⬢ Iron
- ⬢ Nickel
- ⬢ Zinc
- ▮ Oil/gas field
- ▮ Coal field

TOURISM

Tourism gives an important surge to the economies of many countries and territories in Australasia and Oceania. Australia, New Zealand, Fiji, Guam, and the Cook Islands are the most popular destinations.

ULURU (AYERS ROCK)

The large isolated rock called Uluru is a sacred place to Australia's aboriginal peoples. It attracts many tourists, who come to marvel as its color changes during the course of the day.

POLITICAL AUSTRALASIA & OCEANIA

Political structures and systems have been strongly shaped by external influences. The arrival of British settlers in the 1770s led to the building of the first major settlements, first in Australia, and later in New Zealand. Many of the islands were later colonized and became overseas territories of the UK, France, and the US. In the past 40 years, many of them have become independent nations. Economic ties with Europe are less strong today, since links with new Asian trading partners like Japan and South Korea are becoming more important. In Australia and New Zealand, the land rights of native peoples were long ignored, but are now starting to be recognized.

AUSTRALIA

Australia is the world's sixth-largest country, and also the smallest, flattest continent, with the lowest rainfall. Most Australians are of European, mainly British, origin. However, since 1945 almost six million settlers from more than 170 countries have made Australia their home. The Aboriginal people, now only a tiny minority, were the first inhabitants. Recently, there have been several moves to restore their ancient lands.

INDUSTRY

Australia has one of the world's biggest mining industries. Bauxite, coal, copper, gold, and iron ore are mined and exported, especially to Japan. In the cities, service industries, particularly tourism, are growing fast; Australia's sunshine and dramatic scenery are attracting an increasing number of overseas visitors.

STRUCTURE OF INDUSTRY

- Primary 3%
- Services 67%
- Manufacturing 30%

INDUSTRY

- Brewing
- Car manufacturing
- Chemicals
- Electronics
- Engineering
- Food processing
- Coal
- Mining
- Oil and gas
- Tourism
- Major industrial center / area
- Major road

POPULATION

Despite its vast size, Australia is sparsely populated. The desert outback, which covers most of the interior, is too dry and barren to support many people. About 85% of the population live in the cities and towns on the east and southeast coasts, and around Perth in the west.

INHABITANTS PER SQ MILE

- More than 130
- 30–130
- 3–30
- Less than 3
- Capital city
- Major city

URBAN/RURAL POPULATION DIVISION

- Sydney 17.8%
- Melbourne 16%
- Brisbane 7.7%
- Other towns and cities 43.5%
- Rural population 15%

FARMING AND LAND USE

Away from the coasts, much of the land is too dry for agriculture. Fields of sugarcane grow close the east coast, and grapes for the thriving wine industry are cultivated in the south and west, along with wheat. Vast numbers of cattle and sheep are raised for their meat and wool – both of which are major exports. They are grazed in the desert, on huge farms called "stations," and in more fertile areas.

FARMING AND LAND USE

- Cattle
- Sheep
- Wheat
- Sugarcane
- Timber
- Vineyards
- Cropland
- Desert
- Forest
- Pasture
- Major conurbation

LAND USE

- Cropland 6%
- Other (including desert) 21%
- Forest 19%
- Pasture 54%

THE LANDSCAPE

Most of Australia is dry, flat, and barren; all of the wetter, fertile land is found along its coastline. Huge sun-baked deserts, fringed by semiarid plains of scrub and grassland cover most of the west and center of the country. In the east, the land rises to the highlands of the Great Dividing Range, which run the whole length of the east coast. The tropical north coast has rainforests and mangrove swamps.

Blue Mountains (G 6)
The Blue Mountains lie toward the southern end of the Great Dividing Range. They get their name from the blue haze of oil droplets given off by the eucalyptus trees covering their slopes.

Great Barrier Reef (G 2)
This spectacular coral reef, which stretches for over 1,200 miles off the coast of Queensland, is the largest living structure on Earth. The reef has built up over millions of years and its waters are home to thousands of different species of coral and marine animals.

Uluru (Ayers Rock) (D 4)
Uluru is an enormous block of red sandstone, standing almost in the middle of Australia. It is the world's biggest free-standing rock – 5.8 miles around the base, and 2,845 ft high. It is the summit of a sandstone hill that is buried beneath the sands of the desert.

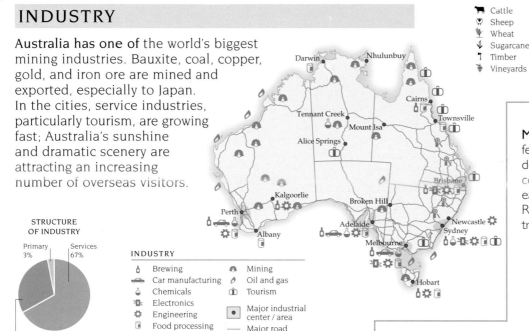

Simpson Desert (E 4)
The Simpson Desert covers around 50,000 sq miles. It contains long, parallel lines of sand dunes and is scattered with large salt pans and salt lakes, which were created when old rivers evaporated. They are now fed by the seasonal rains.

Murray River (F 5)
Together with its tributaries, the Murray River is Australia's main river system. It winds slowly westward for more than 1,562 miles from the Great Dividing Range to the Indian Ocean. It is fed by snow from mountains in the far southeast.

Great Dividing Range (H 5)
These highlands separate the desert regions from the fertile eastern plains. Rivers and streams have eroded them, creating deep valleys and gorges.

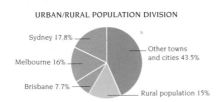

ENVIRONMENTAL ISSUES

Australia's dry climate and low rainfall make it susceptible to desertification. Between 2001 and 2007, southeast Australia experienced one of its worst droughts on record. The Murray-Darling basin, one of Australia's most productive agricultural regions, was very badly affected. During the dry season, vegetation becomes tinder-dry, and bush fires are common, burning huge tracts of land.

2001–2007

ENVIRONMENTAL ISSUES

- Area at risk from bushfires
- Drought
- Existing desert
- Risk of desertification
- Severe risk of desertification

CLIMATE

Much of Australia's climate is continental, and temperatures soar during the day and fall rapidly at night. The climate is also arid and very little rain falls, apart from in the summer months when the north is affected by tropical storms.

January

July

TEMPERATURE AND PRECIPITATION

- More than 95°F
- 86 to 95°F
- 77 to 86°F
- 68 to 77°F
- 59 to 68°F
- 50 to 59°F
- 41 to 50C
- Less than 41°F
- Precipitation (in)

EUROPE ASIA NORTH AMERICA SOUTH AMERICA ANTARCTICA

Map labels

Timor Sea
Arafura Sea
Timor (part of Indonesia)
Melville Island
Croker Island
South Goulburn Island
Badu Island Moa Island
Prince of Wales Island
Cape York
PAPUA NEW GUINEA
Bathurst Island
Van Diemen Gulf
Wessel Islands
Nhulunbuy
Cape Londonderry
Darwin
Arnhem Land
Gulf of Carpentaria
Endeavour Str.
Cape York Peninsula
Princess Charlotte Bay
Coral Sea
Bonaparte Archipelago
Pine Creek
Katherine
Groote Eylandt
Sir Edward Pellew Group
Wyndham
Kununurra
Lake Argyle
Daly Waters
Wellesley Islands
Cooktown
CORAL SEA ISLANDS (Australian external territory)
Kimberley Plateau
King Sound
Victoria River
NORTHERN TERRITORY
Barkly Tableland
Mitchell River
Port Douglas
Mareeba Cairns
Atherton Innisfail
Derby
Fitzroy Crossing
Ord River
Kalkarindji
Burketown
Normanton
Tully
Hinchinbrook Island
Great Barrier Reef
Broome
Fitzroy River
Halls Creek
Tanami Desert
Tennant Creek
Flinders River
Gregory Range
Townsville
Bowen
Whitsunday Group
Eighty Mile Beach
Great Sandy Desert
Cloncurry
Charters Towers
Bloomsbury
Mackay
Port Hedland
Percival Lakes
Mount Isa
Hughenden
Winton
Great Dividing Range
Dampier
Marble Bar
Lake Mackay
AUSTRALIA
Longreach
Clermont
Barrow Island
Exmouth Gulf
Fortescue River
WESTERN
Macdonnell Ranges
Alice Springs
QUEENSLAND
Barcaldine
Emerald
Springsure
Yeppoon
Rockhampton
Onslow
Hamersley Range
Newman
Lake Disappointment
Gibson Desert
Lake Amadeus
Great Artesian Basin
Blackall
Curtis Island
Gladstone
Exmouth
Ashburton River
Little Sandy Desert
Uluru (Ayers Rock) 2,845ft
Simpson Desert
Windorah
Augathella
Biloela
Bundaberg
Barlee Range
Gascoyne River
AUSTRALIA
Musgrave Ranges
Lake Eyre Basin
Cooper Creek
Charleville
Mitchell
Miles
Roma
Murgon
Gayndah
Maryborough
Fraser Island
Gympie
Lake Macleod
Lake Carnegie
Lake Wells
SOUTH AUSTRALIA
Lake Eyre North
Grey Range
Cunnamulla
Bollon
Moonie
Toowoomba
Dalby
Caloundra
Carnarvon
Denham
Meekatharra
Great Victoria Desert
Coober Pedy
Lake Eyre South
Lake Blanche
Saint George
Goondiwindi
Ipswich
Brisbane
Surfers Paradise
Shark Bay
Dirk Hartog Island
Mount Magnet
Lake Carey
Marree
Lake Callabonna
Warwick
Gold Coast
Murwillumbah
Kalbarri
Lake Barlee
Lake Frome
Stanthorpe
Moree
Grafton
Geraldton
Lake Moore
Lake Rebecca
Reid
Tarcoola
Lake Torrens
Flinders Ranges
Barrier Range
Bourke
Walgett
Narrabri
Moora
Southern Cross
Kalgoorlie
Coolgardie
Rawlinna
Barwon River
NEW SOUTH WALES
Armidale
Coffs Harbour
Gingin
Perth
Merredin
Norseman
Balladonia
Nullarbor Plain
Eucla
Penong
Lake Everard
Lake Gairdner
Eyre Peninsula
Wilcannia
Cobar
Nyngan
Gunnedah
Tamworth
Port Macquarie
Fremantle
Northam
Brookton
Lake King
Great Australian Bight
Ceduna
Elliston
Port Augusta
Broken Hill
Ivanhoe
Dubbo
Orange
Taree
Mandurah
Narrogin
Wagin
Esperance
Whyalla
Peterborough
Lachlan River
Parkes
Bathurst
Lithgow
Newcastle
Bunbury
Collie
Katanning
Port Pirie
Port Lincoln
Elizabeth
Murray River
Hay
Blue Mts.
Parramatta
Sydney
Busselton
Manjimup
Adelaide
Murrumbidgee River
Goulburn
Wollongong
Botany Bay
Augusta
Albany
Investigator Strait
Kangaroo Island
Tailem Bend
Keith
Ouyen
Deniliquin
Wagga Wagga
Albury
Wodonga
CANBERRA
AUSTRALIAN CAPITAL TERRITORY
VICTORIA
Horsham
Mildura
Shepparton
Wangaratta
Cooma
Mount Kosciuszko 7,310ft
Australian Alps
Bega
Naracoorte
Bendigo
Ballarat
Mount Gambier
Geelong
Melbourne
Sale
Traralgon
Moe
Portland
Warrnambool
South East Point
King Island
Bass Strait
Flinders Island
Hunter Island
Cape Barren Island
Tasman Sea
Marrawah
Burnie
Bass Strait
Devonport
Launceston
TASMANIA
Hobart
Maria Island
South Bruny Island

LAND HEIGHT

- 6,560–13,120ft
- 3,280–6,560ft
- 1,640–3,280ft
- 820–1,640ft
- 330–820ft
- 0–330ft
- Below sea level

SEA DEPTH

- 0–820ft
- 820–1,640ft
- 1,640–3,280ft
- 3,280–6,560ft
- 6,560–9,840ft
- 9,840–13,120ft
- Below 13,120ft

CITIES AND TOWNS

- Over 500,000 people
- 100,000–500,000
- 50,000–100,000
- Less than 50,000

SCALE BAR

0 km 100 200

0 miles 100 200

INDIAN OCEAN

137

NEW ZEALAND

New Zealand is one of the most remote populated places in the world, and was one of the last places on Earth to be inhabited by people. The first people to settle on the islands were the Maori, a Polynesian people. When European settlers arrived during the 19th century, the Maori became a minority and today make up only about 8% of the population. With few people and rich natural resources, New Zealand's inhabitants have high living standards.

INDUSTRY

High-tech industries such as electronics and computing are growing in the major cities of Auckland and Wellington. Agricultural products such as meat, wool, and milk are still among New Zealand's major exports, and large pine forests supply wood for paper pulp and timber. The magnificent scenery and varied climate draw tourists from all over the world, especially for hiking and other special vacations.

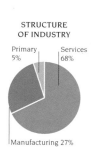

STRUCTURE OF INDUSTRY

Primary 5%
Services 68%
Manufacturing 27%

INDUSTRY
- 🍶 Chemicals
- Electronics
- ⚙ Engineering
- Fish processing
- Food processing
- Iron and steel
- Textiles
- 🌲 Timber
- Tourism

- ▪ Major industrial center / area
- — Major road

POPULATION

Most of the population is descended from European settlers, although immigrants from Asia and the Pacific islands are increasing. About one-third of New Zealand's 4 million people live in Auckland on North Island, which also has the largest Polynesian population of any city in the Pacific. Elsewhere, the population is clustered along the coasts, where the land is lower.

URBAN/RURAL POPULATION DIVISION

Auckland 30.7%
Other towns and cities 36.8%
Wellington 9.3%
Christchurch 9.2%
Rural population 14%

INHABITANTS PER SQ MILE
- More than 130
- 30–130
- 3–30
- Less than 3
- ▪ Capital city
- ● Major city

ENVIRONMENTAL ISSUES

New Zealand is one of the world's least polluted countries, largely due to its small population and lack of heavy industries. Air quality is occasionally poor in Auckland and Christchurch. Environment-friendly geothermal energy is tapped to make electricity in the volcanic region of North Island. Recently, logging companies have begun to exploit the rich forest reserves, although this has been widely opposed.

ENVIRONMENTAL ISSUES
- Geothermal power generation
- Logging activity
- Urban air pollution
- ● Major industrial center

THE LANDSCAPE

Two large, mountainous islands form New Zealand's main land areas. A large crack or fault – the Alpine Fault, in the west of South Island – is the boundary between two plates in the Earth's crust. Land on either side of the fault tends to move, causing earthquakes. Volcanoes, many of them still active, are also found on both islands. South Island has many high peaks, several more than 10,000 ft high.

Geysers and boiling mud

Geysers occur when hot volcanic rocks come into contact with underground water. The water boils and turns to steam, forcing the water above it to burst through the Earth's surface into the air. There are many geysers and boiling mud pools in the areas around Rotorua and Taupo.

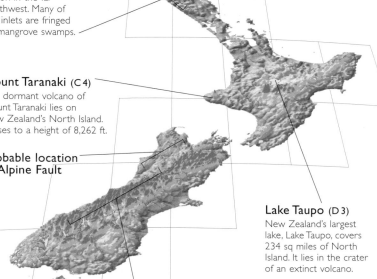

Northland (C 1)
This is a tropical region in the far northwest. Many of the inlets are fringed by mangrove swamps.

Mount Taranaki (C 4)
The dormant volcano of Mount Taranaki lies on New Zealand's North Island. It rises to a height of 8,262 ft.

Probable location of Alpine Fault

Lake Taupo (D 3)
New Zealand's largest lake, Lake Taupo, covers 234 sq miles of North Island. It lies in the crater of an extinct volcano.

Southern Alps
New Zealand's Southern Alps stretch more than 300 miles down the backbone of South Island. They were formed by the collision of the Indo-Australian and Pacific plates. Heavy snowfalls here, brought by westerly winds, feed the Fox Glacier, which moves at a speed of 1.5–15 ft a day.

FARMING AND LAND USE

Large areas of rich, sweet grasslands have made New Zealand one of the world's top regions for rearing sheep. There are around 12 sheep for every person, grazing alongside about ten million cattle. Fruits, including strawberries, apples, oranges, peaches, and the famous kiwi, are cultivated, particularly on South Island, and exported throughout the world. Fish caught off the Pacific coast are another important source of income.

LAND USE

Other 8%
Cropland 14%
Forest 28%
Pasture 50%

FARMING AND LAND USE

- Cattle
- Fishing
- Sheep
- Fruit
- Timber
- Wheat

Cropland
Forest
Mountains
Pasture
● Major conurbation

CLIMATE

North Island has a generally warm climate that becomes tropical – hotter and more humid – toward the far north. South Island is cooler and wetter. There may be heavy snowfall in winter, particularly in the highlands, and many mountains are permanently snow-capped.

TEMPERATURE AND PRECIPITATION

More than 59°F
50 to 59°F
41 to 50°F
32 to 41°F
23 to 32°F
Less than 23°F
4 Precipitation (in)

January

July

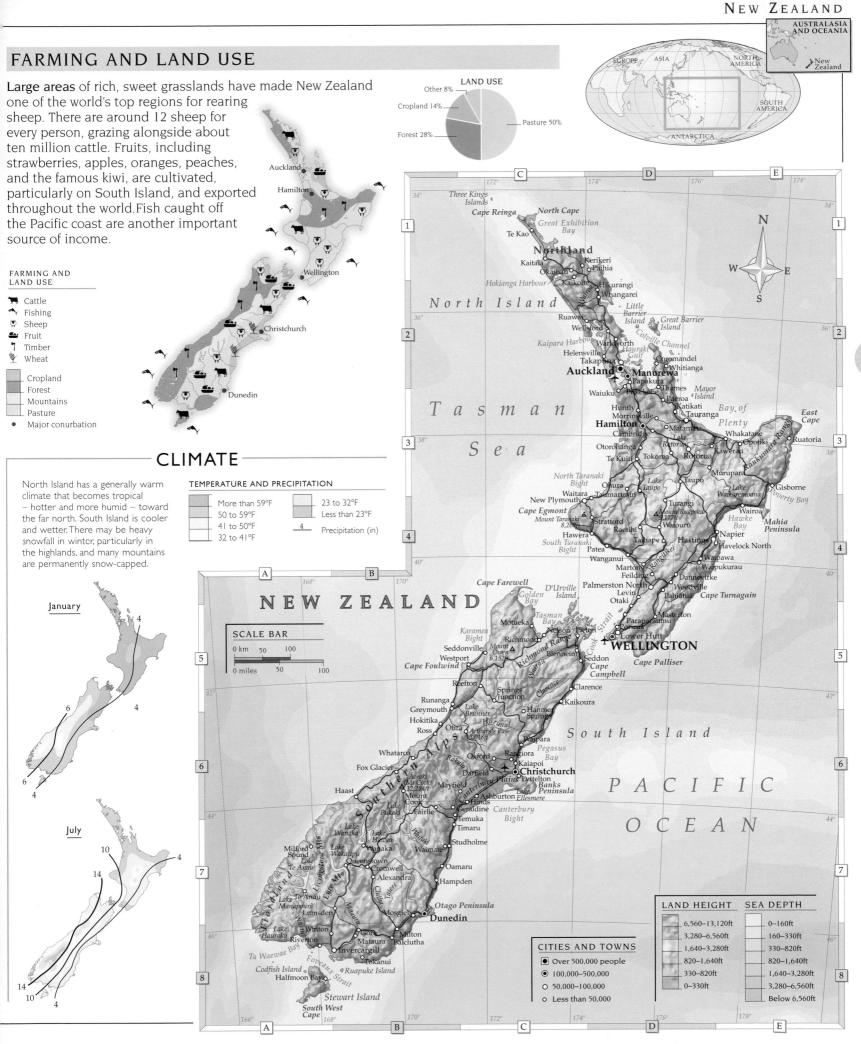

NEW ZEALAND

AUSTRALASIA AND OCEANIA

SCALE BAR
0 km 50 100
0 miles 50 100

LAND HEIGHT
6,560–13,120ft
3,280–6,560ft
1,640–3,280ft
820–1,640ft
330–820ft
0–330ft

SEA DEPTH
0–160ft
160–330ft
330–820ft
820–1,640ft
1,640–3,280ft
3,280–6,560ft
Below 6,560ft

CITIES AND TOWNS
■ Over 500,000 people
◉ 100,000–500,000
◎ 50,000–100,000
○ Less than 50,000

SOUTHWEST PACIFIC

The many thousands of islands in the Pacific Ocean are scattered across an enormous area. The original inhabitants, the Polynesians, Melanesians, and Micronesians, settled the islands following the last Ice Age. In the 1700s Europeans arrived. They colonized all of the Pacific islands, introducing their culture, languages, and religion. Today many, though not all, of the islands have become independent. Their economies are simple, based largely on fishing and agriculture. Many are increasingly relying on their beautiful scenery and tropical climates to attract tourists and give a valuable boost to their economies.

LANDSCAPE

Most of the Pacific islands are extremely small, the largest landmass is the half of the island of New Guinea occupied by Papua New Guinea. The edges of the Indo-Australian and Pacific plates meet on the western edge of the area, leading to much volcanic and earthquake activity. Many of the islands are coral atolls, originally formed by volcanic activity, and some are no more than a few feet above sea level.

New Guinea (A 2)
A mountainous spine runs through the center of the island, separating the northern coast from the dense forests and mangroves found in the south.

Pacific Ocean
The Pacific Ocean is the Earth's oldest and deepest. Its name means peaceful, though it is far from being so; the highest wave ever recorded in open ocean – 112 ft – occurred during a hurricane in the Pacific.

Kavachi
Kavachi is an underwater volcano lying off the coast of New Georgia, in the Solomon Islands. It still erupts every few years.

Ring of Fire
The "Ring of Fire" is the term used to describe the string of volcanoes that surround the entire Pacific Ocean and erupt frequently because of intense stress and movement from within the Earth. The ring crosses the south Pacific, running between Vanuatu and New Caledonia, along the edge of the Solomon Islands, and between New Britain and New Guinea.

Sea trenches
Deep trenches mark the seafloor boundary where the Indo-Australian plate "dives" under the Pacific plate.

Coral atolls
Volcanic activity in the Pacific has led to the creation of many islands. These islands become fringed with a ring of coral. When the islands subside beneath the water once again, only the circle of coral is left, forming an atoll.

INDUSTRY

Today, the main industry for many of the Pacific islands is tourism. Food processing and small-scale textile industries are also common on many islands.

FARMING AND LAND USE

Most farming that takes place on the Pacific islands is at a subsistence level, and many people keep pigs and chickens. A few crops are grown for export, especially oil palms, and coconuts, which are dried in the sun to produce copra. Many islanders make their living from the rich fishing grounds of the Pacific. The thick forests of Papua New Guinea are increasingly cut down for timber.

AUSTRALASIA AND OCEANIA

LAND USE

- Fishing
- Bananas
- Cocoa
- Coconuts
- Coffee
- Oil palms
- Rubber
- Timber

Cropland
Forest
Wetland

• Major conurbation

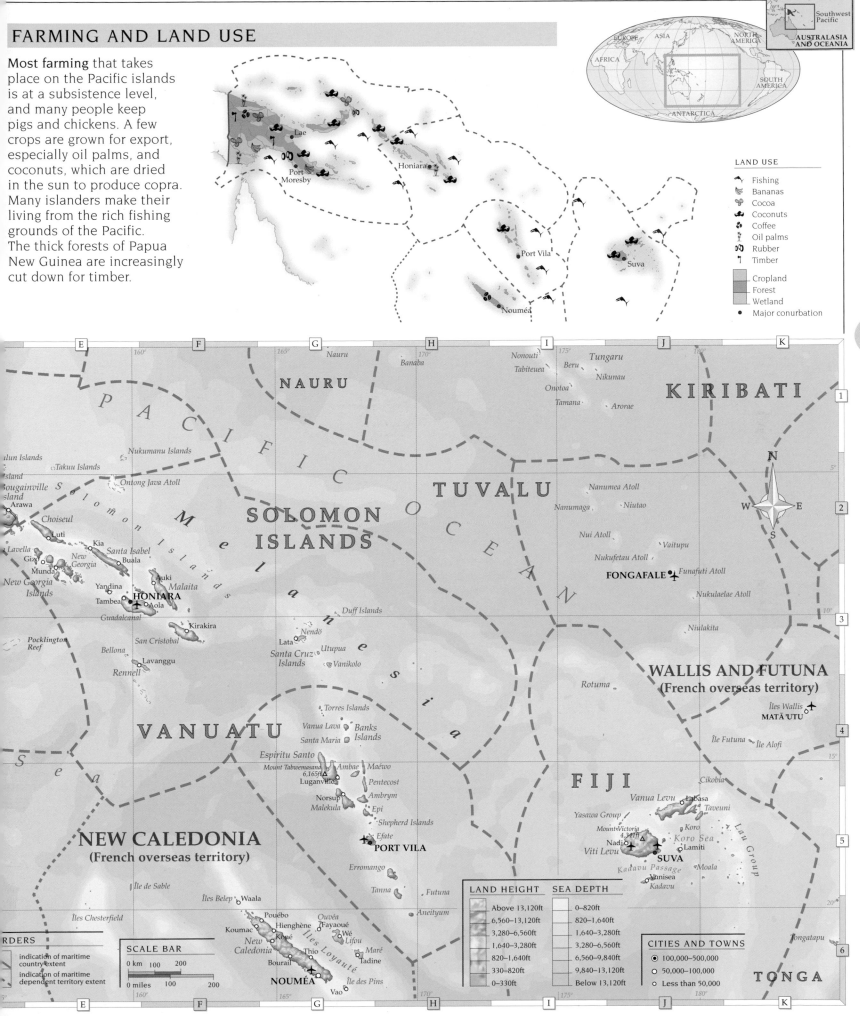

LAND HEIGHT

	Above 13,120ft
	6,560–13,120ft
	3,280–6,560ft
	1,640–3,280ft
	820–1,640ft
	330–820ft
	0–330ft

SEA DEPTH

	0–820ft
	820–1,640ft
	1,640–3,280ft
	3,280–6,560ft
	6,560–9,840ft
	9,840–13,120ft
	Below 13,120ft

CITIES AND TOWNS

⊙ 100,000–500,000
○ 50,000–100,000
○ Less than 50,000

BORDERS

indication of maritime country extent

indication of maritime dependent territory extent

SCALE BAR

0 km   100   200

0 miles   100   200

ANTARCTICA

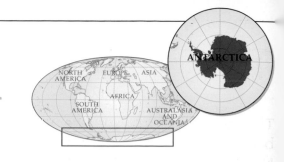

The continent of Antarctica has no permanent human population and very few animals can survive on the frozen land, although the surrounding waters teem with fish and mammals. Even in the summer, the temperature is rarely above freezing and the sea-ice only partly melts; in winter, temperatures plummet to −112°F. The only people who live in Antarctica are teams of scientists who study the wildlife and monitor the ice for changes in the Earth's atmosphere.

THE LANDSCAPE

Frozen seas
During the cold winter months, the water surrounding Antarctica freezes, almost doubling the size of the continent.

Antarctica is the world's most southerly continent. It is also the world's coldest continent and its highest, mainly due to the great ice sheet – up to 1.25 miles thick in parts – that lies over the mountains of the Antarctic Peninsula and the plateau of Greater Antarctica.

Lambert Glacier (E 4)
The Lambert Glacier is the world's largest series of glaciers. It is 50 miles wide at the coast and reaches more than 180 miles inland.

Transantarctic Mountains (C 5)
The Transantarctic Mountains run across the continent, splitting it into Greater and Lesser Antarctica.

Ice sheet
A massive sheet of ice, about 15,700 ft thick at its deepest point, covers almost the entire area of Antarctica. It contains most of the freshwater on Earth. The weight of the ice pushes the land down below sea level.

The Ross Ice Shelf (C 5)
The Ross Sea is part of the Pacific Ocean. This deep bay is covered with a thick sheet of ice that floats on the ocean.

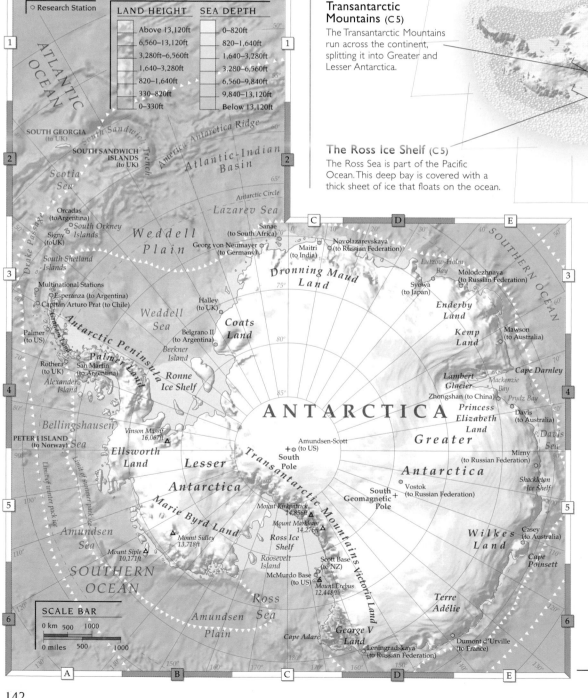

Research Station

LAND HEIGHT	SEA DEPTH
Above 13,120ft	0–820ft
6,560–13,120ft	820–1,640ft
3,280ft–6,560ft	1,640–3,280ft
1,640–3,280ft	3,280–6,560ft
820–1,640ft	6,560–9,840ft
330–820ft	9,840–13,120ft
0–330ft	Below 13,120ft

RESOURCES

The mountains of Antarctica have rich mineral reserves. Gold, iron, and coal are found, and there is natural gas in the surrounding water. The unique and abundant marine wildlife is Antarctica's greatest resource. Colonies of penguins breed on the ice sheet, and whales, seals, and many bird and fish species thrive in the icy waters.

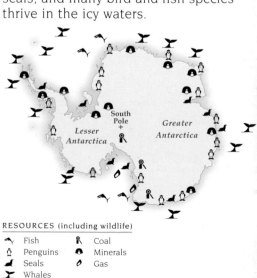

RESOURCES (including wildlife)

Fish	Coal
Penguins	Minerals
Seals	Gas
Whales	

THE ARCTIC

The ice-covered Arctic Ocean is encircled by the most northerly parts of Europe, North America, and Asia. Very few people live in the often-freezing conditions. Those who do, including the Sami of northern Scandinavia, the Siberian Yugyt and Nenet people, and the Canadian Inuit, were nomads who lived by hunting and herding. Some live like this today, but many have now settled in small towns.

THE LANDSCAPE

The Arctic Ocean is the smallest ocean in the world, covering a total area of 5,440,000 sq miles. The ocean is divided into two large basins, divided by three great underwater mountain ranges including the Lomonosov Ridge which is more than 9,842 ft high on average.

THE ARCTIC

Lomonosov Ridge (C 4)

Arctic islands (A 4)
In the far north of Canada, there are many thousands of islands including Baffin Island and Victoria Island. Many of them are almost entirely surrounded by pack ice.

Pack ice
Much of the Arctic Ocean is permanently covered by pack ice. When the ice breaks up, it forms enormous floating ice masses called icebergs.

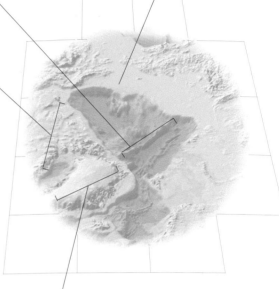

Greenland (A 3)
Greenland is the world's largest island. It is covered by a huge ice sheet, more than 649,960 sq miles across. The weight of the ice has pushed most of the land below sea level.

Sastrugi
Snow, blown by strong winds, can scratch deep patterns in the snow. These patterns are known as sastrugi and line up with the direction of the wind.

RESOURCES

Coal, oil, and gas are found beneath the Arctic Ocean and in Canada, Alaska, and Russia. Fears about damage to the environment and the cost of extracting these resources have restricted the quantities removed. Overfishing has reduced fish stocks to very low levels. Quotas have been put in place to allow them to revive.

SCALE BAR	CITIES AND TOWNS	SEA DEPTH
0 km 250 500	◉ 100,000–500,000	0–820ft
0 miles 250 500	○ 50,000–100,000	820–1,640ft
	○ Less than 50,000	1,640–3,280ft
		3,280–6,560ft
		6,560–9,840ft
		9,840–13,120ft
		Below 13,120ft

RESOURCES
- ⌐ Fish
- ⚒ Coal
- ◭ Minerals
- ◊ Oil and gas
- ● Major town/city

TIME ZONES

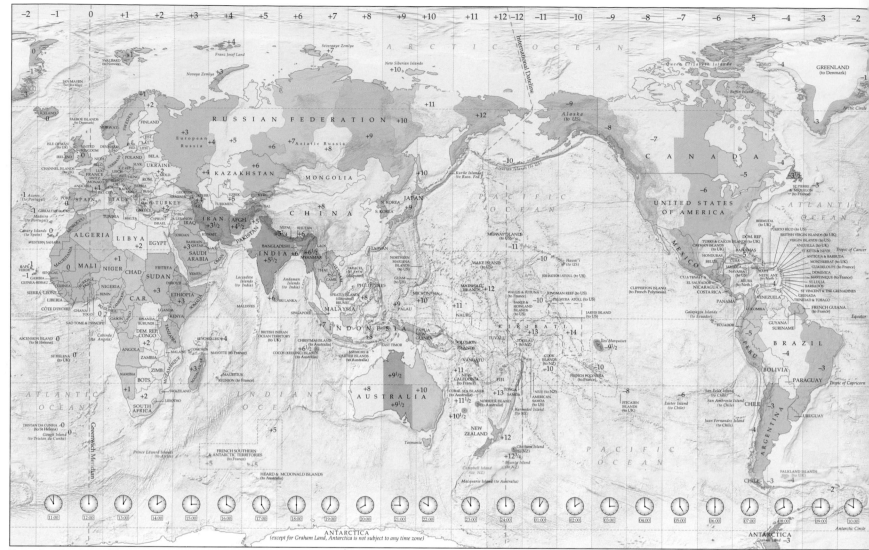

The numbers along the top of the map (+2/-2 etc.), indicate the number of hours each time zone is ahead or behind UTC (Coordinated Universal Time)

The clocks and 24-hour times given at the bottom of the map show time in each time zone when it is 12.00 hours noon UTC

TIME ZONES

The Earth is a rotating sphere, and because of this the Sun only shines on half of its surface at any one time. This means that it is morning, evening, and night time in different parts of the world (*see diagram below*). Because of these differences, each country or part of a country uses a local time. A region of Earth's surface which uses a single local time is called a time zone. There are 24 one-hour time zones around the world, arranged roughly in vertical longitudinal bands.

DAY AND NIGHT AROUND THE WORLD

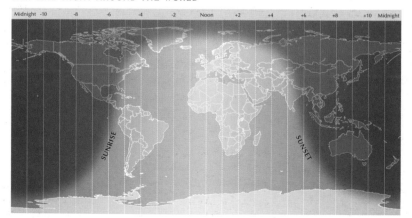

STANDARD TIME

Standard time is the official local time in a particular country or part of a country. Although time zones are arranged roughly in longitudinal bands, in many places the borders of a zone do not fall exactly along a line of longitude, as can be seen on the map, but are determined by geographical factors or by borders between countries.

Most countries have just one time zone, but some large countries (such as the US, Canada, and Russia) are split between several time zones, so standard time varies across those countries. For example, the US mainland crosses four time zones and so has four standard times, called the Eastern, Central, Mountain, and Pacific standard times. China is unusual in that just one standard time is used for the whole country, even though it extends across 60° of longitude from west to east.

COORDINATED UNIVERSAL TIME (UTC)

Coordinated Universal Time (UTC) is an international reference used to set the local time in each time zone. For example, Australian Western Standard Time (the local time in Western Australia) is set 8 hours ahead of UTC (it is UTC+8), so if it were 12.00 noon UTC in London, UK, it would be 8.00pm in Perth, Western Australia. UTC has replaced Greenwich Mean Time (GMT) because UTC is based on an atomic clock, which is more accurate and convenient than GMT. Greenwich Mean Time was determined by the Sun's position in the sky relative to the 0° line of longitude, also known as the Greenwich Meridian, which runs through Greenwich, UK.

THE INTERNATIONAL DATELINE

The International Dateline is an imaginary line from pole to pole that roughly corresponds to the 180° line of longitude. It is an arbitrary marker between calendar days. The dateline is needed because of the use of local times around the world rather than a single universal time. When moving from west to east across the dateline, travelers have to set their watches back one day. Those traveling in the opposite direction, from east to west, must add a day.

DAYLIGHT SAVING TIME

Daylight saving is a summertime adjustment to the local time in a country or region, designed to increase the hours of daylight that occur during people's normal waking hours. To follow the system, clocks are advanced by an hour on a pre-decided date in spring and reverted back in the fall. About half of the world's nations use daylight saving.

LARGEST COUNTRIES

Russian Federation	6,592,735 sq miles (17,075,200 sq km)
Canada	3,854,085 sq miles (9,984,670 sq km)
USA	3,717,792 sq miles (9,629,091 sq km)
China	3,705,386 sq miles (9,596,960 sq km)
Brazil	3,286,470 sq miles (8,511,965 sq km)
Australia	2,967,893 sq miles (7,686,850 sq km)
India	1,269,339 sq miles (3,287,590 sq km)
Argentina	1,068,296 sq miles (2,766,890 sq km)
Kazakhstan	1,049,150 sq miles (2,717,300 sq km)
Sudan	967,493 sq miles (2,505,810 sq km)

SMALLEST COUNTRIES

Vatican City	0.17 sq miles (0.44 sq km)
Monaco	0.75 sq miles (1.95 sq km)
Nauru	8 sq miles (21 sq km)
Tuvalu	10 sq miles (26 sq km)
San Marino	24 sq miles (61 sq km)
Liechtenstein	62 sq miles (160 sq km)
Marshall Islands	70 sq miles (181 sq km)
St. Kitts & Nevis	101 sq miles (261 sq km)
Maldives	116 sq miles (300 sq km)
Malta	122 sq miles (316 sq km)

MOST POPULOUS COUNTRIES

China	1,315,800,000
India	1,103,400,000
USA	298,200,000
Indonesia	222,800,000
Brazil	186,400,000
Cameroon	163,000,000
Pakistan	157,900,000
Russian Federation	143,200,000
Bangladesh	141,800,000
Nigeria	131,500,000

LEAST POPULOUS COUNTRIES

Vatican City	921
Tuvalu	11,630
Nauru	13,048
Palau	20,303
San Marino	28,880
Monaco	32,409
Liechtenstein	33,717
St. Kitts & Nevis	38,958
Marshall Islands	59,071
Antigua & Barbuda	68,722

MOST DENSELY POPULATED COUNTRIES

Monaco	43,212 people per sq mile (16,620 per sq km)
Singapore	18,220 people per sq mile (7049 per sq km)
Vatican City	5418 people per sq mile (2093 per sq km)
Malta	3242 people per sq mile (1256 per sq km)
Maldives	2836 people per sq mile (1097 per sq km)
Bangladesh	2743 people per sq mile (1059 per sq km)
Bahrain	2663 people per sq mile (1030 per sq km)
China	1838 people per sq mile (710 per sq km)
Mauritius	1671 people per sq mile (645 per sq km)
Barbados	1627 people per sq mile (628 per sq km)

MOST SPARSELY POPULATED COUNTRIES

Mongolia	4 people per sq mile (2 per sq km)
Namibia	6 people per sq mile (2 per sq km)
Australia	7 people per sq mile (3 per sq km)
Mauritania	8 people per sq mile (3 per sq km)
Suriname	8 people per sq mile (3 per sq km)
Botswana	8 people per sq mile (3 per sq km)
Iceland	8 people per sq mile (3 per sq km)
Canada	9 people per sq mile (4 per sq km)
Libya	9 people per sq mile (4 per sq km)
Guyana	10 people per sq mile (4 per sq km)

RICHEST COUNTRIES

(GNI PER CAPITA, IN US$)

Luxembourg	56,230
Norway	52,030
Liechtenstein	50,000
Switzerland	48,230
USA	41,400
Denmark	40,650
Iceland	38,620
Japan	37,810
Sweden	35,770
Ireland	34,280

POOREST COUNTRIES

(GNI PER CAPITA, IN US$)

Burundi	90
Ethiopia	110
Liberia	110
Congo, Dem. Rep	120
Somalia	120
Guinea-Bissau	160
Malawi	170
Eritrea	180
Sierra Leone	200
Rwanda	220

MOST WIDELY SPOKEN LANGUAGES

1. Chinese (Mandarin)	6. Arabic
2. English	7. Bengali
3. Hindi	8. Portuguese
4. Spanish	9. Malay-Indonesian
5. Russian	10. French

LARGEST DESERTS

Sahara	3,450,000 sq miles (9,065,000 sq km)
Gobi	500,000 sq miles (1,295,000 sq km)
Ar Rub al Khali	289,600 sq miles (750,000 sq km)
Great Victorian	249,800 sq miles (647,000 sq km)
Sonoran	120,000 sq miles (311,000 sq km)
Kalahari	120,000 sq miles (310,800 sq km)
Garagum	115,800 sq miles (300,000 sq km)
Takla Makan	100,400 sq miles (260,000 sq km)
Namib	52,100 sq miles (135,000 sq km)
Thar	33,670 sq miles (130,000 sq km)

NB – Most of Antarctica is a polar desert, with only 2 inches (50 mm)
of precipitation annually

LARGEST ISLANDS

Greenland	849,400 sq miles (2,200,000 sq km)
New Guinea	312,000 sq miles (808,000 sq km)
Borneo	292,200 sq miles (757,050 sq km)
Madagascar	229,300 sq miles (594,000 sq km)
Sumatra	202,300 sq miles (524,000 sq km)
Baffin Island	183,800 sq miles (476,000 sq km)
Honshu	88,800 sq miles (230,000 sq km)
Britain	88,700 sq miles (229,800 sq km)
Victoria Island	81,900 sq miles (212,000 sq km)
Ellesmere Island	75,700 sq miles (196,000 sq km)

HIGHEST MOUNTAINS

(HEIGHT ABOVE SEA LEVEL)

Everest	29,035 ft (8850 m)
K2	28,253 ft (8611 m)
Kanchenjunga I	28,210 ft (8598 m)
Makalu I	27,767 ft (8463 m)
Cho Oyu	26,907 ft (8201 m)
Dhaulagiri I	26,796 ft (8167 m)
Manaslu I	26,783 ft (8163 m)
Nanga Parbat I	26,661 ft (8126 m)
Annapurna I	26,547 ft (8091 m)
Gasherbrum I	26,471 ft (8068 m)

DEEPEST OCEAN FEATURES

Challenger Deep, Mariana Trench (Pacific)	36,201 ft (11,034 m)
Vityaz III Depth, Tonga Trench (Pacific)	35,704 ft (10,882 m)
Vityaz Depth, Kurile-Kamchatka Trench (Pacific)	34,588 ft (10,542 m)
Cape Johnson Deep, Philippine Trench (Pacific)	34,441 ft (10,497 m)
Kermadec Trench (Pacific)	32,964 ft (10,047 m)
Ramapo Deep, Japan Trench (Pacific)	32,758 ft (9984 m)
Milwaukee Deep, Puerto Rico Trench (Atlantic)	30,185 ft (9200 m)
Argo Deep, Torres Trench (Pacific)	30,070 ft (9165 m)
Meteor Depth, South Sandwich Trench (Atlantic)	30,000 ft (9144 m)
Planet Deep, New Britain Trench (Pacific)	29,988 ft (9140 m)

LARGEST BODIES OF INLAND WATER

(AREA & DEPTH)

Caspian Sea	143,243 sq miles (371,000 sq km)	3215 ft (980 m)
Lake Superior	32,151 sq miles (83,270 sq km)	1289 ft (393 m)
Lake Victoria	26,560 sq miles (68,880 sq km)	328 ft (100 m)
Lake Huron	23,436 sq miles (60,700 sq km)	751 ft (229 m)
Lake Michigan	22,402 sq miles (58,020 sq km)	922 ft (281 m)
Lake Tanganyika	12,703 sq miles (32,900 sq km)	4700 ft (1435 m)
Great Bear Lake	12,274 sq miles (31,790 sq km)	1047 ft (319 m)
Lake Baikal	11,776 sq miles (30,500 sq km)	5712 ft (1741 m)
Great Slave Lake	10,981 sq miles (28,440 sq km)	459 ft (140 m)
Lake Erie	9915 sq miles (25,680 sq km)	197 ft (60 m)

LONGEST RIVERS

Nile (NE Africa)	4160 miles (6695 km)
Amazon (South America)	4049 miles (6516 km)
Yangtze (China)	3915 miles (6299 km)
Mississippi/Missouri (US)	3710 miles (5969 km)
Ob'-Irtysh (Russ. Fed.)	3461 miles (5570 km)
Yellow River (China)	3395 miles (5464 km)
Congo (Central Africa)	2900 miles (4667 km)
Mekong (Southeast Asia)	2749 miles (4425 km)
Lena (Russian Federation)	2734 miles (4400 km)
Mackenzie (Canada)	2640 miles (4250 km)
Yenisey (Russian Federation)	2541 miles (4090 km)

GREATEST WATERFALLS

(MEAN FLOW OF WATER)

Boyoma (Congo)	600,400 cu. ft/sec (17,000 cu.m/sec)
Khône (Laos/Cambodia)	410,000 cu. ft/sec (11,600 cu.m/sec)
Niagara (USA/Canada)	195,000 cu. ft/sec (5500 cu.m/sec)
Grande (Uruguay)	160,000 cu. ft/sec (4500 cu.m/sec)
Paulo Afonso (Brazil)	100,000 cu. ft/sec (2800 cu.m/sec)
Urubupunga (Brazil)	97,000 cu. ft/sec (2750 cu.m/sec)
Iguaçu (Argentina/Brazil)	62,000 cu. ft/sec (1700 cu.m/sec)
Maribondo (Brazil)	53,000 cu. ft/sec (1500 cu.m/sec)
Victoria (Zimbabwe)	39,000 cu. ft/sec (1100 cu.m/sec)
Kabalega (Uganda)	42,000 cu. ft/sec (1200 cu.m/sec)
Churchill (Canada)	35,000 cu. ft/sec (1000 cu.m/sec)
Cauvery (India)	33,000 cu. ft/sec (900 cu.m/sec)

HIGHEST WATERFALLS

Angel (Venezuela)	3212 ft (979 m)
Tugela (South Africa)	3110 ft (948 m)
Utigard (Norway)	2625 ft (800 m)
Mongefossen (Norway)	2539 ft (774 m)
Mtarazi (Zimbabwe)	2500 ft (762 m)
Yosemite (USA)	2425 ft (739 m)
Ostre Mardola Foss (Norway)	2156 ft (657 m)
Tyssestrengane (Norway)	2119 ft (646 m)
*Cuquenan (Venezuela)	2001 ft (610 m)
Sutherland (New Zealand)	1903 ft (580 m)
*Kjellfossen (Norway)	1841 ft (561 m)

* indicates that the total height is a single leap

	GENERAL FACTS				
Country	Capital city	Land area (sq miles)	Main languages spoken	Unit of currency	Population (July 2006, estimate)
NORTH AMERICA					
Antigua and Barbuda	St John's	171	English	East Caribbean dollar	69
Bahamas	Nassau	5 381	English, Creole	Bahamian dollar	303
Barbados	Bridgetown	166	English	Barbados dollar	279
Belize	Belmopan	8 865	English, Spanish	Belezian dollar	287
Canada	Ottawa	3 854 083	English, French	Canadian dollar	33 098
Costa Rica	San José	19 725	Spanish, English	Colón	4 075 2
Cuba	Havana	42 792	Spanish	Cuban peso	11 382 8
Dominica	Roseau	291	English, French patois	East Caribbean dollar	68 9
Dominican Republic	Santo Domingo	18 810	Spanish	Dominican Republic peso	9 183
El Salvador	San Salvador	8 121	Spanish, Nahua	US dollar	6 822 3
Grenada	St George's	133	English, French patois	East Caribbean dollar	89 7
Guatemala	Guatemala City	42 032	Spanish, Amerindian languages	Quetzal, US dollar	12 293 5
Haiti	Port-au-Prince	10 712	French, Creole	Gourde	8 308 5
Honduras	Tegucigalpa	43 267	Spanish	Lempira	7 326 4
Jamaica	Kingston	4 243	English, patois English	Jamaican dollar	2 758 1
Mexico	Mexico City	744 034	Spanish	Mexican peso	107 449 5
Nicaragua	Managua	49 985	Spanish	Gold cordoba	5 570 1
Panama	Panama City	30 185	Spanish, English	Balboa, US dollar	3 191 3
St Kitts and Nevis	Basseterre	101	English	East Caribbean dollar	39 1
St Lucia	Castries	238	English, French patois	East Caribbean dollar	168 4
St Vincent and the Grenadines	Kingstown	150	English, French patois	East Caribbean dollar	117 8
Trinidad and Tobago	Port-of-Spain	2 037	English, Hindi, French, Spanish, Chinese	Trinidad & Tobago dollar	1 065 8
United States of America	Washington, DC	3 717 727	English, Spanish	US dollar	298 444 2
SOUTH AMERICA					
Argentina	Buenos Aires	1 068 020	Spanish	Argentine peso	39 921 8
Bolivia	La Paz/Sucre	424 052	Spanish, Quechua, Aymara	Boliviano	8 989 0
Brazil	Brasília	3 285 618	Portuguese, Spanish	Real	188 078 2
Chile	Santiago	292 183	Spanish	Chilean peso	16 134 2
Colombia	Bogotá	439 619	Spanish	Columbian peso	43 593 0
Ecuador	Quito	109 454	Spanish	US dollar	13 547 5
Guyana	Georgetown	82 978	English, Creole, Amerindian languages	Guyanese dollar	767 2
Paraguay	Asunción	157 006	Spanish, Guarani	Guarani	6 506 4
Peru	Lima	496 095	Spanish, Quechua, Aymara	Nuevo Sol	28 302 6
Suriname	Paramaribo	63 022	Dutch, English, Sranan Tongo	Surinamese dollar	439 1
Uruguay	Montevideo	68 021	Spanish	Uruguayan peso	3 431 9
Venezuela	Caracas	352 051	Spanish	Bolivar	25 730 4
AFRICA					
Algeria	Algiers	919 352	Arabic, French, Berber	Algerian dinar	32 930 09
Angola	Luanda	481 226	Portuguese, Bantu	Kwanza	12 127 07
Benin	Porto-Novo	43 471	French, Fon, Yoruba	CFA franc	7 862 94
Botswana	Gaborone	231 743	Setswana	Pula	1 639 83
Burkina Faso	Ouagadougou	105 841	French	CFA franc	13 902 97
Burundi	Bujumbura	10 742	Kirundi, French, Swahili	Burundi franc	8 090 06
Cameroon	Yaoundé	183 520	English, French	CFA franc	17 340 70
Cape Verde	Praia	1 557	Portuguese, Crioulo	Cape Verdean escudo	420 97
Central African Republic	Bangui	240 472	French, Sangho	CFA franc	4 303 35
Chad	Ndjamena	495 624	French, Arabic, Sara	CFA franc	9 944 20
Comoros	Moroni	838	Arabic, French, Shikomoro	Comoros franc	690 94
Congo, Democratic Republic of the	Kinshasha	905 328	French, Lingala, Kingwana	Congolese franc	62 660 55

Population density per sq mile (July 2006, estimate)	Birth rate per 1000 population (2005, estimate)	Death rate per 1000 population (2005, estimate)	Life expectancy at birth (years; 2006 estimate)		Medical doctors per 100 000 people (country data varies from 1990–2004)	Infant mortality (deaths per 1000 live births; 2006 estimate)	Adult literacy rate (percentage of adults over 15; age of country data varies, 1970–2003)		Average calorie intake per person (2006)	GNI per person (US$; 2004)	Annual electricity consumption (1 000 000 kWh; age of country data varies, 2000–05)	Annual military expenditure (US$1 000 000; age of country data varies, 1999–2004)	Mobile telephones (age of country data varies, 2001–05)	Internet users (age of country data varies, 2001–05)	Television broadcast stations (age of country data varies, 1995–2006)
			Male	Female			Male	Female							
404	17	5	69.78	74.66	17	18.86	-	-	2 349	10 000	93.0	-	38 200	10 000	2
56	18	9	62.24	69.03	106	24.68	94.7	96.5	2 755	14 920	1 683.0	-	121 800	84 000	2
1686	13	9	70.79	74.82	121	11.77	99.7	99.7	3 091	9 270	761.7	-	140 000	100 000	1
32	29	6	66.43	70.26	105	24.89	94.1	94.1	2 869	3 940	111.6	18.0	60 400	30 000	2
9	11	8	76.86	83.74	209	4.69	99.0	99.0	3 589	28 390	520 900.0	9 801.7	13 221 800	16 110 000	80
207	19	4	74.43	79.74	173	9.70	95.9	96.1	2 876	4 670	7 120.0	64.2	528 047	800 000	20
266	12	7	75.11	79.85	591	6.22	97.2	96.9	3 152	-	14 620.0	572.3	17 900	120 000	58
237	16	7	71.95	77.93	49	13.71	94.0	94.0	2 763	3 650	65.1	-	9 400	12 500	1
488	23	7	70.21	73.33	188	28.25	84.6	84.8	2 347	2 080	11 710.0	180.0	2 120 400	500 000	25
840	27	6	67.88	75.28	124	24.39	-	-	2 584	2 350	4 450.0	157.0	1 149 800	550 000	5
674	22	7	63.06	66.68	50	14.27	-	-	2 932	3 760	148.6	-	7 600	15 000	2
292	34	7	67.65	71.18	90	30.94	78.0	63.3	2 219	2 130	6 025.0	201.9	1 577 100	400 000	26
775	37	12	51.89	54.60	25	71.65	54.8	51.2	2 086	390	507.8	26.0	140 000	80 000	2
169	30	7	67.75	70.98	83	25.82	76.1	76.3	2 356	1 030	4 369.0	100.6	326 500	168 600	11
650	17	5	71.54	75.03	85	15.98	84.1	91.6	2 685	2 900	6 124.0	31.2	1 400 000	600 000	7
144	21	5	72.63	78.33	171	20.26	94.0	90.5	3 145	6 770	193 900.0	6 043.0	28 125 000	10 033 000	236
111	25	5	68.55	72.81	164	28.11	67.2	67.8	2 298	790	2 343.0	32.8	202 800	90 000	3
106	20	7	72.68	77.87	168	16.37	93.2	91.9	2 272	4 450	4 870.0	147.0	834 000	120 000	38
387	18	9	69.56	75.42	118	14.12	-	-	2 609	7 600	103.9	-	5 000	10 000	1
708	20	5	70.29	77.65	518	13.17	89.5	90.6	2 988	4 310	261.4	-	14 300	13 000	2
786	16	6	71.99	75.77	88	14.40	96.0	96.0	2 599	3 650	88.4	-	10 000	7 000	1
523	13	9	65.71	67.86	79	25.05	99.1	98.0	2 732	8 580	5 651.0	66.7	361 900	138 000	4
80	14	8	75.02	80.82	549	6.43	99.0	99.0	3 774	41 400	3 656 000.0	370 700.0	158 722 000	159 000 000	1740
37	17	8	72.38	80.05	301	14.73	97.1	97.1	2 992	3 720	83 310.0	4 300.0	6 500 000	4 100 000	42
21	24	8	63.21	68.61	73	51.77	93.1	81.6	2 235	960	3 963.0	132.2	1 401 500	270 000	48
57	17	6	68.02	76.12	-	28.60	86.1	86.6	3 049	3 090	371 400.0	11 000.0	46 373 300	14 300 000	138
55	15	6	73.49	80.21	109	8.58	96.4	96.1	2 863	4 910	44 130.0	3 420.0	6 445 700	3 575 000	63
99	21	6	68.15	75.96	135	20.35	92.4	92.6	2 585	2 000	42 850.0	3 300.0	6 186 200	2 732 200	60
124	23	4	73.55	79.43	148	22.87	94.0	91.0	2 754	2 180	10 550.0	655.0	2 394 400	569 700	7
9	18	8	63.21	68.65	48	32.19	99.1	98.5	2 692	990	724.5	6.5	87 300	125 000	3
41	29	5	72.56	77.78	117	24.78	94.9	93.0	2 565	1 170	3 528.0	53.1	1 770 300	120 000	5
57	21	6	68.05	71.71	117	30.94	93.5	82.1	2 571	2 360	21 090.0	829.3	2 908 800	2 850 000	13
7	18	7	66.66	71.47	45	23.02	92.3	84.1	2 652	2 250	1 873.0	7.5	168 100	20 000	3
50	14	9	73.12	79.65	365	11.61	97.6	98.4	2 828	3 950	7 762.0	257.5	652 000	400 000	23
73	19	5	71.49	77.81	194	21.54	93.8	93.1	2 336	4 020	81 320.0	1 687.0	6 463 600	1 274 400	66
36	17	5	71.68	74.92	85	29.87	78.8	61.0	3 022	2 280	24 900.0	2 480.0	1 447 310	500 000	46
25	45	26	37.47	39.83	8	185.36	82.1	53.8	2 083	1 030	1 782.0	183.6	130 000	41 000	6
181	42	14	51.90	54.22	6	79.56	46.4	22.6	2 548	530	538.2	96.5	236 200	70 000	1
7	23	29	33.90	33.56	29	53.70	76.9	82.4	2 151	4 340	2 641.0	338.5	435 000	60 000	1
131	44	19	47.33	50.42	4	91.35	36.9	16.6	2 462	360	349.3	64.2	227 000	48 000	1
753	40	17	50.07	51.58	5	63.13	58.5	45.2	1 649	90	141.4	38.7	64 000	14 000	1
94	35	15	50.98	51.34	7	63.52	84.7	73.4	2 273	800	2 779.0	221.1	1 077 000	60 000	1
270	25	7	67.41	74.15	17	46.52	85.8	69.2	3 243	1 770	41.1	14.1	53 300	20 400	1
18	35	20	43.46	43.62	4	85.63	63.3	39.9	1 980	310	98.6	15.5	13 000	5 000	1
20	46	16	45.88	49.21	3	91.45	56.0	39.3	2 114	260	111.6	101.3	65 000	15 000	1
825	38	8	60.00	64.72	7	72.85	63.6	49.3	1 754	530	16.7	11.6	2 000	5 000	-
69	44	14	50.01	52.94	7	88.62	76.2	55.1	1 599	120	4 324.0	93.5	1 000 000	50 000	4

Country	Capital city	Land area (sq miles)	Main languages spoken	Unit of currency	Population (July 2006, estimate)
			GENERAL FACTS		
Congo	Brazzaville	132 012	French, Lingala Monokutuba	CFA franc	3 702 3
Côte d'Ivoire	Yamoussoukro	124 470	French	CFA franc	17 654 8
Djibouti	Djibouti	8 878	French, Arabic, Somali, Afar	Djibouti franc	486 5
Egypt	Cairo	386 560	Arabic, English, French	Egyptian pound	78 887 0
Equatorial Guinea	Malabo	10 828	Spanish, French, Fang	CFA franc	540 1
Eritrea	Asmara	46 830	Afar, Arabic	Nakfa	4 786 9
Ethiopia	Addis Ababa	435 071	Amharic, Tigrinya, Oromigna, Guaragigna, Somali, Arabic, English	Birr	74 777 9
Gabon	Libreville	103 319	French, Fang, local languages	CFA franc	1 424 9
Gambia	Banjul	4 362	English, Mandinka, Wolof, Fula	Dalasi	1 641 5
Ghana	Accra	92 432	English, local languages	Cedi	22 409 5
Guinea	Conakry	94 901	French	Guinea franc	9 690 2
Guinea-Bissau	Bissau	13 942	Portuguese, Crioulo	CFA franc	1 442 0
Kenya	Nairobi	224 903	English, Kiswahili	Kenya shilling	34 707 8
Lesotho	Maseru	11 717	Sesotho, English	Loti, South African rand	2 022 3
Liberia	Monrovia	42 989	English	Liberian dollar	3 042 0
Libya	Tripoli	679 182	Arabic, Italian, English	Libyan dinar	5 900 7
Madagascar	Antananarivo	226 597	French, Malagasy	Ariary	18 595 4
Malawi	Lilongwe	45 733	Chichewa, Chinyanja, Chiyao	Malawi kwacha	13 013 9
Mali	Bamako	478 640	French, Bambara	CFA franc	11 716 8
Mauritania	Nouakchott	397 850	Arabic, Pulaar, Soninke, French, Hassaniya, Wolof	Ouguiya	3 177 3
Mauritius	Port Louis	787	Creole	Mauritian rupee	1 240 8
Morocco	Rabat	172 368	Arabic, Berber, French	Dirham	33 241 2
Mozambique	Maputo	309 414	Emakhuwa, Xichangana, Portuguese	Metical	19 686 5
Namibia	Windhoek	318 611	English, Afrikaans, German	Dollar, South African rand	2 044 1
Niger	Niamey	489 062	French, Hausa, Djerma	CFA franc	12 525 09
Nigeria	Abuja	356 574	English, Hausa, Yoruba, Igbo, Fulani	Naira	131 859 7
Rwanda	Kigali	10 166	Kinyarwanda, French, English, Kiswahili	Rwanda franc	8 648 2
São Tomé and Príncipe	São Tomé	386	Portuguese	Dobra	193 4
Senegal	Dakar	75 729	French, Wolof, Pulaar, Jola, Mandinka	CFA franc	11 987 12
Seychelles	Victoria	176	Creole	Seychelles rupee	81 5
Sierra Leone	Freetown	27 692	English, Mende, Temne, Krio	Leone	6 005 2
Somalia	Mogadishu	246 136	Somali, Arabic, Italian, English	Somali shilling	8 863 3
South Africa	Tshwane/Cape Town/Bloemfontein	470 886	IsiZulu, IsiXhosa, Afrikaans, Sepedi, English, Setswana, Sesotho, Xitsonga	Rand	44 187 6
Sudan	Khartoum	967 243	Arabic, Nubian, Ta Bedawie	Sudanese dinar	41 236 37
Swaziland	Mbabane	6 702	English, Siswati	Lilangeni	1 136 33
Tanzania	Dodoma	364 804	Kiswahili, English, Arabic	Tanzanian shilling	37 445 39
Togo	Lomé	21 919	French, Ewe, Mina, Kabye, Dagomba	CFA franc	5 548 70
Tunisia	Tunis	63 153	Arabic, French	Tunisian dinar	10 175 01
Uganda	Kampala	91 111	English, Ganda	Ugandan shilling	28 195 75
Western Sahara	Laâyoune	102 676	Hassaniya Arabic, Moroccan Arabic	Moroccan dirham	273 00
Zambia	Lusaka	290 509	English, Bemba, Kaonda, Lozi, Lunda, Luvale, Nyanja, Tonga	Zambian kwacha	11 502 01
Zimbabwe	Harare	150 764	English, Shona, Sindebele	Zimbabwe dollar	12 236 80
EUROPE					
Albania	Tirana	11 097	Albanian, Greek	Lek	3 581 65
Andorra	Andorra la Vella	181	Catalan, French	Euro	71 20
Austria	Vienna	32 374	German, Croatian, Hungarian, Slovene	Euro	8 192 88
Belarus	Minsk	80 134	Belarussian, Russian	Belarussian rouble	10 293 01
Belgium	Brussels	11 784	Dutch, French, German	Euro	10 379 06
Bosnia and Herzegovina	Sarajevo	19 736	Bosnian, Croatian, Serbian	Marka	4 498 97
Bulgaria	Sofia	42 811	Bulgarian	Lev	7 385 36
Croatia	Zagreb	21 825	Croatian	Kuna	4 494 74

POPULATION · HEALTH AND EDUCATION · ECONOMIC DEVELOPMENT · TECHNOLOGICAL DEVELOPMENT

Population density per sq mile (July 2006, estimate)	Birth rate per 1000 population (2005, estimate)	Death rate per 1000 population (2005, estimate)	Life expectancy at birth (years; 2006 estimate)		Medical doctors per 100 000 people (country data varies from 1990–2004)	Infant mortality (deaths per 1000 live births; 2006 estimate)	Adult literacy rate (percentage of adults over 15; age of country data varies, 1970–2003)		Average calorie intake per person (2006)	GNI per person (US$; 2004)	Annual electricity consumption (1 000 000 kWh; age of country data varies, 2000–05)	Annual military expenditure (US$1 000 000; age of country data varies, 1999–2004)	Mobile telephones (age of country data varies, 2001–05)	Internet users (age of country data varies, 2001–05)	Television broadcast stations (age of country data varies, 1995–2006)
			Male	Female			Male	Female							
28	28	15	51.65	53.98	25	85.29	89.6	78.4	2 162	770	619.0	126.5	330 000	15 000	1
142	36	15	46.24	51.48	9	89.11	57.9	43.6	2 631	770	3 418.0	180.2	1 236 000	90 000	14
55	40	19	41.86	44.52	13	102.44	78.0	58.4	2 220	1 030	223.2	28.6	23 000	6 500	1
204	23	5	68.77	73.93	212	31.33	68.3	46.9	3 388	1 310	78 160.0	2 440.0	8 583 940	4 200 000	98
50	36	12	48.00	51.13	25	89.21	93.3	78.4	-	-	27.4	126.2	41 500	1 800	1
102	39	14	57.44	60.66	3	46.30	69.9	47.6	1 531	180	251.9	151.0	-	9 500	1
172	39	15	47.86	50.24	3	93.62	50.3	35.1	1 857	110	1 914.0	337.1	97 800	75 000	1
14	36	12	53.21	55.81	29	54.51	73.7	53.3	2 637	3 940	1 383.0	184.8	300 000	35 000	4
376	40	12	52.30	56.03	4	71.58	47.8	32.8	2 273	290	130.2	1.0	100 000	25 000	1
242	24	11	58.07	59.69	9	55.02	82.7	67.1	2 667	380	5 081.0	49.2	799 900	170 000	10
102	42	15	48.34	50.70	9	90.00	49:9	21.9	2 409	460	720.8	56.7	111 500	40 000	6
103	38	17	45.05	48.75	17	105.21	58.1	27.4	2 024	160	52.1	8.9	1 300	19 000	-
154	40	15	49.78	48.07	13	59.26	90.6	79.7	2 090	460	4 238.0	177.1	1 590 800	400 000	8
173	27	25	35.55	33.21	5	87.24	74.5	94.5	2 638	740	363.5	32.3	92 000	21 000	1
71	44	18	37.99	41.35	-	155.76	73.3	41.6	1 900	110	473.8	1.5	2 000	1 000	1
9	27	4	74.46	79.02	129	23.71	92.4	72.0	3 320	4 450	13 390.0	1 300.0	100 000	160 000	12
82	42	11	54.93	59.82	9	75.21	75.5	62.5	2 005	300	767.7	44.6	279 500	70 500	1
285	44	23	41.93	41.45	1	94.37	76.1	49.8	2 155	170	1 206.0	11.1	135 100	36 000	1
24	47	19	47.05	51.01	4	107.58	53.5	39.6	2 174	360	762.6	22.4	290 000	25 000	1
8	41	12	50.88	55.42	14	69.48	51.8	31.9	2 772	420	172.6	20.8	300 000	10 000	1
1 577	16	7	68.66	76.66	85	14.59	88.6	82.7	2 955	4 640	1 805.0	12.5	462 400	150 000	2
193	22	6	68.62	73.37	48	40.24	64.1	39.4	3 052	1 520	17 580.0	2 305.6	7 332 800	800 000	35
64	36	21	39.53	40.13	2	129.24	63.5	32.7	2 079	250	10 460.0	117.3	428 900	50 000	1
6	25	18	44.46	42.29	30	48.10	84.4	83.7	2 278	2 370	2 372.0	168.4	223 700	65 000	8
26	48	21	43.80	43.73	3	118.25	25.8	9.7	2 130	230	263.9	33.3	24 000	15 000	3
370	41	17	46.52	47.66	27	97.14	75.7	60.6	2 726	390	14 460.0	544.6	3 149 500	750 000	3
851	41	16	46.26	48.38	2	89.61	76.3	64.7	2 084	220	121.1	50.1	134 000	25 000	2
501	41	7	65.73	68.95	47	41.83	85.0	62.0	2 460	370	14.0	0.7	4 800	15 000	2
158	35	11	57.70	60.85	8	52.94	50.0	30.7	2 279	670	1 239.0	107.3	575 900	225 000	1
463	16	6	66.69	77.63	132	15.14	91.4	92.3	2 465	8 090	224.4	12.3	54 500	11 700	2
217	43	21	38.05	42.46	7	160.39	39.8	20.5	1 936	200	242.4	13.2	67 000	8 000	2
36	46	17	46.71	50.28	-	114.89	49.7	25.8	1 628	-	219.1	18.9	35 000	89 000	4
94	19	21	43.25	42.19	69	60.66	87.0	85.7	2 956	3 630	197 400.0	3 172.0	16 860 000	3 100 000	556
43	35	9	57.69	60.21	16	61.05	71.8	50.5	2 228	530	2 943.0	587.0	650 000	300 000	3
170	28	25	32.10	33.17	18	71.85	82.6	80.8	2 322	1 660	1 161.0	40.5	88 000	27 000	5
103	38	17	44.93	46.37	2	96.48	85.9	70.7	1 975	330	2 959.0	20.6	891 200	250 000	3
253	34	12	55.41	59.49	6	60.63	75.4	46.9	2 345	380	654.3	35.5	220 000	210 000	3
161	16	5	73.40	76.96	70	23.84	83.4	65.3	3 238	2 630	10 760.0	356.0	1 899 900	630 000	26
309	47	13	51.68	53.69	5	66.15	79.5	60.4	2 410	270	1 448.0	170.3	776 200	125 000	8
3	-	-	-	-	-	-	-	-	-	-	83.7	-	-	-	9
40	41	20	39.76	40.31	7	86.84	86.8	74.8	1 927	450	5 345.0	106.8	241 000	68 200	9
81	30	25	40.39	38.16	6	51.71	94.2	87.2	1 943	-	11 220.0	217.0	379 100	500 000	16
323	15	5	74.78	80.34	139	20.75	-	-	2 848	2 080	6 760.0	56.5	1 100 000	30 000	3
393	9	6	80.61	86.61	-	4.04	100.0	100.0	-	-	-	-	23 500	24 500	0
253	9	10	76.17	82.11	324	4.60	-	-	3 673	32 300	57 450.0	1 497.0	7 094 500	3 730 000	10
128	11	14	63.47	74.98	450	13.00	99.8	99.5	3 000	2 120	34 300.0	176.1	1 118 000	1 391 900	47
880	11	10	75.59	82.09	418	4.62	99.0	99.0	3 584	31 030	79 660.0	3 999.0	8 135 500	3 400 000	25
228	13	8	74.39	81.88	134	9.82	98.4	91.1	2 894	2 040	8 849.0	234.3	1 050 000	100 000	33
173	10	14	68.68	76.13	338	19.85	99.1	98.2	2 848	2 740	31 750.0	356.0	2 597 500	630 000	39
206	10	11	71.03	78.53	237	6.72	99.4	97.8	2 799	6 590	15 810.0	620.0	2 553 000	1 014 000	36

Country	Capital city	Land area (sq miles)	Main languages spoken	Unit of currency	Population (July 2006, estimate)
			GENERAL FACTS		
Cyprus	Nicosia	3 571	Greek, Turkish, English	Cyprus pound, Turkish lira	784 3
Czech Republic	Prague	30 442	Czech	Czech Republic koruna	10 235 4
Denmark	Copenhagen	16 634	Danish, English	Danish krone	5 450 6
Estonia	Tallinn	17 457	Estonian, Russian	Kroon	1 324 3
Finland	Helsinki	130 524	Finnish, Swedish	Euro	5 231 3
France	Paris	211 154	French	Euro	60 876 1
Germany	Berlin	137 807	German	Euro	82 422 2
Greece	Athens	50 543	Greek	Euro	10 688 0
Vatican City	Vatican City	0.17	Italian, Latin, French	Euro	9
Hungary	Budapest	35 910	Hungarian	Forint	9 981 3.
Iceland	Reykjavík	39 758	Icelandic, English	Icelandic krona	299 3
Ireland	Dublin	27 128	English, Irish	Euro	4 062 2
Italy	Rome	116 275	Italian	Euro	58 133 5
Latvia	Riga	24 931	Latvian, Russian	Lat	2 274 7.
Liechtenstein	Vaduz	62	German	Swiss franc	33 9
Lithuania	Vilnius	25 167	Lithuanian	Litas	3 585 9
Luxembourg	Luxembourg	998	Luxembourgish, German, French	Euro	474 4
Macedonia	Skopje	9 779	Macedonian	Macedonian denar	2 050 5
Malta	Valletta	122	Maltese, English	Maltese lira	400 2
Moldova	Chişinău	13 063	Moldovan, Russian, Gagauz	Moldovan leu	4 466 70
Monaco	Monaco	0.77	French, English, Italian, Monégasque	Euro	32 5
Montenegro	Podgorica	5 331	Montenegrin, Serbian, Albanian	Euro	620 1
Netherlands	Amsterdam/The Hague	16 029	Dutch, Frisian	Euro	16 491 46
Norway	Oslo	125 149	Bokmal Norwegian, Nynorsk Norwegian	Norwegian krone	4 610 82
Poland	Warsaw	120 696	Polish	Zloty	38 536 86
Portugal	Lisbon	35 663	Portuguese, Mirandese	Euro	10 605 87
Romania	Bucharest	91 675	Romanian, Hungarian, German	Leu	22 303 55
Russian Federation	Moscow	6 591 027	Russian	Rouble	142 893 54
San Marino	San Marino	24	Italian	Euro	29 25
Serbia	Belgrade	34 107	Serbian	Serbian dinar, Euro	9 700 00
Slovakia	Bratislava	18 854	Slovak, Hungarian	Slovakian koruna	5 439 44
Slovenia	Ljubljana	7 825	Slovenian, Serbo-Croatian	Tolar	2 010 34
Spain	Madrid	194 846	Spanish, Catalan, Galician, Basque	Euro	40 397 84
Sweden	Stockholm	173 686	Swedish	Swedish krona	9 016 59
Switzerland	Bern	15 938	German, French, Italian	Swiss franc	7 523 93
Ukraine	Kiev	233 028	Ukrainian, Russian	Hryvnia	46 710 81
United Kingdom	London	94 501	English, Welsh	Pound sterling	60 609 15
ASIA					
Afghanistan	Kabul	249 935	Afghan Persian, Dari, Pashtu	Afghani	31 056 99
Armenia	Yerevan	11 503	Armenian	Dram	2 976 37.
Azerbaijan	Baku	33 428	Azeri	Manat	7 961 619
Bahrain	Manama	257	Arabic, English, Farsi, Urdu	Bahraini dinar	698 585
Bangladesh	Dhaka	55 584	Bengali, English	Taka	147 365 352
Bhutan	Thimphu	18 142	Dzongkha, English	Ngultrum, Indian rupee	2 279 723
Brunei	Bandar Seri Begawan	2 227	Malay, English, Chinese	Brunei dollar	379 444
Cambodia	Phnom Penh	69 881	Khmer	Riel	13 881 427
China	Beijing	3 704 427	Mandarin, Cantonese	Yuan	1 313 973 713
East Timor	Dili	5 793	Tetum, Portuguese, Indonesian, English	US dollar	1 062 777
Georgia	Tbilisi	26 904	Georgian	Lari	4 661 473
India	New Delhi	1 269 010	Hindi, English, local languages	Indian rupee	1 095 351 995

POPULATION					HEALTH AND EDUCATION					ECONOMIC DEVELOPMENT			TECHNOLOGICAL DEVELOPMENT		
Population density per sq mile (July 2006, estimate)	Birth rate per 1000 population (2005, estimate)	Death rate per 1000 population (2005, estimate)	Life expectancy at birth (years; 2006 estimate)		Medical doctors per 100 000 people (country data varies from 1990–2004)	Infant mortality (deaths per 1000 live births; 2006 estimate)	Adult literacy rate (percentage of adults over 15; age of country data varies, 1970–2003)		Average calorie intake per person (2006)	GNI per person (US$; 2004)	Annual electricity consumption (1 000 000 kWh; age of country data varies, 2000–05)	Annual military expenditure (US$1 000 000; age of country data varies, 1999–2004)	Mobile telephones (age of country data varies, 2001–05)	Internet users (age of country data varies, 2001–05)	Television broadcast stations (age of country data varies, 1995–2006)
			Male	Female			Male	Female							
220	13	8	75.44	80.31	298	7.04	98.9	96.3	3 255	17 580	3 535.0	384.0	561 078	210 000	8
336	9	11	72.94	79.69	343	3.89	99.0	99.0	3 171	9 150	56 500.0	2 170.0	9 708 700	27 000 000	150
328	11	10	75.49	80.22	366	4.51	99.0	99.0	3 439	40 650	31 680.0	3 271.6	4 785 300	2 756 000	26
76	10	13	66.58	77.83	316	7.73	99.8	99.8	3 002	7 010	7 024.0	155.0	881 000	444 000	3
40	11	10	74.99	82.17	311	3.55	100.0	100.0	3 100	32 790	78 940.0	1 800.0	4 700 000	2 650 000	120
288	12	9	76.10	83.54	329	4.21	99.0	99.0	3 654	30 090	433 300.0	45 000.0	41 683 100	21 900 000	584
598	8	11	75.81	81.96	362	4.12	99.0	99.0	3 496	30 120	510 400.0	35 063.0	64 800 000	39 000 000	373
211	10	10	76.72	81.91	440	5.43	98.6	96.5	3 721	16 610	53 500.0	5 890.0	8 936 200	1 718 400	36
5 482	-	-	-	-	-	-	100.0	100.0	-	-	-	0.0	-	-	1
278	10	13	68.45	77.14	316	8.39	99.5	99.3	3 483	8 270	39 960.0	1 080.0	6 862 800	1 600 000	35
8	14	7	78.23	82.48	347	3.29	99.0	99.0	3 249	38 620	7 769.0	0.0	279 100	195 000	14
150	15	8	75.11	80.52	237	5.31	99.0	99.0	3 656	34 280	22 970.0	700.0	3 400 000	1 260 000	4
500	9	10	76.88	82.94	606	5.83	99.0	98.3	3 671	26 120	302 200.0	28 182.8	55 918 000	18 500 000	358
91	9	14	66.08	76.85	291	9.35	9.8	99.8	2 938	5 460	5 839.0	87.0	1 219 600	936 000	44
548	10	7	76.10	83.28	-	4.64	-	-	-	-	-	-	11 400	20 000	-
142	9	11	69.20	79.49	403	6.78	99.7	99.6	3 324	5 740	9 109.0	230.8	2 169 900	695 700	27
475	12	8	75.60	82.38	255	4.74	100.0	100.0	3 701	56 230	6 112.0	231.6	473 000	165 000	5
210	12	9	71.51	76.62	-	9.81	98.2	94.1	2 655	2 350	5 289.0	200.0	830 000	100 000	31
3 280	10	8	76.83	81.31	293	3.86	-	-	3 587	12 250	1 936.0	31.1	290 000	120 000	6
278	15	13	61.61	69.88	269	38.38	99.6	98.7	2 806	710	3 036.0	8.7	338 200	150 000	1
42 264	9	13	75.85	83.74	-	5.35	99.0	99.0	-	-	-	-	19 300	16 000	5
116	12	11	72.37	77.75	-	12.52	98.9	94.1	2 678	2 620	36 620.0	654.0	3 634 600	847 000	771
1 029	11	9	76.39	81.67	329	4.96	99.0	99.0	3 362	31 700	101 600.0	9 408.0	12 500 000	8 500 000	21
37	12	9	76.91	82.31	356	3.67	100.0	100.0	3 484	52 030	106 100.0	4 033.5	4 163 400	2 288 000	360
319	11	10	70.95	79.23	220	7.22	99.8	99.7	3 374	6 090	121 300.0	3 500.0	17 401 000	8 970 000	179
297	11	10	74.43	81.20	324	4.98	95.5	91.3	3 741	14 350	44 010.0	3 497.8	9 341 400	3 600 000	62
243	11	12	68.14	75.34	189	25.50	99.1	97.7	3 455	2 920	45 160.0	985.0	6 900 000	4 000 000	48
22	10	15	60.45	74.10	417	15.13	99.7	99.5	3 072	3 410	811 500.0	-	17 608 800	6 000 000	7306
1 219	10	8	78.23	85.50	-	5.63	-	-	-	-	-	0.7	16 800	14 300	1
284	12	11	72.37	77.75	-	12.52	98.9	94.1	2 678	2 620	36 620.0	654.0	3 634 600	847 000	771
288	11	9	70.76	78.89	325	7.26	99.7	99.6	2 889	6 480	25 230.0	406.0	3 678 800	1 375 800	80
257	9	10	72.63	80.29	219	4.40	99.7	99.6	3 001	14 810	12 470.0	370.0	1 739 100	750 000	48
207	10	10	76.32	83.20	320	4.37	98.7	97.2	3 371	21 210	231 200.0	9 906.5	37 506 700	9 789 000	224
52	10	10	78.29	82.87	305	2.76	99.0	99.0	3 185	35 770	131 800.0	5 729.0	7 949 000	5 125 000	169
472	10	9	77.69	83.48	352	4.34	99.0	99.0	3 526	48 230	55 860.0	2 548.0	6 172 000	2 556 000	115
200	11	16	64.71	75.59	297	9.90	99.8	99.6	3 054	1 260	153 100.0	617.9	4 200 000	3 800 000	33
641	11	10	76.09	81.13	166	5.08	99.0	99.0	3 412	33 940	346 100.0	42 836.5	49 677 000	25 000 000	228
124	47	21	43.16	43.53	-	160.23	51.0	21.0	1 539	-	1 042.0	188.4	15 000	1 000	10
259	12	8	68.25	76.02	353	22.47	99.4	98.0	2 268	1 120	4 420.0	135.0	114 400	150 000	3
238	20	10	59.78	68.13	354	79.00	99.5	98.2	2 575	950	20 250.0	121.0	870 000	300 000	2
2 718	18	4	71.97	77.00	160	16.80	91.9	85.0	-	12 410	6 830.0	628.9	443 100	195 700	4
2 651	30	8	62.47	62.45	23	60.83	53.9	31.8	2 205	440	16 200.0	995.3	1 365 000	243 000	15
126	34	13	55.02	54.53	5	98.41	60.0	34.0	-	760	250.3	13.7	22 000	15 000	1
170	19	3	72.57	77.59	101	12.25	96.3	91.4	2 855	-	2 473.0	290.7	137 000	35 000	2
199	27	9	57.35	61.32	16	68.78	84.7	64.1	2 046	320	115.0	112.0	380 000	30 000	7
355	13	7	70.89	74.46	164	23.12	95.1	86.5	2 951	1 290	2 170 000.0	67 490.0	269 000 000	94 000 000	3420
183	27	6	63.96	68.67	-	45.89	-	-	2 806	-	-	4.4	-	-	-
173	10	9	72.80	79.87	391	17.97	100.0	100.0	2 354	1 040	8 630.0	23.0	522 300	150 500	12
863	22	8	63.90	65.57	51	54.63	70.2	48.3	2 459	620	519 900.0	18 860.0	26 154 400	18 481 000	562

			GENERAL FACTS		
Country	**Capital city**	**Land area (sq miles)**	**Main languages spoken**	**Unit of currency**	**Population (July 2006, estimate)**
Indonesia	Jakarta	740 904	Indonesian, English, Dutch	Rupiah	245 452 73
Iran	Tehran	636 128	Persian	Iranian rial	68 688 43
Iraq	Baghdad	168 710	Arabic, Kurdish, Assyrian, Armenian	New Iraqi dinar	26 783 38
Israel	Jerusalem	8 017	Hebrew, Arabic, English	Shekel	6 352 11
Japan	Tokyo	145 844	Japanese	Yen	127 463 61
Jordan	Amman	35 628	Arabic, English	Jordanian dinar	5 906 76
Kazakhstan	Astana	1 048 878	Kazakh, Russian	Tenge	15 233 24
Kuwait	Kuwait	6 879	Arabic, English	Kuwaiti dinar	2 418 39
Kyrgyzstan	Bishkek	76 621	Kyrgyz, Russian	Som	5 213 89
Laos	Vientiane	91 405	Lao, French, English	Kip	6 368 48
Lebanon	Beirut	4 014	Arabic, French, English, Armenian	Lebanese pound	3 874 05
Malaysia	Kuala Lumpur/Putrajaya	127 284	Malay, English, Chinese	Ringgit	24 385 85
Maldives	Male	116	Maldivian Dhivehi, English	Rufiyaa	359 00
Mongolia	Ulan Bator	603 749	Khalkha Mongol	Tögrög/Tugrik	2 832 22
Myanmar	Nay Pyi Taw	265 375	Burmese	Kyat	47 382 63
Nepal	Kathmandu	54 349	Nepali	Nepalese rupee	28 287 14
North Korea	Pyongyang	46 528	Korean	North Korean won	23 113 01
Oman	Muscat	82 010	Arabic, English, Baluchi, Urdu	Omani rial	3 102 22
Pakistan	Islamabad	310 321	Punjabi, English	Pakistani rupee	165 803 56
Philippines	Manila	115 800	Filipino, English	Philippine peso	89 468 67
Qatar	Doha	4 415	Arabic, English	Quatari rial	885 35
Saudi Arabia	Riyadh	756 785	Arabic	Saudi riyal	27 019 73
Singapore	Singapore	267	Mandarin, English, Malay	Singapore dollar	4 492 15
South Korea	Seoul	38 013	Korean, English	South Korean won	48 846 82
Sri Lanka	Colombo	25 325	Sinhala, Tamil	Sri Lanka rupee	20 222 24
Syria	Damascus	71 480	Arabic, Kurdish, Armenian, Aramaic	Syrian pound	18 881 36
Taiwan	Taipei	13 888	Mandarin Chinese, Taiwanese (Min)	Taiwan dollar	23 036 08
Tajikistan	Dushanbe	55 237	Tajik, Russian	Somoni	7 320 81
Thailand	Bangkok	198 404	Thai, English	Baht	64 631 59
Turkey	Ankara	301 304	Turkish, Kurdish, Arabic, Armenian, Greek	Turkish lira	70 413 95
Turkmenistan	Aşgabat	188 407	Turkmen, Russian	Manat	5 042 92
United Arab Emirates	Abu Dhabi	31 992	Arabic, Persian, English, Hindi, Urdu	Dirham	2 602 71
Uzbekistan	Tashkent	172 696	Uzbek, Russian	Soum	27 307 13
Vietnam	Hanoi	127 210	Vietnamese, English	Dong	84 402 96
Yemen	Sana	203 796	Arabic	Yemeni rial	21 456 18

AUSTRALASIA & OCEANIA

Country	**Capital city**	**Land area (sq miles)**	**Main languages spoken**	**Unit of currency**	**Population**
Australia	Canberra	2 967 124	English	Australian dollar	20 264 082
Fiji	Suva	7 052	English, Fijian, Hindustani	Fiji dollar	905 949
Kiribati	Tarawa	313	I-Kiribati, English	Australian dollar	105 432
Marshall Islands	Majuro	70	Marshallese	US dollar	60 422
Micronesia, Federated States of	Palikir	271	English, Trukese, Pohnpeian, Yapese, Kosrean, Ulithian, Woleaian, Nukuoro, Kapingamarangi	US dollar	108 004
Nauru	Yaren District (government offices)	8	Nauruan, English	Australian dollar	13 287
New Zealand	Wellington	103 710	English, Maori	New Zealand dollar	4 076 140
Palau	Koror	177	Palauan	US dollar	20 579
Papua New Guinea	Port Moresby	178 656	Melanesian pidgin, English	Kina	5 670 544
Samoa	Apia	1 136	Samoan, English	Tala	176 908
Solomon Islands	Honiara	10 982	Melanesian pidgin, English	Solomon Islands dollar	552 438
Tonga	Nuku'alofa	289	Tongan, English	Pa'anga	114 689
Tuvalu	Funafuti	10	Tuvaluan, English, Samoan, Kiribati	Australian dollar	11 810
Vanuatu	Port Vila	4 709	English, Bislama, French	Vatu	208 869

POPULATION					HEALTH AND EDUCATION					ECONOMIC DEVELOPMENT			TECHNOLOGICAL DEVELOPMENT		
Population density per sq mile (July 06, estimate)	Birth rate per 1000 population (2005, estimate)	Death rate per 1000 population (2005, estimate)	Life expectancy at birth (years; 2006 estimate)		Medical doctors per 100 000 people (country data varies from 1990–2004)	Infant mortality (deaths per 1000 live births; 2006 estimate)	Adult literacy rate (percentage of adults over 15; age of country data varies, 1970–2003)		Average calorie intake per person (2006)	GNI per person (US$; 2004)	Annual electricity consumption (1 000 000 kWh; age of country data varies, 2000–05)	Annual military expenditure (US$1 000 000; age of country data varies, 1999–2004)	Mobile telephones (age of country data varies, 2001–05)	Internet users (age of country data varies, 2001–05)	Television broadcast stations (age of country data varies, 1995–2006)
			Male	Female			Male	Female							
331	21	6	67.42	72.45	16	34.39	92.5	83.4	2 904	1 140	101 800.0	1 300.0	11 700 000	8 000 000	41
108	17	6	68.86	71.74	105	40.30	85.6	73.0	3 085	2 300	132 100.0	4 300.0	3 376 500	4 300 000	28
159	33	6	67.76	70.31	-	48.64	55.9	24.4	2 197	-	33 300.0	1 300.0	20 000	25 000	21
792	18	6	77.33	81.70	391	6.89	97.3	93.6	3 666	17 380	39 670.0	9 110.0	6 334 000	2 000 000	17
874	10	9	77.96	84.70	201	3.24	99.0	99.0	2 761	37 180	946 300.0	45 841.0	86 658 600	57 200 000	211
166	22	3	75.90	81.05	205	16.76	95.9	86.3	2 673	2 140	7 959.0	1 460.0	1 325 300	457 000	20
15	16	10	61.56	72.52	330	28.30	99.1	97.7	2 677	2 260	52 550.0	221.8	1 027 000	250 000	12
352	22	2	76.13	78.31	153	9.71	85.1	81.7	3 010	17 970	35 520.0	2 584.5	1 420 000	567 000	13
68	23	7	64.48	72.70	268	34.49	99.3	98.1	2 999	400	8 783.0	19.2	53 100	152 000	-
70	36	12	53.45	57.61	59	83.31	77.4	55.5	2 312	390	3 298.0	10.7	55 200	15 000	4
965	19	6	70.41	75.48	325	23.72	93.1	82.2	3 196	4 980	10 670.0	540.6	775 100	400 000	15
192	23	5	69.80	75.38	70	17.16	92.0	85.4	2 881	4 650	73 630.0	1 690.0	11 124 100	8 692 100	1
3 095	35	7	63.08	65.80	78	54.89	97.1	97.3	2 548	2 510	125.6	41.1	41 900	15 000	1
5	22	7	62.64	67.25	267	52.12	98.0	97.5	2 249	590	2 908.0	23.1	404 400	220 000	52
179	18	12	58.07	64.03	-	61.85	89.2	81.4	2 937	-	6 875.0	39.0	66 500	28 000	2
520	31	10	60.43	59.91	5	65.32	62.7	34.9	2 453	260	2 299.0	99.2	50 400	80 000	1
497	16	7	68.92	74.51	-	23.29	99.0	99.0	2 142	-	17 430.0	5 217.4	-	-	4
38	37	4	71.14	75.72	126	18.89	83.1	67.2	-	7 890	9 582.0	253.0	464 900	180 000	13
534	30	8	62.40	64.44	66	70.45	61.7	35.2	2 419	600	71 540.0	3 848.0	2 624 800	1 500 000	22
773	25	6	67.32	73.24	118	22.81	92.5	92.7	2 379	1 170	44 480.0	805.5	15 201 000	3 500 000	225
201	16	5	71.37	76.57	221	18.04	89.1	88.6	-	-	9 053.0	723.0	376 500	126 000	1
36	30	3	73.66	77.78	140	12.81	84.7	70.8	2 844	10 430	134 900.0	18 000.0	7 238 200	1 500 000	117
16 825	10	4	79.13	84.49	140	2.29	96.6	88.6	-	24 220	30 890.0	4 470.0	3 521 800	2 310 000	7
1 285	10	6	73.61	80.75	-	6.16	99.2	96.6	3 058	13 980	303 300.0	20 000.0	33 591 800	29 220 000	64
799	16	7	70.83	76.12	43	13.97	94.8	90.0	2 385	1 010	6 796.0	514.8	931 600	200 000	21
264	28	5	69.01	71.70	140	28.61	89.7	64.0	3 038	1 190	25 280.0	858.0	400 000	220 000	44
1 659	13	6	74.67	80.47	-	6.29	-	-	-	-	206 100.0	7 574.0	25 089 600	13 800 000	29
133	33	8	62.03	68.00	218	106.49	99.6	99.1	1 828	280	15 050.0	35.4	47 600	4 100	13
326	16	7	69.95	74.68	30	19.49	94.9	90.5	2 467	2 540	107 300.0	1 775.0	26 500 000	6 971 500	5
233	17	6	70.18	75.18	124	39.69	94.3	78.7	3 357	3 750	140 300.0	12 155.0	27 887 500	5 500 000	635
27	28	9	58.43	65.41	317	72.56	99.3	98.3	2 742	1 340	8 847.0	90.0	52 000	8 000	4
81	19	4	72.92	78.08	202	14.09	76.1	81.7	3 225	-	38 320.0	1 600.0	2 972 300	1 110 200	15
158	26	8	61.19	68.14	289	69.99	99.6	99.0	2 241	460	48 450.0	200.0	320 800	492 000	4
663	17	6	68.05	73.85	53	25.14	93.9	86.9	2 566	550	36 920.0	650.0	2 742 000	3 500 000	7
105	43	9	60.23	64.11	22	59.88	70.5	30.0	2 038	570	2 827.0	885.5	411 100	100 000	7
7	12	7	77.64	83.52	249	4.63	99.0	99.0	3 054	26 900	200 700.0	16 650.0	14 347 000	9 472 000	104
128	23	6	67.32	72.45	34	12.30	95.5	91.9	2 894	2 690	721.4	36.0	109 900	55 000	-
337	31	8	59.06	65.24	-	47.27	-	-	2 859	970	11.2	-	500	2 000	1
863	34	5	68.33	72.39	-	28.43	93.6	93.7	-	2 370	-	-	600	1 400	2
399	25	5	68.24	71.95	-	29.16	91.0	88.0	-	1 990	178.6	-	1 800	6 000	3
1 661	25	7	59.50	66.84	-	9.78	-	-	-	-	21.4	-	1 500	300	1
39	14	8	75.82	81.93	223	5.76	99.0	99.0	3 219	20 310	37 030.0	1 147.0	2 599 000	2 110 000	41
116	18	7	67.26	73.77	-	14.46	93.0	90.0	-	6 870	-	-	1 000	-	1
32	30	7	63.08	67.58	5	49.96	71.1	57.7	2 193	580	1 481.0	16.9	15 000	75 000	3
156	16	7	68.20	73.94	70	26.85	99.6	99.7	2 945	1 860	107.9	-	2 700	4 000	2
50	31	4	70.40	75.55	13	20.63	-	-	2 265	550	51.2	-	-	2 200	-
397	25	5	67.32	72.45	34	12.30	98.8	99.0	-	1 830	31.6	-	9 000	2 900	3
1 181	22	7	66.08	70.66	-	19.47	-	-	-	-	-	-	0	1 300	0
44	23	8	61.34	64.44	11	53.80	-	-	2 587	1 340	38.1	-	7 800	7 500	1

GLOSSARY

This glossary defines certain geographical and technical terms used in this Atlas.

Acid rain Rain, sleet, snow, or mist that has absorbed waste gases from fossil-fueled power stations and vehicle exhausts, becoming acidic and poisonous.

Alluvium Material deposited by a river, such as silt, sand, and mud.

Archipelago A group, or chain, of islands.

Atoll A circular or horseshoe-shaped coral reef enclosing a shallow area of water (lagoon).

Aquifer A body of rock that can absorb water. It may be a source of water for wells or springs.

Bar, coastal An offshore strip of sand or shingle, either above or below the water.

Biodiversity The quantity of different animal or plant species in a given area.

Birthrate The number of live births per 1,000 individuals annually within a population.

Cash crop Agricultural produce grown for sale, often for foreign export, rather than to be consumed within the country or area in which it was grown.

Climate The long-term trends in weather conditions for an area.

Coniferous forest A type of forest containing trees or shrubs, like pines and firs, that have needles instead of leaves. They are found in temperate zones.

Continental plates The huge interlocking plates that make up the Earth's surface. A plate boundary is an area where two plates meet, and is the point at which earthquakes occur most frequently.

Conurbation A large urban area created by the merging of several towns.

Coral reef An underwater barrier created by colonies of coral polyps. The polyps secrete a protective skeleton of calcium carbonate, and reefs develop as live polyps build on the skeletons of dead generations.

Core The layers of liquid rock and solid iron at the center of the Earth.

Crust The hard, thin outer shell of the Earth. The crust floats on the mantle, which is softer, but more dense.

Deciduous forest A type of broadleaf forest found in temperate regions.

Deforestation Cutting down trees or forest for timber or farmland. It can lead to soil erosion, flooding, and landslides.

Delta A low-lying, fan-shaped area at a river mouth, formed by the deposition of successive layers of sediment. Slowing as it enters the sea, a river deposits sediment and may, as a result, split into many smaller channels called distributaries.

Deposition The laying down of material broken down by erosion or weathering and transported by the wind, water, or gravity.

Desertification The spread of desert conditions into a region that was not previously a desert.

Drainage basin The land drained by a river and its tributaries.

Drought A long period of continuously low rainfall.

Earthquake A trembling or shaking of the ground caused by the sudden movement of rocks in the Earth's crust – and sometimes deeper than the crust. Earthquakes occur most frequently along continental plate boundaries.

Economy The organization of a country's finances, exports, imports, industry, agriculture, and services.

Ecosytem A community of species dependent on each other and on the habitat in which they live.

Equator The 0° line of latitude. Equatorial climates are hot and there is plenty of rain.

Erosion The wearing down of the land surface by running water, waves, moving ice, wind, and weather.

Estuary The mouth of a river, where the saltwater from the sea meets the freshwater of the river.

Fault A crack or fracture in the Earth along which there has been movement of the rock masses relative to one another.

Fjord A coastal valley that was sculpted by glacial action.

Floodplain The broad, flat part of a river valley, next to the river itself, formed by sediment deposited during flooding.

Geyser A fountain of hot water or steam that erupts periodically as a result of underground streams coming into contact with hot rocks.

GDP Gross Domestic Product. The total value of goods and services produced by a country, excluding income from foreign countries.

GIS Geographic Information System. A computerized system for the collection, storage, and retrieval of geographic data.

Glacier A huge mass of ice made up of compacted and frozen snow, that moves slowly, eroding and depositing rock.

Glaciation The molding of the land by a glacier or ice sheet.

GNI Gross National Income. The total value of goods and services produced by a country.

Groundwater Water that has seeped into the pores, cavities, and cracks of rocks or into soil and water held in an aquifer or permeable rock.

Gully A deep, narrow chasm eroded in the landscape by a fast-flowing stream.

Heavy industry Industry that uses large amounts of energy and raw materials to produce heavy goods, such as machinery, ships, or locomotives.

Humidity The moisture content of the air.

Hurricane A violent tropical storm, also known as a cyclone in the Indian Ocean and a typhoon in the Pacific Ocean.

Hydroelectric power Energy produced by harnessing the rapid movement of water down steep mountain slopes to drive turbines to generate electricity.

Ice Age Periods of time in the past when much of the Earth's surface was covered by massive ice sheets. The most recent Ice Age began two million years ago and ended 10,000 years ago.

Iceberg A floating mass of ice that has broken off from a glacier or ice sheet.

Ice sheet A massive area of ice, thousands of feet thick.

Irrigation The artificial supply of water to dry areas – mainly for agricultural use. Water is carried or pumped to the area through pipes or ditches.

Lagoon A shallow stretch of coastal saltwater behind a partial barrier such as a sandbank or coral reef.

Latitude The distance north or south of the equator, measured in degrees, and shown on a globe as imaginary circles running around the Earth parallel to the equator.

Lava The molten rock, magma, that erupts onto the Earth's surface through a volcano, or through a fault or crack in the Earth's crust. Lava refers to the rock both in its liquid and its later, solidified form.

Load The material that is carried by a river or stream.

Longitude The distance, measured in degrees, east or west of the Prime Meridian.

Limestone A type of rock, formed by sediment, through which water can pass.

Magma Underground, molten rock, that is very hot and highly charged with gas. It originates in the Earth's lower crust or mantle.

Mantle The layer of the Earth's interior between the crust and the core. It is about 1,800 miles thick.

Map projection A mathematical formula that is used to show the curved surface of the Earth on a flat map.

Market gardening The intensive growing of fruit and vegetables close to large local markets.

Meander A looplike bend in a river. As a river nears the sea, it tends to wind more and more. The bigger the river and the shallower its slope, the more likely it is that meanders will form.

Mediterranean climate A temperate climate of hot, dry summers and warm, damp winters.

Meltwater Water that has melted from glaciers or ice sheets.

Mestizo A person of mixed native American and European origin.

Mineral A chemical compound that occurs naturally in the Earth.

Monsoon Winds that change direction according to the seasons. They are most common in South and East Asia, where they blow from the southwest in summer, bringing heavy rainfall, and the northeast in winter.

Moraine Sand and gravel that have been deposited by a glacier or ice sheet.

Nomads (nomadic) Wandering communities who move around in search of suitable pasture for their herds of animals.

Oasis A fertile area in a desert, usually watered by an underground aquifer.

Pack ice Ice masses more than 10 ft thick that form on the sea surface and are not attached to a landmass.

Pacific Rim The name given to the economically dynamic countries bordering the Pacific Ocean.

Peat Decomposed vegetation found in bogs. It can be dried and used as fuel.

Per capita A latin term meaning "for each person."

Plantation A large farm on which only one crop is usually grown, e.g, bananas or coffee.

Plain A flat, level region of land, often relatively low-lying.

Plateau A large area of high, flat land. When surrounded by steep slopes it is called a tableland.

Peninsula A thin strip of land surrounded on three of its sides by water. Large examples include Italy, Florida, and Korea.

Permafrost Permanently frozen ground, in which temperatures have remained below 32°F for more than two years.

Precipitation The fall of moisture from the atmosphere onto the surface of the Earth, as dew, hail, rain, sleet, or snow.

Prairie A Spanish-American term for grassy plains, with few or no trees.

Prime Meridian 0° longitude. Also known as the Greenwich Meridian because it runs through Greenwich in England.

Rain forest Dense forests in tropical zones with high rainfall, temperature, and humidity.

Rain shadow An area downwind from high terrain that has little or no rainfall because it has fallen upon the high relief.

Remote-sensing A way of obtaining information about the environment by using unmanned equipment, such as a satellite, that relays the information to a point where it is collected.

Ria A flooded V-shaped river valley or estuary flooded by a rise in sea level or sinking land.

Rift valley A long, narrow depression in the Earth's crust, formed by the sinking of rocks between two faults.

Savanna Open grassland, where an annual dry season prevents the growth of most trees. They lie between the tropical rain forest and hot desert regions.

Scale The relationship between distance on a map and on the Earth's surface.

Sediment Grains of rock transported and deposited by rivers, sea, ice, or wind.

Semiarid Areas between deserts and better-watered areas, where there is sufficient moisture to support a little more vegetation than in a true desert.

Service industry An industry that supplies services, such as banking, rather than producing manufactured goods.

Shanty town An area in or around a city where people live in temporary shacks, usually without basic facilities such as running water.

Silt Small particles, finer than sand, often carried by water and deposited on riverbanks, at river mouths, and harbors.

Soil A thin layer of rock particles mixed with the remains of dead organisms. Soil occurs naturally on the surface of the Earth and provides a medium for plants to grow.

Soil erosion The wearing away of soil more quickly than it is replaced by natural processes. Overgrazing and the clearing of land for farming speeds up the process.

Sorghum A type of grass found in South America, similar to sugarcane.

Spit A narrow bank of pebbles or sand extending out from the seashore. Spits are made out of material transported along the coast by currents, wind, and waves.

Staple crop The main food crop grown in a region, for example, rice in Southeast Asia.

Steppe Large areas of dry grassland in the Northern Hemisphere – particularly found in southeast Europe and central Asia.

Subsistence farming A method of farming in which enough food is produced to feed farmers and their families but not providing any extra to generate an income.

Taiga A Russian name given to the belt of coniferous forest found in Russia, which borders tundra in the north and mixed forests and grasslands in the south.

Temperate The mild, variable climate found in areas between the tropics and cold polar regions.

Terrace Steps cut into steep slopes to create flat surfaces for cultivating crops.

Tropics An area between the equator and the Tropic of Cancer and Tropic of Capricorn that has heavy rainfall and high temperatures, and lacks any clear seasonal variation.

Tundra The land area lying in the very cold northern regions of Europe, Asia, and Canada, where winters are long and cold and the ground beneath the surface is permanently frozen.

U-shaped valley A river valley that has been deepened and widened by a glacier. They are flat-bottomed and steep-sided, and usually much deeper than river valleys.

V-shaped valley A typical valley eroded by a river in its upper course.

Volcano An opening or vent in the Earth's crust where magma erupts. Volcanos are caused by the movement of the Earth's plates. When the plates collide or separate apart, magma is forced to the surface, at or near the place where the plates meet.

Watershed The dividing line between one drainage basin and another.

AREQUIPA

INDEX

A

Aachen 101 A5 W Germany
Aalborg 83 B6 N Denmark
Aalen 101 C6 S Germany
Aalsmeer 84 D4 C Netherlands
Aalst 84 C6 C Belgium
Aalten 84 F4 E Netherlands
Aalter 84 B6 NW Belgium
Äänekoski 83 E4 W Finland
Aare 101 B8 ~ W Switzerland
Aba 76 E1 NE Dem. Rep. Congo
Aba 72 F5 S Nigeria
Abadan 123 D3 SW Iran
Abadan 125 C3 C Turkmenistan
Abadla 70 C2 W Algeria
Abakan 118 E5 S Russian Federation
Abashiri 133 G1 NE Japan
Abbeville 97 D1 N France
Abbeydorney 89 B6 SW Ireland
Abbeyleix 89 D5 C Ireland
Abéché 72 H3 SE Chad
Abengourou 72 D5 E Côte d'Ivoire
Aberaeron 93 B6 SW Wales, United Kingdom
Aberdaron 93 A5 NW Wales, United Kingdom
Aberdeen 91 F4 NE Scotland, United Kingdom
Aberdeen 43 C3 South Dakota, N USA
Aberdeen 49 B2 Washington, NW USA
Aberfeldy 91 D4 C Scotland, United Kingdom
Abergavenny 93 C7 SE Wales, United Kingdom
Aberystwyth 93 B6 W Wales, United Kingdom
Abha 123 B6 SW Saudi Arabia
Abidjan 72 C5 S Côte d'Ivoire
Abilene 44 G3 Texas, SW USA
Abingdon 95 E3 S England, United Kingdom
Åbo see Turku
Aboisso 72 D5 SE Côte d'Ivoire
Abou-Déïa 72 H4 SE Chad
Abrantes 99 B4 C Portugal
Abruzzese, Appennino 103 D5 ▲▲ C Italy
Absaroka Range 47 D3 ▲▲ Montana/Wyoming, NW USA
Abu Dhabi 123 E4 ● test
Abu Hamed 75 C1 N Sudan
Abuja 72 F4 ● C Nigeria
Abunã, Rio 63 D5 ~ Bolivia/Brazil
Abuye Meda 75 D3 ▲ C Ethiopia
Acalayong 72 F6 SW Equatorial Guinea
Acaponeta 53 D4 C Mexico
Acapulco 53 F6 S Mexico
Accra 72 D5 ● SE Ghana
Accrington 93 D4 NW England, United Kingdom
Achacachi 65 A2 W Bolivia
Achill Head 89 A3 headland W Ireland
Achill Sound 89 B3 W Ireland
Acklins Island 57 E3 island SE Bahamas
Aconcagua, Cerro 65 A5 ▲ W Argentina
A Coruña 99 B1 NW Spain
Acre 63 C5 state W Brazil
Ada 43 D8 Oklahoma, C USA
Adamawa Highlands 72 G5 plateau NW Cameroon
Adams, Mount 49 B3 ▲ Washington, NW USA
'Adan see Aden
Adana 121 D5 S Turkey
Adapazarı 120 B2 NW Turkey
Adare, Cape 142 C6 cape Antarctica
Ad Dahna 123 C4 desert E Saudi Arabia
Ad Dammam 123 D4 NE Saudi Arabia
Addis Ababa 75 D3 ● C Ethiopia
Adelaide 137 E6 state capital South Australia
Aden 123 C7 SW Yemen
Aden, Gulf of 75 F2 gulf SW Arabian Sea
Adige 103 C2 ~ N Italy
Adirondack Mountains 37 D3 ▲▲ New York, NE USA
Adis Abeba see Addis Ababa
Adıyaman 121 E4 SE Turkey
Admiralty Islands 141 B1 island group N Papua New Guinea
Adra 99 E6 S Spain
Adrar 70 D3 C Algeria
Adrian 40 E5 Michigan, N USA
Adriatic Sea 112 F2 sea N Mediterranean Sea
Adycha 118 G3 ~ NE Russian Federation
Aegean Sea 107 F5 sea NE Mediterranean Sea
Aeolian Islands 103 D7 island group S Italy
Afareaitu 141 A5 W French Polynesia
Afghanistan 125 D5 ◆ islamic state C Asia
Afmadow 75 E5 S Somalia
Africa 66 continent
Africa, Horn of 66 physical region Ethiopia/Somalia
Afyon 120 B3 W Turkey
Agadez 72 F3 C Niger
Agadir 70 B2 SW Morocco
Agana see Hagåtña
Agaro 75 D4 C Ethiopia
Agat 51 W Guam
Agathónisi 107 F6 island Dodecanese, Greece
Agde 97 D6 S France
Agen 97 C6 SW France
Agialousa see Yenierenköy
Ágios Nikólaos 107 F7 Crete, Greece
Agra 127 D3 N India
Ağrı 121 G3 NE Turkey
Agrigento 103 C8 Sicily, Italy
Agropoli 103 D6 S Italy
Aguadilla 51 W Puerto Rico
Aguadulce 55 G7 S Panama
Aguán, Río 55 D2 ~ N Honduras
Agua Prieta 53 C2 NW Mexico
Aguascalientes 53 E4 C Mexico
Aguilas 99 E5 SE Spain
Aguililla 53 E5 SW Mexico
Ahaggar 70 E4 high plateau region SE Algeria
Ahmadabad 127 C4 W India
Ahmadnagar 127 D5 W India
Ahuachapán 55 B4 W El Salvador
Ahvaz 123 D3 SW Iran
Aiken 39 G4 South Carolina, SE USA
Ailigandí 55 I6 NE Panama
Ailsa Craig 91 C6 island SW Scotland, United Kingdom
'Aïn Ben Tili 72 C1 N Mauritania
Aiquile 65 B2 C Bolivia
Airdrie 91 D6 S Scotland, United Kingdom
Aire 93 D4 ~ N England, United Kingdom
Aïr, Massif de l' 72 F2 ▲▲ NC Niger
Aix-en-Provence 97 E6 SE France
Ajaccio 97 G6 Corsica, France
Aj Bogd Uul 129 D2 ▲ SW Mongolia
Ajdabiya 70 G2 NE Libya
Ajmer 127 D3 N India
Ajo 44 B3 Arizona, SW USA
Akasha 75 C1 N Sudan
Akchâr 72 A2 desert W Mauritania
Akhalts'ikhe 121 G2 SW Georgia
Akhdar, Al Jabal al 70 G2 hill range NE Libya
Akhisar 120 A3 W Turkey
Akhmim 70 I3 C Egypt
Akhtubinsk 111 B7 SW Russian Federation
Akimiski Island 35 C3 island Nunavut, C Canada
Akita 133 F3 C Japan
Akjoujt 72 B2 W Mauritania
Akkeshi 133 H1 NE Japan
Aklavik 33 E3 Northwest Territories, NW Canada
Akmola see Astana
Akpatok Island 35 E1 island Nunavut, E Canada
Akron 40 F6 Ohio, N USA
Akrotiri Sovereign Base Area 112 C6 UK air base S Cyprus
Aksai Chin 129 B3 disputed region China/India
Aksaray 121 D4 C Turkey
Akşehir 120 C4 W Turkey
Aksu He 129 B2 ~ China/Kyrgyzstan
Aktau 118 A5 W Kazakhstan
Aktobe 118 B4 NW Kazakhstan
Akure 72 E5 SW Nigeria
Akureyri 83 A1 N Iceland
Alabama 39 D5 ◈ state S USA
Alabama River 39 D5 ~ Alabama, S USA
Alaca 121 D3 N Turkey
Alacant see Alicante
Alagoas 63 H5 state E Brazil
Alajuela 55 E6 C Costa Rica
Alakanuk 50 D2 Alaska, USA
Al 'Amarah 123 C3 E Iraq
Alamo 47 B6 Nevada, W USA
Alamogordo 44 D3 New Mexico, SW USA
Alamosa 47 F6 Colorado, C USA
Aland Islands 83 D5 island group SW Finland
Aland Sea 83 D5 strait Baltic Sea/Gulf of Bothnia
Alanya 121 C5 S Turkey
Al 'Aqabah 112 K6 SW Jordan
A Laracha 99 B1 NW Spain
Alaşehir 120 A4 W Turkey
Alaska 50 D2 ◈ state NW USA
Alaska, Gulf of 50 D3 gulf Canada/USA
Alaska Peninsula 50 D3 peninsula Alaska, USA
Alaska Range 50 E2 ▲▲ Alaska, USA
Alazeya 118 H2 ~ NE Russian Federation
Albacete 99 E4 C Spain
Al Bāḥah 123 B5 SW Saudi Arabia
Alba Iulia 109 B6 W Romania
Albania 107 C3 ◆ republic SE Europe
Albany 137 B6 Western Australia
Albany 39 F5 Georgia, SE USA
Albany 49 B3 Oregon, NW USA
Albany 35 C4 ~ Ontario, S Canada
Albany 37 E4 state capital New York, NE USA
Al Bayda' 70 H2 NE Libya
Albergaria-a-Velha 99 B3 N Portugal
Albert 97 D1 N France
Alberta 33 F6 ◈ province SW Canada
Albert, Lake 75 B5 ◎ Dem. Rep. Congo/Uganda
Albert Lea 43 E4 Minnesota, N USA
Albi 97 D6 S France
Albuquerque 44 D2 New Mexico, SW USA
Albury 137 G6 New South Wales, SE Australia
Alcácer do Sal 99 B4 W Portugal
Alcalá de Henares 99 D3 C Spain
Alcamo 103 C8 Sicily, Italy
Alcañiz 99 F3 NE Spain
Alcántara, Embalse de 99 B4 ⊠ W Spain
Alcoi see Alcoy
Alcoy 99 F4 E Spain
Aldabra Group 76 G3 island group SW Seychelles
Aldan 118 G3 ~ NE Russian Federation
Alde 95 H2 ~ E England, United Kingdom
Aldeburgh 95 H2 E England, United Kingdom
Alderney 95 H5 island Channel Islands
Aldershot 95 F4 S England, United Kingdom
Aleg 72 B3 SW Mauritania
Aleksin 111 A5 W Russian Federation
Alençon 97 C3 N France
'Alenuihaha Channel 51 D2 channel Hawai'i, USA, C Pacific Ocean
Aleppo 123 B1 NW Syria
Alert 33 H1 Ellesmere Island, Nunavut, N Canada
Alès 97 D6 S France
Alessandria 103 B2 N Italy
Ålesund 83 A4 S Norway
Aleutian Basin 15 undersea feature Bering Sea
Aleutian Islands 50 B2 island group Alaska, USA
Aleutian Trench 15 undersea feature S Bering Sea
Alexander Archipelago 50 E4 island group Alaska, USA
Alexander City 39 E5 Alabama, S USA
Alexander Island 142 A4 island Antarctica
Alexandra 139 B7 South Island, New Zealand
Alexandria 70 I2 N Egypt
Alexandria 39 B5 Louisiana, S USA
Alexandria 43 D3 Minnesota, N USA
Alexandroúpoli 107 F4 NE Greece
Alfeiós 107 D6 ~ S Greece
Alfreton 93 E5 C England, United Kingdom
Alga 118 B4 NW Kazakhstan
Algarve 99 B5 cultural region S Portugal
Algeciras 99 C6 SW Spain
Algemesí 99 F4 E Spain
Algeria 70 C3 ◆ republic N Africa
Al Ghabah 123 F5 C Oman
Alghero 103 A5 Sardinia, Italy
Algiers 70 E1 ● N Algeria
Algona 43 E4 Iowa, C USA
Al Hajar al Gharbi 123 E4 ▲▲ N Oman
Al Hasakah 123 B1 NE Syria
Al Hillah 123 C2 C Iraq
Al Hufuf 123 D4 NE Saudi Arabia
Aliákmonas 107 E4 ~ N Greece
Aliártos 107 E5 C Greece
Ali-Bayramli 121 J2 SE Azerbaijan
Alicante 99 F5 SE Spain
Alice 44 G5 Texas, SW USA
Alice Springs 137 E3 Northern Territory, C Australia
Alindao 72 H5 S Central African Republic
Aliquippa 37 B5 Pennsylvania, NE USA
Al Jaghbub 70 H3 NE Libya
Al Jawf 123 B3 NW Saudi Arabia
Al Jazirah 123 B2 physical region Iraq/Syria
Al Khufrah 70 H4 SE Libya
Al Khums 70 F2 NW Libya
Alkmaar 84 C3 NW Netherlands
Al Kut 123 C2 E Iraq
Al Lādhiqīyah 123 A2 W Syria
Allahabad 127 E3 N India
Allegheny Mountains 39 G2 ▲▲ NE USA
Allegheny Plateau 37 C4 ▲▲ New York/Pennsylvania, NE USA
Allen, Lough 89 D3 ◎ NW Ireland
Allentown 37 D5 Pennsylvania, NE USA
Alleppey 127 D7 SW India
Alliance 43 A4 Nebraska, C USA
Alloa 91 D5 C Scotland, United Kingdom
Alma-Ata see Almaty
Almada 99 A4 W Portugal
Al Mahrah 123 D6 ▲▲ E Yemen
Al Majma'ah 123 C4 C Saudi Arabia
Almansa 99 F4 C Spain
Almaty 118 C6 SE Kazakhstan
Almelo 84 F3 E Netherlands
Almendra, Embalse de 99 C3 ⊠ NW Spain
Almendralejo 99 C4 W Spain
Almere 84 D3 C Netherlands
Almería 99 E6 S Spain
Al'met'yevsk 111 D6 W Russian Federation
Almirante 55 F6 NW Panama
Al Mukalla 123 D7 SE Yemen
Alnwick 93 D1 N England, United Kingdom
Alofi, Île 141 K4 island S Wallis and Futuna
Alónnisos 107 E5 island Vóreioi Sporádes, Greece
Álora 99 D6 S Spain
Alor, Kepulauan 131 F8 island group E Indonesia
Alotau 141 C3 SE Papua New Guinea
Alpena 40 E3 Michigan, N USA
Alpha Cordillera 143 B4 undersea feature Arctic Ocean
Alphen aan den Rijn 84 C4 C Netherlands
Alpine 44 E4 Texas, SW USA
Alps 78 ▲▲ C Europe
Al Qamishli 123 B1 NE Syria
Alqueva, Barragem do 99 B4 ⊠ Portugal/Spain
Al Qunaytirah 123 H5 SW Syria
Alsace 97 F2 cultural region NE France Europe
Alsager 93 D5 W England, United Kingdom
Alsdorf 101 A5 W Germany
Alta 83 D1 N Norway
Altai Mountains 129 C2 ▲▲ Asia/Europe
Altamaha River 39 F5 ~ Georgia, SE USA
Altamira 63 F4 NE Brazil
Altamura 103 E6 SE Italy
Altar, Desierto de 53 A1 desert Mexico/USA
Altay 129 C2 NW China
Altay 129 D2 W Mongolia
Alton 95 F4 S England, United Kingdom
Alton 40 B7 Illinois, N USA
Altoona 37 C5 Pennsylvania, NE USA
Altun Shan 129 C3 ▲▲ NW China
Alturas 49 C5 California, W USA
Altus 43 C8 Oklahoma, C USA
Al 'Uwaynat 70 F4 SW Libya
Alva 43 C7 Oklahoma, C USA
Alvarado 53 G5 E Mexico
Alvin 44 H4 Texas, SW USA
Al Wajh 123 A4 NW Saudi Arabia
Alwar 127 D3 N India
Al Wari'ah 123 C3 N Saudi Arabia
Alytus 83 E7 S Lithuania
Alzette 84 E9 ~ S Luxembourg
Amadeus, Lake 137 D4 seasonal lake Northern Territory, C Australia
Amadi 75 C4 SW Sudan
Amadjuak Lake 33 I3 ◎ Baffin Island, Nunavut, N Canada
Amakusa-nada 133 C8 gulf SW Japan
Åmål 83 C5 S Sweden
Amami-gunto 133 A7 island group SW Japan
Amami-o-shim 133 A7 island S Japan
Amantea 103 E7 SW Italy
Amapá 63 F3 state NE Brazil
Amarapura 131 A2 C Myanmar (Burma)
Amarillo 44 F2 Texas, SW USA
Amay 84 D7 E Belgium
Amazon 63 F3 ~ Brazil/Peru
Amazonas 63 C4 state N Brazil
Amazon Basin 63 E4 basin N South America
Amazon, Mouths of the 63 G3 delta NE Brazil
Ambae 141 G4 island C Vanuatu
Ambam 72 F6 S Cameroon
Ambanja 76 G4 N Madagascar
Ambarchik 118 H2 NE Russian Federation
Ambérieu-en-Bugey 97 E5 E France
Amble 93 D2 N England, United Kingdom
Amboasary 76 G6 S Madagascar
Ambon 131 G7 E Indonesia
Ambositra 76 G5 SE Madagascar
Amboy 49 D8 California, W USA
Ambriz 76 B3 NW Angola
Ambrym 141 G5 island C Vanuatu
Amchitka Island 50 A2 island Aleutian Islands, Alaska, USA
Amdo 129 C4 W China
Ameland 84 D1 island N Netherlands
America-Antarctica Ridge 142 B2 undersea feature S Atlantic Ocean
American Falls Reservoir 47 C4 ⊠ Idaho, NW USA
American Samoa 51 US ◇ W Polynesia
Amersfoort 84 D4 C Netherlands
Ames 43 E5 Iowa, C USA
Amga 118 G4 ~ NE Russian Federation
Amherst 35 F5 Nova Scotia, SE Canada
Amiens 97 D1 N France
Amindivi Islands 127 C7 island group SW India
Amistad Reservoir 44 F4 ⊠ Mexico/USA
Amman 123 A2 ● NW Jordan
Ammassalik 143 A6 S Greenland
Ammochostos see Famagusta
Amol 123 D1 N Iran
Amorgós 107 F6 island Cyclades, Greece
Amos 35 D4 Québec, SE Canada
Amourj 72 C3 SE Mauritania
Ampato, Nevado 63 B6 ▲ S Peru
Amposta 99 F3 NE Spain
Amravati 127 D4 C India
Amritsar 127 D2 N India
Amstelveen 84 D4 C Netherlands
Amsterdam 84 C4 ● C Netherlands
Am Timan 72 H4 SE Chad
Amu Darya 125 D3 ~ C Asia
Amund Ringnes Island 33 H2 island Nunavut, N Canada
Amundsen Gulf 33 F3 gulf Northwest Territories, N Canada
Amundsen Plain 142 B6 undersea feature S Pacific Ocean
Amundsen-Scott 142 C4 US research station Antarctica
Amundsen Sea 142 A5 sea S Pacific Ocean
Amuntai 131 E7 C Indonesia
Amur 118 H5 ~ China/Russian Federation
Amyderya 125 E4 NE Turkmenistan
Anabar 118 F3 ~ NE Russian Federation
Anaconda 47 C2 Montana, NW USA
Anacortes 49 B1 Washington, NW USA
Anadyr' 118 H2 ~ NE Russian Federation
Anadyr, Gulf of 118 I1 gulf NE Russian Federation
Anáfi 107 F6 island Cyclades, Greece
Analalava 76 G4 NW Madagascar
Anamur 121 C5 S Turkey
Anantapur 127 D6 S India
Anápolis 63 G6 C Brazil
Anar 123 E3 C Iran
Anar Darreh 125 D5 W Afghanistan
Anatolia 121 C4 plateau C Turkey
Añatuya 65 B4 N Argentina
Anchorage 50 E3 Alaska, USA
Ancona 103 D4 C Italy
Ancud 65 A7 S Chile
Åndalsnes 83 B4 S Norway
Andalucía 99 D5 cultural region S Spain Europe
Andalucia see Andalusia
Andalusia 39 E6 Alabama, S USA
Andaman Islands 127 H4 island group India, NE Indian Ocean
Andaman Sea 127 H5 sea NE Indian Ocean
Andenne 84 D7 SE Belgium
Anderlues 84 C7 S Belgium
Andersen Air Force Base 51 air base NE Guam
Anderson 40 D6 Indiana, N USA
Andes 63 B5 ▲▲ W South America
Andhra Pradesh 127 E6 cultural region E India
Andijon 125 G3 E Uzbekistan
Andkhvoy 125 E4 N Afghanistan
Andong 133 C6 E South Korea
Andorra 97 C7 ◆ monarchy SW Europe
Andorra la Vella 97 B7 ● C Andorra
Andover 95 E4 S England, United Kingdom
Andøya 83 C2 island C Norway
Andreanof Islands 50 A2 island group Aleutian Islands, Alaska, USA
Andrews 44 F3 Texas, SW USA
Andria 103 E6 SE Italy
Ándros 107 F5 island Cyclades, SE Greece
Andros Island 57 C2 island NW Bahamas
Andros Town 57 D2 NW Bahamas
Aneityum 141 H6 island S Vanuatu
Anepmete 141 C2 E Papua New Guinea
Angara 118 E4 ~ C Russian Federation
Angarsk 118 F5 S Russian Federation
Ånge 83 C4 C Sweden
Ángel de la Guarda, Isla 53 B2 island NW Mexico
Angeles 131 F3 Luzon, N Philippines
Angel Falls 63 D2 waterfall E Venezuela
Ångermanälven 83 D3 ~ N Sweden
Angermünde 101 E3 NE Germany
Angers 97 C3 NW France
Anglesey 93 B4 island NW Wales, United Kingdom
Anglet 97 B6 SW France
Angleton 44 H5 Texas, SW USA
Ang Nam Ngum 131 B3 ◎ C Laos
Angola 76 B3 ◆ republic SW Africa
Angola Basin 15 undersea feature E Atlantic Ocean
Angoram 141 B1 NW Papua New Guinea
Angostura, Presa de la 53 H6 ⊠ SE Mexico
Angoulême 97 C5 W France
Angoumois 97 C5 cultural region W France
Angren 125 G3 E Uzbekistan
Anguilla 57 J4 UK ◇ E West Indies
Anguilla Cays 57 C2 islets SW Bahamas
Animas 44 C3 New Mexico, SW USA
Anjou 97 C3 cultural region NW France
Anjouan 76 G4 island SE Comoros
Anju 133 A5 W North Korea
Ankara 121 C3 ● C Turkey
Ankeny 43 E5 Iowa, C USA
Anklam 101 D2 NE Germany
Annaba 70 E1 NE Algeria
An Nafud 123 B3 desert NW Saudi Arabia
An Najaf 123 C3 S Iraq
Annalee 89 D3 ~ N Ireland
Annalong 89 F3 S Northern Ireland, United Kingdom
Annan 91 E7 S Scotland, United Kingdom
Annapolis 39 H1 state capital Maryland, NE USA
Annapurna 127 F2 ▲ C Nepal
Ann Arbor 40 E5 Michigan, N USA
An Nasiriyah 123 C3 SE Iraq
Annecy 97 E5 E France
Anniston 39 E4 Alabama, S USA
Anqing 129 G4 E China
Anshun 129 E5 S China
Anson 44 G3 Texas, SW USA
Ansongo 72 D3 E Mali
Antakya 121 E5 S Turkey
Antalaha 76 H4 NE Madagascar
Antalya 120 B5 SW Turkey
Antalya, Gulf of 120 B5 gulf SW Turkey
Antananarivo 76 G5 ● C Madagascar
Antarctica 142 C4 continent
Antarctic Peninsula 142 A4 peninsula Antarctica
Antequera 99 D5 S Spain
Antibes 97 F6 SE France
Anticosti, Île d' 35 F4 island Québec, E Canada
Antigua 57 J5 island S Antigua and Barbuda
Antigua and Barbuda 57 J4 ◆ commonwealth republic E West Indies
Antikythira 107 E7 island S Greece
Antofagasta 65 A3 N Chile
Antony 97 D2 N France
Antrim 89 E2 NE Northern Ireland, United Kingdom
Antrim Mountains 89 E1 ▲▲ NE Northern Ireland, United Kingdom
Antsirañana 76 G4 N Madagascar
Antsohihy 76 G4 NW Madagascar
Antwerp 84 C6 N Belgium
Antwerpen see Antwerp
Anuradhapura 127 E7 C Sri Lanka
Anyang 129 F3 C China
A'nyêmaqên Shan 129 D4 ▲▲ C China
Anzio 103 C5 C Italy
Aola 141 F3 C Solomon Islands
Aomori 133 G3 C Japan
Aoraki 139 B6 ▲ South Island, New Zealand
Aosta 103 A2 NW Italy
Aoukâr 72 B2 plateau C Mauritania
Aouk, Bahr 72 H4 ~ Central African Republic/Chad
Aozou 72 G2 N Chad
Apalachee Bay 39 E6 bay Florida, SE USA
Apalachicola River 39 E6 ~ Florida, SE USA
Apaporis, Río 63 C3 ~ Brazil/Colombia
Apatity 111 B2 NW Russian Federation
Apeldoorn 84 E4 E Netherlands
Apennines 103 C3 ▲▲ Italy/San Marino
Apia 141 B5 ● SE Samoa
Apolima Strait 141 A5 strait C Pacific Ocean
Apostle Islands 40 B2 island group Wisconsin, N USA
Appalachian Mountains 39 F3 ▲▲ E USA
Appingedam 84 F2 NE Netherlands
Appleton 40 C4 Wisconsin, N USA
Apra Heights 51 W Guam
Apuseni, Munții 109 B6 ▲▲ W Romania
Aqaba, Gulf of 123 A3 gulf NE Red Sea
Aqchah 125 F4 N Afghanistan
Aquitaine 97 B6 region SW France
'Arabah, Wadi al 123 H7 dry watercourse Israel/Jordan
Arabian Basin 15 undersea feature N Arabian Sea
Arabian Peninsula 123 C4 peninsula SW Asia
Arabian Sea 114 sea NW Indian Ocean
Aracaju 63 I5 E Brazil
'Arad 123 H6 S Israel
Arad 109 A6 W Romania
Arafura Sea 131 H8 sea W Pacific Ocean
Aragón 99 E3 cultural region E Spain
Araguaia, Río 63 F5 ~ C Brazil
Araguari 63 G7 SE Brazil
Arak 123 D2 W Iran
Arakan Yoma 131 A2 ▲▲ W Myanmar (Burma)
Aral Sea 125 D1 inland sea Kazakhstan/Uzbekistan
Aral'sk 118 B5 SW Kazakhstan
Aranda de Duero 99 D2 N Spain
Aran Island 89 C2 island NW Ireland
Aran Islands 89 B4 island group W Ireland
Aranjuez 99 D3 C Spain
Araouane 72 D2 N Mali
'Ar'ar 123 B3 NW Saudi Arabia
Ararat, Mount 121 G3 ▲ E Turkey
Aras 121 I3 ~ SW Asia
Arawa 141 D2 Bougainville Island, NE Papua New Guinea
Arbil 123 C2 N Iraq
Arbroath 91 E5 E Scotland, United Kingdom
Arcachon 97 B5 SW France
Arcata 49 A5 California, W USA
Archangel 111 C3 NW Russian Federation
Archidona 99 D5 S Spain
Arco 103 C2 N Italy
Arco 47 C3 Idaho, NW USA
Arctic Ocean 143 C3 ocean
Arda 107 F3 ~ Bulgaria/Greece
Ardabil 123 D1 NW Iran
Ardara 89 C2 N Ireland
Ardas 107 F3 ~ Bulgaria/Greece
Ardèche 97 D6 cultural region E France Europe
Ardee 89 E3 NE Ireland
Ardennes 84 D8 plateau Belgium/France/Luxembourg W Europe
Ardglass 89 F3 E Northern Ireland, United Kingdom
Ardgroom 89 B7 S Ireland
Ardmore 89 D6 S Ireland
Ardmore 43 D8 Oklahoma, C USA
Ardnamurchan, Point of 91 B4 headland N Scotland, United Kingdom
Ardrahan 89 C4 W Ireland
Ards Peninsula 89 F2 peninsula E Northern Ireland, United Kingdom
Arecibo 51 C Puerto Rico
Arenal, Volcán 55 E6 ⩕ NW Costa Rica
Arendal 83 B6 S Norway
Arenig Fawr 93 B5 ▲ NW Wales, United Kingdom
Arenys de Mar 99 G2 NE Spain
Areópoli 107 E6 S Greece
Arequipa 63 C6 SE Peru

◈ Administrative region ◆ Country ● Country capital ◇ Dependent territory ○ Dependent territory capital ▲▲ Mountain range ▲ Mountain ⩕ Volcano ~ River ◎ Lake ⊠ Reservoir

155

AREZZO

Arezzo 103 C4 C Italy
Argenteuil 97 D2 N France
Argentina 65 A6 ◆ *republic* S South America
Argentine Basin 14 *undersea feature* SW Atlantic Ocean
Arghandab, Darya-ye 125 E5 ≈ SE Afghanistan
Argo 75 C1 N Sudan
Argun 129 F1 ≈ China/Russian Federation
Argyle, Lake 137 D2 *salt lake* Western Australia
Århus 83 B7 C Denmark
Arica 65 A2 N Chile
Arizona 44 A2 ⬖ *state* SW USA
Arkansas 39 B3 ⬖ *state* S USA
Arkansas City 43 D7 Kansas, C USA
Arkansas River 39 B4 ≈ C USA
Arkhangel'sk *see* Archangel
Arklow 89 E5 SE Ireland
Arles 97 E6 SE France
Arlington 44 H3 Texas, SW USA
Arlington 39 H1 Virginia, NE USA
Arlon 84 E9 SE Belgium
Armagh 89 E3 S Northern Ireland, United Kingdom
Armagnac 97 C6 *cultural region* S France
Armenia 63 B2 W Colombia
Armenia 121 H2 ◆ *republic* SW Asia
Armidale 137 H5 New South Wales, SE Australia
Armstrong 35 B4 Ontario, S Canada
Armyans'k 109 F6 S Ukraine
Arnedo 99 E2 N Spain
Arnhem 84 E4 SE Netherlands
Arnhem Land 137 E1 *physical region* Northern Territory, N Australia
Arno 103 C3 ≈ C Italy
Arnold 93 E5 C England, United Kingdom
Arnold 49 C6 California, W USA
Arnold 43 G6 Missouri, C USA
Arorae 141 J1 *atoll* Tungaru, W Kiribati
Arran, Isle of 91 C6 *island* SW Scotland, United Kingdom
Ar Raqqah 123 B2 N Syria
Arras 97 D1 N France
Arriaga 53 G5 SE Mexico
Ar Riyad *see* Riyadh
Arrow, Lough 89 C3 ◎ N Ireland
Ar Rub 'al Khali 123 D6 *desert* SW Asia
Ar Rustaq 123 F4 N Oman
Árta 107 D5 W Greece
Artashat 121 H3 S Armenia
Artemisa 57 B2 W Cuba
Artesia 44 E3 New Mexico, SW USA
Arthur's Pass 139 C6 *pass* C New Zealand
Artigas 65 C5 N Uruguay
Art'ik 121 H2 W Armenia
Artois 97 D1 *cultural region* N France
Artsyz 109 D6 SW Ukraine
Artvin 121 G2 NE Turkey
Arua 75 C5 NW Uganda
Aruba 57 G7 *Dutch* ◇ S West Indies
Aru, Kepulauan 131 H7 *island group* E Indonesia
Arunachal Pradesh 127 F2 *cultural region* NE India Asia
Arusha 75 D6 N Tanzania
Arviat 33 H5 Nunavut, C Canada
Arvidsjaur 83 D3 N Sweden
Arys' 118 C6 S Kazakhstan
Asadabad 125 G5 E Afghanistan
Asahi-dake 133 G1 ▲ Hokkaidō, N Japan
Asahikawa 133 F1 N Japan
Asamankese 72 D5 SE Ghana
Asansol 127 F4 NE India
Ascension Island 26 *St. Helena* ◇ C Atlantic Ocean
Ascoli Piceno 103 D4 C Italy
Aseb 75 E3 SE Eritrea
Aşgabat 125 C3 ● C Turkmenistan
Ashbourne 89 E4 E Ireland
Ashburton 139 C6 South Island, New Zealand
Ashburton River 137 B4 ≈ Western Australia
Ashby de la Zouch 93 D5 C England, United Kingdom
Ashdod 123 G6 W Israel
Asheville 39 F3 North Carolina, SE USA
Ashford 95 G4 SE England, United Kingdom
Ashington 93 D2 N England, United Kingdom
Ashland 49 B4 Oregon, NW USA
Ashland 40 B2 Wisconsin, N USA
Ash Sharah 123 H7 ⛰ W Jordan
Ash Shihr 123 D7 SE Yemen
Ashtabula 40 F5 Ohio, N USA
Asia 114 *continent*
Asinara 103 A5 *island* W Italy
Asipovichy 109 D2 C Belarus
Aşkale 121 F3 NE Turkey
Askersund 83 C6 C Sweden
Asmar 125 G5 E Afghanistan
Asmara 75 D2 ● C Eritrea
Aspermont 44 F3 Texas, SW USA
Assad, Lake 121 E5 ◎ N Syria
Assam 127 G3 *cultural region* NE India Asia
Assamakka 72 E2 NW Niger
As Samawah 123 C3 S Iraq
Assen 84 F2 NE Netherlands
Assenede 84 B6 NW Belgium
As Sulaymaniyah 123 C2 NE Iraq
As Sulayyil 123 C5 S Saudi Arabia
Astana 118 C5 ● N Kazakhstan
Asti 103 B2 NW Italy
Astorga 99 C2 N Spain
Astrakhan' 111 B8 SW Russian Federation
Asturias 99 C1 *cultural region* NW Spain
Astypálaia 107 F6 *island* Cyclades, Greece
Asunción 65 C4 ● S Paraguay
Aswan 70 J4 SE Egypt
Asyut 70 I3 C Egypt
Atacama Desert 65 A3 *desert* N Chile
Atamyrat 125 E4 E Turkmenistan
Atâr 72 B2 W Mauritania
Atas Bogd 129 D2 ▲ SW Mongolia
Atascadero 49 B8 California, W USA
Atatürk Baraji 121 F4 ⊠ S Turkey
Atbara 75 C2 NE Sudan
Atbara 75 D2 ≈ Eritrea/Sudan
Atbasar 118 C5 N Kazakhstan
Atchison 43 E6 Kansas, C USA
Ath 84 B7 SW Belgium
Athabasca 33 G6 Alberta, SW Canada
Athabasca 33 F6 ≈ Alberta, SW Canada
Athabasca, Lake 33 G5 ◎ Alberta/Saskatchewan, SW Canada
Athboy 89 E4 E Ireland
Athens 107 E5 ● C Greece
Athens 39 F4 Georgia, SE USA
Athens 40 F7 Ohio, N USA
Athens 44 H3 Texas, SW USA
Atherton 137 G2 Queensland, NE Australia
Athina *see* Athens
Athlone 89 D4 C Ireland
Ati 72 H3 C Chad
Atikokan 35 A4 Ontario, S Canada
Atka 118 H3 E Russian Federation
Atka 50 B2 Atka Island, Alaska, USA
Atlanta 44 I3 Texas, SW USA
Atlanta 39 E4 *state capital* Georgia, SE USA
Atlantic 39 I3 North Carolina, SE USA
Atlantic City 37 D6 New Jersey, NE USA
Atlantic Ocean 14 *ocean*
Atlas Mountains 70 C2 ⛰ NW Africa
Atlasovo 118 I3 E Russian Federation
Atlas, Tell 70 D2 ⛰ N Algeria
Atlin 33 E5 British Columbia, W Canada
At Ta'if 123 B5 W Saudi Arabia
Attawapiskat 35 C3 Ontario, C Canada
Attawapiskat 35 C3 ≈ Ontario, S Canada
Attu Island 50 A1 *island* Aleutian Islands, Alaska, USA
Atyrau 118 B4 W Kazakhstan
Aubagne 97 E7 SE France
Aubange 84 E9 SE Belgium
Auburn 37 D3 New York, NE USA
Auburn 49 B2 Washington, NW USA
Auch 97 C6 S France
Auckland 139 D2 North Island, New Zealand
Audincourt 97 F3 E France
Augathella 137 G4 Queensland, E Australia
Augsburg 101 C7 S Germany
Augusta 137 B6 Western Australia
Augusta 39 F4 Georgia, SE USA
Augusta 37 G3 *state capital* Maine, NE USA
Augustów 105 G2 NE Poland
Auki 141 F3 Malaita, N Solomon Islands
Aunu'u Island 51 *island* W American Samoa
Auob 76 C6 ≈ Namibia/South Africa
Aurangabad 127 D5 C India
Auray 97 B3 NW France
Aurès, Massif de l' 112 D4 ⛰ NE Algeria
Aurillac 97 D5 C France
Aurora 47 F5 Colorado, C USA
Aurora 40 C5 Illinois, N USA
Aurora 43 E7 Missouri, C USA
Aus 76 B6 SW Namibia
Austin 43 E4 Minnesota, N USA
Austin 47 B5 Nevada, W USA
Austin 44 G4 *state capital* Texas, SW USA
Australes, Îles 135 *island group* SW French Polynesia
Australia 137 D3 ◆ *commonwealth republic*
Australian Alps 137 G6 ⛰ SE Australia
Australian Capital Territory 137 G6 ⬖ *territory* SE Australia
Austria 101 E8 ◆ *republic* C Europe
Auvergne 97 D5 *cultural region* C France Europe
Auxerre 97 D3 C France
Avarua 135 ○ Rarotonga, S Cook Islands
Aveiro 99 B3 W Portugal
Avellino 103 D6 S Italy
Avesta 83 C5 C Sweden
Aveyron 97 C6 ≈ S France
Avezzano 103 D5 C Italy
Aviemore 91 D4 N Scotland, United Kingdom
Avignon 97 E6 SE France
Ávila 99 D3 C Spain
Avilés 99 C1 NW Spain
Avon 95 D4 ≈ SW England, United Kingdom
Avon 95 E4 ≈ C England, United Kingdom
Avonmouth 95 D4 SW England, United Kingdom
Avranches 97 B2 N France
Awaji-shima 133 E6 *island* SW Japan
Awash 75 E3 NE Ethiopia
Awbari 70 F3 SW Libya
Awe, Loch 91 C5 ◎ W Scotland, United Kingdom
Axe 95 D5 ≈ SW England, United Kingdom
Axel 84 B6 SW Netherlands
Axel Heiberg Island 33 G1 *island* Nunavut, N Canada
Ayacucho 63 C6 S Peru
Ayagoz 118 D6 E Kazakhstan
Ayamonte 99 B5 SW Spain
Aydarko'l Ko'li 125 F3 ◎ C Uzbekistan
Aydın 120 A4 SW Turkey
Ayers Rock *see* Uluru
Aylesbury 95 F3 SE England, United Kingdom
Ayorou 72 D3 W Niger
'Ayoûn el 'Atroûs 72 B3 SE Mauritania
Ayr 91 D6 W Scotland, United Kingdom
Ayr 91 D6 ≈ W Scotland, United Kingdom
Ayre, Point of 93 A3 *headland* N Isle of Man
Ayteke Bi 118 B5 SW Kazakhstan
Aytos 107 F3 E Bulgaria
Ayvalık 120 A3 W Turkey
Azahar, Costa del 99 F4 *coastal region* E Spain
Azaouâd 72 D2 *desert* C Mali
Azerbaijan 121 I2 ◆ *republic* SE Asia
Azoum, Bahr 72 H4 *seasonal river* SE Chad
Azov 118 A4 SW Russian Federation
Azov, Sea of 109 F6 *sea* NE Black Sea
Aztec 44 C1 New Mexico, SW USA
Azuaga 99 C5 W Spain
Azuero, Península de 55 G7 *peninsula* S Panama
Azul 65 C6 E Argentina
Az Zarqā' 123 A2 NW Jordan
Az Zāwiyah 70 F2 NW Libya

B

Baardheere 75 E5 SW Somalia
Baarle-Hertog 84 D5 N Belgium
Baarn 84 D4 C Netherlands
Babayevo 111 B4 NW Russian Federation
Babeldaob 131 H5 *island* N Palau
Bab el Mandeb 123 B7 *strait* Gulf of Aden/Red Sea
Babruysk 109 D3 E Belarus
Babuyan Channel 131 F3 *channel* N Philippines
Babuyan Island 131 F3 *island* N Philippines
Bacabal 63 G4 E Brazil
Bacău 109 C6 NE Romania
Bacheykava 109 D2 N Belarus
Back 33 G4 ≈ Nunavut, N Canada
Bacton 95 H1 E England, United Kingdom
Badajoz 99 B4 W Spain
Baden-Baden 101 B6 SW Germany
Bad Freienwalde 101 E3 NE Germany
Badgastein 101 D8 NW Austria
Bad Hersfeld 101 C5 C Germany
Bad Homburg vor der Höhe 101 B5 W Germany
Bad Ischl 101 E7 N Austria
Bad Krozingen 101 B7 SW Germany
Badlands 43 A4 *physical region* North Dakota/South Dakota, N USA
Badu Island 137 F1 *island* Queensland, NE Australia
Bad Vöslau 101 F7 NE Austria
Badwater Basin 49 D7 *depression* California, W USA
Bafatá 72 A4 C Guinea-Bissau
Baffin Bay 33 I2 *bay* Canada/Greenland
Baffin Island 33 I3 *island* Nunavut, NE Canada
Bafing 72 B4 ≈ W Africa
Bafoussam 72 F5 W Cameroon
Bafra 121 D2 N Turkey
Bagaces 55 E5 NW Costa Rica
Bagé 63 F9 S Brazil
Baghdad 123 C2 ● C Iraq
Baghlan 125 F4 NE Afghanistan
Baghran 125 E5 S Afghanistan
Bagoé 72 C4 ≈ Côte d'Ivoire/Mali
Baguio 131 F3 Luzon, N Philippines
Bagzane, Monts 72 F3 ▲ N Niger
Bahamas 57 D2 ◆ *commonwealth republic* N West Indies
Baharly 125 C3 C Turkmenistan
Bahawalpur 127 C2 E Pakistan
Bahia 63 G5 *state* E Brazil
Bahía Blanca 65 B6 E Argentina
Bahir Dar 75 D3 N Ethiopia
Bahraich 127 E3 N India
Bahrain 123 D4 ◆ *monarchy* SW Asia
Bahushewsk 109 D2 NE Belarus
Baia Mare 109 B5 NW Romania
Baïbokoum 72 G5 SW Chad
Baie-Comeau 35 F4 Québec, SE Canada
Baikal, Lake 118 F5 ◎ S Russian Federation
Bailén 99 D5 S Spain
Ba Illi 72 G4 SW Chad
Bainbridge 39 E6 Georgia, SE USA
Bairiki 135 ● Tarawa, NW Kiribati
Bairnsdale 137 G6 Victoria, SE Australia
Baishan 129 H2 NE China
Baiyin 129 E3 N China
Baja 105 E8 S Hungary
Baja, Punta 141 C6 *headland* Easter Island, Chile
Bajram Curri 107 D3 N Albania
Bakala 72 H5 C Central African Republic
Baker 49 C3 Oregon, NW USA
Baker and Howland Islands 135 *US* ◇ W Polynesia
Baker Lake 33 H4 Nunavut, N Canada
Bakersfield 49 C8 California, W USA
Bakhtaran *see* Kermanshah
Baki *see* Baku
Bakony 105 D8 ⛰ W Hungary
Baku 121 J2 ● E Azerbaijan
Bala 93 B5 NW Wales, United Kingdom
Balabac Strait 131 E5 *strait* Malaysia/Philippines
Balaguer 99 G2 NE Spain
Balaitous 97 B7 ▲ France/Spain
Balakovo 111 C7 W Russian Federation
Bala Morghab 125 E4 NW Afghanistan
Balashov 111 B6 W Russian Federation
Balaton, Lake 105 D8 ◎ W Hungary
Balbina, Represa 63 E3 ⊠ NW Brazil
Balboa 55 H6 C Panama
Balbriggan 89 E4 E Ireland
Balcarce 65 C6 E Argentina
Balclutha 139 B8 South Island, New Zealand
Baldy Mountain 47 D1 ▲ Montana, NW USA
Baldy Peak 44 C3 ▲ Arizona, SW USA
Baleares, Islas *see* Balearic Islands
Balearic Islands 99 G4 *island group* Spain, W Mediterranean Sea
Baleine, Rivière à la 35 E2 ≈ Québec, E Canada
Balen 84 D6 N Belgium
Baleshwar 127 F4 E India
Bali 131 E8 *island* C Indonesia
Balıkesir 120 A3 W Turkey
Balikpapan 131 E7 C Indonesia
Balkanabat 125 B3 W Turkmenistan
Balkan Mountains 107 E3 ⛰ Bulgaria/Serbia
Balkh 125 F4 N Afghanistan
Balkhash 118 C6 SE Kazakhstan
Balkhash, Lake 118 C6 ◎ SE Kazakhstan
Balladonia 137 C5 Western Australia
Ballaghmore 89 D5 C Ireland
Ballantrae 91 C7 W Scotland, United Kingdom
Ballarat 137 F6 Victoria, SE Australia
Ballater 91 E4 NE Scotland, United Kingdom
Ballina 89 C3 W Ireland
Ballinasloe 89 C4 W Ireland
Ballindine 89 C4 NW Ireland
Ballinger 44 G4 Texas, SW USA
Ballinhassig 89 C7 S Ireland
Ballinskelligs 89 A6 SW Ireland
Ballinskelligs Bay 89 A7 *inlet* SW Ireland
Ballinspittle 89 C7 S Ireland
Ballintra 89 D2 NW Ireland
Ballybofey 89 D2 NW Ireland
Ballybunnion 89 B5 SW Ireland
Ballycastle 89 E1 N Northern Ireland, United Kingdom
Ballyclare 89 F2 E Northern Ireland, United Kingdom
Ballyconneely 89 B4 W Ireland
Ballycotton 89 C7 S Ireland
Ballycroy 89 B3 NW Ireland
Ballydehob 89 B7 S Ireland
Ballydonegan 89 A7 S Ireland
Ballyduff 89 B5 SW Ireland
Ballyferriter 89 A6 SW Ireland
Ballyhaunis 89 C3 W Ireland
Ballyhoura Mountains 89 C6 ⛰ S Ireland
Ballymena 89 E2 NE Northern Ireland, United Kingdom
Ballymoe 89 C4 W Ireland
Ballymoney 89 E1 NE Northern Ireland, United Kingdom
Ballynafid 89 D4 C Ireland
Ballyshannon 89 C2 NW Ireland
Ballywalter 89 F2 E Northern Ireland, United Kingdom
Balrath 89 E4 E Ireland
Balsas 63 G4 E Brazil
Balsas, Río 53 E5 ≈ S Mexico
Baltasound 91 B5 NE Scotland, United Kingdom
Bălţi 109 D5 N Moldova
Baltic Sea 83 D7 *sea* N Europe
Baltimore 89 B7 S Ireland
Baltimore 39 H1 Maryland, NE USA
Baltinglass 89 E5 E Ireland
Baluchistan 127 B3 *province* SW Pakistan
Balykchy 125 H2 NE Kyrgyzstan
Bam 123 F3 SE Iran
Bamako 72 C4 ● SW Mali
Bambari 72 H5 C Central African Republic
Bamberg 101 C5 SE Germany
Bamburgh 93 D1 N England, United Kingdom
Bamenda 72 F5 W Cameroon
Banaba 141 H1 *island* W Kiribati
Bananga 127 H6 Nicobar Islands, India
Banbridge 89 E3 SE Northern Ireland, United Kingdom
Banbury 95 E3 S England, United Kingdom
Banchory 91 F4 NE Scotland, United Kingdom
Bandaaceh 131 A5 Sumatra, W Indonesia
Bandama 72 C5 ≈ S Côte d'Ivoire
Bandarbeyla 75 G3 NE Somalia
Bandar-e 'Abbas 123 E4 S Iran
Bandar-e Būshehr 123 D3 S Iran
Bandar-e Kangan 123 D3 S Iran
Bandar Lampung 131 B7 W Indonesia
Bandar Seri Begawan 131 D5 ● N Brunei
Banda Sea 131 G7 *sea* E Indonesia
Bandırma 120 A2 NW Turkey
Bandon 89 B7 ≈ S Ireland
Bandundu 76 B2 W Dem. Rep. Congo
Bandung 131 C8 Java, C Indonesia
Banff 91 E3 NE Scotland, United Kingdom
Bangalore 127 D5 S India
Bangassou 72 I5 SE Central African Republic
Banggai, Kepulauan 131 F6 *island group* C Indonesia
Banghazi *see* Benghazi
Bangka, Pulau 131 C7 *island* W Indonesia
Bangkok 131 B4 ● C Thailand
Bangladesh 127 G3 ◆ *republic* S Asia
Bangor 93 B5 NW Wales, United Kingdom
Bangor 89 F2 E Northern Ireland, United Kingdom
Bangor 37 G2 Maine, NE USA
Bangui 72 H5 ● SW Central African Republic
Bangweulu, Lake 76 D3 ◎ N Zambia
Bani 72 C4 ≈ S Mali
Banja Luka 107 C2 Republika Srpska, NW Bosnia and Herzegovina
Banjarmasin 131 E7 C Indonesia
Banjul 72 B3 ● W Gambia
Banks Island 33 F3 *island* Northwest Territories, NW Canada
Banks Islands 141 G4 *island group* N Vanuatu
Banks Lake 49 C2 ⊠ Washington, NW USA
Banks Peninsula 139 C6 *peninsula* South Island, New Zealand
Banks Strait 137 G7 *strait* SW Tasman Sea
Bankura 127 F4 NE India
Banmauk 131 A2 N Myanmar (Burma)
Bann 89 E2 ≈ N Northern Ireland, United Kingdom
Ban Nadou 131 C3 S Laos
Bansha 89 C6 S Ireland
Banská Bystrica 105 E6 C Slovakia
Banteer 89 C6 S Ireland
Bantry 89 B7 SW Ireland
Bantry Bay 89 B7 *bay* SW Ireland
Banyak, Kepulauan 131 A6 *island group* NW Indonesia
Banyo 72 F5 NW Cameroon
Banyoles 99 H2 NE Spain
Baoji 129 E4 C China
Baoro 72 G5 W Central African Republic
Baoshan 129 D5 SW China
Baotou 129 F3 N China
Ba'qubah 123 C2 C Iraq
Baraawe 75 E5 S Somalia
Baranavichy 109 C3 SW Belarus
Barbados 57 K6 ◆ *commonwealth republic* SE West Indies
Barbastro 99 F2 NE Spain
Barbate de Franco 99 C6 S Spain
Barbuda 57 J4 *island* N Antigua and Barbuda
Barcaldine 137 G3 Queensland, E Australia
Barcelona 99 G2 E Spain
Barcelona 63 D1 NE Venezuela
Barcs 105 D9 SW Hungary
Bardaï 72 G2 N Chad
Bardejov 105 F6 E Slovakia
Bareilly 127 E3 N India
Barendrecht 84 C4 SW Netherlands
Barentin 97 C2 N France
Barents Sea 111 C2 *sea* Arctic Ocean
Bar Harbor 37 G2 Mount Desert Island, Maine, NE USA
Bari 103 E6 SE Italy
Barikowt 125 G4 NE Afghanistan
Barillas 55 A2 NW Guatemala
Barinas 63 C2 W Venezuela
Barisal 127 G4 S Bangladesh
Barisan, Pegunungan 131 B7 ⛰ Sumatera, W Indonesia
Barito, Sungai 131 E7 ≈ Borneo, C Indonesia
Barkly Tableland 137 E2 *plateau* Northern Territory/Queensland, N Australia
Bârlad 109 C6 E Romania
Bar-le-Duc 97 E2 NE France
Barlee, Lake 137 B5 ◎ Western Australia
Barlee Range 137 B4 ⛰ Western Australia
Barletta 103 E5 SE Italy
Barlinek 105 C3 W Poland
Barmouth 93 B5 NW Wales, United Kingdom
Barnard Castle 93 D3 N England, United Kingdom
Barnaul 118 D5 C Russian Federation
Barnsley 93 D4 N England, United Kingdom
Barnstaple 95 B4 SW England, United Kingdom
Barnstaple Bay 95 B4 *bay* SW England, United Kingdom
Baroghil Pass 125 G4 *pass* Afghanistan/Pakistan
Barquisimeto 63 C1 NW Venezuela
Barra 91 A4 *island* NW Scotland, United Kingdom
Barra de Río Grande 55 E4 E Nicaragua
Barranca 63 B5 W Peru
Barrancabermeja 63 B2 N Colombia
Barranquilla 63 B1 N Colombia
Barreiro 99 A4 W Portugal
Barrier Range 137 F5 *hill range* New South Wales, SE Australia
Barrier Reef 55 C1 *reef* E Belize
Barrow 50 E1 Alaska, USA
Barrow 89 D6 ≈ SE Ireland
Barrow-in-Furness 93 C3 NW England, United Kingdom
Barrow Island 137 A3 *island* Western Australia
Barry 93 C7 S Wales, United Kingdom
Barstow 49 D8 California, W USA
Bartang 125 G4 ≈ SE Tajikistan
Bartın 121 C2 NW Turkey
Bartlesville 43 D7 Oklahoma, C USA
Barton-upon-Humber 93 F4 N England, United Kingdom
Bartoszyce 105 E2 NE Poland
Baruun-Urt 129 F2 E Mongolia
Barú, Volcán 55 F6 ☼ W Panama
Barva, Volcán 55 E6 ☼ NW Costa Rica
Barwon River 137 G5 ≈ New South Wales, SE Australia
Barysaw 109 D2 NE Belarus
Basarabeasca 109 D6 SE Moldova
Basel 101 B7 NW Switzerland
Basilan 131 F5 *island* SW Philippines
Basildon 95 G3 E England, United Kingdom
Basingstoke 95 E4 S England, United Kingdom
Basque Country, The 99 E1 *cultural region* N Spain Europe
Basra 123 D3 SE Iraq
Bassano del Grappa 103 C2 NE Italy
Bassein 131 A3 SW Myanmar (Burma)
Bassenthwaite Lake 93 C2 ◎ NW England, United Kingdom
Basseterre 57 J4 ● C Saint Kitts and Nevis
Basse-Terre 57 J5 ○ SW Guadeloupe
Bassett 43 C4 Nebraska, C USA
Bassikounou 72 C3 SE Mauritania
Bass Strait 137 F7 *strait* SE Australia
Bassum 101 B3 NW Germany
Bastia 97 G5 Corsica, France
Bastogne 84 E8 SE Belgium
Bata 72 F6 NW Equatorial Guinea
Batangas 131 F4 Luzon, N Philippines
Batdambang 131 C4 NW Cambodia
Batéké, Plateaux 76 B2 *plateau* S Congo
Bath 95 D4 SW England, United Kingdom
Bath 37 G3 Maine, NE USA
Bathinda 127 D2 NW India
Bathurst 137 G6 New South Wales, SE Australia
Bathurst 35 F4 New Brunswick, SE Canada
Bathurst Island 137 C1 *island* Northern Territory, N Australia
Bathurst Island 33 G2 *island* Parry Islands, Nunavut, N Canada
Batin, Wadi al 123 C3 *dry watercourse* SW Asia
Batman 121 G4 SE Turkey
Batna 70 E1 NE Algeria
Baton Rouge 39 C6 *state capital* Louisiana, S USA
Batticaloa 127 E8 E Sri Lanka
Battipaglia 103 D6 S Italy
Battle Mountain 47 B5 Nevada, W USA
Bat'umi 121 G2 W Georgia
Batu Pahat 131 C6 W Malaysia
Bauchi 72 F4 NE Nigeria
Bautzen 101 E4 E Germany
Bavaria 101 C7 *cultural region* SE Germany Europe
Bavarian Alps 101 C7 ⛰ Austria/Germany
Bavispe, Río 53 C2 ≈ NW Mexico
Bawiti 70 I3 N Egypt
Bawku 72 D4 N Ghana
Bayamo 57 D3 E Cuba
Bayamón 51 E Puerto Rico
Bayan Har Shan 129 D4 ⛰ C China
Bayanhongor 129 D2 C Mongolia
Bayano, Lago 55 H6 ◎ E Panama
Bayard 44 C3 New Mexico, SW USA
Bay City 40 E4 Michigan, N USA
Bay City 44 H5 Texas, SW USA
Baydhabo 75 E5 SW Somalia
Bayern *see* Bavaria
Bayeux 97 C2 N France
Bay Islands 55 D2 *island group* N Honduras
Baymak 111 D7 W Russian Federation
Bayonne 97 B6 SW France
Bayramaly 125 D4 S Turkmenistan
Bayreuth 101 C5 SE Germany
Baytown 44 I4 Texas, SW USA
Baza 99 E5 S Spain
Beachy Head 95 G5 *headland* SE England, United Kingdom
Beacon 37 E4 New York, NE USA
Beacon Hill 93 C6 *hill* E Wales, United Kingdom
Beagle Channel 65 B9 *channel* Argentina/Chile
Bear Lake 47 D4 ◎ Idaho/Utah, NW USA
Beas de Segura 99 E5 S Spain
Beata, Isla 57 F5 *island* SW Dominican Republic
Beatrice 43 D5 Nebraska, C USA
Beatty 47 B6 Nevada, W USA
Beaufort Sea 50 F1 *sea* Arctic Ocean
Beaufort West 76 C7 SW South Africa
Beauly 91 D3 N Scotland, United Kingdom
Beaumont 44 I4 Texas, SW USA
Beaune 97 E4 C France
Beauvais 97 D2 N France
Beaver Falls 37 A5 Pennsylvania, NE USA
Beaver Island 40 C3 *island* Michigan, N USA
Beaver River 43 B7 ≈ Oklahoma, C USA
Beaverton 49 B3 Oregon, NW USA
Beawar 127 D3 N India
Beccles 95 H2 E England, United Kingdom
Béchar 70 D2 W Algeria
Beckley 39 G2 West Virginia, NE USA
Bedford 95 F2 E England, United Kingdom
Bedford 40 D7 Indiana, N USA
Bedford Level 95 F2 *physical region* E England, United Kingdom
Bedum 84 F2 NE Netherlands
Bedworth 93 D6 C England, United Kingdom
Be'er Menuha 123 H7 S Israel
Beernem 84 B6 NW Belgium
Be'ér Sheva' 123 G6 S Israel
Beesel 84 E5 SE Netherlands

⬖ Administrative region ◆ Country ● Country capital ◇ Dependent territory ○ Dependent territory capital ⛰ Mountain range ▲ Mountain ☼ Volcano ≈ River ◎ Lake ⊠ Reservoir

Administrative region   ◆ Country   ● Country capital   ◇ Dependent territory   ○ Dependent territory capital   ▲ Mountain range   ▲ Mountain   ℞ Volcano   ∽ River   ◎ Lake   ▣ Reservoir

D

◆ Administrative region   ◆ Country   ● Country capital   ◇ Dependent territory   O Dependent territory capital   ▲ Mountain range   ▲ Mountain   ☸ Volcano   ᴧ River   ◎ Lake   ▤ Reservoir

◆ Administrative region   ● Country   ○ Country capital   ◇ Dependent territory   ○ Dependent territory capital   ▲ Mountain range   ▲ Mountain   ☆ Volcano   ✍ River   ● Lake   ◎ Reservoir

◆ Administrative region ◆ Country ■ Country capital ◇ Dependent territory ○ Dependent territory capital ▲ Mountain range ▲ Mountain ⊼ Volcano ⊿ River ⊘ Lake ⊞ Reservoir

161

GEORGE, LAKE

George, Lake 39 G7 ◎ Florida, SE USA
Georgetown 63 E2 ● N Guyana
George Town 57 D2 C Bahamas
George Town 57 B4 ○ SW Cayman Islands
George Town 131 B5 C Malaysia
Georgetown 39 H4 South Carolina, SE USA
George V Land 142 C6 *physical region* Antarctica
Georgia 121 G1 ◆ *republic* SW Asia
Georgia 39 E5 ◐ *state* SE USA
Georgian Bay 40 F3 *lake bay* Ontario, S Canada
Georgia, Strait of 49 A1 *strait* British Columbia, W Canada
Georg von Neumayer 142 B3 *German research station* Antarctica
Gera 101 D5 E Germany
Geraldine 139 C6 South Island, New Zealand
Geraldton 137 B5 Western Australia
Gerede 121 C2 N Turkey
Gereshk 125 E6 SW Afghanistan
Gering 43 A5 Nebraska, C USA
Gerlach 47 A5 Nevada, W USA
Gerlachovský štít 105 E6 ▲ N Slovakia
Germany 101 B5 ◆ *federal republic* N Europe
Gerona *see* Girona
Gerpinnes 84 C7 S Belgium
Gerze 121 D2 N Turkey
Getafe 99 D3 C Spain
Gevaş 121 H4 SE Turkey
Ghana 72 D5 ◆ *republic* W Africa
Ghanzi 76 C5 W Botswana
Ghardaïa 70 E2 N Algeria
Gharyan 70 F2 NW Libya
Ghazni 125 F5 E Afghanistan
Ghent 84 B6 NW Belgium
Ghudara 125 G3 SE Tajikistan
Ghurian 125 D5 W Afghanistan
Giannitsá 107 E4 N Greece
Gibraltar 99 C6 *UK* ◇ SW Europe
Gibraltar, Strait of 99 *strait* Atlantic Ocean/Mediterranean Sea
Gibson Desert 137 C4 *desert* Western Australia
Giedraičiai 83 F7 E Lithuania
Giessen 101 B5 W Germany
Giffnock 91 D6 C Scotland, United Kingdom
Gifu 133 F6 SW Japan
Giganta, Sierra de la 53 B3 ⛰ W Mexico
Gigha Island 91 B6 *island* SW Scotland, United Kingdom
G'ijduvon 125 E3 C Uzbekistan
Gijón 99 C1 NW Spain
Gila River 44 A3 ≈ Arizona, SW USA
Gilf Kebir Plateau 70 H4 *plateau* SW Egypt
Gilford 89 E3 SE Northern Ireland, United Kingdom
Gillette 47 F3 Wyoming, C USA
Gillingham 95 G4 SE England, United Kingdom
Gilroy 49 B7 California, W USA
Giluwe, Mount 141 B2 ▲ W Papua New Guinea
Gingin 137 B5 Western Australia
Giresun 121 E2 NE Turkey
Girne 112 C6 N Cyprus
Girona 99 H2 NE Spain
Girvan 91 D6 W Scotland, United Kingdom
Gisborne 139 E3 NE New Zealand
Gissar Range 125 F3 ⛰ Tajikistan/Uzbekistan
Giulianova 103 D4 C Italy
Giurgiu 109 C7 S Romania
Gizo 141 E2 NW Solomon Islands
Gjirokastër 107 D4 S Albania
Gjoa Haven 33 H3 King William Island, Nunavut, NW Canada
Gjøvik 83 B5 S Norway
Glace Bay 35 G5 Cape Breton Island, Nova Scotia, SE Canada
Glacier Peak 49 B2 ▲ Washington, NW USA
Gladstone 137 H4 Queensland, E Australia
Glåma 83 B5 ≈ S Norway
Glasgow 91 D6 S Scotland, United Kingdom
Glastonbury 95 D4 SW England, United Kingdom
Glazov 111 D5 NW Russian Federation
Glenamoy 89 B3 NW Ireland
Glen Coe 91 C4 *valley* N Scotland, United Kingdom
Glendale 44 B3 Arizona, SW USA
Glendale 49 C8 California, W USA
Glendive 47 F2 Montana, NW USA
Glengad Head 89 D1 *headland* N Ireland
Glengarriff 89 B7 S Ireland
Glenluce 91 D7 SW Scotland, United Kingdom
Glen Mor 91 D4 *valley* NW Scotland, United Kingdom
Glenrothes 91 E5 E Scotland, United Kingdom
Glens Falls 37 E3 New York, NE USA
Glenties 89 C2 NW Ireland
Glin 89 B5 SW Ireland
Glittertind 83 B4 ▲ S Norway
Gliwice 105 D5 S Poland
Globe 44 B3 Arizona, SW USA
Głogów 105 C4 SW Poland
Gloucester 141 C2 E Papua New Guinea
Gloucester 95 D3 C England, United Kingdom
Glovers Reef 55 C2 *reef* E Belize
Głowno 105 E3 C Poland
Gniezno 105 D3 C Poland
Gobabis 76 C5 E Namibia
Gobi 129 E3 *desert* China/Mongolia
Gobo 133 E7 SW Japan
Godalming 95 F4 SE England, United Kingdom
Godavari 127 E5 ≈ C India
Godhra 127 D4 W India
Godoy Cruz 65 A5 W Argentina
Goeree 84 B5 *island* SW Netherlands
Goes 84 B5 SW Netherlands
Gogebic Range 40 B2 *hill range* Michigan/Wisconsin, N USA
Goiânia 63 G6 C Brazil
Goiás 63 F5 C Brazil
Gojome 133 F3 NW Japan
Gökdepe 125 C3 C Turkmenistan
Göksun 121 E4 C Turkey
Gol 83 B5 S Norway
Golan Heights 123 H5 ⛰ SW Syria
Gołdap 105 F2 NE Poland
Gold Beach 49 A4 Oregon, NW USA
Gold Coast 137 H5 ◐ *cultural region* Queensland, E Australia
Golden Bay 139 C4 *bay* South Island, New Zealand
Goldfield 47 B6 Nevada, W USA
Goldsboro 39 H3 North Carolina, SE USA
Goleniów 105 B2 NW Poland
Golmud 129 D3 C China
Goma 76 D2 NE Dem. Rep. Congo
Gombi 72 G4 E Nigeria
Gómez Palacio 53 D3 C Mexico
Gonaïves 57 F4 N Haiti
Gonâve, Île de la 57 E4 *island* C Haiti
Gonder 75 D3 NW Ethiopia
Gondia 127 E4 C India
Gongola 72 F4 ≈ E Nigeria
Good Hope, Cape of 76 B7 *cape* SW South Africa
Goodland 43 B6 Kansas, C USA
Goodwick 93 A6 SW Wales, United Kingdom
Goole 93 E4 E England, United Kingdom
Goondiwindi 137 G5 Queensland, E Australia
Goor 84 F4 E Netherlands
Goose Green 65 C9 E Falkland Islands
Goose Lake 49 B5 ◎ California/Oregon, W USA
Göppingen 101 C6 SW Germany
Gorakhpur 127 F3 N India
Goré 72 G5 S Chad
Gore 75 D4 C Ethiopia
Gore 139 B8 South Island, New Zealand
Gorey 89 E5 SE Ireland
Gorey 95 H6 Jersey, Channel Islands
Gorgan 123 E1 N Iran
Gori 121 H1 C Georgia
Gorinchem 84 D5 C Netherlands
Goris 121 I3 SE Armenia
Görlitz 101 E4 E Germany
Goroka 141 B2 C Papua New Guinea
Gorontalo 131 F6 Celebes, C Indonesia
Gorssel 84 E4 E Netherlands
Gort 89 C5 W Ireland
Gorzów Wielkopolski 105 C3 W Poland
Goshogawara 133 F3 C Japan
Gosport 95 E5 S England, United Kingdom
Göteborg *see* Gothenburg
Gotha 101 C5 C Germany
Gothenburg 83 B6 S Sweden
Gotland 83 D6 *island* SE Sweden
Goto-retto 133 C8 *island group* SW Japan
Gotsu 133 D6 SW Japan
Göttingen 101 C4 C Germany
Gouda 84 C4 C Netherlands
Gouin, Réservoir 35 D4 ☒ Québec, SE Canada
Goulburn 137 G6 New South Wales, SE Australia
Goundam 72 D3 NW Mali
Gouré 72 F3 SE Niger
Governador Valadares 63 H7 SE Brazil
Govi Altayn Nuruu 129 E2 ⛰ S Mongolia
Gower 93 B7 *peninsula* S Wales, United Kingdom
Gowran 89 D5 SE Ireland
Goya 65 C4 NE Argentina
Goz Beïda 72 H4 SE Chad
Gozo 112 A6 *island* N Malta
Gradačac 107 C2 N Bosnia and Herzegovina
Gradaús, Serra dos 63 F5 ⛰ C Brazil
Grafton 137 H5 New South Wales, SE Australia
Grafton 43 D1 North Dakota, N USA
Graham Land 142 A4 *physical region* Antarctica
Grajewo 105 F2 NE Poland
Grampian Mountains 91 D4 ⛰ C Scotland, United Kingdom
Granada 55 D5 SW Nicaragua
Granada 99 D5 S Spain
Gran Chaco 65 B3 *lowland plain* South America
Grand Bahama Island 57 C1 *island* N Bahamas
Grand Canal 89 C4 *canal* C Ireland
Grand Canyon 44 B1 *canyon* Arizona, SW USA
Grand Cayman 57 C4 *island* SW Cayman Islands
Grande, Bahía 65 B8 *bay* S Argentina
Grande Comore 76 G4 *island* NW Comoros
Grande de Matagalpa, Río 55 E4 ≈ C Nicaragua
Grande Prairie 33 F6 Alberta, W Canada
Grand Erg Occidental 70 D2 *desert* W Algeria
Grand Erg Oriental 70 E3 *desert* Algeria/Tunisia
Grande, Rio 44 G5 ≈ Mexico/USA
Grande Terre 57 K5 *island* E Guadeloupe
Grand Falls 35 H4 Newfoundland, Newfoundland and Labrador, SE Canada
Grand Forks 43 D2 North Dakota, N USA
Grand Island 43 C5 Nebraska, C USA
Grand Junction 47 E5 Colorado, C USA
Grand Rapids 40 D4 Michigan, N USA
Grand Rapids 43 E2 Minnesota, N USA
Grand Union Canal 95 E2 *canal* SE England, United Kingdom
Grange 89 C2 N Ireland
Grangemouth 91 D5 C Scotland, United Kingdom
Granite City 40 B7 Illinois, N USA
Granite Peak 47 B4 ▲ Nevada, W USA
Gran Paradiso 103 A2 ▲ NW Italy
Grantham 93 E6 E England, United Kingdom
Grantown-on-Spey 91 E3 N Scotland, United Kingdom
Grants 44 D2 New Mexico, SW USA
Grantsburg 40 A3 Wisconsin, N USA
Grants Pass 49 B4 Oregon, NW USA
Granville 97 B2 N France
Graulhet 97 C6 S France
Grave 84 E5 SE Netherlands
Gravesend 95 G4 SE England, United Kingdom
Grayling 50 D2 Alaska, USA
Graz 101 E8 SE Austria
Great Abaco 57 D1 *island* N Bahamas
Great Artesian Basin 137 F4 *lowlands* Queensland, C Australia
Great Australian Bight 137 D5 *bight* S Australia
Great Barrier Island 139 D2 *island* N New Zealand
Great Barrier Reef 137 G2 *reef* Queensland, NE Australia
Great Basin 47 B5 *basin* W USA
Great Bear Lake 33 F4 ◎ Northwest Territories, NW Canada
Great Belt 83 B7 *channel* Baltic Sea/Kattegat
Great Bend 43 C6 Kansas, C USA
Great Dividing Range 134 ⛰ NE Australia
Greater Antarctica 142 D4 *physical region* Antarctica
Greater Antilles 57 E5 *island group* West Indies
Great Exhibition Bay 139 C1 *inlet* North Island, New Zealand
Great Exuma Island 57 D2 *island* C Bahamas
Great Falls 47 D2 Montana, NW USA
Great Hungarian Plain 105 D8 *plain* SE Europe
Great Inagua 57 F3 *island* S Bahamas
Great Karoo 76 C7 *plateau region* S South Africa
Great Khingan Range 129 G1 ⛰ NE China
Great Lakes 40 *lakes* Canada/USA
Great Malvern 93 D6 W England, United Kingdom
Great Nicobar 127 H6 *island* SE India
Great Ouse 93 F6 ≈ E England, United Kingdom
Great Plains 43 C5 *plains* Canada/USA
Great Rift Valley 65 *depression* Asia/Africa
Great Ruaha 75 D7 ≈ S Tanzania
Great Saint Bernard Pass 103 A1 *pass* Italy/Switzerland
Great Salt Lake 47 C4 *salt lake* Utah, W USA
Great Salt Lake Desert 47 C5 *plain* Utah, W USA
Great Salt Plains 43 C7 *plain* Oklahoma, C USA
Great Sand Sea 70 H3 *desert* Egypt/Libya
Great Sandy Desert 137 C3 *desert* Western Australia
Great Slave Lake 33 G5 ◎ Northwest Territories, NW Canada
Great Torrington 95 B4 SW England, United Kingdom
Great Victoria Desert 137 C4 *desert* South Australia/Western Australia
Great Wall of China 129 E3 *ancient monument* N China Asia
Great Yarmouth 95 H2 E England, United Kingdom
Gredos, Sierra de 99 C3 ⛰ W Spain
Greece 107 D5 ◆ *republic* SE Europe
Greeley 47 F5 Colorado, C USA
Green Bay 40 C3 Wisconsin, N USA
Green Bay 40 C3 *lake bay* Michigan/Wisconsin, N USA
Greencastle 89 E3 S Northern Ireland, United Kingdom
Greeneville 39 F3 Tennessee, S USA
Greenfield 37 E4 Massachusetts, NE USA
Green Islands 141 D2 *island group* NE Papua New Guinea
Greenland 28 *Danish* ◇ NE North America
Greenland Sea 143 C5 *sea* Arctic Ocean
Green Mountains 37 E3 ⛰ Vermont, NE USA
Greenock 91 D5 W Scotland, United Kingdom
Green River 141 A1 NW Papua New Guinea
Green River 47 D5 Utah, W USA
Green River 47 D4 Wyoming, C USA
Green River 47 D5 ≈ W USA
Green River 39 D2 ≈ Kentucky, C USA
Greensboro 39 G3 North Carolina, SE USA
Greensburg 37 B5 Pennsylvania, NE USA
Green Valley 44 B3 Arizona, SW USA
Greenville 39 C4 Mississippi, S USA
Greenville 39 H3 North Carolina, SE USA
Greenville 39 F4 South Carolina, SE USA
Greenville 44 H3 Texas, SW USA
Greenwood 39 C4 Mississippi, S USA
Greenwood 39 F4 South Carolina, SE USA
Gregory Range 137 G3 ⛰ Queensland, E Australia
Greifswald 101 D2 NE Germany
Grenada 39 C4 Mississippi, S USA
Grenada 57 J6 ◆ *commonwealth republic* SE West Indies
Grenadines, The 57 K6 *island group* Grenada/St Vincent and the Grenadines
Grenoble 97 E5 E France
Gresham 49 B3 Oregon, NW USA
Gretna 91 E7 SW Scotland, United Kingdom
Grevenmacher 84 E9 E Luxembourg
Greybull 47 E3 Wyoming, C USA
Greymouth 139 B6 South Island, New Zealand
Grey Range 137 F4 ⛰ New South Wales/Queensland, E Australia
Greystones 89 E4 E Ireland
Griffin 39 E5 Georgia, SE USA
Grimari 72 H5 C Central African Republic
Grimsby 93 F4 E England, United Kingdom
Groesbeek 84 E5 SE Netherlands
Grójec 105 F4 C Poland
Groningen 84 F2 NE Netherlands
Groote Eylandt 137 E2 *island* Northern Territory, N Australia
Grootfontein 76 C5 N Namibia
Groot Karasberge 76 C6 ⛰ S Namibia
Grosseto 103 C4 C Italy
Grossglockner 101 D8 ▲ W Austria
Groznyy 111 B9 SW Russian Federation
Grudziądz 105 D2 C Poland
Grums 83 C5 C Sweden
Gryazi 111 B6 W Russian Federation
Gryfice 105 C2 NW Poland
Guabito 55 F6 NW Panama
Guadalajara 53 D5 C Mexico
Guadalajara 99 D3 C Spain
Guadalcanal 141 E3 *island* C Solomon Islands
Guadalquivir 99 C5 ≈ W Spain
Guadalupe 53 D4 C Mexico
Guadalupe Peak 44 E4 ▲ Texas, SW USA
Guadalupe River 44 H5 ≈ SW USA
Guadarrama, Sierra de 99 E3 ⛰ C Spain
Guadeloupe 57 K5 *French* ◇ E West Indies
Guadiana 99 B4 ≈ Portugal/Spain
Guadix 99 D5 S Spain
Guaimaca 55 D3 C Honduras
Gualaco 55 D3 C Honduras
Gualán 55 B3 C Guatemala
Gualeguaychú 65 C5 E Argentina
Guam 51 *US* ◇ W Pacific Ocean
Guamúchil 53 C3 C Mexico
Guanabacoa 57 B2 W Cuba
Guanajuato 53 E4 C Mexico
Guanare 63 C2 N Venezuela
Guangyuan 129 E4 C China
Guangzhou 129 F6 S China
Guantánamo 57 E4 SE Cuba
Guaporé, Rio 63 D5 ≈ Bolivia/Brazil
Guarda 99 B3 N Portugal
Guarumal 55 F6 S Panama
Guasave 53 C3 C Mexico
Guasopa 141 D3 SE Papua New Guinea
Guatemala 55 A3 ◆ *republic* Central America
Guatemala Basin 14 *undersea feature* E Pacific Ocean
Guatemala City 55 B3 ● C Guatemala
Guaviare, Río 63 C2 ≈ E Colombia
Guayama 51 E Puerto Rico
Guayaquil 63 A4 SW Ecuador
Guayaquil, Gulf of 63 A4 *gulf* SW Ecuador
Guaymas 53 B3 NW Mexico
Guaynabo 51 E Puerto Rico
Gubadag 125 D2 N Turkmenistan
Guben 101 E4 E Germany
Gubkin 111 A6 W Russian Federation
Gudaut'a 121 F1 NW Georgia
Guéret 97 D4 C France
Guernsey 95 G6 *UK* ◇ Channel Islands, NW Europe
Guerrero Negro 53 A3 W Mexico
Guiana Basin 14 *undersea feature* W Atlantic Ocean
Guiana Highlands 63 E3 ⛰ N South America
Guider 72 G4 N Cameroon
Guidimouni 72 F3 S Niger
Guildford 95 F4 SE England, United Kingdom
Guilin 129 F5 S China
Guimarães 99 B2 N Portugal
Guinea 72 B4 ◆ *republic* W Africa
Guinea-Bissau 72 A4 ◆ *republic* W Africa
Guinea, Gulf of 72 E6 *gulf* E Atlantic Ocean
Guiyang 129 E5 S China
Gujarat 127 C4 *cultural region* W India, Asia
Gujranwala 127 D2 NE Pakistan
Gujrat 127 D2 E Pakistan
Gulbarga 127 D5 C India
Gulfport 39 C6 Mississippi, S USA
Gulf, The *see* Persian Gulf
Guliston 125 F3 E Uzbekistan
Gulkana 50 E3 Alaska, USA
Gulu 75 C5 N Uganda
Gümüşhane 121 F2 NE Turkey
Güney Doğu Toroslar 121 F4 ⛰ SE Turkey
Gunnbjørn Fjeld 143 A6 ▲ C Greenland
Gunnedah 137 G5 New South Wales, SE Australia
Gunnison 47 E6 Colorado, C USA
Gunnison 47 D5 Utah, W USA
Gurbansoltan Eje 125 D2 N Turkmenistan
Gurbantünggüt Shamo 129 C2 *desert* NW China
Gurktaler Alpen 101 E8 ⛰ S Austria
Gürün 121 E3 C Turkey
Gusau 72 E4 NW Nigeria
Gusev 83 E7 W Russian Federation
Gustavus 50 F4 Alaska, USA
Güstrow 101 D2 NE Germany
Gütersloh 101 B4 W Germany
Guthrie 44 F3 Texas, SW USA
Guwahati 127 G3 NE India
Guyana 63 E2 ◆ *republic* N South America
Guymon 43 B7 Oklahoma, C USA
Güzelyurt 112 C6 N Cyprus
Gwadar 127 A3 SW Pakistan
Gwalior 127 E3 C India
Gwanda 76 D5 SW Zimbabwe
Gweedore 89 C1 NW Ireland
Gyangzê 129 C5 W China
Gyaring Co 129 C4 ◎ W China
Gympie 137 H4 Queensland, E Australia
Gyomaendrőd 105 F8 SE Hungary
Gyöngyös 105 E7 NE Hungary
Győr 105 D7 NW Hungary
Gyumri 121 G2 W Armenia

H

Haacht 84 C6 C Belgium
Haaksbergen 84 F4 E Netherlands
Haarlem 84 C3 W Netherlands
Haast 139 B6 South Island, New Zealand
Hachijo-jima 133 G7 *island* Izu-shoto, SE Japan
Hachinohe 133 G3 C Japan
Haddington 91 E5 SE Scotland, United Kingdom
Hadejia 72 F4 N Nigeria
Hadejia 72 F4 ≈ N Nigeria
Hadleigh 95 G3 SE England, United Kingdom
Ha Dong 131 C2 N Vietnam
Hadramaut 123 D7 ⛰ S Yemen
Haeju 133 A5 S North Korea
Hagåtña 51 ○ NW Guam
Hagerman 47 C4 Idaho, NW USA
Hagerstown 39 H1 Maryland, NE USA
Hagondange 97 F2 NE France
Hag's Head 89 B5 *headland* W Ireland
Haguenau 97 F2 NE France
Hague, The 84 C4 ● W Netherlands
Haicheng 129 G3 NE China
Haifa 123 G5 N Israel
Haikou 129 F6 S China
Ha'il 123 B3 NW Saudi Arabia
Hailar 129 G1 N China
Hailsham 95 G4 SE England, United Kingdom
Hailuoto 83 E3 *island* W Finland
Hainan Dao 129 F6 *island* S China
Haines 50 G3 Alaska, USA
Hainichen 101 D5 E Germany
Hai Phong 131 C2 N Vietnam
Haiti 57 F4 ◆ *republic* C West Indies
Haiya 75 D2 NE Sudan
Hajdúhadház 105 F7 E Hungary
Hakodate 133 F2 NE Japan
Halberstadt 101 C4 C Germany
Halden 83 B5 S Norway
Halfmoon Bay 139 B8 Stewart Island, Southland, New Zealand
Halifax 35 G5 *province capital* Nova Scotia, SE Canada
Halifax 93 D4 N England, United Kingdom
Halkirk 91 E2 N Scotland, United Kingdom
Halladale 91 D2 ≈ N Scotland, United Kingdom
Halle 84 C7 C Belgium
Halle 101 D4 C Germany
Halle-Neustadt 101 D4 C Germany
Halley 142 B3 *UK research station* Antarctica
Halls Creek 137 D2 Western Australia
Halmahera, Pulau 131 G6 *island* E Indonesia
Halmahera Sea 131 G6 *sea* E Indonesia
Halmstad 83 C6 S Sweden
Haltwhistle 93 C2 N England, United Kingdom
Hamada 133 D6 SW Japan
Hamadan 123 D2 W Iran
Hamah 123 B3 W Syria
Hamamatsu 133 F6 S Japan
Hamar 83 B5 S Norway
Hamburg 101 C3 N Germany
Hamd, Wadi al 123 A4 *dry watercourse* W Saudi Arabia
Hämeenlinna 83 E5 S Finland
Hamersley Range 137 B3 ⛰ Western Australia
Hamgyong-sanmaek 133 B4 ⛰ N North Korea
Hamhung 133 B4 C North Korea
Hami 129 D2 NW China
Hamilton 35 D6 Ontario, S Canada
Hamilton 139 D3 North Island, New Zealand
Hamilton 91 D6 S Scotland, United Kingdom
Hamilton 39 D4 Alabama, S USA
Hamim, Wadi al 70 G3 ≈ NE Libya
Hamm 101 B4 W Germany
Hammamet, Golfe de 112 E4 *gulf* NE Tunisia
Hammar, Hawr al 123 C3 ◎ SE Iraq
Hammond 40 C5 Indiana, N USA
Hampden 139 B7 South Island, New Zealand
Hamrun 112 B6 C Malta
Hanalei 51 A1 Kaua'i, Hawai'i, USA
Handan 129 F4 E China
Hanford 49 C7 California, W USA
Hangayn Nuruu 129 D2 ⛰ C Mongolia
Hangö *see* Hanko
Hangzhou 129 G4 SE China
Hanko 83 E5 SW Finland
Hanley 93 D5 C England, United Kingdom
Hanmer Springs 139 C6 South Island, New Zealand
Hannibal 43 F6 Missouri, C USA
Hannover *see* Hanover
Hanöbukten 83 C7 *bay* S Sweden
Hanoi 131 C2 ● N Vietnam
Hanover 101 C4 NW Germany
Han Shui 129 F4 ≈ C China
Hanzhong 129 E4 C China
Haora 127 G4 NE India
Haparanda 83 E3 N Sweden
Haradok 109 D1 N Belarus
Haramachi 133 G4 E Japan
Harare 76 E4 ● NE Zimbabwe
Harbel 72 B5 W Liberia
Harbin 129 H2 NE China
Hardangerfjorden 83 A5 *fjord* S Norway
Hardangervidda 83 B5 *plateau* S Norway
Hardenberg 84 F3 E Netherlands
Harelbeke 84 B6 W Belgium
Haren 84 F2 NE Netherlands
Harer 75 E3 E Ethiopia
Hargeysa 75 E3 NW Somalia
Harima-nada 133 E6 *sea* S Japan
Harirud 125 E5 ≈ Afghanistan/Iran
Harlan 43 D5 Iowa, C USA
Harlech 93 B5 NW Wales, United Kingdom
Harlingen 84 D2 N Netherlands
Harlingen 44 H6 Texas, SW USA
Harlow 95 G3 E England, United Kingdom
Harney Basin 49 C4 *basin* Oregon, NW USA
Härnösand 83 D4 C Sweden
Har Nuur 129 D2 ◎ NW Mongolia
Harpenden 95 F3 E England, United Kingdom
Harper 72 C5 NE Liberia
Harricana 35 D4 ≈ Québec, SE Canada
Harris 91 B3 *physical region* NW Scotland, United Kingdom
Harrisburg 40 C8 Illinois, N USA
Harrisburg 37 C5 *state capital* Pennsylvania, NE USA
Harrisonburg 39 H2 Virginia, NE USA
Harrison, Cape 35 G2 *cape* Newfoundland and Labrador, E Canada
Harris, Sound of 91 B3 *strait* NW Scotland, United Kingdom
Harrogate 93 D3 N England, United Kingdom
Harrow 95 F3 SE England, United Kingdom
Harstad 83 C2 N Norway
Hartford 37 E4 *state capital* Connecticut, NE USA
Hartland Point 95 B4 *headland* SW England, United Kingdom
Hartlepool 93 E2 N England, United Kingdom
Hartwell Lake 39 F4 ☒ Georgia/South Carolina, SE USA
Har Us Gol 129 D2 ◎ W Mongolia
Har Us Nuur 129 C2 ◎ NW Mongolia
Harvey 43 C2 North Dakota, N USA
Harwich 95 H3 E England, United Kingdom
Haryana 127 D2 *state* N India
Harz 101 C4 ⛰ C Germany
Haslemere 95 F4 SE England, United Kingdom
Hasselt 84 D6 NE Belgium
Hastings 139 E4 North Island, New Zealand
Hastings 95 G4 SE England, United Kingdom
Hastings 43 C5 Nebraska, C USA
Hatch 44 D3 New Mexico, SW USA
Hatfield 95 F3 E England, United Kingdom
Hattem 84 E3 E Netherlands
Hatteras, Cape 39 I3 *headland* North Carolina, SE USA
Hattiesburg 39 C6 Mississippi, S USA
Hat Yai 131 B5 SW Thailand
Haugesund 83 A5 S Norway
Haukeligrend 83 B5 S Norway
Haukivesi 83 F4 ◎ SE Finland
Hauraki Gulf 139 D2 *gulf* North Island, N New Zealand
Hauroko, Lake 139 A8 ◎ SW New Zealand
Hautes Fagnes 84 E7 ⛰ E Belgium
Hauts Plateaux 70 D2 *plateau* Algeria/Morocco
Hauzenberg 101 E6 SE Germany

◐ Administrative region ◆ Country ● Country capital ◇ Dependent territory ○ Dependent territory capital ⛰ Mountain range ▲ Mountain ⛰ Volcano ≈ River ◎ Lake ☒ Reservoir

JARDINES DE LA REINA

Havana 57 B2 ● W Cuba
Havant 95 F5 S England, United Kingdom
Havelock 39 H4 North Carolina, SE USA
Havelock North 139 E4 North Island, New Zealand
Haverfordwest 93 A7 SW Wales, United Kingdom
Haverhill 95 G2 E England, United Kingdom
Havířov 105 D5 E Czech Republic
Havre 47 D1 Montana, NW USA
Havre-St-Pierre 35 F4 Québec, E Canada
Hawi 51 D2 Hawaii, USA
Hawai'i 51 C1 ◈ *state* USA, C Pacific Ocean
Hawai'i 51 D3 *island* USA, C Pacific Ocean
Hawea, Lake 139 B7 ◎ South Island, New Zealand
Hawera 139 D4 North Island, New Zealand
Hawes 93 D3 N England, United Kingdom
Hawick 91 E6 SE Scotland, United Kingdom
Hawke Bay 139 E4 *bay* North Island, New Zealand
Hawthorne 47 A6 Nevada, W USA
Hay 137 F6 New South Wales, SE Australia
Hayden 44 B3 Arizona, SW USA
Hayes 35 A2 ≈ Manitoba, C Canada
Hay-on-Wye 93 C6 E Wales, United Kingdom
Hay River 33 G5 Northwest Territories, W Canada
Hays 43 C6 Kansas, C USA
Haysyn 109 D5 C Ukraine
Haywards Heath 95 G4 SE England, United Kingdom
Hazar 125 B3 W Turkmenistan
Hearne 44 H4 Texas, SW USA
Hearst 35 C4 Ontario, S Canada
Hebbronville 44 G6 Texas, SW USA
Hebrides, Sea of the 91 B4 *sea* NW Scotland, United Kingdom
Hebron 123 H6 S West Bank
Heemskerk 84 C3 W Netherlands
Heerde 84 E3 E Netherlands
Heerenveen 84 E2 N Netherlands
Heerhugowaard 84 D3 NW Netherlands
Heerlen 84 E6 SE Netherlands
Hefa *see* Haifa
Hefei 129 G4 E China
Hegang 129 H1 NE China
Heide 101 B2 N Germany
Heidelberg 101 B6 SW Germany
Heidenheim an der Brenz 101 C6 S Germany
Heilbronn 101 B6 SW Germany
Heilong Jiang *see* Amur
Heiloo 84 C3 NW Netherlands
Heimdal 83 B4 S Norway
Hekimhan 121 E3 C Turkey
Helena 47 D2 *state capital* Montana, NW USA
Helensburgh 91 D5 W Scotland, United Kingdom
Helensville 139 D2 North Island, New Zealand
Helgoländer Bucht 101 B2 *bay* NW Germany
Hellevoetsluis 84 C5 SW Netherlands
Hellín 99 E4 C Spain
Hells Canyon 49 D3 *valley* Idaho/Oregon, NW USA
Helmand, Darya-ye 125 D6 ≈ Afghanistan/Iran
Helmond 84 E5 S Netherlands
Helmsdale 91 E2 N Scotland, United Kingdom
Helmsley 93 E3 N England, United Kingdom
Helsingborg 83 C7 S Sweden
Helsinki 83 E5 ● S Finland
Helston 95 A6 SW England, United Kingdom
Helvellyn 93 C3 ▲ NW England, United Kingdom
Henderson 47 C7 Nevada, W USA
Henderson 44 H3 Texas, SW USA
Hengduan Shan 129 D5 ▲▲ SW China
Hengelo 84 F4 E Netherlands
Hengyang 129 F5 S China
Heniches'k 109 F6 S Ukraine
Henley-on-Thames 95 F3 C England, United Kingdom
Hennebont 97 B3 NW France
Henzada 131 A3 SW Myanmar (Burma)
Herat 125 D5 W Afghanistan
Heredia 55 E6 C Costa Rica
Hereford 93 C6 W England, United Kingdom
Hereford 44 F2 Texas, SW USA
Herford 101 B4 NW Germany
Herk-de-Stad 84 D6 NE Belgium
Herm 95 G6 *island* Channel Islands
Herma Ness 91 B5 *headland* NE Scotland, United Kingdom
Hermansverk 83 B5 S Norway
Hermiston 49 C3 Oregon, NW USA
Hermit Islands 141 B1 *island group* N Papua New Guinea
Hermon, Mount 123 H5 ▲ S Syria
Hermosillo 53 B2 NW Mexico
Herrera del Duque 99 C4 W Spain
Herselt 84 D6 C Belgium
Herstal 84 E7 E Belgium
Hessen 101 C5 *state* C Germany
Hessle 93 F4 N England, United Kingdom
Hettinger 43 B3 North Dakota, N USA
Hexham 93 D2 N England, United Kingdom
Hidalgo del Parral 53 D3 N Mexico
Hida-sanmyaku 133 E5 ▲▲ Honshū, S Japan
Hienghène 141 G6 C New Caledonia
High Atlas 70 C2 ▲▲ C Morocco
High Point 39 G3 North Carolina, SE USA
High Willhays 95 C5 ▲ SW England, United Kingdom
High Wycombe 95 F3 SE England, United Kingdom
Higüero, Punta 51 *headland* W Puerto Rico
Hiiumaa 83 D6 *island* W Estonia
Hikurangi 139 D2 North Island, New Zealand
Hildesheim 101 C4 N Germany
Hill Bank 55 B1 N Belize
Hillegom 84 C4 W Netherlands
Hillsborough 89 E2 E Northern Ireland, United Kingdom
Hilo 51 D3 Hawai'i, USA, C Pacific Ocean
Hilversum 84 D4 C Netherlands
Himalayas 127 E2 ▲▲ S Asia
Himeji 133 E6 SW Japan
Hims 123 B2 C Syria
Hinchinbrook Island 137 G2 *island* Queensland, NE Australia
Hinds 139 C6 SW New Zealand
Hindu Kush 125 F4 ▲▲ Afghanistan/Pakistan
Hinesville 39 G5 Georgia, SE USA
Hinnøya 83 C2 *island* C Norway
Hirfanlı Barajı 121 C3 ⊞ C Turkey
Hirosaki 133 F3 C Japan
Hiroshima 133 D7 SW Japan
Hirson 97 E2 N France
Hisiu 141 B3 SW Papua New Guinea
Hispaniola 57 F4 *island* Dominion Republic/Haiti
Hitachi 133 G5 S Japan
Hitra 83 B4 *island* S Norway
Hjälmaren 83 C6 ◎ C Sweden
Hjørring 83 B6 N Denmark
Hkakabo Razi 131 A1 ▲ Myanmar (Burma)/China
Hlukhiv 109 E3 NE Ukraine
Hlybokaye 109 C2 N Belarus
Hoang Lien Son 131 C2 ▲▲ N Vietnam
Hobart 137 G7 *state capital* Tasmania, SE Australia
Hobbs 44 E3 New Mexico, SW USA
Hobro 83 B6 N Denmark
Ho Chi Minh 131 C4 S Vietnam
Hocking River 40 F7 ≈ Ohio, N USA
Hodeida 123 B6 W Yemen
Hódmezővásárhely 105 E8 SE Hungary
Hodna, Chott El 112 D4 *salt lake* N Algeria
Hodonín 105 D6 SE Czech Republic
Hoeryong 133 C3 NE North Korea
Hof 101 D5 SE Germany
Hofu 133 D7 SW Japan
Hohenems 101 C7 W Austria
Hohe Tauern 101 D8 ▲▲ W Austria
Hohhot 129 F3 N China
Hokianga Harbour 139 C2 *inlet* SE Tasman Sea
Hokitika 139 B6 South Island, New Zealand
Hokkaido 133 F1 *island* NE Japan
Holbrook 44 C2 Arizona, SW USA
Holden 47 D5 Utah, W USA
Holguín 57 D3 SE Cuba
Hollabrunn 101 F6 NE Austria
Holland *see* Netherlands
Holly Springs 39 C4 Mississippi, S USA
Hollywood 39 G8 Florida, SE USA
Holman 33 G3 Victoria Island, Northwest Territories, N Canada
Holmsund 83 D4 N Sweden
Holon 123 G6 C Israel
Holstebro 83 B6 W Denmark
Holt 95 H1 E England, United Kingdom
Holycross 89 D5 S Ireland
Holyhead 93 A4 NW Wales, United Kingdom
Holy Island 93 D1 *island* NE England, United Kingdom
Holyoke 37 E4 Massachusetts, NE USA
Hombori 72 D3 S Mali
Homyel' 109 D3 SE Belarus
Hondo 44 G5 Texas, SW USA
Hondo 55 B1 ≈ Central America
Honduras 55 C3 ◆ *republic* Central America
Honduras, Gulf of 55 C2 *gulf* W Caribbean Sea
Hønefoss 83 B5 S Norway
Honey Lake 49 B6 ◎ California, W USA
Hong Gai 131 C2 N Vietnam
Hong Kong 129 H6 S China
Honiara 141 E3 ● C Solomon Islands
Honiton 95 C5 SW England, United Kingdom
Honjo 133 F4 C Japan
Honolulu 51 B1 *state capital* O'ahu, Hawai'i, USA
Honshu 133 G5 *island* SW Japan
Hoogeveen 84 E3 NE Netherlands
Hoogezand-Sappemeer 84 F2 NE Netherlands
Hoorn 84 D3 NW Netherlands
Hoover Dam 47 C7 *dam* Arizona/Nevada, W USA
Hopa 121 G2 NE Turkey
Hope 33 D4 British Columbia, SW Canada
Hope 50 E3 Alaska, USA
Hopedale 35 F2 Newfoundland and Labrador, NE Canada
Hopkinsville 39 D3 Kentucky, S USA
Horasan 121 G3 NE Turkey
Horki 109 D2 E Belarus
Horley 95 F4 SE England, United Kingdom
Horlivka 109 G5 E Ukraine
Hormuz, Strait of 123 E4 *strait* Iran/Oman
Horn, Cape 65 B9 *cape* S Chile
Horncastle 93 F5 E England, United Kingdom
Hornsea 93 F4 E England, United Kingdom
Horoshiri-dake 133 G2 ▲ Hokkaidō, N Japan
Horseleap 89 D4 C Ireland
Horsham 137 F6 Victoria, SE Australia
Horsham 95 F4 SE England, United Kingdom
Horst 84 E5 SE Netherlands
Horten 83 B5 S Norway
Horyn' 109 C4 ≈ NW Ukraine
Hosingen 84 E8 NE Luxembourg
Hotan 129 B3 NW China
Hotazel 76 C6 N South Africa
Hoting 83 C4 C Sweden
Hot Springs 39 B4 Arkansas, C USA
Houayxay 131 B2 N Laos
Houghton 40 C2 Michigan, N USA
Houghton Lake 40 D4 Michigan, N USA
Houilles 97 C6 N France
Houlton 37 G1 Maine, NE USA
Houma 39 C6 Louisiana, S USA
Houston 44 H4 Texas, SW USA
Hovd 129 C2 W Mongolia
Hove 95 F5 SE England, United Kingdom
Hoverla, Hora 109 B5 ▲ W Ukraine
Hövsgöl Nuur 129 D1 ◎ N Mongolia
Howar, Wadi 75 B2 ≈ Chad/Sudan
Howth 89 E4 E Ireland
Hoy 91 E1 *island* N Scotland, United Kingdom
Hoyerswerda 101 E4 E Germany
Hradec Králové 105 C5 N Czech Republic
Hranice 105 D6 E Czech Republic
Hrodna 109 B2 W Belarus
Huaihua 129 F5 S China
Huajuapan 53 F5 SE Mexico
Hualapai Peak 44 A2 ▲ Arizona, SW USA
Huambo 76 B4 C Angola
Huancayo 63 B5 C Peru
Huangshi 129 G4 C China
Huánuco 63 B5 C Peru
Huanuni 65 C4 W Bolivia
Huaraz 63 B5 W Peru
Huatabampo 53 C3 NW Mexico
Hubli 127 D6 SW India
Huch'ang 133 B4 N North Korea
Hucknall 93 D5 C England, United Kingdom
Huddersfield 93 D4 N England, United Kingdom
Hudiksvall 83 D4 C Sweden
Hudson Bay 35 B2 *bay* NE Canada
Hudson River 37 E4 ≈ New Jersey/New York, NE USA
Hudson Strait 33 J4 *strait* Northwest Territories/Québec, NE Canada
Hue 131 C3 C Vietnam
Huehuetenango 55 A3 W Guatemala
Huelva 99 B5 SW Spain
Huesca 99 F2 NE Spain
Huéscar 99 E5 S Spain
Hughenden 137 G3 Queensland, NE Australia
Hugo 43 D9 Oklahoma, C USA
Huich'on 133 B4 C North Korea
Huíla Plateau 76 B4 *plateau* S Angola
Huixtla 53 H6 SE Mexico
Hulingol 129 G2 N China
Hull 35 D5 Québec, SE Canada
Hull 93 E4 ≈ N England, United Kingdom
Hulst 84 C6 SW Netherlands
Hulun Nur 129 F2 ◎ NE China
Humacao 51 E Puerto Rico
Humaitá 63 D4 N Brazil
Humber 93 F4 *estuary* E England, United Kingdom
Humboldt River 47 B5 ≈ Nevada, W USA
Humphreys Peak 44 A2 ▲ Arizona, SW USA
Humpolec 105 C6 C Czech Republic
Hunedoara 109 B6 SW Romania
Hünfeld 101 C5 C Germany
Hungary 105 D8 ◆ *republic* C Europe
Hunstanton 95 G1 E England, United Kingdom
Hunter Island 137 F7 *island* Tasmania, SE Australia
Huntingdon 95 F2 E England, United Kingdom
Huntington 39 F2 West Virginia, NE USA
Huntington Beach 49 C9 California, W USA
Huntly 139 D3 North Island, New Zealand
Huntly 91 E3 NE Scotland, United Kingdom
Huntsville 39 E4 Alabama, S USA
Huntsville 44 H4 Texas, SW USA
Huon Gulf 141 B2 *gulf* E Papua New Guinea
Hurghada 70 J3 E Egypt
Huron 43 C3 South Dakota, N USA
Huron, Lake 40 E3 ◎ Canada/USA
Hurunui 139 C6 ≈ South Island, New Zealand
Húsavík 83 A1 NE Iceland
Husum 101 B2 N Germany
Hutchinson 43 C6 Kansas, C USA
Huy 84 D7 E Belgium
Hvannadalshnúkur 83 B1 ☄ S Iceland
Hvar 107 B3 *island* S Croatia
Hwange 76 D5 W Zimbabwe
Hyargas Nuur 129 D2 ◎ NW Mongolia
Hyderabad 127 E5 C India
Hyderabad 127 B3 SE Pakistan
Hyères 97 E7 SE France
Hyères, Îles d' 97 E7 *island group* S France
Hyesan 133 B4 NE North Korea
Hythe 95 H4 SE England, United Kingdom
Hyvinkää 83 E5 S Finland

I

Ialomița 109 C7 ≈ SE Romania
Iași 109 C6 NE Romania
Ibadan 72 E5 SW Nigeria
Ibar 107 D2 ≈ C Serbia
Ibarra 63 B3 N Ecuador
Iberian Peninsula 78 *physical region* Portugal/Spain
Ibérico, Sistema 99 E2 ▲▲ NE Spain
Ibiza 99 G4 *island* Balearic Islands, Spain
Ica 63 B6 SW Peru
Iceland 83 A1 ◆ *republic* N Atlantic Ocean
Iceland Plateau 143 B6 *undersea feature* S Greenland Sea
Idabel 43 E9 Oklahoma, C USA
Idaho 49 D3 ◈ *state* NW USA
Idaho Falls 47 D3 Idaho, NW USA
Idfu 70 J3 E Egypt
Idini 72 A2 W Mauritania
Idlib 123 B2 NW Syria
Idre 83 C4 C Sweden
Ieper 84 A6 W Belgium
Iferouâne 72 F2 N Niger
Ifôghas, Adrar des 72 E2 ▲▲ NE Mali
Igarka 118 E3 N Russian Federation
Iglesias 103 A6 Sardinia, Italy
Igloolik 33 I3 Nunavut, N Canada
Igoumenitsa 107 D5 W Greece
Iguaçu, Rio 63 F8 ≈ Argentina/Brazil
Iguala 53 F5 S Mexico
Iguazu Falls 65 D4 *waterfall* Brazil/Argentina
Iguidi, 'Erg 70 C3 *desert* Algeria/Mauritania
Ihosy 76 G5 S Madagascar
Iisalmi 83 E4 C Finland
IJssel 84 E4 ≈ Netherlands
IJsselmeer 84 D3 ◎ N Netherlands
IJsselmuiden 84 E3 E Netherlands
Ijzer 84 A6 ≈ W Belgium
Ikaría 107 F6 *island* Dodecanese, Greece
Ikela 76 C2 C Dem. Rep. Congo
Iki 133 C7 *island* SW Japan
Ilagan 131 F3 Luzon, N Philippines
Iława 105 E2 NE Poland
Ilebo 76 C2 W Dem. Rep. Congo
Île-de-France 97 D3 *region* N France
Ilford 95 G3 SE England, United Kingdom
Ilfracombe 95 B4 SW England, United Kingdom
Ílhavo 99 B3 N Portugal
Iliamna Lake 50 D2 ◎ Alaska, USA
Iligan 131 F5 S Philippines
Ilkeston 95 E1 C England, United Kingdom
Ilkley 93 D4 N England, United Kingdom
Illapel 65 A5 C Chile
Illichivs'k 109 E6 SW Ukraine
Illinois 40 B7 ◈ *state* C USA
Illinois River 40 B6 ≈ Illinois, N USA
Iloilo 131 F4 Panay Island, C Philippines
Ilorin 72 E4 W Nigeria
Ilovlya 111 B7 SW Russian Federation
Imatra 83 F4 SE Finland
Imisli 121 I2 C Azerbaijan
Imola 103 C3 N Italy
Imperatriz 63 G4 NE Brazil
Imperia 103 A3 NW Italy
Imphal 127 H3 NE India
Inagh 89 B5 W Ireland
Inarajan 51 SE Guam
Inarijärvi 83 E1 ◎ N Finland
Inawashiro-ko 133 F5 ◎ Honshu, C Japan
İncesu 121 D4 Turkey
Inch'on 133 B5 NW South Korea
Independence 43 E6 Missouri, C USA
Independence Mountains 47 B4 ▲▲ Nevada, W USA
India 127 D4 ◆ *republic* S Asia
Indiana 37 B5 Pennsylvania, NE USA
Indiana 40 C6 ◈ *state* N USA
Indianapolis 40 D7 *state capital* Indiana, N USA
Indian Church 55 B1 N Belize
Indian Ocean 15 *ocean*
Indianola 43 E5 Iowa, C USA
Indigirka 118 G2 ≈ NE Russian Federation
Indonesia 131 C7 ◆ *republic* SE Asia
Indore 127 D4 C India
Indus 127 B3 ≈ S Asia
Indus, Mouths of the 127 B3 *delta* S Pakistan
İnebolu 121 D2 N Turkey
Infiernillo, Presa del 53 E5 ⊞ S Mexico
Ingleborough 93 C4 ▲ N England, United Kingdom
Ingolstadt 101 C6 S Germany
Inhambane 76 E6 SE Mozambique
Inishannon 89 C7 S Ireland
Inishbofin 89 A4 *island* W Ireland
Inishcrone 89 C3 N Ireland
Inishkea North 89 A3 *island* NW Ireland
Inishkea South 89 A3 *island* NW Ireland
Inishmore 89 B4 *island* W Ireland
Inishshark 89 A4 *island* W Ireland
Inishtrahull 89 D1 *island* NW Ireland
Inishturk 89 A3 *island* W Ireland
Inn 101 D7 ≈ C Europe
Inner Hebrides 91 B5 *island group* W Scotland, United Kingdom
Inner Sound 91 C3 *strait* NW Scotland, United Kingdom
Innisfail 137 G2 Queensland, NE Australia
Innsbruck 101 C7 W Austria
Inowrocław 105 D3 C Poland
I-n-Sakane, 'Erg 72 D2 *desert* N Mali
I-n-Salah 70 D3 C Algeria
Inta 111 E3 NW Russian Federation
Interlaken 101 B8 SW Switzerland
International Falls 43 E1 Minnesota, N USA
Inukjuak 35 D2 Québec, NE Canada
Inuvik 33 F4 Northwest Territories, NW Canada
Inver 89 C2 N Ireland
Inveraray 91 C5 W Scotland, United Kingdom
Inverbervie 91 F4 NE Scotland, United Kingdom
Invercargill 139 B8 Sw New Zealand
Invergordon 91 D3 N Scotland, United Kingdom
Inverness 91 D3 N Scotland, United Kingdom
Inverurie 91 F3 NE Scotland, United Kingdom
Investigator Strait 137 E6 *strait* South Australia
Inyangani 76 E5 ▲ NE Zimbabwe
Ioánnina 107 D5 W Greece
Iola 43 E7 Kansas, C USA
Iona 91 B5 *island* W Scotland, United Kingdom
Iónia Nisiá *see* Ionian Islands
Ionian Islands 107 D5 *island group* W Greece
Ionian Sea 112 G3 *sea* C Mediterranean Sea
Íos 107 F6 *island* Cyclades, Greece
Iowa 43 E5 ◈ *state* C USA
Iowa City 43 F5 Iowa, C USA
Iowa Falls 43 E4 Iowa, C USA
Iowa River 40 A5 ≈ Iowa, C USA
Ipel' 105 E7 ≈ Hungary/Slovakia
Ipoh 131 B5 W Malaysia
Ippy 72 H5 C Central African Republic
Ipswich 137 H5 Queensland, E Australia
Ipswich 95 H2 E England, United Kingdom
Iqaluit 33 J3 *province capital* Baffin Island, Nunavut, NE Canada
Iquique 65 A3 N Chile
Iquitos 63 C4 N Peru
Irákleio 107 F7 Crete, Greece
Iran 123 E2 ◆ *republic* SW Asia
Iranian Plateau 123 E3 *plateau* N Iran
Irapuato 53 E4 C Mexico
Iraq 123 B2 ◆ *republic* SW Asia
Irbid 123 A2 N Jordan
Ireland 89 C4 ◆ *republic* NW Europe
Irian Jaya *see* Papua
Iringa 75 D7 C Tanzania
Iriomote-jima 133 A8 *island* Sakishima-shoto, SW Japan
Iriona 55 D2 NE Honduras
Irish Sea 87 C6 *sea* C British Isles
Irkutsk 118 F5 S Russian Federation
Iroise 97 A2 *sea* NW France
Iron Mountain 40 C3 Michigan, N USA
Ironwood 40 B2 Michigan, N USA
Irrawaddy 131 A2 ≈ W Myanmar (Burma)
Irrawaddy, Mouths of the 131 A3 *delta* SW Myanmar (Burma)
Irtysh 118 D4 ≈ C Asia
Irún 99 E1 N Spain
Iruña *see* Pamplona
Irvine 91 D6 W Scotland, United Kingdom
Irvinestown 89 D2 W Northern Ireland, United Kingdom
Isabela, Isla 63 A7 *island* Galapagos Islands, Ecuador
Isabella, Cordillera 55 D4 ▲▲ NW Nicaragua
Isachsen 33 G2 Ellef Ringnes Island, Nunavut, N Canada
Ísafjördhur 83 A1 NW Iceland
Isbister 91 A6 NE Scotland, United Kingdom
Ise 133 F6 SW Japan
Isère 97 E5 ◈ *state* E France
Isernia 103 D5 C Italy
Ise-wan 133 F6 *bay* S Japan
Isfahan 123 D2 C Iran
Ishigaki-jima 133 A8 *island* Sakishima-shoto, SW Japan
Ishikari-wan 133 F2 *bay* Hokkaidō, NE Japan
Ishim 118 C4 C Russian Federation
Ishim 118 D4 ≈ Kazakhstan/Russian Federation
Ishinomaki 133 G4 C Japan
Ishkoshim 125 G4 S Tajikistan
Isiro 76 D1 NE Dem. Rep. Congo
İskenderun 121 E5 S Turkey
Iskur 107 E3 ≈ NW Bulgaria
Iskur, Yazovir 107 E3 ⊞ W Bulgaria
Isla Cristina 99 B5 SW Spain
Islamabad 127 D1 ● NE Pakistan
Islay 91 B6 *island* SW Scotland, United Kingdom
Isle 97 C5 ≈ W France
Isle of Man 93 B3 *UK* ◇ NW Europe
Isle of Wight 95 E5 *island* , United Kingdom
Isles of Scilly 95 A3 *island group* SW England, United Kingdom
Isma'iliya 70 I2 N Egypt
Isna 70 J3 SE Egypt
Isoka 76 E3 NE Zambia
Isparta 120 B4 SW Turkey
İspir 121 F2 NE Turkey
Israel 123 G6 ◆ *republic* SW Asia
Issoire 97 D5 C France
Issyk-Kul', Ozero 125 H2 ◎ E Kyrgyzstan
Istanbul 120 B2 NW Turkey
Istra 107 A1 *cultural region* NW Croatia
Itabuna 63 H6 E Brazil
Itagüí 63 B2 W Colombia
Itaipú Dam 65 C4 *dam* Brazil/Paraguay
Itaipú, Represa de 63 F7 ⊞ Brazil/Paraguay
Itaituba 63 F4 NE Brazil
Italy 103 C4 ◆ *republic* S Europe
Ithaca 37 D4 New York, NE USA
Itoigawa 133 F5 C Japan
Iturup, Ostrov 118 I5 *island* Kurile Islands, SE Russian Federation
Itzehoe 101 C2 N Germany
Ivalo 83 E2 N Finland
Ivanhoe 137 F5 New South Wales, SE Australia
Ivano-Frankivs'k 109 B5 W Ukraine
Ivanovo 111 B5 W Russian Federation
Ivoire, Côte d' 72 C5 ◆ *republic* W Africa
Ivory Coast *see* Ivoire, Côte d'
Ivujivik 35 D1 Québec, NE Canada
Iwaki 133 G5 N Japan
Iwakuni 133 D7 SW Japan
Iwanai 133 F2 NE Japan
Iwate 133 G3 N Japan
Ixtapa 53 E5 S Mexico
Ixtepec 53 G5 SE Mexico
Iyo-nada 133 D7 *sea* S Japan
Izabal, Lago de 55 B3 ◎ E Guatemala
Izad Khvast 123 D3 C Iran
Izegem 84 B6 W Belgium
Izhevsk 111 D6 NW Russian Federation
Izmayil 109 D7 SW Ukraine
İzmir 120 A4 W Turkey
İzmit 120 B2 NW Turkey
İznik Gölü 120 B2 ◎ NW Turkey
133 G6 *peninsula* Honshu, S Japan
Izu-hanto 133 G6 *peninsula* Honshu, S Japan
Izu-shoto 133 G6 *island group* S Japan

J

Jabal ash Shifa 123 A3 *desert* NW Saudi Arabia
Jabalpur 127 F4 C India
Jaca 99 F2 NE Spain
Jacaltenango 55 A3 W Guatemala
Jackman 37 F2 Maine, NE USA
Jackpot 47 C4 Nevada, W USA
Jackson 43 G7 Missouri, C USA
Jackson 39 D3 Tennessee, S USA
Jackson 39 C5 *state capital* Mississippi, S USA
Jacksonville 39 G6 Florida, SE USA
Jacksonville 40 B6 Illinois, N USA
Jacksonville 39 H4 North Carolina, SE USA
Jacksonville 44 H3 Texas, SW USA
Jacmel 57 F4 S Haiti
Jacobabad 127 C3 SE Pakistan
Jaén 99 D5 S Spain
Jaffna 127 E7 N Sri Lanka
Jagdalpur 127 E5 C India
Jagdaqi 129 G1 N China
Jaipur 127 D3 N India
Jaisalmer 127 C3 NW India
Jakarta 131 C7 ● Java, C Indonesia
Jakobstad 83 E4 W Finland
Jalalabad 125 G5 E Afghanistan
Jalandhar 127 D2 N India
Jalapa 55 D3 NW Nicaragua
Jalpa 53 E4 C Mexico
Jalu 70 H3 NE Libya
Jamaame 75 E5 S Somalia
Jamaica 57 C5 ◆ *commonwealth republic* W West Indies
Jamaica Channel 57 E4 *channel* Haiti/Jamaica
Jambi 131 C7 Sumatra, W Indonesia
James Bay 35 C3 *bay* Ontario/Québec, E Canada
James River 43 C4 ≈ North Dakota/South Dakota, N USA
James River 39 H2 ≈ Virginia, NE USA
Jamestown 37 B4 New York, NE USA
Jamestown 43 C2 North Dakota, N USA
Jammu 127 D2 NW India
Jammu and Kashmir 127 D2 *disputed region* India/Pakistan
Jamnagar 127 C4 W India
Jamshedpur 127 F4 NE India
Jamuna 127 G4 ≈ C Bangladesh
Janesville 40 B5 Wisconsin, N USA
Jan Mayen 143 C6 *Norwegian* ◇ N Atlantic Ocean
Jánoshalma 105 E8 S Hungary
Japan 133 G4 ◆ *monarchy* E Asia
Japan, Sea of 133 D5 *sea* NW Pacific Ocean
Japiim 63 C5 W Brazil
Japurá, Rio 63 C3 ≈ Brazil/Colombia
Jaqué 55 I7 SE Panama
Jardines de la Reina, Archipiélago de los 57 C3 *island group* C Cuba

◈ Administrative region ◆ Country ● Country capital ◇ Dependent territory ○ Dependent territory capital ▲▲ Mountain range ▲ Mountain ☄ Volcano ≈ River ◎ Lake ⊞ Reservoir

163

K

◆ Administrative region ◆ Country ● Country capital ◇ Dependent territory ○ Dependent territory capital ▲ Mountain range ▲ Mountain ◣ Volcano ≈ River ● Lake ◙ Reservoir

◆ Administrative region   ◆ Country   ● Country capital   ◇ Dependent territory   ○ Dependent territory capital   ▲ Mountain range   ▲ Mountain   ℞ Volcano   ↝ River   ⊚ Lake   ☒ Reservoir

165

LIMASSOL

Limassol 112 C6 SW Cyprus
Limavady 89 E1 NW Northern Ireland, United Kingdom
Limerick 89 C5 SW Ireland
Límnos 107 F4 island E Greece
Limoges 97 C4 C France
Limón 55 F6 E Costa Rica
Limón 55 D2 NE Honduras
Limon 47 F5 Colorado, C USA
Limousin 97 C5 cultural region C France Europe
Limoux 97 D7 S France
Limpopo 76 E5 ≈ S Africa
Linares 65 A6 C Chile
Linares 53 E3 NE Mexico
Linares 99 D5 S Spain
Lincoln 93 E5 E England, United Kingdom
Lincoln 37 G2 Maine, NE USA
Lincoln 43 D5 state capital Nebraska, C USA
Lincoln Edge 93 E4 ridge E England, United Kingdom
Lincoln Sea 143 B4 sea Arctic Ocean
Linden 63 E2 E Guyana
Lindi 75 E7 SE Tanzania
Líndos 107 G6 Rhodes, Dodecanese, Greece
Line Islands 135 island group E Kiribati
Lingen 101 B3 NW Germany
Lingga, Kepulauan 131 C6 island group W Indonesia
Linköping 83 C6 S Sweden
Linnhe, Loch 91 C5 inlet W Scotland, United Kingdom
Linton 43 C2 North Dakota, N USA
Linz 101 E7 N Austria
Lion, Gulf of 97 D7 gulf S France
Lipari 103 D7 island Aeolian Islands, Italy
Lipetsk 111 B6 W Russian Federation
Lira 75 C5 N Uganda
Lisala 76 C1 N Dem. Rep. Congo
Lisboa see Lisbon
Lisbon 99 A4 ● W Portugal
Lisburn 89 E2 E Northern Ireland, United Kingdom
Lisdoonvarna 89 B5 W Ireland
Lisieux 97 C2 N France
Liski 111 A6 W Russian Federation
Lisnaskea 89 D3 W Northern Ireland, United Kingdom
Lisse 84 C4 W Netherlands
Listowel 89 B5 SW Ireland
Litang 129 D5 C China
Lithgow 137 G6 New South Wales, SE Australia
Lithuania 83 E7 ◆ republic NE Europe
Little Alföld 105 D7 plain Hungary/Slovakia
Little Andaman 127 H5 island Andaman Islands, SE India
Little Barrier Island 139 D2 island N New Zealand
Little Cayman 57 C4 island E Cayman Islands
Little Colorado River 47 D7 ≈ Arizona, SW USA
Little Falls 43 E3 Minnesota, N USA
Littlefield 44 F3 Texas, SW USA
Littlehampton 95 F5 SE England, United Kingdom
Little Inagua 57 E3 island S Bahamas
Little Minch, The 91 B3 strait NW Scotland, United Kingdom
Little Missouri River 43 A3 ≈ NW USA
Little Nicobar 127 H6 island Nicobar Islands, SE India
Little Ouse 95 G2 ≈ E England, United Kingdom
Little Rock 39 B4 state capital Arkansas, C USA
Little Saint Bernard Pass 97 F5 pass France/Italy
Little Sandy Desert 137 B4 desert Western Australia
Littleton 47 F5 Colorado, C USA
Littleton 37 F3 New Hampshire, NE USA
Liuzhou 129 F5 S China
Liverpool 35 F5 Nova Scotia, SE Canada
Liverpool 93 C4 NW England, United Kingdom
Liverpool Bay 93 E1 bay England/Wales, United Kingdom
Livingston 91 E5 C Scotland, United Kingdom
Livingston 47 D3 Montana, NW USA
Livingston 44 H4 Texas, SW USA
Livingstone 76 D4 S Zambia
Livingstone Mountains 139 A7 ▲▲ South Island, New Zealand
Livingston, Lake 44 H4 ⊠ Texas, SW USA
Livojoki 83 E3 ≈ C Finland
Livonia 40 E5 Michigan, N USA
Livorno 103 B3 C Italy
Lizard Point 95 A6 headland SW England, United Kingdom
Ljubljana 101 E8 ● C Slovenia
Ljungby 83 C6 S Sweden
Ljusdal 83 C4 C Sweden
Ljusnan 83 C4 ≈ C Sweden
Llandeilo 93 B7 S Wales, United Kingdom
Llandovery 93 B6 S Wales, United Kingdom
Llandrindod Wells 93 C6 E Wales, United Kingdom
Llandudno 93 B4 N Wales, United Kingdom
Llanes 99 D1 N Spain
Llanos 63 C2 physical region Colombia/Venezuela
Llanwrtyd Wells 93 B6 C Wales, United Kingdom
Lleida 99 F2 NE Spain
Lleyn Peninsula 93 A5 peninsula NW Wales, United Kingdom
Llucmajor 99 H4 Majorca, Spain
Lobatse 76 D6 SE Botswana
Löbau 101 E4 E Germany
Lobito 76 B4 W Angola
Locarno 101 B8 S Switzerland
Lochboisdale 91 A4 NW Scotland, United Kingdom
Lochdon 91 C5 W Scotland, United Kingdom
Lochem 84 E4 E Netherlands
Lochgilphead 91 C5 W Scotland, United Kingdom
Lochinver 91 C2 N Scotland, United Kingdom
Lochmaddy 91 B3 NW Scotland, United Kingdom
Lochnagar 91 E4 ▲ C Scotland, United Kingdom
Lochy, Loch 91 C4 ◎ N Scotland, United Kingdom
Lockerbie 91 E7 S Scotland, United Kingdom
Lockport 37 C3 New York, NE USA
Lodja 76 C2 C Dem. Rep. Congo
Lodwar 75 D5 NW Kenya
Lodz 105 E4 C Poland
Lofoten 83 C2 island group C Norway
Logan 47 D4 Utah, W USA
Logan, Mount 33 E5 ▲ Yukon Territory, W Canada
Logansport 40 D6 Indiana, N USA
Logroño 99 E2 N Spain
Loibl Pass 101 E8 pass Austria/Slovenia
Loire 97 C3 ≈ C France
Loja 63 B4 S Ecuador
Lokitaung 75 D4 NW Kenya
Lokoja 72 E5 C Nigeria
Lola, Mount 49 B6 ▲ California, W USA
Lolland 83 B7 island S Denmark
Lom 107 E2 NW Bulgaria
Lomami 76 D2 ≈ C Dem. Rep. Congo
Lomas de Zamora 65 C5 E Argentina
Lombardia see Lombardy
Lombardy 103 C2 cultural region N Italy
Lombok, Pulau 131 E8 island Nusa Tenggara, C Indonesia
Lomé 72 D5 ● S Togo
Lomela 76 C2 C Dem. Rep. Congo
Lommel 84 D6 N Belgium
Lomond, Loch 91 D5 ◎ C Scotland, United Kingdom
Lomonosov Ridge 143 C4 undersea feature Arctic Ocean
Lompoc 49 C8 California, W USA
Łomża 105 F2 NE Poland
Loncoche 65 A6 C Chile
London 95 G4 ● SE England, United Kingdom
London 35 C6 Ontario, S Canada
London 39 F3 Kentucky, S USA
Londonderry 89 D2 NW Northern Ireland, United Kingdom
Londonderry, Cape 137 C1 cape Western Australia
Londrina 63 F7 S Brazil
Lone Pine 49 C7 California, W USA
Long Bay 39 H4 bay North Carolina/South Carolina, E USA
Long Beach 49 C9 California, W USA
Long Eaton 93 E5 C England, United Kingdom
Longford 89 D4 C Ireland
Long Island 57 E2 island C Bahamas
Long Island 37 E5 island New York, NE USA
Long Island Sound 37 F5 sound NE USA
Longlac 35 B4 Ontario, S Canada
Longmont 47 F5 Colorado, C USA
Longreach 137 G3 Queensland, E Australia
Long Strait 118 H1 strait NE Russian Federation
Longview 44 H3 Texas, SW USA
Longview 49 B3 Washington, NW USA
Longyan 129 G5 SE China
Longyearbyen 143 C5 ○ W Svalbard
Lons-le-Saunier 97 E4 E France
Loop Head 89 A5 promontory W Ireland
Lop Nur 129 C3 seasonal lake NW China
Loppersum 84 F2 NE Netherlands
Lorca 99 E5 S Spain
Lorengau 141 B1 Manus Island, N Papua New Guinea
Loreto 53 B3 W Mexico
Lorient 97 B3 NW France
Lorn, Firth of 91 B5 inlet W Scotland, United Kingdom
Lörrach 101 B7 S Germany
Lorraine 97 F2 cultural region NE France Europe
Los Alamos 44 D2 New Mexico, SW USA
Los Amates 55 B3 E Guatemala
Los Ángeles 65 A6 C Chile
Los Angeles 49 C8 California, W USA
Lošinj 107 A2 island W Croatia
Los Mochis 53 C3 C Mexico
Los Roques, Islas 57 H7 island group N Venezuela
Lossiemouth 91 E3 NE Scotland, United Kingdom
Los Testigos, Islas 57 J7 island NE Venezuela
Lot 97 C5 cultural region C France Europe
Lot 97 C6 ≈ S France
Lotagipi Swamp 75 D4 wetland Kenya/Sudan
Louangphabang 131 B3 N Laos
Loudéac 97 B2 NW France
Loudi 129 F5 S China
Louga 72 A3 NW Senegal
Loughborough 93 E5 C England, United Kingdom
Loughrea 89 C4 W Ireland
Louisburgh 89 B3 NW Ireland
Louisiade Archipelago 141 D3 island group SE Papua New Guinea
Louisiana 39 A5 ◈ state S USA
Louisville 39 E2 Kentucky, S USA
Louisville Ridge 14 undersea feature S Pacific Ocean
Loup River 43 C5 ≈ Nebraska, C USA
Lourdes 97 C6 S France
Louth 89 E3 NE Ireland
Louth 93 F4 E England, United Kingdom
Loutrá 107 E4 N Greece
Louvain-la Neuve 84 C7 C Belgium
Louviers 97 D2 N France
Loveland 47 F5 Colorado, C USA
Lovelock 47 A5 Nevada, W USA
Lovosice 105 B5 NW Czech Republic
Lóvua 76 C3 NE Angola
Lowell 47 C2 Idaho, NW USA
Lowell 37 F4 Massachusetts, NE USA
Lower California 53 B3 peninsula NW Mexico
Lower Hutt 139 D5 North Island, New Zealand
Lower Lough Erne 89 D2 ◎ SW Northern Ireland, United Kingdom
Lower Red Lake 43 E2 ◎ Minnesota, N USA
Lower Tunguska 118 E4 ≈ N Russian Federation
Lowestoft 95 H2 E England, United Kingdom
Loyauté, Îles 141 G6 island group S New Caledonia
Lualaba 76 D2 ≈ SE Dem. Rep. Congo
Luanda 76 B3 ● NW Angola
Luangwa 76 E4 ≈ Mozambique/Zambia
Luanshya 76 D4 C Zambia
Luarca 99 C1 N Spain
Lubaczów 105 G5 SE Poland
Lubań 105 B4 SW Poland
Lubango 76 B4 SW Angola
Lubao 76 D2 C Dem. Rep. Congo
Lübben 101 E4 E Germany
Lübbenau 101 E4 E Germany
Lubbock 44 F3 Texas, SW USA
Lübeck 101 C2 N Germany
Lubelska, Wyżyna 105 F4 plateau SE Poland
Lubin 105 C4 SW Poland
Lublin 105 F4 E Poland
Lubliniec 105 D5 S Poland
Lubny 109 E4 NE Ukraine
Lubsko 105 B4 W Poland
Lubumbashi 76 D3 SE Dem. Rep. Congo
Lucan 89 E4 E Ireland
Lucano, Appennino 103 E6 ▲▲ S Italy
Lucapa 76 C3 NE Angola
Lucca 103 C3 C Italy
Luce Bay 91 C7 inlet SW Scotland, United Kingdom
Lucena 131 F4 Luzon, N Philippines
Lucena 99 D5 S Spain
Lučenec 105 E7 C Slovakia
Lucknow 127 E3 N India
Luda Kamchiya 107 F3 ≈ E Bulgaria
Lüderitz 76 B6 SW Namibia
Ludhiana 127 D2 N India
Ludington 40 D4 Michigan, N USA
Ludlow 93 C6 W England, United Kingdom
Ludvika 83 C5 C Sweden
Ludwigsburg 101 B6 SW Germany
Ludwigsfelde 101 D4 NE Germany
Ludwigshafen 101 B6 W Germany
Ludwigslust 101 C3 N Germany
Ludza 83 F6 E Latvia
Luena 76 C3 E Angola
Lufira 76 D3 ≈ SE Dem. Rep. Congo
Lufkin 44 I4 Texas, SW USA
Luga 111 A4 NW Russian Federation
Lugano 101 B8 S Switzerland
Luganville 141 G4 C Vanuatu
Lugenda, Rio 76 F4 ≈ N Mozambique
Lugnaquillia Mountain 89 E5 ▲ E Ireland
Lugo 99 B1 NW Spain
Lugoj 109 A6 W Romania
Luhans'k 109 G5 E Ukraine
Lukenie 76 C2 ≈ C Dem. Rep. Congo
Łuków 105 F4 E Poland
Lukuga 76 D3 ≈ SE Dem. Rep. Congo
Luleå 83 D3 N Sweden
Luleälven 83 D3 ≈ N Sweden
Lulimba 76 D2 E Dem. Rep. Congo
Lulonga 76 C1 ≈ NW Dem. Rep. Congo
Luma 51 E American Samoa
Lumberton 39 H4 North Carolina, SE USA
Lumbo 76 F4 NE Mozambique
Lumi 141 A1 NW Papua New Guinea
Lumsden 139 B7 South Island, New Zealand
Lund 83 C7 S Sweden
Lundy 95 B4 island SW England, United Kingdom
Lüneburg 101 C3 N Germany
Lungué-Bungo 76 C4 ≈ Angola/Zambia
Luninyets 109 C3 SW Belarus
Lunteren 84 D4 C Netherlands
Luoyang 129 F4 C China
Lurgan 89 E2 S Northern Ireland, United Kingdom
Lúrio 76 F4 NE Mozambique
Lúrio, Rio 76 F4 ≈ NE Mozambique
Lusaka 76 D4 ● SE Zambia
Lut, Dasht-e 123 F3 desert E Iran
Luti 141 E2 NW Solomon Islands
Luton 95 F3 E England, United Kingdom
Łutselk'e 33 G5 Northwest Territories, W Canada
Luts'k 109 C4 NW Ukraine
Lutzow-Holm Bay 142 D3 bay Antarctica
Luuq 75 E4 SW Somalia
Luwego 75 D7 ≈ S Tanzania
Luxembourg 84 E9 ● S Luxembourg
Luxembourg 84 E8 ◆ monarchy NW Europe
Luxor 70 J3 E Egypt
Luza 111 C4 NW Russian Federation
Luzern 101 B8 C Switzerland
Luzon 131 F3 island N Philippines
Luzon Strait 131 F3 strait Philippines/Taiwan
L'viv 109 B4 W Ukraine
Lycksele 83 D3 N Sweden
Lyepyel' 109 D2 N Belarus
Lyme Bay 95 C5 bay S England, United Kingdom
Lyme Regis 95 D5 S England, United Kingdom
Lymington 95 E5 S England, United Kingdom
Lynchburg 39 G2 Virginia, NE USA
Lynn 37 F4 Massachusetts, NE USA
Lynn Lake 33 H6 Manitoba, C Canada
Lynton 95 C4 SW England, United Kingdom
Lyon 97 E5 E France
Lysychans'k 109 G4 E Ukraine
Lytham St Anne's 93 C4 NW England, United Kingdom
Lyttelton 139 C6 South Island, New Zealand

M

Maamturk Mountains 89 B4 ▲▲ W Ireland
Maaseik 84 E6 NE Belgium
Maastricht 84 E6 SE Netherlands
Mablethorpe 93 F4 E England, United Kingdom
Macao 129 G6 S China
Macapá 63 F3 N Brazil
Macclesfield 93 D5 C England, United Kingdom
Macdonnell Ranges 137 D3 ▲▲ Northern Territory, C Australia
Macduff 91 F3 NE Scotland, United Kingdom
Macedonia 107 D4 ◆ republic SE Europe
Maceió 63 I5 E Brazil
Macgillycuddy's Reeks 89 B6 ▲▲ SW Ireland
Machala 63 A4 SW Ecuador
Machanga 76 E5 E Mozambique
Machilipatnam 127 E5 E India
Machynlleth 93 B6 C Wales, United Kingdom
Mackay 137 G3 Queensland, NE Australia
Mackay, Lake 137 D3 salt lake Northern Territory/Western Australia
Mackenzie 33 F4 ≈ Northwest Territories, NW Canada
Mackenzie Bay 142 E4 bay Antarctica
Mackenzie Mountains 33 E4 ▲▲ Northwest Territories, NW Canada
Macleod, Lake 137 A4 ◎ Western Australia
Macomb 40 B6 Illinois, N USA
Macomer 103 A6 Sardinia, Italy
Mâcon 97 E4 C France
Macon 39 F5 Georgia, SE USA
Macon 43 F6 Missouri, C USA
Macroom 89 B6 SW Ireland
Macuspana 53 H5 SE Mexico
Ma'daba 123 A2 NW Jordan
Madagascar 76 G5 ◆ republic W Indian Ocean
Madang 141 B2 N Papua New Guinea
Made 84 C5 S Netherlands
Madeira, Rio 63 E4 ≈ Bolivia/Brazil
Madeleine, Îles de la 35 F4 island group Québec, E Canada
Madeline 49 C5 California, W USA
Madera 49 C7 California, W USA
Madhya Pradesh 127 E4 state C India
Madison 43 D4 South Dakota, N USA
Madison 40 B4 state capital Wisconsin, N USA
Madisonville 39 D2 Kentucky, S USA
Madiun 131 D8 C Indonesia
Madras see Chennai
Madre de Dios, Río 65 A1 ≈ Bolivia/Peru
Madre del Sur, Sierra 53 F5 ▲▲ S Mexico
Madre, Laguna 53 F3 lagoon NE Mexico
Madre, Laguna 44 H6 lagoon Texas, SW USA
Madre Occidental, Sierra 53 C3 ▲▲ C Mexico
Madre Oriental, Sierra 53 E4 ▲▲ C Mexico
Madrid 99 D3 ● C Spain
Madrid 99 D3 cultural region C Spain
Madurai 127 D7 S India
Madura, Pulau 131 E8 island C Indonesia
Maebashi 133 G5 S Japan
Mae Nam Nan 131 B3 ≈ NW Thailand
Maéwo 141 G4 island C Vanuatu
Mafia 75 E7 island E Tanzania
Magadan 118 H3 E Russian Federation
Magarida 141 C3 SW Papua New Guinea
Magdalena 65 B1 N Bolivia
Magdalena 53 B2 NW Mexico
Magdalena, Isla 53 B4 island W Mexico
Magdalena, Río 63 B3 ≈ C Colombia
Magdeburg 101 D4 C Germany
Magee, Island 89 F2 island E Northern Ireland, United Kingdom
Magelang 131 C8 C Indonesia
Magellan, Strait of 65 B9 strait Argentina/Chile
Magerøya 83 D1 island N Norway
Maggiore, Lake 103 B1 ◎ Italy/Switzerland
Maghera 89 E2 C Northern Ireland, United Kingdom
Maglie 103 F6 SE Italy
Magna 47 D5 Utah, W USA
Magnitogorsk 118 C4 C Russian Federation
Magnolia 39 B4 Arkansas, C USA
Magta' Lahjar 72 B3 SW Mauritania
Magtymguly 125 G3 W Turkmenistan
Mahajanga 76 G4 NW Madagascar
Mahakam, Sungai 131 E6 ≈ Borneo, C Indonesia
Mahalapye 76 D5 SE Botswana
Mahanādi 127 F4 ≈ E India
Mahārāshtra 127 D5 state W India
Mahbubnagar 127 D5 C India
Mahia Peninsula 139 E4 peninsula North Island, New Zealand
Mahilyow 109 D2 E Belarus
Mahmud-e Raqi 125 F5 NE Afghanistan
Mahón 99 H3 Minorca, E Spain
Maidenhead 95 F3 S England, United Kingdom
Maidens, The 89 F2 island group E Northern Ireland, United Kingdom
Maidstone 95 G4 SE England, United Kingdom
Maiduguri 72 G4 NE Nigeria
Main 101 C5 ≈ C Germany
Mai-Ndombe, Lac 76 C2 ◎ W Dem. Rep. Congo
Maine 97 C2 cultural region NW France
Maine 37 F2 ◈ state NE USA
Maine, Gulf of 37 G3 gulf NE USA
Mainland 91 E1 island N Scotland, United Kingdom
Mainland 91 A6 island NE Scotland, United Kingdom
Mainz 101 B5 SW Germany
Maitri 142 C3 Indian research station Antarctica
Maizhokunggar 129 C4 W China
Majorca 99 H4 island E Spain
Makarov Basin 143 C4 undersea feature Arctic Ocean
Makassar 131 E7 Celebes, C Indonesia
Makassar Straits 131 E7 strait C Indonesia
Makay 76 G5 ▲▲ SW Madagascar
Makeni 72 B4 C Sierra Leone
Makhachkala 111 B9 SW Russian Federation
Makiyivka 109 G5 E Ukraine
Makkovik 35 G2 Newfoundland and Labrador, NE Canada
Makó 105 F8 SE Hungary
Makoua 76 B2 C Congo
Makran Coast 123 F4 coastal region SE Iran
Makrany 109 B3 SW Belarus
Makurdi 72 F5 C Nigeria
Malabo 72 F6 ● Isla de Bioco, NW Equatorial Guinea
Malacca, Strait of 131 B6 strait Indonesia/Malaysia
Malacky 105 C7 W Slovakia
Maladzyechna 109 C2 C Belarus
Málaga 99 D6 S Spain
Malahide 89 E4 E Ireland
Malaita 141 F3 island N Solomon Islands
Malakal 75 C3 S Sudan
Malang 131 D8 Java, C Indonesia
Malanje 76 B3 NW Angola
Mälaren 83 D5 ◎ C Sweden
Malatya 121 E4 SE Turkey
Malawi 76 E4 ◆ republic S Africa
Malay Peninsula 131 B5 peninsula Malaysia/Thailand
Malaysia 131 C5 ◆ monarchy SE Asia
Malbork 105 E2 N Poland
Malchin 101 D2 N Germany
Malden 43 G7 Missouri, C USA
Malden Island 135 atoll E Kiribati
Maldives 127 C9 ◆ republic N Indian Ocean
Male 127 C8 ● C Maldives
Malekula 141 G5 island W Vanuatu
Malheur Lake 49 C4 ◎ Oregon, NW USA
Malheur River 49 C4 ≈ Oregon, NW USA
Mali 72 D3 ◆ republic W Africa
Mali Kyun 131 A4 island Mergui Archipelago, S Myanmar (Burma)
Malin 89 D1 NW Ireland
Malindi 75 E6 SE Kenya
Malin Head 89 D1 headland NW Ireland
Mallaig 91 C4 N Scotland, United Kingdom
Mallawi 70 I3 C Egypt
Mallorca see Majorca
Mallow 89 C6 SW Ireland
Malmberget 83 D2 N Sweden
Malmédy 84 E7 E Belgium
Malmö 83 C7 S Sweden
Malone 37 E2 New York, NE USA
Małopolska, Wyżyna 105 F5 plateau S Poland
Malozemel'skaya Tundra 111 D3 physical region NW Russian Federation
Malta 47 E1 Montana, NW USA
Malta 112 A6 ◆ republic C Mediterranean Sea
Malta Channel 103 D9 strait Italy/Malta
Malton 93 E4 N England, United Kingdom
Maluku see Moluccas
Malung 83 C5 C Sweden
Malvern Hills 93 C6 hill range W England, United Kingdom
Mamberamo, Sungai 131 I7 ≈ Papua, E Indonesia
Mamonovo 83 D7 W Russian Federation
Mamoré, Rio 65 B1 ≈ Bolivia/Brazil
Mamou 72 B4 W Guinea
Mamoudzou 76 G4 ○ C Mayotte
Mamuno 76 C5 W Botswana
Manacor 99 H4 Spain
Manado 131 F6 Celebes, C Indonesia
Managua 55 D5 ● W Nicaragua
Managua, Lake 55 D4 ◎ W Nicaragua
Manakara 76 G5 SE Madagascar
Manama 123 D4 ● N Bahrain
Mananjary 76 G5 SE Madagascar
Manapouri, Lake 139 A7 ◎ South Island, New Zealand
Manas, Gora 125 F2 ▲ Kyrgyzstan/Uzbekistan
Manau 141 C2 S Papua New Guinea
Manaus 63 E4 NW Brazil
Manavgat 121 C5 SW Turkey
Manbij 123 B1 N Syria
Manchester 93 D4 NW England, United Kingdom
Manchester 37 F3 New Hampshire, NE USA
Mandalay 131 A2 C Myanmar (Burma)
Mandan 43 B2 North Dakota, N USA
Mand, Rud-e 123 D3 ≈ S Iran
Mandurah 137 B5 Western Australia
Manduria 103 F6 SE Italy
Mandya 127 D6 C India
Manfredonia 103 E5 SE Italy
Mangai 76 C2 W Dem. Rep. Congo
Mangalmé 75 B3 SE Chad
Mangalore 127 D6 W India
Mangerton Mountain 89 B6 ▲ SW Ireland
Mangoky 76 F5 ≈ W Madagascar
Manhattan 43 D6 Kansas, C USA
Manicouagan, Réservoir 35 E4 ◎ Québec, E Canada
Manihiki 135 atoll N Cook Islands
Manila 131 F4 ● N Philippines
Manisa 120 A3 W Turkey
Manistee River 40 D4 ≈ Michigan, N USA
Manitoba 33 H6 ◈ province S Canada
Manitoba, Lake 33 H6 ◎ Manitoba, S Canada
Manitoulin Island 35 C5 island Ontario, S Canada
Manizales 63 B2 W Colombia
Manjimup 137 B6 Western Australia
Mankato 43 E3 Minnesota, N USA
Manlleu 99 G2 NE Spain
Manmad 127 D4 W India
Mannar 127 E7 NW Sri Lanka
Mannar, Gulf of 127 D8 gulf India/Sri Lanka
Mannheim 101 B6 SW Germany
Manokwari 131 H6 E Indonesia
Manono 76 D3 SE Dem. Rep. Congo
Manorhamilton 89 C3 NW Ireland
Manosque 97 E6 SE France
Mansa 76 D3 N Zambia
Mansel Island 33 I4 island Nunavut, NE Canada
Mansfield 93 E5 C England, United Kingdom
Mansfield 40 E6 Ohio, N USA
Mansfield 37 C4 Pennsylvania, NE USA
Mantova 103 C2 NW Italy
Manua Islands 51 island group E American Samoa
Manurewa 139 D2 North Island, New Zealand
Manus Island 141 B1 island N Papua New Guinea
Manzanares 99 D4 C Spain
Manzanillo 57 D3 E Cuba
Manzanillo 53 D5 SW Mexico
Manzhouli 129 F1 N China
Mao 72 G3 W Chad
Maoke, Pegunungan 131 I7 ▲▲ Papua, E Indonesia
Maoming 129 F6 S China
Maputo 76 E6 ● S Mozambique
Maraa 141 A6 W French Polynesia
Marabá 63 G4 NE Brazil
Maracaibo 63 C1 NW Venezuela
Maracaibo, Lake 63 B2 inlet NW Venezuela
Maradah 70 G3 N Libya
Maradi 72 F3 S Niger
Maragheh 123 C1 NW Iran
Marajó, Baía de 63 G3 bay N Brazil
Marajó, Ilha de 63 F3 island N Brazil
Maranhão 63 G4 state E Brazil
Marañón, Río 63 B4 ≈ N Peru
Marathon 35 B4 Ontario, S Canada
Marathon 44 E4 Texas, SW USA
Maraza 121 I2 E Azerbaijan
Marbella 99 D6 S Spain
Marble Bar 137 B3 Western Australia
Marburg an der Lahn 101 B5 W Germany
March 95 G2 E England, United Kingdom
Marche 97 D4 cultural region C France
Marche-en-Famenne 84 D8 SE Belgium
Mar Chiquita, Laguna 65 B5 ◎ C Argentina
Marcy, Mount 37 E3 ▲ New York, NE USA
Mardan 127 C1 N Pakistan
Mar del Plata 65 C6 E Argentina
Mardin 121 F5 SE Turkey
Maré 141 G6 island Îles Loyauté, E New Caledonia

◈ Administrative region ◆ Country ● Country capital ◇ Dependent territory ○ Dependent territory capital ▲▲ Mountain range ▲ Mountain Volcano ≈ River ◎ Lake ⊠ Reservoir

MOSQUITO GULF

Mareeba 137 G2 Queensland, NE Australia
Maree, Loch 91 C3 ◎ N Scotland, United Kingdom
Marfa 44 E4 Texas, SW USA
Margarita, Isla de 63 D1 *island* N Venezuela
Margate 95 H4 SE England, United Kingdom
Margherita, Lake 75 D4 ◎ SW Ethiopia
Margow, Dasht-e 125 D6 *desert* SW Afghanistan
Mari 141 A3 SW Papua New Guinea
María Cleofas, Isla 53 C5 *island* C Mexico
Maria Island 137 G7 *island* Tasmania, SE Australia
María Madre, Isla 53 C4 *island* C Mexico
María Magdalena, Isla 53 C4 *island* C Mexico
Mariana Islands 15 *island group* Guam/Northern Mariana Islands
Mariana Trench 15 *undersea feature* W Pacific Ocean
Mariánské Lázně 105 A5 W Czech Republic
Maribor 101 F8 NE Slovenia
Maridi 75 B4 SW Sudan
Marie Byrd Land 142 B5 *physical region* Antarctica
Marie-Galante 57 K5 *island* SE Guadeloupe
Mariental 76 C6 SW Namibia
Mariestad 83 C6 S Sweden
Marietta 39 E4 Georgia, SE USA
Marietta 40 F7 Ohio, N USA
Marília 63 F7 S Brazil
Marín 99 B2 NW Spain
Maringá 63 F7 S Brazil
Marion 40 B8 Illinois, N USA
Marion 43 F4 Iowa, C USA
Marion 40 E6 Ohio, N USA
Mariscal Estigarribia 65 C3 NW Paraguay
Maritsa 107 F3 ≈ SW Europe
Mariupol' 109 G5 SE Ukraine
Marka 75 F5 S Somalia
Market Harborough 93 E6 C England, United Kingdom
Markham, Mount 142 C5 ▲ Antarctica
Markounda 72 H5 NW Central African Republic
Marktredwitz 101 D5 E Germany
Marmande 97 C5 SW France
Marmara, Sea of 120 A2 *sea* NW Turkey
Marmaris 120 A5 SW Turkey
Marne 97 E2 *cultural region* N France Europe
Marne 97 E3 ≈ N France
Maro 72 H4 S Chad
Maroantsetra 76 G4 NE Madagascar
Maromokotro 76 G4 ▲ N Madagascar
Maroni 63 F2 ≈ French Guiana/Surinam
Maroua 72 G4 N Cameroon
Marquesas Islands 135 *island group* N French Polynesia
Marquette 40 C2 Michigan, N USA
Marrakech 70 C2 W Morocco
Marrawah 137 F7 Tasmania, SE Australia
Marree 137 E5 South Australia
Marsa al Burayqah 70 G3 N Libya
Marsabit 75 D5 N Kenya
Marsala 103 C8 Sicily, Italy
Marsberg 101 B4 W Germany
Marseille 97 E7 SE France
Marshall 43 D3 Minnesota, N USA
Marshall 44 I3 Texas, SW USA
Marshall Islands 135 ◆ *republic* W Pacific Ocean
Marsh Harbour 57 D1 Great Abaco, W Bahamas
Martigues 97 E6 SE France
Martin 105 E6 N Slovakia
Martinique 57 K5 *French* ◇ E West Indies
Martinique Passage 57 K5 *channel* Dominica/Martinique
Marton 139 D4 North Island, New Zealand
Martos 99 D5 S Spain
Mary 125 D4 S Turkmenistan
Maryborough 137 H4 Queensland, E Australia
Maryland 39 I2 ◐ *state* NE USA
Maryville 43 E5 Missouri, C USA
Maryville 39 F3 Tennessee, S USA
Masai Steppe 75 D6 *grassland* NW Tanzania
Masaka 75 C5 SW Uganda
Masan 133 C6 S South Korea
Masasi 75 D7 SE Tanzania
Masaya 55 D5 W Nicaragua
Maseru 76 D6 ● W Lesotho
Mashhad 123 F1 NE Iran
Masindi 75 C5 W Uganda
Masira, Gulf of 123 F5 *bay* E Oman
Mask, Lough 89 B4 ◎ W Ireland
Mason 44 G4 Texas, SW USA
Mason City 43 E4 Iowa, C USA
Masqat *see* Muscat
Massa 103 B3 C Italy
Massachusetts 37 F4 ◐ *state* NE USA
Massawa 75 D2 E Eritrea
Massena 37 D2 New York, NE USA
Massenya 72 G4 SW Chad
Massif Central 97 D5 *plateau* C France
Masterton 139 D5 North Island, New Zealand
Masuda 133 D7 SW Japan
Masvingo 76 E5 SE Zimbabwe
Matadi 76 B3 W Dem. Rep. Congo
Matagalpa 55 D4 C Nicaragua
Matale 127 E8 C Sri Lanka
Matamata 139 D3 North Island, New Zealand
Matamoros 53 F3 NE Mexico
Matane 35 F4 Québec, SE Canada
Matanzas 57 B2 NW Cuba
Matara 127 E8 S Sri Lanka
Mataram 131 E8 C Indonesia
Mataró 99 G2 E Spain
Matātula, Cape 51 *headland* W American Samoa
Mataura 139 B8 South Island, New Zealand
Mataura 139 B7 ≈ South Island, New Zealand
Matautu 141 B5 C Samoa
Matā'utu 141 K4 ○ N Wallis and Futuna
Mataveri 141 C6 Easter Island, Chile
Matera 103 E6 S Italy
Matías Romero 53 G5 SE Mexico
Matlock 93 D5 C England, United Kingdom
Mato Grosso 63 E6 *state* W Brazil
Mato Grosso do Sul 63 E7 *state* S Brazil
Matosinhos 99 B3 NW Portugal
Matsue 133 D6 SW Japan
Matsumoto 133 F5 S Japan
Matsuyama 133 D7 Shikoku, SW Japan
Matterhorn 101 B9 ▲ Italy/Switzerland
Matthew Town 57 E3 S Bahamas
Maturín 63 D1 NE Venezuela
Mau 127 E3 N India
Maui 51 D2 *island* Hawai'i, USA
Maun 76 C5 C Botswana
Mauna Loa 51 D3 ▲▲ Hawai'i, USA
Mauritania 72 A2 ◆ *republic* W Africa
Mauritius 66 ◆ *republic* W Indian Ocean
Mawson 142 E4 *Australian research station* Antarctica
Maya 55 B2 ≈ E Russian Federation
Mayaguana 57 F3 *island* SE Bahamas
Mayaguana Passage 57 E3 *passage* SE Bahamas
Mayagüez 57 H4 W Puerto Rico
Maybole 91 D6 W Scotland, United Kingdom
Maych'ew 75 D3 N Ethiopia
Maydan Shahr 125 F5 E Afghanistan
Mayfield 139 C6 South Island, New Zealand
May, Isle of 91 F5 *island* E Scotland, United Kingdom
Maykop 111 A8 SW Russian Federation
Maymyo 131 A2 C Myanmar (Burma)
Mayor Island 139 D3 *island* NE New Zealand
Mayotte 76 G4 *French* ◇ E Africa
Mazabuka 76 D4 S Zambia
Mazar-e Sharif 125 F4 N Afghanistan
Mazatlán 53 D4 C Mexico
Mazury 105 F2 *physical region* NE Poland
Mazyr 109 D3 SE Belarus
Mbabane 76 E6 ● NW Swaziland
Mbala 76 E3 NE Zambia
Mbale 75 C5 E Uganda
Mbandaka 76 C2 NW Dem. Rep. Congo
M'Banza Congo 76 B3 NW Angola
Mbanza-Ngungu 76 B2 W Dem. Rep. Congo
Mbarara 75 C5 SW Uganda
Mbé 72 G5 N Cameroon
Mbeya 75 C7 SW Tanzania
Mbuji-Mayi 76 C3 S Dem. Rep. Congo
McAlester 43 D8 Oklahoma, C USA
McAllen 44 G6 Texas, SW USA
McCamey 44 F4 Texas, SW USA
McCammon 47 D4 Idaho, NW USA
McClintock Channel 33 G3 *channel* Nunavut, N Canada
McComb 39 C6 Mississippi, S USA
McCook 43 B5 Nebraska, C USA
McDermitt 47 B4 Nevada, W USA
McKinley, Mount 50 D2 ▲ Alaska, USA
McKinley Park 50 E2 Alaska, USA
McLaughlin 43 B3 South Dakota, N USA
McMinnville 49 B3 Oregon, NW USA
McMurdo 142 C6 *US research station* Antarctica
McNary 44 D4 Texas, SW USA
McPherson 43 D6 Kansas, C USA
Mdantsane 76 D7 SE South Africa
Mead, Lake 47 C7 ⊠ Arizona/Nevada, W USA
Meadville 37 B4 Pennsylvania, NE USA
Mecca 123 B5 W Saudi Arabia
Mechelen 84 C6 C Belgium
Mecklenburger Bucht 101 C2 *bay* N Germany
Mecsek 105 D8 ▲▲ SW Hungary
Medan 131 B6 E Indonesia
Medellín 63 B2 NW Colombia
Médenine 70 F2 SE Tunisia
Medford 49 B4 Oregon, NW USA
Mediaş 109 B6 C Romania
Medicine Hat 33 G7 Alberta, SW Canada
Medina 123 B4 W Saudi Arabia
Medinaceli 99 E3 N Spain
Medina del Campo 99 D3 N Spain
Mediterranean Sea 112 D4 *sea* Africa/Asia/Europe
Médoc 97 B5 *cultural region* SW France
Medvezh'yegorsk 111 B3 NW Russian Federation
Medway 95 G4 ≈ SE England, United Kingdom
Meekatharra 137 B4 Western Australia
Meerssen 84 E5 SE Netherlands
Meerut 127 D2 N India
Mehtar Lām 125 G5 E Afghanistan
Mejillones 65 A3 N Chile
Mek'ele 75 D2 N Ethiopia
Meknès 70 C1 N Morocco
Mekong 131 C4 ≈ SE Asia
Mekong, Mouths of the 131 C5 *delta* S Vietnam
Melaka 131 B6 SW Malaysia
Melanesia 141 G3 *island group* W Pacific Ocean
Melbourne 39 G7 Florida, SE USA
Melbourne 137 F6 *state capital* Victoria, SE Australia
Melghir, Chott 70 E2 *salt lake* E Algeria
Melilla 69 D1 S Spain
Melita 33 H7 Manitoba, S Canada
Melitopol' 109 F6 SE Ukraine
Melle 84 B6 NW Belgium
Melleray, Mount 89 D6 ▲ S Ireland
Mellerud 83 C6 S Sweden
Mellieha 112 B6 E Malta
Mellizo Sur, Cerro 65 A8 ▲ S Chile
Melo 65 D5 NE Uruguay
Melsungen 101 C5 C Germany
Melton Mowbray 93 E5 C England, United Kingdom
Melun 97 D3 N France
Melville Island 137 D1 *island* Northern Territory, N Australia
Melville Island 33 G2 *island* Parry Islands, Northwest Territories, NW Canada
Melville, Lake 35 G3 ◎ Newfoundland and Labrador, E Canada
Melville Peninsula 33 H3 *peninsula* Nunavut, NE Canada
Memmingen 101 C7 S Germany
Memphis 39 C3 Tennessee, S USA
Menai Bridge 93 B5 NW Wales, United Kingdom
Ménaka 72 E3 E Mali
Menaldum 84 D2 N Netherlands
Mende 97 D6 S France
Mendeleyev Ridge 143 C3 *undersea feature* Arctic Ocean
Mendi 141 B2 W Papua New Guinea
Mendip Hills 95 D4 *hill range* S England, United Kingdom
Mendocino, Cape 49 A5 *headland* California, W USA
Mendoza 65 A5 W Argentina
Menemen 120 A3 W Turkey
Menengiyn Tal 129 F2 *plain* E Mongolia
Menongue 76 B4 C Angola
Menorca *see* Minorca
Mentawai, Kepulauan 131 B7 *island group* W Indonesia
Meppel 84 E3 NE Netherlands
Merano 103 C1 N Italy
Mercedes 65 C4 NE Argentina
Mercedes 44 G6 Texas, SW USA
Meredith, Lake 44 E2 ⊠ Texas, SW USA
Mergui 131 B4 S Myanmar (Burma)
Mérida 53 H4 SE Mexico
Mérida 99 C4 W Spain
Mérida 63 C2 W Venezuela
Meridian 39 D5 Mississippi, S USA
Mérignac 97 B5 SW France
Merizo 51 SW Guam
Merowe 75 C2 *desert* W Sudan
Merredin 137 B5 Western Australia
Merrick 91 D7 ▲ S Scotland, United Kingdom
Merrimack River 37 F4 ≈ Massachusetts/New Hampshire, NE USA
Mersey 93 C4 ≈ NW England, U K
Mersin 121 D5 S Turkey
Merthyr Tydfil 93 C7 S Wales, United Kingdom
Merton 95 F4 SE England, United Kingdom
Meru 75 D5 C Kenya
Merzifon 121 D2 N Turkey
Merzig 101 A6 SW Germany
Mesa 44 B3 Arizona, SW USA
Messalo, Rio 76 F4 ≈ NE Mozambique
Messina 103 D8 Sicily, Italy
Messina *see* Musina
Messina, Strait of 103 E8 *strait* SW Italy
Mestia 121 G1 N Georgia
Mestre 103 D2 NE Italy
Metairie 39 C6 Louisiana, S USA
Metán 65 B4 N Argentina
Metapán 55 B3 NW El Salvador
Meta, Río 63 C2 ≈ Colombia/Venezuela
Métsovo 107 D4 C Greece
Metz 97 F2 NE France
Meulaboh 131 A6 Sumatra, W Indonesia
Meuse 97 E2 ≈ W Europe
Mexborough 93 E4 N England, United Kingdom
Mexicali 53 A1 NW Mexico
Mexico 43 F6 Missouri, C USA
Mexico 53 D3 ◆ *federal republic* N Central America
Mexico City 53 E5 ● C Mexico
Mexico, Gulf of 28 G3 *gulf* W Atlantic Ocean
Meymaneh 125 E4 NW Afghanistan
Mezen' 111 C3 ≈ NW Russian Federation
Mezőtúr 105 F8 E Hungary
Mġarr 112 A6 N Malta
Miahuatlán 53 G6 SE Mexico
Miami 39 G9 Florida, SE USA
Miami 43 E7 Oklahoma, C USA
Miami Beach 39 G8 Florida, SE USA
Mianyang 129 E4 C China
Miastko 105 C2 N Poland
Michalovce 105 F6 E Slovakia
Michigan 40 D4 ◐ *state* N USA
Michigan, Lake 40 C4 ◎ N USA
Michurinsk 111 B6 W Russian Federation
Micronesia 135 ◆ *federation* W Pacific Ocean
Mid-Atlantic Ridge 14 *undersea feature* Atlantic Ocean
Middelburg 84 B5 SW Netherlands
Middelharnis 84 C5 SW Netherlands
Middelkerke 84 A6 W Belgium
Middle Andaman 127 H5 *island* SE India
Middle Atlas 70 C2 ▲▲ N Morocco
Middlesboro 39 F3 Kentucky, S USA
Middlesbrough 93 E3 N England, United Kingdom
Middletown 37 D6 Delaware, NE USA
Middletown 37 E5 New Jersey, NE USA
Middletown 37 E4 New York, NE USA
Middlewich 93 C5 W England, United Kingdom
Mid-Indian Ridge 15 *undersea feature* C Indian Ocean
Midland 35 D5 Ontario, S Canada
Midland 40 E4 Michigan, N USA
Midland 43 B4 South Dakota, N USA
Midland 44 F3 Texas, SW USA
Midleton 89 C6 SW Ireland
Mid-Pacific Mountains 15 *undersea feature* NW Pacific Ocean
Midway Islands 27 *US* ◇ C Pacific Ocean
Miechów 105 E5 S Poland
Międzyrzec Podlaski 105 G3 E Poland
Międzyrzecz 105 C3 W Poland
Mielec 105 F5 SE Poland
Miercurea-Ciuc 109 C6 C Romania
Mieres del Camino 99 C1 NW Spain
Mī'ēso 75 E3 C Ethiopia
Miguel Asua 53 D3 C Mexico
Mijdrecht 84 D4 C Netherlands
Mikhaylovka 111 B7 SW Russian Federation
Mikun' 111 D4 NW Russian Federation
Mikura-jima 133 G6 *island* E Japan
Milan 103 B2 N Italy
Milano *see* Milan
Milas 120 A4 SW Turkey
Mildenhall 95 G2 E England, United Kingdom
Mildura 137 F5 Victoria, SE Australia
Miles 137 G4 Queensland, E Australia
Miles City 47 F2 Montana, NW USA
Milford Haven 93 A7 SW Wales, United Kingdom
Milford Haven 93 A7 *inlet* SW Wales, United Kingdom
Milford Sound 139 A7 South Island, New Zealand
Mil'kovo 118 I3 E Russian Federation
Milk River 33 G7 Alberta, SW Canada
Milk River 47 E1 ≈ Montana, NW USA
Milk, Wadi el 75 B2 ≈ C Sudan
Milledgeville 39 F5 Georgia, SE USA
Mille Lacs Lake 43 E2 ◎ Minnesota, N USA
Millennium Island 135 *atoll* Line Islands, E Kiribati
Millerovo 111 A7 SW Russian Federation
Millford 89 D1 NW Ireland
Millville 37 D6 New Jersey, NE USA
Mílos 107 F6 *island* Cyclades, Greece
Milton 139 B8 South Island, New Zealand
Milton Keynes 95 F3 SE England, United Kingdom
Milwaukee 40 C4 Wisconsin, N USA
Minas Gerais 63 H7 *state* E Brazil
Minatitlán 53 G5 E Mexico
Minbu 131 A2 W Myanmar (Burma)
Minch, The 91 C2 *strait* NW Scotland, United Kingdom
Mindanao 131 G5 *island* S Philippines
Mindelheim 101 C7 S Germany
Minden 101 B4 NW Germany
Mindoro 131 F4 *island* N Philippines
Mindoro Strait 131 E4 *strait* W Philippines
Minehead 95 C4 SW England, United Kingdom
Mineral Wells 44 G3 Texas, SW USA
Mingäçevir 121 I2 C Azerbaijan
Mingaora 127 C1 N Pakistan
Mingulay 91 A4 *island* NW Scotland, United Kingdom
Minho 99 B2 ≈ Portugal/Spain
Minicoy Island 127 C7 *island* SW India
Minna 72 E4 C Nigeria
Minneapolis 43 E3 Minnesota, N USA
Minnesota 43 D3 ◐ *state* N USA
Miño 99 B2 ≈ Portugal/Spain
Minorca 99 H3 *island* Balearic Islands, Spain
Minot 43 B1 North Dakota, N USA
Minsk 109 C2 ● C Belarus
Minskaya Wzvyshsha 109 C2 ▲▲ C Belarus
Minto, Lac 35 D2 ◎ Québec, C Canada
Miraflores 53 C4 W Mexico
Miranda de Ebro 99 E2 N Spain
Miri 131 D5 E Malaysia
Mirim Lagoon 65 D5 *lagoon* Brazil/Uruguay
Mirjaveh 123 F3 SE Iran
Mirny 142 D5 *Russian research station* Antarctica
Mirnyy 118 F4 NE Russian Federation
Mirpur Khas 127 C3 SE Pakistan
Mirtoan Sea 107 E6 *sea* S Greece
Miskitos, Cayos 55 F3 *island group* NE Nicaragua
Miskolc 105 F7 NE Hungary
Misool, Pulau 131 G7 *island* Maluku, E Indonesia
Misratah 70 F2 NW Libya
Mission 43 B4 South Dakota, N USA
Mississippi 39 C5 ◐ *state* SE USA
Mississippi Delta 39 C7 *delta* Louisiana, S USA
Mississippi River 39 C4 ≈ C USA
Missoula 47 C2 Montana, NW USA
Missouri 43 E6 ◐ *state* C USA
Missouri River 43 C4 ≈ C USA
Mistassini, Lac 35 D4 ◎ Québec, SE Canada
Mistelbach an der Zaya 101 F6 NE Austria
Misti, Volcán 63 C6 ⛰ S Peru
Mitchell 137 G4 Queensland, E Australia
Mitchell 49 C3 Oregon, NW USA
Mitchell 43 C4 South Dakota, N USA
Mitchell, Mount 39 F3 ▲ North Carolina, SE USA
Mitchell River 137 F2 ≈ Queensland, NE Australia
Mito 133 G5 S Japan
Mitú 63 C3 SE Colombia
Mitumba Range 76 D3 ▲▲ E Dem. Rep. Congo
Miyako 133 G3 C Japan
Miyako-jima 133 G6 *island* SW Japan
Miyakonojo 133 D8 SW Japan
Miyazaki 133 D8 SW Japan
Mizen Head 89 A7 *headland* SW Ireland
Mizpe Ramon 123 G7 S Israel
Mjøsa 83 B5 ◎ S Norway
Mława 105 E3 C Poland
Mljet 107 C3 *island* S Croatia
Moab 47 D6 Utah, W USA
Moa Island 137 F1 *island* Queensland, NE Australia
Moala 141 J5 *island* S Fiji
Moanda 76 B2 SE Gabon
Moate 89 D4 C Ireland
Moba 76 D3 E Dem. Rep. Congo
Mobaye 72 H5 S Central African Republic
Moberly 43 F6 Missouri, C USA
Mobile 39 D6 Alabama, S USA
Mochudi 76 D6 SE Botswana
Mocímboa da Praia 76 F3 N Mozambique
Môco 76 B4 ▲ W Angola
Mocuba 76 F4 NE Mozambique
Modena 103 C3 N Italy
Modesto 49 B7 California, W USA
Modica 103 D8 Sicily, Italy
Modimolle 76 D6 NE South Africa
Moe 137 F6 Victoria, SE Australia
Moffat 91 E6 S Scotland, United Kingdom
Mogadishu 75 F5 ● S Somalia
Mogilno 105 D3 C Poland
Mogollon Rim 44 B2 *cliff* Arizona, SW USA
Mohammedia 70 C1 NW Morocco
Mohawk River 37 D4 ≈ New York, NE USA
Mohéli 76 F4 *island* S Comoros
Mohoro 75 D7 E Tanzania
Moi 83 A6 S Norway
Mo i Rana 83 C3 C Norway
Mõisaküla 83 E6 S Estonia
Moissac 97 C6 S France
Mojácar 99 E5 S Spain
Mojave 49 C8 California, W USA
Mojave Desert 49 D8 *plain* California, W USA
Mokp'o 133 B7 SW South Korea
Mol 84 D6 N Belgium
Mold 93 C5 NE Wales, United Kingdom
Moldavia *see* Moldova
Molde 83 B4 S Norway
Moldo-Too, Khrebet 125 H2 ▲▲ C Kyrgyzstan
Moldova 109 ◆ *republic* SE Europe
Molfetta 103 E6 SE Italy
Mölndal 83 B6 S Sweden
Molodezhnaya 142 E3 *Russian research station* Antarctica
Moloka'i 51 C1 *island* Hawai'i, USA
Molopo 76 C6 *seasonal river* Botswana/South Africa
Moluccas 131 G7 *island group* E Indonesia
Molucca Sea 131 F6 *sea* E Indonesia
Mombacho, Volcán 55 D5 ⛰ SW Nicaragua
Mombasa 75 E6 SE Kenya
Møn 83 B7 *island* SE Denmark
Monach Islands 91 A3 *island group* NW Scotland, United Kingdom
Monaco 97 F6 ● S Monaco
Monaco 97 F6 ◆ *monarchy* W Europe
Monadhliath Mountains 91 D4 ▲▲ N Scotland, United Kingdom
Monaghan 89 E3 N Ireland
Monahans 44 E4 Texas, SW USA
Mona, Isla 57 H4 *island* W Puerto Rico
Mona Passage 57 H4 *channel* Dominican Republic/Puerto Rico
Monbetsu 133 G1 NE Japan
Moncalieri 103 A2 NW Italy
Monchegorsk 111 B2 NW Russian Federation
Monclova 53 E3 NE Mexico
Moncton 35 F5 New Brunswick, SE Canada
Mondovì 103 A3 NW Italy
Moneygall 89 D5 C Ireland
Moneymore 89 E2 C Northern Ireland, United Kingdom
Monfalcone 103 D2 NE Italy
Monforte de Lemos 99 B2 NW Spain
Mongo 72 H4 C Chad
Mongolia 129 D2 ◆ *republic* E Asia
Mongu 76 C4 W Zambia
Monkey Bay 76 E4 SE Malawi
Monkey River Town 55 C2 SE Belize
Monmouth 93 C7 SE Wales, United Kingdom
Mono Lake 49 C7 ◎ California, W USA
Monovar 99 F5 E Spain
Monroe 39 B5 Louisiana, S USA
Monrovia 72 B5 ● W Liberia
Mons 84 C7 S Belgium
Monselice 103 C2 NE Italy
Montana 107 E2 NW Bulgaria
Montana 47 D2 ◐ *state* NW USA
Montargis 97 D3 C France
Montauban 97 C6 S France
Montbéliard 97 F3 E France
Mont Cenis, Col du 97 F5 *pass* E France
Mont-de-Marsan 97 B6 SW France
Monteagudo 65 B3 S Bolivia
Monte Caseros 65 C5 NE Argentina
Monte Cristi 57 F4 NW Dominican Republic
Montego Bay 57 D4 W Jamaica
Montélimar 97 E6 E France
Montemorelos 53 E3 NE Mexico
Montenegro 107 C3 ◆ *republic* SW Europe
Monte Patria 65 A5 N Chile
Monterey 49 B7 California, W USA
Monterey Bay 49 B7 *bay* California, W USA
Montería 63 B2 NW Colombia
Montero 65 B2 C Bolivia
Monterrey 53 E3 NE Mexico
Montes Claros 63 G6 SE Brazil
Montevideo 65 C6 ● S Uruguay
Montevideo 43 D3 Minnesota, N USA
Montgenèvre, Col de 97 F5 *pass* France/Italy
Montgomery 93 C6 E Wales, United Kingdom
Montgomery 39 E5 *state capital* Alabama, S USA
Monthey 101 A8 SW Switzerland
Monticello 37 D4 New York, NE USA
Monticello 47 E6 Utah, W USA
Montluçon 97 D4 C France
Montoro 99 D5 S Spain
Montpelier 47 D4 Idaho, NW USA
Montpelier 37 E3 *state capital* Vermont, NE USA
Montpellier 97 D6 S France
Montréal 35 E5 Québec, SE Canada
Montrose 91 F4 E Scotland, United Kingdom
Montrose 47 E6 Colorado, C USA
Montserrat 57 J5 *UK* ◇ E West Indies
Monywa 131 A2 C Myanmar (Burma)
Monza 103 B2 N Italy
Monze 76 D4 S Zambia
Monzón 99 F2 NE Spain
Moonie 137 G4 Queensland, E Australia
Moora 137 B5 Western Australia
Moore 43 D8 Oklahoma, C USA
Moorea 141 A5 *island* Îles du Vent, W French Polynesia
Moore, Lake 137 B5 ◎ Western Australia
Moorhead 43 D2 Minnesota, N USA
Moose 47 D3 Wyoming, C USA
Moose 35 C4 ≈ Ontario, S Canada
Moosehead Lake 37 F1 ◎ Maine, NE USA
Moosonee 35 C4 Ontario, SE Canada
Mopti 72 C3 C Mali
Mora 83 C5 C Sweden
Morales 55 B3 E Guatemala
Morar, Loch 91 C4 ◎ N Scotland, United Kingdom
Moratalla 99 E5 Spain
Morava 105 D6 ≈ C Europe
Moravia 105 D6 *cultural region* E Czech Republic
Moray Firth 91 D3 *inlet* N Scotland, United Kingdom
Moreau River 43 B3 ≈ South Dakota, N USA
Morecambe 93 C3 NW England, United Kingdom
Morecambe Bay 93 C3 *inlet* NW England, United Kingdom
Moree 137 G5 New South Wales, SE Australia
Morelia 53 E5 S Mexico
Morena, Sierra 99 C5 ▲▲ S Spain
Mórfou *see* Güzelyurt
Morgan City 39 B6 Louisiana, S USA
Morghab, Darya-ye 125 E4 ≈ Afghanistan/Turkmenistan
Moriarty 44 D2 New Mexico, SW USA
Morioka 133 G3 C Japan
Morlaix 97 A2 NW France
Morocco 70 B2 ◆ *monarchy* N Africa
Morogoro 75 D6 E Tanzania
Moro Gulf 131 F5 *gulf* S Philippines
Morón 57 D3 C Cuba
Mörön 129 D1 N Mongolia
Morondava 76 G5 W Madagascar
Moroni 76 F4 ● Grande Comore, NW Comoros
Morotai, Pulau 131 G6 *island* Moluccas, E Indonesia
Morpeth 93 D2 N England, United Kingdom
Morrinsville 139 D3 North Island, New Zealand
Morris 43 D3 Minnesota, N USA
Morris Jesup, Kap 143 C4 *headland* N Greenland
Morvan 97 E4 *physical region* C France
Moscow 111 B5 ● W Russian Federation
Moscow 47 B2 Idaho, NW USA
Mosel 97 F2 ≈ W Europe
Moselle 97 F3 ≈ W Europe
Mosgiel 139 B7 South Island, New Zealand
Moshi 75 D6 NE Tanzania
Mosjøen 83 C3 C Norway
Moskva 125 F4 SW Tajikistan
Moskva *see* Moscow
Mosonmagyaróvár 105 D7 NW Hungary
Mosquito Coast 55 E4 *coastal region* E Nicaragua
Mosquito Gulf 55 G6 *gulf* N Panama

◐ Administrative region ◆ Country ● Country capital ◇ Dependent territory ○ Dependent territory capital ▲▲ Mountain range ▲ Mountain ⛰ Volcano ≈ River ◎ Lake ⊠ Reservoir

Moss 83 B5 S Norway
Mosselbaai 76 C7 SW South Africa
Mossendjo 76 B2 SW Congo
Mossoró 63 I4 NE Brazil
Most 105 B5 NW Czech Republic
Mosta 112 B6 C Malta
Mostaganem 70 D1 NW Algeria
Mostar 107 C2 S Bosnia and Herzegovina
Mosul 123 C2 N Iraq
Mota del Cuervo 99 E4 C Spain
Motagua, Río 55 B3 ≈ Guatemala/Honduras
Motherwell 91 D6 C Scotland, United Kingdom
Motril 99 D6 S Spain
Motueka 139 C5 South Island, New Zealand
Motul 53 H4 SE Mexico
Motu Nui 141 C6 *island* Easter Island, Chile
Mouila 76 A2 C Gabon
Mould Bay 33 G2 Prince Patrick Island, Northwest Territories, N Canada
Moulins 97 D4 C France
Moulmein 131 B3 S Myanmar (Burma)
Moundou 72 G4 SW Chad
Mountain Home 39 B3 Arkansas, C USA
Mountain Home 47 B4 Idaho, NW USA
Mountbellew Bridge 89 C4 C Ireland
Mount Desert Island 37 G3 *island* Maine, NE USA
Mount Gambier 137 F6 South Australia
Mount Hagen 141 B2 C Papua New Guinea
Mount Isa 137 F3 Queensland, C Australia
Mount Magnet 137 B4 Western Australia
Mount Pleasant 43 F5 Iowa, C USA
Mount Pleasant 40 D4 Michigan, N USA
Mount's Bay 95 A6 *inlet* SW England, United Kingdom
Mount Vernon 40 B7 Illinois, N USA
Mount Vernon 49 B1 Washington, NW USA
Mourne Mountains 89 E3 ▲▲ SE Northern Ireland, United Kingdom
Mouscron 84 B7 W Belgium
Moussoro 72 G3 W Chad
Moycullen 89 B4 W Ireland
Mo'ynoq 125 D1 NW Uzbekistan
Moyynkum, Peski 125 G1 *desert* S Kazakhstan
Mozambique 76 E5 ◆ *republic* S Africa
Mozambique Channel 76 F5 *strait* W Indian Ocean
Mpama 76 B2 ≈ C Congo
Mragowo 105 F2 NE Poland
Mtwara 75 E7 SE Tanzania
Muar 131 B6 W Malaysia
Muck 91 B4 *island* W Scotland, United Kingdom
Muckle Roe 91 A6 *island* NE Scotland, United Kingdom
Mucojo 76 F4 N Mozambique
Mudanjiang 129 H2 NE China
Muddy Gap 47 E4 Wyoming, C USA
Mufulira 76 D4 C Zambia
Muğla 120 A4 SW Turkey
Muine Bheag 89 E5 SE Ireland
Mukacheve 109 B5 W Ukraine
Mula 99 E5 SE Spain
Muleshoe 44 E2 Texas, SW USA
Mulhacén 99 D5 ▲ S Spain
Mulhouse 97 E3 NE France
Mullaghmore 89 C2 N Ireland
Mullan 89 D3 W Northern Ireland, United Kingdom
Mullaranny 89 B3 NW Ireland
Muller, Pegunungan 131 D6 ▲▲ Borneo, C Indonesia
Müllheim 101 B7 SW Germany
Mullingar 89 D4 C Ireland
Mull, Isle of 91 B5 *island* W Scotland, United Kingdom
Mulongo 76 D3 SE Dem. Rep. Congo
Multan 127 C2 E Pakistan
Multinational Station 142 A3 *multinational research station* Antarctica
Mumbai 127 C5 W India
Münchberg 101 D5 E Germany
München *see* Munich
Muncie 40 D6 Indiana, N USA
Munda 141 E2 NW Solomon Islands
Mungbere 76 D1 NE Dem. Rep. Congo
Munich 101 D7 SE Germany
Munster 101 B4 NW Germany
Munster 89 B6 *cultural region* S Ireland
Muonio 83 E2 N Finland
Muonionjoki 83 D2 ≈ Finland/Sweden
Muqdisho *see* Mogadishu
Mur 101 F8 ≈ C Europe
Muradiye 121 H3 E Turkey
Murchison River 137 B4 ≈ Western Australia
Murcia 99 F5 SE Spain
Murcia 99 E5 *cultural region* SE Spain
Mureş 109 A6 ≈ Hungary/Romania
Murfreesboro 39 E3 Tennessee, S USA
Murgap 125 D4 S Turkmenistan
Murgap 83 D4 ≈ Afghanistan/Turkmenistan
Murghob 125 H3 SE Tajikistan
Murgon 137 H4 Queensland, E Australia
Müritz 101 D3 ◎ NE Germany
Murmansk 111 C2 NW Russian Federation
Murmashi 111 B2 NW Russian Federation
Murom 111 B5 W Russian Federation
Muroran 133 F2 NE Japan
Muros 99 A1 NW Spain
Murray, Lake 141 A2 ◎ SW Papua New Guinea
Murray River 137 F5 ≈ SE Australia
Murrumbidgee River 137 F6 ≈ New South Wales, SE Australia
Murska Sobota 101 F8 NE Slovenia
Murupara 139 E3 North Island, New Zealand
Mururoa 135 *atoll* Îles Tuamotu, SE French Polynesia
Murwara 127 E4 N India
Murwillumbah 137 H5 New South Wales, SE Australia
Murzuq, Idhan 70 F4 *desert* SW Libya
Mürzzuschlag 101 F7 E Austria
Muş 121 G3 E Turkey
Musa, Gebel 70 I3 ▲ NE Egypt
Musala 107 E3 ▲ W Bulgaria
Muscat 123 F4 ● NE Oman
Muscatine 43 F5 Iowa, C USA
Musgrave Ranges 137 D4 ▲▲ South Australia
Musina 76 D5 NE South Africa
Muskegon 40 D4 Michigan, N USA
Muskegon River 40 D4 ≈ Michigan, N USA
Muskogee 43 E8 Oklahoma, C USA
Musoma 75 C5 N Tanzania
Musselshell River 47 E2 ≈ Montana, NW USA
Musters, Lago 65 A7 ◎ S Argentina
Muswellbrook 137 G5 New South Wales, SE Australia
Mut 121 C5 S Turkey
Mutare 76 E5 E Zimbabwe
Muy Muy 55 D4 C Nicaragua
Mwanza 75 C6 NW Tanzania
Mweelrea 89 A4 ▲ W Ireland
Mweka 76 C2 C Dem. Rep. Congo
Mwene-Ditu 76 C3 S Dem. Rep. Congo
Mweru, Lake 76 D3 ◎ Dem. Rep. Congo/Zambia
Myadzyel 109 C2 N Belarus
Myanmar 131 A2 ◆ *military dictatorship* SE Asia
Myingyan 131 A2 C Myanmar (Burma)
Myitkyina 131 B1 N Myanmar (Burma)
Mykolayiv 109 E6 S Ukraine
Mykonos 107 F6 *island* Cyclades, Greece
Mýrina 107 F4 Limnos, Greece
Myrtle Beach 39 H4 South Carolina, SE USA
Myślibórz 105 B3 NW Poland
Mysore 127 D6 W India
My Tho 131 C4 S Vietnam
Mytilíni 107 F5 Lesbos, Greece
Mzuzu 76 E3 N Malawi

N

Nā'ālehu 51 D3 Hawai'i, USA
Naas 89 E4 C Ireland
Naberezhnyye Chelny 111 D6 W Russian Federation
Nacala 76 F4 NE Mozambique
Nacogdoches 44 I3 Texas, SW USA
Nadi 141 J5 Viti Levu, W Fiji
Nadur 112 A6 N Malta
Nadvoitsy 111 B3 NW Russian Federation
Nadym 118 D3 N Russian Federation
Náfpaktos 107 D5 C Greece
Náfplio 107 E6 S Greece
Naga 131 F4 N Philippines
Nagano 133 F5 S Japan
Nagaoka 133 F5 C Japan
Nagasaki 133 C8 SW Japan
Nagato 133 D7 Honshu, SW Japan
Nagercoil 127 D7 SE India
Nagles Mountains 89 C6 ▲▲ S Ireland
Nagorno-Karabakh 121 H2 *former autonomous region* SW Azerbaijan
Nagoya 133 F6 SW Japan
Nagpur 127 E4 C India
Nagqu 129 C4 W China
Nagykálló 105 F7 E Hungary
Nagykanizsa 105 C8 SW Hungary
Nagykörös 105 E8 C Hungary
Naha 133 A8 Okinawa, SW Japan
Nahariyya 123 H5 N Israel
Nahuel Huapí, Lago 65 A7 ◎ W Argentina
Nain 35 F2 Newfoundland and Labrador, NE Canada
Nairn 91 D3 N Scotland, United Kingdom
Nairobi 75 D5 ● S Kenya
Najin 133 C3 NE North Korea
Najran 123 C6 S Saudi Arabia
Nakamura 133 E7 Shikoku, SW Japan
Nakatsugawa 133 F6 SW Japan
Nakhodka 118 H6 SE Russian Federation
Nakhon Ratchasima 131 B3 E Thailand
Nakhon Sawan 131 B3 W Thailand
Nakhon Si Thammarat 131 B5 SW Thailand
Nakuru 75 D5 SW Kenya
Nal'chik 111 A8 SW Russian Federation
Nalut 70 F2 NW Libya
Namangan 125 G3 E Uzbekistan
Nam Co 129 C4 ◎ W China
Nam Dinh 131 C2 N Vietnam
Namhae-do 133 B7 *island* S South Korea
Namib Desert 76 B5 *desert* W Namibia
Namibe 76 B4 SW Angola
Namibia 76 B5 ◆ *republic* S Africa
Nam Ou 131 B2 ≈ N Laos
Nampa 47 B3 Idaho, NW USA
Namp'o 133 A5 SW North Korea
Nampula 76 F4 NE Mozambique
Namsan-ni 133 A4 NW North Korea
Namsos 83 C3 C Norway
Namur 84 D7 SE Belgium
Namwon 133 B6 S South Korea
Nanaimo 33 E7 Vancouver Island, British Columbia, SW Canada
Nanchang 129 F5 S China
Nancy 97 F3 NE France
Nandaime 55 D5 SW Nicaragua
Nanded 127 D5 C India
Nandyal 127 E6 E India
Nangnim-sanmaek 133 B4 ▲▲ C North Korea
Nanjing 129 G4 E China
Nanning 129 F6 S China
Nanping 129 G5 SE China
Nansen Basin 143 D4 *undersea feature* Arctic Ocean
Nansen Cordillera 143 C4 *undersea feature* Arctic Ocean
Nanterre 97 D2 N France
Nantes 97 B3 NW France
Nantucket Island 37 G4 *island* Massachusetts, NE USA
Nantwich 93 C5 W England, United Kingdom
Nanumaga 141 I2 *atoll* NW Tuvalu
Nanumea Atoll 141 I2 *atoll* NW Tuvalu
Nanyang 129 F4 C China
Napa 49 B6 California, W USA
Napier 139 E4 North Island, New Zealand
Naples 103 D6 S Italy
Naples 39 G8 Florida, SE USA
Napoli *see* Naples
Napo, Río 63 B3 ≈ Ecuador/Peru
Naracoorte 137 F6 South Australia
Nara Visa 44 E2 New Mexico, SW USA
Narbonne 97 D7 S France
Nares Strait 33 H1 *strait* Canada/Greenland
Narew 105 F3 ≈ E Poland
Narowlya 109 D3 SE Belarus
Närpes 83 D4 W Finland
Närpiö *see* Närpes
Narrabri 137 G5 New South Wales, SE Australia
Narrogin 137 B5 Western Australia
Narva 83 F5 NE Estonia
Narvik 83 D2 C Norway
Nar'yan-Mar 111 D3 NW Russian Federation
Naryn 125 H2 C Kyrgyzstan
Nashik 127 D5 W India
Nashua 37 F4 New Hampshire, NE USA
Nashville 39 D3 *state capital* Tennessee, S USA
Näsijärvi 83 E4 ◎ SW Finland
Nassau 57 D2 ● New Providence, N Bahamas
Nasser, Lake 70 J4 ◎ Egypt/Sudan
Nata 76 D5 NE Botswana
Natal 63 I4 E Brazil
Natchez 39 B5 Mississippi, S USA
Natchitoches 39 B5 Louisiana, S USA
Natitingou 72 D4 NW Benin
Natuna, Kepulauan 131 C6 *island group* W Indonesia
Nauru 141 G1 ◆ *republic* W Pacific Ocean
Navan 89 E4 E Ireland
Navapolatsk 109 D1 N Belarus
Navarra 99 E2 *cultural region* N Spain
Navassa Island 57 D4 *US* ◇ C West Indies
Navoiy 125 E3 C Uzbekistan
Navojoa 53 C3 NW Mexico
Navolato 53 C3 C Mexico
Nawabshah 127 B3 S Pakistan
Naxcivan 121 H3 SW Azerbaijan
Náxos 107 F6 *island* Cyclades, Greece
Nayoro 133 G1 NE Japan
Nay Pyi Taw 130 A3 ● C Myanmar (Burma)
Nazareth 123 H5 N Israel
Nazca Ridge 14 *undersea feature* E Pacific Ocean
Naze 133 B7 SW Japan
Nazilli 120 A4 SW Turkey
Nazret 75 D3 C Ethiopia
N'Dalatando 76 B3 NW Angola
Ndélé 72 H4 N Central African Republic
Ndendé 76 A2 S Gabon
Ndindi 76 A2 S Gabon
Ndjamena 72 G4 ● W Chad
Ndola 76 D4 C Zambia
Neagh, Lough 89 E2 ◎ E Northern Ireland, United Kingdom
Neápoli 107 D4 N Greece
Neápoli 107 E6 S Greece
Near Islands 50 A1 *island group* Aleutian Islands, Alaska, USA
Neath 93 B7 S Wales, United Kingdom
Nebaj 55 A3 W Guatemala
Neblina, Pico da 63 C3 ▲ NW Brazil
Nebraska 43 B5 ⬖ *state* C USA
Nebraska City 43 D5 Nebraska, C USA
Neches River 44 I4 ≈ Texas, SW USA
Neckar 101 B6 ≈ SW Germany
Necochea 65 C6 E Argentina
Neder Rijn 84 D4 ≈ C Netherlands
Nederweert 84 E6 SE Netherlands
Neede 84 F4 E Netherlands
Needles 49 E8 California, W USA
Neerpelt 84 D6 NE Belgium
Neftekamsk 111 D6 W Russian Federation
Negele 75 E4 C Ethiopia
Negev 123 G6 *desert* S Israel
Negombo 127 E8 SW Sri Lanka
Negotin 107 D2 E Serbia
Negra, Punta 63 A4 *point* NW Peru
Negro, Río 65 B6 ≈ E Argentina
Negro, Río 63 D3 ≈ N South America
Negros 131 F5 *island* C Philippines
Neijiang 129 E5 C China
Nellore 127 E6 E India
Nelson 139 C5 South Island, New Zealand
Nelson 33 H6 ≈ Manitoba, C Canada
Néma 72 C3 SE Mauritania
Neman 83 E7 ≈ NE Europe
Nemours 97 D3 N France
Nemuro 133 H1 NE Japan
Nenagh 89 C5 C Ireland
Nendö 141 G3 *island* Santa Cruz Islands, E Solomon Islands
Nene 95 G2 ≈ E England, United Kingdom
Nepal 127 E3 ◆ *monarchy* S Asia
Nepean 35 D5 Ontario, SE Canada
Nephin 89 B3 ▲ W Ireland
Neretva 107 C2 ≈ Bosnia and Herzegovina/Croatia
Neris 109 C2 ≈ Belarus/Lithuania
Nerva 99 C5 SW Spain
Neryungri 118 G4 NE Russian Federation
Neskaupstadhur 83 B1 E Iceland
Ness, Loch 91 D4 ◎ N Scotland, United Kingdom
Néstos 107 E4 ≈ Bulgaria/Greece
Netanya 123 G6 C Israel
Netherlands 84 D3 ◆ *monarchy* NW Europe
Netherlands Antilles 57 G7 *Dutch* ◇ S Caribbean Sea
Nettilling Lake 33 I3 ◎ Baffin Island, Nunavut, N Canada
Neubrandenburg 101 D3 NE Germany
Neuchâtel 101 A8 W Switzerland
Neuchâtel, Lac de 101 A8 ◎ W Switzerland
Neufchâteau 84 D8 SE Belgium
Neumünster 101 C2 N Germany
Neunkirchen 101 A6 SW Germany
Neuquén 65 A6 SE Argentina
Neuruppin 101 D3 NE Germany
Neusiedler See 101 F7 ◎ Austria/Hungary
Neustadt an der Weinstrasse 101 A6 SW Germany
Neustrelitz 101 D3 NE Germany
Neu-Ulm 101 C7 S Germany
Neuwied 101 B5 W Germany
Nevada 47 B5 ⬖ *state* W USA
Nevers 97 D4 C France
Nevinnomyssk 111 A8 SW Russian Federation
Nevşehir 121 D4 C Turkey
Newala 75 D7 SE Tanzania
New Albany 40 D7 Indiana, N USA
New Amsterdam 63 E2 E Guyana
Newark 37 E5 New Jersey, NE USA
Newark-on-Trent 93 E5 C England, United Kingdom
New Bedford 37 F4 Massachusetts, NE USA
New Bern 39 H3 North Carolina, SE USA
New Braunfels 44 G4 Texas, SW USA
Newbridge 89 C4 W Ireland
Newbridge on Wye 93 B6 C Wales, United Kingdom
New Britain 141 C2 *island* E Papua New Guinea
New Brunswick 35 F5 ⬖ *province* SE Canada
Newbury 95 E4 S England, United Kingdom
New Caledonia 141 D5 *French* ◇ SW Pacific Ocean
Newcastle 137 G5 New South Wales, SE Australia
Newcastle 89 F3 SE Northern Ireland, United Kingdom
New Castle 37 B5 Pennsylvania, NE USA
Newcastle 47 F3 Wyoming, C USA
Newcastle-under-Lyme 93 D5 C England, United Kingdom
Newcastle upon Tyne 93 D2 NE England, United Kingdom
Newcastle West 89 B5 SW Ireland
New Delhi 127 D3 ● N India
New England 37 F3 ⬖ *cultural region* NE USA
New Forest 95 E5 *physical region* S England, United Kingdom
Newfoundland 35 G4 *island* Newfoundland and Labrador, SE Canada
Newfoundland and Labrador 35 G3 ⬖ *province* E Canada
New Georgia 141 E2 *island* New Georgia Islands, NW Solomon Islands
New Georgia Islands 141 D3 *island group* NW Solomon Islands
New Glasgow 35 G5 Nova Scotia, SE Canada
New Guinea 141 A2 *island* Indonesia/Papua New Guinea
New Hampshire 37 E2 ⬖ *state* NE USA
New Hanover 141 C1 *island* NE Papua New Guinea
Newhaven 95 G5 SE England, United Kingdom
New Haven 37 E5 Connecticut, NE USA
New Iberia 39 B6 Louisiana, S USA
New Ireland 141 C1 *island* NE Papua New Guinea
New Jersey 37 E5 ⬖ *state* NE USA
Newman 137 B3 Western Australia
Newmarket 95 G2 E England, United Kingdom
Newmarket on Fergus 89 C5 W Ireland
New Mexico 44 D2 ⬖ *state* SW USA
New Orleans 39 C6 Louisiana, S USA
New Plymouth 139 D4 North Island, New Zealand
Newport 95 E5 S England, United Kingdom
Newport 93 C7 SE Wales, United Kingdom
Newport 39 E1 Kentucky, S USA
Newport 37 F4 Rhode Island, NE USA
Newport 37 F2 Vermont, NE USA
Newport News 39 I2 Virginia, NE USA
Newport Pagnell 95 F3 SE England, United Kingdom
New Providence 57 D1 *island* N Bahamas
Newquay 95 A5 SW England, United Kingdom
New Ross 89 E6 SE Ireland
Newry 89 E3 SE Northern Ireland, United Kingdom
New Siberian Islands 118 F2 *island group* N Russian Federation
New South Wales 137 F5 ⬖ *state* SE Australia
Newton 43 E5 Iowa, C USA
Newton 43 D7 Kansas, C USA
Newton Abbot 95 C5 SW England, United Kingdom
Newton Stewart 91 D7 S Scotland, United Kingdom
Newtown 89 C6 S Ireland
Newtownabbey 89 E2 E Northern Ireland, United Kingdom
Newtown St Boswells 91 E6 S Scotland, United Kingdom
Newtownstewart 89 D2 W Northern Ireland, United Kingdom
New Ulm 43 E3 Minnesota, N USA
New York 37 E5 New York, NE USA
New York 37 C4 ⬖ *state* NE USA
New Zealand 139 A5 ◆ *commonwealth republic* SW Pacific Ocean
Neyveli 127 E7 SE India
Ngangze Co 129 B4 ◎ W China
Ngaoundéré 72 G5 N Cameroon
N'Giva 76 B4 S Angola
Ngo 76 B2 SE Congo
Ngoko 72 G6 ≈ Cameroon/Congo
Ngourti 72 G3 E Niger
Nguigmi 72 G3 SE Niger
Nguru 72 F4 NE Nigeria
Nha Trang 131 D4 S Vietnam
Nhulunbuy 137 E1 Northern Territory, N Australia
Niagara Falls 35 D6 Ontario, S Canada
Niagara Falls 37 B3 New York, NE USA
Niagara Falls 37 B3 *waterfall* Canada/USA
Niamey 72 D3 ● SW Niger
Niangay, Lac 72 D3 ◎ E Mali
Nia-Nia 76 D1 NE Dem. Rep. Congo
Nias, Pulau 131 A6 *island* W Indonesia
Nicaragua 55 D4 ◆ *republic* Central America
Nicaragua, Lake 55 E5 ◎ S Nicaragua
Nice 97 F6 SE France
Nicholls Town 57 D1 NW Bahamas
Nicobar Islands 127 H6 *island group* SE India
Nicosia 112 C6 ● C Cyprus
Nicoya 55 D6 W Costa Rica
Nicoya, Golfo de 55 E6 *gulf* W Costa Rica
Nicoya, Península de 55 D6 *peninsula* NW Costa Rica
Nida 83 E7 SW Lithuania
Nidzica 105 E2 NE Poland
Nieuw-Bergen 84 E5 SE Netherlands
Nieuwegein 84 D4 C Netherlands
Nieuw Nickerie 63 E2 NW Suriname
Niğde 121 D4 C Turkey
Niger 72 E3 ◆ *republic* W Africa
Niger 72 E4 ≈ W Africa
Niger Delta 66 *delta* S Nigeria
Nigeria 72 E4 ◆ *federal republic* W Africa
Niger, Mouths of the 72 E5 *delta* S Nigeria
Niigata 133 F4 C Japan
Niihama 133 E7 Shikoku, SW Japan
Ni'ihau 51 A1 *island* Hawai'i, USA
Nii-jima 133 G6 *island* E Japan
Nijkerk 84 D4 C Netherlands
Nijlen 84 C6 N Belgium
Nijmegen 84 E4 SE Netherlands
Nikel' 111 B2 NW Russian Federation
Nikiniki 131 F8 S Indonesia
Nikopol' 109 F5 SE Ukraine
Nikšić 107 C3 SW Montenegro
Nile 70 I3 ≈ N Africa
Nile Delta 70 I2 *delta* N Egypt
Nimes 97 E6 S France
Nine Degree Channel 127 C7 *channel* India/Maldives
Ninetyeast Ridge 15 *undersea feature* E Indian Ocean
Ningbo 129 G4 SE China
Ninigo Group 141 A1 *island group* N Papua New Guinea
Niobrara River 43 C4 ≈ Nebraska/Wyoming, C USA
Nioro 72 B3 W Mali
Niort 97 C4 W France
Nipigon 35 B4 Ontario, S Canada
Nipigon, Lake 35 B4 ◎ Ontario, S Canada
Niš 107 D2 SE Serbia
Nisko 105 F5 SE Poland
Nísyros 107 G6 *island* Dodecanese, Greece
Nith 91 D6 ≈ S Scotland, United Kingdom
Nitra 105 D7 SW Slovakia
Nitra 105 D7 ≈ W Slovakia
Niue 135 *Self-governing* ◇ S Pacific Ocean
Niulakita 141 J3 *atoll* S Tuvalu
Niutao 141 J2 *atoll* NW Tuvalu
Nivernais 97 D4 *cultural region* C France
Nizamabad 127 D5 C India
Nizhnekamsk 111 C6 W Russian Federation
Nizhnevartovsk 118 D4 C Russian Federation
Nizhniy Novgorod 111 B5 W Russian Federation
Nizhniy Odes 111 D4 NW Russian Federation
Nizhyn 109 E4 NE Ukraine
Njombe 75 D7 S Tanzania
Nkayi 76 B2 S Congo
Nkongsamba 72 F5 W Cameroon
Nmai Hka 131 B1 ≈ N Myanmar (Burma)
Nobeoka 133 D8 SW Japan
Noboribetsu 133 F2 NE Japan
Nogales 53 B2 NW Mexico
Nogales 44 B4 Arizona, SW USA
Nokia 83 E5 W Finland
Nokou 72 G3 W Chad
Nola 72 G5 SW Central African Republic
Nolinsk 111 C5 NW Russian Federation
Nome 143 B1 Alaska, USA
Noord-Beveland 84 B5 *island* SW Netherlands
Noordwijk aan Zee 84 C4 W Netherlands
Nora 83 C5 C Sweden
Norak 125 F3 W Tajikistan
Norddeutsches Tiefland 105 A2 *plain* N Germany
Norden 101 B3 NW Germany
Norderstedt 101 C3 N Germany
Nordfriesische Inseln *see* North Frisian Islands
Nordhausen 101 C4 C Germany
Nordhorn 101 A3 NW Germany
Nordkapp *see* North Cape
Nore 89 D5 ≈ S Ireland
Norfolk 43 D5 Nebraska, C USA
Norfolk 39 I2 Virginia, NE USA
Norfolk Island 135 *Australian* ◇ SW Pacific Ocean
Norias 44 H6 Texas, SW USA
Noril'sk 118 E3 N Russian Federation
Norman 43 D8 Oklahoma, C USA
Normandie *see* Normandy
Normandy 97 C2 *cultural region* N France
Normanton 137 F2 Queensland, NE Australia
Norrköping 83 C6 S Sweden
Norrtälje 83 D5 C Sweden
Norseman 137 C5 Western Australia
Norsup 141 G5 Malekula, C Vanuatu
Northallerton 93 D3 N England, United Kingdom
Northam 137 B5 Western Australia
North America 28 *continent*
North American Basin 14 *undersea feature* W Sargasso Sea
Northampton 95 F2 C England, United Kingdom
North Andaman 127 H4 *island* Andaman Islands, SE India
North Bay 35 D5 Ontario, S Canada
North Berwick 91 E5 SE Scotland, United Kingdom
North Canadian River 44 G2 ≈ Oklahoma, C USA
North Cape 139 C1 *headland* North Island, New Zealand
North Cape 83 E1 *headland* N Norway
North Carolina 39 F3 ⬖ *state* SE USA
North Channel 40 E3 *lake channel* Canada/USA
North Channel 91 B6 *strait* Northern Ireland/Scotland, United Kingdom
North Charleston 39 G5 South Carolina, SE USA
North Dakota 43 B2 ⬖ *state* N USA
Northeim 101 C4 C Germany
Northern Cook Islands 135 *island group* N Cook Islands
Northern Dvina 111 C4 ≈ NW Russian Federation
Northern Ireland 87 C5 ⬖ *national region* United Kingdom
Northern Mariana Islands 135 *US* ◇ W Pacific Ocean
Northern Sporades 107 E5 *island group* E Greece
Northern Territory 137 D2 ⬖ *territory* N Australia
North Esk 91 E4 ≈ E Scotland, United Kingdom
North European Plain 78 *plain* N Europe
Northfield 43 E3 Minnesota, N USA
North Foreland 95 H3 *headland* SE England, United Kingdom
North Frisian Islands 101 B2 *island group* N Germany
North Geomagnetic Pole 143 A4 *pole* Arctic Ocean
North Island 139 B2 *island* N New Zealand
North Korea 133 C4 ◆ *republic* E Asia
Northland 139 C1 *cultural region* North Island, New Zealand
North Las Vegas 47 B7 Nevada, W USA
North Little Rock 39 C4 Arkansas, C USA
North Platte 43 B5 Nebraska, C USA
North Platte River 43 B5 ≈ C USA
North Pole 143 C4 *pole* Arctic Ocean
North Ronaldsay 91 F1 *island* NE Scotland, United Kingdom
North Saskatchewan 33 G6 ≈ Alberta/Saskatchewan, S Canada
North Sea 78 *sea* NW Europe
North Siberian Lowland 118 E3 *lowlands* N Russian Federation
North Sound 89 B4 *sound* W Ireland
North Sound, The 91 E1 *sound* N Scotland, United Kingdom

⬖ Administrative region ◆ Country ● Country capital ◇ Dependent territory ○ Dependent territory capital ▲▲ Mountain range ▲ Mountain ⩙ Volcano ≈ River ◎ Lake ▣ Reservoir

PAVLOHRAD

North Taranaki Bight 139 C3 gulf North Island, New Zealand
North Tyne 93 D2 ≈ N England, United Kingdom
North Uist 91 A3 island NW Scotland, United Kingdom
North West Highlands 91 C3 ▲▲ N Scotland, United Kingdom
Northwest Pacific Basin 15 undersea feature NW Pacific Ocean
Northwest Territories 33 F4 ◈ territory NW Canada
Northwich 93 C5 C England, United Kingdom
Northwind Plain 143 B2 undersea feature Arctic Ocean
North York Moors 93 E3 moorland N England, United Kingdom
Norton Sound 50 D1 inlet Alaska, USA
Norway 83 A4 ◆ monarchy N Europe
Norwegian Sea 83 A4 sea NE Atlantic Ocean
Norwich 95 H2 E England, United Kingdom
Noshiro 133 F3 C Japan
Nossob 76 C6 ≈ E Namibia
Noteć 105 D3 ≈ NW Poland
Nottingham 93 E5 C England, United Kingdom
Nouâdhibou 72 A2 W Mauritania
Nouakchott 72 A2 ● SW Mauritania
Nouméa 141 G6 ○ S New Caledonia
Nova Gorica 101 E8 W Slovenia
Nova Iguaçu 63 G7 SE Brazil
Novara 103 B2 NW Italy
Nova Scotia 37 H2 ◈ province SE Canada
Novaya Sibir', Ostrov 118 G2 island NE Russian Federation
Novaya Zemlya 111 E1 island group N Russian Federation
Novi Sad 107 D1 N Serbia
Novoazovs'k 109 G5 E Ukraine
Novocheboksarsk 111 C6 W Russian Federation
Novocherkassk 111 A7 SW Russian Federation
Novodvinsk 111 C3 NW Russian Federation
Novokuznetsk 118 E5 S Russian Federation
Novolazarevskaya 142 C3 Russian research station Antarctica
Novo mesto 101 E9 SE Slovenia
Novomoskovsk 111 B6 W Russian Federation
Novomoskovs'k 109 F5 E Ukraine
Novorossiysk 111 A8 SW Russian Federation
Novoshakhtinsk 111 A7 SW Russian Federation
Novosibirsk 118 D5 C Russian Federation
Novotroitsk 111 D7 W Russian Federation
Novyy Buh 109 E5 S Ukraine
Nowogard 105 C2 NW Poland
Nowy Dwór Mazowiecki 105 E3 C Poland
Nowy Sącz 105 F6 S Poland
Nowy Tomyśl 105 C3 C Poland
Noyon 97 D2 N France
Ntomba, Lac 76 B2 ◎ NW Dem. Rep. Congo
Nubian Desert 75 C1 desert NE Sudan
Nueces River 44 G5 ≈ Texas, SW USA
Nueva Gerona 57 B3 NW Cuba
Nueva Guinea 55 E5 SE Nicaragua
Nueva Ocotepeque 55 B3 W Honduras
Nueva Rosita 53 E2 NE Mexico
Nuevitas 57 D3 E Cuba
Nuevo Casas Grandes 53 C2 N Mexico
Nuevo, Golfo 65 B7 gulf S Argentina
Nuevo Laredo 53 E2 NE Mexico
Nui Atoll 141 I2 atoll W Tuvalu
Nuku'alofa 135 ● Tongatapu, S Tonga
Nukufetau Atoll 141 I2 atoll C Tuvalu
Nukulaelae Atoll 141 J3 atoll E Tuvalu
Nukumanu Islands 141 E1 island group NE Papua New Guinea
Nukus 125 D2 W Uzbekistan
Nullarbor Plain 137 D5 plateau South Australia/Western Australia
Nunavut 33 H4 ◈ territory N Canada
Nuneaton 93 D6 C England, United Kingdom
Nunivak Island 50 C2 island Alaska, USA
Nunspeet 84 E4 E Netherlands
Nuoro 103 A6 Sardinia, Italy
Nuremberg 101 C6 S Germany
Nurmes 83 F4 E Finland
Nürnberg see Nuremberg
Nurota 125 E3 C Uzbekistan
Nusaybin 121 G4 SE Turkey
Nyagan' 118 D3 N Russian Federation
Nyainqentanglha Shan 129 C4 ▲▲ W China
Nyala 75 B3 W Sudan
Nyamtumbo 75 D7 S Tanzania
Nyandoma 111 B4 NW Russian Federation
Nyantakara 75 C6 NW Tanzania
Nyasa, Lake 76 E4 ◎ Malawi/Mozambique/Tanzania/Zambia
Nyeri 75 D5 C Kenya
Nyima 129 C4 W China
Nyíregyháza 105 F7 NE Hungary
Nykøbing 83 B7 SE Denmark
Nyköping 83 D6 S Sweden
Nylstroom see Modimolle
Nyngan 137 G5 New South Wales, SE Australia
Nyurba 118 F4 NE Russian Federation
Nzega 75 C6 C Tanzania
Nzérékoré 72 B5 SE Guinea
N'Zeto 76 B3 NW Angola

O

Oahe, Lake 43 C3 ⊠ North Dakota/South Dakota, N USA
Oa'hu 51 B1 island Hawai'ian Islands, Hawai'i, USA
Oakham 93 E5 C England, United Kingdom
Oak Harbor 49 B2 Washington, NW USA
Oakland 49 B7 California, W USA
Oakley 43 B6 Kansas, C USA
Oamaru 139 B7 South Island, New Zealand
Oa, Mull of 91 B6 headland W Scotland, United Kingdom
Oaxaca 53 F5 SE Mexico
Ob' 118 D3 ≈ C Russian Federation
Oban 91 C5 W Scotland, United Kingdom
Ob', Gulf of 118 D3 gulf N Russian Federation
Obihiro 133 G2 NE Japan
Obo 72 I5 E Central African Republic
Obock 75 E3 E Djibouti
Oborniki 105 C3 W Poland
Ocala 39 F7 Florida, SE USA
Ocaña 99 D3 C Spain
O Carballiño 99 B2 NW Spain
Occidental, Cordillera 65 A2 ▲▲ Bolivia/Chile
Ocean Falls 33 E6 British Columbia, SW Canada
Oceanside 49 D9 California, W USA
Och'amch'ire 121 G1 W Georgia
Ochil Hills 91 E5 ▲▲ C Scotland, United Kingdom
Ocotal 55 D4 NW Nicaragua
Ocozocuautla 53 G5 SE Mexico
October Revolution Island 118 F2 island N Russian Federation
Ocú 55 G7 S Panama
Odate 133 G3 C Japan
Ödemiş 120 A4 SW Turkey
Odense 83 B7 C Denmark
Oder 101 E3 ≈ C Europe
Oderhaff 105 B2 bay Germany/Poland
Odesa 109 E6 SW Ukraine
Odessa 44 F4 Texas, SW USA
Odienné 72 C4 NW Côte d'Ivoire
Odoorn 84 F2 NE Netherlands
Of 121 F2 NE Turkey
Ofanto 103 E6 ≈ S Italy
Offenbach 101 B5 W Germany
Offenburg 101 B7 SW Germany
Ofu 51 island E American Samoa
Ogaden 75 F4 plateau Ethiopia/Somalia
Ogaki 133 F6 SW Japan
Ogallala 43 B5 Nebraska, C USA
Ogbomosho 72 E5 W Nigeria
Ogden 47 D5 Utah, W USA
Ogdensburg 37 D2 New York, NE USA
Ohio 40 E6 ◈ state N USA
Ohio River 40 F7 ≈ N USA
Ohrid, Lake 107 D4 ◎ Albania/Macedonia
Ohura 139 D3 North Island, New Zealand
Oil City 37 B4 Pennsylvania, NE USA
Oirschot 84 D5 S Netherlands
Oise 97 D2 ≈ N France
Oita 133 D7 Kyushu, SW Japan
Ojinaga 53 D2 N Mexico
Ojos del Salado, Cerro 65 A4 ▲ W Argentina
Okaihau 139 C1 North Island, New Zealand
Okanogan River 49 C1 ≈ Washington, NW USA
Okara 127 D2 E Pakistan
Okavango 76 C5 ≈ S Africa
Okavango Delta 76 C5 wetland N Botswana
Okayama 133 E6 SW Japan
Okazaki 133 F6 C Japan
Okeechobee, Lake 39 F8 ◎ Florida, SE USA
Okefenokee Swamp 39 F6 wetland Georgia, SE USA
Okehampton 95 C5 SW England, United Kingdom
Okhotsk 118 H3 E Russian Federation
Okhotsk, Sea of 118 H4 sea NW Pacific Ocean
Okhtyrka 109 F4 NE Ukraine
Okinawa 133 A8 SW Japan
Okinawa-shoto 133 A8 island group SW Japan
Oki-shoto 133 D6 island group SW Japan
Oklahoma 43 C8 ◈ state C USA
Oklahoma City 43 D8 state capital Oklahoma, C USA
Okmulgee 43 D8 Oklahoma, C USA
Oko, Wadi 75 D1 ≈ NE Sudan
Oktyabr'skiy 111 D6 SW Russian Federation
Okushiri-to 133 F2 island NE Japan
Öland 83 D7 island S Sweden
Olavarría 65 C6 E Argentina
Oława 105 D4 SW Poland
Olbia 103 B5 Sardinia, Italy
Oldebroek 84 E3 E Netherlands
Oldenburg 101 B3 NW Germany
Oldenburg 101 C2 N Germany
Oldenzaal 84 F4 E Netherlands
Oldham 93 D4 NW England, United Kingdom
Old Head of Kinsale 89 C7 headland SW Ireland
Olëkma 118 G4 ≈ C Russian Federation
Olëkminsk 118 G4 NE Russian Federation
Oleksandriya 109 E5 C Ukraine
Olenegorsk 111 B2 NW Russian Federation
Olenek 118 F3 NE Russian Federation
Olenëk 118 F3 ≈ NE Russian Federation
Oléron, Île d' 97 B4 island W France
Olevs'k 109 C4 N Ukraine
Ölgiy 129 C1 W Mongolia
Olhão 99 B5 S Portugal
Olifa 76 B4 NW Namibia
Oliva 99 F4 E Spain
Olivet 97 D3 C France
Olmaliq 125 F3 E Uzbekistan
Olomouc 105 D6 E Czech Republic
Olonets 111 B4 NW Russian Federation
Olosega 51 island E American Samoa
Olovyannaya 118 G5 S Russian Federation
Olpe 101 B5 W Germany
Olsztyn 105 E2 N Poland
Olt 109 B7 ≈ S Romania
Olvera 99 C6 SW Spain
Olympia 49 B2 state capital Washington, NW USA
Olympic Mountains 49 A2 ▲▲ Washington, NW USA
Olympus, Mount 107 D4 ▲ N Greece
Omagh 89 D2 W Northern Ireland, United Kingdom
Omaha 43 D5 Nebraska, C USA
Oman 123 E6 ◆ monarchy SW Asia
Oman, Gulf of 123 F4 gulf N Arabian Sea
Omboué 76 A2 W Gabon
Omdurman 75 C2 C Sudan
Ometepe, Isla de 55 D5 island S Nicaragua
Ommen 84 E3 E Netherlands
Omsk 118 D5 C Russian Federation
Omuta 133 D7 SW Japan
Onda 99 F3 E Spain
Öndörhaan 129 F2 E Mongolia
Onega 111 B3 NW Russian Federation
Onega 111 B4 ≈ NW Russian Federation
Onega, Lake 111 B4 ◎ NW Russian Federation
Oneida Lake 37 D3 ◎ New York, NE USA
O'Neill 43 C4 Nebraska, C USA
Oneonta 37 D4 New York, NE USA
Onex 101 A8 SW Switzerland
Ongjin 133 A5 SW North Korea
Ongole 127 E6 E India
Onitsha 72 F5 S Nigeria
Onon Gol 129 F2 ≈ N Mongolia
Onslow 137 A3 Western Australia
Onslow Bay 39 H4 bay North Carolina, E USA
Ontario 35 B4 ◈ province S Canada
Ontario, Lake 37 C3 ◎ Canada/USA
Ontinyent 99 F4 E Spain
Ontong Java Atoll 141 E2 atoll N Solomon Islands
Oostakker 84 B6 NW Belgium
Oostburg 84 B5 SW Netherlands
Oostende see Ostend
Oosterbeek 84 E4 SE Netherlands
Oosterhout 84 D5 S Netherlands
Opava 105 D5 E Czech Republic
Opelika 39 E5 Alabama, S USA
Opelousas 39 B6 Louisiana, S USA
Opmeer 84 D3 NW Netherlands
Opochka 111 A4 W Russian Federation
Opole 105 D5 S Poland
Oporto 99 B3 NW Portugal
Opotiki 139 E3 North Island, New Zealand
Oqtosh 125 E3 C Uzbekistan
Oradea 109 B6 NW Romania
Oran 70 D1 NW Algeria
Orange 137 G5 New South Wales, SE Australia
Orange 97 E6 SE France
Orangeburg 39 G4 South Carolina, SE USA
Orange River 76 C6 ≈ S Africa
Orange Walk 55 C1 N Belize
Oranienburg 101 D3 NE Germany
Oranjemund 76 B6 SW Namibia
Oranjestad 57 G7 ○ W Aruba
Oranmore 89 C4 W Ireland
Orbetello 103 C4 C Italy
Orcadas 142 A2 Argentinian research station South Orkney Islands, Antarctica
Orchard Homes 47 C2 Montana, NW USA
Ord River 137 D2 ≈ N Australia
Ordu 121 E2 N Turkey
Örebro 83 C5 C Sweden
Oregon 49 B4 ◈ state NW USA
Oregon City 49 B3 Oregon, NW USA
Orël 111 A6 W Russian Federation
Orem 47 D5 Utah, W USA
Ore Mountains 101 D5 ▲▲ Czech Republic/Germany
Orenburg 111 D7 W Russian Federation
Orense see Ourense
Orford Ness 95 H2 cape E England, United Kingdom
Organ Peak 44 D3 ▲ New Mexico, SW USA
Oriental, Cordillera 65 B3 ▲▲ Bolivia/Peru
Orihuela 99 F5 E Spain
Orikhiv 109 F5 SE Ukraine
Orin 47 F4 Wyoming, C USA
Orinoco, Río 63 D2 ≈ Colombia/Venezuela
Oriomo 141 A3 SW Papua New Guinea
Orissa 127 F5 state NE India
Oristano 103 A6 Sardinia, Italy
Orkney Islands 91 D1 island group N Scotland, United Kingdom
Orlando 39 G7 Florida, SE USA
Orléanais 97 D3 cultural region C France
Orléans 97 D3 C France
Orleans 37 G4 Massachusetts, NE USA
Ormskirk 93 C4 NW England, United Kingdom
Örnsköldsvik 83 D4 C Sweden
Orohena, Mont 141 B6 ⛰ Tahiti, W French Polynesia
Oromocto 35 F5 New Brunswick, SE Canada
Orsha 109 D2 NE Belarus
Orsk 111 D7 W Russian Federation
Orthez 97 B6 SW France
Ortona 103 D5 C Italy
Oruro 65 A2 W Bolivia
Orwell 95 H2 ≈ E England, United Kingdom
Osaka 133 E6 SW Japan
Osa, Península de 55 E7 peninsula S Costa Rica
Osborne 43 C6 Kansas, C USA
Osh 125 G3 SW Kyrgyzstan
Oshakati 76 B5 N Namibia
Oshawa 35 D6 Ontario, SE Canada
Oshikango 76 B4 N Namibia
O-shima 133 G6 island S Japan
Oshkosh 40 C4 Wisconsin, N USA
Osijek 107 C1 E Croatia
Oskaloosa 43 F5 Iowa, C USA
Oskarshamn 83 C6 S Sweden
Oslo 83 B5 ● S Norway
Osmaniye 121 E5 S Turkey
Osnabrück 101 B4 NW Germany
Osorno 65 A7 C Chile
Oss 84 D5 S Netherlands
Ossa, Serra d' 99 B4 ▲▲ SE Portugal
Ossora 118 I3 E Russian Federation
Ostend 84 A6 NW Belgium
Östersund 83 C4 C Sweden
Ostfriesische Inseln see East Frisian Islands
Ostiglia 103 C2 N Italy
Ostrava 105 D5 E Czech Republic
Ostróda 105 E2 NE Poland
Ostrołęka 105 F3 C Poland
Ostrov 111 A4 W Russian Federation
Ostrowiec Świętokrzyski 105 F4 C Poland
Ostrów Mazowiecka 105 F3 NE Poland
Ostrów Wielkopolski 105 D4 C Poland
Osumi-shoto 133 A7 island group SW Japan
Osumit, Lumi i 107 D4 ≈ SE Albania
Osuna 99 C5 SW Spain
Oswego 37 D3 New York, NE USA
Oswestry 93 C5 W England, United Kingdom
Otago Peninsula 139 B7 peninsula South Island, New Zealand
Otaki 139 D5 North Island, New Zealand
Otaru 133 F2 NE Japan
Otavi 76 B5 N Namibia
Otira 139 C6 South Island, New Zealand
Otjiwarongo 76 B5 N Namibia
Otley 93 D4 N England, United Kingdom
Otorohanga 139 D3 North Island, New Zealand
Otranto 112 G3 SE Italy
Otranto, Strait of 103 F7 strait Albania/Italy
Otrokovice 105 D6 E Czech Republic
Ōtsu 133 E6 Honshu, SW Japan
Ottawa 35 D5 ● Ontario, SE Canada
Ottawa 40 B5 Illinois, N USA
Ottawa 43 E6 Kansas, C USA
Ottawa Islands 35 C2 island group Nunavut, C Canada
Otterburn 93 D2 N England, United Kingdom
Ottignies 84 C7 C Belgium
Ottumwa 43 F5 Iowa, C USA
Ouachita Mountains 39 A3 ▲▲ Arkansas/Oklahoma, C USA
Ouachita River 39 B5 ≈ Arkansas/Louisiana, C USA
Ouagadougou 72 D4 ● C Burkina Faso
Ouahigouya 72 D3 NW Burkina
Oualâta 72 C3 SE Mauritania
Ouanda Djallé 72 I4 NE Central African Republic
Ouarâne 72 B2 desert C Mauritania
Ouargla 70 E2 NE Algeria
Ouarzazate 70 C2 S Morocco
Oubangui 72 H5 ≈ C Africa
Ouessant, Île d' 97 A2 island NW France
Ouésso 76 B1 NW Congo
Oughterard 89 B4 W Ireland
Oujda 70 D1 NE Morocco
Oujeft 72 B2 C Mauritania
Oulu 83 E3 C Finland
Oulujärvi 83 E3 ◎ C Finland
Oulujoki 83 E3 ≈ C Finland
Ounasjoki 83 E2 ≈ N Finland
Ounianga Kébir 72 H2 N Chad
Oupeye 84 D7 E Belgium
Our 84 E8 ≈ NW Europe
Ourense 99 B2 NW Spain
Ourique 99 B5 S Portugal
Ourthe 84 E8 ≈ E Belgium
Ou-sanmyaku 133 G3 ▲▲ Honshū, C Japan
Ouse 93 E4 ≈ N England, United Kingdom
Outer Hebrides 91 A3 island group NW Scotland, United Kingdom
Outes 99 B1 NW Spain
Out Skerries 91 B6 island group NE Scotland, United Kingdom
Ouvéa 141 G6 island Îles Loyauté, NE New Caledonia
Ouyen 137 F6 Victoria, SE Australia
Ovalle 65 A5 N Chile
Ovar 99 B3 N Portugal
Overflakkee 84 C5 island SW Netherlands
Overijse 84 C7 C Belgium
Oviedo 99 C1 NW Spain
Owando 76 B2 C Congo
Owase 133 F6 SW Japan
Owatonna 43 E4 Minnesota, N USA
Owen, Mount 139 C5 ▲ South Island, New Zealand
Owensboro 39 D2 Kentucky, S USA
Owens Lake 49 D7 salt flat California, W USA
Owen Stanley Range 141 B3 ▲▲ S Papua New Guinea
Owerri 72 F5 S Nigeria
Owyhee River 49 D4 ≈ Idaho/Oregon, NW USA
Oxford 139 C6 South Island, New Zealand
Oxford 95 E3 S England, United Kingdom
Oxford Canal 95 E2 canal S England, United Kingdom
Oxkutzcab 53 H4 SE Mexico
Oxnard 49 C8 California, W USA
Oyama 133 G5 Honshu, S Japan
Oyem 76 A1 N Gabon
Oykel 91 D3 ≈ N Scotland, United Kingdom
Oyo 76 B2 C Congo
Oyo 72 E5 W Nigeria
Ozark 39 E6 Alabama, S USA
Ozark Plateau 43 E7 plain Arkansas/Missouri, C USA
Ozarks, Lake of the 43 F6 ⊠ Missouri, C USA
Ózd 105 E7 NE Hungary
Ozieri 103 A5 Sardinia, Italy

P

Pabbay 91 A3 island NW Scotland, United Kingdom
Pabna 127 G3 W Bangladesh
Pachuca 53 F5 C Mexico
Pacific Ocean 14 ocean
Padang 131 B6 Sumatra, W Indonesia
Paderborn 101 B4 NW Germany
Padova see Padua
Padre Island 44 H6 island Texas, SW USA
Padua 103 C2 NE Italy
Paducah 39 D2 Kentucky, S USA
Paektu-san 133 B3 ▲ China/North Korea
Paengnyong-do 133 A5 island NW South Korea
Paeroa 139 D3 North Island, New Zealand
Páfos 112 C6 W Cyprus
Pag 107 B2 island C Croatia
Page 44 B1 Arizona, SW USA
Pago Pago 135 ○ W American Samoa
Pāhala 51 D3 Hawai'i, USA
Pahiatua 139 D4 North Island, New Zealand
Pāhoa 51 D3 Hawai'i, USA
Paignton 95 C5 SW England, United Kingdom
Paihia 139 D1 North Island, New Zealand
Päijänne 83 E4 ◎ S Finland
Pailolo Channel 51 C2 channel Hawai'i, USA
Paine, Cerro 65 A9 ▲ S Chile
Painted Desert 47 D7 desert Arizona, SW USA
Paisley 91 D6 W Scotland, United Kingdom
País Valenciano 99 F3 cultural region NE Spain
País Vasco see Basque Country, The
Pakistan 127 B2 ◆ republic S Asia
Pakokku 131 A2 C Myanmar (Burma)
Pakruojis 83 E7 N Lithuania
Paks 105 E8 S Hungary
Pakwach 75 C5 NW Uganda
Pakxe 131 C3 S Laos
Palafrugell 99 H2 NE Spain
Palagruža 107 B3 island SW Croatia
Palamós 99 H2 NE Spain
Palanpur 127 C4 W India
Palapye 76 D5 SE Botswana
Palatka 39 G6 Florida, SE USA
Palau 131 H6 ◆ republic W Pacific Ocean
Palawan 131 E5 island W Philippines
Palawan Passage 131 E4 passage W Philippines
Palembang 131 C7 W Indonesia
Palencia 99 D2 NW Spain
Palermo 103 C7 Sicily, Italy
Palestine 44 H3 Texas, SW USA
Pali 127 C3 N India
Palikir 135 ● Pohnpei, E Micronesia
Palk Strait 127 E7 strait India/Sri Lanka
Palliser, Cape 139 D5 headland North Island, New Zealand
Palma 99 H4 Balearic Islands, E Spain
Palma del Río 99 C5 S Spain
Palmar Sur 55 F6 SE Costa Rica
Palma Soriano 57 E4 E Cuba
Palmer 37 F4 Massachusetts, NE USA
Palmer 142 A4 US research station Antarctica
Palmer Land 142 B4 physical region Antarctica
Palmerston North 139 D4 North Island, New Zealand
Palmi 103 E8 SW Italy
Palm Springs 49 D9 California, W USA
Palmyra Atoll 135 US ◇ C Pacific Ocean
Palo Alto 49 B7 California, W USA
Palu 131 E6 Celebes, C Indonesia
Pamiers 97 C7 S France
Pamir 125 G4 ≈ Afghanistan/Tajikistan
Pamirs 125 G4 ▲▲ C Asia
Pamlico Sound 39 I3 sound North Carolina, SE USA
Pampa 44 F2 Texas, SW USA
Pampas 65 B6 plain C Argentina
Pamplona 99 E2 N Spain
Panaji 127 C6 W India
Panama 55 G7 ◆ republic Central America
Panama Canal 55 G6 shipping canal E Panama
Panama City 55 H6 ● C Panama
Panama City 39 E6 Florida, SE USA
Panama, Gulf of 55 H7 gulf S Panama
Panama, Isthmus of 55 H6 isthmus E Panama
Panay Island 131 E4 island C Philippines
Pančevo 107 D2 N Serbia
Panevėžys 83 E7 C Lithuania
Pangkalpinang 131 C7 W Indonesia
Panguitch 47 C6 Utah, W USA
Pantanal 63 E6 swamp SW Brazil
Pantelleria 103 B8 Sicily, Italy
Pantelleria, Isola di 112 F4 island SW Italy
Pánuco 53 F4 E Mexico
Paola 112 B6 E Malta
Papagayo, Golfo de 55 D5 gulf NW Costa Rica
Papakura 139 D2 North Island, New Zealand
Papantla 53 F4 E Mexico
Papa Stour 91 A6 island NE Scotland, United Kingdom
Papa Westray 91 E1 island NE Scotland, United Kingdom
Papeete 141 A5 ○ W French Polynesia
Papillion 43 D5 Nebraska, C USA
Papua 131 I7 province E Indonesia
Papua, Gulf of 141 B3 gulf S Papua New Guinea
Papua New Guinea 141 B2 ◆ commonwealth republic NW Melanesia
Papuk 107 C1 ▲▲ NE Croatia
Pará 63 F4 state NE Brazil
Paracel Islands 131 C3 Disputed ◇ SE Asia
Paraguay 65 B3 ◆ republic C South America
Paraguay 65 C3 ≈ C South America
Paraíba 63 I5 state E Brazil
Parakou 72 E4 C Benin
Paramaribo 63 F2 ● N Suriname
Paramushir, Ostrov 118 I4 island SE Russian Federation
Paraná 65 C5 E Argentina
Paraná 63 F8 state S Brazil
Paraná 65 C5 ≈ C South America
Paraparaumu 139 D5 North Island, New Zealand
Parchim 101 D3 N Germany
Parczew 105 G4 E Poland
Pardubice 105 C5 C Czech Republic
Parecis, Chapada dos 65 B1 ▲▲ W Brazil
Parepare 131 E7 Celebes, C Indonesia
Paria, Gulf of 57 J7 gulf Trinidad and Tobago/Venezuela
Paris 97 D2 ● N France
Paris 44 H2 Texas, SW USA
Parkersburg 39 F1 West Virginia, NE USA
Parkes 137 G5 New South Wales, SE Australia
Parma 103 C3 N Italy
Parnaíba 63 H4 E Brazil
Pärnu 83 E6 SW Estonia
Páros 107 F6 island SE Greece
Parral 65 A6 C Chile
Parramatta 137 G6 New South Wales, SE Australia
Parras 53 E3 NE Mexico
Parrett 95 D4 ≈ SW England, United Kingdom
Parsons 43 E7 Kansas, C USA
Partney 93 F5 E England, United Kingdom
Partry 89 B3 NW Ireland
Partry Mountains 89 B4 ▲▲ W Ireland
Pasadena 49 C8 California, W USA
Pasadena 44 H4 Texas, SW USA
Pasco 49 C3 Washington, NW USA
Pasewalk 101 E3 NE Germany
Pasinler 121 G3 NE Turkey
Pasłęk 105 E2 NE Poland
Pasni 127 A3 SW Pakistan
Paso de Indios 65 A7 S Argentina
Passau 101 D6 SE Germany
Passo Fundo 63 F8 S Brazil
Pasto 63 B3 SW Colombia
Patagonia 65 B7 semi arid region Argentina/Chile
Patea 139 D4 North Island, New Zealand
Paterson 37 E5 New Jersey, NE USA
Pátmos 107 F6 island Dodecanese, Greece
Patna 127 F3 N India
Patnos 121 G3 E Turkey
Patos, Lagoa dos 63 F9 lagoon S Brazil
Pátra 107 D5 S Greece
Patrickswell 89 C5 SW Ireland
Patuca, Río 55 E3 ≈ E Honduras
Pau 97 B6 SW France
Paulatuk 33 F3 Northwest Territories, NW Canada
Pavia 103 B2 N Italy
Pavlodar 118 D5 NE Kazakhstan
Pavlohrad 109 F5 E Ukraine

◈ Administrative region ◆ Country ● Country capital ◇ Dependent territory ○ Dependent territory capital ▲▲ Mountain range ▲ Mountain ⛰ Volcano ≈ River ◎ Lake ⊠ Reservoir

Pawn *131 B3* ≈ C Myanmar (Burma)
Paxoí *107 D5 island* Ionian Islands, Greece
Paysandú *65 C5* W Uruguay
Pazar *121 F2* NE Turkey
Pazardzhik *107 E3* C Bulgaria
Peach Springs *44 A2* Arizona, SW USA
Peak District *93 D5 physical region* C England, United Kingdom
Pearl City *51 B1* O'ahu, Hawai'i, USA
Pearl Harbor *51 B2 inlet* O'ahu, Hawai'i, USA, C Pacific Ocean
Pearl Islands *55 H6 island group* SE Panama
Pearl Lagoon *55 F4 lagoon* E Nicaragua
Pearl River *39 C6* ≈ Louisiana/ Mississippi, S USA
Pearsall *44 G5* Texas, SW USA
Peawanuk *35 C3* Ontario, C Canada
Peć *107 D3* S Serbia
Pechora *111 D4* NW Russian Federation
Pechora *111 D3* ≈ NW Russian Federation
Pechora Sea *111 D2 sea* NW Russian Federation
Pecos *44 E4* Texas, SW USA
Pecos River *44 F4* ≈ New Mexico/Texas, SW USA
Pécs *105 D9* SW Hungary
Pedro Juan Caballero *65 C3* E Paraguay
Peebles *91 E6* SE Scotland, United Kingdom
Peel *93 A3* W Isle of Man
Peer *84 D6* NE Belgium
Pegasus Bay *139 C6 bay* South Island, New Zealand
Pegu *131 A3* SW Myanmar (Burma)
Pehuajó *65 B6* E Argentina
Peine *101 C4* C Germany
Peipus, Lake *83 E5* ◎ Estonia/Russian Federation
Peiraías *see* Piraeus
Pekalongan *131 D7* Java, C Indonesia
Pekanbaru *131 B6* Sumatra, W Indonesia
Pekin *40 B6* Illinois, N USA
Peking *see* Beijing
Pelagie *103 C9 island group* SW Italy
Pelly Bay *33 H3* Nunavut, N Canada
Peloponnese *107 D6 peninsula* S Greece
Pematangsiantar *131 A6* Sumatra, W Indonesia
Pemba *76 F4* NE Mozambique
Pemba *75 E6 island* E Tanzania
Pembroke *35 D5* Ontario, SE Canada
Pembroke *93 A7* SW Wales, United Kingdom
Pembroke Dock *93 A7* SW Wales, United Kingdom
Penas, Golfo de *65 A8 gulf* S Chile
Pendleton *49 C3* Oregon, NW USA
Pend Oreille, Lake *47 B1* ◎ Idaho, NW USA
Peniche *99 A4* W Portugal
Penn Hills *37 B5* Pennsylvania, NE USA
Pennine Alps *101 A8* ▲▲ Italy/Switzerland
Pennines *93 D3* ▲▲ N England, United Kingdom
Pennsylvania *37 C5* ⬖ *state* NE USA
Penobscot River *37 G2* ≈ Maine, NE USA
Penong *137 E5* South Australia
Penonomé *55 G6* C Panama
Penrhyn *135 atoll* N Cook Islands
Penrith *93 C2* NW England, United Kingdom
Pensacola *39 D6* Florida, SE USA
Pentecost *141 H4 island* C Vanuatu
Pentland Firth *91 E1 strait* N Scotland, United Kingdom
Pentland Hills *91 E6 hill range* S Scotland, United Kingdom
Pen y Fan *93 B7* ▲ SE Wales, United Kingdom
Pen-y-ghent *93 D3* ▲ N England, United Kingdom
Penza *111 B6* W Russian Federation
Penzance *95 A6* SW England, United Kingdom
Peoria *40 B6* Illinois, N USA
Perchtoldsdorf *101 F7* NE Austria
Percival Lakes *137 C3 lakes* Western Australia
Perdido, Monte *99 F2* ▲ NE Spain
Pergamino *65 C5* E Argentina
Périgueux *97 C5* SW France
Perito Moreno *65 A8* S Argentina
Perleberg *101 D3* N Germany
Perm' *111 D5* NW Russian Federation
Pernambuco *63 H5 state* E Brazil
Pernik *107 E3* W Bulgaria
Perote *53 F5* E Mexico
Perpignan *97 D7* S France
Perryton *44 F1* Texas, SW USA
Perryville *43 G7* Missouri, C USA
Persian Gulf *123 D3 Gulf* SW Asia
Perth *91 E5* C Scotland, United Kingdom
Perth *137 B5 state capital* Western Australia
Peru *65 A2* ◆ *republic* W South America
Peru Basin *14 undersea feature* E Pacific Ocean
Peru-Chile Trench *14 undersea feature* E Pacific Ocean
Perugia *103 C4* C Italy
Péruwelz *84 B7* SW Belgium
Pervomays'k *109 E5* S Ukraine
Pervyy Kuril'skiy Proliv *118 I4 strait* E Russian Federation
Pesaro *103 D3* C Italy
Pescara *103 D5* C Italy
Peshawar *127 C1* N Pakistan
Pessac *97 B5* SW France
Petah Tiqwa *123 H6* C Israel
Pétange *84 E9* SW Luxembourg
Petén Itzá, Lago *55 B2* ◎ N Guatemala
Peterborough *137 E5* South Australia
Peterborough *35 D6* Ontario, SE Canada
Peterborough *95 F2* E England, United Kingdom
Peterhead *91 F3* NE Scotland, United Kingdom
Peter I Island *142 A4 Norwegian* ◇ Antarctica
Peterlee *93 E3* N England, United Kingdom
Petersburg *39 H2* Virginia, NE USA
Petersfield *95 F4* S England, United Kingdom
Peto *53 H4* SE Mexico
Petrich *107 E4* SW Bulgaria
Petrodvorets *111 A4* NW Russian Federation
Petropavlovsk *118 C4* N Kazakhstan
Petropavlovsk-Kamchatskiy *118 I3* E Russian Federation
Petrozavodsk *111 B4* NW Russian Federation
Pevek *118 H2* NE Russian Federation
Pezinok *105 D7* W Slovakia
Pforzheim *101 B6* SW Germany
Pfungstadt *101 B6* W Germany
Phangan, Ko *131 B4 island* SW Thailand
Phenix City *39 E5* Alabama, S USA
Phetchaburi *131 B4* SW Thailand
Philadelphia *37 D5* Pennsylvania, NE USA
Philippines *131 D4* ◆ *republic* SE Asia
Philippine Sea *131 F3 sea* W Pacific Ocean
Philippine Trench *15 undersea feature* W Philippine Sea
Phitsanulok *131 B3* C Thailand
Phnom Penh *131 C4* ● S Cambodia
Phoenix *44 B3 state capital* Arizona, SW USA
Phoenix Islands *135 island group* C Kiribati
Phra Thong, Ko *131 A5 island* SW Thailand
Phuket *131 B5* SW Thailand
Phuket, Ko *131 A5 island* SW Thailand
Piacenza *103 B2* N Italy
Piatra-Neamț *109 C6* NE Romania
Piauí *63 G5 state* E Brazil
Picardie *see* Picardy
Picardy *97 D2 cultural region* N France Europe
Pichilemu *65 A5* C Chile
Pickering *93 E3* N England, United Kingdom
Picos *63 H4* E Brazil
Picton *139 D5* South Island, New Zealand
Piedmont *103 A2 cultural region* NW Italy
Piedmont *39 G3 escarpment* E USA
Piedras Negras *53 E2* NE Mexico
Pielavesi *83 E4* C Finland
Pielinen *83 F4* ◎ E Finland
Piemonte *see* Piedmont
Pierre *43 C3 state capital* South Dakota, N USA
Piešťany *105 D6* W Slovakia
Pietarsaari *see* Jakobstad
Pietermaritzburg *76 D6* E South Africa
Pietersburg *see* Polokwane
Pigs, Bay of *57 C3 bay* SE Cuba
Pijijiapán *53 H6* SE Mexico
Pikes Peak *47 E6* ▲ Colorado, C USA
Pikeville *39 F2* Kentucky, S USA
Piła *105 C3* C Poland
Pilar *65 C4* S Paraguay
Pilcomayo, Rio *65 C3* ≈ C South America
Pillsbury Sound *51 strait* C Virgin Islands (US) North America Caribbean Sea Atlantic Ocean
Pinar del Río *57 B2* W Cuba
Pindus Mountains *107 D5* ▲▲ C Greece
Pine Bluff *39 B4* Arkansas, C USA
Pine Creek *137 D1* Northern Territory, N Australia
Pinega *111 C4* ≈ NW Russian Federation
Pineiós *107 E4* ≈ C Greece
Pineland *44 I4* Texas, SW USA
Pingdingshan *129 F4* C China
Ping, Mae Nam *131 B3* ≈ W Thailand
Pinotepa Nacional *53 F6* SE Mexico
Pins, Île des *141 G6 island* E New Caledonia
Pinsk *109 C3* SW Belarus
Piombino *103 B4* C Italy
Piotrków Trybunalski *105 E4* C Poland
Piraeus *107 E5* C Greece
Pirata, Monte *51* ▲ E Puerto Rico
Piripiri *63 H4* E Brazil
Pirna *101 E5* E Germany
Pisa *103 B3* C Italy
Pisco *63 B6* SW Peru
Písek *105 B6* S Czech Republic
Pishan *129 B3* NW China
Pistoia *103 C3* C Italy
Pisz *105 F2* NE Poland
Pita *72 B4* NW Guinea
Pitcairn Islands *135 UK* ◇ C Pacific Ocean
Piteå *83 D3* N Sweden
Pitești *109 B7* S Romania
Pitlochry *91 D4* C Scotland, United Kingdom
Pit River *49 B5* ≈ California, W USA
Pittsburg *43 E7* Kansas, C USA
Pittsburgh *37 B5* Pennsylvania, NE USA
Pittsfield *37 E4* Massachusetts, NE USA
Piura *63 A4* NW Peru
Pivdennyy Buh *109 E5* ≈ S Ukraine
Placetas *57 C3* C Cuba
Plainview *44 F2* Texas, SW USA
Plano *44 H3* Texas, SW USA
Plasencia *99 C3* W Spain
Plate, River *65 C5 estuary* Argentina/Uruguay
Platinum *50 D2* Alaska, USA
Platte River *43 D5* ≈ Nebraska, C USA
Plattsburgh *37 E2* New York, NE USA
Plauen *101 D5* E Germany
Play Cu *131 C4* C Vietnam
Plenty, Bay of *139 E3 bay* North Island, New Zealand
Plérin *97 B2* NW France
Plesetsk *111 C4* NW Russian Federation
Pleszew *105 D4* C Poland
Pleven *107 E2* N Bulgaria
Płock *105 E3* C Poland
Plöcken Pass *101 D8 pass* SW Austria
Ploiești *109 C7* SE Romania
Płońsk *105 E3* C Poland
Plovdiv *107 F3* C Bulgaria
Plymouth *57 J5* Trinidad and Tobago
Plymouth *95 B5* SW England, United Kingdom
Plynlimon *93 B6* ▲ C Wales, United Kingdom
Plzeň *105 A5* W Czech Republic
Po *103 C3* ≈ N Italy
Pobedy, Pik *129 B2* ▲ China/Kyrgyzstan
Pocahontas *39 C3* Arkansas, C USA
Pocatello *47 C4* Idaho, NW USA
Pochinok *111 A5* W Russian Federation
Pocking *101 D7* SE Germany
Pocklington Reef *141 E3 reef* SE Papua New Guinea
Poděbrady *105 B5* C Czech Republic
Podgorica *107 C3* ● S Montenegro
Podil's'ka Vysochyna *109 C5* ▲▲ SW Ukraine
Podol'sk *111 A5* W Russian Federation
P'ohang *133 C6* E South Korea
Poinsett, Cape *142 E5 cape* Antarctica
Pointe-à-Pitre *57 J5* C Guadeloupe
Pointe-Noire *76 A2* S Congo
Point Lay *50 E1* Alaska, USA
Poitiers *97 C4* W France
Poitou *97 B4 cultural region* W France
Pokhara *127 F3* C Nepal
Pola de Lena *99 C1* N Spain
Poland *105 D4* ◆ *republic* C Europe
Polatlı *121 C3* C Turkey
Polatsk *109 D1* N Belarus
Pol-e Khomrī *125 F4* NE Afghanistan
Pólis *112 C6* W Cyprus
Pollença *99 H3* Majorca, Spain
Polokwane *76 D6* NE South Africa
Poltava *109 F4* NE Ukraine
Polyarnyy *111 C2* NW Russian Federation
Polynesia *135 island group* C Pacific Ocean
Pomerania *105 C2 cultural region* Germany/Poland
Pomeranian Bay *101 E2 bay* Germany/Poland
Pomio *141 C2* E Papua New Guinea
Pomorskiy Proliv *111 D3 strait* NW Russian Federation
Pompano Beach *39 G8* Florida, SE USA
Ponca City *43 D7* Oklahoma, C USA
Ponce *57 H4* C Puerto Rico
Pondicherry *127 E6* SE India
Pond Inlet *143 A4* Baffin Island, Nunavut, NE Canada
Ponferrada *99 C2* NW Spain
Poniatowa *105 F4* E Poland
Ponta Grossa *63 F8* S Brazil
Pontarlier *97 F4* E France
Pontearéas *99 B2* NW Spain
Ponte da Barca *99 B2* N Portugal
Pontevedra *99 B2* NW Spain
Pontiac *40 E5* Michigan, N USA
Pontianak *131 D6* C Indonesia
Pontivy *97 B3* NW France
Pontoise *97 D2* N France
Pontypool *93 C7* SE Wales, United Kingdom
Pontypridd *93 C7* S Wales, United Kingdom
Ponziane Island *103 C6 island* C Italy
Poole *95 E5* S England, United Kingdom
Poole Bay *95 E5 bay* S England, United Kingdom
Popayán *63 B3* SW Colombia
Poperinge *84 A6* W Belgium
Poplar Bluff *43 G7* Missouri, C USA
Popocatépetl *53 F5* △ S Mexico
Popondetta *141 C3* S Papua New Guinea
Poprad *105 E6* C Slovakia
Poprád *105 E6* ≈ Poland/Slovakia
Porbandar *127 C4* W India
Pordenone *103 D2* NE Italy
Pori *83 E5* SW Finland
Porirua *139 D5* C New Zealand
Porkhov *111 A4* W Russian Federation
Póros *107 D5* Kefallonía, Greece
Porsangenfjorden *83 E1 fjord* N Norway
Porsgrunn *83 B5* S Norway
Portadown *89 E2* S Northern Ireland, United Kingdom
Portaferry *89 F3* E Northern Ireland, United Kingdom
Portalegre *99 B4* E Portugal
Port Alexander *50 F4* Baranof Island, Alaska, USA
Port Alfred *76 D7* S South Africa
Port Angeles *49 B2* Washington, NW USA
Port Arthur *44 I4* Texas, SW USA
Port Askaig *91 B6* W Scotland, United Kingdom
Port Augusta *137 E5* South Australia
Port-au-Prince *57* ● C Haiti
Port Blair *127 H5* Andaman Islands, SE India
Port Charlotte *39 F8* Florida, SE USA
Port Douglas *137 G2* Queensland, NE Australia
Port Elizabeth *76 D7* S South Africa
Port Ellen *91 B6* W Scotland, United Kingdom
Port Erin *93 A4* SW Isle of Man
Porterville *49 C8* California, W USA
Port-Gentil *76 A2* W Gabon
Port Harcourt *72 E5* S Nigeria
Port Hardy *33 E7* Vancouver Island, British Columbia, SW Canada
Port Hedland *137 B3* Western Australia
Port Huron *40 E4* Michigan, N USA
Portimão *99 B5* S Portugal
Port Isaac Bay *95 A5 bay* SW England, United Kingdom
Portishead *95 D4* SW England, United Kingdom
Portland *137 F6* Victoria, SE Australia
Portland *37 F3* Maine, NE USA
Portland *49 B3* Oregon, NW USA
Portland *44 H5* Texas, SW USA
Portland Bill *95 D5 headland* S England, United Kingdom
Portland, Isle of *95 D5 island* SW England, United Kingdom
Port Laoise *89 D5* C Ireland
Port Lavaca *44 H5* Texas, SW USA
Port Lincoln *137 E6* South Australia
Port Louis *67* ● NW Mauritius
Port Macquarie *137 H5* New South Wales, SE Australia
Port Moresby *141 B3* ● New Guinea, SW Papua New Guinea
Porto *see* Oporto
Porto Alegre *63 F8* S Brazil
Portobelo *55 H6* N Panama
Port O'Connor *44 H5* Texas, SW USA
Portoferraio *103 B4* C Italy
Port of Ness *91 B2* NW Scotland, United Kingdom
Port-of-Spain *57 K7* ● C Trinidad and Tobago
Portogruaro *103 D2* NE Italy
Porto-Novo *72 E5* ● S Benin
Porto Torres *103 A5* Sardinia, Italy
Porto Velho *63 D5* W Brazil
Portoviejo *63 A4* W Ecuador
Port Pirie *137 E5* South Australia
Portree *91 B3* N Scotland, United Kingdom
Portrush *89 E1* N Northern Ireland, United Kingdom
Port Said *70 I2* N Egypt
Portskerra *91 D2* N Scotland, United Kingdom
Portsmouth *95 F5* S England, United Kingdom
Portsmouth *37 F3* New Hampshire, NE USA
Portsmouth *40 E7* Ohio, N USA
Portsmouth *39 I2* Virginia, NE USA
Port Sudan *75 D1* NE Sudan
Portugal *99 A3* ◆ *republic* SW Europe
Port-Vila *141 H5* ● Éfaté, C Vanuatu
Porvenir *65 A1* NW Bolivia
Porvenir *65 B9* S Chile
Porvoo *83 E5* S Finland
Posadas *65 C4* NE Argentina
Post *44 F3* Texas, SW USA
Posterholt *84 E6* SE Netherlands
Postojna *101 E9* SW Slovenia
Potenza *103 E6* S Italy
P'ot'i *121 G1* W Georgia
Potiskum *72 F4* NE Nigeria
Potomac River *39 H1* ≈ NE USA
Potosí *65 B3* S Bolivia
Potsdam *101 D3* NE Germany
Potsdam *37 D2* New York, NE USA
Pottsville *37 D5* Pennsylvania, NE USA
Pouébo *141 G6* C New Caledonia
Poulton-le-Fylde *93 C4* NW England, United Kingdom
Po Valley *103 C3 valley* N Italy
Považská Bystrica *105 D6* W Slovakia
Poverty Bay *139 E4 inlet* North Island, New Zealand
Póvoa de Varzim *99 B2* NW Portugal
Powder River *47 F3* ≈ Montana/ Wyoming, NW USA
Powell *47 E3* Wyoming, C USA
Powell, Lake *47 D6* ◎ Utah, W USA
Poza Rica *53 F4* E Mexico
Poznań *105 C3* C Poland
Pozoblanco *99 D5* S Spain
Pozzallo *103 D9* Sicily, Italy
Prachatice *105 B6* S Czech Republic
Prague *105* ● NW Czech Republic
Praha *see* Prague
Praia *67* ● Santiago, S Cape Verde
Prairie du Chien *40 B4* Wisconsin, N USA
Prato *103 C3* C Italy
Pratt *43 C7* Kansas, C USA
Prattville *39 E5* Alabama, S USA
Pravia *99 C1* N Spain
Prenzlau *101 D3* NE Germany
Přerov *105 D6* E Czech Republic
Prescott *44 B2* Arizona, SW USA
Preseli, Mynydd *93 A6* ▲▲ SW Wales, United Kingdom
Presidio *44 E5* Texas, SW USA
Prešov *105 F6* E Slovakia
Prespa, Lake *107 D4* ◎ SE Europe
Presque Isle *37 G1* Maine, NE USA
Prestatyn *93 C4* N Wales, United Kingdom
Preston *93 C4* NW England, United Kingdom
Prestwick *91 D6* W Scotland, United Kingdom
Pretoria *see* Tshwane
Préveza *107 D5* W Greece
Pribilof Islands *50 B2 island group* Alaska, USA
Price *47 D5* Utah, W USA
Prichard *39 D6* Alabama, S USA
Prilep *107 D4* S Macedonia
Prince Albert *33 G6* Saskatchewan, S Canada
Prince Edward Island *35 G5* ⬖ *province* SE Canada
Prince George *33 F6* British Columbia, SW Canada
Prince of Wales Island *137 F1 island* Queensland, E Australia
Prince of Wales Island *33 H3 island* Queen Elizabeth Islands, Nunavut, NW Canada
Prince Patrick Island *33 F2 island* Parry Islands, Northwest Territories, NW Canada
Prince Rupert *33 E6* British Columbia, SW Canada
Princess Charlotte Bay *137 G1 bay* Queensland, NE Australia
Princess Elizabeth Land *142 D4 physical region* Antarctica
Príncipe *72 E6 island* N Sao Tome and Principe
Prinzapolka *55 E4* NE Nicaragua
Pripet *109 C3* ≈ Belarus/Ukraine
Pripet Marshes *109 C3 forested and swampy region* Belarus/Ukraine
Priština *107 D3* S Serbia
Privas *97 E5* E France
Prizren *107 D3* S Serbia
Probolinggo *131 D8* C Indonesia
Progreso *53 H4* SE Mexico
Prokhladnyy *111 B8* SW Russian Federation
Prome *131 A3* C Myanmar (Burma)
Promyshlennyy *111 E3* NW Russian Federation
Prostějov *105 D6* E Czech Republic
Provence *97 E6 cultural region* SE France
Providence *37 F4 state capital* Rhode Island, NE USA
Provideniya *143 C1* NE Russian Federation
Provo *47 D5* Utah, W USA
Prudhoe Bay *50 F1* Alaska, USA
Pruszków *105 E3* C Poland
Prut *109 D6* ≈ E Europe
Prydz Bay *142 E4 bay* Antarctica
Pryluky *109 E4* NE Ukraine
Przemyśl *105 G5* C Poland
Psará *107 F5 island* E Greece
Psël *109 F4* ≈ Russian Federation/Ukraine
Pskov *111 A4* W Russian Federation
Ptsich *109 D3* ≈ SE Belarus
Ptuj *101 F8* NE Slovenia
Pucallpa *63 B5* C Peru
Puck *105 D1* N Poland
Pudasjärvi *83 E3* C Finland
Puebla *53 F5* S Mexico
Pueblo *47 F6* Colorado, C USA
Puerto Acosta *65 A2* W Bolivia
Puerto Aisén *65 A7* S Chile
Puerto Ángel *53 F6* SE Mexico
Puerto Ayacucho *63 D2* SW Venezuela
Puerto Baquerizo Moreno *63 B7* Galapagos Islands, Ecuador
Puerto Barrios *55 C2* E Guatemala
Puerto Cabezas *55 E3* NE Nicaragua
Puerto Cortés *55 C2* NW Honduras
Puerto Deseado *65 B8* SE Argentina
Puerto Escondido *53 F6* SE Mexico
Puerto Lempira *55 E3* E Honduras
Puertollano *99 D4* C Spain
Puerto Maldonado *63 C5* E Peru
Puerto Montt *65 A7* C Chile
Puerto Natales *65 A9* S Chile
Puerto Obaldía *55 I6* NE Panama
Puerto Plata *57 G4* N Dominican Republic
Puerto Princesa *131 E4* Palawan, W Philippines
Puerto Rico *51 US* ◇ C West Indies
Puerto San Julián *65 B8* SE Argentina
Puerto Suárez *65 C2* E Bolivia
Puerto Vallarta *53 D5* SW Mexico
Puerto Varas *65 A7* C Chile
Puerto Viejo *55 E5* NE Costa Rica
Puget Sound *49 B2 sound* Washington, NW USA
Pukaki, Lake *139 B6* ◎ SW New Zealand
Pukatikei, Maunga *141 D6* △ Easter Island, Chile
Pukch'ong *133 B4* E North Korea
Pukekohe *139 D3* North Island, New Zealand
Pula *107 A2* NW Croatia
Pulaski *39 G2* Virginia, NE USA
Puławy *105 F4* E Poland
Pullman *49 D2* Washington, NW USA
Pultusk *105 E3* C Poland
Pune *127 C5* W India
Punjab *127 D2 cultural region* India/Pakistan
Puno *63 C6* SE Peru
Punta Alta *65 B6* E Argentina
Punta Arenas *65 A9* S Chile
Punta, Cerro de *51* ▲ C Puerto Rico
Punta Gorda *55 B2* SE Belize
Punta Gorda *55 E5* SE Nicaragua
Puntarenas *55 E6* W Costa Rica
Puntland *75 F3 cultural region* NE Somalia
Pupuya, Nevado *65 A2* ▲ W Bolivia
Puri *127 F5* E India
Purmerend *84 D3* C Netherlands
Purus, Rio *63 D4* ≈ Brazil/Peru
Pusan *133 C6* SE South Korea
Püspökladány *105 F7* E Hungary
Putney *37 E3* Vermont, NE USA
Putorana Mountains *118 E3* ▲▲ N Russian Federation
Putrajaya *131 B6* ● Peninsular Malaysia
Puttalam *127 E7* W Sri Lanka
Puttgarden *101 C2* N Germany
Putumayo, Río *63 C4* ≈ NW South America
Pu'u 'Ula'ula *51 C2* ▲ Maui, Hawai'i, USA
Pu'uwai *51 A1* Ni'ihau, Hawai'i, USA
Pwllheli *93 B5* NW Wales, United Kingdom
Pyatigorsk *111 A8* SW Russian Federation
Pyongyang *133 A5* ● SW North Korea
Pyramid Lake *47 A5* ◎ Nevada, W USA
Pyrenees *99 F2* ▲▲ SW Europe
Pyrgos *107 D6* S Greece
Pyrzyce *105 B3* NW Poland

Q

Qaidam Pendi *129 D3 basin* C China
Qal'aikhum *125 G3* S Tajikistan
Qalat *125 F6* S Afghanistan
Qal'eh-ye Now *125 E4* NW Afghanistan
Qamdo *129 D4* China
Qarokul *125 G3* E Tajikistan
Qarshi *125 E3* S Uzbekistan
Qasr Farafra *70 I3* W Egypt
Qatar *123 D4* ◆ *monarchy* SW Asia
Qattara Depression *70 I3 desert* NW Egypt
Qausuittuq *see* Resolute
Qazimämmäd *121 J2* SE Azerbaijan
Qazvin *123 D2* N Iran
Qena *70 J3* E Egypt
Qilian Shan *129 D3* ▲▲ N China
Qingdao *129 G3* E China
Qinghai Hu *129 D3* ◎ C China
Qinhuangdao *129 G3* E China
Qinzhou *129 F6* S China
Qiqihar *129 G2* NE China
Qira *129 B3* NW China
Qitai *129 C2* NW China
Qizilrabot *125 H4* SE Tajikistan
Qom *123 D2* N Iran
Qo'ng'irot *125 D2* NW Uzbekistan
Qo'qon *125 G3* E Uzbekistan
Quang Ngai *131 D3* C Vietnam
Quanzhou *129 G5* SE China
Quanzhou *129 F5* S China
Qu'Appelle *33 H7* ≈ Saskatchewan, S Canada
Quarles, Pegunungan *131 E7* ▲▲ Sulawesi, C Indonesia
Quartu Sant' Elena *103 A6* Sardegna, Italy
Quba *121 I2* N Azerbaijan
Québec *35 D3 province capital* Québec, SE Canada
Québec *35 E5* ⬖ *province* SE Canada
Queen Charlotte Islands *33 D6 island group* British Columbia, SW Canada
Queen Charlotte Sound *33 D6 sea area* British Columbia, W Canada
Queen Elizabeth Islands *33 G2 island group* Nunavut, N Canada
Queensland *137 F3* ⬖ *state* N Australia
Queenstown *139 B7* South Island, New Zealand
Queenstown *76 D7* S South Africa
Quelimane *76 E5* NE Mozambique
Quemado *44 C2* New Mexico, SW USA
Quepos *55 E6* S Costa Rica
Querétaro *53 E4* C Mexico
Quesada *55 E6* N Costa Rica
Quetta *127 B2* SW Pakistan
Quezaltenango *55 A3* W Guatemala
Quilon *127 D7* SW India
Quilty *89 B5* W Ireland
Quimper *97 A2* NW France
Quimperlé *97 A3* NW France
Quinault *49 B2* Washington, NW USA
Quincy *40 A6* Illinois, N USA
Quito *63 B3* ● N Ecuador
Qurghonteppa *125 F4* SW Tajikistan
Quy Nhon *131 D4* C Vietnam

R

Raahe *83 E3* W Finland
Raalte *84 E3* E Netherlands
Raamsdonksveer *84 D5* S Netherlands
Raasay *91 B3 island* NW Scotland, United Kingdom
Rába *105 C8* ≈ Austria/Hungary
Rabat *70 C1* ● NW Morocco
Rabat *112 A5* W Malta
Rabaul *141 D1* E Papua New Guinea
Rabinal *55 B3* C Guatemala
Rabka *105 E6* S Poland
Rabyanah Ramlat *70 G4 desert* SE Libya
Race, Cape *35 H4 cape* Newfoundland, E Canada
Rach Gia *131 C4* S Vietnam
Racine *40 C5* Wisconsin, N USA
Radom *105 F4* C Poland

⬖ Administrative region ◆ Country ● Country capital ◇ Dependent territory ○ Dependent territory capital ▲▲ Mountain range ▲ Mountain △ Volcano ≈ River ◎ Lake ▣ Reservoir

SALZBURG

Radomsko 105 E4 C Poland
Radzyń Podlaski 105 F4 E Poland
Raetihi 139 D4 North Island, New Zealand
Rafaela 65 B5 E Argentina
Raga 75 B4 SW Sudan
Ragged Island Range 57 D3 *island group* S Bahamas
Ragusa 103 D8 Sicily, Italy
Rahimyar Khan 127 C3 SE Pakistan
Raichur 127 D5 C India
Rainier, Mount 49 B2 ⋀ Washington, NW USA
Rainy Lake 43 E1 ◎ Canada/USA
Raipur 127 E4 C India
Rajahmundry 127 E5 E India
Rajang, Batang 131 D6 ≈ East Malaysia
Rajapalaiyam 127 D7 SE India
Rajasthan 127 C3 *state* NW India
Rajkot 127 C4 W India
Rajshahi 127 G3 W Bangladesh
Rakaia 139 C6 ≈ South Island, New Zealand
Raleigh 39 H3 *state capital* North Carolina, SE USA
Râmnicu Vâlcea 109 B7 C Romania
Ramree Island 131 A3 *island* W Myanmar (Burma)
Ramsey 93 B3 NE Isle of Man
Ramsgate 95 H4 SE England, United Kingdom
Rancagua 65 A5 C Chile
Ranchi 127 F4 N India
Randers 83 B6 C Denmark
Rangiora 139 C6 South Island, New Zealand
Rangitikei 139 D4 ≈ North Island, New Zealand
Rangoon 131 A3 S Myanmar (Burma)
Rangpur 127 G3 N Bangladesh
Rankin Inlet 33 H4 Nunavut, C Canada
Rannoch Moor 91 D4 *heathland* C Scotland, United Kingdom
Rapid City 43 A3 South Dakota, N USA
Räpina 83 F6 SE Estonia
Rarotonga 135 *island* S Cook Islands
Rasht 123 D1 NW Iran
Ratän 83 C4 C Sweden
Rathfriland 89 E3 SE Northern Ireland, United Kingdom
Rathkeale 89 C5 SW Ireland
Rathlin Island 89 E1 *island* N Northern Ireland, United Kingdom
Ráth Luirc 89 C6 S Ireland
Rathmelton 89 D1 N Ireland
Rathmore 89 B6 SW Ireland
Rathmullan 89 D1 N Ireland
Rathnew 89 E5 E Ireland
Rat Islands 50 A1 *island group* Aleutian Islands, Alaska, USA
Ratlam 127 D4 C India
Ratnapura 127 E8 S Sri Lanka
Raton 44 E1 New Mexico, SW USA
Rättvik 83 C5 C Sweden
Raufarhöfn 83 B1 NE Iceland
Raukumara Range 139 E3 ⛰ North Island, New Zealand
Räurkela 127 F4 E India
Rauma 83 D5 SW Finland
Ravenglass 93 B3 NW England, United Kingdom
Ravenna 103 C3 N Italy
Ravi 127 C2 ≈ India/Pakistan
Rawalpindi 127 D1 NE Pakistan
Rawa Mazowiecka 105 E4 C Poland
Rawicz 105 C4 C Poland
Rawlinna 137 C5 Western Australia
Rawlins 47 E4 Wyoming, C USA
Rawson 65 B7 SE Argentina
Rayong 131 B4 S Thailand
Razazah, Buhayrat ar 123 B2 ◎ C Iraq
Razgrad 107 F2 N Bulgaria
Razim, Lacul 109 D7 *lagoon* NW Black Sea
Reading 95 F4 S England, United Kingdom
Reading 37 D5 Pennsylvania, NE USA
Real, Cordillera 58 ⛰ C Ecuador
Realicó 65 B5 C Argentina
Rebecca, Lake 137 C5 ◎ Western Australia
Rebun-to 133 F1 *island* NE Japan
Recife 63 I5 E Brazil
Recklinghausen 101 A4 W Germany
Recogne 84 D8 SE Belgium
Reconquista 65 C4 C Argentina
Red Bluff 49 B5 California, W USA
Redcar 93 E2 N England, United Kingdom
Red Deer 33 G7 Alberta, SW Canada
Redding 49 B5 California, W USA
Redditch 93 D6 W England, United Kingdom
Redhill 95 F4 SE England, United Kingdom
Redon 97 B3 NW France
Red River 43 D1 ≈ Canada/USA
Red River 131 B2 ≈ China/Vietnam
Red River 44 G2 ≈ S USA
Red River 39 B6 ≈ Louisiana, S USA
Redruth 95 A6 SW England, United Kingdom
Red Sea 123 A4 *sea* Africa/Asia
Red Wing 43 F3 Minnesota, N USA
Reefton 139 C5 South Island, New Zealand
Ree, Lough 89 D4 ◎ C Ireland
Reese River 47 B5 ≈ Nevada, W USA
Refahiye 121 F3 C Turkey
Regensburg 101 D6 SE Germany
Regenstauf 101 D6 SE Germany
Reggane 70 D3 C Algeria
Reggio di Calabria 103 E8 SW Italy
Reggio nell'Emilia 103 C3 N Italy
Regina 33 H7 *province capital* Saskatchewan, S Canada
Rehoboth 76 B5 C Namibia
Rehovot 123 G6 C Israel
Reid 137 D5 Western Australia
Ré, Île de 97 B4 *island* W France
Reims 97 E2 N France
Reindeer Lake 33 H5 ◎ Manitoba/Saskatchewan, C Canada
Reinga, Cape 139 C1 *headland* North Island, New Zealand
Reinosa 99 D1 N Spain
Reliance 33 G5 Northwest Territories, C Canada
Rendsburg 101 C2 N Germany
Rengat 131 B6 Sumatra, W Indonesia
Rennell 141 E3 *island* S Solomon Islands
Rennes 97 B3 NW France
Reno 47 A5 Nevada, W USA
Republican River 47 G5 ≈ Kansas/Nebraska, C USA
Repulse Bay 33 I3 Northwest Terretories, N Canada
Resistencia 65 C4 NE Argentina
Reşiţa 109 A7 W Romania
Resolute 33 H2 Cornwallis Island, Nunavut, N Canada
Resolution Island 35 E1 *island* Nunavut, NE Canada
Réthymno 107 F7 SE Greece
Réunion 76 H6 *French* ◇ W Indian Ocean
Reus 99 G3 E Spain
Reutlingen 101 B7 S Germany
Reuver 84 E6 SE Netherlands
Revillagigedo, Islas 53 B5 *island group* W Mexico
Rexburg 47 D3 Idaho, NW USA
Reyes 65 A2 NW Bolivia
Rey, Isla del 55 H6 *island* Archipiélago de las Perlas, SE Panama
Reykjavík 83 A1 ● W Iceland
Reynosa 53 F3 C Mexico
Rezé 97 B3 NW France
Rhein *see* Rhine
Rheine 101 B4 NW Germany
Rheinisches Schiefergebirge 101 A5 ⛰ W Germany
Rhine 84 E4 ≈ W Europe
Rhinelander 40 B3 Wisconsin, N USA
Rho 103 B2 N Italy
Rhode Island 37 F5 ⬖ *state* NE USA
Rhodes 107 G6 *island* Dodecanese, Greece
Rhodope Mountains 107 E3 ⛰ Bulgaria/Greece
Rhône 97 E6 ≈ France/Switzerland
Rhossili 93 B7 S Wales, United Kingdom
Rhum 91 B4 *island* W Scotland, United Kingdom
Ribble 93 C4 ≈ NW England, United Kingdom
Ribeira 99 A2 NW Spain
Ribeirão Preto 63 G7 S Brazil
Riberalta 65 B1 N Bolivia
Rice Lake 40 A3 Wisconsin, N USA
Richard Toll 72 A3 N Senegal
Richfield 47 D6 Utah, W USA
Richland 49 C3 Washington, NW USA
Richmond 139 C5 South Island, New Zealand
Richmond 93 D3 N England, United Kingdom
Richmond 39 E2 Kentucky, S USA
Richmond 39 H2 *state capital* Virginia, NE USA
Richmond Range 139 C5 ⛰ South Island, New Zealand
Ricobayo, Embalse de 99 B2 ⊠ NW Spain
Ridgecrest 49 D8 California, W USA
Ridsdale 93 D2 N England, United Kingdom
Ried im Innkreis 101 D7 NW Austria
Riemst 84 D7 NE Belgium
Riesa 101 D4 E Germany
Riga 83 E6 ● C Latvia
Riga, Gulf of 83 E6 *gulf* Estonia/Latvia
Rigestan 125 E6 *desert region* S Afghanistan
Riggins 47 B3 Idaho, NW USA
Riihimäki 83 E5 S Finland
Rijeka 107 B1 NW Croatia
Rijn *see* Rhine
Rijssen 84 E4 E Netherlands
Rimah, Wadi ar 123 C4 *dry watercourse* C Saudi Arabia
Rimini 103 D3 N Italy
Rimouski 35 E4 Québec, SE Canada
Ringebu 83 B4 S Norway
Ringkøbing Fjord 83 A7 *fjord* W Denmark
Ringvassøya 83 C1 *island* N Norway
Ringwood 95 E5 S England, United Kingdom
Rio Branco 63 D5 W Brazil
Río Bravo 53 F3 C Mexico
Río Cuarto 65 B5 C Argentina
Rio de Janeiro 63 H7 SE Brazil
Río Gallegos 65 B9 S Argentina
Río Grande 65 B9 S Argentina
Rio Grande 63 F9 S Brazil
Río Grande 53 D4 C Mexico
Rio Grande 47 F7 ≈ Texas, SW USA
Rio Grande do Norte 63 I4 *state* E Brazil
Rio Grande do Sul 63 F8 *state* S Brazil
Ríohacha 63 C1 N Colombia
Río Lagartos 53 I4 SE Mexico
Riom 97 D5 C France
Río Verde 53 E4 C Mexico
Ripoll 99 G2 NE Spain
Ripon 93 D3 N England, United Kingdom
Rishiri-to 133 F1 *island* NE Japan
Ritidian Point 51 *headland* N Guam
Rivas 55 D5 SW Nicaragua
Rivera 65 C5 NE Uruguay
River Falls 40 A3 Wisconsin, N USA
Riverside 49 D9 California, W USA
Riverstown 89 C6 S Ireland
Riverton 139 A8 South Island, New Zealand
Riverton 47 E4 Wyoming, C USA
Riviera 44 G6 Texas, SW USA
Rivière-du-Loup 35 E5 Québec, SE Canada
Rivne 109 C4 NW Ukraine
Rivoli 103 A2 NW Italy
Riyadh 123 C4 ● C Saudi Arabia
Rize 121 F2 NE Turkey
Rkîz 72 A3 W Mauritania
Road Town 57 I4 ○ C British Virgin Islands
Roag, Loch 91 A2 *inlet* NW Scotland, United Kingdom
Roanne 97 E4 E France
Roanoke 39 G2 Virginia, NE USA
Roanoke River 39 H3 ≈ North Carolina/Virginia, SE USA
Roatán 55 D2 N Honduras
Robin Hood's Bay 93 E3 N England, United Kingdom
Robson, Mount 33 F6 ▲ British Columbia, SW Canada
Robstown 44 H5 Texas, SW USA
Roca Partida, Isla 53 B5 *island* W Mexico
Rocas, Atol das 63 I4 *island* E Brazil
Rochdale 93 D4 NW England, United Kingdom
Rochefort 84 D8 SE Belgium
Rochefort 97 B4 W France
Rochester 43 F4 Minnesota, N USA
Rochester 37 F3 New Hampshire, NE USA
Rochester 37 C3 New York, NE USA
Rockford 40 B5 Illinois, N USA
Rockhampton 137 H4 Queensland, E Australia
Rock Hill 39 G4 South Carolina, SE USA
Rock Island 40 B5 Illinois, N USA
Rock Sound 57 E2 Eleuthera Island, C Bahamas
Rock Springs 47 E4 Wyoming, C USA
Rocky Mount 39 H3 North Carolina, SE USA
Rocky Mountains 28 ⛰ Canada/USA
Roden 84 E2 NE Netherlands
Rodez 97 D6 S France
Rodos *see* Rhodes
Roermond 84 E6 SE Netherlands
Roeselare 84 B6 W Belgium
Rogers 39 B3 Arkansas, C USA
Roi Et 131 C3 E Thailand
Rokiškis 83 F7 NE Lithuania
Rokycany 105 B5 W Czech Republic
Rolla 43 F6 Missouri, C USA
Roma 137 G4 Queensland, E Australia
Roma *see* Rome
Roman 109 C6 NE Romania
Romania 109 B6 ◆ *republic* SE Europe
Rome 103 C5 ● C Italy
Rome 39 E4 Georgia, SE USA
Romford 95 G3 SE England, United Kingdom
Romney Marsh 95 G4 *physical region* SE England, United Kingdom
Romny 109 E4 NE Ukraine
Rømø 83 A7 *island* SW Denmark
Romsey 95 E4 S England, United Kingdom
Ronda 99 C6 S Spain
Rondônia 63 D5 *state* W Brazil
Rondonópolis 63 F6 W Brazil
Rønne 83 C7 E Denmark
Ronne Ice Shelf 142 B4 *ice shelf* Antarctica
Roosendaal 84 C5 S Netherlands
Roosevelt Island 142 C6 *island* Antarctica
Roraima 63 D3 *state* N Brazil
Roraima, Mount 63 D2 ▲ N South America
Røros 83 B4 S Norway
Rosa, Lake 57 E3 ◎ S Bahamas
Rosalia, Punta 141 C5 *headland* Easter Island, Chile
Rosario 65 C5 C Argentina
Rosario 65 C3 C Paraguay
Rosarito 53 A1 NW Mexico
Roscommon 89 C4 C Ireland
Roscommon 40 D4 Michigan, N USA
Roscrea 89 D5 C Ireland
Roseau 57 K5 ● SW Dominica
Roseburg 49 B4 Oregon, NW USA
Rosenberg 44 H4 Texas, SW USA
Rosengarten 101 C3 N Germany
Rosenheim 101 D7 S Germany
Roslavl' 111 A5 W Russian Federation
Rosmalen 84 D5 S Netherlands
Ross 139 B6 SW New Zealand
Rossano 103 E7 SW Italy
Ross Carbery 89 B7 S Ireland
Ross Ice Shelf 142 C5 *ice shelf* Antarctica
Rosslare 89 E6 SE Ireland
Rosslare Harbour 89 E6 SE Ireland
Rosso 72 A3 SW Mauritania
Ross-on-Wye 93 C6 W England, United Kingdom
Rossosh' 111 A7 W Russian Federation
Ross Sea 142 C6 *sea* Antarctica
Rostock 101 D2 NE Germany
Rostov-na-Donu 111 A7 SW Russian Federation
Roswell 44 E3 New Mexico, SW USA
Rother 95 F4 ≈ S England, United Kingdom
Rothera 142 A4 *UK research station* Antarctica
Rotherham 93 E4 N England, United Kingdom
Rothesay 91 C6 W Scotland, United Kingdom
Rotorua 139 D3 North Island, New Zealand
Rotorua, Lake 139 D3 ◎ NE New Zealand
Rotterdam 84 C4 SW Netherlands
Rottweil 101 B7 S Germany
Rotuma 141 I4 *island* NW Fiji
Roubaix 97 D1 N France
Rouen 97 D2 N France
Round Rock 44 G4 Texas, SW USA
Roundstone 89 B4 W Ireland
Roundwood 89 E5 E Ireland
Rousay 91 E1 *island* N Scotland, United Kingdom
Roussillon 97 D7 *cultural region* S France
Rouyn-Noranda 35 D5 Québec, SE Canada
Rovaniemi 83 E3 N Finland
Rovigo 103 C3 NE Italy
Rovuma, Rio 76 F4 ≈ Mozambique/Tanzania
Roxas City 131 F4 C Philippines
Royale, Isle 40 C1 *island* Michigan, N USA
Royal Leamington Spa 93 D6 C England, United Kingdom
Royal Tunbridge Wells 95 G4 SE England, United Kingdom
Royan 97 B4 W France
Royston 95 G3 E England, United Kingdom
Rožňava 105 E6 E Slovakia
Ruapehu, Mount 139 D4 ▲ North Island, New Zealand
Ruapuke Island 139 B8 *island* SW New Zealand
Ruatoria 139 E3 North Island, New Zealand
Ruawai 139 D2 North Island, New Zealand
Rubizhne 109 G4 E Ukraine
Ruby Mountains 47 C5 ⛰ Nevada, W USA
Rudnyy 118 C4 N Kazakhstan
Rufiji 75 D7 ≈ E Tanzania
Rufino 65 B5 C Argentina
Rugby 93 E6 C England, United Kingdom
Rugeley 93 D5 C England, United Kingdom
Rügen 101 D2 *cape* NE Germany
Ruhr Valley 101 A4 *industrial region* W Germany
Rukwa, Lake 75 C7 ◎ SE Tanzania
Rumbek 75 B4 S Sudan
Rum Cay 57 E2 *island* C Bahamas
Rumia 105 D1 N Poland
Runanga 139 C5 South Island, New Zealand
Runcorn 93 C4 C England, United Kingdom
Rundu 76 C5 NE Namibia
Ruoqiang 129 C3 NW China
Rupel 84 C6 ≈ N Belgium
Rupert, Rivière de 35 D4 ≈ Québec, C Canada
Ruse 107 F2 N Bulgaria
Rushden 95 F2 C England, United Kingdom
Rushmore, Mount 43 A4 ▲ South Dakota, N USA
Russellville 39 B3 Arkansas, C USA
Russian Federation 118 D4 ◆ *republic* Asia/Europe
Rust'avi 121 H2 SE Georgia
Ruston 39 B5 Louisiana, S USA
Rutland 37 E3 Vermont, NE USA
Rutland Water 93 E5 ◎ C England, United Kingdom
Rutög 129 A4 W China
Ruvuma 75 D7 ≈ Mozambique/Tanzania
Ruwenzori 75 B5 ⛰ Dem. Rep. Congo/Uganda
Ružomberok 105 E6 N Slovakia
Rwanda 75 B6 ◆ *republic* C Africa
Ryazan' 111 B6 W Russian Federation
Rybinsk 111 B5 W Russian Federation
Rybnik 105 D5 S Poland
Rye 95 G4 SE England, United Kingdom
Rye 93 E3 ≈ N England, United Kingdom
Ryki 105 F4 E Poland
Rypin 105 E3 C Poland
Rysy 105 E6 ▲ S Poland
Ryukyu Islands 133 A7 *island group* SW Japan
Rzeszów 105 F5 SE Poland
Rzhev 111 A5 W Russian Federation

S

Saale 101 D4 ≈ C Germany
Saalfeld 101 C5 C Germany
Saarbrücken 101 A6 SW Germany
Saaremaa 83 D6 *island* W Estonia
Saariselkä 83 E2 N Finland
Šabac 107 D2 W Serbia
Sabadell 99 G2 E Spain
Sabah 131 E5 *cultural region* Borneo, E Malaysia Asia
Sab'atayn, Ramlat as 123 C7 *desert* C Yemen
Sabaya 65 A3 S Bolivia
Saberi, Hamun-e 123 F3 ◎ Afghanistan/Iran
Sabha 70 F3 C Libya
Sabinas 53 E2 NE Mexico
Sabinas Hidalgo 53 E3 NE Mexico
Sabine Lake 39 A6 ◎ Louisiana/Texas, S USA
Sabine River 44 I4 ≈ Louisiana/Texas, SW USA
Sable, Cape 39 G9 *headland* Florida, SE USA
Sable, Île de 141 E5 *island* NW New Caledonia
Sable Island 35 G5 *island* Nova Scotia, SE Canada
Sabzevar 123 E1 NE Iran
Sachsen *see* Saxony
Sachs Harbour 33 F3 Banks Island, Northwest Territories, N Canada
Sacramento 49 B6 *state capital* California, W USA
Sacramento Mountains 44 D3 ⛰ New Mexico, SW USA
Sacramento River 49 B6 ≈ California, W USA
Sacramento Valley 49 B6 *valley* California, W USA
Sa'dah 123 C6 NW Yemen
Sado 133 F4 *island* C Japan
Säffle 83 C5 C Sweden
Safford 44 C3 Arizona, SW USA
Saffron Walden 95 G3 SE England, United Kingdom
Safi 70 B2 W Morocco
Safid Kuh, Selseleh-ye 125 D5 ⛰ W Afghanistan
Saga 133 D7 Kyūshū, SW Japan
Sagaing 131 A2 C Myanmar (Burma)
Sagami-nada 133 G6 *inlet* SW Japan
Saganaga Lake 43 F1 ◎ Minnesota, N USA
Sagar 127 E4 C India
Saginaw 40 E4 Michigan, N USA
Saginaw Bay 40 E4 *lake bay* Michigan, N USA
Sagua la Grande 57 C2 C Cuba
Sagunt *see* Sagunto
Sagunto 99 F4 E Spain
Sahara 72 D2 *desert* Libya/Algeria
Saharan Atlas 70 D2 ⛰ Algeria/Morocco
Sahel 72 E3 *physical region* C Africa
Sahiwal 127 D2 E Pakistan
Saidpur 127 F3 NW Bangladesh
Saimaa 83 F4 ◎ SE Finland
St Albans 95 F3 E England, United Kingdom
Saint Albans 39 F2 West Virginia, NE USA
St Aldhelm's Head 95 E5 *headland* S England, United Kingdom
St Andrews 91 E5 E Scotland, United Kingdom
St Anne 95 H5 Alderney, Channel Islands
St. Anthony 35 G3 Newfoundland, SE Canada
Saint Augustine 39 G6 Florida, SE USA
St Austell 95 B5 SW England, United Kingdom
St Austell Bay 95 B6 *bay* SW England, United Kingdom
St-Barthélemy 57 J4 *island* N Guadeloupe
St Bees Head 93 B3 *headland* NW England, United Kingdom
St-Brieuc 97 B2 NW France
St. Catharines 35 D6 Ontario, S Canada
St Catherine's Point 95 E5 *headland* S England, United Kingdom
St-Chamond 97 E5 E France
Saint Clair, Lake 37 A4 ◎ Canada/USA
St-Claude 97 E4 E France
Saint Cloud 43 E3 Minnesota, N USA
St Croix 51 *island* S Virgin Islands (US)
Saint Croix River 40 A3 ≈ Minnesota/Wisconsin, N USA
St David's 93 A7 SW Wales, United Kingdom
St-Dié 97 F3 NE France
St-Egrève 97 E5 E France
Saintes 97 B4 W France
St-Étienne 97 E5 E France
St-Flour 97 D5 C France
St-Gaudens 97 C6 S France
Saint George 137 G4 Queensland, E Australia
Saint George 47 C6 Utah, W USA
St. George's 57 K7 ● SW Grenada
St-Georges 35 E5 Québec, SE Canada
St George's Channel 89 F6 *channel* Ireland/Wales, United Kingdom
Saint Helena 26 *UK* ◇ C Atlantic Ocean
St. Helena Bay 76 B7 *bay* SW South Africa
St Helens 93 C4 NW England, United Kingdom
Saint Helens, Mount 49 B2 ⋀ Washington, NW USA
St Helier 95 H6 ○ S Jersey, Channel Islands
Saint Ignace 40 D3 Michigan, N USA
St Ives 95 A6 E England, United Kingdom
St Ives 95 B3 SW England, United Kingdom
St-Jean, Lac 35 E4 ◎ Québec, SE Canada
St. John 35 F5 New Brunswick, SE Canada
St John 95 H6 N Jersey
St John 51 *island* Virgin Islands (US)
Saint John River 37 G1 ≈ Canada/USA
St John's 57 J4 ● Antigua, Antigua and Barbuda
St. John's 35 H4 Newfoundland, E Canada
Saint Johns 44 C2 Arizona, SW USA
St John's Point 89 C2 *headland* N Ireland
Saint Joseph 43 E6 Missouri, C USA
St Julian's 112 B6 N Malta
Saint Kitts and Nevis 57 I5 ◆ *commonwealth republic* E West Indies
St. Lawrence, Gulf of 35 F4 *gulf* NW Atlantic Ocean
Saint Lawrence Island 50 C1 *island* Alaska, USA
Saint Lawrence River 37 D2 ≈ Canada/USA
St. Lawrence Seaway 35 F4 *seaway* Canada/USA North America Gulf of St.Lawrence N Atlantic Ocean
St-Lô 97 C2 N France
St-Louis 97 F3 NE France
Saint Louis 72 A3 NW Senegal
Saint Louis 43 G6 Missouri, C USA
St Lucia 57 J6 ◆ *commonwealth republic* SE West Indies
St. Lucia Channel 57 K6 *channel* Martinique/Saint Lucia North America Atlantic Ocean
St Magnus Bay 91 A6 *bay* N Scotland, United Kingdom
St-Malo 97 B2 NW France
St-Malo, Golfe de 97 B2 *gulf* NW France
St Margaret's Hope 91 E1 NE Scotland, United Kingdom
St-Martin 57 J4 *island* N Guadeloupe
St Mary 95 H6 Jersey, Channel Islands
St. Matthias Group 141 C1 *island group* NE Papua New Guinea
St. Moritz 101 C8 SE Switzerland
St-Nazaire 97 B3 NW France
St Neots 95 F2 E England, United Kingdom
St-Omer 97 D1 N France
Saint Paul 43 E3 *state capital* Minnesota, N USA
St Peter Port 95 G6 ○ C Guernsey, Channel Islands
Saint Petersburg 111 A4 NW Russian Federation
Saint Petersburg 39 F7 Florida, SE USA
St-Pierre and Miquelon 35 G4 *French* ◇ NE North America
St-Quentin 97 D2 N France
St Thomas 51 *island* Virgin Islands (US)
Saint Vincent 57 J6 *island* N Saint Vincent and the Grenadines
Saint Vincent and the Grenadines 57 I6 ◆ *commonwealth republic* SE West Indies
Saint Vincent Passage 57 K6 *passage* Saint Lucia/Saint Vincent and the Grenadines
Sajama, Nevado 65 A2 ▲ W Bolivia
Sajószentpéter 105 F7 NE Hungary
Sakakawea, Lake 43 B2 ⊠ North Dakota, N USA
Sakata 133 F4 C Japan
Sakhalin 118 I4 *island* SE Russian Federation
Saki 121 I2 NW Azerbaijan
Sakishima-shoto 133 A8 *island group* SW Japan
Sala 83 C5 C Sweden
Sala Consilina 103 E6 S Italy
Salado, Río 65 B4 ≈ E Argentina
Salado, Río 65 B5 ≈ C Argentina
Salalah 123 E6 SW Oman
Salamá 55 B3 C Guatemala
Salamanca 65 A5 C Chile
Salamanca 99 C3 NW Spain
Salang Tunnel 125 F4 *tunnel* C Afghanistan Asia
Salantai 83 E7 NW Lithuania
Salavat 111 D6 W Russian Federation
Šalčininkai 83 F7 SE Lithuania
Salcombe 95 C6 SW England, United Kingdom
Sale 137 G6 Victoria, SE Australia
Salé 70 C1 NW Morocco
Salekhard 118 D3 N Russian Federation
Salelologa 141 A5 C Samoa
Salem 127 D7 SE India
Salem 49 B3 *state capital* Oregon, NW USA
Salerno 103 D6 S Italy
Salerno, Gulf of 103 D6 *gulf* S Italy
Salford 93 D4 NW England, United Kingdom
Salihorsk 109 C3 S Belarus
Salina 43 D6 Kansas, C USA
Salina 47 D6 Utah, W USA
Salina Cruz 53 G6 SE Mexico
Salinas 49 B7 California, W USA
Salisbury 95 E4 S England, United Kingdom
Salisbury Plain 95 E4 *plain* S England, United Kingdom
Salmon 47 C3 Idaho, NW USA
Salmon River 47 B3 ≈ Idaho, NW USA
Salmon River Mountains 47 B3 ⛰ Idaho, NW USA
Salo 83 E5 SW Finland
Salon-de-Provence 97 E6 SE France
Salonica 107 E4 N Greece
Sal'sk 111 A8 SW Russian Federation
Salta 65 B4 NW Argentina
Saltash 95 B5 SW England, United Kingdom
Saltillo 53 E3 NE Mexico
Salt Lake City 47 D5 *state capital* Utah, W USA
Salto 65 C5 N Uruguay
Salton Sea 49 D9 ◎ California, W USA
Salvador 63 H6 E Brazil
Salween 131 B2 ≈ SE Asia
Salyan 127 E3 W Nepal
Salzburg 101 D7 N Austria

⬖ Administrative region ◆ Country ● Country capital ◇ Dependent territory ○ Dependent territory capital ⛰ Mountain range ▲ Mountain ⋀ Volcano ≈ River ◎ Lake ⊠ Reservoir

◆ Administrative region   ◆ Country   ◆ Country capital   ◇ Dependent territory   ○ Dependent territory capital   ▲ Mountain range   ▲ Mountain   ☞ Volcano   ☞ River   ⊚ Lake   ⊡ Reservoir

173

WAUSAU

Turnhout 84 D6 N Belgium
Turnov 105 B5 N Czech Republic
Turpan 129 C2 NW China
Turriff 91 F3 NE Scotland, United Kingdom
Tuscaloosa 39 D5 Alabama, S USA
Tuscany 103 C4 *cultural region* C Italy Europe
Tuticorin 127 D7 SE India
Tutuila 51 *island* W American Samoa
Tuvalu 141 H2 ◆ *commonwealth republic* SW Pacific Ocean
Tuwayq, Jabal 123 C5 ⛰ C Saudi Arabia
Tuxpan 53 E5 C Mexico
Tuxpan 53 D4 C Mexico
Tuxpán 53 F4 E Mexico
Tuxtepec 53 G5 S Mexico
Tuxtla 53 H5 SE Mexico
Tuy Hoa 131 D4 S Vietnam
Tuzla 107 C2 NE Bosnia and Herzegovina
Tuz, Lake 121 C3 ◎ C Turkey
Tver' 111 A5 W Russian Federation
Tweed 91 E6 ≈ England/Scotland, United Kingdom
Tweedmouth 93 D1 N England, United Kingdom
Twin Falls 47 C4 Idaho, NW USA
Tychy 105 E5 S Poland
Tyler 44 H3 Texas, SW USA
Tympáki 107 F7 Crete, Greece
Tynda 118 G5 SE Russian Federation
Tyne 91 F7 ≈ N England, United Kingdom
Tynemouth 93 D2 NE England, United Kingdom
Tyrrhenian Sea 103 B6 *sea* N Mediterranean Sea
Tyumen' 118 C4 C Russian Federation
Tyup 125 I2 NE Kyrgyzstan
Tywi 93 B6 ≈ S Wales, United Kingdom
Tywyn 93 B6 W Wales, United Kingdom
Tziá 107 F6 *island* Cyclades, SE Greece

U

Ubangi *see* Oubangui
Ube 133 D7 SW Japan
Ubeda 99 D5 S Spain
Uberaba 63 G7 SE Brazil
Uberlândia 63 F7 SE Brazil
Ubon Ratchathani 131 C3 E Thailand
Ubrique 99 C6 SW Spain
Ucayali, Río 63 B4 ≈ C Peru
Uchiura-wan 133 F2 *bay* NW Pacific Ocean
Uchquduq 125 E2 N Uzbekistan
Uckfield 95 G4 SE England, United Kingdom
Uçtagan Gumy 125 C2 *desert* NW Turkmenistan
Udaipur 127 D3 N India
Uddevalla 83 B6 S Sweden
Udine 103 D2 NE Italy
Udon Thani 131 B3 N Thailand
Udupi 127 D6 SW India
Uele 76 C1 ≈ NE Dem. Rep. Congo
Uelzen 101 C3 N Germany
Ufa 111 D6 W Russian Federation
Uganda 75 C5 ◆ *republic* E Africa
Uglovka 111 A4 W Russian Federation
Uig 91 B3 N Scotland, United Kingdom
Uíge 76 B3 NW Angola
Uinta Mountains 47 D5 ⛰ Utah, W USA
Uitenhage 76 D7 S South Africa
Uithoorn 84 D4 C Netherlands
Ukhta 111 D4 NW Russian Federation
Ukiah 49 B6 California, W USA
Ukmergė 83 E7 C Lithuania
Ukraine 109 C4 ◆ *republic* SE Europe
Ulaanbaatar *see* Ulan Bator
Ulaangom 129 D1 NW Mongolia
Ulan Bator 129 E2 ● C Mongolia
Ulanhot 129 G2 N China
Ulan-Ude 118 F5 S Russian Federation
Ulft 84 E4 E Netherlands
Ullapool 91 C3 N Scotland, United Kingdom
Ullswater 93 C3 ◎ NW England, United Kingdom
Ulm 101 C7 S Germany
Ulsan 133 C6 SE South Korea
Ulsta 91 B6 NE Scotland, United Kingdom
Ulster 89 D2 *cultural region* N Ireland
Ulungur Hu 129 C2 ◎ NW China
Uluru 137 D4 *rocky outcrop* Northern Territory, C Australia
Ulverston 93 C4 NW England, United Kingdom
Ul'yanovsk 111 C6 W Russian Federation
Umán 53 H4 SE Mexico
Uman' 109 D5 C Ukraine
Umbro-Marchigiano, Appennino 103 D4 ⛰ C Italy
Umeå 83 D4 N Sweden
Umeälven 83 D3 ≈ N Sweden
Umiat 50 E1 Alaska, USA
Umm Buru 75 A2 W Sudan
Umm Ruwaba 75 C3 C Sudan
Umnak Island 50 B2 *island* Aleutian Islands, Alaska, USA
Umtata 76 D7 SE South Africa
Una 107 B1 ≈ Bosnia and Herzegovina/Croatia
Unac 107 B2 ≈ W Bosnia and Herzegovina
Unalaska Island 50 B3 *island* Aleutian Islands, Alaska, USA
Uncía 65 B2 C Bolivia
Uncompahgre Peak 47 E6 ▲ Colorado, C USA
Ungava Bay 35 E2 *bay* Québec, E Canada
Ungava Peninsula 35 D1 *peninsula* Québec, SE Canada
Üngüz Angyrsyndaky Garagum 125 C3 *desert* N Turkmenistan
Unimak Island 50 B3 *island* Aleutian Islands, Alaska, USA
Union City 39 D3 Tennessee, S USA
Uniontown 37 B5 Pennsylvania, NE USA
United Arab Emirates 123 E4 ◆ *federation* SW Asia
United Kingdom 87 D5 ◆ *monarchy* NW Europe
United States of America 29 ◆ *federal republic* North America
Unst 91 B5 *island* NE Scotland, United Kingdom
Ünye 121 E2 W Turkey
Upala 55 E5 NW Costa Rica
Upemba, Lac 76 D3 ◎ SE Dem. Rep. Congo
Upolu 141 B5 *island* SE Samoa
Upper Darby 37 D5 Pennsylvania, NE USA
Upper Klamath Lake 49 B4 ◎ Oregon, NW USA
Upper Lough Erne 89 D3 ◎ Ireland/United Kingdom
Upper Red Lake 43 E2 ◎ Minnesota, N USA
Uppsala 83 D5 C Sweden
Ural 118 B4 ≈ Kazakhstan/Russian Federation
Ural Mountains 118 C3 ⛰ Kazakhstan/Russian Federation
Ural'sk 118 B4 NW Kazakhstan
Ural'skiye Gory *see* Ural Mountains
Urbandale 43 E5 Iowa, C USA
Ure 93 D3 ≈ N England, United Kingdom
Uren' 111 C5 W Russian Federation
Urganch 125 D2 W Uzbekistan
Urgut 125 F3 C Uzbekistan
Urlingford 89 D5 SE Ireland
Urmia, Lake 123 C1 ◎ NW Iran
Uroteppa 125 F3 NW Tajikistan
Uruapan 53 E5 SW Mexico
Uruguay 65 C5 ◆ *republic* E South America
Uruguay 65 C5 ≈ E South America
Ürümqi 129 C2 NW China
Urup, Ostrov 118 I4 *island* Kurile Islands, Russian Federation
Uruzgan 125 F5 C Afghanistan
Usa 111 E3 ≈ NW Russian Federation
Uşak 120 B3 W Turkey
Ushuaia 65 B9 S Argentina
Usinsk 111 D3 NW Russian Federation
Usk 93 B6 ≈ SE Wales, United Kingdom
Usol'ye-Sibirskoye 118 F5 C Russian Federation
Ussel 97 D5 C France
Ussuriysk 118 H6 SE Russian Federation
Ustica 103 C7 Sicily, Italy
Ust'-Ilimsk 118 F4 C Russian Federation
Ústí nad Labem 105 B5 NW Czech Republic
Ustka 105 C1 N Poland
Ust'-Kamchatsk 118 I3 E Russian Federation
Ust'-Kamenogorsk 118 D5 E Kazakhstan
Ust'-Kut 118 F5 C Russian Federation
Ustyurt Plateau 125 C1 *plateau* Kazakhstan/Uzbekistan
Usulután 55 C4 SE El Salvador
Usumacinta, Río 55 A2 ≈ Guatemala/Mexico
Utah 47 C5 ⬖ *state* W USA
Utah Lake 47 C5 ◎ Utah, W USA
Utica 37 D3 New York, NE USA
Utrecht 84 D4 C Netherlands
Utsunomiya 133 G5 S Japan
Uttaranchal 127 E2 *state* N India
Uttar Pradesh 127 E3 *state* N India
Uttoxeter 93 D5 C England, United Kingdom
Utupua 141 G3 *island* E Solomon Islands
Uulu 83 E6 SW Estonia
Uvalde 44 G5 Texas, SW USA
Uvs Nuur 129 D1 ◎ Mongolia/Russian Federation
'Uwaynāt, Jabal al 75 B1 ▲ Libya/Sudan
Uyo 72 F5 S Nigeria
Uyuni 65 B3 W Bolivia
Uzbekistan 125 D2 ◆ *republic* C Asia
Uzhhorod 109 B5 W Ukraine

V

Vaal 76 D6 ≈ C South Africa
Vaals 84 E7 SE Netherlands
Vaasa 83 D4 W Finland
Vaassen 84 E4 E Netherlands
Vác 105 E7 N Hungary
Vadodara 127 D4 W India
Vaduz 101 C8 ● W Liechtenstein
Váh 105 D6 ≈ W Slovakia
Vaitogi 51 W American Samoa
Vaitupu 141 J2 *atoll* C Tuvalu
Valdai Hills 111 A5 *hill range* W Russian Federation
Valday 111 A4 W Russian Federation
Valdecañas, Embalse de 99 C4 ⊠ W Spain
Valdepeñas 99 D4 C Spain
Valdés, Península 65 B7 *peninsula* SE Argentina
Valdez 50 E3 Alaska, USA
Valdivia 65 A6 C Chile
Val-d'Or 35 D5 Québec, SE Canada
Valdosta 39 F6 Georgia, SE USA
Valence 97 E5 E France
Valencia 99 F4 E Spain
Valencia 63 D1 N Venezuela
Valencia, Gulf of 99 F4 *gulf* E Spain
Valencia Island 89 A6 *island* SW Ireland
Valenciennes 97 E1 N France
Valentine 43 B4 Nebraska, C USA
Valjevo 107 D2 W Serbia
Valkenswaard 84 D5 S Netherlands
Valladolid 53 I4 SE Mexico
Valladolid 99 D2 NW Spain
Vall d'Uxó 99 F4 E Spain
Vallejo 49 B6 California, W USA
Vallenar 65 A4 N Chile
Valletta 112 B6 ● E Malta
Valley City 43 C2 North Dakota, N USA
Válljohka 83 E1 N Norway
Valls 99 G3 NE Spain
Valparaíso 65 A5 C Chile
Valparaiso 40 C5 Indiana, N USA
Valverde del Camino 99 C5 SW Spain
Van 121 G3 E Turkey
Vanadzor 121 H2 N Armenia
Van Buren 37 G1 Maine, NE USA
Vanceboro 37 H2 Maine, NE USA
Vancouver 33 F7 British Columbia, SW Canada
Vancouver 49 B3 Washington, NW USA
Vancouver Island 33 E7 *island* British Columbia, SW Canada
Van Diemen Gulf 137 D1 *gulf* Northern Territory, N Australia
Vänern 83 C6 ◎ S Sweden
Vangaindrano 76 G6 SE Madagascar
Van Gölü *see* Van, Lake
Van Horn 44 E4 Texas, SW USA
Vanikolo 141 G3 *island* Santa Cruz Islands, E Solomon Islands
Vanimo 141 A1 NW Papua New Guinea
Van, Lake 121 G4 *salt lake* E Turkey
Vannes 97 B3 NW France
Vantaa 83 E5 S Finland
Vanua Lava 141 G4 *island* Banks Islands, N Vanuatu
Vanua Levu 141 J5 *island* N Fiji
Vanuatu 141 E4 ◆ *republic* SW Pacific Ocean
Van Wert 40 D6 Ohio, N USA
Vao 141 G6 S New Caledonia
Varanasi 127 F3 N India
Varangerfjorden 83 F1 *fjord* N Norway
Varangerhalvøya 83 E1 *peninsula* N Norway
Varaždin 107 B1 N Croatia
Varberg 83 B6 S Sweden
Vardar 107 E4 ≈ FYR Macedonia/Greece
Varde 83 B7 W Denmark
Varese 103 B2 N Italy
Vârful Moldoveanu 109 B6 ▲ C Romania
Varkaus 83 F4 C Finland
Varna 107 G2 E Bulgaria
Varnenski Zaliv 120 A1 *bay* E Bulgaria
Vasa *see* Vaasa
Vasilikí 107 D5 Lefkáda, Ionian Islands, W Greece
Vaslui 109 D6 C Romania
Västerås 83 C5 C Sweden
Vatican City 103 C5 ◆ *papal state* S Europe
Vatnajökull 83 A1 *glacier* SE Iceland
Vättern 83 C6 ◎ S Sweden
Vaughn 44 D2 New Mexico, SW USA
Vaupés, Río 63 C3 ≈ Brazil/Colombia
Vavuniya 127 E7 N Sri Lanka
Vawkavysk 109 B3 W Belarus
Växjö 83 C6 S Sweden
Vaygach, Ostrov 111 E2 *island* NW Russian Federation
Veendam 84 F2 NE Netherlands
Veenendaal 84 D4 C Netherlands
Vega 83 C3 *island* C Norway
Veisiejai 83 E7 S Lithuania
Vejer de la Frontera 99 C6 SW Spain
Veldhoven 84 D5 S Netherlands
Velebit 107 B2 ⛰ C Croatia
Velenje 101 E8 N Slovenia
Velika Morava 107 D2 ≈ C Serbia
Velikiye Luki 111 A5 W Russian Federation
Velikiy Novgorod 111 A4 W Russian Federation
Veliko Turnovo 107 F3 N Bulgaria
Vel'ký Krtíš 105 E7 C Slovakia
Vella Lavella 141 D2 *island* New Georgia Islands, NW Solomon Islands
Vellore 127 E6 SE India
Velsen-Noord 84 C3 W Netherlands
Vel'sk 111 C4 NW Russian Federation
Vendôme 97 C3 C France
Venezia *see* Venice
Venezuela 63 C2 ◆ *republic* N South America
Venezuela, Gulf of 63 C1 *gulf* NW Venezuela
Venice 103 D2 NE Italy
Venice 39 C7 Louisiana, S USA
Venice, Gulf of 103 D3 *gulf* N Adriatic Sea
Venlo 84 E5 SE Netherlands
Venta 83 E6 ≈ Latvia/Lithuania
Vent, Îles du 141 A6 *island group* Archipel de la Société, W French Polynesia
Ventimiglia 103 A3 NW Italy
Ventspils 83 E6 NW Latvia
Vera 65 C4 C Argentina
Veracruz 53 F5 E Mexico
Vercelli 103 B2 NW Italy
Verdalsøra 83 C4 C Norway
Verde, Costa 99 D1 *coastal region* N Spain
Verden 101 B3 NW Germany
Verkhoyanskiy Khrebet 118 G3 ⛰ NE Russian Federation
Vermillion 43 D4 South Dakota, N USA
Vermont 37 E3 ⬖ *state* NE USA
Vernal 47 D5 Utah, W USA
Vernon 44 G2 Texas, SW USA
Verona 103 C2 NE Italy
Versailles 97 D2 N France
Verviers 84 E7 E Belgium
Vesdre 84 E7 ≈ E Belgium
Vesoul 97 F3 E France
Vesterålen 83 C2 *island* NW Norway
Vestfjorden 83 C2 *fjord* C Norway
Vestmannaeyjar 83 A2 S Iceland
Vesuvius 103 D6 🌋 S Italy
Veszprém 105 D8 W Hungary
Veurne 84 A6 W Belgium
Viacha 65 A2 W Bolivia
Viana do Castelo 99 B2 NW Portugal
Vianen 84 D4 C Netherlands
Viareggio 103 C4 C Italy
Viborg 83 B6 NW Denmark
Vic 99 G2 NE Spain
Vicenza 103 C2 NE Italy
Vichy 97 D4 C France
Vicksburg 39 C5 Mississippi, S USA
Victoria 67 ● SW Seychelles
Victoria 33 E7 *province capital* Vancouver Island, British Columbia, SW Canada
Victoria 112 A6 NW Malta
Victoria 44 H5 Texas, SW USA
Victoria 137 F6 ⬖ *state* SE Australia
Victoria Falls 76 C5 *waterfall* Zambia/Zimbabwe
Victoria Island 33 G3 *island* Northwest Territories/Nunavut, NW Canada
Victoria, Lake 75 C5 ◎ Kenya/Tanzania/Uganda
Victoria Land 142 D6 *physical region* Antarctica
Victoria, Mount 141 I5 ▲ Viti Levu, W Fiji
Victoria River 137 D2 ≈ Western Australia
Victorville 49 D8 California, W USA
Vidalia 39 F5 Georgia, SE USA
Vidin 107 E2 NW Bulgaria
Viedma 65 B7 E Argentina
Vienna 101 F7 ● NE Austria
Vienne 97 E5 E France
Vienne 97 C4 ≈ W France
Vientiane 131 B3 ● C Laos
Vieques 51 E Puerto Rico
Vieques, Isla de 51 *island* E Puerto Rico
Vierzon 97 D3 C France
Vietnam 131 C4 ◆ *republic* SE Asia
Vieux Fort 57 K6 S Saint Lucia
Vigo 99 B2 NW Spain
Vijayawada 127 E5 SE India
Vila do Conde 99 B2 NW Portugal
Vilafranca del Penedès 99 G2 NE Spain
Viļaka 83 F6 NE Latvia
Vilalba 99 B1 NW Spain
Vila Nova de Gaia 99 B3 NW Portugal
Vila Real 99 B3 N Portugal
Vilhelmina 83 C3 N Sweden
Viliya 109 C2 ≈ W Belarus
Villa Acuña 53 E2 NE Mexico
Villa Bella 65 B1 N Bolivia
Villacarrillo 99 E5 S Spain
Villach 101 E8 S Austria
Villacidro 103 A6 Sardinia, Italy
Villafranca de los Barros 99 C4 W Spain
Villahermosa 53 H5 SE Mexico
Villajoyosa 99 F4 E Spain
Villa María 65 B5 C Argentina
Villa Martín 65 A3 SW Bolivia
Villanueva 53 E4 C Mexico
Villanueva de la Serena 99 C4 W Spain
Villanueva de los Infantes 99 E4 C Spain
Villarrica 65 C4 SE Paraguay
Villavicencio 63 C2 C Colombia
Villaviciosa 99 C1 N Spain
Villazón 65 B3 S Bolivia
Villena 99 F4 E Spain
Villeurbanne 97 E5 E France
Villingen-Schwenningen 101 B7 S Germany
Vilnius 83 F7 ● SE Lithuania
Vilvoorde 84 C6 C Belgium
Vilyuy 118 G4 ≈ NE Russian Federation
Viña del Mar 65 A5 C Chile
Vinaròs 99 F3 E Spain
Vincennes 40 C7 Indiana, N USA
Vindhya Range 127 D4 ⛰ N India
Vineland 37 D6 New Jersey, NE USA
Vinh 131 C3 N Vietnam
Vinita 43 E7 Oklahoma, C USA
Vinnytsya 109 D5 C Ukraine
Vinson Massif 142 A4 ▲ Antarctica
Viranşehir 121 F4 SE Turkey
Virginia 89 D3 N Ireland
Virginia 43 E2 Minnesota, N USA
Virginia 39 H2 ⬖ *state* NE USA
Virginia Beach 39 I2 Virginia, NE USA
Virgin Islands (US) 51 *US* ◇ E West Indies
Virgin Passage 51 *passage* Puerto Rico/Virgin Islands (US)
Virovitica 107 C1 NE Croatia
Virton 84 D9 SE Belgium
Vis 107 B3 *island* S Croatia
Visakhapatnam 127 F5 SE India
Visalia 49 C7 California, W USA
Visby 83 D6 SE Sweden
Viscount Melville Sound 33 G2 *sound* Northwest Territories, N Canada
Visé 84 E7 E Belgium
Viseu 99 B3 N Portugal
Vistula 105 E2 ≈ C Poland
Vistula Lagoon 105 E1 *lagoon* Poland/Russian Federation
Viterbo 103 C4 C Italy
Vitiaz Strait 141 B2 *strait* NE Papua New Guinea
Viti Levu 141 I5 *island* W Fiji
Vitim 118 G5 ≈ C Russian Federation
Vitória 63 H7 SE Brazil
Vitória da Conquista 63 H6 E Brazil
Vitoria-Gasteiz 99 E2 N Spain
Vitré 97 B3 NW France
Vitsyebsk 109 D2 NE Belarus
Vittoria 103 D8 Sicily, Italy
Vizianagaram 127 F5 E India
Vlaardingen 84 C4 SW Netherlands
Vladikavkaz 111 B9 SW Russian Federation
Vladimir 111 B5 W Russian Federation
Vladivostok 118 H6 SE Russian Federation
Vlagtwedde 84 F2 NE Netherlands
Vlieland 84 C2 *island* Waddeneilanden, N Netherlands
Vlijmen 84 D5 S Netherlands
Vlissingen 84 B5 SW Netherlands
Vlorë 107 C4 SW Albania
Vöcklabruck 101 E7 NW Austria
Vohimena, Tanjona 76 F6 *headland* S Madagascar
Voiron 97 E5 E France
Vojvodina 107 D1 *cultural region* N Serbia
Volga 111 B7 ≈ NW Russian Federation
Volga Uplands 111 B6 ⛰ W Russian Federation
Volgodonsk 111 A7 SW Russian Federation
Volgograd 111 B7 SW Russian Federation
Volkhov 111 A4 NW Russian Federation
Volnovakha 109 G5 SE Ukraine
Volodymyr-Volyns'kyy 109 B4 NW Ukraine
Vologda 111 B4 W Russian Federation
Vólos 107 E5 C Greece
Vol'sk 111 C6 W Russian Federation
Volta 72 D5 ≈ SE Ghana
Volta, Lake 72 D5 ⊠ SE Ghana
Volturno 103 D5 ≈ S Italy
Volzhskiy 111 B7 SW Russian Federation
Voorst 84 E4 E Netherlands
Vorderrhein 101 B8 ≈ SE Switzerland
Vorkuta 111 E3 NW Russian Federation
Voronezh 111 A6 W Russian Federation
Võrtsjärv 83 E6 ◎ SE Estonia
Võru 83 F6 SE Estonia
Vosges 97 F3 ⛰ NE France
Vostok 142 D5 *Russian research station* Antarctica
Vranov nad Topľou 105 F6 E Slovakia
Vratsa 107 E3 NW Bulgaria
Vrbas 107 C1 NW Serbia
Vrbas 107 C2 ≈ N Bosnia and Herzegovina
Vršac 107 D1 NE Serbia
Vsetín 105 D6 E Czech Republic
Vukovar 107 C1 E Croatia
Vulcano, Isola 103 D7 *island* Aeolian Islands, Italy
Vung Tau 131 C4 S Vietnam
Vunisea 141 J5 SE Fiji
Vyatka 111 C5 ≈ NW Russian Federation
Vyborg 111 A4 NW Russian Federation

W

Wa 72 D4 NW Ghana
Waal 84 D4 ≈ S Netherlands
Waala 141 F6 W New Caledonia
Wabash 40 D6 Indiana, N USA
Wabash River 40 D6 ≈ N USA
Waco 44 H4 Texas, SW USA
Waddan 70 G3 NW Libya
Waddeneilanden *see* West Frisian Islands
Waddenzee 84 D2 *sea* SE North Sea
Waddington, Mount 33 E7 ▲ British Columbia, SW Canada
Wadebridge 95 B5 SW England, United Kingdom
Wadi Halfa 75 C1 N Sudan
Wad Medani 75 C3 C Sudan
Waflia 131 G7 E Indonesia
Wagga Wagga 137 G6 New South Wales, SE Australia
Wagin 137 B5 Western Australia
Wah 127 C1 NE Pakistan
Wahai 131 G7 E Indonesia
Wahiawā 51 B1 O'ahu, Hawai'i, USA
Wahībah Sands 123 E5 *desert* N Oman
Wahpeton 43 D2 North Dakota, N USA
Waiau 139 A8 ≈ South Island, New Zealand
Waigeo, Pulau 131 G6 *island* Maluku, E Indonesia
Waikaremoana, Lake 139 E3 ◎ North Island, New Zealand
Wailuku 51 C2 Maui, Hawai'i, USA
Waimate 139 B7 South Island, New Zealand
Waimea 51 D2 Hawai'i, USA
Waiouru 139 D4 North Island, New Zealand
Waipara 139 C6 South Island, New Zealand
Waipawa 139 D4 North Island, New Zealand
Waipukurau 139 D4 North Island, New Zealand
Wairau 139 C5 ≈ South Island, New Zealand
Wairoa 139 E4 North Island, New Zealand
Wairoa 139 D2 ≈ North Island, New Zealand
Waitaki 139 B7 ≈ South Island, New Zealand
Waitara 139 C4 North Island, New Zealand
Waiuku 139 D3 North Island, New Zealand
Wakasa-wan 133 E6 *bay* C Japan
Wakatipu, Lake 139 B7 ◎ South Island, New Zealand
Wakayama 133 E6 SW Japan
Wakefield 93 D4 N England, United Kingdom
Wakkanai 133 F1 NE Japan
Wałbrzych 105 C5 SW Poland
Walcourt 84 C8 S Belgium
Wałcz 105 C2 NW Poland
Wales 50 D1 Alaska, USA
Wales 93 B6 ⬖ *national region* Wales, United Kingdom
Walgett 137 G5 New South Wales, SE Australia
Walker Lake 47 A6 ◎ Nevada, W USA
Wallace 47 B2 Idaho, NW USA
Wallachia 109 B7 *cultural region* S Romania
Wallasey 93 C4 NW England, United Kingdom
Walla Walla 49 C3 Washington, NW USA
Wallis and Futuna 141 I4 *French* ◇ C Pacific Ocean
Wallis, Îles 141 K4 *island group* N Wallis and Futuna
Walney, Isle of 93 C3 *island* NW England, United Kingdom
Walnut Ridge 39 C3 Arkansas, C USA
Walsall 93 D6 C England, United Kingdom
Walvis Bay 76 B5 NW Namibia
Wanaka 139 B7 South Island, New Zealand
Wanaka, Lake 139 A7 ◎ South Island, New Zealand
Wandel Sea 143 C5 *sea* Arctic Ocean
Wanganui 139 D4 North Island, New Zealand
Wangaratta 137 G6 Victoria, SE Australia
Wanlaweyn 75 F5 SW Somalia
Wanzhou 129 F4 C China
Warangal 127 E5 C India
Warburg 101 B4 W Germany
Ware 33 E6 British Columbia, W Canada
Waremme 84 D7 E Belgium
Waren 101 D3 NE Germany
Warkworth 139 D2 North Island, New Zealand
Warminster 95 D4 S England, United Kingdom
Warm Springs 47 B6 Nevada, W USA
Warnemünde 101 D2 NE Germany
Warner 43 E8 Oklahoma, C USA
Warnes 65 B2 C Bolivia
Warrego River 137 G5 *seasonal river* New South Wales/Queensland, E Australia
Warren 40 E5 Michigan, N USA
Warren 40 F6 Ohio, N USA
Warren 37 B4 Pennsylvania, NE USA
Warri 72 E5 S Nigeria
Warrington 93 C4 C England, United Kingdom
Warrnambool 137 F6 Victoria, SE Australia
Warsaw 105 F3 ● C Poland
Warszawa *see* Warsaw
Warta 105 D4 ≈ W Poland
Warwick 137 H5 Queensland, E Australia
Warwick 93 D6 C England, United Kingdom
Warwick 37 F4 Rhode Island, NE USA
Washington 93 D2 NE England, United Kingdom
Washington 40 C7 Indiana, N USA
Washington 49 B2 ⬖ *state* NW USA
Washington DC 39 H1 ● District of Columbia, NE USA
Washington, Mount 37 F3 ▲ New Hampshire, NE USA
Wash, The 95 G1 *inlet* E England, United Kingdom
Waspam 55 E3 NE Nicaragua
Waterbury 37 E4 Connecticut, NE USA
Waterford 89 D6 S Ireland
Waterloo 43 F4 Iowa, C USA
Watersmeet 40 B2 Michigan, N USA
Watertown 37 D3 New York, NE USA
Watertown 43 D3 South Dakota, N USA
Waterville 89 A6 SW Ireland
Waterville 37 G2 Maine, NE USA
Watford 95 F3 E England, United Kingdom
Watford City 43 A2 North Dakota, N USA
Watrous 44 E2 New Mexico, SW USA
Watsa 76 D1 NE Dem. Rep. Congo
Watts Bar Lake 39 E3 ⊠ Tennessee, S USA
Wau 75 B4 S Sudan
Waukegan 40 C5 Illinois, N USA
Waukesha 40 C4 Wisconsin, N USA
Wausau 40 B3 Wisconsin, N USA

⬖ Administrative region ◆ Country ● Country capital ◇ Dependent territory ○ Dependent territory capital ⛰ Mountain range ▲ Mountain 🌋 Volcano ≈ River ◎ Lake ⊠ Reservoir

175

X

Y

Z

◈ Administrative region ◆ Country ● Country capital ◇ Dependent territory ○ Dependent territory capital ▲ Mountain range ▲ Mountain ☒ Volcano ⌇ River ◎ Lake ⊞ Reservoir